ARISTOTLE'S ETHICAL THEORY

BY

W. F. R. HARDIE

SECOND EDITION

CLARENDON PRESS · OXFORD

Oxford University Press, Walton Street, Oxford OX2 6DP

Oxford New York Toronto
Delhi Bombay Calcutta Madras Karachi
Kuala Lumpur Singapore Hong Kong Tokyo
Nairobi Dar es Salaam Cape Town
Melbourne Auckland

and associated companies in
Beirut Berlin Ibadan Nicosia

Oxford is a trade mark of Oxford University Press

Published in the United States
by Oxford University Press, New York

First Edition 1968
Second Edition 1980

Reprinted 1985

British Library Cataloguing in Publication Data

Hardie, William Francis Ross
Aristotle's Ethical Theory.—2nd ed.
1. Aristotle — Ethics 2. Ethics
I. Title
170'.92'4   B491.E7   79-41243

ISBN 0-19-824633-1

Printed in Great Britain by
Antony Rowe Ltd,
Chippenham

ARISTOTLE'S
ETHICAL THEORY

TO

I. St. M. H.

PREFACE (1968)

I HAVE tried in this book to give an account of Aristotle's main ethical doctrines, and to justify my interpretations by the detailed scrutiny of particular passages, often very familiar passages. In the study of Aristotle familiarity can be an obstacle to understanding; we are prone to think we know what he means before we do. I hope that I have avoided some misunderstandings by making the analyses of particular passages part of a continuous account of the whole relevant doctrine.

The book contains some independent discussions of philosophical questions which I take to be raised by Aristotle's work. A historian of philosophy may be tempted to think that his whole task is to discover what questions his author was asking and how he answered them, and not himself to discuss philosophical questions. But he cannot avoid discussing philosophical questions if he finds that what is said in the text he studies is intelligible only as a step towards saying something different and better. He must place his author in a historical sequence but also on a map of the subject. Interpretation involves risks, but the risks are less if they are taken openly.

I have not assumed in readers any knowledge of Greek. When I have mentioned Greek words I have transliterated them as well as translated. Translated passages are usually quotations from the Oxford Translation of Aristotle.[1]

I am grateful to many with whom I have discussed Aristotelian questions, in particular to Professor G. E. L. Owen who read some of the chapters in typescript.

My obligations to commentators, and to the writers of books and articles, will be obvious to readers who read only the Index. I regret if I have anywhere failed to acknowledge what

---

[1] Works of Aristotle. Translated into English under the editorship of J. A. Smith and W. D. Ross.

I have appropriated. My greatest obligation is to the works of Sir David Ross.

I have to make some acknowledgements of permission to use work previously published.

Chapter VII ('Virtue is a Mean') was published in the *Proceedings of the Aristotelian Society*, 1964–5. I am grateful to the editor for his permission to print it again here.

I have used some of the material contained in two other articles: 'Aristotle's Treatment of the Relation between the Soul and the Body' published in the *Philosophical Quarterly*, 1964, and 'The Final Good in Aristotle's Ethics' published in *Philosophy*, 1965. I thank the editors of these journals for their permission.

I thank also the editor of the *Listener* for his permission to use (in the Appendix to Chapter V) paragraphs from a Third Programme talk ('Bodies and Minds') which was published in his paper on 14 April 1960.

I acknowledge the courtesy of the Librarian of Balliol College, Oxford, in allowing me to borrow some manuscripts by the late Professor J. A. Smith.

Finally, I wish to express my gratitude to the publishers and printers, and to their reader, whose acute queries and suggestions were always reasonable and almost always accepted.

Corpus Christi College   W. F. R. H.
Oxford

PREFACE TO THE SECOND EDITION
(1980)

THIS book was published in 1968 and has been out of print for a number of years. It is now reprinted with the pagination unchanged but with additional matter in the form of Appended Notes. These notes are printed continuously at the end of the book in an order determined by the order of the chapters or pages to which they primarily refer. The Bibliography has been rearranged and brought up to date. The revised Index has been enlarged by the inclusion of references to the Appended Notes, and an index of Aristotelian passages has been added.

In writing the notes I have had two main objectives in view: to correct or supplement some of the interpretations which I now think were wrong or inadequate in the book and to take account of some recent contributions to the study of the *Ethics*. Some of the points made in the notes have been anticipated in articles. In particular I thank the editor of *Philosophy* for allowing me to use my article, 'Aristotle on the best life for a man' (1979). Points argued in it reappear with modifications in the notes to chapter II (The Final Good) and chapter XVI (Theoretical Activity).

I have come to think differently on two questions which I have found puzzling in Aristotle's doctrine on ethical virtue. What has Aristotle in mind when he speaks, most explicitly in his introduction to *EN* VII but not only there, of extraordinary or heroic virtue? The first note appended to XIII (Moral Weakness) is a second version, written two years later, of the Appendix ('Continence, Virtue, Heroic Virtue') which I was allowed to add to my chapter VII ('Virtue is a Mean') when the greater part of that chapter was reprinted in *Articles on Aristotle*, 2 (1977). The second puzzle has some connection with the first. What was Aristotle's purpose in IV 3 where he gives a description of the magnanimous man (*megalopsuchos*) which has evoked hostile and disrespectful reactions? I have discussed *megalopsuchia* and the interpretations of commentators in an article in *Phronesis* (1978), and have found room here only for a short note to chapter VI.

The notes on V (The Nature of Man) are based on, but not transcribed from, parts of an article, 'Concepts of Consciousness in Aristotle', in *Mind* (1976).

Two major books were published after I had, as I thought, completed my Appended Notes: the edition of the *De Motu Animalium* (1978) by Martha Craven Nussbaum and *The Aristotelian Ethics* (1978) by Anthony Kenny. Beyond adding to my Bibliography I could react only by writing two short 'postscripts': one to my chapter XII (Practical Syllogism) suggested by the fourth of Nussbaum's five Interpretive Essays ('Practical Syllogisms and Practical Science') and one in response to the second of Kenny's philosophical chapters ('Happiness in the Aristotelian Ethics').

W. F. R. H.

Corpus Christi College
Oxford

CONTENTS

I

INTRODUCTORY NOTE: ARISTOTLE'S ETHICAL WRITINGS

THIS book examines Aristotle's ethical doctrines as they are expounded in the work known as the *Nicomachean Ethics*. Two other works on ethics have come down to us as Aristotle's, the *Eudemian Ethics* and the *Great Ethics* or *Magna Moralia*. Later in this note I shall refer briefly to the general character of these other two treatises, and to the variety of the opinions which have been held by scholars about their relations to the *Nicomachean Ethics*. But I shall first say something about the characteristics of the *Nicomachean Ethics*. I am assuming that the reader may never have read an Aristotelian treatise and may not know Greek. Such a reader, if he approaches the work expecting it to resemble a modern book, planned as a whole and written for publication, will find in it features which should surprise him and cause him to wonder how the work came to be written in its present form.[1]

The *EN* is divided into ten 'books' of roughly similar length, a length (twenty pages or so) which makes it natural to think of them as analogous to the chapters of a modern book. But the analogy fails in more than one way. In a modern book it is normal for each chapter to deal with a single topic and hence we expect the chapters to vary considerably in length. It is true that, if a chapter threatens to exceed a certain length, the author may allow one topic to spread over two chapters, just as in the *EN* the topic

[1] I shall refer to the *Nicomachean Ethics* as *EN* (*Ethica Nicomachea*), to the *Eudemian Ethics* as *EE* (*Ethica Eudemia*), and to the *Magna Moralia* as *MM*. In referring to particular passages in Aristotle it is customary to give the page, column (a or b), and line of Bekker's text (see the Select List of Books and Articles at the end of this book). I have usually given also the name of the work and the numbers of the book and chapter. As regards the *EN* I have followed the division of the books into chapters which is used in the Oxford Text and Translation.

of *philia* (friendship) spreads over two books (VIII and IX). In the *EN* some of the books deal with a single topic, or a set of closely connected topics, as V with justice and VI with the intellectual excellencies. But sometimes there is a transition from one topic to another in the middle of a book. It is as if a book had to be of a certain approximate length, perhaps the length convenient for a single roll of papyrus.

When we look at the over-all arrangement of the contents of the *EN* we notice a more important difference between the treatise and a modern book: there are signs that the treatise was not planned and composed as a unitary whole by the author of its parts or that, if it was, it was planned to have a looser structure than a modern book. It need not surprise us to find separate discussions of the final good or end, happiness, in both the first and the last books (I and X); for it is natural to separate preliminary outlines from final conclusions. But it is disconcerting that there is no clear reference in I to the doctrine of X that the highest form of happiness is intellectual 'contemplation' (*theōria*), although in X we are reminded of what has been said in I.[1] Again the reader may be surprised to find two whole books[2] dealing with friendship and only one[3] book covering, in a rather untidy form, the important topics of the virtues of the intellect and the intellectual aspect of right conduct. Again the formulas of transition are often mechanical, e.g. at the beginning of VII: 'let us now make a fresh start and point out . . .'[4] Such formulas suggest the stitching together of sections which might have been composed without an eye on an over-all plan.

There is one very conspicuous anomaly in the arrangement of the treatise. It contains two separated treatments of pleasure which are not made to seem consistent and neither of which refers to the other.[5] At the end of the first treatment our text says: 'we have discussed pleasure and pain . . . ; it remains to speak of friendship.'[6] Then the section on friendship (VIII and IX) ends with the words: 'so much, then, for friendship; our next task must be to discuss

---

[1] 1176 a30–5. [2] VIII and IX, 44 pages of the Oxford Text.
[3] VI, 17 pages of the Oxford Text. [4] 1145 a15.
[5] VII. 11–14 and X. 1–5. [6] 1154 b32–5.

pleasure.'[1] It is difficult to suppose that Aristotle could have planned this sequence. The two treatments of pleasure cover similar ground in their criticisms of the views which they reject but x contains also an elaborate exposition of a positive doctrine. A possible inference is that the discussion of pleasure and pain in vii was inserted by an editor who might have felt that the piece dealt with the subject from an angle different from that of the discussion in x and made points not repeated there. We can be grateful for his clumsiness if it preserved an essay by Aristotle which would otherwise have been lost. A modern editor producing posthumously the work of the author might have printed the earlier less finished treatment of pleasure as an appendix.

So much on the general arrangement of the contents of the work. There are, moreover, considerable variations in the texture of the argument, in the degree of finish and elaboration with which the points are made. Some passages are highly condensed or sketchy. Here, for example, is a complete argument from the attack in I. 6 on the Platonic doctrine of the good: 'but again it will not be good any the more for being eternal, since that which lasts long is no whiter than that which perishes in a day.'[2] Sometimes an argument is mentioned rather than stated: one passage in the *Metaphysics* mentions three Platonic arguments and three Aristotelian refutations in four lines.[3] A man preparing a lecture may need to write down only a word or two to remind him of an argument which he knows will trip from his tongue.

There are other ways in which the composition is unequal. Sometimes the sequence of thought is unclear. Sometimes passages are repeated in an apparently pointless way with minor variations. Commentators would like to change the order of paragraphs or sentences in order to make the argument more consecutive and more intelligible. Modern editors have sometimes actually practised such surgery. An eminent scholar once went so far as to compare the contents of an Aristotelian treatise with the contents of a waste-paper basket. Two explanations of this kind of roughness or disorder might suggest themselves. One is that a basic text, amended from time to time by Aristotle, has

---

[1] 1172 a14–15.   [2] 1096 b3–5.   [3] *A* 9, 990 b11–15.

accumulated variants and accretions but has never been finished and polished. Another is that an editor in producing a text has at some points conflated two or more versions of sections dealing with the same points, and has been over-anxious that nothing significant or valuable should be lost. Sometimes both causes may be at work. This source of difficulty is specially frequent in the central books of the *EN* (v–vii).

The description I have given of some of the ways in which the *EN* is, from our point of view, a work of an unexpected and unfamiliar form would be misleading if it were taken to imply that the treatise is not a methodical and carefully written exposition of Aristotle's ethical views. The philosophy of morals is a set of more and less closely connected topics. Hence both the selection of topics to be discussed and the order in which they are discussed, whether in a book or in a course of lectures, are inevitably arbitrary to some extent. Thus the fact that we cannot be sure how far the work in its present form was planned by Aristotle himself is not inconsistent with the assurance of Rackham that 'the *Nicomachean Ethics* is the authoritative statement of Aristotle's system'.[1] It has always over the centuries been so regarded. Again the observation that the state of the text is at some points confused must not be understood as suggesting that there is, in general, anything loose or slipshod in the style and manner of the writing.

Aristotle resembles most philosophers in not being a literary artist in the class of Plato. His prose is dry, precise, and business-like, but it is artful as well. He exploits with resource, in pursuit of clarity, the flexibility of the Greek language. He enriched the language of philosophy by the invention of many technical expressions and usages which serve to consolidate conceptual advances. His vocabulary is large.[2] Sometimes new words are coined to make it easier to follow the thought.[3] His sentences are usually short, but sometimes they are long and complicated.

[1] Text with Translation (Loeb Classical Library 1926, revised 1934), p. xiii.
[2] Düring tells us that Bonitz's index to Aristotle contains 13,150 words (excluding proper names), while Ast's index to Plato contains 10,316 words (*Aristoteles*, p. 20 n. 106).
[3] *EN* ii. 7, 1108 a16–19.

In his most characteristic vein he is pungent and condensed. Sometimes indeed he chooses to offer us glimpses of the obvious, as when he remarks that to win an athletic competition it is necessary not only to be a good athlete but to be a competitor, the winners being a sub-class of the competitors.[1] Very occasionally we are tempted to suspect him, perhaps mistakenly, of having his tongue in his cheek, as when he suggests that the truly noble and unselfish person can show his quality by relinquishing to others opportunities of doing noble actions and not grabbing them for himself.[2] While his style is in general austere, his words can on occasion glow with feeling. Speaking of 'philosophy' he tells us that its pleasures are 'marvellously pure and lasting', and that a man, though mortal, should not, as the moralists advise, think mortal thoughts but should 'practise immortality as best he can'.[3]

The claim of the *EN* to be the 'authoritative statement' of Aristotle's ethical theory is not invalidated by the existence of the two other Aristotelian treatises on ethics mentioned at the beginning of this chapter, the *EE* and the *MM*. The *MM*, in spite of its title (*Great Ethics*), is a relatively short work which offers a succinct account of Aristotle's ethical views. Scholars are in disagreement on the question whether it was written, or at least written in part, by Aristotle himself. It is not within my scope to discuss the authenticity and date of this work. It will be enough to list the conclusions reached by some leading scholars in the present century. In his edition of the *EN* (1900) Burnet claimed the agreement of 'all competent judges' for the view that the *MM* is 'a Peripatetic handbook written after Aristotle's time'.[4] He stated that, 'as it shows no traces of Stoic influence or of opposition to Stoic views, it cannot well be later than the third century B.C.'. Thomas Case in the *Encyclopaedia Britannica* (1910) argued that it is an early work of Aristotle giving a 'more rudimentary' account of his ethical system than the *EN*. Ross (1923) said that the work is based on the *EE* and 'apparently dates from the late third or from the second century B.C.', that it shows the influence

---

[1] I. 8, 1099 a3–5.   [2] IX. 8, 1169 a32–4.   [3] *EN* x. 7.
[4] p. x.

of Theophrastus, Aristotle's successor as head of the Lyceum, and
that there are traces in it of Stoic terminology.[1] Jaeger (also 1923)
took a similar view and argued, mainly on the evidence of the
general character of the work and its language, for a date in the
generation immediately following Aristotle's death in 322 B.C.
It was maintained against Jaeger by H. von Arnim (1924 and
later) that the *MM* is a genuine work of Aristotle and earlier than
the *EE* and the *EN*. Von Arnim's thesis was attacked by critics
including Jaeger himself and R. Walzer (1929).[2] But the view
that the *MM* is substantially an early work of Aristotle was
defended again by F. Dirlmeier in his commentary on the work
(1958). Dirlmeier's arguments have been endorsed by I. Düring
in his *Aristoteles* (1966). Düring claims that the *MM* can no longer
be dismissed as merely a later compendium.[3] There is thus at
present no agreed view on the character of the treatise or on the
date of its composition. In this book I shall refer only occasionally
to formulations of Aristotelian doctrine in the *MM*.

The *Eudemian Ethics* has always received much less attention
from editors and commentators than the *Nicomachean*, and our
manuscript evidence for the text is less good. Scholars in the
nineteenth century doubted or denied its authenticity. The title
suggested the idea that the work was written by Aristotle's pupil,
Eudemus of Rhodes. Both Grant and Burnet in their editions of
the *EN* accepted this attribution. But, if this were a correct
interpretation of the title, we should have to suppose that Aristotle's son Nicomachus, who was a child when his father died
and is said to have died young in battle, wrote the *EN*. Cicero
indeed suggests that he might have done so, pointing out that
clever fathers sometimes have clever sons,[4] but this only shows
that in his time the work already had its present title and was
taken to be a work of Aristotle. An early suggestion was that the
works were dedicated to Nicomachus and Eudemus respectively,
and this idea is reflected in the French form of the titles.[5] Ross

---

[1] *Aristotle*, p. 15.

[2] *Magna Moralia und aristotelische Ethik*, Berlin, 1929 (=*Neue philologische Untersuchungen* 7).

[3] pp. 438, 443-4.   [4] *De Finibus* v. 5. 12.

[5] 'L'Éthique à Nicomaque', 'à Eudème'.

thinks that 'the most natural explanation of the titles' is that the works are 'editions' by Eudemus and Nicomachus of 'two courses on ethics by Aristotle'.[1] Rackham, the translator in the Loeb Classical Library of both the *EN* and the *EE*, agrees that Eudemus and Nicomachus 'may' have been 'editors' or 'compilers' of the treatises.[2]

The authenticity of the *EE* is defended by W. Jaeger in his book on the development of Aristotle's philosophy. Jaeger believed that Aristotle as a young man accepted from Plato the 'theory of forms' and an ethical doctrine based on that metaphysical theory. He finds evidence for this Platonic stage in Aristotle's development in passages quoted by ancient writers from Aristotle's dialogues and other literary works (none of which has survived), especially the *Protrepticus* and the *Eudemus*. Jaeger argues that the characteristic doctrine of the *EE* represents an intermediate stage in the development of Aristotle's ethics between the Platonism of his youth and the mature doctrine formulated in the *EN*. It will be sufficient to mention here one of the points in Jaeger's case. In Platonism the wisdom of the philosopher who knows the Forms is also the authoritative guide to what is right in practice. But in the *EN* Aristotle separates practical wisdom (*phronēsis*) from theoretical or philosophic wisdom (*sophia*). In *EE* I, on the other hand, we find two passages in which the life of philosophy is linked with *phronēsis*.[3] This is taken as evidence that, when he wrote the *EE*, Aristotle was not yet fully emancipated, as he was when he wrote the *EN*, from the influence of Plato.[4] Jaeger's arguments convinced Ross and also Burnet. In a lecture given in 1924 to the British Academy Burnet gave up the view assumed in his edition of the *EN* (1900) that the *EE* was written by Eudemus and spoke of it as having been 'finally disproved by Jaeger'. Jaeger's thesis entails the authenticity of the *EE*. But acceptance of the tradition that both 'courses', the *EE* and the *EN*, are works of Aristotle does not

---

[1] *Aristotle*, p. 14.   [2] *EN* Translation, p. xiii.

[3] 1214 a30–b5, 1215 b1–6.

[4] The view that the *EE* represents an earlier, and the *EN* a later, stage in the development of Aristotle's ethical theory had been maintained for similar reasons by Thomas Case (1910).

entail acceptance of Jaeger's theory of their places in an evolution
of Aristotle's views.

What I have said so far will have suggested that the *EE* and the
EN are two quite separate works both surviving intact and complete and both covering the whole ground of Aristotelian ethics.
But this is not strictly speaking the case. The question how the
two works are related is complicated by the fact that, according
to the tradition conveyed by the manuscripts of the *EE*, the three
central books are common to them both. At the end of Book III
of the *EE* the manuscripts state that the next three books are
identical with *EN* v, vi, and vii, and the remaining books of the
EE are numbered accordingly in the manuscripts as vii and viii.[1]
Scholars have argued both ways on the question whether, as
regards style and doctrine, the affinities of the common or disputed books are with the other books of the *EN* or with the other
books of the *EE*. Of the English commentators on the *EN* Grant
argued that the common books belonged originally to the *EE*[2]
and Stewart agreed with him.[3] So did Henry Jackson in his
edition of *EN* v.[4] Burnet left the central books with the *EN*,[5] and
Greenwood argued that VI belongs to the *EN*.[6] Ross also argued for
assigning the disputed books to the *EN*.[7] An intermediate view
was taken in the middle of the nineteenth century by two German
scholars,[8] who held that of the common books only *EN* v (= *EE*
IV) on justice belongs to the *EN*.

Scholars taking part in the argument over the common books
have usually assumed or implied that the treatise to which the
books do not properly belong must originally have contained a
section covering the same ground, a section the loss of which
created the gap which the books belonging to the other treatise
were imported to fill. But the need to make this assumption seems
questionable when we reflect on the differences which we have
noted between an Aristotelian treatise and a modern book. If it is

---

[1] Details of what is said and not said in the manuscripts are given in the Berlin
Aristotle on *EE* 1234 b14 and in Susemihl's edition of the *EE*, p. ix n. 5. There is a
discussion of the evidence in G. Lieberg's *Die Lehre von der Lust in den Ethiken
des Aristoteles* (1958), pp. 4–6.

[2] Essay I.   [3] ii, p. 217.   [4] pp. xxii–xxxii.   [5] pp. xi–xv.
[6] pp. 1–20.   [7] *Aristotle*, p. 15.   [8] Fischer and Fritzsche.

right to think of the EE as an earlier and the EN as a later course of instruction by Aristotle, we can simply accept as a fact that the middle books were common to the two courses. It is not unusual for a lecturer who sets out to rewrite a course of lectures to succeed in rewriting or revising only part of the course. I take this to be the suggestion of Rackham in the introduction to his translation: 'Aristotle left only one course of lectures on these portions of the subject.'[1]

My purpose in this introductory chapter has been to anticipate some of the questions which the non-specialist reader is likely to have in mind about Aristotle's ethical writings. I have described the way in which the contents of the EN are arranged and some of the features of Aristotle's manner and style of writing. I have reported on the opinions of scholars about the date and authenticity of the EE and the MM. I have not discussed the questions to which the experts have given different answers, and have indicated only briefly what sorts of arguments are used in support of these answers. Not all the questions which it is reasonable to ask about Aristotle's writings can be given answers which are known to be true. In the case of some questions it may not be possible to say of any of the possible answers that it is more probable than any other. As I understand, we do not know exactly when or how the EN was put together. But we know that it is one of Aristotle's more finished works, that it is an important document for the history of thought on a wide range of questions, and that it is found interesting and helpful by contemporary philosophers in their study of these questions.

We know that Aristotle was an organizer of research and a writer of treatises. We can be sure that he gave courses of instruction or lectures. I have pointed to characteristics of the EN which suggest that it is a course written out by a lecturer for delivery sometimes verbatim and sometimes in the form of notes of points to be developed or illustrated in a fuller exposition. It is open to any reader, if he wishes, to form his own mental image of Aristotle as a lecturer. Some suggestive clues are offered by Henry Jackson in his stimulating essay, 'Aristotle's Lecture Room

[1] p. xiv.

and Lectures'.[1] We learn that the lecture room was furnished with a three-legged table, sofas made of wood, a white board for diagrams,[2] a bronze statue and a bronze globe, and on the walls various tabular summaries including lists of virtues and vices.[3] The decorations of the room included pictures representing Socrates in scenes from the *Phaedo* and the *Protagoras*. All this information, and a good deal about the lectures themselves, is deduced by Jackson from the text of Aristotle's works.

BIBLIOGRAPHICAL NOTE

The text and doctrine of the *EN* has through the ages been the subject of paraphrase and discussion in sentence-by-sentence commentaries, and in modern times also in articles and notes in learned periodicals, in books on Aristotle, and in books on moral philosophy. The edition and commentary by R. A. Gauthier and J. Y. Jolif (1958–9) gives a list of books and articles mainly published since 1912 and for earlier work refers to the bibliography in the edition of Susemihl revised by O. Apelt (1912).[4] There is a bibliography also in Dirlmeier's commentary (1956).[5] A 'short', up-to-date general bibliography of works on Aristotle,[6] prefaced by directions for finding fuller information and longer lists, will be found at the end of Ingemar Düring's *Aristoteles* (1966).[7] The English translation from which I have usually quoted is the Oxford Translation by W. D. Ross. It has a useful table of contents. The translation in the Everyman Library by D. P. Chase has a good Introduction by J. A. Smith. The large commentaries mentioned above, and that of J. A. Stewart (1892), will help the student who already has some acquaintance with the *EN*. On a first reading of the Greek text a shorter commentary may be more helpful. Joachim's commentary (1951) is a useful guide, especially on doctrines of Aristotle in other works relevant to the *EN*. Burnet's edition and commentary (1900) is crisp and readable and often illuminating. But he is sometimes unclear on philosophical issues and on some questions of interpretation I shall argue against his views. Grant's Introductory Essays were valuable in their time. Ross's *Aristotle* (1923) gives an account of Aristotle's doctrines in all his works, and the chapter (vii)

---

[1] *Journal of Philology*, vol. xxxv, no. 70, 1920. [2] Cf. *EN* v. 5.
[3] Cf. *EN* 1107 a33, *EE* 1220 b37. [4] pp. 917–40.
[5] pp. 255–64. [6] *Kleine Aristoteles-Bibliographie.* [7] pp. 623–40.

on Ethics is outstanding. Some of the ground covered in other chapters is more fully explored in the introductions to his commentaries on the *Metaphysics*, the *Physics*, the *Prior* and *Posterior Analytics*, the *Parva Naturalia*, and the *De Anima*.

II

THE FINAL GOOD FOR MAN

ARISTOTLE, in describing the nature of his inquiry, tries to persuade his hearers to accept at the outset the doctrine that there is one supreme end of action, a final good for man. He seems to suggest that, when this central doctrine has been grasped, there will be a clear programme for what remains to be done, like the filling in of the details in a map when the main lines have been drawn. He makes this comparison in *EN* I. 7. 'Let the above serve as an outline of the good; for we must presumably first sketch it roughly and then fill in the details. It would seem that anyone is capable of carrying out and articulating what has once been well outlined, and that time is a good discoverer or partner in such a work' (1098 a20–4). But it is seldom possible in philosophy to get the central concepts and doctrines clear at the outset. The opening chapters, which we have now to examine, do not in fact make clear what Aristotle meant by an 'end' (*telos*), but reflection on the ambiguity of the term is a good way of starting the study of his ethical theory.

Aristotle states in chapter 1 that every human activity aims at some good, i.e. some end, and that the end in view may be either the activity itself or something produced by the activity and distinct from it (1094 a1–5). On this division of ends the comment seems obvious that activities in which we engage only because we enjoy them, such as listening to music or playing golf, have no end in view. There is an end only when we engage in the activity in order to produce a desired result, as when we go to a concert in order to please somebody or play golf for money. Seeking an end implies taking appropriate means. But, as Aristotle uses end (*telos*), an end does not imply a means. An activity, looking at a picture or following an argument, is an end if it is desired for itself. To say that it is an end does not imply the finding or adopting of means leading to the enjoyable activity of seeing or understanding. Aristotle's second class of ends, the ends which are desired results of activities, coincides with what we commonly understand by the 'ends' of actions. An example, typical for us as for Aristotle, is the use of massage as a means of producing warmth and so health.[1] His examples in *EN* I. 1 and 2 are taken from the productive arts and skills, because he wishes to expound the concept of politics as an architectonic art ruling over other arts. But he speaks of actions as well as of arts and sciences (1094 a1, a7); and the account in III. 3 of the process of discovering means to ends shows that he there has in mind taking steps to an end where no technical skill need be involved.

When we speak of choosing means, or of taking steps, to an end we often combine two distinct, and not necessarily connected, ideas. The first is the idea of a series of steps planned in order to bring into existence some object, e.g. a boat, or some state of affairs, e.g. an enjoyment or restored health. It should be added that, in speaking of living things, Aristotle is willing to say that they develop, by a series of stages, towards an end, or aim at an end, and this way of speaking does not seem to imply design. An acorn does not plan to be an oak. The second is the idea that the steps taken towards the terminus are desired and chosen only because they lead to the terminus; the dependent desire for the means is wholly parasitic on the independent desire for the end. To speak of an end in this sense is to ascribe a motive. Aristotle says here that it is in the nature of ends produced to be 'better than' the activities which produce them (1094 a5–6, cf. a15–16). Similarly in the *Metaphysics* he says that a course of action which has a limit (*peras*) or terminus, like slimming, is not itself an end (Θ 6, 1048 b18). Here Aristotle's primary point is that slimming is a process (*kinēsis*) and not what he calls an *energeia* (activity), but he assumes that the process is desired for the sake of the terminus which is its end and is at its end. These passages show that Aristotle tended to run together the two ideas which I have distinguished. But examples show that they are separable as well as distinct. Our activities in playing a game have victory as the

[1] *Metaphysics Z* 7, 1032 b6–10, b18–26.

end in view. A golfer plays to win. But, if he loses, he does not feel that his day has been wasted, that he has laboured in vain, as he would if his sole reason for playing had been to win a prize or to mortify his opponent or just to win. Similarly philosophy is desired for itself as a worthwhile activity even if the problems which we take steps to solve remain unsolved. It would not be as attractive as it is if only results mattered. What can be shown by these and other examples is that an activity which aims at producing a result may itself be an object either of aversion or of indifference or of a positive desire which may be less or greater than the desire for its product. Again an activity of a kind capable of being desired both for itself and for its results, e.g. physical exercise, may on some occasions be desired primarily or solely for its results and on others primarily or solely for itself. To travel may be a bore but may also be better than to arrive. Aristotle did not indeed fail to see and mention that an object may be desired both for itself and for its results (7, 1097 a30-4; cf. 6, 1096 b16-19). But he sometimes ignores this and his doing so can have unfortunate consequences. It leads, as we shall see, to his failure to specify adequately the architectonic function of the statesman. It is connected also, although only as one consideration among others, with his curious insistence, when recommending the pursuit of science and philosophy, on the joys of knowing rather than the joys of research (EN x. 7, 1177 a25-7; cf. VII. 14, 1154 b26-8). He tends to think that seeking, if desired for the sake of finding, cannot also be desired for itself.

In the second part of chapter 1 (1094 a6 ff.) Aristotle introduces the relation between arts of subordinate to superordinate and the doctrine that there is a supreme art, statesmanship. As Burnet points out (pp. xxiv-xxv), there are Platonic sources of these ideas. In the Politicus (304 b-305 e) the art of the statesman is described as 'ruling over' other arts, in particular the arts of the orator (304 d), the general (304 e), and the judge (305 b, c). The idea that the user of a product has authority over the maker is in the Cratylus (390 c), and the example of bridle-making in relation to horsemanship is given in the Republic (601 c). The relation of a subordinate to a superordinate art is defined in terms of means

and ends. An art is subordinate if what it does, or what it produces, is used as a means by another art. In the series, bridle-
making horsemanship strategy statesmanship, each is subordinate
to its successor, and statesmanship, being the most authoritative, is
subordinate to none (a27).[1] This should mean that an order for so
many bridles is given by the chief cavalry officer, who, in turn,
has been ordered by the supreme commander to organize a force
of cavalry as part of an army the size of which has been fixed by
the commander in the light of instructions from the statesman to
make the state safe from invaders. Statesmanship 'ordains which
of the sciences should be studied in a state, and which each class
of citizens should learn and up to what point they should learn
them' (1094 a28–b2). The ends of superordinate (architectonic)
arts are more desirable than the ends of subordinate arts, as means
are pursued for the sake of ends (a14–16). Aristotle does not here
anticipate his answer to the question what end the statesman has
in view. An obvious but vague answer would be the happiness of
the citizens (x. 7, 1177 b14). A more definite, but partial, answer
is that the function of statesmanship is to promote the conditions
of the study of mathematics, physical science, and philosophy by
those of the citizens who are capable of such studies (vi. 13,
1145 a6–9). On this view the authority and business of the statesman would be like that of a bursar in a research institute, or, as is
said in the *MM* of practical wisdom generally, that of a steward
who so arranges things that his master has leisure for his high
vocation (*A* 34, 1198 b12–17).

   Now it is no doubt true that some human activities, and even
the exercise of some skills, are valued only as means. Even making
bridles might be fun compared with digging coal or a repeated
operation on a production line. But the ladder, or pyramid, of
ends can be made to look like a tidy scheme only by ignoring the
fact already mentioned that many activities are attractive both for
themselves and for the results they produce. Since riding is an
enjoyable sport it would be wrong to provide bridles only for the
cavalry. Again two arts may each be, in Aristotle's sense, under
the other. Riders use bridles, but a bridle-maker may ride to his

---

[1] Cf. vi. 8, 1141 b23–5.

work. The engineer uses techniques invented by the mathematician, but also promotes the wealth and leisure in which pure
mathematics can flourish. Two craftsmen might each make
tools for the other. An activity may be valuable as having more
than one kind of effect, as military training might promote both
the safety of the state and the health of its citizens. These complexities are relevant to the account which Aristotle gives of
statesmanship. The account is too simple: it is not easy to think of
any political problem which is merely one of finding means to a
fixed end. Thus a Local Authority should employ enough, but
not more than enough, sweepers to keep the streets clean. But, if
labour and money are short, it may be doubtful how clean to
keep the streets. A political authority is more often an arbitrator
between conflicting claims than a technician devising means to
ends. Aristotle tries to make means-finding cover too large a part
of practical thinking, whether of the statesman or of the private
citizen.

After his introductory remarks about ends, and about the
subordination of some ends to others, Aristotle proceeds in
chapter 2 to formulate as follows the idea that there is a 'good for
man'.

If, then, there is some end of the things we do which we desire for
its own sake, everything else being desired for the sake of this, and if
we do not choose everything for the sake of something else (for at that
rate the process would go on to infinity, so that our desire would be
empty and vain), clearly this must be the good and the chief good.
Will not the knowledge of it, then, have a great influence on life?
Shall we not, like archers who have a mark to aim at (*skopos*), be more
likely to hit upon what is right? (1094 a18–24.)

I understand Aristotle in this passage to be saying two things,
but without separating them from each other as sharply as he
should. He is saying first that, in order to avoid an infinite regress,
it must be allowed that, if there is anything which is desired but
not desired for itself, there must be something which is desired for
itself. He is saying secondly that, if there were one such object and
one only, this fact would be important for the conduct of life.

It would put a man in the position of an archer with a definite target. So read, the passage has a coherent meaning. But, if we interpret the passage as claiming to *prove* that there is only one ultimate end, it is open to the criticism neatly stated by Miss Anscombe, who finds here 'an illicit transition' from 'all chains must stop somewhere' to 'there is somewhere where all chains must stop'.[1] I am inclined to acquit Aristotle of this fallacy in view of the fact that the possibility of a plurality of ends is mentioned in chapter 7 (1097 a22–4) and that he certainly knew that men enjoy and desire many different objects. Even philosophers have pleasures outside philosophy, and many men are not philosophers. Any sense in which there is a single end for all actions must be one which allows for these obvious facts.

The single end which is 'the good and the best' (1094 a22) is represented in the *EN* as the goal of statesmanship or political science in the exercise of its architectonic function (a27–8). While the good for the state and the good for the individual are the same, the end of the state is 'something greater and more complete'. 'Though it is worth while to attain the end merely for one man, it is finer and more godlike to attain it for a nation or for city-states' (1094 b7–10). This seems to imply that the thinking required for a man's arrangement of his own life is of the same kind, although on a smaller scale, as the thinking of the statesman. It must also, since the *Ethics* is a political treatise (b10–11), be of the same kind as Aristotle's thinking when he wrote the *Ethics* as well as the *Politics*. We must defer discussion of the questions raised by these implications. Our immediate need is to understand the doctrine that there is a single end in its application to the planning by the individual of his own life. We find a statement of the doctrine in this application at the beginning of the *EE*.

Everyone who has the power to live according to his own choice (*prohairesis*) should dwell on these points and set up for himself some object (*skopos*) for the good life to aim at, whether honour or reputation or wealth or culture, by reference to which he will do all he does, since not to have one's life organized in view of some end is a sign of

---

[1] G. E. M. Anscombe, *Intention* (1957), § 21.

great folly. Now above all we must define to ourselves without hurry or carelessness in which of our possessions the good life (*to eu zēn*) consists, and what for men are the conditions of its attainment. (*EE A* 2, 1214 b6–14.)

The statement that it is foolish 'not to have one's life organized in view of some end' suggests the following comments. If the statement is true, the man who fails to organize and plan his life shows lack of wisdom on two distinct counts; first in not planning his life, and secondly in not giving a paramount place in his plan to one particular object or aim. The thesis that a man is foolish if he does not plan his own life might be amplified as follows. Every man has, and knows that he has, a number of desires and interests, and knows also that these interests may compete and interfere with each other and sometimes promote each other. He will inevitably sometimes, and to some extent, be a planner of his own life, and he is foolish if he does not try to plan sensibly and to get his priorities right. So far we can surely agree. The second contention, that a good planner will always give a paramount place to one dominant interest, is more questionable. Perhaps it is exceptional for a life to be unified by dedication to one end. We might, if asked for examples, think of Disraeli's political ambition, of Henry James's devotion to the art of the novel, or of Wordsworth's concentration on conveying in poetry his feelings about nature and man. Aristotle might admit that his prescription was for a minority. But he might also claim that the life of the philosopher or scientist or scholar or artist was preferable to other lives just because it has this kind of unity and continuity.

What is the significance of Aristotle's insistence in *EN* I. 2 that the end of the city-state (*polis*), or of a nation (*ethnos*), is greater and more complete, finer and more godlike, than the end of the single man? It is not indeed surprising that this should be said. If it is a fine thing that a man should fulfil the potentialities of his nature, then the more who achieve this the better. Such achievement is impossible without the security, the economic resources, and the educative agencies of a politically organized society. Self-development, as conceived by Aristotle, covers family life and friendship as well as intellectual pursuits. In *EN* I. 7 he says that

the good life must be sufficient by itself, and that a solitary life
will not satisfy human nature. 'Now by self-sufficient we do not
mean that which is sufficient for a man by himself, for one who
lives a solitary life, but also for parents, children, wife, and in
general for friends and fellow citizens, since man is born for
citizenship' (*phusei politikon*) (1097 b7–11). Aristotle stresses the
fact that men have social needs and interests, but he does not suggest that there is any reason for political institutions beyond the
fact that they promote the ends and enjoyments of individuals.
This is implied in *EN* VI. 8. 'The man who knows and concerns
himself with his own interests is thought to have practical wisdom,
while politicians are thought to be busybodies . . . Yet perhaps
one's own good cannot exist without household management,
nor without a form of government' (1142 a1–10). Political science has in view an end more fair and godlike than the end of
the individual. Politicians are thought to be busybodies, but we
cannot do without them. The two passages differ in their tone of
voice. There is no conflict of doctrine.

In chapter 3 Aristotle tells us that ethics is not an exact science,
that its purpose is practical, and that it is a subject which cannot
profitably be studied by the very young or by those who have not
learnt to control their passions. A man who has not had a good
moral training will get nothing from lectures on ethics (1095
a30–b13). Aristotle returns in the last part of chapter 7 (1098 a26)
to the inexactness of ethics and to the question how first principles
come to be grasped. These doctrines are important, and not all the
difficulties in the way of understanding them appear on the surface. They must be reserved for a separate discussion[1] in which
different aspects of Aristotle's view of ethical science can be considered together.

At the beginning of chapter 4 the treatment of the final good is
resumed from the point reached at the end of chapter 2. We have
learnt that political science aims at 'the highest of all goods
achievable by action', and we have to ask what this good is.
'Verbally there is very general agreement; for both the general
run of men and people of superior refinement say that it is

[1] See Chapter III below.

happiness (*eudaimonia*), and identify living well and doing well (*eu prattein*) with being happy; but with regard to what happiness is they differ, and the many do not give the same account as the wise' (1095 a17–22). Aristotle is saying, it would seem, that many different views are held on the question what it is in life that is most worth having, desirable in the highest degree. But, whatever it is, everyone is prepared to say that its possessor is 'doing well', is *eudaimōn*, that fortune has blessed him and he is to be felicitated. Aristotle does not propose to examine all the views, only 'the most prevalent and the most plausible' (1095 a28–30). Of the answers given by the many he selects for mention pleasure, wealth, and honour (a22–3). Of philosophical answers he mentions the Platonic doctrine of the self-subsistent good which he discusses in chapter 6. His own answer, reached by considering the specific nature of man, is formulated in chapter 7: 'the good for man turns out to be activity of soul in accordance with virtue, and if there is more than one virtue, in accordance with the best and most complete; but we must add "in a complete life" ' (1098 a16–18).

My account of what Aristotle says in chapter 4 has implied that we can accept what he says as an adequate formulation of his question. To say that the supremely desirable end is *eudaimonia* does not settle what it is that is supremely desirable. This interpretation conflicts with the view of H. A. Prichard that Aristotle in chapter 4 misdescribes his own position.

He certainly did not think that anyone ever meant by *eudaimonia* either honour (*timē*) or wealth (*ploutos*); and he certainly did not himself mean by it activity of the soul in accordance with complete virtue. What he undoubtedly meant and thought others meant by the word *eudaimonia* is happiness. Plainly, too, what he thought men differed about was not the nature of happiness but the conditions of its realization, and when he says that *eudaimonia is* activity of the soul in accordance with complete virtue, what he really means is that the latter is what is required for the realization of happiness. Consideration of the *Ethics* by itself should be enough to convince us of this, but if it is not, we need only take into account his elucidation of the question 'what is?' to be sure that, when he asks 'what is *eudaimonia*?' his meaning is similar to that of a man who, when he asks 'what is colour?' or 'what is sound?' really means 'what are the conditions necessary for its realization?' We must, therefore, understand Aristotle in chapter 4 to be in effect contending that, while it is universally admitted that our ultimate aim is happiness, there is great divergence of view about the conditions, or more precisely the proximate conditions, of its realization.[1]

When Prichard speaks here of Aristotle's 'elucidation of the question "what is?"' he is referring to the doctrine in the *Posterior Analytics* (II. 8 and 9, cf. 2) that the scientific definition of an attribute states what causes it to belong to the subject. Aristotle's example is thunder which is produced in the clouds by the quenching of fire. The definition of thunder is given in one passage as 'noise produced by quenching of fire in clouds' (94 a3–7) and in another as 'quenching of fire in clouds' (93 b8). The second states only the 'condition necessary for its realization' but this is just a loose abbreviation of the first, which mentions, as a definition should, the genus as well as the differentia. Prichard assumes wrongly that the second is the standard formulation. Thus, if we assume that Aristotle in *EN* I. 4 has in mind this doctrine about definition, this evidence is against Prichard's interpretation.

The point at issue which is important for the interpretation of Aristotle's argument in *EN* I can be stated very briefly. Aristotle says that the supremely desirable end, the highest good, is a certain sort of activity or certain sorts of activity. He says that the highest good (1095 a16–17), the good for which we are seeking, is desired as being what it is and not because of anything produced by it (1096 a6–7).[2] For Aristotle the word *agathon* (good), in the use to which he refers in the first sentence of the *EN* (1094 a1–3), implies being desired or chosen for its own sake.[3] Prichard, on the other hand, says that, whatever Aristotle may have said, what he 'really means' is that the activity is desired not for itself but as being 'required for the realisation of happiness'. He implies that the happiness is something different from the activity which is

---

[1] *Moral Obligation*, pp. 51–2 (reprinted from *Philosophy*, 1935).
[2] Cf. 7, 1097 a30 ff.; *EE* I. 2, 1214 b24–7.
[3] Cf. *Rhetoric* I. 5, 1362 a21–4; 6, 1363 b12–15.

required to produce it, as the purchase of a house is different from
the possession of the money required for the transaction, or as
colour, to take Prichard's example, is different from the physical
and physiological conditions necessary for its realization. Now, if
we say that a philosopher 'really means' something which he has
not said, we imply that what he has said is, as it stands, so absurd
or so obviously false that, when this is pointed out, the need for
a revised statement will be admitted. I can see no˙such absurdity
in what Aristotle here says. Prichard appears to think that he is
pointing to such an absurdity when he says that Aristotle 'certainly
did not himself mean' by *eudaimonia* a certain sort of activity.
But this remark takes us no further since the question what is
'meant' by *eudaimonia* itself needs elucidation. The right course
is to accept provisionally Aristotle's account in chapter 4 of the
question which he sets himself to discuss in these chapters of
the *Ethics*. Any other course would demand a full examination
of the concepts of pleasure, enjoyment, and happiness.

Aristotle's exposition in chapter 7 of his own view falls into two
sections. In the first (1097 a15–b21) he argues that the 'good
achievable by action' must be final (*teleion*), self-sufficient
(*autarkes*) in the sense of being something which 'when isolated
makes life desirable and lacking in nothing' (1097 b14–15), and
'most desirable of all things, without being counted as one good
thing among others' (b16–17). In the second section of the chapter (1097 b22–1098 a20) Aristotle arrives at a definition of the
human good by considering what is the function (*ergon*) of man.

In the first section of the chapter Aristotle comes near to
facing, but does not quite face, the fact that, within the human
good, there are many activities desired for themselves and not one
only. This is certainly his own conviction. There is a place, and a
paramount place, in the good life for 'theory', i.e. for philosophy
and science. But there is a place also for family and friends and the
active life of the citizen (1097 b8 ff.). In x. 8 he explicitly asserts
that human happiness has these two main forms. Now in I. 7 he
admits, and indeed insists, that the 'human good' must be an
inclusive whole: it would not be final and self-sufficient if any
addition would make it better (1097 b16–18). In agreement with

this he says that we must be ready to allow a plurality of ends (1097 a22–4). But a few lines later he puzzles us by saying that, if there is more than one final end, the object of our search is the most final (a28–30). Similarly his definition of *eudaimonia* as activity in accordance with virtue contains the clause: 'if there are more than one virtue, in accordance with the best and most complete' (1098 a17–18; cf. 1099 a30). Thus in speaking of the good for man Aristotle hesitates between an inclusive and an exclusive formulation. As we saw earlier, it is consistent to hold both that a wise man will plan his life so as to make room for many different enjoyments and that he will give a paramount place to one kind of activity or enjoyment. What is unsatisfactory in Aristotle's treatment is his failure to make explicit the distinction between the comprehensive plan and the paramount end. In the planning of life at all levels, especially the highest, it is necessary to decide priorities between ends as well as to devise means for achieving ends. Aristotle tends to speak as if all that was needed was to set up a paramount end and then work out plans for attaining it.

The second section starts from the notion that man has an *ergon* (function).

Just as for a flute-player, a sculptor, or any artist and, in general, for all things that have a function (*ergon*) or activity (*praxis*), the good . . . is thought to reside in the function, so it would seem to be for man if he has a function. Have the carpenter, then, and the cobbler certain functions or activities, and has man none? Is he born without a function (*argon*)? Or as eye hand foot and in general each part evidently has a function, may one lay it down that man similarly has a function apart from all these? (1097 b25–33.)

The obvious answer is that one may not, unless one is prepared to compare a man with an instrument designed for some use. In *Republic* I the notion of function is illustrated by a pruning-hook, by the eye and ear, and hence, by a curious transition, applied to the soul. It is intelligible that the eye or the hand, or even the brain, should be regarded as analogous to instruments. Plato first spoke of eyes and ears as 'organs' (tools).[1] The idea that they are instruments is difficult unless we think that they were designed.

---

[1] *Theaetetus* 184 a; cf. *Republic* 508 b.

It is natural again to think of the carpenter and the cobbler as instrumental to the needs which they supply. But it is not natural to speak as if the fact that the eye can be thought of as having a function, or the fact that a cobbler has one, creates a presumption that the whole man is not functionless (1097 b30). On the contrary, it is only the fact that a cobbler is an abstraction that makes it possible to think of him as a means. It is only the fact that the eye and hand are parts of the body that makes it possible to think of them as tools. My whole body is not like a tool; still less my soul. I may misuse my hands in playing a golf shot; but I do not use, or misuse, my body to play golf with. That is not what it is for. It is not for anything.

The best way to find out what is the function of something is to ask its designer or his customer. Even if a man were an instrument made by God for a purpose, this inquiry would not be open. The *Republic* suggests a criterion (353 a9). If it is true of something that it could be used to produce certain desirable results, and if anything else would produce them, if at all, less effectively, then the thing is probably a tool and producing these results is probably its function. Aristotle, applying a similar principle, proceeds on the assumption that it is best for man to exercise the powers which are peculiar to him. 'Life seems to be common even to plants, but we are seeking what is peculiar (*idion*) to man. Let us exclude, therefore, the life of nutrition and growth. Next there would be a life of perception, but it also seems to be common to the horse, the ox, and every animal. There remains, then, an active life (*praktikē*) of the element that has a rational principle' (*logos*) (1097 b33–98 a4). So he draws the conclusion that the good for man is activity in accordance with virtue, or the most complete of the virtues, in a complete life. 'For one swallow does not make a summer, nor does one day; and so too one day, or a short time, does not make a man blessed and happy' (1098 a18–20).

Only very brief comment is needed at this stage. As Aristotle indicates, the outline will be filled up in detail later (1098 a20 ff.). The reference to the three grades of soul must be understood in the light of Aristotle's teaching, in *De Anima B*, on the relation of the soul to the body and of the various grades of soul to each other. Aristotle remarks later that the student of politics must study psychology up to the point required for the questions he is discussing (I. 13, 1102 a18–26). An account of the relevant doctrine is given by Ross.[1] The main point to notice in connection with the definition of the best life is that the 'exclusion' of the lower levels of soul is not to be taken as meaning more than that the distinctive nature of man does not lie in them taken by themselves. It does not mean that the lower levels are worthless or that they are not essential to the functioning of the higher. Sense-perception is possible only in a living body. Aristotle speaks of the grades of soul as a series in which each term contains 'potentially' its predecessor. Thus the nutritive soul is contained in the perceptual soul, as the triangle in the quadrilateral.[2] On the same principle the functioning of the intellect, with the difficult and doubtful exception of the divine element in man's nature, is based on sense-perception. Thus Aristotle's rejection here of the nutritive soul, and his assertion in I. 13 that it 'has by its nature no share in human excellence' (1102 b11–12), are not to be taken as meaning that the satisfaction of bodily desires has no place in the best lives. The ethical virtue of moderation (sōphrosunē) is concerned with desires which have their source in the nutritive soul, and Aristotle's doctrine of ethical virtue is incompatible with the doctrine of asceticism, that such pleasures should be reduced to a minimum.

When Aristotle speaks here of the specifically human life as 'practical' (1098 a3), the word is not to be understood as excluding the exercise of the intellect in the theoretical sciences.[3] As we have noted, the 'best and most complete virtue' is naturally taken as a reference to theoretical wisdom (sophia) (1098 a17–18; cf. 8, 1099 a29–31). Aristotle's language in this chapter straddles, as we have seen, between the concept of the best life generally as one lived according to a reasonable plan and the more determinate idea of concentration on a paramount end. The principle from which he argues points to the wider interpretation. What is common and peculiar (idion) to men is rationality in a general sense, not theoretical insight, which is one specialized way of

---

[1] *Aristotle*, ch. 5.   [2] *De Anima B* 3, 414 b29–32.
[3] Cf. *Politics*, VII. 3, 1325 b16–23.

being rational. A man differs from other animals not primarily in being a natural metaphysician, or a natural artist, but rather in being capable of planning his own life.

Aristotle believes that his account of the good for man can be corroborated by showing what are the partial truths conveyed by other accounts, whether popular or held by eminent thinkers. 'It is not probable that either of them should be entirely mistaken, but rather that they should be right in at least some one respect or even in most respects' (8, 1098 b28–9). In the chapters which follow (8–12) he tries to show how these other views confirm his own, and deals with some questions arising out of the definition of happiness (eudaimonia). He maintains that his own view is a satisfactory synthesis of the data which have impressed plain men and philosophers. I do not propose to enumerate and discuss the points which he makes. I shall note only one problem to which he refers more than once and which evidently causes him uneasiness. This arises from the fact that, in order to be happy, it is not enough for a man to be virtuous. He must also achieve a 'complete life' (1098 a18, 1100 a4), and for this he needs good fortune as well as good conduct. Aristotle has said in chapter 5 that we divine the good to be 'something proper (oikeion) to a man and not easily taken from him' (1095 b25–6). He says in chapter 9 that it should be something 'widely shared': 'for all who are not maimed for virtue can win it by study and practice' (1099 b18–20). 'But if it is better to be happy thus than by chance, it is reasonable that the facts should be so, since everything that depends on the action of nature is by nature as good as it can be' (1099 b20–2). Unfortunately the facts conflict with this optimistic fancy. Good men may prosper for a time and then come to miserable ends, like Priam (1100 a5–9). Some kinds of noble actions require money or political power as instruments (1099 a33–b2). 'The man who is very ugly in appearance or ill-born or solitary and childless is not exactly happy, and perhaps even less if he has thoroughly bad children or friends or has lost good children or friends by death' (b3–6). Such facts lead some to say that happiness is a matter of luck (b7–8). Aristotle's comments on this aspect of the human situation come uncomfortably close to the suggestion that a good man can indeed be happy on the rack, if he is a very good man on a very bad rack. Moderate misfortunes will not make too much difference; real disasters can destroy happiness (1100 b21–30; cf. 1101 a6–13). Yet even in disaster 'nobility shines through, when a man bears with resignation many great misfortunes, not through insensibility to pain but through nobility and greatness of soul' (1100 b30–3). The wise and good man 'bears all the chances of life becomingly and always makes the best of circumstances . . . as a good shoemaker makes the best possible shoes out of the hides that are given him' (1100 b35–1101 a5). It is difficult for any moralist to say more. But there is here a suggestion, not developed by Aristotle, that there are two different ways of measuring human excellence. By one measure the man who makes good use of splendid opportunities is at the summit of achievement. By another measure he may be no better, or less good, than the man who tries nobly to make the best of what will unavoidably be a bad job. The question whether there is anything in human life and conduct which cannot be put down to good fortune, and cannot be taken from a man (dusaphaireton), is one which we shall meet again in Aristotle's ethics.

III

THE NATURE OF THE INQUIRY

WE have seen that for Aristotle, because the good for man can be achieved only in political societies, ethics is 'a political inquiry' (*politikē tis*) (1. 2, 1094 b11).[1] Ross translates 'political science in one sense of the term'; but Aristotle does not seem to suggest that there are different senses of 'political science' or different kinds, as opposed to branches, of political science. Aristotle's position seems to be correctly stated by the writer of the *MM*: 'the treatment of character (*ēthē*) is, it seems, a part (*meros*) and starting-point (*archē*) of political science, but the whole is rightly called politics not ethics' (*A* 1, 1181 b25–82 a1). The expression 'ethics' (*ta ēthika*) occurs in the *Politics* and also 'ethical discourses' (*ēthikoi logoi*). It would be unprofitable to discuss how far Aristotle moved towards separating ethics from politics, or how, within politics, the province of 'ethical discourses' is demarcated. There is no sharp or fixed boundary. In the *MM* ethics is described both as part of politics and as its starting-point. It is not clear what this means, but it may be a reference to Aristotle's view, which I shall discuss, that, unless a man has been trained to have a good moral character, he will not be able to grasp what for him are the starting-points in the study of politics (1. 4, 1095 b4–8). In what follows I shall sometimes use the terms 'ethics' and 'politics' as if they were for Aristotle the names of separate but related inquiries; branches, as one might say, of 'eudaimonics'. But I shall be using 'ethics' merely as a convenient way of referring to those parts of what Aristotle calls politics (*politikē*) which deal with the subjects considered in the *EN*.

Aristotle says in the *Metaphysics* that all thinking (*dianoia*) is 'either practical or productive (*poiētikē*) or theoretical'.[2] This

---

[1] Cf. *Rhetoric A* 2, 1356 a25–7.
[2] *E* 1, 1025 b25–6; cf. *Topics* VI. 6, 145 a15.

threefold division is mentioned in *EN* VI. 2 (1139 a27–8). Aristotle speaks of production (*poiēsis*) in VI. 4, where an art (*technē*), e.g. the art of building, is defined as a 'rational state of capacity to produce' (1140 a6–10), i.e. the producer must be able to give a correct account (*logos*) of his own performance. The product (*poiēma*) is not necessarily a material thing, a house or a pair of shoes. It may be a poem. In the *Metaphysics* (*Z* 7) medicine is classed with building as an art; here the product is a qualitative state, health, of a living body (1032 b9–14). The evidence suggests that the three members of the division are not strictly co-ordinate. For in the *Metaphysics* he opposes physics, the subject-matter of which 'has the principle of its movement and rest present in itself', to practical and productive intelligence taken together as being themselves principles of change, the changes being initiated by the activity, guided by intelligence, of the agent or the craftsman.[1] It is stated in the *EN* that practical intelligence 'rules over' productive intelligence (1139 a35–b1), and in the opening chapters the subordination of productive arts to the practical science of politics is exhibited. Again in Book VI the various excellencies of the intellect are grouped under two heads: practical wisdom (*phronēsis*) and theoretical wisdom (*sophia*). Different views may be taken about the precise significance and value of Aristotle's classification, or bifurcation, of intellectual functions. These views cannot all be considered at this stage. But there is one possible misunderstanding which should be noted now.

It would be natural, at first sight, to suppose that Aristotle has in mind a distinction between the intelligence shown by a man immersed in practical affairs and the reflective intelligence of the student of moral or political science, or again between the poetic activity (*poiētikē*) of Sophocles in writing the *Oedipus* and Aristotle's theoretical study of poetry in the *Poetics*. Aristotle's use of technical terms often falls short of precision, or at least of pedantry, and he does occasionally use the word *sophia* or *philosophia* of ethical and political science (*EN* x. 9, 1181 b15). Again in the *Politics* he speaks of 'political theory' (VII. 2, 1324 a20).

[1] 1025 b18–25; cf. Θ 2, 1046 b2–4.

But these expressions must not mislead us into thinking that Aristotle thought of the *Ethics* and the *Politics*, or indeed the *Poetics*, as exercises of the 'theoretical' intellect. This view about the *Ethics* was held by some scholars in the nineteenth century.[1] But it is shown to be wrong by Aristotle's insistence in the early chapters of the *EN* on the practical nature of his inquiry, and is explicitly contradicted by a passage in *EN* VI. 8: 'political science and practical wisdom (*phronēsis*) are the same state of mind, although not defined in the same way; as regards the city the practical wisdom which exercises authority is legislative wisdom . . .' (1141 b23 ff.). This makes it clear that for Aristotle the *Ethics* itself, being a political treatise (1094 b11), is an exercise of the practical intellect. Some moral philosophers would say that their business was the analysis of moral concepts and that their conclusions could not point, or not directly, to any practical morals. This is not Aristotle's view of what he was doing. His inquiry is directed to finding out how happiness can be achieved. Analogously the *Poetics* is a manual on playwriting. It is not, of course, to be assumed that what Aristotle, or any other thinker, says he is doing is necessarily an accurate or adequate account of what he achieves.

'The end is not knowledge but action' (I. 3, 1095 a5–6). 'We are inquiring not in order to know what virtue is, but in order to become good, since otherwise our inquiry would have been of no use' (II. 2, 1103 b27–9).[2] It is natural to find these statements paradoxical and to think that they conflict in spirit with the opening assertion of the *Metaphysics* that 'all men by nature desire to know' (980 a21). Joachim in particular gives a hostile account of the doctrine that ethics is practical, and takes the doctrine to imply that thought about human conduct and character, because it is 'subordinate to practice', is 'necessarily curtailed and perverted', can aim only at 'such a rough and distorted version of the truth as is required for action' (p. 15). It is difficult to see anything in what Aristotle says which justifies the words 'perverted' and 'distorted'. Joachim implies that Aristotle's theory of ethics

---

[1] See T. Ando, *Aristotle's Theory of Practical Cognition* (1958), pp. 210 ff.

[2] Cf. x. 9, 1179 a35–b2.

required him to sacrifice truth to utility, although admittedly his investigation in the *Ethics* and *Politics* was in fact 'free and unperverted' (p. 16). But this is not quite fair to Aristotle. His doctrine is about the logical structure of an inquiry directed to finding out how such a creature as man in such a world as this can best organize his life. He is not talking about motives which lead to the curtailing of curiosity; for he is not talking about motives but about methods. Ethics is practical in the sense that, starting from concepts of ends to be achieved, it concludes, or should conclude, with the formulation of rules for achieving ends, e.g. with an account of the ideal political constitution.[1] To say this is not to deny that the inquiry can be of theoretical interest to the student and gratify his desire for knowledge and clear thinking. There are passages in the *Politics* which admit a theoretical interest in practical topics (III. 8, 1279 b12–15). 'To aim at utility everywhere is utterly unbecoming to high-minded and liberal spirits' (VIII. 3, 1338 b2–4). But I do not wish to overstate the defence of Aristotle against the suggestion that his doctrine about the nature of ethics is too narrowly pragmatic. He does not distinguish clearly, when he says that the end is action, between the nature of the inquiry (methodology) and our motives for pursuing it (psychology). Again he seems over-anxious to warn the student of politics against excursions into psychology unless they are strictly pertinent to the practical aim of political science (*EN* I. 13, 1102 e23–6).

What methods and procedures are proper in a science depends on its purpose, on what are the questions to which answers are sought, but depends also on the nature of its subject-matter. Aristotle speaks of the subject-matter of ethics as being variable (I. 3, 1094 b14 ff.), as 'capable of being otherwise' (VI. 1, 1139 a6–8), and says that a man who is educated (*pepaideumenos*) will not expect mathematical precision (*akribeia*) in a science which has a concrete subject-matter (1094 b23–95 a1).[2] An 'educated' man in this context means one with sufficient training in logic ('analytics') to know what propositions need to be proved, and

[1] Cf. *EN* x. 9, 1181 b20–3.
[2] Cf. *Metaphysics* 995 a14–16; *EN* vi. 8, 1142 a18–19.

what sort of proof they need or admit.[1] For example, it would show lack of education (*apaideusia*) to demand a proof of a logical axiom such as the principle of contradiction.[2] General education or culture in this sense is to be distinguished from the specialized culture which enables an amateur to form a judgement on the soundness of work in a particular science such as medicine.[3]

How are we to understand Aristotle's doctrine that in ethics, because the subject-matter is variable, complete precision is not to be expected? In I. 3 he offers the following explanation. 'Now fine and just actions, which political science investigates, admit of much variety and fluctuation of opinion, so that they may be thought to exist only by convention (*nomos*), and not by nature (*phusis*). And goods also give rise to a similar fluctuation because they bring harm to many; for before now men have been undone by reason of their wealth, and others by reason of their courage' (1094 b14–19). There appear to be two distinct points here. The first is that there are conflicts of opinion about what is right and good. Aristotle does not, of course, himself admit that rules of right are only arbitrary conventions, as is clear in Book v (7, 1134 b18–35 a5). He would presumably hold that those who have had a good moral training, which is a requirement for students of politics (1095 b4–6), agree broadly in their judgements on conduct. His second point is that, because the subject-matter is complex and empirical, generalizations in ethics are not true without exceptions, but only roughly and generally (1094 b19–22; 1142 a18–19). Thus, as regards things which are good because their consequences are good, there will be circumstances in which the consequences are not good. There are occasions on which it is neither expedient nor right to tell the truth. It is reasonable to think that, in holding this view, Aristotle is right as against those philosophers who have believed that moral rules can be demonstrated as in geometry, a company which includes Locke[4] as well as Spinoza. But we might expect Aristotle to say also that, even

---

[1] See Burnet's Introduction, pp. xxxi–xxxiv.
[2] *Metaphysics* Γ 4, 1006 a5–7; cf. *EE A* 6, 1217 a7–10.
[3] *De Partibus Animalium* I. 1, 639 a1.
[4] *Essay on the Human Understanding*, IV. 3, § 18.

if we cannot formulate a rule which has no exceptions, we can reduce the number of the exceptions if we restrict the claims of the rule by incorporating exceptions in its formulation: tell the truth except when to do so would lead to loss of life or cause acute and unnecessary distress, etc. Aristotle does indeed make substantially this point in two later passages: II. 7, 1107 a29–32 and X. 9, 1180 b7–13. In the second of these passages he remarks that in medicine a greater degree of scientific precision (*akribeia*) is possible in the treatment of an individual patient than in the formulation of rules which can be only roughly applicable to classes of patients.

The argument we have considered is perhaps sufficient to justify Aristotle's doctrine that practical rules always admit of exceptions; but it is not his only reason for holding this. As J. A. Smith puts it in his Introduction to the Everyman translation, exceptions may 'arise not from the mere complexity of the facts, but from the liability of the facts to a certain unpredictable variation' (p. xi). And Ross: 'In human actions at all events there is actual contingency.'[1] In deciding whether to act on some rule or not it may be relevant to consider how what is done would affect what other human agents would do. If human actions are the effects of causes, uncertainty about these consequences could be eliminated in principle even if not in practice. But, if human actions or some of them are uncaused, the uncertainty cannot be eliminated even in principle. Aristotle discusses elaborately in the *De Interpretatione* (ch. 9) the contingency of future events which depend on human decisions. While scholars are not agreed on what is the correct analysis of his argument in this much discussed chapter, it is clear that his problem arises because he thinks of human decisions as uncaused. Moreover there is an explicit statement in the *Metaphysics* of the doctrine that a human action, e.g. eating something pungent, is the uncaused cause of a chain of effects (*E* 3, 1027 a29–b14): 'the process goes back to a certain starting-point, but this no longer points to something further; this then will be the starting-point for the fortuitous, and will have nothing else as cause of its coming to be' (b11–14).[2] We shall

---

[1] *Aristotle*, p. 188.   [2] Cf. *K* 8, 1065 a6–21.

find that the question whether human actions are necessitated is raised, but only in a tentative form and not answered, when Aristotle discusses choice (*prohairesis*) in *EN* III. 1–5.

Aristotle thinks that the student of ethics, or of politics generally, can usefully be told at the outset certain facts about the general nature of the inquiry. He should know that its purpose is practical and that its subject matter is variable. I have discussed the meaning of these statements. We must now consider the important remarks in the last section of *EN* I. 4 on what he calls principles or starting points (*archai*) (1095 a30–b13). It is important, he says, not to overlook the distinction between arguments on their way from principles and arguments on their way to principles. Plato's practice of asking in which of these two directions an argument was moving was salutary. Starts must be made from what is known, but to say this is ambiguous: what comes first in our order of knowledge may not be what comes first in an absolute sense (*haplōs*). The Greek here is very concise and allusive, but the meaning is clear in the light of other passages in Aristotle.

In the *Posterior Analytics* he says that for us, but not in the natural order of knowledge, particulars come before universals (I. 2, 71 b33–72 a5). An example of this would be the fact that, in learning to understand '2+2 = 4', a child would start from counting fingers or tables. Burnet quotes an example from the *Topics* (VI. 4). The order, point line plane solid, is the absolute or natural order of knowledge, and a mathematician would derive each term from its predecessor, just as he would treat the unit as 'the *prius* (*proteron*) and starting-point (*archē*) of numbers'. But for us, on the other hand, the solid comes first because it 'falls under perception most of all' (141 b3–14). What is the application of this distinction for a student starting a course on ethics?

He starts from what he knows as a result of having been 'brought up in good habits' (1095 b4–6): he must understand and accept the moral rules of his political society if he belongs to the right sort of political society. For the fact (*to hoti*) is the starting-point, and if this is sufficiently plain to him, he will not at the start need the reason (*to dihoti*) as well' (b6–7). I take the 'fact' here to be a particular moral rule or perhaps the definition of a particular moral virtue.[1] Burnet seems to take it as 'the fact that the definition of Happiness is whatever we may find it to be'. But the definition of Happiness is the starting-point of ethics in the absolute and not in the subjective sense. 'We must start from what we know.' A student who understands the definition of happiness, so far as he really understands it, is learning what Aristotle calls 'the reason' and not merely a 'fact'. For in Aristotle's view a rule of conduct is justified and explained only when it is seen to be required for the achievement of the final good. But it takes more than a good moral training to prepare the mind for Aristotle's definition of happiness.

In the account I have given of what Aristotle says here about 'starting-points' I have tried to bring out clearly not only what he says but what he does not say. I think that commentators have run into difficulties by supposing that Aristotle's remarks have a wider scope than they in fact have. The trouble has begun already when the passage is described, as it is by Grant, as being a digression on 'the method of Ethics'. Aristotle is assumed to be asking, and even answering, the question whether ethics is a science in which the reasoning is 'from' or 'to' first principles. But, as we have seen, there is nothing in the text which implies that arguments in each of these directions will not have their appropriate places in a treatise, or course of lectures, on ethics. Clearly Aristotle gave a place in his lectures to arguments 'to principles'. At least some of his arguments in approaching the definition of happiness can be so classed. But the suggestion that ethics as a whole, the science of politics, is a discipline which proceeds towards and not from principles is one which, so far as I can see, would to Aristotle seem to be not so much false as unintelligible. Politics, the supreme practical science, has its own 'proper principles' (*oikeiai archai*) which are basic in an objective, and not merely relative, sense. In the nature of the case a systematic treatise on the subject would reason from these principles. This is not to say that the reasoning would have the form of strict demonstration. It would not. But it would start from the concept of a good and proceed to the detailed description of its elements

[1] Cf. VI. 12, 1144 a34–6.

and the elaboration of means for its attainment. It is, of course, a further question how far Aristotle's ethical discourses, as they have come to us, have the form of a systematic treatise. I shall have something to say about this when I discuss shortly Burnet's paradox that the *Ethics*, as we have it, is 'dialectical throughout' (p. v).

I hope that what I have said about this passage on method in ethics (not the Method of Ethics) will be accepted by most readers as being uncontroversial and even obvious. But, in order to show that there is an issue, I must briefly justify the suggestion I have made above that what is said by some of the commentators, and not only by Burnet, shows misunderstanding. Here, then, first is a quotation from what the latest commentators, Gauthier and Jolif, have to say: 'il s'agit donc pour lui de savoir si la méthode de la morale doit être la démonstration ou l'induction, et le sens de sa réponse ne fait aucun doute: c'est l'induction' (ii. 19). Stewart finds in the passage an assertion by Aristotle that 'moral science must be prosecuted on the inductive method'.[1] Ross, with reference to this passage, writes: 'Ethics reasons not from but to first principles; it starts not with what is intelligible in itself but with what is familiar to us, i.e. with the bare facts, and works back from them to the underlying reasons.'[2] Aristotle does indeed say that the student must start in this way, working *towards* first principles. But he does not deny that politics, as a special science, derives consequences *from* its own first principles. It should be clear that, if I have given a correct account of the passage, the scholars whom I have quoted have attributed to Aristotle an answer which he could not have given to a question which he did not ask.

I have discussed the passage about principles (*archai*) in I. 4 in detail because it is important for the understanding, or removal of misunderstanding, of Aristotle's doctrine of method in ethics. There are other passages in the *EN* about first principles in scientific inquiries, theoretical or practical, but on these there is no need for detailed comment at least in this context. In VI. 6 there is a statement of the doctrine that the first principles of the demon-

---

[1] *Notes on the NE of Aristotle* (1892), i. 48.   [2] *Aristotle*, p. 189.

strative sciences are apprehended by intuitive reason (*nous*). The different kinds of principles, axioms, hypotheses, and definitions, are distinguished in the *Posterior Analytics*.[1] In *EN* I. 7 Aristotle speaks again of the apprehension of first principles, and says that we come to understand them 'some by induction (*epagōgē*), some by perception (*aisthēsis*), some by a certain habituation (*ethismos*), and others too in other ways' (1098 b3-4). In Aristotle's view a principle is seen by reason to be true and necessary when it is clearly and accurately formulated. But it has first to be disengaged by abstraction from the world of concrete objects known to sense-perception. Hence various preliminary processes, and faculties other than reason, are involved in the approach to first principles. An important passage for Aristotle's general view of the way in which the mind grows to a knowledge of universal propositions is in the *Posterior Analytics* II. 19.[2] In ethical matters the faculty of insight and understanding can develop only in those who have learned how to conduct themselves and have acquired a character formed by habituation (*ethismos*). The various faculties and processes mentioned by Aristotle as connected with the knowledge of principles are not mutually exclusive. Thus the use of 'induction' (*epagōgē*) involves the exercise of perception. For induction is a process in which someone is 'induced' to direct his attention on some particular object, or set of objects, in the hope that he will come to understand the general principle of which they are examples.[3] It need hardly be said that induction in this sense is related only very distantly to the use of 'induction' in modern logic to refer to the procedures, based on observation and experiment, of the natural sciences.

We must now look more closely at the question what sort of arguments are appropriate, according to Aristotle, when the movement of thought on ethical subjects is 'towards first principles'. In his approach to the definition of happiness in Book I, and also when he discusses incontinence (*akrasia*) in Book VII and in other places, for example, in the discussion of pleasure, Aristotle

---

[1] See Ross, *Aristotle*, pp. 42 ff.
[2] See ibid., pp. 54-5; cf. *Metaphysics* A 1.
[3] But see Ross's edition of *Prior and Posterior Analytics* pp. 481-5; cf. pp. 47-51.

makes considerable use of procedures which are 'dialectical' in the sense that they start, not from premisses formulated and defended by himself, but from received opinions (*endoxa*). *Endoxa* are of two main kinds: opinions held by all or most men, by the plain man as we might say, and opinions held by some or most of the wise, by philosophers.[1] According to Aristotle an opinion backed by either of these kinds of authority is never sheer error and indeed is likely to be 'right in at least some one respect or even in most respects' (*EN* I. 8, 1098 b27–9; cf. 4, 1095 a28–30). Such opinions, as Aristotle puts it elsewhere, are 'true but not clear': they may be expressed in a confused way, and so need correction or qualification, but there is always *something* in them.[2] Hence the methodical examination (*exetasmos*) of received opinions is likely to be profitable. But it should be noted that Aristotle's profession of respect for the opinions of 'the many' is somewhat misleading. For he believes that the mass of mankind have no conception of the best kind of life and make pleasure their paramount aim (*EN* I. 5, 1095 b16; b19–22).

The examination of opinions is not casual but systematic, and makes use of general logical notions or 'commonplaces' (*topoi*). These tools of dialectic suggest ways in which an opinion can be attacked, or qualified so as to make it acceptable, or again how the impasse (*aporia*) produced by the conflict of two opinions might be resolved. Aristotle gives an account of dialectical discussion in a separate work, the *Topics*, and some of the same ground is covered in the *Rhetoric*. Burnet's Introduction gives a short account of the method (pp. xl–xliii). An important 'topic' is the distinction between essential and accidental: thus a thing said to be good or bad, with the implication that it is good or bad essentially, may be so only *per accidens* or in certain circumstances. Another is that of 'opposition' (*enantion*) which is used by Eudoxus to show that pleasure, being the opposite of pain which is bad, must be good (*EN* X. 2, 1172 b18–20).[3] In the dialectical discussions of the end for man and of incontinence Aristotle starts from an enumeration of received opinions (*endoxa*). A

---

[1] *Topics A* 1, 100 b21–3.   [2] Cf. *EE A* 6, 1216 b28–35.
[3] Cf. *Topics B* 2, 117 b3–9.

passage in the *EN* gives a compact summary of the procedure: 'we must, as in other cases, set out the data and, having formulated the difficulties, go on to prove if possible all the received opinions —or, failing this, most of them and the most authoritative; for if we both refute the objections and leave the received opinions undisturbed, we shall have proved the case sufficiently' (VII. 1, 1145 b2–7).

As our account has already made clear, Aristotle associates with his dialectical method a considerable variety of technical, or semi-technical, terms. These terms spring from at least two distinct metaphors. The mind, confronted by a conflict between opinions, or between an opinion and observed facts, is said to be blocked, as when traffic streams meet, and can find no way out (*aporia*). It then has to 'shift its ground' (*metabainein*).[1] Again the mind is said to be 'bound' and seeks release (*lusis*) from its chains (VII. 2, 1146 a24–7). These metaphors are freely combined, as in the passage just mentioned and in Aristotle's expression for the solution of an impasse, *lusis tēs aporias* (1146 b6–8).

Dialectical arguments, then, have, in Aristotle's view, an important and useful part to play in ethical discussions. But there is no suggestion in the text of the *Ethics* that dialectic is the only kind of treatment which is available to him or the only kind which he proposes to use. For the most part Aristotle argues from premisses which state his own views or views which he has made his own. Burnet, who held that the *EN* is 'dialectical throughout' (p. v), exaggerates the extent to which Aristotle starts from the opinions of others, especially Plato and the Academy. Thus he represents the doctrine of the categories, used by Aristotle in his criticism of Plato (I. 6), as 'simply part of his heritage from the Academy'.[2] Greenwood shows clearly and in detail that, in many passages where Burnet represents Aristotle as using borrowed premisses, the views expressed are in fact his own.[3] Moreover, even in those sections of the *Ethics* in which the treatment is most overtly dialectical, it is not the case that the treatment is 'dialectical throughout'. The definition of happiness in I. 7 is based on the

---

[1] *EN* I. 7, 1097 a24 and Burnet's note; cf. *EE A* 6, 1216 b30.
[2] Introduction, p. l.   [3] *EN* VI, pp. 138 ff.

doctrine that man has a function (*ergon*) and on Aristotle's account, similar to that of the *De Anima*, of the different levels of
'soul'. Of these the second is certainly Aristotle's; and I know of no
adequate reason for suggesting that he did not himself assert that
man has a function.[1] Again Aristotle himself represents his discussion of incontinence (*akrasia*) as only in part dialectical. For at
a crucial point he says that we may 'also view' the matter 'with
reference to the facts of human nature', *phusikōs* (VII. 3, 1147
a24–5). As Burnet points out, the 'physical' (*phusikōs*) treatment of
a question is regularly opposed to a dialectical (*logikōs*) treatment.
Dialectical examinations of a question use principles and distinctions which have applications in more than one science, while a
physical explanation is in terms of the principles proper to the
special science concerned. In the treatment of *akrasia* the line
between dialectical and physical solutions is perhaps not very
clear or definite. But this does not affect the point I am making;
that there is an explicit transition from the dialectical examination
of the topic to a solution based, as Joachim puts it, 'on grounds
appropriate to the phenomena to be explained'.[2]

I have referred to Burnet's view that the *Ethics* is 'dialectical
throughout' (p. v), that it 'is, and from the nature of the case
must be, a dialectical and not a demonstrative work' (p. xvii).
We have seen that this sweeping assertion is not supported by
what we find when we look at Aristotle's arguments in the *EN*.
But Burnet's interpretation must be rejected for a further reason,
similar to the reason we have already given for denying that, in
Aristotle's view, the movement of thought in ethics is always
'towards first principles'. Ethics is a special science and as such
has its own 'proper principles', and to say that it is necessarily and
wholly dialectical would be to deny it the status of a special
science. Burnet quotes the passage in the *Topics* (I. 2) which
enumerates the uses of dialectic, and he implies that the passage
supports and explains his thesis. In fact it has implications which
are inconsistent with his thesis, and these implications are even

---

[1] Greenwood, p. 134.
[2] Commentary, p. 266; cf. *Physics* 204 b4 and 10; *De Generatione et Corruptione*
316 a10; *Topics* 105 b21; *Posterior Analytics* 84 a7–9.

more explicit in a passage in the *Rhetoric* (I. 2) which he does not quote.

Aristotle in the *Topics* distinguishes three uses of dialectic: as a kind of mental training or gymnastics; as enabling us to argue with people whom we meet from their own premisses; and thirdly as having a place in the study of the sciences. We need consider only the third use, which Aristotle describes as follows.

It is useful because the ability to raise difficulties on both sides of a subject will make us detect more easily the truth and error about the several points that arise. It has a further use in relation to the bases of the principles used in the several sciences. For it is impossible to discuss them at all from the principles proper to the particular science (*oikeiai archai*), seeing that the principles are prior to everything else: it is through the opinions generally held (*endoxa*) on the particular points that these have to be discussed, and this task belongs properly, or most appropriately, to dialectic: for dialectic is a process of criticism which leads to the principles of all systematic inquiries (*methodoi*). (101 a34–b4.)

We learn from this passage that every special science, or independent 'method', has its own proper first principles; and that, in the case of any science, the dialectical examination of *endoxa* may be useful in the process of arriving at a formulation of first principles. It is implied that, when this process has been completed, a systematic exposition of the science, starting from its first principles, can begin. It is true that in this passage ethics, or politics, is not mentioned as an example of a special science. But this gap, if it needs filling, is filled in the *Rhetoric*.

Here Aristotle explains, as in the *Topics*, that dialectical and rhetorical arguments use 'commonplaces' (*topoi*) which are applicable to different subject-matters, and that such 'topics' are to be distinguished from those which cannot be transferred from one subject to another. I quote the sentences which follow.

There are, for example, propositions about physics which can furnish neither enthymemes [rhetorical syllogisms] nor syllogisms about ethics, and there are propositions concerned with ethics which will be useless for furnishing conclusions about physics; and the same holds good in all cases. The first kind of topics will not make a man wise about any particular class of things, because they do not deal with any particular subject-matter, but as to the specific topics, the happier a man is in his choice of premisses [*protaseis*], the more he will unconsciously produce a science quite different from dialectic and rhetoric. For if once he hits upon first principles, it will no longer be dialectic or rhetoric, but that science whose principles he has arrived at (I. 2, 1358 a17–26).

This passage makes it clear that, in Aristotle's theory of the matter, an inquiry which starts by being dialectical may be expected, at the stage when principles have been found, to cease to be dialectical and become scientific. This is, indeed, a statement of methodological principle which might, or might not, accord with what is contained in the works of Aristotle as they have come down to us. It might have been the case, though it would have been surprising, that in these works, or in some of them, the treatment was wholly or mainly dialectical. But I have already adduced evidence that what we actually find in the *EN* is not a treatment of the subject which is 'dialectical throughout'.

It should be noted that Burnet himself, in the paragraph (§ 26) of his Introduction which immediately follows his account of the dialectical method and quotation from the *Topics*, makes a remark which is difficult to reconcile with his view that the *Ethics* is 'dialectical throughout'. For he states that, when the definition of the human good has been reached by dialectic, 'the procedure becomes quite different'. 'Our analysis of it, though it is deliberative and not demonstrative, will proceed through middle terms and can only be expressed adequately in the form of a series of practical syllogisms' (p. xliii). We can ignore in this context Burnet's assertion that deliberation for Aristotle is properly expressed in 'a series of practical syllogisms'. Burnet is here implying that political thought as such is an 'analytic' regress from end to means, and that such deliberation could or should be expressed as a sorites or series of syllogisms. To give reasons for rejecting these implications, or for accepting them only with very large reservations, would be to anticipate the discussion of later books, in particular the account of practical wisdom (*phronēsis*) in Book VI. What alone I am here concerned to point out is that

Burnet, while insisting that Aristotle proposes a procedure 'quite different' from that used in his (at least partly) dialectical approach to the definition of happiness, nevertheless refrains from raising the question whether this 'quite different' procedure is itself dialectical. If, as is indeed the case, it is not dialectical, Burnet cannot justify his contention that the treatise is 'dialectical throughout'.

It is difficult to understand why Burnet does not face this question. But there is a clue to a possible explanation in an earlier passage of the Introduction (§ 5) in which he states in an extreme form the view that the *Ethics* 'must be a dialectical and not a demonstrative work'. He maintains that Aristotle's view of the appropriate method was 'to give as many solutions of the difficulties which arise as can be given, without any regard to the real philosophical validity of these solutions'. Aristotle is not committed to any of the solutions given. 'Nor can we even assume that the true solution is necessarily given at all. It often is given; but it was contrary to Aristotle's own principles to base the exposition of Politics on his metaphysical system' (p. xvii). Burnet is here assuming that, if the *Ethics* were a 'demonstrative work', it would have to be based on Aristotle's metaphysics, and assuming further that, if it is not a demonstrative work, it must be a dialectical work. Similarly he supposed, when he wrote the later passage (p. xliii), that the fact that the deliberative procedure is not 'demonstrative' leaves it within the field of dialectic. But Burnet's assumptions in the earlier passage cannot be defended. That Aristotle does not base his ethics on his metaphysics has no tendency to show that the *Ethics* is a dialectical work in reading which we should not expect to find doctrines defended as true. For, on Aristotle's principles, no special science is 'based' on metaphysics in any sense which would imply that it had not its own proper and ultimate first principles. This is indeed perhaps the main issue on which Aristotle firmly dissents from Plato in *EN* I. 6. In Aristotle's view a special science would not be scientific unless it were both non-dialectical and independent of metaphysics. Both these attributes are implied by the claim that a special science has its own proper principles. I should add that, in saying this, I have no intention of broaching, at this point in the discussion of Aristotle's views, the question what connections there are between his ethical and his metaphysical doctrines. There are connections.

I have tried to make clear the sense of 'dialectical' in which Burnet maintains that the *Ethics* is dialectical throughout, and to show that in this sense the *Ethics* is not dialectical throughout. The most detailed criticism known to me of Burnet on this question is the essay by Greenwood on dialectic method.[1] As we have seen, Greenwood rejects, as regards Book VI, Burnet's view that Aristotle is arguing from borrowed premisses which he does not himself accept. On Greenwood's view generally I have only two comments. First, I do not think that he makes clear the difficulty of reconciling Burnet's view with the claim of ethics or politics to be a systematic inquiry with the status of a special science. Secondly, he appears to concede a partial validity to Burnet's thesis when he suggests that there is a weaker sense of 'dialectical' in which any reasoning which does not proceed from strictly necessary premisses to strictly necessary conclusions, as in mathematics and perhaps in what Aristotle calls 'first philosophy', is dialectical. He implies that the fact that generalizations in ethics are 'not truly universal' is a reason for admitting that, in this weaker sense, ethics is for Aristotle dialectical.[2] Similarly Joachim says that, outside the sphere of necessity, 'dialectic is the only possible method not only for bringing home the first principles to the pupil, but also for deducing the derivative truths from first principles'.[3] Joachim gives no supporting reason or evidence for the second part of this assertion. Nor does Greenwood offer evidence for the suggestion that, in Aristotle's view, the fact that reasoning in a science leads to conclusions not strictly necessary is sufficient ground for saying that the reasoning is dialectical. The suggestion is paradoxical since, as Joachim points out, the subject-matter of physics also is to a large extent indeterminate.[4] But I do not know of any sense of 'dialectical' such that it follows from this that arguments in these parts of physics are dialectical. We have

---

[1] *EN* VI, pp. 127–44.   [2] *EN* VI, p. 133; cf. p. 131, etc.
[3] Commentary, p. 30.
[4] Commentary, p. 15; cf. *Prior Analytics A* 13, 32 b4; *Metaphysics K* 8, 1065 a 4

seen that, when Aristotle in the *Topics* and the *Rhetoric* defines the scope of dialectic, he makes it clear that, while dialectic is often useful to the student of a special science in the approach to first principles through the examination of received opinions, no special science could be, in this sense, dialectical throughout. He does not suggest that there is some other sense of 'dialectical' in which a special science might be dialectical throughout. If, as is implied by Greenwood and by Joachim, there is such a wider and weaker sense of 'dialectical', the only comment needed is that to assert that, in this wider sense, ethics is dialectical is merely to restate the doctrine, which I have already discussed, that the subject-matter of ethics is variable or contingent.

IV

THE PLATONIC IDEA OF THE GOOD

THE doctrine that there is a good which is universal and self-subsistent and transcendent is mentioned first in chapter 4 of Book I. I quote the opening sentences of the chapter in Ross's translation:

Let us resume our inquiry and state, in view of the fact that all knowledge and every pursuit aims at some good, what it is that we say political science aims at and what is the highest of all goods achievable by action. Verbally there is very general agreement; for both the general run of men and people of superior refinement say that it is happiness, and identify living well and doing well with being happy; but with regard to what happiness is they differ, and the many do not give the same account as the wise. For the former think it is some plain and obvious thing, like pleasure, wealth, or honour; they differ, however, from one another—and often even the same man identifies it with different things, with health when he is ill, with wealth when he is poor; but, conscious of their ignorance, they admire those who proclaim some great ideal that is above their comprehension. Now some thought that apart from those many goods there is another which is self-subsistent (*kath' hauto*) and causes the goodness of all these as well. (1095 a14–28.)

Aristotle is here giving a list of answers to a practical question; what is the highest good achievable by (or in) action, or alternatively, in what does happiness consist. Some of the answers suggest ways of living or interests which can dominate a life and determine its pattern; the life of a pleasure-seeker or the life of a man with political ambitions. We are given another list, explicitly in terms of ways of life, at the beginning of the following chapter (5). 'To judge from the lives that men lead, most men, and men of the most vulgar type, seem (not without some ground) to identify the good, or happiness, with pleasure; which is the reason why they love the life of enjoyment. For there are, we may say, three prominent types of life—that just mentioned, the political, and thirdly the contemplative life' (1095 b14-19).

How does the transcendent self-subsistent good, the good which makes other goods good, come into this list of ways of life all claiming to be the best and the happiest? The doctrine does not tell us how to be happy but rather, perhaps, how to find out how to be happy. This claim, made by those who hold the doctrine, is mentioned in chapter 6. 'For having this as a sort of pattern (*paradeigma*) we shall know better the goods that are good for us, and if we know them shall attain them' (1097 a1-3). Why then does Aristotle imply in chapter 4 that the doctrine is itself an attempted answer to the question in what happiness consists? Perhaps he would expect his hearers to know, or assume, that the Platonists who have held this doctrine are among the advocates of the *theoretic* life. The guardian in Plato's republic, if he sought only his own personal happiness, would make it his first object to rise, by dialectic, to the contemplation of the Form of the Good. To run the state, descending into the Cave, involves the self-sacrifice of the individual for the good of the community. Aristotle would himself allow, since he holds the theorist to be supremely happy, that, if *per impossible* there were a kind of knowledge which answered to the description of the Platonists, such knowledge would be the greatest of all goods. But in the *Ethics* Aristotle simply refers to the doctrine of the transcendent good as one of the views to be considered in connection with the question what is the highest of all goods achievable by action (1095 a16-17). He does not explain how acceptance of the doctrine determines an answer to the question.

The doctrine, formulated as we have seen in chapter 4, is discussed elaborately in chapter 6. Aristotle professes reluctance to attack it because 'the Forms were brought in by our friends'; but a philosopher must prefer truth to friendship even if he has to destroy the tenets of his own school (1096 a11-17). Plato is not mentioned here. But the theory of Forms is ascribed to Plato in the *Metaphysics* (987 a29 ff.). Some of the arguments used in the chapter are used elsewhere in contexts where Plato is named or is clearly intended. The *Republic* teaches that the Form of the Good has a unique status. Stewart thinks that the arguments of the chapter are not relevant ('entirely beside the mark') to the doctrine of the *Republic*, and draws the unacceptable conclusion that Aristotle is attacking 'not Plato's theory but the formalism of the Platonic school' (i. 74). In so far as the arguments of the chapter are aimed at the theory of Forms generally Aristotle would certainly have held that they were damaging to ·the *Republic* as well as other dialogues. It is true that Aristotle does not in the chapter refer to the peculiar doctrines of the *Republic* about the Idea of the Good. It is perhaps unlikely, therefore, that he had the *Republic* specially in mind. But it would be surprising if the *Republic* were Aristotle's only source for this celebrated doctrine of Plato, mentioned in comedies as a paradigm of philosophic abstruseness. According to Aristoxenus,[1] Plato gave a lecture on the subject which was attended by Aristotle, who reported that the audience found the lecture difficult and mathematical, not the revelation which they had expected of the secret of happiness. There is a tradition that Aristotle, and other pupils of Plato, 'published their notes or transcripts of the lecture'.[2] But the assumption that, in this chapter, Aristotle aims his criticism at Plato, and not only at Platonists, does not need to be supported by evidence that Plato was famous for a doctrine about the Good. For the Good is discussed here as a Form, and Aristotle represents Plato as the author of the theory of Forms.

The Good under criticism is a Form. When first mentioned in chapter 4 it is said to be *kath' hauto*, translated 'self-subsistent'. In chapter 6 what is self-subsistent, or exists *per se* (*kath' hauto*) is identified with the category of substance (*ousia*). The expression 'substantial form' can be made to convey the same idea. These phrases are not illuminating. What they mean is that Plato, at least according to Aristotle, asserts, or at least implies, that a Form is a substance in the sense in which a lump of gold, or a horse, or a physical atom is a substance; a subject of predicates which endures and is liable to change—except that a Form is not liable to change.

---

[1] *Harmonics* 30–1 (ed. H. S. Macran).
[2] Cherniss, *The Riddle of the Early Academy* (1945), p. 12 and notes.

This is the third of the senses of *kath' hauto* which Aristotle distinguishes in the *Posterior Analytics* (I. 4, 73 b5–10). In chapter 6 it is implied that Man and Good are Forms which have predicates, and that the Form Man can be said, according to the theory, to be human and the Form Good good. 'And one might ask the question, what in the world they *mean* by "a thing itself", if (as is the case) in "man himself" and in a particular man the account of man is one and the same. For in so far as they are man, they will in no respect differ; and if this is so neither will "good itself" and particular goods, in so far as they are good. But again it will not be good any the more for being eternal (*aïdion*), since that which lasts long (*poluchronion*) is no whiter than that which perishes in a day' (1096 a34–b5). It is clear that, as Plato himself noted in the *Parmenides* (132 a1–b2, 132 d5–133 a7), the theory so understood leads, in so far as the Form is posited to explain predication, to a vicious infinite regress: a man and 'man himself' will be related to 'man himself himself' and so on. The account of the doctrine in the *Eudemian Ethics* similarly implies that the Good is a good thing. The Good itself is 'first of the goods' (I. 8, 1217 b4). The Form of the good is also said to be 'separate', like other forms, from the things which participate in it (1217 b14–15). In the *Metaphysics* also Aristotle finds fault with the Platonic theory for making the Form both a universal predicate and an individual substance: 'no universal is a substance'.[1]

Thus the chapter (I. 6) repeats a familiar criticism of the theory of Forms, that it makes the universal, or common predicate, a superior or perfect particular. But the more interesting sections of the chapter deal with a different question, the question what sort of predicate 'good' is. Does it refer to a characteristic which is identical in all the things that are good? Several of the rather vague phrases used by Aristotle when he refers to the doctrine under fire contain the word 'common'. The opening words of the chapter speak of 'the universal good' (1096 a11). Later we have other phrases: 'a common idea (*koinē ideä*) set over all these goods' (1096 a23); 'something universally present in all cases (*koinon ti katholou*) and single' (1096 a28); 'called good by

[1] Z 16, 1041 a3; cf. Z 16, 1040 b32–4, *Topics* 179 a9, *EE* 1218 a10–15.

reference to a single idea' (*kath' hen eidos*) (1096 b10, b15–16); 'some common element answering to one idea' (1096 b25–6). In one passage he comes near to implying that there are two distinct doctrines to be considered; a theory of substantial forms and a theory of goodness as a single identical characteristic—'. . . if there is some one good which is universally predicable of goods or is capable of separate and independent existence . . .' (1096 b32–3). Why does Aristotle not say that there are two views to be considered, perhaps the two views distinguished, in a later jargon, as *universalia ante res* and *universalia in rebus*? The answer must be that, in his view, the theory which he rejects holds, however confusedly, that the Form is both a universal predicate and an individual substance. The theory, according to Aristotle, is nonsense; 'meaningless noises' he says in the *Posterior Analytics* (83 a32–5), 'dialectical and futile' in the *EE* (1217 b19–23). The substantial form being a chimera, what the Platonists must have in mind is the common character, 'universally present in all cases and single' (1096 a28).

One further comment is needed before we start our examination of the main argument of the chapter. Aristotle, as we have seen, seeks to refute the Platonic doctrine considered as offering, or suggesting, an answer to the question what is the highest good that can be achieved in human action (1095 a15–17). The intrinsic goods mentioned in the chapter are specific human goods; intelligence, sight, and certain pleasures and honours (1096 b17–18). Thus he is concerned with the question whether 'good' is univocally applicable to various human goods rather than with the question whether it is univocally applicable to human and to non-human goods. He says elsewhere that the good for man is not the same as the good for other species of living things. Thus it is different for men and for fish (*EN* VI. 7, 1141 a22–3). In the *Metaphysics* he remarks that 'good and evil indicate quality especially in living things, and among them especially in those which have purpose (*prohairesis*)' (Δ 14 1020 b23–5). In the *EE* he draws a distinction between the good which is practicable (*prakton*), i.e. the end (*hou heneka*), and the good which is not, i.e. the good in things unchanging (1218 b4–6).

We have sufficiently discussed the opening lines of the chapter, Aristotle's apologia for attacking a famous doctrine of Plato and the Platonists (1096 a11-17). The following passage contains two similar and connected arguments which should be considered together.

(1) The men who introduced this doctrine did not posit Ideas of classes within which they recognised priority and posteriority (which is the reason why they did not maintain the existence of an Idea embracing all numbers); but the term 'good' is used both in the category of substance and in that of quality and in that of relation, and that which is *per se*, i.e. substance, is prior in nature to the relative (for the latter is like an offshoot and accident of being); so that there could not be a common Idea set over all these goods. (2) Further, since 'good' has as many senses as 'being' (for it is predicated both in the category of substance, as of God and of reason, and in quality, i.e. of the virtues, and in quantity, i.e. of that which is moderate, and in relation, i.e. of the useful, and in time, i.e. of the right opportunity, and in place, i.e. of the right locality and the like), clearly it cannot be something universally present in all cases and single; for then it could not have been predicated in all the categories but in one only. (1096 a17-29.)

In both arguments, or in both versions of the argument, Aristotle argues from the fact that 'good' is predicated both of substances and of subjects which are not substances, e.g. qualities and relations. But in the first he uses as a premiss a principle which he attributes to the Platonists, that there is no Form corresponding to terms related as prior and posterior, as are substance and relation. In the second he uses as a premiss his own doctrine of categories, the doctrine that 'being' has a number of senses.[1]

---

[1] Burnet says that this doctrine is 'not Aristotle's at all, but simply part of his heritage from the Academy' (Introduction, pp. xlviii-lii). But I think there is general agreement that this statement greatly exaggerates the extent to which Aristotle's doctrine had been anticipated. Ross gives a brief account of the doctrine in his *Aristotle* (pp. 21-4), and a fuller one in his edition of the *Metaphysics* (pp. lxxxii-xciii). On Plato's doctrine about numbers it is necessary to read the article by Cook Wilson in the *Classical Review*, xviii (1904), pp. 247-60. See also Cherniss, *Aristotle's Criticism of Plato and the Platonists*, pp. 513-24. G. E. L. Owen's article, 'Logic and Metaphysics in some earlier Works of Aristotle', published in *Aristotle and Plato in the mid-fourth century* (Göteborg, 1960) discusses the differences in the treatment of this topic between the *Nicomachean* and the *Eudemian Ethics*

Aristotle's works contain many passages in which different senses of 'prior' and 'posterior' are elucidated. One of them in *Metaphysics Δ* 11 attributes a definition to Plato: there are things which are prior and posterior 'in respect of nature and substance, i.e. those which can be without other things, while the others cannot be without *them*—a distinction which Plato used' (*Δ* 11, 1019 a2–4). It is, no doubt, questionable whether, in this sense, substance is prior to relation (1096 a20–1), but we can see how it might come to be said that it is: if John is taller than James, the relation between them in respect of height could not exist without them, but either could exist without the other and, therefore, without the relation. The same definition of priority is found in a passage in the *Categories* which gives as an example of such priority that of a number to its successor.

Secondly, one thing is said to be 'prior' to another when the sequence of their being cannot be reversed. In this sense 'one' is prior to 'two'. For if 'two' exists, it follows directly that 'one' must exist, but if 'one' exists, it does not follow necessarily that 'two' exists: thus the sequence subsisting cannot be reversed. It is agreed, then, that when the sequence of two things cannot be reversed, then that one on which the other depends is called prior to that other. (14 a29–35.)[1]

It is in this sense that, according to the *EE* (*A* 8, 1218 a4–5), the separate Form is prior to that which falls under it: the Form can exist without the particular but not the particular without the Form. Priority in this sense may be called 'natural' priority.

Natural priority is distinguished by Aristotle from 'logical' priority, priority in definition (*logǭ*). *A* is logically prior to *B* when the definition of *B* mentions *A* but the definition of *A* does not mention *B*. In *Metaphysics Z* 1 Aristotle says that substance is the first category both in the sense that it alone can exist independently and also in definition, since the definition of substance enters into the definition of any other category (1028 a33–b2). Thus, as Ross puts it (in his note on 1028 a34), 'all attributes involve in the end substances and cannot be defined without

---

(*A* 8). See also D. J. Allan, 'Aristotle's Criticism of Platonic Doctrine concerning Goodness and the Good', in the *Proceedings of the Aristotelian Society*, 1963–4.

[1] Cf. *Physics* 260 b18.

including their definition'. For example, you 'cannot define white without including the definition of surface nor surface without including the definition of body'. The priority of a number to its successor is logical as well as natural. For example, it is impossible to define two without mentioning one, e.g. by saying that there are two when, and only when, it is the case both that there is one, and that there is one, and only one, other. In the *Metaphysics* Aristotle points out that logical priority does not entail natural priority, since in respect of definition white is prior to white man although, being an attribute, it cannot exist apart from a man or some other subject.[1] Ross's note on 1028 a34 (quoted above) shows how this can be reconciled with the logical priority of substance as a category.

The Platonists, Aristotle tells us, 'did not maintain the existence of an Idea embracing all numbers' (1096 a18-19). In his account of Platonic doctrine Aristotle distinguishes two kinds of number, ideal numbers or Forms and mathematical numbers. We need not discuss this distinction here. It is enough to refer to the evidence that the numbers here are Forms, and that what Aristotle is saying that the Platonists denied is not that the numbers, i.e. the members of the series of integers, are Forms but that there is a Form of number in general. The expression in the *EE* (*A* 8) which corresponds to 'Idea embracing all numbers' here is the common predicate, multiple (*to pollaplasion*) (1218 a6-7). If plurality were a separate Form, the first of the numbers which it would cover would be two, i.e. the double. It is clear that two is here what later was called a universal and what Plato called a Form. This interpretation is confirmed by passages in the *Metaphysics*. 'Some say that both kinds of number exist, that which has a before and after being identical with the Ideas, and mathematical numbers being different from the Ideas and from sensible things, and both being separable from sensible things . . .' (*M* 6, 1080 b11-14). In *B* 3 we seem to have a reference to an argument stated in the *EE*: 'Further, in the case of things in which the distinction of prior and posterior is present, that which is predicable of these things cannot be something apart from them; e.g. if two (*hē duas*) is the

[1] *M* 2, 1077 a36-b11; cf. *Δ* 11, 1018 b34-7.

first of the numbers, there will not be a Number apart from the kinds of numbers' (999 a6–9). 'Number' and 'the dyad' in this passage correspond to 'multiplicity' and 'duplicity' in the *EE*. In view of this evidence we can confidently reject the eccentric opinion of Stewart that the numbers in *EN* I. 6 are mathematical numbers and not Ideas.

We have seen that the material supplied by Aristotle enables us to formulate senses in which the numbers form a series connected by a relation of prior and posterior. There is indeed a confusion in the evidence on the question whether the first term in the series is one or two. In the *Categories* (14 a29–35) Aristotle makes one a number, or at least implies that one is prior to two in the sense in which two is prior to three, and so on. In the *EE* (1218 a1–8) he makes duplicity the first kind of numerical multiplicity, as indeed it is. Is this apparent contradiction merely a verbal variation in the use of 'number'? A man might give one as the number of his sisters, the answer to 'how many?', but also, in answer to the question whether he had a number of sisters, might say 'no—only one'. But Aristotle does not merely decide not to call one a number; he argues that it is not a number. 'For "the one" means the measure of some plurality, and "number" means a measured plurality and a plurality of measures. Thus it is natural that one is not a number; for the measure is not measures, but both the measure and the one are starting points.'[1]

In the *EN* Aristotle does not report any arguments either for the general thesis, attributed to the Platonists, that there are no Ideas embracing terms related as prior and posterior, or for the particular thesis that there is no Idea embracing all numbers. In the *EE* Aristotle reports an argument for the particular thesis which purports to show that the assumption of an Idea of Number leads to a self-contradiction, to the assertion that there is a term prior to the first term of the series of numbers. 'For the common and separable element would be prior, because with its destruction the first would be destroyed as well: e.g. if the double is the first of the multiples, then the universal multiple cannot be separable, for it would be prior to the double, if the common element turns

---

[1] *Metaphysics N* 1, 1088 a4–8; cf. *Δ* 1020 a13 with Ross's note and *Z* 1039 a12.

out to be the Idea, as it would be if one made the common element separable' (I. 8, 1218 a1–9). This is not a convincing argument against a separate Idea, or substantial Form, of number. First, it is difficult to make sense of the suggestion that, if there were a separable comprehensive Idea of number, this Idea would be prior to two in the sense of being its immediate predecessor. For, even if we are not to say that one is a number on the ground that a single entity is not numerous, we can surely not refuse to say that, as two precedes three, so one precedes two. Thus, in order to make sense of the argument, it would be necessary to say that one, or perhaps nought, and not two, is the first term of the numerical series. But the argument is anyhow invalid, and the alleged contradiction does not arise, for a reason which was pointed out in a lecture by J. L. Austin. The assumption of the separate Idea would lead to the contradiction only if the Idea would be prior to the first term of the series in the sense of being its immediate predecessor. But the Idea would be prior not to the first term of the series but rather to the series as a whole.

Aristotle, then, does not in the *EN* attempt to tell us the reasons for the Platonic doctrine that there is no Form embracing the terms of a series, and in particular the series of numbers. And what he tells us in the *EE* does not seem to make sense. But Aristotle speaking for himself states the same doctrine, or a doctrine verbally similar. Thus in *Metaphysics B* 3 (already quoted)[1] he says that what is predicable of things related as prior and posterior 'cannot be something apart from them' (999 a6–7). After mentioning Number and Figure (*schēma*) he adds that 'if the genera of these things do not exist apart from the species, the genera of other things will scarcely do so; for genera of these things are thought to exist if any do' (999 a10–12). Aristotle does indeed hold, as a universal proposition, that the generic nature of anything is not something apart from its specific nature; he compares the generic nature to formless matter (*Z* 12, 1038 a5–9). Thus Aristotle notices that a 'determinable' is related to its 'determinates' otherwise than the determinate or specific nature is related to its instances. Something red is not red *and* coloured;

[1] See p. 53 above.

red and green are alternative ways of being coloured; a generic concept is a disjunctive concept. It is not clear why Aristotle should argue *a fortiori* from Number and Figure to other genera.[1] For in the *De Anima* he implies that the fact that the kinds of soul, like the kinds of rectilinear figure, are in a serial order constitutes a special difficulty in the way of framing a common definition (414 b20–33). In *Politics Γ* 1, where he is looking for a definition of citizenship, we find a more explicit assertion of the principle that, when species are in a serial order, it is difficult to frame a definition, unless one which is thin and uninformative, of the genus; 'we must not forget that subjects which differ in species and are related as first, second, third, have nothing or hardly anything common to them' (1275 a34–8). A possible criticism of what Aristotle is saying here is that he is failing to drive home his own doctrine that the generic nature is indeterminate. He is trying to think of it as a thin essence extracted from the species. But the concept of number is the concept of the series of numbers. Colour is not a factor common to colours but what is differentiated as the colours of the rainbow. Perhaps something similar could be said, if less confidently, about the general concept of soul or life. There is not much in being alive if it is only a property shared by cabbages and men. But, if the concept is taken as disjunctive, it does not exclude, but rather embraces, the varieties within the plant and animal kingdoms.

I turn now to Aristotle's second argument. Here he maintains that, since 'good' has as many senses as 'being', goodness cannot be 'something universally present in all cases and single' (1096 a23–9) The words *to agathon legetai isachōs tō onti* are understood by Joachim as meaning that a subject which is good is called good in a number of senses corresponding to the senses in which something which is is said to be. In the phrase '*to on pollachōs legetai*' I think that '*to on*' means 'what has being' and not ' "being" '. Joachim's way of taking the words seems preferable, therefore, to that of Ross in his translation. But the decision between them does not make any difference to the doctrine. In the examples which Aristotle gives of predication in the different categories I take it that

[1] *Metaphysics B 3.*

the sentences implied are: 'God is good', 'courage (for example) is good', 'the useful is good', not 'God is the good', etc. They are sentences with 'good' as predicate and entities which are instances of various categories as subjects. But to say that 'good' is predicated *in* different categories surely cannot mean merely that it is predicated of subjects which are in different categories. Aristotle seems to be making an unstated assumption about the members of the set of sentences which he adduces as evidence that 'good' is predicated in different categories; the assumption that the common predicate of these sentences, 'good', has categorial multisignificance, a plurality of meanings which correspond to the categorial differences between the subjects of these sentences. The question arises how Aristotle, if he was aware of this hiatus in his argument, would have defended the proposition needed to bridge the gap. The difficulty of the notion of predication in a category seems to be overlooked by the English commentators except Joachim.

In his note on 1096 a23 ff. (p. 41) Joachim writes:

> God is called good: his goodness constitutes his substance: 'being good' as predicated of God is, therefore, a predication in the category of substance. The useful is called good: its goodness means its contribution to something valued *per se*, i.e. 'being good' as predicated of the useful indicates a certain essential relatedness, and therefore is a predicate under the category of the relative or related.

I agree with this account of what Aristotle means by saying that the good is predicated in different categories. But the point can, perhaps, be put more sharply by saying that the statements adduced by Aristotle are not simply propositions in which good is a predicate asserted of various subjects; they are definitions. The predicate expresses the essence, or part of the essence, of the subject; and it is, therefore, inevitably in the same category as the subject. That the distinction between definitory and non-definitory is applicable to statements about subjects in different categories is said explicitly by Aristotle in the *Metaphysics*:

> Definition, like 'what a thing is', has several meanings; 'what a thing is' in one sense means substance and the individual, in another, one

or other of the predicands, quantity, quality, and the like. For as 'is' (*to estin*) is predicable of all things, not however in the same sense, but of one sort of thing primarily and of others in a secondary way, so too then 'what' (*to ti estin*) belongs in the full sense to substance, but in a limited sense (*pōs*) to the other categories.[1]

Thus the statement that good has as many senses as being (1096 a23–4), read in the light of what Aristotle says elsewhere about the definition of subjects in different categories, can be expanded as follows: when the essence of the *definiendum* includes goodness, then the goodness specified in the *definiens* is of the kind appropriate to the category of the *definiendum*, i.e. the sense in which it is or the kind of being which it has, i.e. substantial, qualitative, relational, etc.

Aristotle's third argument against the Platonic Idea hinges on the question whether, or in what sense, there is 'one science of all the goods'. 'Further, since of the things answering to one Idea there is one science, there would have been one science of all the goods; but as it is there are many sciences even of the things that fall under one category, e.g. of opportunity, for opportunity in war is studied by strategics and in disease by medicine, and the moderate in food is studied by medicine and in exercise by the science of gymnastics' (1096 a29–34). There is another version of the same argument in the *EE*. 'As then being is not one in all that we have just mentioned, so neither is good; nor is there one science of being or of the good; not even things named good in the same category are the objects of a single science, e.g. opportunity or moderation' (I. 8, 1217 b33–7). The examples are similar to those in the *EN*. In regard to food opportunity and moderation are studied by medicine and gymnastics; in military matters by strategy. The main difference between the two versions of the argument is that the explicit statement in the *EE* that there is no single science of being is not repeated in the *EN*. But it is perhaps implied, if the fact that there is no single science of goods depends on the fact that there are categorially different kinds of goodness.

---

[1] Z 4, 1030 a17–23, cf. 1028 b1–2, *Topics* 103 b27–39.

It is puzzling to find, in both versions, the statement that there are many sciences of goods *even* when those goods are in one category. For this seems to suggest that, if goods are in different categories, it is natural to expect them to be objects of different sciences, and that it would be surprising if they were objects of the same science. But the suggestion that a scientist could be concerned with a class of things, but not with their qualities and relations, or with qualities but not with the things that have them, or with relations without the things related, is evidently absurd. Aristotle's own doctrine insists on the dependence of the other categories on substances.[1] Again, the very examples which Aristotle here gives of sciences dealing with distinct objects in the same categories are also examples of sciences which straddle, as all sciences must, over a number of categories. Medicine, gymnastics, and strategy all deal with both the moderate in quality and the opportune in time. It is, therefore, not surprising that in the *Metaphysics* Aristotle uses the doctrine of the categories in order to vindicate, not to undermine, the possibility of a single science of being. Things that are said to 'be' have not merely the name in common but are related to one central point (*pros hen*) (*Γ* 2, 1003 a33–4). 'For not only in the case of things which have one common notion (*kath' hen*) does the investigation belong to one science, but also in the case of things which are related to one common nature; for even these in a sense have one common notion' (1003 b12–15).[2]

In the *EN* Aristotle is aware of the fact that, when a word has a plurality of meanings, there may be one meaning which is central and primary and others which involve a reference to this central meaning and are derived from it (*pros hen*, *aph' henos*). Later in the chapter (1. 6) he refers to this as a possible view about the meanings of good (1096 b27–8). G. E. L. Owen, in the article already mentioned,[3] uses the expression 'focal meaning' for this kind of systematic ambiguity, or systematic relationship between the

---

[1] *Metaphysics Z* 1, 1028 a33–6.
[2] Cf. *K* 3, 1060 b31–1061 a8, where the phrase corresponding to 'common notion' (*kath' hen*) is 'in virtue of some common nature'.
[3] See above, p. 51 n. 1.

different senses of a term. We find the idea of focal meaning, with a reference to Aristotle's stock example ('medical'), applied to friendship in the *EE* (*H* 2, 1236 a16–20). Since in the *Metaphysics* the possibility of a general science of being is based on focal meaning it is surprising, at first sight, to find in the *Ethics* both focal meaning and the rejection of a general science of being. But the Platonic science of being, if it resembled the dialectical knowledge of the Good in the *Republic*, would be very different both from Aristotelian metaphysics as the science of being *qua* being and from Aristotelian politics as a comprehensive practical science of goods. It may be true also, as Owen maintains, that Aristotle, in the *EE* at least, had not yet seen clearly the application of focal meaning to being and good, and had not seen that this application involves the possibility of a science of being (p. 169). But I confess that the difference between the doctrine of the categories without focal meaning and the doctrine as elaborated in terms of focal meaning is not clear to me. The development of Aristotle's metaphysical thought, or thought about metaphysics, is a subject outside the scope of this discussion. The question on which, as students of the *Ethics*, we should like to know more than Aristotle tells us is what he is rejecting when he denies that there is 'one science of all the goods'.

The rejection of a universal science of being and of good is part of a polemic against Plato and Platonists. Thus Aristotle is to be understood as attacking Platonic conceptions of a universal science. The idea or ideal of a universal science is propounded in the *Republic*, and, in the absence of other usable evidence, it is reasonable for us to think here of that idea. It is the idea, if we may ignore all the difficulties which would arise in any attempt to make coherent sense in detail of Plato's doctrine, of a science which has the form of a deductive system based on a single 'unhypothetical' principle (510b, 511b). Within this universal system the 'hypotheses' which are the principles of the special sciences would be included as deduced propositions. If it is something of this kind which is the object of Aristotle's attack, his rejection of a universal science is consistent with the claim which he would make for the universal science which he vindicates in

Metaphysics Γ. For the science of being *qua* being does not involve a denial that the principles and proofs of a special science like geometry are independent and self-justifying. In Owen's words, 'the new enterprise is not cast in the form of a deductive system and it does not dictate premisses to the special sciences' (p. 179).

The rejection of a universal science, in the Platonic sense, is consistent also with the claims which Aristotle makes in the *EE* for politics as the science of the end of all human actions (*A* 8, 1218 b11–19) and in the *EN* for politics as the supreme architectonic science which 'ordains which of the sciences should be studied in a state, and which each class of citizens should learn and up to what point they should learn them' (1. 2, 1094 a26–b7). But, just as metaphysics does not 'dictate premisses to the special sciences', so the statesman cannot tell a general how to win a campaign or a doctor how to control an epidemic. In the exercise of its authority over the sciences, politics dictates only the occasions of their application; but each is an independent technique. Direction *ab extra* does not involve internal interference. 'It is hard to see how a weaver or a carpenter will be benefited in regard to his own craft by knowing the "good itself" . . .' (1097 a8–9).

The next section of the chapter (1096 a34–b7, cf. *EE A* 8, 1218 a10–15) has already been quoted, except for the brief reference at the end to the views of Speusippus and the Pythagoreans (on which see the commentators, e.g. Burnet). Aristotle here makes a brief statement of some of his stock objections to Platonic Forms, not the Form of Good in particular. It would be out of place, in an examination of Aristotle's ethical doctrine, to discuss the questions raised by these arguments.

In the section which follows (1096 b7–26) the argument is stated with characteristic terseness. In the following paraphrase I try to show what I take the argument to be. Aristotle proceeds to consider a possible rejoinder by the Platonists. They will object, he says, that they distinguish between (*a*) goods pursued for their own sake, and (*b*) things which produce or preserve such goods or prevent the opposite, and will hold that only (*a*) are called good by reference to a single Form (*kath' hen eidos*). But they can be faced with a dilemma. (1) If things good in themselves are taken to include goods pursued both when isolated and for the sake of something else, e.g. intelligence, sight, and certain pleasures and honours, then in all these the definition of the good must be the same, like that of whiteness in snow and white lead; but it is not the same since they differ *qua* good. (2) If only the Idea is good in itself, it will be superfluous. (It would be idle to postulate an Idea under which nothing falls.) The good, therefore, is not some common element answering to one Idea (*kata mian idean*).

Aristotle proceeds to make some brief, and, as they stand, cryptic, suggestions for possible answers to the question how the different senses of 'good' are connected; or, as he puts the question, how the things that are good are said to be good... (*pōs dē legetai*) (1096 b26). He has just rejected one possible answer, which he takes to be the answer implied by the Platonic doctrine, that the subjects said to be good are 'synonymous', i.e. have a common name which refers to a common identical nature of which an account (*logos*) or definition can be given, 'as that of whiteness is identical in snow and white lead' (1096 b22-3). In chapter 1 of the *Categories* the example given of things that are synonymous is a man and an ox which are both 'animals' (1 a6-10). But if goods are not synonymous neither are they merely 'homonymous', 'like the things that only chance to have the same name' (1096 b26-7). An example of homonymy is 'the ambiguity in the use of *kleis* for the collar-bone of an animal and for that with which we lock a door' (*EN* v. 1, 1129 a29-31). In the *Categories* the example is the use of 'animal' for both a living animal and one in a picture (1 a1-6). Goods, then, while not owners of a common nature as well as name, are not mere namesakes. Aristotle implies that there may be an intermediate view, or a number of possible intermediate views. 'Are goods one, then, by being derived from one good or by all contributing to one good, or are they rather one by analogy?' (1096 b27-8). An example of 'analogy' is given: 'as sight is in the body, so is reason in the soul, and so on in other cases' (1096 b28-9). Aristotle adds a reference to a treatment of the subject elsewhere, perhaps in the *Metaphysics*: 'precision on these subjects would be more appropriate to another branch of philosophy' (1096 b30-1).

As we saw earlier, Aristotle holds that some words have a meaning which is central or, to use Owen's word, focal and also other meanings which are connected as all being related to the focal meaning. There are different ways in which secondary meaning may be related to primary meaning. One of these ways is the way in which the other categories are related to the category of substance. One of Aristotle's favourite examples of focal meaning is 'medical'; another is 'healthy'. In the *Metaphysics* (*K* 3) the systematic ambiguity of these terms is used to illustrate the systematic ambiguity of 'being'.

The term seems to be used in the way we have mentioned, like 'medical' and 'healthy'. For each of these also we use in many senses; and each is used in this way because the former refers somehow to medical science and the latter to health. Other terms refer to other central concepts, but each term refers to one identical concept. For a prescription and a knife are called medical because the former proceeds from medical science, and the latter is useful to it. And a thing is called healthy in the same way; one thing because it is indicative of health, another because it is productive of it. (1060 b36-1061 a7.)

The same comparison is made in *Z* 4: 'a patient and an operation and an instrument are called medical neither by an ambiguity (*homōnumōs*) nor with a single meaning (*kath' hen*) but with a common reference (*pros hen*).'[1] According to Aristotle, the primary or central meaning is an element in the definition of the secondary or peripheral meanings. In *Metaphysics Z* 1, as we have seen, this is one of the ways in which the category of substance is primary (1028 a33-b2). The same point is stated in the passage in the *EE* (*H* 2) on the varieties of friendship or love.

There must, then, be three kinds of love, not all being so named for one thing or as species of one genus, nor yet having the same name by accident. For all the senses of love are related to one which is the primary, just as is the case with the word 'medical', and just as we speak

---

[1] 1030 b2-4; cf. 2, 1003 a33-b15, a passage from which I quoted earlier (p. 59 above).

of a medical soul, body, instrument, or act, but properly the name belongs to that primarily so called. The primary is that of which the definition is implied in the definition of all; e.g. a medical instrument is one that a medical man would use, but the definition of the instrument is not implied in that of 'medical man'. Everywhere, then, we seek for the primary. (1236 a16–23.)

Aristotle, then, gives a variety of examples of 'focal meaning', that is, of terms referred to by a word used in different but connected senses. He does not make explicit the fact that the terms to which a word refers in secondary senses may be related in a number of different ways to the terms to which a word refers in its primary sense. What these different ways are can be seen at a glance if we consider Aristotle's favourite example; the subjects of which we predicate the words 'healthy', and 'medical'. In one kind of secondary meaning the relation involved is causality: a diet is healthy if it is the cause, a complexion is healthy if it is an effect or a sign, of health in a man (K 3, 1061 a6–7).[1] It is the living animal, or man, which is healthy in the central or primary sense. So in the chapter we are discussing (EN I. 6) Aristotle points out that both ends and the means by which ends are realized and protected are said to be good (1096 b10–16). But the relation between the different kinds of subject of which 'healthy' is predicated is not always causal. It may be the relation between one category and another. Thus both a living body and the state or condition of that living body can be said to be healthy. The relation is categorial also in the slide from medical science to medical man. In other cases the connection involved is neither causal nor categorial but, as Aristotle says here, analogy (1096 b28) and elsewhere metaphor or metaphor by analogy.[2] Thus by analogy or metaphor a society, or a condition of a society, can be said to be healthy.

The list just given of kinds of systematic multisignificance is not, of course, to be taken as being exhaustive, either in fact or in the opinion of Aristotle. In the passage quoted from the EE (1236 a16–23) the two inferior kinds of friendship are said to be related to one which is primary, viz., friendship based not on usefulness or on pleasure but on virtue. Aristotle rejects without

---

[1] Cf. 1003 a33–b10.   [2] *Rhetoric* 1410 b36, 1412 b34.

argument the obvious suggestion that the varieties of friendship are species, or rather co-ordinate species, of a genus. If the suggestion were accepted, 'friend' would not be ambiguous any more than 'coloured' means something different when applied to red things from what it means when applied to green things. Why should not 'friend' similarly be applicable without multi-significance to soul-mates or partners or companions? Aristotle appears to imply that the kinds of friendship are related as prior and posterior while the colours are not so related to each other. But it is not obvious that the kinds of friendship are in fact so related. Moreover, as we saw earlier,[1] Aristotle does not offer clear or convincing reasons for his denial, in any case half-hearted, that we can frame a generic concept or definition when the species falling under it are in an order of prior and posterior.

We have seen that one of the kinds of focal meaning, one of the ways in which a word can be systematically multisignificant, is the multisignificance of being, the variety of categories. Hence, if good is multisignificant in the same way as being, it is not to be expected that the general notion of focal meaning should throw light on the systematic ambiguity of good. The types of ambiguity which fall under the general or collective notion do not illuminate each other. What Aristotle's treatment suggests, and no doubt correctly, is that, while it is true that good has different meanings corresponding to different categories, this is not the only way in which 'good' is multisignificant. There may be many ways in which 'good' is multisignificant. Among them certainly is the difference between the goodness of means and the goodness of ends. And Aristotle suggests here, although he does not explain or defend the suggestion, that different ends, goods pursued and loved for themselves (1096 b10–11), are good in different senses of 'good'. 'But of honour, wisdom, and pleasure, just in respect of their goodness, the accounts are distinct and diverse . . .' (1096 b23–5). Perhaps what Aristotle has in mind is that they are objects of different kinds of desire, and that these kinds of desire are related as prior and posterior.

Aristotle's last suggestion is that different goods are so called

[1] See pp. 55–6 above.

by analogy. He gives as an example of analogy that reason is in the soul as sight is in the body. Thus we might say of a statesman that he was acute and far-sighted. The meanings of 'acute' and 'far-sighted' are analogous to the meanings of these words when they refer literally to sight. Other examples of identical generic meanings based on analogy are given in the *Topics* (108 b22–31): 'calm' is applied both to absence of movement in air and absence of movement in water; the unit is the 'starting-point' of number and the point of the line. Aristotle does not explain how the notion of analogical meaning applies to the meanings of good. Some of the commentators seem to think that this notion expresses Aristotle's own view on the question discussed. But this is a pointless speculation unless the suggestion that the uses of good are related by analogy is significant and at least interesting. Burnet tells us that the suggestion represents Aristotle's own view, and Stewart says that it is Aristotle's 'final answer'. In explaining what this answer is Stewart says: 'Different things are called good, not because they all contribute well to *one* end, but because they all contribute to *their respective ends*.'[1] This could be at most part of Aristotle's answer. For nothing is said in Stewart's elucidation about the goodness of ends. But Aristotle certainly thinks that ends, 'goods that are pursued and loved for themselves' (1096 b10–11), are good and not only the means by which these ends are achieved. Moreover it is not clear why Aristotle should think that 'good', as applied to means, should be made variously significant by the fact that ends are various. According to Ross[2] the proportion (*analogia*) intended is: 'The good in one category is to other things in that category as the good in a second category is to other things in it'—e.g., as opportunity is to time, so is the moderate to quantity. This proportion mathematically entails, and is entailed by, the proportion expressed by saying that 'good has as many senses as being' (1096 a23–4): the good in one category is to the good in another category as things in the first category are to things in the second category. In other words the multisignificance of 'good' is similar to the multisignificance of 'being'. Thus the suggestion of analogy has not taken us any further. It

---

[1] *Notes*, i. 88.   [2] *Aristotle*, p. 191.

does not tell us how 'being' is multisignificant. The answer that it is so by analogy would be viciously circular if we agree with Ross that to say that goodness is predicated by analogy is to say that it is multisignificant in the same way as being. I think that any commentator who holds that analogy is Aristotle's own answer to his question about the meanings of good is implicitly involved in this absurdity. Rodier,[1] without perhaps being aware of it, makes the absurdity explicit. For, having stated Ross's account of the proportion, he goes on to ask whether the meanings of being vary analogically in the same way. As the question is logically vicious, it is not surprising that he fails to find an answer.

The concluding section of the chapter raises no further problems of interpretation, and needs only a brief paraphrase (1096 b31–1097 a14). Aristotle argues that, even if the doctrine of the absolute good could be defended, it would not be relevant to practical human activities. 'Even if there is some one good which is universally predicable of goods or is capable of separate and independent existence, clearly it could not be achieved or attained by man; but we are now seeking something attainable' (1096 b32–5). It may be suggested that, even if the absolute good is itself unattainable, knowledge of it would help men to achieve the goods that are attainable: 'for having this as a sort of pattern (paradeigma) we shall know better the goods that are good for us, and if we know them shall attain them' (1097 a1–3). This suggestion has a certain plausibility, but 'seems to clash with the procedure of the sciences which leave on one side knowledge of the good, each aiming at its own particular good' (1097 a3–6). If the absolute good is relevant, why do all the particular arts ignore it? (1097 a6–8). 'It is hard, too, to see how a weaver or a carpenter will be benefited in regard to his own craft by knowing this "good itself", or how the man who has viewed the idea itself will be a better doctor or general thereby. For a doctor seems not even to study health in this way, but the health of man, or perhaps rather the health of a particular man; it is individuals that he is healing. But enough of these topics' (1097 a8–14).

[1] G. Rodier, Études de philosophie grecque (Paris, 1926), pp. 167–9.

V

THE NATURE OF MAN

THE 'good which we are seeking' when, as students of political science, we try to define happiness (*eudaimonia*) is the 'human good', the good for man, '*to anthrōpinon agathon*' (*EN* I. 2, 1094 b7, 10–11; 5, 1096 a6–7). Human virtue, Aristotle says in I. 13, is the virtue 'not of the body but of the soul', and happiness has been defined as an activity of the soul in accordance with virtue (1102 a14–18). It is, therefore, reasonable to assume that the study of politics will be based on a methodical study of the human soul. Man is 'composite' (*sunthetos*) and the elements in the composition are body and soul (*psuchē*). This is true not only of man but of all animals, and indeed of plants, since plants too have souls in the sense of being alive (*empsucha*). At the beginning of the *De Anima* Aristotle finds fault with earlier psychologists for confining their attention to the human soul (*A* 1, 402 b3–5). He thought of man as a member of the animal kingdom: 'in most of the other animals there are traces of psychical qualities which in men are more clearly differentiated'.[1] Soul is a genus of which the souls of plants, non-human animals, and men are species, and each of these kinds of soul has its own definition.[2]

Aristotle recognizes in *EN* I. 13 that knowledge of the nature of man is relevant to an inquiry which seeks to determine the good for man; that ethics must have an adequate basis or backing in psychology. But he conveys this recognition in terms which are puzzling and which some readers have misunderstood.

The student of politics, then, must study the soul (*psuchē*), and must study it with these objects in view, and do so just to the extent which is sufficient for the questions we are discussing; for further precision is perhaps something more laborious than our purpose requires. Some

---

[1] *Historia Animalium* Θ 1, 588 a18–20.   [2] *De Anima* B 3, 414 b32–3.

things are said about it, adequately enough, even in the discussions outside our school (*exōterikoi logoi*), and we must use these; e.g. that one element in the soul is irrational and one has a rational principle. Whether these are separated as the parts of the body or anything divisible are, or are distinct by definition but by nature inseparable, like convex and concave in the circumference of a circle, does not affect the present question. (*EN* I. 13, 1102 a23–32.)

He proceeds to use this consciously unprecise division of the soul as a basis for the classification of human excellencies (*aretai*) as ethical and intellectual (1103 a3–10).

What are these 'exoteric discussions' which we are advised to 'use'? The word 'exoteric' is translated by Ross, in the Oxford Translation, as 'outside our school'; but this makes the reference too definite. For, while the expression can be used to refer to such discussions,[1] it is probable that in some of the places in which it occurs the reference is to dialogues or other literary works of Aristotle himself.[2] A critical account of the various opinions which have been held by scholars on the meaning of the expression has been given by Paul Moraux.[3] Burnet thought that the reference here was 'certainly' to the writings of the Academic school (p. 58). But, at the time (1900) when he published his commentary, Burnet believed that the *EE* was written by Eudemus, one of Aristotle's disciples. So long as this attribution was accepted the references could not naturally be taken as being to a class of Aristotle's writings. But Jaeger persuaded most scholars, including Burnet, that the *EE* is a version of Aristotle's Ethics earlier than the *EN*. He also pointed out that, if this view is accepted, 'there is no longer anything against Bernays's conjecture that the exoteric discussions were definite writings, and in fact the literary works of Aristotle.'[4] Jaeger thinks that the reference here is to the *Protrepticus*.[5] Why are we referred to a popular work and not to Aristotle's systematic exposition of his psychology in the *De Anima*?

---

[1] e.g. *Physics* Δ 10, 217 b30–1.

[2] *Metaphysics M* 1, 1076 a28–9; *EE A* 8, 1217 b22; *B* 1, 1218 b32–4; *Politics H* 1, 1323 a21–3; *EN* VI. 4, 1140 a1–3.

[3] *Le dialogue sur la justice* (1957), pp. 16–22.

[4] *Aristotle* (1923), pp. 248–9.

[5] Cf. also the note in Gauthier–Jolif on 1102 a26–7.

The explanation might be simply that the *De Anima* was written later, although some doctrines of the *De Anima* are taken for granted in the *EN*. But, even if the *De Anima* had already been written, Aristotle might prefer to use easier and more accessible works. I shall examine later the opinion, which I do not accept, that Aristotle's view of the soul in the *EN* is radically different from his view in the *De Anima*.

It is not surprising to find Burnet, who believes, as we have seen, that Aristotle's method in the *EN* is 'dialectical throughout' (p. v), holding that the distinction made here between the rational and the irrational soul is 'the popular psychology of the Academy' and that Aristotle is appealing to a doctrine which he no longer held himself (p. 65). But Burnet is not alone in this opinion. Jaeger, for example, says that the doctrine, although it appears in Aristotle's *Protrepticus*, is 'simply Plato's' and speaks of it as 'a very primitive theory of the soul'. Aristotle's own psychology, he suggests, had not 'reached the level at which we know it', although from the use of the primitive theory 'no errors followed serious enough to vitiate the ethical result' (pp. 332–3). Jaeger argues, as Burnet had argued (p. 58), that Aristotle did not himself believe that the soul has 'parts'. But this argument overlooks the reservations which Aristotle makes in i. 13 when he proposes to assume that there are rational and irrational elements in the soul. He is careful to say that he is not assuming that the soul has parts which are separable, or separately located, but only that the soul as rational and the soul as non-rational are 'distinct by definition' (1102 a30; cf. b25). This is a proposition which he would himself accept,[1] although he would add that, in this sense, the soul can be divided into an indefinite number of parts (432 a22 ff.). Again, when he says that 'further precision' would be excessively laborious, he is not implying that there is anything erroneous in the doctrine as he states it. He is saying only that, in the systematic study of the soul, much of the detail has no relevance or interest for the student of ethics. For example, the ethical virtues of courage (*andreia*) and gentleness (*praotēs*) are concerned with the emotions of fear and anger. We learn in the *De Anima*

---

[1] Cf. *De Anima* B 2, 413 b27–32; cf. Γ 9, 432 a20; 10, 433 b24.

that these emotions are intimately connected with processes in the body (A 1, 403 a16 ff.). But the definitions of the virtues are not affected by detailed information about the physiological aspects of desires and emotions. Such information, if available, could not be used in ethics. Aristotle might have added that physiological psychology is a progressive inquiry in which it is difficult to reach firm conclusions. We do not know, for example, when, or with what degree of firmness, Aristotle himself arrived at the theory, prominent in the *Parva Naturalia* but not in the *De Anima*, that the heart is a central organ of perception, imagination, and movement.

Thus neither the reference to 'exoteric discussions' nor the disclaimer of detailed precision is to be understood as implying that Aristotle would be willing to argue from psychological premisses which he did not himself accept. But this conclusion leaves open the question whether Aristotle's doctrine in the *EN* implies, or at least is in harmony with, the view of the nature of man, and in particular the view of the relation of soul to body, which we find in the *De Anima*. I have already said that I do not think that the differences are radical, and that some doctrines of the *De Anima* are taken for granted in the *EN*. To say this is perhaps not inconsistent with the opinion I have quoted from Jaeger that, when he wrote the *EN*, Aristotle's psychology had not 'reached the level' of the *De Anima*. But the view I take does need to be defended against the view held by some scholars that the *EN* implies a doctrine of the soul, of the nature of man, radically different from that of the *De Anima*. In one of his early literary works, the *Eudemus*, Aristotle expounded a Platonic concept of the soul. The view which I shall now briefly consider is that, in the *EN* and in some of his biological treatises, Aristotle implies a doctrine on the relation of the soul to the body which is intermediate, in a sense to be explained, between his early Platonism and his own mature doctrine as it is expounded in the *De Anima*.

The *Eudemus* follows Plato's *Phaedo* in maintaining that the soul is an incorporeal thing which can exist independently of the body and which survives bodily death. The soul's capacity for knowledge and happiness is curtailed by its temporary association with the body which is its prison or tomb. There is a clear contrast between this view of soul and body as two separable things and the doctrine expressed in the *De Anima* by the description of the soul as the form (*eidos*) or essence (*ousia*) or definition (*logos*) or actuality (*energeia* or *entelecheia*) of the body. A man is not two things but one; a besouled body or embodied soul, formed matter or enmattered form. What we call states of the soul are, properly speaking, states of the man. 'To say thàt it is the soul which is angry is like saying that it is the soul that weaves webs or builds houses. It is doubtless better to avoid saying that the soul pities or learns or thinks and rather to say that it is the man who does this with his soul.'[1] Let us call this the 'entelechy' theory. The theory is stated with force and conviction in the *De Anima*, but with an important reservation. In the third book (Γ) Aristotle expounds the doctrine that there is an element in the soul, reason (*nous*), which, being separable, is not the entelechy of the body or of any part of the body (Γ 4 and 5). This doctrine is not confined to the third book. It is defended in the first book (*A* 4, 408 b18–29) and is mentioned in a number of other passages in both the first and second books.[2] A comparable doctrine about 'reason' is stated in *EN* x.[3] When he wrote these passages Aristotle was in partial agreement with the Platonic way of thinking about the soul. There is no evidence that he ever maintained the entelechy doctrine without this important reservation. I shall discuss this doctrine of reason in my last chapter.

The view that we can find in the surviving works of Aristotle a theory of soul and body intermediate between the Platonism of the *Eudemus* and the entelechy theory was maintained by Nuyens in a book on the development of Aristotle's psychology.[4] He does not claim that there is any exposition in Aristotle of the transitional theory, but finds it expressed in 'brief assertions and incidental remarks'[5] in the biological works, except the *De Generatione Animalium*, and in the *EE* and *EN*. The theory is described as

---

[1] *A* 4, 408 b11–15; cf. *A* 1, 403 a16 ff.

[2] *A* 1, 403 a3–12; *B* 1, 413 a5–7; 2, 413 b24–7; 3, 415 a11–12.

[3] 7, 1177 a13–17; 8, 1178 a20–3; cf. also *De Generatione Animalium* 736 b27, 737 a10, 744 b21.

[4] *L'Évolution de la psychologie d'Aristote.*   [5] Op. cit., p. 57.

transitional or intermediate because, while it agrees with the *Eudemus* in holding that the soul is a thing distinct from the body, each acting on the other, it differs from the *Eudemus* in no longer holding that the soul's association with the body is unnatural and degrading. The soul collaborates with the body as a ruler with a willing subject or a workman with a friendly tool. Ross, in his Dawes Hicks Lecture, expresses the view as follows: 'The soul is no longer the prisoner of the body, and has its seat in a particular organ, the heart; and soul and body are described as acting on one another.'[1] Ross himself in the Lecture, and in his editions of the *Parva Naturalia* and the *De Anima*, expresses the opinion that Nuyens was successful in his attempt to show that there was an intermediate stage. The view is accepted also by Gauthier and Jolif, among other scholars, who go so far as to assert that Aristotle, when he wrote the *EN*, had not 'even an inkling' ('ne la soupçonnait même') of the entelechy theory.[2] On the other hand, it has been argued by Irving Block that there are no good reasons for believing that Aristotle ever held an intermediate theory.[3] I agree with Block, and have stated elsewhere[4] my reasons for thinking that Nuyens fails to prove his interesting thesis. Here I need only comment briefly on the application to the *EN* of the view that there was a period when Aristotle held a transitional theory about soul and body to be sharply distinguished from the entelechy theory. I do not wish to maintain that all the doctrines of the *De Anima* were in Aristotle's mind when he wrote the *EN*. I wish only to justify the opinion that, as regards the specific nature of the human animal, the two works broadly agree. I am sure also that, in the study of the *EN*, it is often necessary to refer to the *De Anima* in order to understand Aristotle's thought and the terms he uses. Aristotle does not say that the student of ethics will find *all* the psychology he needs in 'exoteric' works.

Aristotle holds that his generic definition of soul as the 'actuality' (*entelecheia*) of the body has distinct specific meanings as

[1] 'The Development of Aristotle's Thought', p. 57.
[2] Commentary, p. 34.
[3] 'The Order of Aristotle's Psychological Writings', *American Journal of Philology*, 1961.
[4] *Philosophical Quarterly*, 1964.

applied to plants, non-human animals, and men (*B* 3, 414 b32–3; b22–5; *A* 1, 402 b5–8). Hence in considering whether the entelechy doctrine is expressed or implied in the *EN* we must distinguish soul as the principle of nutrition and growth, soul as the capacity to perceive and feel, and soul as manifested in the various aspects of man's rational nature. In its application to plants, and to the nutritive (*threptikē*) level of soul in animals, the entelechy doctrine asserts that life in a living body is not an extra entity but its form, the way it lives and moves and has its being. The nutritive soul is mentioned in *EN* I. 13 and treated as a familiar concept. There is no reason for suggesting that it is not conceived in terms of the entelechy doctrine. The scholars who find the transitional theory, formulated in terms of a soul seated in a central citadel, in Aristotle's biological works, seem sometimes to forget that this cannot be Aristotle's account of the plant soul. It cannot be suggested that Aristotle ever thought of the life of a cabbage as a thing separable from the cabbage and confined to one part of it. The entelechy theory of the *psuchē* is an easily acceptable statement about the subject-matter of biology. When we turn to processes which are 'psychical' in our sense, as biological processes are not, the theory becomes more elusive. We have to empty our minds of preconceptions and make ourselves receptive of Aristotle's elucidations.

He explains the application of the entelechy theory to the animal soul in a discussion of the question whether what we call 'affections of the soul' are strictly speaking affections of the complex of body and soul.[1] With the usual reservation about the activity of the theoretical intellect he answers the question affirmatively. 'It seems that all the affections of soul involve a body—passion, gentleness, fear, pity, courage, joy, loving, and hating; in all these there is a concurrent affection of the body.'[2] Feelings and emotions are not, of course, the only 'affections of the soul' which involve a 'concurrent affection of the body'. The dependence of sense-perception on bodily organs is obvious.[3] Aristotle holds that imagination (*phantasia*), and hence thinking

---

[1] *De Anima A* 1, 403 a3–b9.   [2] 403 a16–19.
[3] *De Sensu I*, 436 b6–7.

in so far as thinking depends on imagination, and memory (*mnēmē*) are also conditioned by processes in the body.[1] He proceeds in the De Anima (*A* 1), taking anger as an example, to link the fact that there are concurrent affections of the body with the entelechy theory. That anger is a boiling of the blood or warm substance round the heart is a statement of its matter (*hulē*); that it is a desire to return pain for pain is its essence or form (*eidos*) (403 a29–b2). A true and adequate statement of the nature of anger will mention both since anger is an 'essence involving matter' (403 b7–9; a25). Thus the cash value, so to say, of the entelechy theory in its application to mental states and processes is that these occur only in conjunction with processes in the living body. As Ross expresses it in his edition of the Parva Naturalia, 'all psychological phenomena are essentially psycho-physical' (p. 14). So also Nuyens: 'c'est précisément sur le caractère psychophysique des manifestations de la vie qu'Aristote a fondé sa définition de l'âme' (p. 251).

Aristotle's 'psychophysical' doctrine, that the besouled body is a substance, carries with it the rejection of the idea that the soul, conceived as the subject of feelings and desires, of perception, imagination, and memory, is itself a substance. Our bodies are the continuous and enduring, and in this sense substantial, basis of our minds. From birth to death there is no interruption in the existence of the body, and something is always going on in it. But, prima facie at least, there are no actual mental states or processes going on when we are asleep and not dreaming. Thus the soul or mind is not one thing and the body another thing. There is no soul-thing or *res cogitans*. For it is inconsistent with our concept of thinghood that a thing should keep popping in and out of existence; should lose and resume its existence as an actively conscious being, persisting in the intervals as no more than a permanent possibility of consciousness.

Are we to suppose that Aristotle, when he wrote the *EN*, took for granted the entelechy theory in its application to the second level of soul, the soul which is capable of sense-perception and

---

[1] De Anima A 1, 403 a8–10; De Insomniis 461 b2, cf. 461 a14–25, 462 a8; De Sensu 436 a6–10; De Memoria 450 a25–b11, 453 a14–23.

imagination, which is susceptible to pleasures and pains, desires and emotional states? There are two questions here. The first is the question whether he assumed that, when a man has these experiences, there are 'concurrent affections of the body'. In the case of sense-perception and of many pleasures and pains the concurrence is obvious and does not have to be demonstrated by scientists or philosophers: we know that we see with our eyes; we are sure that toothache is caused by the state of a tooth. What of other 'affections' (pathē)? In EN II. 5 we have the following list: 'appetite, anger, fear, confidence, envy, joy, friendly feeling, hatred, longing, emulation, pity, and in general the feelings that are accompanied by pleasure and pain' (1105 b19–23). Nuyens (p. 191) contrasts this passage with the passage in the De Anima (A 1) where a similar list is connected with the assertion that there are bodily concomitants (403 a16–19). But the passage in the EN does not deny, or imply a denial, that there are bodily concomitants. In the case of anger and fear, for example, we all know that there are. Aristotle refers in general terms to the bodily concomitants of emotions in x. 7 (1178 a14–16), and in other passages mentions particular examples: fear and shame in IV. 9 (1128 b10–15); anger, sexual desire, etc., in VII. 3 (1147 a14–18, cf. 1147 b6–9). But he might have accepted and taken for granted the fact that 'psychological phenomena are psychophysical' without having come to express the fact by saying that the soul is the form (eidos), essence (logos, ousia), or entelechy of the body. Our second question, therefore, is whether, when he wrote the EN, his thinking had made this move.

There is in the EN no formulation of the entelechy theory. But in EN x. 7 and 8 he describes man as a 'composition' (suntheton) of body and soul. 'Being connected with the passions also, the moral virtues must belong to our composite nature, and the virtues of our composite nature are human' (1178 a19–21; cf. 1177 b26–9). In the Metaphysics the expression 'composite being' (sunthetos ousia) is regularly applied to the union of form and matter.[1] I think that scholars who have faced the question have usually concluded, as did Bonitz and Stewart, that the

---

[1] Δ 24, 1023 a31 ff.; H 3, 1043 a29–b4, b28–32.

'composition' in the *EN* is a composition of matter and form. If they are right, Aristotle's language in these passages presupposes the entelechy doctrine.[1] Nuyens strangely does not discuss these passages or note them in his index, but he mentions them in a footnote as supporting his opinion that Aristotle's views in the *EN* on the relation between the soul and the body are not in accord with those in the *De Anima* (p. 192 n. 140). Gauthier and Jolif, defending the view of Nuyens, point out that the term 'composite' does not necessarily imply a union of matter and form. Thus in the *Phaedo* (78b–c) the word is used to express a very different view of the combination of soul and body, 'the accidental union of a substantial intellect and a substantial body' (p. 895). But, apart from the exceptional status of theoretical reason which is affirmed also in the *De Anima*, there is nothing in the *EN* to suggest this Platonic conception. I think that the burden of proof lies on those who deny that Aristotle in the *EN* had in his mind the entelechy doctrine. Gauthier and Jolif try but fail to sustain the burden. Perhaps they would not have tried if they had not already been convinced, mistakenly as I believe, that Nuyens had made good his claim to have discovered in Aristotle, and in the *EN*, a view of human nature intermediate between the *Eudemus* and the *De Anima*.

I have said what I take to be asserted by the entelechy theory. It is important to notice also what the doctrine does not assert or imply. It does not assert that, when we speak about a state or process in the soul, all that we say can be expressed in terms of bodily processes alone. There is nothing in Aristotle's doctrine which would require him to deny that, when a prick causes a pain, the prick and the pain are events of different kinds. Nor would he have to deny that, when a decision, or a decision with its neural concomitants, indirectly causes the movement of a finger, the decision is something different in kind from the bodily movements. Psychophysical dualism is built into the convictions and language of ordinary men. Aristotle has no qualms about speaking in terms of dualism, as he does when he says that 'the body is affected at the same time' (403 a18–19), i.e. physical

[1] Cf. P. Léonard, *Le Bonheur chez Aristote*, pp. 204–5.

processes are contemporaneous with psychical processes.[1] Aristotle's account of soul (or mind) and body is monistic in so far as he said that a besouled body is only one thing. It is not monistic in the sense of denying that there is a difference of kind between physical and mental or conscious processes. He draws, as we do, a line between plants and animals, on the assumption that the latter but not the former are capable of consciousness, can at least feel and perceive. If it were objected that I have not quoted from Aristotle any explicit assertion of psychophysical dualism, I should agree that he made no such explicit assertion; but I should add that, in his time, no one had yet been clever enough to think of the corresponding denial.

It may be suggested that, when Aristotle speaks of the soul as the form, essence, or actuality of the body, his language implies a more intimate union of soul and body than my account of the entelechy doctrine has so far admitted. Surely such a unity cannot be adequately defined in terms of concomitances and causal connections between physical and psychical events. I shall now consider briefly two passages which might be quoted in support of this suggestion. The first is the remark quoted earlier from *A* 4 where Aristotle observes that 'to say that it is the soul which is angry is like saying that it is the soul that weaves webs or builds houses' (408 b11–13). The second is the passage in *B* 1 in which, having defined the soul as the entelechy of the body, he says that 'there is no need to inquire whether the soul and the body are one any more than there is to inquire whether the wax and the shape given to it by the stamp are one, or generally the matter of anything and that of which it is the matter' (412 b6–8).

Aristotle does not explain what similarity he sees between saying that a man's soul or mind, as opposed to a man, weaves webs and saying that it is the soul which is angry. Weaving is by definition a capacity to execute bodily movements, although the fact that the weaver must move with care and attention, keeping his eyes and mind on the task, means that psychical processes are involved as well. The suggestion that an unembodied soul might weave is thus logically absurd in the sense of self-contradictory.

[1] Cf. p. 79 below.

In Aristotle's view the suggestion that an unembodied soul might be angry is similarly absurd since anger has by definition a bodily aspect: anger is 'a certain mode of movement of such and such a body (or part or faculty of a body) by this or that cause and for this or that end' (*A* 1, 403, a25-7). If 'anger' is so defined the statement that anger involves the body becomes analytic. But this does not mean that the connections between kinds of physical and kinds of psychical process are not synthetic and factual. For observation of the connections is prior to the convention or decision to use 'anger' in a psychophysical sense, straddling, like 'weave', both kinds of event. Did Aristotle fail to see this point? What we can say is that he had not a vocabulary in which it could be simply stated. For, in his language, *psuchē* covered life as well as consciousness. He had no single word to which he gave the job for which I have been employing 'psychical' and 'consciousness'. To say this is not to imply that he did not have the concept implicitly.[1] On the contrary, when, for example, he says that 'perception as an activity is a movement of the soul through the body',[2] his use of *psuchē* in effect corresponds to our psychical. Again he had only a limited logical vocabulary for distinguishing between different kinds of proposition and different kinds of definition. He had, for example, no inverted commas. He had not invented ways of saying clearly all that needs to be said on the mind-body problem. Hence he does not make a clear diagnosis of what is wrong with the attribution of states or activities to the soul and not to the man.

I shall not comment at length on the passage in which Aristotle compares the relation of the soul to the body with the relation between the shape imprinted on the wax and the wax (412 b6-8). To do so would involve discussing questions about Aristotle's metaphysics connected only remotely with his psychology and his ethics. The shapeless marble has the potentiality of being shaped into a statue. Human eyes and nervous systems have the potentiality of actual seeing. The comparison takes us as far as it takes us, and that is not far. For the shape of the statue is related to the marble in a way quite different from the way in which seeing

---

[1] Cf. pp. 77-8 above.   [2] *De Somno* 1, 454 a7-11.

is related to its physiological conditions, or acts of recollection to processes in the brain. All that we need note here is that in Aristotle's theorizing the words *eidos* and *hulē* are used more widely than we find it natural to use the words 'form' and 'matter'. His wider use is connected with his interest in the connections between two very different pairs of terms: form and matter, actual and potential.[1] We shall encounter the latter pair again in our study of the Ethics.

The following further point should be kept in mind when we reflect on what Aristotle says about the unity of the embodied soul or besouled body. Laws of coexistence and sequence are not the only ways in which states of the soul, e.g. pains or fits of temper, are connected with our bodies. A pain in the foot is not only caused indirectly by physical changes in the foot; it is also felt in the foot. The second statement may be true when the first is false, since an identical experience may be had when the foot has been amputated. What makes the word 'toothache' appropriate for a certain ache is the fact that the ache is felt in the tooth rather than the fact that it is caused by something happening in the tooth. Similarly, when we say that our hair stands on end, our flesh creeps, or our blood boils, we are describing not processes in our bodies but what it feels like to be panic-stricken or furious. The descriptions of some occurrences in the soul necessarily include mentions of (sometimes hallucinatory) occurrences in the body. This fact may well be in Aristotle's mind when he gives psychophysical definitions of emotional states. It is the connection in description rather than the causal connection which is suggested to our minds by his remark that 'there is no need to ask whether the soul and the body are one'. For the former connection is a familiar fact of experience, whereas the causal connection, while it may be suggested by experience, has to be verified by physiologists.

I have tried to suggest that Aristotle's entelechy theory or formula expresses important insights. Its originality and value lies in the adoption of a biological approach to the study of man, and in the way in which Aristotle brings out the difficulty of

---

[1] Cf. *Metaphysics* Θ 8, 1050 a15–16; *De Anima* B 1, 412 a9–11.

accepting without qualification a Platonic doctrine of the soul. But we should note also that Aristotle's formula is indeterminate and flexible, leaving open many questions about soul and body, about the connections between mental states and their bodily concomitants. Aristotle himself recognizes this by the reservation which we have found him making, and which we shall discuss in connection with the doctrine of Book x, as regards the special status of theoretical reason. He recognizes it, in another way, in a passage at the end of De Anima B 1 which commentators have rightly found difficult. I shall conclude my account of Aristotle's doctrine with a brief discussion of the difficulty.

'Further, we have no light on the problem whether the soul may not be the actuality of the body in the sense in which the sailor is the actuality of the ship' (413 a8–9). I have quoted the Oxford Translation (1931). But the Oxford Text (1956) inserts the Greek word for 'or' (ē) before the mention of the sailor and the ship. The word is not in the manuscripts but its insertion is supported by the paraphrases of two ancient commentators, Themistius (fourth century) and Philoponus (sixth century). Two interpretations are possible of the amended text. According to the first, and most natural, the point said to be unclear is whether the soul is the entelechy of the body in the sense discussed or in the sense in which the sailor is the entelechy of the ship. On this interpretation, the amendment of the text makes no significant difference to the meaning of the sentence as rendered in the Oxford Translation. According to the second interpretation the question is whether the soul is the entelechy of the body or is related to it as the sailor to his ship. Ross holds that the sailor–ship analogy is not a possible specification of the entelechy theory. He adopts, therefore, the second interpretation. He says in his commentary (1961) that the sailor–ship analogy is 'the suggestion of a completely different theory of the soul from that presented in the rest of the chapter' (p. 21), and again that the suggestion 'flatly contradicts the thesis Aristotle has been maintaining' (p. 214). If we are not satisfied that there is a contradiction we can either adhere to the reading of the manuscripts or accept the first interpretation of the amended text.

The contradiction asserted by Ross is between a metaphorical analogy on the one hand and an indeterminate generic definition on the other. It is not easy to demonstrate a flat contradiction between such opposites. It is true that the analogy is capable of suggesting ideas inconsistent with the entelechy definition. It might suggest, for example, that the soul is confined to one part of the body, as the steersman to one part of the ship. But the entelechy theory implies that all parts of the body are besouled (alive), although not all in the same way. Again the analogy might suggest that soul and body are two separable things, or that a soul could migrate from one body to another, as a pilot can be transferred to another ship. Aristotle strongly repudiates the idea that any soul can go into any body.[1] But surely the analogy does not commit its user to these implications, any more than Aristotle was committed to all the implications which might be read into his saying that the soul is related to the body as the imprinted shape to the wax. What suggests the sailor analogy is the voluntary or deliberate origination of bodily movements in accordance with wishes and intentions. Aristotle gives his own physiological account of such origination in the *De Motu Animalium* (ch. 8). He makes the heart the central organ and the source of movement in peripheral parts of the body. At one point he uses the analogy of the steersman: 'it is not hard to see that a small change occurring at the centre makes great and numerous changes at the circumference, just as by shifting the rudder a hair's breadth you get a wide deviation at the prow' (701 b24–8). There is a shorter treatment of the same subject in the *De Anima* itself (Γ 9–11) and it contains a reference (10, 433 b19–21) to a longer discussion, probably that in the *De Motu Animalium*. It would not do to suggest on behalf of Ross that the doctrine of the heart as a central organ is inconsistent, as Nuyens maintained, with the entelechy theory. It is true that the fact that both doctrines are in the *De Anima* is not conclusive since the treatise, as we have it, might contain inconsistent parts put together by an editor. But among the reasons for rejecting Nuyens's theory of the 'transitional' doctrine is the fact that in the *Metaphysics* Aristotle explicitly

[1] *A* 3, 407 b15–26; *B* 2, 414 a20–5.

combines the entelechy doctrine with the doctrine that the most important functions of the soul are primarily connected with a central organ, the heart or brain (*Z* 10, 1035 b25–7).

Aristotle maintains both that the soul is the actuality of the body and that the soul is involved in the origination of bodily movement. We shall consider his view of the origination of movement and action when we discuss his account of choice (*prohairesis*) in *EN* III. His adherence to the entelechy theory involved, if my account is right, denying that the soul is a separable thing and denying that the psychical processes to which the theory applies, including those involved in the origination of bodily movements, occur without physiological concomitants. These denials are, if true, important. They are part of Aristotle's deviation from Platonism. But they do not, so far as I can see, oblige him to contradict flatly all that Plato had meant when he said that the soul rules the body or that it uses the body as an instrument. Hence, as regards the sentence in *De Anima B* 1 which has suggested these comments (413 a8–9), I am inclined to think that we need not emend the text and that, if we do emend it, we need not accept the interpretation which Ross proposes. I suggest that discussion of the passage has confirmed the view for which I have argued, that the entelechy formula is indeterminate and flexible, and that it is not to be understood as a clear-cut rejection of other ways of speaking about soul and body or as having meanings and implications not explicitly noted by Aristotle himself in the *De Anima*.

APPENDIX

Bodies which have souls

IN the preceding chapter I have been discussing Aristotle's opinions on the question sometimes formulated, perhaps misleadingly, as the question how a mind (or soul) is related to its body or conversely how a body which has a mind (or soul) is related to its mind. I shall be discussing another part of Aristotle's doctrine on this question in the final chapter (XVI), which is on the nature of reason (*nous*). The discussion so far has been about what I have called Aristotle's 'entelechy' theory of the soul. I have taken as a paradigmatic expression of this theory Aristotle's assertion in the first chapter of the *De Anima*, with reference to emotional states such as anger and cognitive acts such as perceiving, that the material or physiological process involved stands to the mental or psychical process involved as matter (*hulē*) to form (*eidos*).

Now we can regard, or attempt to regard, this assertion as giving information, or throwing light, in either of two opposed senses or directions. We can start by considering how Aristotle uses the word *eidos* (form) and other words which can replace it or are used in similar or connected senses, and then go on to use our understanding of these words in order to elucidate Aristotle's view of what Ross calls, as we have seen, 'psycho-physical phenomena'. But we can also reverse the direction of our search. We can start by noting how Aristotle applies such a word as *eidos* (form) to the phenomena, or apparent facts, and take this application as elucidating his concept of form and matter, as showing how the range of the concept can be extended.

Perhaps we can benefit as we should from the study of Aristotle only if we allow our thought to move freely in both directions. But in the preceding chapter I have found it natural and helpful to proceed in the second of these two opposed senses: I have treated the facts as throwing light on the terminology rather than the terminology as throwing light on the facts. But, unless it is clear how I see the facts, it will not be clear how I understand the terms. In the rest of this appendix I shall try, leaving Aristotle, to give a general and elementary description of the apparent facts; to say what it is for a body to have a soul or mind, the kind of soul or mind which embodied is a man.

When we speak of a man as having, or being, a mind or soul (*psuchē*) we are speaking of his psychical capacities, of the fact that he can, for example, feel pleasure or pain, be angry or afraid, ask questions and draw conclusions. We do not doubt that at least some non-human animals have some of these, or at least of analogous, capacities. Plants, we suppose, have not; they do not even feel. Hence there is no psychology of plants; the processes which occur in them, growth for example, are not psychical but physical.

The physical and psychical processes which occur in a man, while different and distinct, are variously connected. The connections can be described under three heads: the unique position of a man's body in his perceptual experience; the causal dependence of a man's experiences on his body, in particular on his sense-organs and his brain; the influence of psychical processes on physical processes, and especially a man's voluntary control of his own bodily movements. The apparent facts falling under these heads explain how a man comes to think of one particular body as his own body, and what is involved in this thought.

A man's perception of his own body differs in two main ways from his perception of other bodies. First, he has sensations which he locates in definite parts of his body; pains in his teeth, ears, head, etc.; tastes in his mouth, tactual feelings on the surface of his skin. Secondly, his body has a central position in the world as he perceives it by sight and touch. He sees the world around him from the place where his eyes are, and, whenever he can see anything, he can see his own body or at least the clothes he is wearing. Again, his own body is the only one which, if he can touch anything, he can always touch; it is always within reach. In these ways a man's body is privileged as an *object* of perception. But it also has a special position as a *causal condition* of perception, and of experience generally.

We cannot see when our eyes are shut, or hear when our ears are plugged, or smell without a nose. But, in order that a man should see and hear, it is not enough that his eyes should be exposed to light rays and his ears to sound waves. Impulses, which are accompanied by electrical effects, must be carried along the optic and auditory nerves to regions at the base of the brain. Moreover, as we are told, '. . . it is only when the impulses have been relayed from the base of the brain to a much more complicated mechanism in the grey matter on the surface of the brain—the central cortex—that a conscious sensation becomes possible'.[1] Anatomists and physiologists, using microscopes and electrodes and studying the effects of local injuries to the brain on the working of the mind, are finding it 'possible to define in more and more detail the particular anatomical dispositions which appear to be necessary as a basis for mental activity'.[2] The broadcast talks by eminent physiologists which were published in the book from which I have quoted give a clear outline of what was then (in 1952) known about processes in the brain. I shall return later to the function of the brain as a 'basis for mental activity'.

A very important element in a man's thought of a certain body as being his, or as being himself, is the voluntary control he can exercise

[1] W. E. Le Gros Clark, in *The Physical Basis of Mind* (Basil Blackwell, Oxford, 1952), p. 14.　　　　　　　　　[2] Ibid., p. 24.

over some of its movements. When such control extends to tools and implements, they too come to feel as if they were parts of his body. Thus, if I poke the ground with a walking-stick, I seem to have a feeling of hardness which I actually locate at the end of the stick.

These facts are among those which have led some psychologists and philosophers to say that there is two-way causal 'interaction' between minds and bodies. The body acts on the mind when, for example, lack of food causes a pang of hunger or a process in a sense-organ and brain causes the hearing of a noise or the seeing of a view. The mind acts on the body when, for example, a decision to take a walk leads to our going out of the house or a state of anxiety inhibits digestion or shame produces a blush. Now these causal connections are as well supported as any in our experience. It seems obvious to common sense that our bodies and our minds do produce effects on each other. But the word 'interaction' suggests something more, viz. that mind–body and body–mind causation are comparable with the action of one body on another body, as when a billiard-ball causes by impact a movement in another billiard-ball or ice is melted by the sun. We are, however, made uneasy by the suggestion that a man's body is one thing and his mind another thing. There are good reasons for this uneasiness. For there are facts which suggest that minds lack some of the essential elements in our concept of a thing, that perhaps we ought, if we are not to be misled, to avoid speaking of minds at all but only of mental, or psychical, processes. These facts might be summarized by saying that psychical processes are not continuous and independent, as physical processes are.

If we consider the events, physical and psychical, which happen in a man between the time of his birth and the time of his death, we are inclined to say that, while in any stretch of time, however short, within this period physical processes occur, there are stretches of time, within the period, when no psychical processes occur, for example when we are in a state of dreamless sleep. I have said that we are inclined to assert that there are gaps. Some would assert this more confidently. E. D. Adrian speaks of 'the abrupt departure of the mind in the fainting fit when the blood supply to the brain is suddenly reduced', and re-marks that 'we have only to be given gas by the dentist to realise that the mind can be turned on and off as abruptly as the B.B.C. news by agencies which modify the general level of brain activity'.[1] This interpretation of the facts is natural, but hardly inevitable. It might be

---

[1] *The Physical Background of Perception*, pp. 6, 7.

suggested that the apparent gaps are filled by psychical processes of a subdued or dim kind, such as occur in dreams. We certainly forget most of our dreams very quickly, and we might have others which we never remember at all. But, while this suggestion cannot be refuted, it would be paradoxical, unless there are positive arguments on its side, to deny that our experience is discontinuous, that our minds come and go, lapsing regularly into non-existence. Are there such arguments?

'The mind', Adrian tells us, 'can be turned on and off.' But, when it is turned on again, it starts roughly where it left off. A man emerging from a fainting fit or sleep is what he was; he has the same ambitions and fears, the same tastes for, and aversions from, particular pursuits, the same tendencies to be interested and happy or bored and sad, the same dispositions to love and hate, like and dislike, the same corpus of knowledge and portfolio of opinions, the same memories. Does this continuity of traits and abilities suggest that the discontinuity of psychical process is apparent rather than real? The question has different aspects. At this stage of the argument I am concerned with its causal aspect. We look for causal explanations of the continuity of a man's dispositions and capacities, including his capacity to remember his own past experiences. The act which contributes to forming a disposition or habit is a causal ancestor of the act or state which manifests the disposition. But physiologists at least tend to assume that the intermediate links are physical and not psychical: they are modifications or 'traces', produced by disciplinary or habit-forming acts, in the ten billion or so nerve-cells in the brain.

Now the hypothesis that mental habits and capacities depend on physical traces in the brain is supported by some evidence; for example, by the way memory is affected when certain parts of the brain are removed or injured.[1] But the theory is still largely an unverified assumption. Scientists do not claim to be able to show what sort of arrangements in the brain could account for the variety of the mind's abilities; there are many unsolved problems. The nature of traces is largely unknown. Adrian tells us that 'we really do not know what sort of change takes place in the brain when a memory is established',[2] that 'what actually happens in the nerve cells is still quite uncertain'.[3] With these large reservations it is reasonable to accept the assumption of physical traces, and it is very difficult to make sense of any alternative

[1] *The Physical Basis of Mind*, pp. 6, 7.   [2] Ibid., p. 6.
[3] Ibid., p. 7.

assumption. If the assumption is made, the answer to our question is plain: the continuity of a man's psychical *characteristics* is not a reason for denying the discontinuity of his psychical *processes*. We do not need to suppose, in the gaps between psychical processes, the continuous existence of a soul or mind, if indeed we can conceive such a thing, to be the recipient of the modifications or traces, whatever they would be, which must be assumed to account for the formation of habits and capacities.

There is at the level of common sense no question whether physical processes exist independently of psychical processes. In the universe life is rare, and mind rarer. And it seems obvious that, in the body of an animal or a man, there occur countless processes which have no psychical conditions or accompaniments. On the other hand, there does not seem to be any evidence for the occurrence of any psychical process except in close association with some physical process. Physiologists assume that all sensations and thoughts, and all voluntary activity, are inseparable from contemporaneous processes in the nervous system. The mind, as Adrian puts it, is 'anchored to the brain'.[1]

We can now see, in more detail than before, what is true, and what is at least questionable, in the assertion of the interactionist that both body acts on mind and mind acts on body. The interactionist is right when he insists on the apparent absurdity of denying that physical causes have psychical effects and that psychical causes have physical effects. He is wrong, or at least rash, in so far as he ignores or denies the differences and asymmetries which we have been discussing between the physical and the psychical processes which occur in a man. For these differences involve, or include, differences between the way in which body acts on mind and the way in which mind acts on body. So far as I can see, the facts, as we have so far taken them to be, conflict in two main respects with the implications of the interactionist's model of explanation.

First, when the mind acts on the body it produces a change in a pre-existing thing; when the body acts on the mind, there is, or need be, no such pre-existing mental thing, as when a blow wakes a man from sleep and causes a pain. Secondly, when the body acts on the mind it acts, or may act, by itself; when the mind acts on the body it does not act by itself, but with the body; for it never, so far as we know, acts by itself. We might summarize the position, as we have described it, by saying that in body–mind action a physical process brings into existence

[1] *The Physical Background of Perception*, p. 6.

or modifies a psychical process, while in mind–body action a psychical process in conjunction with a physical process causes a process of change in a physical thing. The interactionist does not provide for these asymmetries. He is apt to speak as if a mind and a body, like two billiard-balls, were things in the same sense of 'thing'.

My account so far includes two main assertions. The first is that the processes which occur in a man, and indeed in the world, are of two radically different kinds, physical and psychical—i.e. dualism. The second is that the mind is not a thing but is incidental to the body. I shall refer to this latter assertion as 'epiphenomenalism', although most epiphenomenalists have denied, as I have not, that psychical processes are factors in causes as well as effects. Hence this denial is usually part of what is meant by 'epiphenomenalism' (as in chapter VI, p. 115).

Some philosophers would like, if they could, to reject dualism. Gilbert Ryle, for example, says:

> When we read novels, biographies, and reminiscences, we do not find the chapters partitioned into section 'A', covering the hero's 'bodily' doings, and section 'B', covering his 'mental' doings. We find unpartitioned accounts of what he did and thought and felt, of what he said to others and to himself, of the mountains he tried to climb and the problems he tried to solve.[1]

Now it is not, in fact, true that biographical narratives are uniformly unpartitioned. A section or bulletin on the illness of a man may well be couched in purely 'bodily' terms. And it is not clear why any 'bodily doings' should by any logical necessity be included in a section on what he 'thought and felt'. But it is quite true that biographical accounts are, for the most part, unpartitioned. They are unpartitioned because so much of the vocabulary employed refers both to bodily and to mental transactions. To say that a statesman developed tooth-ache is to say something about his tooth and also something about his sensations; about his thoughts as well if the toothache is a diplomatic toothache. When I say that I went for a walk what I report is not exclusively the occurrence of certainly bodily movements; seeing sights and having bodily sensations are part of taking a walk. We may say, then, that much of our vocabulary refers jointly both to physical and to psychical processes. That it does so is a natural consequence of the intimate connections between bodies and minds. It is not always obvious whether a word, or a phrase, is thus jointly referent or

[1] *The Physical Basis of Mind*, p. 77.

not. It may straddle in one use but not in another; thus the word 'climb' implies experiences if used of a man but not if used of a mechanical toy. The physical reference of 'hungry' is clearer than that of 'angry'. But Aristotle implied that 'angry' is jointly referent when he remarked that 'to say that it is the soul which is angry is as inexact as it would be to say that the soul weaves webs or builds houses'.[1]

Thus words which ostensibly describe mental states and activities often refer also to bodily doings. Conversely words which ostensibly describe bodies often refer also to mental doings. Suppose that Ryle's unpartitioned biographical account states that the mountain climbed by the hero was covered with green vegetation and that its snowy summit glistened in the sun. In this statement 'climbed' is jointly referent. But so also are 'green' and 'glistened'. For to mention the colour of a thing is to say what it looks like; and to talk about the looks of things is to talk about visual experiences. Hence to speak of green grass and glistening snow is to refer to psychical processes as well as to physical processes. The same can, of course, be said of any description of things which refers to the appearances they present, to their so-called secondary qualities.

We must now consider the epiphenomenalist part of the view which I described as being supported by the facts so far considered. I used 'epiphenomenalism' as a term for the doctrine that the mind, being discontinuous and dependent on the body, is not a thing in its own right but is incidental to a body which has a certain degree and kind of complexity. The soul or mind, on this view, is not a permanent and continuously existing *owner* of experiences, but only a permanent *possibility* of experiences. No doubt all experiences must and do have owners: my experiences are mine and yours are yours. But what account is the epiphenomenalist to give of what is meant by saying that this experience is mine and that one is yours? He will be tempted to say that my experiences are just those based on one particular body and yours are those based on another particular body. But, if he says this, he will find himself in a difficulty when he considers the question how he comes to know that his experiences are based on his body. Consider, for example, the fact that we see with our eyes. We have to find out that it is so. I have shut my eyes and cannot see, but I remember that earlier my eyes were open and I was seeing. Any such account presupposes that I can identify past experiences as mine independently of coming to know that they are connected with my body. That they are

---

[1] *De Anima A* 4, 408 b11-15.

so connected is an empirical discovery. But if my ownership of experiences were correctly defined in terms of connection with a particular body, it could not be an empirical discovery. For to say that my experiences are connected with a particular body would be to utter the empty tautology that the experiences connected with a particular body are the experiences connected with a particular body. In short, there is a fundamental sense, not definable in terms of connection with a particular body, in which my experiences are mine; the epiphenomenalist would like to evade this but, like everyone else, he has to assume it when he is off his guard.

This argument purports to show that what is meant when it is said that two experiences, occurring at different times, belong to the same person cannot be defined in terms of their connection with the same physical organism. This conclusion is confirmed by reflection on what is involved in a man's concern with his own past and future. We have to ask whether the epiphenomenalist's account of the identity of a person does justice to the familiar, if puzzling, sense in which a man's experiences are his own.

A man looking back at some action of his own in the past may congratulate himself that he did so well or feel sorry that he did so ill. Again he may look forward with pleasure, or with fear, to an experience which he expects to enjoy, or to endure, in the future. Now the past activities for which a man claims to be responsible, and the future experiences to which he looks forward, certainly were and will be based on the bodily organism which is the basis of his present retrospective and prospective thoughts and feelings. But, if a man is asked why he accepts responsibility for activities connected with his bodily organism, he will reply, if he takes the question seriously, that it is because they are *his* activities. If he is asked why he is specially interested in the experiences which will occur in connection with his bodily organism, he will again answer that it is because they will be *his* experiences; it will be he who enjoys or endures them. In both cases he will seem to himself to be giving a *reason* for his own exclusive responsibility and concern. He will say that his answer is indeed a truism or platitude, but certainly not that it is an empty tautology. To say that the experiences which were or will be based on my body were or will be mine is not just to say that they were or will be based on my body.

I can see no convincing way of defending the view which I have called epiphenomenalism against this argument. Unless a defence can be found, it is necessary to give up the view that the persistent owner of a set of experiences which are the experiences of one person is simply the living body on which they are based. It becomes necessary to suggest that the soul or mind of Smith is, after all, something more or other than a permanent possibility of Smithian experiences. When I rehearse the arguments against epiphenomenalism I am tempted to say that the mind is a persisting subject or owner of experiences. But to this temptation there are strong counter-temptations. For, in the first place, it is very difficult to attach any clear meaning to the notion of a persisting non-physical subject of experiences. In the second place the facts which make epiphenomenalism a plausible view remain facts: our experience is dependent on our bodies and is interrupted by gaps. Hence epiphenomenalism continues to attract us even after we have become convinced that what it maintains is in clear conflict with what we all believe about ourselves.

The reader may ask how the above excursus helps towards an understanding and assessment of Aristotle's doctrine of human nature. My intention is to make it easier to follow what I have said in this chapter (V) about the entelechy doctrine and what I shall say in the following chapter (VI) about dispositions and in the final chapter (XVI) about the nature of reason (*nous*). The technical terms which have been commonly used in discussing the mind–body problem, terms such as monism and dualism, interaction and epiphenomenalism, can be convenient; but they are highly ambiguous. So I have tried to make as clear as I can in what senses I take such terms to be applicable to Aristotle's views. If I have expressed or implied personal opinions on the problem itself, my object has been not to buttress my interpretations of the Aristotelian texts, but rather to declare an interest or prejudice.

In what Aristotle says about human nature we find combined or juxtaposed a biological view of man as one animal among others and a Platonic, or near-Platonic, view of man as a spiritual or mental entity in association with a living body. It has been thought that Aristotle could not have adopted the former view without abandoning the latter. The two views are, therefore, to be regarded not as two elements in one doctrine but as two doctrines held at different times. This interpretation has plausibility. But my prejudice is against accepting it, at least without first trying out the idea that Aristotle never regarded acceptance of the biological view or point of view as involving the rejection of the doctrine that a man's mind, or an element in it, is in some sense independent of his body. My reason for this prejudice is that the phenomena to be saved, the apparent facts, do not point clearly to any single, and certainly to no simple, solution of the problem. It should not, therefore, surprise us to find Aristotle implying that, if we are to 'save the appearances', we must try to have it both ways.

VI

THE GENERAL NATURE OF ETHICAL VIRTUE

ARISTOTLE defines ethical virtue as 'a state of character concerned with choice, lying in a mean, i.e. the mean relative to us, this being determined by a rational principle, and by that principle by which the man of practical wisdom would determine it' (*EN* II. 6, 1106 b36–1107 a2). What, according to Aristotle, is a 'state of character' (*hexis*)? What is his account of choice (*prohairesis*)? How are we to interpret the doctrine that virtue lies 'in a mean'? What is 'practical wisdom' (*phronēsis*), and what are the 'principles' (*logoi*) which its possessor applies in his own actions and in prescribing the actions of others? There is very little in Aristotle's treatise which would not have to be considered in any adequate discussion of these questions. I shall here consider the doctrine that virtue is 'a state of character concerned with choice'. But I shall reserve for separate treatment the problems involved in the interpretation and criticism in detail of Aristotle's doctrine of choice.

To say of someone that he is virtuous is to say that he has a certain quality. Quality is the kind or category of being to which virtue, as being a state of character (*hexis*), belongs. Aristotle's treatment of virtue in the *EN* does not mention explicitly the doctrine of categories. He does not say that being a state of character is one way of being a quality (*poiotēs*). But that he implies this is clear when we consider the argument in II. 5 which leads to the conclusion that virtue is a state of character along with the classification of kinds of quality in chapter 8 of the *Categories*.

In the *EN* he says that 'things that are found in the soul are of three kinds—passions, faculties, states of character' (1105 b20). He reaches by elimination the conclusion that virtue is a state of character. Virtues are not 'passions' (pathē). For men are not judged good or bad, praised or blamed, for being in emotional states like anger and fear (1105 b28–1106 a2). Again virtues, unlike passions, 'are modes of choice or involve choice' (1106 a2–4). Further, in respect of the passions we are said to be moved (kineisthai), but in respect of the virtues and the vices we are said not to be moved but to be disposed in a particular way (1106 a4–6). So much for the elimination in II. 5 of the suggestion that virtues might be 'passions'. The second suggestion is that they might be 'faculties'. Faculties are 'the things in virtue of which we are said to be capable' of feeling passions, e.g. of becoming angry, or being pained, or feeling pity (1105 b23–5). We have faculties by nature and we are not good or bad in respect of them. So virtues are not faculties. Not being either passions or faculties they must be states of character.

Before we turn to the list of kinds of quality in *Categories* 8 we should ask whether the three kinds of 'things that are found in the soul' according to *EN* are different kinds of qualities. Prima facie there is an important difference between passions and affections on the one hand and both faculties and states of character on the other; the difference marked by the technical terms, 'occurrent' and 'dispositional', as applied to physical or mental states. In general, dispositions are defined in terms of occurrences; brittleness in terms of breaking under certain conditions, irritability in terms of feeling angry and of acting in certain ways if and when provoked. Being angry in an occurrent sense is not a quality. In Aristotle's list of categories being-affected (paschein) is a category on its own.[1] But 'angry' has itself a dispositional as well as an occurrent sense. When we say that Smith is angry with Brown we need not be implying that Smith is now thinking of Brown and feeling hot under the collar; Smith may be asleep or attending to something else. In *EN* II. 5 Aristotle gives the following list of passions: 'appetite, anger, fear, confidence, envy, joy, friendly feeling, hatred, longing, emulation, pity, and in general the feelings that are accompanied by pleasure or pain' (1105 b21–3). Most of the words in this list may refer, according to context,

[1] *Categories* 4, 1 b25–7.

either to actual feelings, a thrill or a throb, and occurrent thoughts or to a temporary proneness to have an actual feeling or thought, and to behave in certain characteristic ways; for example, in the case of the appetite for food, either an empty feeling and salivation or the liability to suffer these affections when food is seen or mentioned. This ambiguity in the notion of an affection perhaps helps to account for the apparent contradiction concerning its categorial classification. When the affection is thought of as an occurrent transaction in which the subject is passive, it is not a quality, as Aristotle remarks in the *EE* (*B* 2). This is illustrated in the *Categories* by the remark that, when a man blushes for shame or turns pale from fear, he is not qualified as of a ruddy or pallid complexion (9 b30–2). Nevertheless an affection can be regarded as qualifying its subject. When we say that a man is ashamed we are not referring only to the occurrence of a single blush. But we are referring to something less permanent than a virtue or a vice. As Joachim points out, passions, faculties, and states fall into an order which depends upon 'the extent to which the thing's own being is involved in the qualification: the degree in which the thing itself contributes to the quality or character affirmed to belong to it in the judgement in question: and, therefore, also the permanence or transitoriness, the necessity or accidental character, of the inherence of the predicate in the subject'.[1]

In chapter 8 of the *Categories*, Aristotle tells us that quality is 'one of the things spoken of in a number of ways' (8 b25–6). As J. L. Ackrill points out, 'he does not mean that the word "quality" is ambiguous but only that there are different kinds of quality'.[2] Aristotle distinguishes four kinds. (i) A member of the first kind (8 b26–9 a13) may be called a 'state' (*hexis*) or a 'condition' (*diathesis*). 'Condition' is generic. States are always conditions, but conditions are not always states (9 a10–13). A state is a condition which is relatively stable and enduring (8 b27–8); for example, a virtue or a branch of knowledge (8 b29). As examples of conditions Aristotle gives 'hotness and chill and sickness and health and the like' (8 b36–7). (ii) The second kind of quality (9 a14–27) is a 'natural capacity or incapacity'. Health reappears under this

---

[1] Commentary, p. 82.   [2] Translation and Notes, p. 104.

head along with the capacities to which we refer when we speak of men as boxers or runners. Ackrill complains of Aristotle's lack of precision and thoroughness in his 'mapping of this territory' (p. 105). For example, is the 'capacity' of the boxer ability to fight without training or ability to acquire skill through training? Hardness and softness are also classed as capacities, being respectively a capacity and an incapacity not to be divided easily (9 a24–7). The 'faculties' of *EN* II. 5, e.g. the liability to feel anger or pity, might fall under this head. Under this head also, or under the head of conditions which are not states, would fall what Aristotle in *EN* VI. 13 calls 'natural virtues', the tendencies towards virtues which men have from birth (1144 b1 ff.). But they might also be placed under Aristotle's third head, 'affective qualities'. These classifications are vague in two distinct ways. First, some of the terms, in particular 'capacity' and 'condition' or 'disposition', can be used in both wider and narrower senses; in their widest senses both can be used to cover anything which is potential not actual, dispositional not occurrent. Thus in the *Rhetoric* (I. 9) virtue is said to be a power, 'a faculty of providing and preserving good things, or a faculty of conferring many great benefits, and benefits of all kinds on all occasions' (1366 a36–b1). Secondly, the kinds of quality are not definitely demarcated species but rather cross-sections of a continuum. (iii) Aristotle's third kind of quality (9 a28–10 a10) consists of 'affective qualities and affections'. We have anticipated the most important points to be made about these in discussing the 'passions' of *EN* II. 5. As instances of affective qualities Aristotle gives first 'sweetness, bitterness, sourness, and all their kin, and also hotness and coldness and paleness and darkness' (9 a29–31). Most of these qualities are called 'affective' not in respect of any affection of the things that have the qualities, but 'because each of the qualities mentioned is productive of an affection of the senses' (9 a35–b7). 'For sweetness produces a certain affection of taste, hotness one of touch, and the rest likewise' (9 b7–9). In some cases, however, the term 'affective quality' is appropriate for a different reason, because the quality has been 'brought about by an affection', as when a man's complexion is pale as a result of illness or tanned by the sun (9 b9–27).

Aristotle contrasts such lasting conditions, as we have seen, with the pallor of fear and the blush of shame (9 b30–2). He adds that affective qualities may be psychical as well as physical: 'with regard to the soul also we speak of affective qualities and affections' (9 b33–5); for example, madness and irascibility which may be present from birth as the result of certain affections. (iv) The fourth kind of quality (10 a11–26) is 'shape and the external form of each thing, and in addition straightness and curvedness and anything like these' (10 a11–13). Aristotle raises the question whether 'open-textured' and 'close-textured', 'rough' and 'smooth', signify qualities; he gives a negative answer on the ground that these terms refer to the relative position of the parts composing a whole. But, as Ackrill remarks (p. 107), if these predicates are not qualities, it is hard to see in what category they fall. Moreover, the same objection could be made to classing shape as a quality.

We have now set beside each other the division, in *EN* ii. 5, of psychical states into passions, faculties, and states of character, and the division, in *Categories* 8, of qualities into states and conditions, natural capacities and incapacities, affective qualities and affections, shapes, etc. We have seen that nearly all the types of quality, whether physical or psychical, which Aristotle distinguishes resemble each other in a certain important respect; to have a quality is to have, or to lack, a capacity or liability or tendency, whether natural or acquired, to respond in certain ways, whether actively or passively, to environmental conditions. There are two apparent exceptions to this generalization about Aristotle's doctrines in these chapters. The first is that, when we predicate an affection or a passion, we may be reporting some particular event or transaction; a fit of temper not irritability, a fracture not brittleness. But this exception is only apparent since, as we have seen, this kind of predicate is not in the category of quality. The second exception, or apparent exception, is Aristotle's fourth kind of quality in the *Categories*; square, spherical, straight. A thing is said to be sweet or hot because it 'produces an affection of the senses' (9 a35–b9). Sugar is sweet; a lump, if put in the mouth, would produce a sensation of sweetness. A similar account might be offered of physical shape. This penny is round. If seen, it would cause a certain kind of visual experience, present a round appearance. But we find it natural to think that there is a difference between sweetness or colour or sound on the one hand and shape on the other; a difference of the kind explained by Locke when he said that secondary qualities, which include sweetness and colour, are 'powers', while primary qualities, which include 'figure', are not. We are inclined to think, when we reflect on the causal processes involved in perception, that sweetness and colour just *are* powers. But we are also inclined to think that a penny *both* looks round and elliptical *and* has a roughly round *physical* shape, this not being merely a power. If this distinction between primary and secondary qualities is right in principle, we must allow that there are non-dispositional qualities, or at least predicates, as well as dispositional ones. There is thus an important way in which Aristotle's fourth kind of quality is a different kind of predicate from the rest: it is, or in certain contexts may be, non-dispositional. One further remark may be made at this point. Locke's use of the terms 'primary' and 'secondary' suggests, and is doubtless intended to suggest, that the fact that something has a certain disposition depends on facts which are not of this form, on facts about the non-dispositional nature of things. This is a difficult idea; but it is deeply rooted, if not fundamental, in the thinking of common sense and of science. We shall return to it later in our discussion of Aristotle's theory of those dispositions of human beings which we call virtues and vices.

We have seen that the most general category to which the virtues and vices belong is that of potentiality or power, and that Aristotle's name for the kind of power which they are is *hexis*, state of character or state of mind. In *EN* I. 13 the states with which Aristotle is concerned in the *Ethics* are divided into intellectual (*dianoētikai*) and moral (*ēthikai*). Both are acquired and not natural or innate. In II. 1 Aristotle tells us that intellectual virtues come into existence and develop as the result of teaching and need experience and time, while moral virtues are the result of habituation (1103 a14–18). Reflection on the facts shows that this contrast is somewhat misleading. Habituation, like instruction, requires time and experience, and is not confined to moral virtues. In the *Metaphysics* flute-playing is said to be acquired by habituation. Again the trainer in moral virtues does not rely on habituation only, but also gives verbal instruction, the word itself being used later in the chapter (1103 b12 *tou didaxontos*) in connection with moral virtue. In *EN* x. 9 we learn that the moral education in virtue given through laws should consist in the first place of exhortation or protreptic by the law-makers, and that threats of punishment are needed for 'those who disobey and are of inferior nature' (1180 a1–10). This point is important, as we shall see, in connection with Aristotle's treatment of the paradox of habituation in *EN* ii. 4: how men can become virtuous by doing virtuous actions if, to do virtuous actions, they must first be virtuous.

In *EN* ii. 1 Aristotle contrasts the virtues, as being acquired powers, first with the powers of 'things that exist by nature', his instance being the natural tendency of a stone to fall: you cannot train a stone to fly up or fire to fall down (1103 a19–23). There is no natural tendency to virtuous behaviour, but this does not mean that virtue is contrary to nature. What is natural is the capacity to acquire virtue by habituation (a 23–6). Aristotle secondly contrasts the virtues with capacities which are innate in human beings, e.g. the kinds of sense-perception: we had the senses before we used them, while the virtues and the arts are acquired by exercising them (1103 a26–b2). The powers of non-rational beings, and the natural or innate powers of rational beings, are alike non-rational. Non-rational powers can be exercised, or actualized, only in one way. Rational powers, or at least arts and sciences, can be exercised in opposite ways. This division of powers into rational and non-rational, which is briefly indicated in *EN* ii. 1, is stated more fully in *Metaphysics* (Θ 2 and 5).

Since some such principles are present in soulless things, and others in things possessed of soul, and in soul and in the rational part of the soul, clearly some potencies will be non-rational and some will be accompanied by knowledge of a rational formula. This is why all arts, i.e. all productive forms of knowledge, are potencies; they are principles of change in another thing or in the artist himself considered as other. And each of those which are accompanied by reason is alike capable of contrary effects, but one non-rational power produces one effect; e.g. the hot is capable only of heating, but the medical art can produce both disease and health. The reason is that science is a rational formula, and the same rational formula explains a thing and its privation (sterēsis), only not in the same way; and in a sense it applies to both, but in a sense it applies rather to the positive fact. Therefore such sciences must deal with contraries. (Θ 2, 1046 a36–b11.)

The doctrine is developed further in chapter 5. Non-rational powers are exercised necessarily whenever 'the agent and the patient meet in the way appropriate to the potency in question' (1048 a5–8). In the case of rational powers there is no such necessity. 'For the non-rational potencies are all productive of one effect each, but the rational produce contrary effects, so that if they produced certain effects necessarily they would produce contrary effects at the same time; but this is impossible. That which decides, then, must be something else; I mean by this desire or choice' (1048 a8–11). Aristotle adds that, when desire is present decisively, action occurs (a11–16).

The ethical virtues, as defined by Aristotle, do not fit in any simple way into the classification of powers, in the Metaphysics, as rational or irrational. Ross, in his Introduction to his edition of the Metaphysics (p. cxxv), says that Aristotle classes the moral virtues, along with the arts or productive forms of knowledge, as rational powers. They are not innate but are acquired by exercise, and they involve conformity to rational principles. On the other hand, in the way in which the art of medicine is a power to do either of two contrary things, a moral virtue is not an ambivalent power. For, whereas it requires the external intervention of 'something else', desire or choice, to determine whether the art of medicine is used to cure or to kill, a moral virtue is itself a disposition to desire or choose and not merely a capacity to know; it is not neutral but, by definition, on the side of the angels. On its cognitive side, indeed, it might be held, although Aristotle does not say so, to be a 'power of opposites' for the same reason as Aristotle gives for the ambivalence of an art: 'the same rational formula explains a thing and its privation' (1046 b7–10). Unless a man knows which road is right he cannot point infallibly to the wrong road. A vicious man might do the right thing by mistake. Perhaps only a polite man has the delicacy of perception required for really exquisite rudeness, and only a just man can make no mistake about what it would be most unjust to do. But if we omit, as Ross here does, to note the sense in which moral virtue is *not* a power of opposites, we are failing to credit Aristotle with the discovery of an important dissimilarity between virtue and any art. Joachim, in his commentary, also attempts to connect Aristotle's doctrine of rational and irrational powers with his account of ethical virtue in *EN* ii. But he does so in a curious way: 'We are born with a mere capacity for feeling and reacting to feeling either rightly or wrongly, and we have to convert this capacity, which is indeterminately a capacity for opposites, into an established habit of feeling and reacting rightly, into a *hexis* which is a moral virtue' (p. 72). I know of no authority for this use of the Aristotelian expression 'capacity for opposites'. It has nothing to do with the use of the expression found, as we have seen, in *Metaphysics* Θ.

Thus virtue for Aristotle is a state of character which manifests itself in choice or preference (*hexis prohairetikē*). Any translation of this crucial expression inevitably begs questions the discussion of which must be based on an analysis of Aristotle's set treatment of preference in the early chapters, especially chapter 5, of *EN* iii. In the preceding paragraph I have spoken evasively of 'a disposition to desire or choose'. I have quoted an expression from Joachim, 'an established habit of feeling and reacting rightly'. In *EN* iii. 3 *prohairesis* is defined as a 'deliberate desire of things in our own power' (1113 a10–11). 'For when we have decided as a result of deliberation, we desire in accordance with our deliberation'. Preference is thus a desire, following on deliberation, to initiate a change judged to be in our power. But there is much in what Aristotle says about preference which suggests that he has in mind, not a desire which precedes action, but rather the action itself considered, in abstraction from its aspect as an event in the physical world, as the experienced activity of the agent. Preference, Aristotle says in *EN* iii. 2, 'is thought to be most closely bound up with virtue and to discriminate characters better than actions do' (1111 b5–6). The thought here seems to be that it is a man's intention and purpose in acting, rather than the actual result achieved, which is correlated with his character. As a manifestation of character the pulling of the trigger of a gun which misfires is equivalent to murder. Preference is apparently thought of as purposive activity rather than mere desire. Again in *EN* VI. 2 Aristotle says, rather mysteriously, that preference is 'either desiderative reason or ratiocinative desire, and such an origin of action is a man' (1139 b4–5). Ross[1] treats Aristotle's doctrine of choice as an attempt to formulate a 'conception of the will'. Aristotle's statement that choice 'may be called either desireful reason or reasonable desire implies that desire is not its genus, that it is a new thing different from either of its preconditions'. Aristotle's 'preference', so understood, is an act of choosing or willing, an initiation which, when it issues in change or in the prevention of change, is what we call an action. Here again we are confronted by a difficult question of interpretation. In what sense, according to Aristotle, is a man's choice or will 'an origin of action'? Is choice, as the expression (*hexis prohairetikē*) suggests, the causally necessary manifestation in appropriate conditions of a formed character?[2] Or is it, as Aristotle sometimes (e.g. in *De Interpretatione* 9) seems to imply, a spontaneous initiation, a fresh start, undetermined by pre-existent causes? In the *Ethics* the place where this issue between the freedom of indeterminism and determinism comes nearest to the surface is Aristotle's tentative but searching treatment of responsibility in the first five chapters of *EN* III.

'State', 'disposition', 'habit'—these are the words which suggest themselves as translations of *hexis*. 'Habit' is specially tempting as being the Latin for the Greek, and because habits, like *hexeis*, are the products of repetitive lessons, of habituation. But there are important differences between the results in different cases of learning lessons. Sometimes the learner ends with a capacity to do something which he had not been able to do at all; to drive a car or mend shoes or play a violin. Sometimes he learns to do quickly,

---

[1] *Aristotle*, pp. 199–200.   [2] Cf. *Metaphysics* 1048 a11–16.

and without attending to what he is doing, what he started by being able to do only slowly and attentively; putting on his clothes or brushing his teeth, for example, or presenting arms. We tend to label as habitual, or as merely habitual, activities which are performed without effort and also without attention and care. Actions which proceed from a *hexis* are effortless but careful and attentive. As in the case of an accomplished tennis player, the things which are done automatically are the basis of heedful performances at a higher level. Here virtue, as conceived by Aristotle, resembles the virtuosity of the accomplished games player or craftsman. Mere drill teaches a man to do the same thing in the same circumstances without attending to what he is doing; but virtuosity, like virtue, involves doing the appropriately different thing attentively in varying circumstances. The virtuous action is second nature and not against the grain; but it is not mechanical. The agent must have knowledge and he must choose (*EN* II. 4, 1105 a31–2). There is a nice discrimination in his actions and a fine appropriateness in his feelings: 'but to feel at the right times, with reference to the right objects, towards the right people, with the right motives, and in the right way, is what is both intermediate and best, and this is characteristic of virtue. Similarly with regard to actions also' (*EN* II. 6, 1106 b21–3).

How do habituation and training produce virtuous dispositions? Aristotle recognizes that we find this question difficult. In *EN* II. 4 he formulates the following puzzle. We are inclined to say both (*a*) that we become virtuous by doing virtuous actions and (*b*) that, unless we are already virtuous, we cannot do virtuous actions. The virtuous actions which produce virtue must clearly be different from the actions which manifest virtue. 'The question might be asked what we mean by saying that we must become just by doing just acts, and temperate by doing temperate acts; for if men do just and temperate acts, they are already just and temperate, exactly as, if they do what is in accordance with the laws of grammar and of music, they are grammarians and musicians' (1105 a17–21). Aristotle escapes without difficulty from this contradiction, although his solution still leaves him with a problem. He points out that the performances which produce a virtue or a technical accomplishment, while not strictly virtuous or accomplished, have an external similarity to the performances which manifest a virtue or an accomplishment. We learn by 'going through the motions'. 'It is possible to do something that is in accordance with the laws of grammar, either by chance or at the suggestion of another. A man will be a grammarian, then, only when he has both done something grammatical and done it grammatically; and this means doing it in accordance with the grammatical knowledge in himself' (1105 a22–6). Aristotle next asserts that there are certain differences between an art and a virtue. In the arts the goodness lies in the product. But in virtuous action the agent must be in a certain state: he must have knowledge, he must choose the act and choose it for its own sake, and his action must 'proceed from a firm and unchangeable character' (1105 a26–33). This passage is puzzling in two ways. First, it exaggerates the difference between an art and a virtue. For an artistic performance, just as much as a virtuous action, manifests, unless it is a mere fluke, an established disposition, in the case of the artist a skill. Indeed, with reference to grammar and music, Aristotle has just pointed this out. Secondly the relevance to what has preceded of this contrast between arts and virtues is not made clear. The point seems to be that, because a virtuous action requires disciplined desire and rightness of motive, not knowledge alone, there is a greater difference between the acts performed before and after learning. Hence the fact that we learn by repeatedly going through the motions is more puzzling in the case of the virtues than in the case of the arts.

The question then remains how non-virtuous actions, actions done under direction or even under compulsion, produce virtues. To say, as Aristotle does in *EN* II. 1, that, while virtue is not an endowment of nature, we have a natural tendency to acquire virtue is, perhaps, only a way of saying that the thing does happen: 'we are adapted by nature to receive them, the virtues, and are made perfect by habit' (1103 a23–6). We have an aptitude for understanding and obeying rules. Hence moral training is not merely, and not necessarily, the inculcating of patterns of behaviour by the use of rewards and punishments, the carrot and the stick. It is also, as we saw earlier, an appeal to our power to see the difference between right and wrong, the better and the worse, and our tendency to prefer the better when we see it. Aristotle expounds this in *EN* x. 9, and stresses the educational function of the laws (1179 b31–2). 'This is why some think that legislators ought to stimulate men to virtue and urge them forward by the motive of the noble, on the assumption that those who have been well advanced by the formation of habits will attend to such influences; and that punishments and penalties should be imposed on those who disobey and are of inferior nature, while the incurably bad should be completely banished'.[1] Aristotle is here referring to the view expressed by Plato in the *Laws* (718–23) where he suggests that each law should have a protreptic preface, and formulates a marriage law as an example. It is difficult to find any general or radical fault in Aristotle's theory of moral training. A person who starts by obeying a rule through fear of penalties, or hope of rewards, may end by obeying it, thinking it right and reasonable, for better reasons. And perhaps he would not end as he does, choosing to conform for the good of his soul or of the city, if he had not begun, and been induced to begin, at a lower level. Our understanding of the process may be helped by reflection on the variety of possible motives, or motive-factors. There are motives and sentiments which would generally be regarded as higher than the mere desire to avoid material penalties but still as falling short of the true moral motive: patriotism, for example, and the desire to be well thought of by others, especially one's own immediate circle of relatives, friends, and professional colleagues, and perhaps by oneself. Plato had recognized in the love of honour such an intermediate motive. So Aristotle in III. 8 describes 'political courage', of which the motive is the desire for honour and the fear of disgrace, as being a near approach to true virtue. 'This kind of courage is most like that which we described earlier, because it is due to virtue; for it is due to shame and to desire of a noble object, i.e. honour, and avoidance of disgrace which is ignoble' (1116 a27–9). Perhaps the highest motive for right conduct seldom operates with both purity and strength. Its develop-

---

[1] 1180 a5–10; cf. a21–2 and *Politics* 1287 a32.

ment may be assisted by these other quite respectable motives, the desire to excel and the desire to be esteemed. Moreover, when the highest motive has been developed, other motives can reinforce it and make the good life less a matter of tears and sweat than it would otherwise be.

We have seen that, according to Aristotle, virtues and vices are acquired dispositional qualities. A dispositional quality can be defined only in terms of its actual manifestations, and such a definition is expressed in hypothetical statements mentioning the conditions of these manifestations. For example, to say that glass is brittle is to say that, if it is (were) struck with a hammer, it breaks (would break). To say that something is elastic is to say that, if pushed and pulled, it will change in shape but will revert to its original shape if the pushing and pulling is discontinued. Brittleness and elasticity are physical dispositions in the sense that the changes which have to be mentioned in defining these qualities are all physical changes. Shyness, on the other hand, would not be classed as a physical quality or disposition. It is true that a shy man will dodge to avoid a meeting or blush when addressed. But the manifestations of shyness include thoughts and feelings as well as bodily changes and movements. Let us speak of dispositions as psychical when their manifestations are not exclusively physical. Plainly virtues and vices are psychical dispositions, states of the soul.

Consider now the following question. When we say that something has a dispositional quality, are we saying only that, under certain conditions, it will change or act in a certain way? To say that glass is brittle is to say that when hit in a certain way it breaks. To say that a man is generous is to say that, in suitable circumstances, he will act generously. This will not do. To say that this piece of glass is brittle is not to say that it will be broken. To say that glass is brittle is not to say that any piece of glass ever was or will be broken, but rather that, under certain conditions, glass *would* break. In order to elucidate the concept of a disposition we need not 'when' but 'if' and the 'if' of unfulfilled conditions. To say that something has a dispositional quality is to say that it is such that, if certain things happened, certain other things would happen to it or be done by it. The distinction may be expressed as that between what is said by 'all *X*s are *y*' and 'all the *X*s are in fact *y*'. Some philosophers would express it by saying that the notion of a disposition involves the notion of natural law or natural necessity.

Glass, then, is brittle when it is not broken: it is such that it might be broken. Similarly Aristotle tells us that man is virtuous when 'asleep or in some other way quite inactive' (*EN* i. 8, 1098 b33–1099 a2). It might be thought that the point just made is at the back of Plato's mind when in the *Republic* he makes the cryptic remark that 'powers' are 'a kind of existent thing' (477 c1). It may be attributed more confidently to Aristotle when, in the *Metaphysics*, he criticizes the Megarian view that powers have no existence except when they are being exercised (Θ 3, 1046 b29). Aristotle objects that, on this view, a man will not have a technical capacity when he is not exercising it, e.g. will not be a builder when he is not actually building. He objects further that things will not have sensible qualities when no one is perceiving them. 'Nothing will be either cold or hot or sweet or perceptible at all if people are not perceiving it' (1047 a4–6). The implication is that things *are* indeed cold, hot, sweet, etc., when no one is perceiving them, but that to say that they have these qualities is to say that they have certain powers. This is also Locke's account of sensible qualities. We saw earlier that qualities which are powers are called by Locke 'secondary'. We must now consider more closely the meaning and justification of this term.

When we say of two men that the one is brave and unselfish the other cowardly and selfish what difference, if any, are we asserting that there is between them other than the differences described by the conditional assertions which would elucidate what it is for them to have these dispositional qualities? Do we assert that there are differences on which the differences between their dispositions depend? To this Ross gives the following answer:

But, it may be said, all that exists when the two men are not behaving is potentialities of behaving, or tendencies to behave. The answer to this is that there is no such thing as potentiality that is not rooted in actuality. That which potentially has the characteristic *a* can have it only by actually having some characteristic *b*. We have no means of knowing what is the actual characteristic that distinguishes the selfish man from the unselfish man, when neither is behaving selfishly or unselfishly; we can only say that there must be some difference between the two characters which actually exists, and becomes the cause of their different behaviours when the occasion arises. The man who habitually behaves bravely is in some sense really brave even when he is asleep, or when no occasion for bravery is present; and his bravery has moral goodness when it is dormant no less than when it is being exercised.[1]

The doctrine of this passage is not easy to follow. Bravery and cowardice are characteristics of the kind we have called dispositional. If these characteristics and the difference between them must depend on other characteristics and the difference between them we should have a regress which could be terminated only by characteristics which were not dispositional. It seems, then, that by the 'actual characteristic' on which bravery depends, the 'real bravery' which is actual even in sleep, Ross must mean something non-dispositional. But, if so, it is something of which Ross says that 'we have no means of knowing what it is'. How then can he assert that it is known to 'have moral goodness'? Surely it can have moral goodness only in a sense derivative from the sense in which the behaviour which it 'causes' has moral goodness.

The principle which Ross is expressing in what he says here about dormant virtues can be made more clear by reflection on dispositions which are purely physical, i.e. whose manifestations are exclusively physical. If we are told that a mushroom is edible and a toadstool is not, we assume that this difference must depend on some further difference between the two substances, say in respect of their biochemical constitution. Such further differences may be themselves in part dispositional, e.g. the difference between the dispositional properties of molecules pertaining respectively to mushrooms and toadstools. But we assume that, in the end, dispositional differences between one thing and another depend on differences which are not differences between dispositions but between characteristics which may be called

---

[1] *Foundations of Ethics*, p. 292.

'intrinsic'. The distinction here indicated between dispositional and intrinsic characteristics is the same as the distinction, to which I have referred earlier, drawn by Locke between secondary and primary qualities. The principle that dispositional characteristics are secondary, dependent on characteristics which are primary, is formulated as follows by C. D. Broad: 'Now dispositional properties themselves are, no doubt, merely conditional propositions or facts. But we always tend to assume that such conditional facts have a categorical basis in the more or less permanent *internal structure* of the continuant which is their subject'.[1]

A virtue is a disposition acquired by learning. We must consider the application of what has been said about dispositions in general to acquired dispositions, learned powers. Take the case of a man who spends a day learning for the first time to skate. He finds on a following day that he can perform better on his skates, and that he remembers the efforts he made and the mishaps he suffered on the earlier day. He has acquired two powers; a rudimentary ability to skate and an ability to remember certain events. Now we have obvious and good reasons for believing that the events of the earlier day account for the man's present possession and exercise of these powers. Further, since we reject causal action at a distance in time, we think it necessary to conclude that these events have in some enduring way altered the nature of the man, and that this altered nature accounts for the fact that he possesses now these powers which formerly he lacked. What sort of change in the man? An answer which is plausible, and to many seems obvious, is that it is a change in his body and, at least mainly, in his brain and nervous system. This answer is plausible partly because it is difficult to think of any other, but partly also because we have evidence of connections between mental capacities, such as memory, and the state of the brain: for example, damage to the brain may destroy or impair such capacities. If these ideas are accepted, we shall say that the 'categorical basis' of the power to remember yesterday's events on the ice includes as a standing condition the general integrity of the nervous system and as a differentiating condition the modification made in the system by

[1] *Examination of McTaggart's Philosophy*, II. i, p. 145.

yesterday's events. Broad speaks of these modifications as 'traces'. I have tried in this paragraph to state briefly the important distinction between dispositions and traces which he expounds in *Mind and its Place in Nature*.[1]

The idea that powers like the power to skate and the power to remember skating depend on physical traces, modifications of the brain and nervous system, is a reasonable assumption even if little or nothing is known in detail about the nature of the traces. Virtues and vices resemble such powers in being also psychical dispositions, but they are dispositions of a different kind. The differences might well make us hesitate to suggest without reservations that virtues and vices also depend on modifications of the brain and nervous system. But that they do so depend is boldly asserted by an eminent philosopher and psychologist, William James, in the following passage:

Could the young but realise how soon they will become mere walking bundles of habits, they would give more heed to their conduct while in the plastic state. We are spinning our own fates, good and evil, and never to be undone. Every smallest stroke of virtue or of vice leaves its never so little scar [cf. 'trace']. The drunken Rip van Winkle, in Jefferson's play, excuses himself for every fresh dereliction by saying, 'I won't count this time'. Well! he may not count it, and a kind heaven may not count it; but it is being counted none the less. Down among his nerve-cells and fibres the molecules are counting it, registering and storing it up to be used against him when the next temptation comes. Nothing we ever do is, in strict scientific literalness, wiped out. Of course, this has its good side as well as its bad one. As we become permanent drunkards by so many separate drinks, so we become saints in the moral, and authorities and experts in the practical and scientific spheres, by so many acts and hours of work.[2]

The view that powers and tendencies in the soul have a basis in the body is in general agreement with the doctrine about the soul which Aristotle stated in the *De Anima* when he said that the soul is the form or 'entelechy' of the body.[3] We have discussed this celebrated definition in the preceding chapter. We saw that at

---

[1] See Section C, chapter x. [2] *Textbook of Psychology* (1906), p. 149.
[3] B 1, 412 a27–8; 2, 414 a12–14.

least a very important part of what the definition affirms, in its application to the souls of men and other animals, is that corresponding to, and in connection with, every psychical and mental process there occurs at the same time a process in the body. According to Aristotle, as Ross puts it in his edition of the *Parva Naturalia*, 'all psychological phenomena are essentially psychophysical' (p. 14). At the beginning of the *De Anima* (*A* 1, 403 a3 ff.) Aristotle asks whether the affections (*pathē*) of the soul are all common to the soul and the body. That some are is, in Aristotle's view, an obvious fact of experience. For example, the dependence of sense-perception on bodily organs is evident.[1] Again we are familiar with the bodily side of emotional states, with blushing and trembling. We can say of anger, as Aristotle goes on to point out, both with the 'physicist' that it is 'a boiling of the blood or warm substance surrounding the heart' and with the 'dialectician' that it is 'the desire to return pain for pain'; the former gives the matter, the latter the form or essence.[2] But in answer to the question whether there is always a bodily side Aristotle, as we saw, gives only a qualified affirmative: emotions, desires, sensation, imagination, all involve the body, but thought is a possible exception, although the body will be involved in thought also if thought is a kind of imagination or if it involves imagination (403 a5–10). Aristotle does indeed maintain in the *EN* that mind, the faculty of metaphysical theorizing, has an exceptional status (*EN* x. 7, 1177 a12–18; 8, 1178 a22–3). A similar doctrine, and a refinement of it, is part of the teaching of the *De Anima*, not only in *Γ*4 and 5 but also in passages in *A* and *B*.[3] This doctrine attributes to the nature of man a discontinuity which it is difficult to reconcile with the apparent continuity of cognitive experience, and indeed with Aristotle's own recognition of this continuity in *Post. An.* II. 19.[4] But we have no evidence that Aristotle ever ceased to hold the doctrine. On the other hand, he does not offer any solution of the difficulties raised by his own assertion that imagination and memory are to be classed, along

---

[1] *De Sensu* 1, 436 b6–7.   [2] *De Anima A* 1, 403 a29–b2.
[3] *A* 1, 403 a3–12; *B* 1, 413 a5–7; *B* 2, 413 b24–7; *B* 3, 415 a11–12.
[4] Cf. *Metaphysics A* 1.

with desire and emotion and sense-perception, as affections dependent on the body. This admission makes it difficult to form any positive concept of the contemplative activity of a 'separate' or disembodied mind.

Aristotle's view that, broadly speaking, every psychical process has a physical aspect, or physical concomitant, might be expected to lead him to suppose that the permanent changes made by experience in a being capable of learning from experience are physical changes. For, while psychical process is prima facie discontinuous or gappy, physical process in the body is taken to be continuous. Hence prima facie the living body is the only possible receptacle of the 'traces' on which learning and habituation depend. But we can go further. In the De Memoria Aristotle asserts explicitly that memory depends on physical traces. 'We must conceive that which is generated through sense-perception in the sentient soul, *and in the part of the body which is its seat*, as a sort of picture the having of which is memory.[1] The process of movement involved in the act of perception stamps in, as it were, a sort of impression of the percept, just as persons do who make an impression with a seal' (450 a27–32). That it is right to emphasize the reference here to the part played by the body is confirmed by a passage near the end of the De Memoria when Aristotle discusses the fact that recollection is involuntary: 'The reason why recollection is not under the control of their will is that, as those who throw a stone cannot stop it at their will when thrown, so he who tries to recollect and "hunts" sets up a process in a material part in which resides the affection' (453 a20–3). These passages make it clear that, in Aristotle's view, physical traces in the human body are an essential factor in what Broad refers to as the 'categorical basis' of a man's powers of memory, and more generally of his capacity to learn from experience.

Both in the De Anima and in the EN Aristotle refers, when it is relevant to do so, to the importance of the condition of our bodies as a factor affecting our tendencies to fly or lapse into states of emotional excitement. According to the condition of the body the same stimulus or provocation may produce reactions of

---

[1] Omit *to pathos* as Ross suggests.

widely varying intensity. 'Sometimes on the occasion of violent and striking occurrences there is no excitement or fear felt, on others faint and feeble stimulations produce these emotions, viz. when the body is already in a state of tension resembling its condition when we are angry. Here is a still clearer case: in the absence of any external cause of terror we find ourselves experiencing the feelings of a man in terror.'[1] In these cases the bodily tension is the 'categorical basis' of the emotional disposition, the irritability or nervousness. In *EN* iv. 9 Aristotle notes the connections between shame and blushing, fear and turning pale, and remarks that both seem to be in a sense bodily conditions (*sōmatika*), 'which is thought to be characteristic of feeling rather than of a state of character' (1128 b13–15). In x. 8 he points out that virtue of character is concerned with passions as well as actions. 'Some of them seem even to arise from the body, and virtue of character to be in many ways bound up with the passions' (1178 a14–16). In vii. 3 he assimilates incontinence to the condition of being mad or drunk. 'For outbursts of anger and sexual appetites and some other such passions, it is evident, actually alter our bodily condition, and in some men even produce fits of madness. It is plain, then, that incontinent people must be said to be in a similar condition to men asleep, mad, or drunk' (1147 a14–18).

I have argued that, if we are to understand Aristotle's doctrine that virtues and vices are states of character, it is helpful, and indeed necessary, to keep in mind his general view that mental or psychical states and activities, with the possible exception of theoretical reason, are intimately connected with bodily states and processes. For this side of his doctrine Aristotle would claim, and would be justified in claiming, the support of common sense and common experience. But it is important that, in our account of what Aristotle has to say, we should not rashly attribute to him doctrines of later philosophers which go beyond, and perhaps contradict, common sense and common experience; doctrines which, moreover, may be answers to questions which Aristotle did not explicitly ask. In saying this I have two such doctrines in mind.

[1] *De Anima A* 1, 403 a19–24.

The first asserts that, whereas physical events are often causes of mental or psychical effects, as in sense-perception or the sensation of pain caused by a blow or stab, mental events are never causes, or partial causes, of effects. The accepted name for this doctrine is epiphenomenalism. The proposition which it asserts appears to be inconsistent with common sense, since we all believe, for example, that our decisions have effects in the world and that our thoughts and emotions may affect the state of our bodies. Nothing that I have said about Aristotle's views, and so far as I know nothing said by Aristotle, would justify the suggestion that he was, or was inclined to be, an epiphenomenalist in this sense. As regards human actions, epiphenomenalism is so paradoxical that only incontrovertible evidence could justify its attribution to Aristotle or to anyone else. Again, the statement in *EN* vii. 3 quoted at the end of the last paragraph, that anger, for example, may alter our bodily condition, is prima facie inconsistent with epiphenomenalism.

The second doctrine which I have in mind as one which we should not be in a hurry to attribute to Aristotle asserts that all events, including human decisions and actions, are effects of causes, happen in accordance with natural necessity. The accepted name for this doctrine is, of course, determinism. Now it is true in general that we think of the manifestations of a disposition, the actualizations of a potentiality, as being caused events. Thus the thought that glass is brittle involves the thought that, if it were hit by a stone, its fracture would be an effect of the impact of the stone on a substance having the nature of glass. Similar remarks could be made with truth about at least some psychical dispositions. For example, it would be natural to say that, in an irritable man, a fit of temper was the effect of an insult. Moreover, as we have seen,[1] Aristotle himself seems to say, in *Metaphysics* Θ 5, that the manifestation of a disposition is the necessary consequence of the appropriate stimulus: 'When the agent and the patient meet in the way appropriate to the potency in question, the one must (*ananke*) act and the other be acted on' (1048 a5–7). But, as we have also seen,[2] a virtue, being 'a state of character concerned with

---

[1] pp. 100–1 above.   [2] pp. 101–3 above.

choice', is a special kind of disposition and one which does not fit into Aristotle's classification of powers in the *Metaphysics* (Θ 2 and 5). Before we could decide whether the fact that Aristotle classes virtue as a disposition justifies us in saying that he was explicitly or implicitly a determinist, we should have to answer two questions: first, what exactly is the meaning and application in Aristotle of the word translated 'choice' (*prohairesis*); and secondly, what Aristotle's doctrine is concerning the 'necessity' of events dependent on human decisions. As has been said,[1] these are difficult questions which can be discussed further only in connection with Aristotle's treatment of freedom and responsibility in *EN* III. 1–5 and with his discussion in *De Interpretatione* 9 of the application to future events of the Law of Excluded Middle.

According to Aristotle, vice as well as virtue is a state of character concerned with choice. He proceeds, in *EN* II. 6, to discuss the question what sort of state virtue is and how it differs from vice, his answer being that virtue lies in a mean and vice in extremes. Before we discuss this famous doctrine, there are some further comments to be made on Aristotle's general treatment of virtue. Ross has said justly that 'what is true in Aristotle has become part, and no small part, of the heritage of all educated men'.[2] The remark is applicable to Aristotle's account of moral virtue and moral habituation. But his account has also, as is to be expected, had its share of criticism and depreciation. Some reference to these criticisms may be helpful as throwing light on the limitations of Aristotle's treatment of the subject. It is convenient to start from a consideration of his division of virtue into virtues.

Aristotle enumerates and discusses particular ethical virtues and vices in two and a half books of the *EN* (from III. 6). In the second part of Book III he deals with courage and temperance; in Book IV with a number of less important virtues and vices; in Book V with justice. The fact that Aristotle describes each virtue separately must not be taken to imply that he thinks that a man can have one virtue without having others as well. On the contrary he tells us in VI. 13 that, while a man may have the

---

[1] p. 103 above.   [2] *Aristotle*, p. v.

natural endowment which fits him for one virtue but not for another, virtue in the proper sense is a unity. It is impossible to have ethical goodness in the strict sense (*kuriōs*) without practical wisdom (*phronēsis*) or practical wisdom without ethical goodness (1144 b30–2); and the presence of practical wisdom carries with it all the virtues (1145 a1–2). This is a rather surprising assertion and can be discussed only in connection with his account of practical wisdom. Aristotle gives several reasons for undertaking a detailed, and, as he claims, exhaustive enumeration and description of the ethical virtues. Thus in iv. 7 he claims that the enumeration will increase our knowledge of character, and that an exhaustive review will strengthen our confidence in the doctrine that the virtues are means (1127 a14–17). At the outset of his treatment he makes the claim to exhaustiveness: 'it will become plain how many they are' (1115 a5). An enumeration which claims to be exhaustive should be based on some single principle. Now Aristotle has said in ii. 6 that ethical virtue is 'concerned with passions and actions' (1106 b16–17). Thus we should expect him to base a classification of virtues either on a classification of passions or on a classification of actions. In fact, as Ross points out, 'their scope is defined sometimes by reference to a type of feeling, sometimes by reference to a type of action'.[1] He adds that 'no attempt is made at an exhaustive logical division of either feelings or actions' and that 'the order is haphazard'. Perhaps these criticisms are unnecessarily stern. For it might be said that no method of classifying feelings or actions could guarantee its own exhaustiveness, as does the classification of triangles into equilateral, isosceles, and scalene. Thus it is hard to see how any order could fail to be in some degree arbitrary. And it is clear that the order is not merely haphazard. Joachim ingeniously finds an 'underlying' plan based on a classification of the pleasures and pains with which the various virtues are concerned: bodily pleasures and pains; pleasures and pains of which man is susceptible as an owner of property, and as a civic person; the refined pleasures and pains of social intercourse and conversation.[2]

The order in which Aristotle in fact treats the virtues is the

[1] *Aristotle*, p. 202.   [2] *Commentary*, p. 115.

following. Having discussed first courage (III. 6-9), he goes on next to temperance (III. 10-12), giving as a reason for this transition that 'these seem to be the virtues of the irrational parts' (1117 b23-4). This is almost the only indication he gives of a principle of order or classification. Courage is 'a mean with regard to feelings of fear and confidence' (1115 a6-7). Temperance is 'concerned with the kind of pleasures that the other animals share in, which therefore appear slavish and brutish; these are touch and taste' (1118 a23-6). We might expect Aristotle to deal next, or between courage and temperance, with good temper (*praotēs*) which is 'a mean with respect to anger' (IV. 5, 1125 b26). But he goes on instead to analyse certain virtues and corresponding vices which are defined by reference not to passions but to actions. Liberality (IV. 1) is praised 'with regard to the giving and taking of wealth, and especially in respect of giving' (1119 b25-6). Magnificence (IV. 2) is also concerned with wealth; 'but it does not, like liberality, extend to all the actions that are concerned with wealth, but only to those that involve expenditure; and in those it surpasses liberality in scale' (1122 a19-22). Aristotle next (IV. 3) describes the proud man (*megalopsuchos*) whose virtue has as its sphere 'honours and dishonours' (1123 b21-2). After this celebrated or notorious portrait comes (IV. 4) another virtue, also concerned with honour, the nameless mean (1125 b17) between ambition and unambitiousness, 'which would appear to be related to pride as liberality is to magnificence' (1125 b2-4). Next Aristotle deals with good temper, a mean between irascibility and its opposite. This is followed by descriptions of three virtues of social intercourse: friendliness (IV. 6), truthfulness (IV. 7), and ready wit (IV. 8). These three virtues are 'all concerned with an interchange of words and deeds of some kind'. 'They differ, however, in that one is concerned with truth, and the other two with pleasantness. Of those concerned with pleasure, one is displayed in jests, the other in the general social intercourse of life' (1128 b 4-9). The concluding chapter (9) of Book IV deals with shame, which is more like a feeling than a state of character (1128 b11). The whole of Book V is taken up with the treatment of justice, and this concludes Aristotle's survey of the ethical virtues. Justice, being an ethical virtue, is a mean, 'but not in the same way as the other virtues' (1133 b32–3). Aristotle begins his discussion by drawing a distinction between universal justice and particular justice, and then examines in detail the varieties of particular justice. In the later chapters (8–11) of the book he discusses a number of questions about the inner nature of just action considered as involving choice.

Aristotle's description of particular virtues and vices is an analysis of contemporary society and ideas; 'a lively and often amusing account of the qualities admired or disliked by cultivated Greeks of Aristotle's time'.[1] In I. 7 happiness (*eudaimonia*) was defined as 'activity of the soul in accordance with virtue' (1098 a16–18), and Aristotle said that the details of the 'rough sketch' would be filled in later. This is what he is doing in his description of the virtues. It is perhaps hardly appropriate for a modern critic to feel either surprise or indignation when he finds that he does not always admire the qualities which were admired by 'cultivated Greeks of Aristotle's time'. Yet Aristotle's account in particular of the proud man (*megalopsuchos*) has had a bad press. 'A prig with the conceit and bad manners of a prig' was the verdict of one Oxford lecturer. Even Ross speaks disapprovingly of 'the self-absorption which is the bad side of Aristotle's ethics'.[2] 'The offensiveness of the picture is mitigated, but not removed, if we remember that the man who behaves like this is supposed to have, to start with, the highest possible merits.' Russell, in his *History of Western Philosophy*, after quoting Aristotle's description of the proud or magnanimous man, remarks: 'one shudders to think what a vain man would be like' (p. 198). Indeed Russell writes of Aristotle's views on ethics in a tone almost of exasperation. 'Aristotle's opinions on moral questions are always such as were conventional in his day' (p. 196). 'There is something unduly smug and comfortable about Aristotle's speculations on human affairs; everything that makes men feel a passionate interest in each other seems to be forgotten. Even his account of friendship is tepid. He shows no sign of having had any of those experiences which make it difficult to preserve sanity; all the more profound

[1] Ross, *Aristotle*, p. 202.   [2] *Aristotle*, p. 208.

aspects of the moral life are apparently unknown to him' (p. 206). These are surprising complaints. Was it 'conventional' to say, as Aristotle does, of the life of the philosopher that 'it is not in so far as he is a man that he will live so but in so far as something divine is present in him' (x. 7, 1177 b27–8)? The good man, according to Aristotle, 'does many acts for the sake of his friends and his country, and if necessary dies for them', 'gaining for himself nobility' (ix. 8, 1169 a18–22). 'As the virtuous man is to himself, he is to his friend also; for his friend is another self' (1170 b5–7). Is this a 'tepid' conception of friendship or of patriotism?

Aristotle's moral ideas and moral ideals are, in some degree, the product of his time, and cannot be expected to be adequate in the world of today. Scientific and material progress have extended man's moral horizons. His increasing power to determine his own environment, including now the power to make human survival impossible, has produced problems which Aristotle could not envisage. The history of moral ideas is not a subject in which philosophers, at least recently, have shown as much interest as perhaps they should. But a careful discussion of the differences between the Greek and the modern conceptions of virtue will be found in T. H. Green's *Prolegomena to Ethics*. Among the points considered by Green are the development, under the influence of Christian ideas, of the concept of self-denial, the need for an account more sophisticated than Aristotle's of the motives leading to excess in the sphere of physical appetites, and the extension of the sphere of morality to include all human beings as such. 'Where the Greek saw a supply of possible labour, having no end or function but to be made really serviceable to the privileged few, the Christian citizen sees a multitude of persons who, in their actual present condition, may have no advantage over the slaves of an ancient state, but who, in undeveloped possibility and in the claims which arise out of that possibility, are all that he himself is.'[1]

One reason, then, why Aristotle's account of the good man cannot be expected to satisfy us is that moral ideas have an historical context in the societies of their time. But there is a

[1] iii, ch. 5, § 270.

further reason for the fact that Aristotle's descriptions of virtues and vices may strike us as deficient in profundity and insight. This is that the effective constituents of a personality, the moving forces, are not virtues and vices, but sentiments such as attachment to family or friends or to a society, and interests in, for example, a science or music or a game. It is not possible to describe a personality in terms of virtuous and vicious qualities and the lack of such qualities. This is a fact familiar to the writers of testimonials. To say of a man that he has courage, industry, and sobriety is not to say anything very significant about him. He might be stupid or wicked or both. Hitler was abstemious. Mussolini, for all I know, was industrious. Both were brave. There is a further paradox to be mentioned. This is that the eulogistic terms of our moral vocabulary, especially 'conscientious', often have a depressing impact, because we tend to think of virtue as a sort of long stop, something in reserve which should not be needed. Thus a person fully interested in his work does not have to show industry; he may have to be persuaded to stop for food or sleep. Similarly we think of courage as something which has to be screwed to the sticking place and of conscience as a sad substitute for effortless efficiency and enjoyment. I should be prepared to argue that these are bad and muddled reasons for depreciating moral goodness; but that is another story.

If the 'character' of a man is that in him which will enable us to understand his conduct, it should mean primarily a 'system of sentiments' and interests not a system or collection of virtues and vices.[1] We know that this is what matters about ourselves. Novelists know it about their 'characters'. Psychologists and philosophers sometimes lag behind, perhaps because they are looking or waiting for a science and 'ethology', as J. S. Mill hopefully called it, is not yet a science. A 'sentiment' is an 'organised concentration of interests' round one object.[2] It involves not a uniform range of emotion, as does an Aristotelian virtue, but an interconnected variety of emotions appropriate to a variety of relationships. Thus anyone who has a sentiment of attachment to a society, such

[1] Cf. McDougall, *Character and the Conduct of Life*, e.g. pp. 95, 99.
[2] See W. J. H. Sprott, *General Psychology*, pp. 144–6.

as a college, will be pleased by its successes, saddened by its failures, and gratified by the misfortunes of its rivals. If we know what are a man's dominant sentiments and interests, we can make a reasonable estimate of the way in which he will respond to specified demands and opportunities. We can write an informative testimonial. But the information will not be conveyed by an inventory of more or less virtuous attributes.

Must we, then, say that Aristotle, in his theory of character, offers or suggests the wrong sort of map of human nature? Such a judgement would be unfair if it implied that Aristotle's description of virtues and vices is all that he has to say about human nature. The *Ethics* starts with a consideration of 'ends'. Aristotle thus recognizes that the most important difference between one man and another is a difference between the objects which they value and seek to achieve. This defence of Aristotle is valid so far as it goes. But it does not go very far. For it must be admitted that the portrait gallery of virtuous and vicious characters in Books III and IV stands alongside of his account in Book I of human nature in terms of ends without the two accounts' being integrated; their mutual relations are not made clear. In this sense Aristotle's view of conduct and character is a patchwork rather than a unified whole. As we have seen, his theory of moral education and development is sketchy. It consists of the observation that repeated performances make tasks easier together with some casual indications of the motives which may play a part in the acquisition of virtue. But, if there is a gap here in Aristotle's theory, it is a gap which the philosophers and educationists who have succeeded him have not satisfactorily filled. We know enough to doubt the wisdom of our ancestors, but not enough to feel confidence in new prescriptions. Perhaps the main advance in educational theory made in this century has been that we have come to understand more clearly the difficulty of discovering how best to prepare the young for the successful pursuit of happiness.

In Chapter X of this book I shall examine Aristotle's treatment in *EN* v of the ethical virtue of justice (*dikaiosunē*). In Chapter VII the discussion of the doctrine that virtue lies in a mean will require reference to the ethical virtues of courage (*andreia*) and temperance (*sōphrosunē*). Otherwise I shall not comment further on the particular ethical virtues and vices in Aristotle's lists. But I shall conclude this chapter by taking notice of a general issue, or complex of issues, which has to be faced in the study of Aristotle's ethics. I have quoted Ross's remark that Aristotle's virtues are qualities admired by Greeks and Green's remark on the restricted range of responsibilities in the moral thinking of the Greeks. Aristotle spent most of his working life in Athens and it was natural for him to think that, if men are to live well and be happy, they should live in city states. Is it only the content of morality which is determined by a particular historical and cultural context? Or does this relativity extend also to form or structure and basic concepts? The comments I have quoted suggest, or at least are compatible with, a negative answer to this last question. They suggest that Aristotle in the *EN* is at least in part an interpreter of Greek experience, but they do not deny that he may also be an acute and wise commentator on the human situation. The distinction between the basic universal elements in the moral life and its varying content is not simple and not to be accepted without argument; but there is at least a prima facie case for some such distinction.

In different kinds of society men have different stations and duties; but all men are alike in having responsibilities, duties to which they are attentive or which they neglect. Nelson in his signal before Trafalgar said that England expected every man to do his duty. He wished his sailors to think and feel very much as the Spartans at Thermopylae when they willingly obeyed the laws of Sparta. Again it is difficult to see how the differences between social life in ancient Athens and in modern England are relevant to the question, elaborately treated by Aristotle, whether, or within what limits, a man is a free agent in a sense which makes it reasonable to hold him responsible, to praise or blame him, for what he does or omits to do.

So much seems clear or at least credible. But perhaps not all students of the history of moral ideas are willing to accept the distinction between the variable and the invariant aspects of morality. They might accept it in a sense which would reduce the universal element to very small proportions. I have in mind in particular the acute and learned book by Professor Arthur W. H. Adkins, *Merit and Responsibility, A Study in Greek Values* (1960). Adkins makes the concept of moral responsibility the 'connecting thread' of his discussion not because he thinks that the concept was important in 'the Greek moral scene' but because, in his view, the concept was intimately connected with, coloured and confused by, a concept of virtue (*aretē*) which is strange to us. 'If we can discover why the concept of moral responsibility is so unimportant to the Greek, we shall go far towards understanding the difference between our moral systems, and discovering the nature of each' (p. 3). In the last hundred pages of his book Adkins discusses the ethical and political doctrines of Plato and Aristotle. He approaches this discussion by way of a comprehensive survey of the meanings and applications of words in the Greek moral vocabulary, 'key terms of value'. The survey embraces Homer and the tragedians, other writers before Plato, and also the Athenian law courts. I cannot attempt here to summarize this illuminating investigation. But I wish to say briefly why I have found it hard to follow, so far as Aristotle is concerned, the plot of the book.

I begin by quoting some further passages which seem to convey an important part of Adkin's main thesis.

For any man brought up in a western democratic society the related concepts of duty and responsibility are the central concepts of ethics; and we are inclined to take it as an unquestionable truth, though there is abundant evidence to the contrary, that the same must be true of all societies. In this respect at least we are all Kantians now (p. 2). That there should exist a society so different from our own as to render it impossible to translate 'duty' in the Kantian sense with its ethical terminology at all—impossible, that is to say, to translate 'duty' by a word not only of equivalent connotation but also of equivalent status and emotive power—is, despite the evidence, a very difficult idea to accept. (2-3)

The absence of duty, or Duty, from 'the Greek moral scene' is asserted again in a later chapter (xii).

It is evident—indeed, the point hardly requires making—that no Kantian idea of 'Duty' can exist in such a system of values as this:

what one 'ought' to do is what it is necessary to do in order to be *eudaimōn* (happy) (253). The Greek moral scene does not provide, and never has provided, even the raw material from which a categorical imperative could be fabricated. (253)

The expression 'the Greek moral scene' is unhappily or conveniently vague. The repeated references to Kant suggest that part of what Adkins has in mind is a contrast between Kantian ethical theories and the ethical theories of Plato and Aristotle. If he finds in Aristotle a failure to separate rules of prudence from principles, or the principle, of duty, I agree with him. I shall say so in my own way, and without bringing in Kant, in this book. But it seems clear in the passages which I have quoted that Adkins means more than this. He seems to be saying that ancient Athens and Sparta were societies so different from our own that, while we western democrats can all distinguish our duty from our interest, the Athenians, Socrates, for example, when he refused to escape from prison, and the Spartans, those, for example, who chose to die at Thermopylae, could not—not because they were bad philosophers but because of their limited experience. What sort of evidence would support such a denial? Not the alleged impossibility of translating 'duty'. In English and German as well as Greek linguistic habits are confusing and untidy. 'Ought' in English as well as *dei* in Greek straddles obscurely over different kinds of 'imperative'. It may be doubted whether even 'duty', in spite of the persuasion exercised by Kant and Wordsworth, has quite the 'status and emotive power' with which it is invested by the philosopher and the poet. Nor would it be difficult to suggest lines of thought which would render unsurprising the idea that the Greeks did not have a word for it. Perhaps at some times in all societies, and at all times in some societies, patriotism is enough, in the sense that virtually all duties have reference to the survival and welfare of the family and the city and the state. If so, an expression like 'the laws of Sparta' would naturally appropriate the 'emotive power' which, for those of us who are sufficiently Kantian, belongs to 'duty'.

Adkins's two concluding chapters (xv and xvi) are about Aristotle's ethical theory and, as the title of the book suggests, they are concerned ostensibly with Aristotle's concept of 'moral responsibility'. Adkins can hardly maintain that Aristotle treats the concept as if it were 'unimportant'. For, as we shall see when we come to *EN* III, Aristotle's discussion of the topic is elaborate and searching. Adkins states in his first chapter that Aristotle's analysis 'seems fully adequate', but adds that it cannot be identical with ours because Aristotle's 'system of ethics' does not permit the application of the analysis in all cases in which we should apply it (8). For further elucidation we have to turn to the two concluding chapters of the book. In chapter xv Adkins gives credit to Aristotle for his account, under the head of the voluntary (*hekousion*), of imputability: a man, when he knows what he is doing, is responsible for what he originates. But Adkins adds that we cannot expect Aristotle to discuss the 'classic' free will problem (324), and implies that Aristotle fails to consider whether the bad man is to be exempted from blame on the ground that his moral blindness, being determined by his innate constitution, is 'in some sense involuntary' (328). But in fact Aristotle discusses just this problem in *EN* III. 5. Surprisingly this chapter is ignored by Adkins; there are no references to it in his Index Locorum.

Adkins asserts that the apparent success and modernity of Aristotle's account of responsibility is deceptive. The account involves 'inevitable concomitant disadvantages' (328), as he promises to show in his final chapter. His main thesis in this chapter (xvi) may be stated as follows. Aristotle's concept of virtue (*aretē*) covers, in addition to the quiet 'co-operative' virtue of justice, those more spectacular qualities which, from Homer onwards, were admired and valued by the Greeks because they were needed for the protection of the household and the city state. Among the most important of these qualities were courage, military prowess, leadership, liberality in the use of wealth. This concept of *aretē* is 'the chief impediment in the way of the development of a satisfactory concept of moral responsibility' (332). The traditional concept of virtue 'is inimical to' (337), 'can only confuse' (340), the concept of moral responsibility. But I cannot see that the traditional values, so far as Aristotle accepts them, do in fact confuse his treatment of responsibility in the *EN*.

Nor has Adkins convinced me that the traditional concept need have any strong tendency to confuse him. I give here only one example of my difficulty. Adkins argues that, in a Greek city state, the 'enforcement of strict justice' against a leading man might result 'in the loss of the services or goodwill of a valuable citizen who might well turn the scale by his presence or absence at the next crisis' (349). 'The claims of individual merit are undeniable: those of responsibility cannot override them.' I do not see anything peculiarly Greek in this kind of conflict. It could happen in any state in which there is a privileged and powerful class or party. A German might have thought, or said, that a blind eye should be turned on the lawlessness of a leading Nazi because a strong and successful Nazi movement was needed for national morale and recovery. But to argue in this way, however it may shock us, is not necessarily to fall into conceptual confusion about responsibility. It is possible to remain clear about the concept of responsibility while allowing that sometimes, when a man has been responsible for injustice, nothing should be done to remedy the injury. Adkins thinks it 'inevitable' that, because 'the basic system of Greek values' is different from ours, the Greek concept of responsibility must be different from ours. It does not seem to me that he has shown either in general that a Greek thinker's concept of moral responsibility *must be* different from ours or that Aristotle's concept *is* different and, if it is, how its different character is determined by elements strange to us in his concept of virtue (*aretē*).

If these comments are justified, we must conclude that Adkins's arguments fail to show that Aristotle's thought about responsibility was confused or unsatisfactory. This is not, of course, to deny that Aristotle's theory was un-Kantian. And it is true that the question of responsibility does not arise in the same direct way in an un-Kantian as in a Kantian theory. When the idea of duty is central, the idea of responsibility is also central, the idea that it is reasonable to praise people for doing their duty and blame or even punish them for not doing it. When the central ideas are happiness and virtue, as a condition or constituent of happiness, the topic of moral accountability is not in the foreground. For reflection soon shows that a man's possessing or not possessing admirable qualities which make him useful to the state or agreeable to his friends and his family depends on many factors over which he has no control. A man is not held responsible, is not the subject of blame, merely because he is no great asset in a battle or at a party. But, if he is not cut out for a battle or not at home at a party, he should still do the best he can. And this, as Aristotle would allow, is all that we can ask of him.[1]

[1] Cf. EN i. 10, 1101 a2–5.

VII

VIRTUE IS A MEAN

'WE must, however, not only describe virtue as a state of character, but also say what sort of state it is' (*EN* II. 6, 1106 a14–15). Aristotle's answer is that it is a state concerned with choice (*prohairetikē*), lying in a mean (*en mesotēti*) relative to us and determined by a rational principle (*logǫ*), the principle by which the man of practical wisdom (*phronimos*) would determine it (1106 b36–1107 a2). Each phrase in this statement of the differentia of virtue is difficult. We have to look further on in the *EN* for much of the explanation needed: Aristotle's account of choice is in Book III, his account of practical wisdom in Book VI. I shall consider now the statement that virtue is, or lies in, a mean.

Commentators and critics have had a great deal to say about and around this celebrated doctrine. Not surprisingly, Aristotle's view that moderation is good, and excess to be avoided, had been anticipated by popular morality and by poets as well as by Plato. Also not surprisingly, the concept of a mathematical mean, especially if allowed to expand to cover any sort of quantitative rule or formula, has many applications in the philosophy of Aristotle himself and of his predecessors: applications for the theory of what is good and bad in art and in the condition, healthy or unhealthy, of living bodies; applications, in Aristotle's works, to the physiology of perception and the constitution of physical bodies. Hence the student of the *EN* is bombarded with quotations from, and references to, the works of Plato and other works of Aristotle. The student is faced also by the widely ranging criticisms which have been directed against the doctrine of the mean. Aristotle is accused of spoiling Plato and of failing to anticipate Kant. All this comment and criticism is usually relevant and sometimes helpful. But it is not always needed to enable us to understand what Aristotle says in the *EN* and it is sometimes only distantly relevant and sometimes confused. It is important, therefore, to start from what Aristotle says in the *EN*. If and so far as what he says can be understood, the pursuit and disentangling of similar and connected ideas in the works of Plato, and in other works of Aristotle, is not essential for the study of Aristotle's moral philosophy.

We have had a preliminary statement of the doctrine in *EN* II. 2. Aristotle has just warned us that, in the sphere of action as in medicine or navigation, any general account must lack detail and precision (1103 b34–1104 a10). He then offers the generalization that, as in the case of strength and health, it is 'the nature of such things to be destroyed by defect and excess' (1104 a11–14). Thus, if an athlete takes either too much exercise or too little, he destroys his strength; similarly health can be impaired by eating or drinking too much or too little, while that which is proportionate (*summetron*) both produces and increases and preserves it (1104 a 15–18). The same principle applies to the virtues of courage and temperance. To fear everything is to be a coward; to fear nothing is to be rash. It is self-indulgent to abstain from no pleasure, insensible to abstain from all. Thus courage and temperance 'are destroyed by excess and defect, and preserved by the mean' (1104 a18–27). Aristotle adds that the same kind of activity as produces a certain state, whether the strength of the athlete or an ethical virtue, is also the manifestation or actualization of the state when it has been produced (1104 a27–b3). Now in at least one obvious respect this statement of the doctrine does indeed lack detail and precision. A quantitative idea is applied to virtue and to vice with only a vague indication of how it can be applicable. Quantities of food and drink can be weighed and measured; exercise can be timed. But the quantities involved in virtuous and vicious action, which must at least be roughly measurable if the analogy with athletic training is to hold, are indicated only by reference to fearing everything or nothing, indulging in all pleasures or in none.

Chapter 6 gives a more explicit and definite answer to the question what, in relation to ethical virtue and vice, are the variable quantities excess or defect of which constitutes vice. The matter will become clear, Aristotle says, if we consider the specific nature of virtue. 'In everything that is continuous and divisible (*suneches kai diaireton*) it is possible to take more, less, or an equal amount, and that either in terms of the thing itself or relatively to us; and the equal is an intermediate between excess and defect' (1106 a26-9). Note first the precise meaning of the phrase 'continuous and divisible'. Quantity which is continuous is not merely divisible, but divisible *ad infinitum*: it has no indivisible, atomic, parts. This is the definition of continuous (*suneches*) in *De Caelo* 268 a6 and *Physics* 231 b16.[1] Thus the sense conveyed by the whole phrase is that of 'continuous, i.e. divisible *ad infinitum*'. Grant and Stewart very strangely take the phrase to mean 'continuous and discrete'. Quantity which is discrete is quantity which is *not* divisible *ad infinitum*; and, if the number of indivisible units is odd, it cannot be divided at the half-way point. Having asked us to consider the nature of continuous quantity, Aristotle proceeds to try to explain the distinction between 'the intermediate in the object' and 'the intermediate relative to us' (1106 a29-b7). Before we consider his explanation, it is desirable to see what answer Aristotle gives us, in this chapter, to the main question not so far answered, viz. what are the quantities with which virtue and vice are concerned.

Ethical virtue 'is concerned with passions and actions, and in these there is excess, defect, and the intermediate' (1106 b16-18). It is a mean between two vices, and the vices 'respectively fall short of or exceed what is right in both passions and actions, while virtue both finds and chooses that which is intermediate' (1107 a2-6). Similarly, in the summary of the doctrine at the beginning of chapter 9, virtue is said to be a mean 'because its character is to aim at what is intermediate in passions and in actions' (1109 a20-4). The natural meaning of these statements is that in the case of *every* virtue, the virtuous man conforms to the mean, avoids excess and defect, in respect *both* of passions *and* of actions. This is asserted by Gauthier-Jolif: 'On peut donc tenir pour assuré que *toutes* les vertus, et pas seulement la justice, ont pour domaine les activités extérieures, en ce sens qu'elles assurent l'accomplissement d'œuvres pourvues de certaines qualités. Mais elles ne peuvent

---

[1] Cf. 232 b24, 233 a25.

le faire sans modérer aussi les passions intérieures' (II, pp. 141–2).
But it is not clear how strictly this should be taken. As regards
one important virtue, justice, Aristotle himself tells us that it
is 'a kind of mean but not in the same way as the other virtues'
(v. 5, 1133 b32–3). We are not concerned at present with the
meaning of this statement. The main point probably is that there
is no single range of passions with which justice, in the sense in
which justice is a particular virtue, is concerned. As regards the
virtues generally the following point is important. One of the
ways in which an action can conform, or fail to conform, to
the mean is in respect of the feeling or emotion which is expressed
in it and accompanies it. Thus a brave man will go into battle
feeling some fear, but not too much. A temperate man at a party
will desire and enjoy the good things that are going round, but not
too much. Two further points should be in our minds. In the case
of some classes of virtuous actions, but not of all, quantitative
variables, other than degrees of feeling, are involved. For the
temperate man it may be a question of how much to eat or
drink; for the liberal man of how much money to give away.
But in the case of other virtues there may be no such quantitative
aspect. A man is not called brave because he kills neither too many
nor too few of the enemy. A man does not avoid the extremes
of buffoonery (bōmolochia) and boorishness (agroikia) by making
neither too many jokes nor too few (iv. 8). The second point is
that all virtuous actions, including those in which external divisible
objects are involved, can be right or wrong in respects which
are not quantitative at all. They must be done, for example, 'at
the right times, with reference to the right objects, towards the
right people'. Aristotle makes this statement in the very centre
of his exposition of the doctrine of the mean (1106 b21–4).
There may be much that is unsatisfactory and unclear in Aristotle's
doctrine that virtue lies in a mean. But it is wrong to criticize
him in a way which would imply that this doctrine is the whole
of what he has to say about virtue. What the doctrine does
assert is that virtue is manifested in feelings and emotions, and
also in actions, which avoid excess and defect, and that, where
action is concerned with extensive quantities, virtue again shows

itself in avoiding excess and defect. The second part of the doctrine as thus stated is comparatively trivial and obvious. But, in
its application to 'passions' (*pathē*), the doctrine is important and
an important *part* of the truth about moral goodness. As we shall
find, not all of Aristotle's critics have seen this clearly or have
given him the credit which is his due. I return now to Aristotle's
exposition of his doctrine in II. 6.

Both fear and confidence and appetite and anger and pity and in
general pleasure and pain may be felt both too much and too little,
and in both cases not well; but to feel them at the right times, with
reference to the right objects, towards the right people, with the right
motive, and in the right way, is what is both intermediate and best,
and this is characteristic of virtue. Similarly with regard to actions also
there is excess, defect, and the intermediate (1106 b18–24.)

In the application of the mean to athletic training the reference
was to continuous extensive quanta, i.e. quanta with spatial or
temporal dimensions. When two such quanta, i.e. extensive
quanta, differ in size the lesser is equal to part of the greater. What
is measured in the case of passions, at least in their psychical as
opposed to physical aspect, is intensive quantity, degree of intensity. The assertion that quantity of this kind is continuous
means, in the case of feelings, that there is no smallest interval
between one degree of the feeling and another. Thus, if it is said
that a pleasure or pain is becoming continuously more intense,
this means that the change does not occur in jumps from one
degree of intensity to the next: there is no next, any more than, if
an extensive quantity is continuous, there is a next size. Having
referred to degrees of the passions, Aristotle remarks that there is
a mean, as well as excess and defect, 'similarly, with regard to
actions' (1106 b23–4). This is not explained. It might, as we have
seen, refer to the degree of the passion which is felt in the performance of the action. At least in some cases the reference might
be to extensive quanta involved in the action as an external transaction, e.g. to the amount of food consumed or the amount of
goods transferred from one owner to another. The parallel
passage in the *EE* (*B*3) appears to offer an explanation in the
remark that 'movement is continuous, and action is movement'

(1220 b26). But the explanation is surely not intelligible; it would suggest that an action achieves the mean by being neither too fast nor too slow.

We return now to Aristotle's explanation, earlier in the chapter, of the distinction between the mean 'in terms of the thing itself' and the mean 'relatively to us' (1106 a28). The first point to notice is that the word which Aristotle starts by using, in his opening statement on continuous quantity, is not mean or intermediate (*meson*) but equal (*ison*). Equal to what? There can be no answer except 'equal to the amount which is right'. This at once gives rise to a puzzle. If we have to know what amount is right before we know that this is the amount which is intermediate, then surely the statement that it is of the essence of virtue to aim at and hit the intermediate does not tell us anything which has practical significance. We shall return to this question. In order to answer it we must decide how far Aristotle claims to find a resemblance between the ethical mean and the mean in the mathematical sense of a quantity intermediate between a larger and a smaller quantity and calculated from a prior knowledge of the extremes. The resemblance or analogy for which we might look is that knowledge of what is intermediate might be reached, though not strictly calculated, from a prior knowledge of what would be too much or too little. But, if Aristotle did mean to imply this, his use of the word equal instead of intermediate in 1106 a27 would be misleading.

Aristotle now tells us that by the 'intermediate in the object' he means 'that which is equidistant from each of the extremes, which is one and the same for all men' (1106 a29–31). By the 'intermediate relatively to us' he means 'that which is neither too much nor too little'. This may well not be the half-way point between two extremes, and it is 'not one, nor the same for all' (1106 a31–2). Aristotle illustrates again from the training of athletes. If a ration of ten pounds (of meat) is too much and two pounds too little, it does not follow that the trainer will order six pounds. This might be too much for the beginner but too little for Milo, a wrestler of whom Athenaeus[1] tells us that he once ate a whole ox

[1] x. 412–13.

in the course of a day (1106 a33–b5). Thus a master of any art chooses 'the intermediate not in the object but relatively to us' (1106 b5–7).

There is nothing, so far as I can see, abstruse or elusive in the doctrine conveyed by this passage: that the ethical mean must be appropriate to circumstances including facts about the agent himself. The mean is not 'one and the same' for all (1106 a32). The mathematical terms in which Aristotle chooses to express himself need not, and indeed cannot, be taken very seriously. It is a lecturer's patter. Do not imagine, he is saying, that finding the mean is a matter simply of 'splitting the difference' between opposing over- and under-estimates. It is not as easy as that. On the evidence of this passage, there is no suggestion of any quasi-mathematical derivation of the mean from prior knowledge of the extremes. This is made obvious by the fact that the extremes mentioned, ten pounds and two pounds of meat, are quite arbitrary. If the extremes named had been ten pounds and six pounds, the mean for the man beginning his training, a quantity less than six pounds, would not have been intermediate at all.

Since I find nothing either obscure or profound in Aristotle's distinction here between the 'mean in the object' and the 'mean relative to us', I do not agree with the commentators who make heavy weather of this passage. I have in mind Joachim in particular (pp. 85–9). He extracts from the passage a 'geometrical proportion', i.e. an equation of the form $a : b :: c : d$ of which the terms are the amount of a passion 'embodied in this act' by a given agent, the amount which the man of practical wisdom would embody, the nature of the agent, and the nature of the wise man. The mean to be determined is 'the *meson* (mean) in a geometrical proportion, and therefore the range of its variations is determined by precise limits' (p. 87). I do not find any of this in the text. Moreover, I do not think that the expression 'mean in a geometrical proportion' is significant: as there are four terms in the proportion as formulated by Joachim there is no middle term (when $a : b :: b : c$, b is the 'geometrical mean' between a and c). Aristotle is not saying that the ethical mean, while not an arithmetical mean $(a - b = b - c)$, is some other kind of mathematical mean.

The next step in Aristotle's exposition of the doctrine is a suggestion that the principle of the mean is exemplified in the successful products of the arts. 'We often say of good works of art that it is not possible either to take away or to add anything, implying that excess and defect destroy the goodness of works of art, while the mean preserves it' (1106 b8–14). This remark again is surely a popular illustration, a lecturer's aside, rather than an essential part of the exposition. The idea of spoiling a work of art by adding or removing a part is remote from the idea of excess and defect in action constituted by choosing too much or too little from a continuous range of quantities, whether extensive as amounts of food or intensive as 'amounts', in terms of degree, of a passion. Aristotle, in expounding the mean, allows himself to range over a wide territory. But for the student of the *EN* the important passages are those in which he formally and explicitly applies the doctrine to virtuous and vicious passions and actions.

There are two further passages which should be noticed in Aristotle's exposition of the mean in II. 6. They are important not because they add any new points to the doctrine, or because they modify points which have been made, but rather because they indicate implications of the doctrine which have to be stated in order to anticipate or eliminate misunderstanding. The first is the statement that ethical virtue, while in its essence a mean, is an extreme 'with regard to what is best and right' (1107 a6–8); cf. 1107 a23: 'what is intermediate is in a sense an extreme' (*pōs akron*). Aristotle is pointing out that, on a scale of merit, a virtue is above both the corresponding vices and not between them. Thus to be in a state of excess or deficiency in relation to a virtue is to have a vice; it is not to have too much or too little of a virtue. Similarly in IV. 3 Aristotle says of the proud man that he is 'an extreme in respect of the greatness of his claims, but a mean in respect of the rightness of them' (1123 b13–14). This point is closely connected with the point made in the second, and immediately following, passage which we have to consider.

'But not every action nor every passion admits of a mean; for some have names (*ōnomastai*) that already imply that badness is included in them (*suneilēmmena meta tēs phaulotētos*), e.g. spite, shamelessness, envy, and in the case of actions adultery, theft, murder; for all of these and such like things imply by their names that they are themselves bad, and not the excesses or deficiencies of them' (1107 a9–14). The opening words of this passage might suggest that Aristotle was asserting or admitting that there are exceptions to the doctrine of the mean, ranges of actions or passions to which it does not apply. But he is making a purely logical point which arises from the fact that certain words are used to name not ranges of action or passion but determinations within a range with the implication, as part of the meaning of the word, that they are excessive or defective, and therefore wrong. Thus envy is never right and proper because 'envy' conveys that it is wrong and improper. Again it does not make sense to ask when murder is right because to call a killing 'murder' is to say that it is wrong. Most of the commentators get this point right, but Stewart at least is wrong or confused when he says: 'There are certain passions and actions which cannot be so modified as to form parts of an orderly character and life, but must be eradicated by education' (i. 120). This may be true, but it is not the point which Aristotle is making in this passage. There is a point about the vocabulary of the passage which should be noticed because of its significance for the doctrine. Aristotle says that some words name combinations of elements with the implication that badness is included. The word corresponding to 'combinations' is *suneilēmmena* (1107 a10).[1] The word is applied in the *Metaphysics* to the combination of matter and form. Thus in Z 10 he speaks of 'things in which the form and matter are taken together' (*suneilēmmena*) (1035 a25–6). The standard example of a term which refers to both form and matter is 'the snub' (*simon*). ' "Snub" is bound up with matter (*suneilēmmenon*) (for what is snub is a concave *nose*)' (1025 b32). We can now restate, making use of the Aristotelian notions of form and matter, the point which Aristotle is making in the *EN*. In our vocabulary for referring to actions and passions there are words which name misformations; and, in such cases, there is no sense in asking what is the right formation of the object named. This, and no more than this, is what Aristotle

[1] Cf. *EE B* 3, 1221 b18–26.

means when he says that 'not every action nor every passion admits of a mean' (1107 a8–9).

I have claimed that the doctrine of the mean states 'an important part of the truth about moral goodnes'.[1] I wish now to amplify this statement, and, in connection with it, to comment on a criticism of Aristotle's doctrine made by Ross in his *Aristotle*. The discovery for which I wish to give Aristotle credit is that of the distinction between two different kinds of moral goodness, the goodness of the man who does what is right in spite of desires which incline him strongly not to do it and the goodness of the man who does what is right without any resistance from unruly or discordant desires, the man whose inclinations are in harmony with his concept of the life he ought to lead. It would, perhaps, be more correct to speak of this as a distinction between classes of good actions than between men. For most men, sometimes at least, find that duty and inclination coincide; and most men, sometimes at least, find that they do not coincide. If we ask ourselves which of these two kinds of goodness is the better, we find ourselves distracted by a difficulty. In one way we admire the man who behaves well in a battle without undue distress more than the man who has to overcome obvious terror. In one way a man naturally moderate in his appetites is better than a man who has to struggle to control them. On the other hand, the merit of moral victory seems to be enhanced when there have been obstacles to overcome. Is the saint, or moral hero, the man who is not tempted or the man who struggles successfully with temptations?

The man who does what is right in spite of opposing desires is given by Aristotle the name conventionally translated 'continent' (*enkratēs*). He is distinguished from the man who is temperate (*sōphrōn*), whose desires are in harmony with the right rule, being neither excessive nor defective. I quote from *EN* vii. 9: 'for both the continent man and the temperate man are such as to do nothing contrary to the rule for the sake of the bodily pleasures, but the former has and the latter has not bad appetites, and the latter is such as not to feel pleasure contrary to the rule, while the former is such as to feel pleasure but not to be led by it' (1151 b34–1152 a3).

[1] See p. 133 above.

To make this distinction so clearly was a major achievement in the reflective study of human conduct. If it has become a platitude, this is what happens to many discoveries in philosophy. As to the relative ranking of these two kinds of moral goodness, Aristotle, I think, takes it for granted that 'continence' is a second best to 'temperance' or virtue: it is better not to have bad or excessive desires. He does not formulate and face the problem, and there is still no agreed solution. But Aristotle's doctrine of the mean, taken along with his treatment in Book VII of continence (*enkrateia*) and incontinence (*akrasia*), brings the problem into the light.

Ross's chapter vii ('Ethics') in his *Aristotle* has much that is interesting and suggestive to say on the doctrine of the mean.[1] But, in an important section of his criticism, he appears to take insufficient account of the distinction between virtue and continence, which I have held to be the vital centre of the doctrine. Ross writes: 'The essential thing is not that feelings should have some particular intensity, but that they should be thoroughly subjugated to the "right rule" or, as we might say, to the sense of duty' (p. 195). At this point Ross does not press his criticism; he points out that Aristotle's definition of virtue does include 'determined by a rational principle'. But he returns to the attack in a passage later in the chapter where he contends that 'the trinitarian scheme of virtues and vices is mistaken', and that 'each virtue has but one opposite vice'. 'Must not this be so from the nature of the distinction between virtue and vice? Vice is passive obedience to natural instinct, virtue the controlling of instinct by sense of duty or by some other high motive—as Aristotle says, by the rule discerned by reason. There can be too little of such control but there cannot be too much' (p. 206). It is clear that Aristotle has a reply to this criticism. The criticism lumps together two states of character which Aristotle has been anxious to distinguish, continence and virtue, both of which are manifested in the control of natural instinct. In order to distinguish them it is essential, as the doctrine of the mean affirms, 'that feelings should have some particular intensity'.

Ross goes on to say that what Aristotle has seen, though he has

[1] See pp. 194–6, and, with reference to particular virtues, pp. 202–8.

not expressed it very well, is that, in many cases at all events, 'natural reactions to stimulus go in pairs of opposites' (p. 206). Thus, in Aristotle's account of courage two types of feeling are involved, fear and 'cheer' or love of danger.[1] Both must be controlled. So, Ross suggests, we must substitute for Aristotle's trinity 'not one duality but two'. Courage is control of fear and cowardice the lack of control. Discretion is the control of cheer and rashness the lack of control. Again the distinction between virtue and continence disappears in this corrected version of Aristotle. The distinction requires us, if there are two distinct ranges of feeling, to recognize not two vices but four, and this is just what Aristotle does in his treatment of courage in EN III. 7. In principle at least, even if some types of character are too rare to have been given a name, as in the case of the man who has no fear (1115 b24–8), there is excess and defect of both fear and its opposite. It would be natural to suppose that this implies two virtues, even if 'courage' (andreia) is the name for both. But N. Hartmann in his Ethics suggests that for Aristotle there is one virtue with two aspects, i.e. virtue, as he puts it, is a 'synthesis of values' (Wertsynthese).[2] In this he seems to be right. Aristotle appears to hold that courage and discretion, in the sense given to it by Ross, are aspects of a single virtue.

I have argued that Aristotle's 'trinitarian scheme' is a necessary deduction from the important distinction which he makes between virtue and continence. But Ross finds in Aristotle's treatment of temperance (sōphrosunē) confirmation of the view that each virtue should be opposed to only one vice. The vice which consists in the excessive indulgence of physical appetites is profligacy (akolasia). Aristotle admits that the vice of defect has no name.

People who fall short with regard to pleasures and delight in them less than they should are hardly found; for such insensibility (anaisthēsia) is not human. Even the other animals distinguish different kinds of food and enjoy some and not others; and if there is anyone who finds nothing pleasant and nothing more attractive than anything else, he must be something quite different from a man; this sort of person has not received a name because he hardly occurs. (III. 11, 1119 a5–11.)

[1] See J. L. Stocks in Mind, 1919.   [2] Ch. 61, pp. 517–18.

Ross is surely not justified in suggesting that, in this passage, we see 'the breakdown of the doctrine of the mean' (p. 207). Even if complete insensibility would be inhuman, it may be claimed that defective degrees of sensibility are not uncommon. But is such a defect vicious? In the sense that it is a deviation from a reasonable standard of human excellence it surely is. Ross will not allow this. 'There is here no *vice* of defect; the "defect" can only be either an innate insensibility for which one cannot be blamed, or asceticism, which is not enslavement to instinct but subjugation of instinct to a rule, though perhaps not to the "right rule"' (p. 207).

There are two comments to be made on these arguments. First, the suggestion that a man 'cannot be blamed' for 'innate insensibility' would, if pursued, have wide-ranging implications for Aristotle's whole theory of ethical virtue and vice. The profligate man might claim to be the victim of innate sensibility. Again a similar argument might be used against the appropriateness of praising a man for courage and temperance, if these virtues can be developed only on the basis of normal and healthy innate tendencies. The argument might thus lead to the conclusion that, from a moral point of view, what should be blamed is incontinence not vice, and what should be praised is continence, control of 'instinct' when control is difficult, not effortless virtue. Secondly, Aristotle would not accept the descriptions which Ross gives of vice as 'passive obedience to natural instinct' (p. 206), or 'enslavement to instinct' (p. 207). According to Aristotle the vicious man deliberately pursues his ill-judged end. If, then, an ascetic is a man in whose 'end', or plan of life, there is no place, or not an adequate place, for bodily pleasures, Aristotle would surely reject Ross's assumption that asceticism is not a vice. The ascetic follows a rule which, as Ross says, is not the right rule. No doubt some deviations from right rules are much more serious than others. But the following of wrong rules is, in Aristotle's view, the essence of vice.

We have already seen, in considering Aristotle's doctrine that the mean is 'relative to us' (1106 a29 ff.), that he does not make clear how close an analogy he wishes to suggest between the ethical mean and the various types of mean in mathematics. Does the ethical doctrine assert only that deviations from what is right may be either excessive or defective, or does it assert also that, just as in mathematics the extremes are data from which the mean is calculated, so, with due allowance for the fact that ethics is not mathematical, there is in moral thinking a movement of thought from the extremes to the mean? Aristotle does not explicitly make this second assertion, but Ross implies that it was in his mind. 'Even in the light of Aristotle's disclaimer of the suggestion that any mere arithmetical calculation will tell us what we should do, to describe virtue as essentially a mean suggests that we first know the extremes and from them infer the mean' (p. 195). Ross suggests that we do sometimes reach decisions in this way, e.g. in deciding how much to give to a charity we might start by thinking that £100 was too much and £5 too little, and then work inwards. In this way a man might 'finally decide what it would be right to give' (p. 196). But Ross thinks that normally 'we recognize what is too much and too little by recognizing what is right'. Similarly, as Ross might have added, we recognize what is false by first finding what is true.

Have we any grounds for attributing to Aristotle the idea that, at least sometimes, we 'work inwards' from the extremes to the mean? I think that Ross could have put his case more strongly if he had connected the suggestion with Aristotle's doctrine that ethical knowledge is only approximate, that it lacks mathematical precision (*akribeia*) (I. 7, 1098 a26–32; cf. I. 3, 1094 b11–27). In the example of the subscription to charity we are, in fact, unlikely to decide that some determinate sum, say £25, is right. We are more likely to decide not to give more than £30 or less than £20, and then quite arbitrarily fix on £26. 5s. od. The brackets are brought closer, but they remain separated. And so what is right is defined as coming between certain limits, and in this sense is a mean. The idea is expressed accurately by the words of Horace,

> sunt certi denique fines
> quos ultra citraque nequit consistere rectum.

In *EN* IX. 10 Aristotle considers the question whether there is 'a limit to the number of one's friends, as there is to the size of a city'. 'You cannot make a city of ten men, and if there are a hundred thousand it is a city no longer. But the proper number is presumably not a single number, but anything that falls between certain fixed points' (1170 b29-33). Similarly in x. 3, in a discussion of the argument that pleasure cannot be good because it is indeterminate (*aoristos*), Aristotle points out that health, while determinate, nevertheless admits of greater and less. 'The same proportion (*summetria*) is not found in all things, nor a single proportion always in the same thing, but it may be relaxed and yet persist up to a point, and it may differ in degree' (1173 a23-8). Ethical virtue, like health, 'may be relaxed and yet persist'. In a given situation there is no precisely determinate intensity of feeling which is characteristic of courage or temperance. Any degree within a limited range is good enough to avoid the vices of excess and defect. It is not merely that we do not know which degree within that range is the right degree. There is no one right degree. Any degree within the range is right, just as any subscription between £20 and £30 would be right. I suggest that, in the passages to which I have referred, the doctrine of the approximateness of non-mathematical knowledge and the doctrine of the mean are interconnected and help each to elucidate the other.

In the account which I have given of the doctrine of the mean, as Aristotle explains it in *EN* II. 6, I have made no reference to the view of those commentators who say that it is important to take account of certain physical doctrines in the exposition of which Aristotle makes use of the term *mesotēs*. It is claimed that, in these other uses of the term, we find clues to the interpretation of the ethical doctrine, and that without these clues the doctrine cannot be fully understood. I think that the most important of the passages adduced are the treatment of sense perception in *De Anima B* and the theory, in *De Generatione et Corruptione* II. 7, of the combination or fusion of elements to form compound bodies. This approach to the doctrine of ethical virtue was explored by Burnet, and is expounded in his Introductory Note to Book II. Burnet's views appear to have influenced Mure's account of the mean in his *Aristotle*,[1] and also Joachim's treatment of the subject

---

[1] See pp. 141, 142, and n. 1 on p. 107.

in his commentary on the *EN*. There are some critical comments on Burnet's interpretation in Joseph's *Essays in Ancient and Modern Philosophy*.[1] Burnet was clearly right to raise the question whether Aristotle's use of the term *mesotēs* in other works throws light on the doctrine of the *Ethics*. But I do not think that he succeeds in showing that it does. I think that his attempt fails in two ways. First, he fails to produce evidence that the idea on which he lays most stress is, in fact, part of Aristotle's doctrine in the *Ethics*. This is the idea of the combination, or blending, of opposites in determinate ratios. It is not easy to find this in the doctrine of the ethical mean. Secondly, the doctrines to which Burnet refers belong to Aristotle's now obsolete speculations in physics and physiology. They are, if intelligible at all, more obscure than the doctrine of the *Ethics*. Thus, if they were helpfully relevant to the interpretation of the *EN*, they would throw only a murky light.

Burnet tells us that 'we must go to the *Physics* for Aristotle's moral philosophy' (p. 69), but does not give us a clear account of what we find when we go there. He says that the Greek word *mesotēs* does not 'mean only or even primarily the arithmetical mean', but is 'the oldest word for a proportion of any kind however determined' (p. 70). In the following paragraph he speaks of the mean as a 'ratio between opposites' (p. 71). This makes it likely that he is using 'proportion' as a synonym for 'ratio', but he does not say what he has in mind when he speaks of a 'proportion of any kind'. What are the different kinds of ratio? Moreover the sentences which immediately follow, although presumably intended to elucidate the determination of a proportion, do not in fact mention any ratios. 'We must admit that a feeling like fear is capable of such determination; for we must fear either more or less or equally. And the same is true of an act like giving away money; for we must give away either more or less or an equal sum' (p. 70). As we saw earlier, 'equal' in 1106 a26 ff. is a surprising substitute for 'intermediate' (*meson*). But how is any ratio involved? Burnet says that, in the theory of goodness as a mean, the ratio is between opposites. Joachim seems to imply the same idea when he translates *hōrismenē logō* (1107 a1) in Aristotle's definition of virtue as

[1] vi, pp. 156–8 and footnote on pp. 170–1.

'determined by a proportion'. But the idea of a ratio between opposites has, so far as I can see, no possible application to the example of giving away greater or smaller sums of money: the right sum is not a ratio *between* a larger and a smaller sum. What of Burnet's other example? Does Aristotle's analysis of courage involve a mean which is a 'ratio between opposites'? It is true that courage has for its sphere the opposed feelings of fear (*phobos*) and cheer (*tharros*) (*EN* III. 6 ff.). But, as D. J. Allan correctly states, Aristotle treats these feelings 'not as opposite points on a single scale, so related that to exceed in one is to fall short in the other (like hot and cold), but as distinct emotions each admitting of excess, moderation, and deficiency'.[1] Aristotle does not say that courage lies in a ratio between amounts or degrees of fear and amounts or degrees of cheer. He describes it rather as involving appropriate, and intermediate, degrees of both these ranges of feeling. This fact makes it impossible to understand the mean as an equipoise, determined by a ratio, between the opposed feelings or qualities. As we have seen, it is not clear how these two means are connected or integrated in courage as Aristotle conceives it. But, even if it were possible to give sense to the suggestion that courage essentially involves a ratio between opposite passions and to produce evidence that Aristotle maintained this, the general assertion that the ethical mean is a ratio between opposites could not be maintained. It is not applicable to excessive and defective sums of money, to the mean in action in respect of divisible goods. And, on the side of feeling, not every virtue is concerned, as courage is, with ranges of contrary passions. Aristotle tells us that temperance is concerned primarily with bodily pleasures, and with pains only in the sense of the 'pain' caused by the absence of such pleasures.[2] I can see here no possibility of interpreting the mean as being 'determined by a ratio' between opposites.

I have argued that Aristotle's ethical mean is not as such a ratio of opposites. But Burnet, as we have seen, asserts that *mesotēs* is 'the oldest word for a proportion', apparently in the sense of ratio. If *mesotēs* means ratio, we must look for a ratio in the mean.

---

[1] *The Philosophy of Aristotle*, p. 173.
[2] *EN* III. 10, 11, especially 1118 b27–33.

But *mesotēs* means a state of being between or in the middle. It does not mean 'ratio', for which the Greek word is *logos* in one of its senses (not, in my opinion, the sense it has in the definition of ethical virtue). But it is, of course, true that any ratio, being a quantity, lies between ratios which are larger and ratios which are smaller. Burnet reports correctly that, in his physical and physiological doctrines, Aristotle emphasizes the intermediate character of certain ratios. Although these ideas are not as closely relevant to the ethical doctrine of the mean as Burnet thought, it will be helpful to follow some further steps in Burnet's exposition. Consider the following passage. 'Now the form which is the cause of all becoming is always a ratio (*logos*) or mean (*mesotēs*) between the two opposites, it is a definite "interval" as musicians call it, a fixed proportion in which the opposites neutralize one another and give rise to a new product' (p. 71). Burnet next suggests that 'a chemical formula like H_2O is the most typical instance of what he calls a *logos* or *mesotēs*' (pp. 71–2). It is not clear why Burnet is so pleased with the example of the chemical formula. For, although this is a ratio, it is not a ratio of opposites. But his reference to intervals in music does lead us to an Aristotelian application of the idea of a ratio of opposites, the application of the idea to ranges of sensible qualities. The doctrine of the formation of 'homoeomerous' substances, such as flesh and bone, is another instance which Burnet adduces at the end of his Introductory Note (pp. 72–3).

I have shown that Burnet appears to use the word 'proportion' as a synonym for 'ratio'. How else might he have used it? What other meaning might be present to his mind? 'Proportion' in mathematics is used in the sense of equality of ratios, i.e. $a/b = b/c$ if the proportion is 'continuous', and $a/b = c/d$ if it is 'discrete'. The Greek term for proportion in this sense is *analogia*, defined by Aristotle in *EN* v. 3 as *isotēs logōn* (1131 a31). Aristotle here says that a proportion 'involves four terms at least', since a continuous proportion 'uses one term as two and mentions it twice' (1131 a31–b3). He points out that *analogia* in this sense is called 'geometrical' in mathematics (1131 b12–13), and he distinguishes it, in his treatment of justice, from 'arithmetical proportion', e.g.

$a-b = b-c$ (1131 b32–1132 a2; cf. II. 6, 1106 a35–6). There is a certain vagueness in Burnet's use of 'proportion' which suggests that he may not have been clearly aware of its ambiguity. Whether this is so or not, I think that in Joachim's commentary 'proportion' is equivalent sometimes to *analogia*, equality of ratios, not *logos*, ratio. When he translates *hōrismenē logō* (1107 a1) in Aristotle's definition of ethical virtue as 'determined by a proportion', 'proportion' seems to mean ratio (p. 89). But, when he uses the expression '*meson* (mean) in a geometrical proportion' (p. 87), the context, especially the 'rule' formulated at the bottom of p. 88, implies that 'proportion' has the meaning 'equality of ratios'.[1]

The way in which the musical 'interval' involves a ratio of opposites is not made clear by Burnet. The pitch of a note in music depends on the length of the string in the lyre, or more directly on the frequency of the sound waves, and hence the interval between two notes is correlated with a numerical ratio. The Pythagoreans discovered that the intervals between notes in the scale are correlated with simple rational fractions, that for the octave being 1/2, for the fifth 3/2, etc. So far there is no ratio of contraries. But we find, in Aristotle's account of sensible qualities, a theory that determinate qualities within a range are the product, in some sense, of a blending of opposites in a ratio.[2] The opposites for hearing are the sharp and the flat,[3] for sight white and black, for taste sweet and bitter.[4] A sufficient excess of one opposite in the object of sense can make perception impossible, and perception, therefore, depends on a ratio (*logos*) which is a mean (*mesotēs*) between extremes. According to Aristotle, there is a corresponding, or identical, ratio in the faculty or organ of sense. It is not, I think, possible to find in the *De Anima* any clear and consistent account of the sense in which sensation is a ratio (*logos*) or mean (*mesotēs*). Some of the difficulties in the way of making the doctrine intelligible were pointed out acutely by J. L. Stocks in an article '*Logos* and *Mesotēs* in the *De Anima* of Aristotle'.[5] But, at least in some passages, Aristotle seems committed to

---

[1] See p. 135 above on Joachim's view.
[2] *De Anima* III. 2, 426 a27 ff.: cf. 423 b27–424 b3, 407 b30–1.
[3] 426 a30–1.   [4] 426 b8–12.   [5] *Journal of Philology*, 1914.

a doctrine that all sensible forms are ratios in the sense of being blends, according to a ratio, of opposed qualities. As regards hearing, the doctrine is stated in the following passage.[1] 'If voice (*phōnē*) always implies a concord (*sumphōnia*), and if the voice and the hearing of it are in one sense one and the same, and if concord always implies a ratio, hearing as well as what is heard must be a ratio. That is why the excess of either the sharp or the flat destroys the hearing' (426 a27–31). Ross quotes a statement of this difficult doctrine from Simplicius 194, 15–19: The actual object of hearing is said to be in a concord (*sumphōnia*) of extremes, so that it avoids excess or defect; concord is defined as being, as it were, a blending of extremes (*krasis tōn akrōn*). This evidence shows that Aristotle *might* have tried to exhibit the ethical mean as a mixture of opposites according to a ratio. But he does not in fact do so. By not doing so he avoids serious difficulties, if not absurdities.

It has been suggested that the way in which the concept of a mean (*mesotēs*) enters into Aristotle's account of sense-perception helps us to understand what Aristotle says in the *Nicomachean Ethics* about the role of perception (*aisthēsis*) in ethical cognition. The suggestion was elaborated by E. Harris Olmsted in an article entitled 'The "Moral Sense" Aspect of Aristotle's Ethical Theory'.[2] The object of the article is defined at the outset as being 'to bring into relation the use of the term *mesotēs* (i) in Aristotle's theory of perception as stated in the *De Anima* and (ii) in his account of the differentia of virtue in the *Nicomachean Ethics*' (p. 42). The writer does not claim to show a close connection, and such a claim would lack initial plausibility. For the application of the term in Aristotle's theory of perception is, at least primarily, to the perception of objects perceptible by one sense only, colour, sound, taste;[3] and Aristotle insists that practical sense is not like this kind of sense (*EN* VI. 8, 1142 a25–30). And Aristotle is right. Seeing what should be done is not like seeing a colour.

Harris Olmsted starts from the account of 'the physiological side of sense-perception' in the *De Anima* (423 b30–424 a7). The

---

[1] See Ross's notes on the text and its interpretation.
[2] *American Journal of Philology*, 1948.   [3] *De Anima* 418 a7–16.

sense-organ is 'sensitive to a set of qualities ranging between extremes, and to be sensitive to the whole range it must itself be a kind of mixture of the opposed qualities, in which neither extreme unduly predominates' (p. 43). In its application to temperature this account says that, for an object to be felt as warm or cold, it must be warmer or colder than the organ. But the article points out that this account cannot be applied to the senses generally. 'Sight and hearing, far from having a neutral spot, are most acute in the middle of their range'; and 'we perceive by touch what is just as hard or soft as we are' (p. 44). Moreover the writer does not try to explain, still less defend, the idea that the sense-organ is 'a kind of mixture' (what kind?) of the opposed qualities. Nor does he, as I understand, claim that the ethical mean is a mixture of opposed emotions, or of pleasures and opposed pains. He discusses helpfully some crucial passages about sense-perception in the *De Anima*[1] and about 'moral sense' in the *EN*.[2] It is right to stress the importance, in Aristotle's account of virtuous conduct, of the doctrine that the virtuous man exercises intuitive judgement in particular situations. But Harris Olmsted wished to hold that the doctrine of the ethical mean is primarily a doctrine about moral sense. I do not think he has shown this. But, if he had, it would still be questionable whether the doctrine of the mean in sense-perception helps us to understand the doctrine of moral sense. He hardly claims that it does. As we have seen, he himself points acutely to obscurities and weaknesses in the doctrine of the perceptual mean. It would not be profitable, he tells us, to try to 'interpret moral perception rigidly' in terms of Aristotle's theory of sense-perception (p. 58). Hence the theory of the ethical mean, as seen in the light of the *De Anima*, seems in the end, for Harris Olmsted, to fade out into the broad and innocuous assertion that to be virtuous is to be 'able to deal with the particular moral situation clear-sightedly' (p. 61).

Aristotle's theory of the 'chemical' composition of homoeo-merous bodies, minerals and tissues, by fusion of the physical elements is stated in *De Generatione et Corruptione* II. 7, 334 b2–30,

[1] 424 a17–b3, 431 a8–20.
[2] 1142 a25–30 and 1143 a35–b10; cf. 1109 b22–3, 1126 b3–4.

and is explained in Joachim's commentary. The whole passage is quoted as being 'specially instructive' by Burnet (pp. 72–3). Flesh and bones, for example, are formed as the result of 'the reciprocal action–passion of a completely-hot and a completely-cold which were present in amounts approximately balanced or equal'.[1] The opposites, dry and moist and hot and cold, produce flesh and bone and the remaining compounds 'in accordance with a mean', i.e. according to a ratio which is a mean (334 b28–30). If one of the contraries is present in sufficient excess, blending will not occur; the result, according to Aristotle, will be either bare matter or the one extreme 'existing in its full reality without qualification' (334 b8 ff.). But, when there is no such excess, then in the process of mixing the contraries 'destroy one another's excesses' and produce something intermediate (*metaxu*), 'which, according as it is potentially more hot than cold or *vice versa*, will possess a power-of-heating that is double or triple its power-of-cooling, or in some other ratio' (334 b13–16).

It is important to notice the following point about these speculations of Aristotle. The theory of the ratio of opposites must be stated, if it is to be intelligible, in terms of opposites which are absolute not relative, i.e. not just cross-sections of a range of qualities or of intensities. If this were not so, the theory would involve a vicious infinite regress since the extremes them-selves would be constituted by ratios. In Aristotle's philosophy of nature the two pairs of primary qualities, hot and cold and dry and fluid, are indeed absolute. The possible combinations of them, excluding the coupling of contraries, constitute the simple bodies of which what we call fire (hot and dry), air (hot and fluid), water (cold and fluid), and earth (cold and dry) 'are impure or exaggerated forms'.[2] Similarly Aristotle's theory of sensible qualities as ratios of opposites presupposes, for example, the notion of an absolute low and an absolute high in pitch, and the notion of the absolutely sweet and the absolutely bitter. The difficulty of these notions might well be taken to be a fatal weak-ness in the theories. In the case of the ethical mean the difficulties are so obvious and glaring as to constitute in themselves a serious

---

[1] Joachim, p. 241.   [2] Ross, *Aristotle*, p. 106.

objection to Burnet's interpretation of the doctrine. As we have already seen, the mean in the case of divisible goods, such as money or food, cannot be a ratio of opposites because it would not make sense to speak of ratios between amounts of the absolutely large and the absolutely small. Joseph elucidates the difficulty clearly, with reference to passions (*pathē*), in his criticism of Burnet. He argues that the *logos* by which the *mesotēs* is determined cannot be a ratio of contrary impulses. 'For these impulses would themselves be capable of varying in degree of strength, and it is difficult to see how the ratio in which they are to be combined, in order to secure the "mean" required, can be fixed unless the strength of each is first fixed. Yet this strength might in turn be regarded as involving a combination of contraries in a certain ratio, and so *ad infinitum*.'[1] Burnet tells us to 'go to the *Physics* for Aristotle's moral philosophy' (p. 69). I have argued that Aristotle did not in fact import into his ethics the 'physical' ideas which Burnet finds there. I think we should be glad that he did not do so. For, if he had, he would have spoiled his ethical doctrine by introducing into it confusions and mistakes from which it is in fact free.

[1] *Essays in Ancient and Modern Philosophy*, p. 171.

VIII

THE DISTINCTION BETWEEN THE VOLUNTARY AND THE INVOLUNTARY

A T the beginning of Book III Aristotle gives reasons for discussing the distinction between the 'voluntary' (*hekousion*) and the 'involuntary' (*akousion*). It is necessary to notice that the Greek words, although in some contexts they may be synonyms of the words used in translating them, have in general a wider or vaguer meaning. Thus in chapter 2 Aristotle says that 'both children and the lower animals share in voluntary action' (1111 b8–9; cf. a25–6). To say that some action was done, some effect produced, 'voluntarily' normally implies that there was an 'intention' to produce it. About children, except when they are very young indeed, we do not hesitate to speak in these ways. As regards animals, there is indeed a difference analogous to the difference between the voluntary and the involuntary production of an effect. Thus a dog may bite a man either viciously or inadvertently in play. On the other hand, we are inclined to say that a creature which, not being a user of language, cannot talk to itself about its expectations or intentions or aims cannot be said, in the fullest sense, to have expectations or intentions or aims. Of a barking dog we do not say seriously that 'he only does it to annoy'. So animal behaviour can more easily be described as *hekousion* in Greek than as 'voluntary' in English.

For the reader of this chapter of the *EN* the difference of meaning between 'voluntary' and *hekousion* which is important lies in the fact that the Greek words can mean what is meant by 'willing' and 'unwilling' as well as what is meant by 'voluntary' and 'involuntary'. When we say of someone that he did something 'involuntarily' we convey that some result which he produced was not intended. When we say that he did what he did 'unwillingly' we convey that the result was intended but not desired. Aristotle sometimes uses *akōn* to mean 'unwilling' not 'involuntary' (e.g. 1110 b12). Moreover, the unrecognized ambiguity seems to underlie some of the things which we find perverse or confusing in the text: e.g. the description of a certain class of actions as a 'mixture' (1110 a11) of the voluntary and the involuntary, and the suggestion that a man whose action is plainly involuntary cannot be said to have acted *akōn* unless he regrets it afterwards (1110 b18–24). It is best at the outset to stand clear of these complications. I shall, therefore, begin by stating in my own words the main doctrine of chapter 1.

Aristotle is formulating the criteria of imputability. He discusses two reasons which may be adduced for denying responsibility, whether what is disclaimed is the merit of a good action or the demerit of a bad one. A man may say that there was compulsion. This disclaimer or excuse covers both cases in which he would say that he did not act at all and cases in which he would say that he acted but was 'compelled' to act as he did. Secondly, a man may deny responsibility on the ground that the result which he is praised or blamed for producing was not intended, in the sense that it was not before his mind when he acted. Here I am going beyond Aristotle's words. What Aristotle says is that there is no responsibility when the result is due to innocent ignorance of some particular fact or facts. He implies that, because the fact, e.g. that some water had been poisoned, was not something which the agent knew, or could be expected to envisage, there could not have been any intention on his part to cause a certain result, e.g. someone's death.

Aristotle at the outset gives two reasons for thinking it 'necessary' (1109 b33) to discuss the voluntary and the involuntary: first, praise and blame are awarded to voluntary transactions, while involuntary transactions earn pardon or pity; secondly, the inquiry is 'useful also for legislators with a view to the assigning both of honours and punishments' (1109 b30–5). Aristotle does not say whether, or how, the criteria relevant to praise or blame in general differ from those relevant to rewards and punishments authorized by law. It is clear that there are differences. For example, information which is relevant to moral appraisal, e.g. about a man's upbringing or about his emotional tendencies, may be treated as irrelevant by a judge. Conversely, in a case of an attempted crime, e.g. murder, the question whether the attempt was successful may be important for the judge in court but irrelevant at the last judgement. Aristotle may have this in mind when he says that choice (*prohairesis*) is thought 'to discriminate characters better than actions do' (1111 b5–6).[1] Although for Aristotle the juristic interest is secondary, his discussion here starts from a juristic standpoint. The student of moral ideas must be interested in discovering what considerations are treated in the courts as relevant to guilt or innocence, or to degrees of guilt or innocence. But Aristotle's main interest, as is clear in chapter 5, is in the appropriateness and significance of the praise and blame awarded to human actions, and particularly actions which manifest ethical dispositions.

Aristotle's first division of 'the compulsory' presents no problem. The so-called agent is completely inactive, 'contributes nothing' (1110 a2; b16–17), e.g. 'if he were to be carried somewhere by a wind or by men who had him in their power' (1110 a3–4). Aristotle gives an example in v. 8: one man seizes the arm of another and uses it to strike a third person (1135 a27–8). The plea of compulsion in this sense is, if made good, conclusive: if there was no action, there was no illegal or blameworthy action.

Aristotle's second division of 'the compulsory' is described as consisting of 'things that are done from fear of greater evils or for some noble object, e.g. if a tyrant were to order one to do something base, having one's parents and children in his power, and if one did the action they were to be saved, but otherwise would be put to death' (1110 a4–7). Aristotle assimilates to this case the case of the captain who jettisons his cargo in order to save the lives of himself and his crew (a8–11). According to Aristotle 'it may be debated whether such actions are voluntary or involuntary' (1110 a7–8). But his description covers a wide range of different cases, and the kind of 'debate' which is possible is different

---

[1] Cf. I. 10, 1100 b35–1101 a5; *EE B* 11, 1228a 1–5; *Rhetoric* I. 9, 1367 b26–36.

at the two ends of the range. At one end it is plausible to compare the 'compulsion' involved with compulsion in the literal physical sense already considered. This is the case in which the 'fear of greater evils' is so extreme as to impose, as Aristotle suggests, 'pressure which overstrains human nature and which no one could withstand' (1110 a23–6). In the case of mental or physical torture it may be doubtful whether the victim has acted voluntarily or even, as in the case of literal physical compulsion, whether he has acted at all. But Aristotle suggests that, if what the tyrant requires us to do is sufficiently bad, the plea of compulsion cannot be accepted: 'we cannot be forced but ought rather to face death after the most fearful sufferings' (a26–7). It is clear that Aristotle's opinion on this point is questionable. The fact that the plea is sometimes used improperly, as in the case of Alcmaeon's killing his mother (a27–9), is not conclusive.

The plea of compulsion, in the sense of extreme psychological pressure, even if not conclusive, is certainly strong enough to justify pity and pardon (1110 a24). But at the other end of the range of Aristotle's so-called 'mixed actions' there is no pressure of this kind. The agent, as in the case of the prudent captain, is in full command of his faculties and acts freely although after what is often a difficult assessment of pros and cons (1110 a8–11, a29–30). The plea of compulsion is not that it would require a miracle of heroism for a man to hold out but that, in the special circumstances, any sensible man would have done the same. The only question for debate is not whether the action was voluntary but whether it was justified. Aristotle admits in effect that such actions are voluntary, and indeed that they are chosen freely (1110 a11–19, b5–7). Why, then, is he tempted to speak of them as 'mixed' or as 'in the abstract' or 'in themselves' (*haplōs*) involuntary (a18, b5)? Partly because they are done 'under compulsion' in a sense, and actions which are done under 'compulsion' in other senses are involuntary. Again, Aristotle has in mind the fact that, except in a storm, no one would voluntarily throw a cargo overboard (a9–10). But, as I suggested earlier, Aristotle's way of talking here is influenced by the fact that *akōn* can mean 'unwilling' as well as 'involuntary'. The man who acts from 'fear of greater evils' has feelings which make him actually reluctant or unwilling to act as he does.

Aristotle concludes the discussion of compulsion by dismissing the suggestion that a man who is attracted by a pleasant or noble object is 'compelled' by his own desire to do what he wants to do (1110 b9–10). The suggestion is in conflict with ordinary language. To say that a man is compelled to do something implies that he finds doing it painful (b11–13). Again 'it is absurd to make external circumstances responsible, and not oneself, as being easily caught by such attractions' (b13–14). Further, this line of thought is made suspect by the fact that it is commonly used as an argument for denying demerit to bad actions while still claiming merit for good ones (b14–15). Aristotle has more to say in chapter 5 on the questions raised by this dialectical move.

Having discussed 'compulsion' in its various senses and applications Aristotle goes on (1110 b18 ff.) to consider cases in which actions are made 'involuntary' by the fact that they are 'due to ignorance' (*di'agnoian*). His main point can be stated most shortly by saying that a man can defend himself against blame or punishment on the ground that he did not know what he was doing but not on the ground that he did not know that what he was doing was wrong. Socrates is not mentioned here, but Aristotle must have in mind the Socratic paradox, which he discusses in Book VII, that no one does what is wrong if he knows that it is wrong, so that wrong actions are 'due to ignorance' (VII. 2, 1145 b26–7). Aristotle insists that the ignorance which excuses is ignorance of fact not ignorance of rules or principles.

Before he comes to his main point (1110 b28) he makes two preliminary remarks. A man whose action is due to ignorance may or may not be sorry afterwards that the accident happened. Aristotle suggests that his action is involuntary (*akousion*) only if he is sorry; if he is not, the action is non-voluntary (1110 b18–24; cf. 1111 a19–21). This terminological proposal seems perverse, but I have suggested that it is to be connected with the fact that *akousion* has a wider range of meaning than 'involuntary'. Secondly, Aristotle distinguishes between actions 'due to ignorance' and actions done 'in ignorance'. A man who is drunk or in a rage may not know what he is doing, may produce effects which he did not intend, but the unfortunate outcome is regarded as 'due' not to his ignorance but to his drunkenness or rage (1110 b24–7). Later Aristotle refers to the law of Pittacus which imposed a double penalty for crimes committed when drunk (1113 b31–2).[1]

Every bad man is ignorant of what he ought to do and what he ought to abstain from, and it is due to error of this kind that men come to be unjust and generally bad. But the term 'involuntary' is not applicable if a man is ignorant of what is expedient. For it is not ignorance in his choice (*hē en tē prohairesei agnoia*) that causes the involuntary (it causes badness), nor ignorance of the universal (men are blamed for this) but ignorance of particulars, i.e. of the circumstances of the action and the objects with which it is concerned. In the case of this kind of ignorance pity is felt and pardon given. For the person who is ignorant of one of these circumstances acts involuntarily. (1110 b28–1111 a2.)

The ignorance in respect of which a man is bad, and which does not make his actions involuntary, is here variously described: ignorance of what he ought to do and abstain from doing, ignorance of the expedient, ignorance in the choice, ignorance of the universal. I agree with the view of nearly all the modern commentators that these are alternative descriptions of one kind of ignorance not descriptions of different kinds of ignorance, or even by intention different elements in one kind of ignorance. A bad man is one who acts on wrong principles, who follows rules of conduct suggested by ends which are misconceived. No doubt we think that there are obvious and important differences between universal rules which formulate duties and rules which express prudent counsels, and it is fair to ask whether Aristotle's ethical theory wrongly assimilates, or fails to contrast, things so different. But these large issues have no special relevance in the present context.

The only one of the phrases used to describe the ignorance contrasted with ignorance of circumstances which need detain us is 'ignorance in the choice' (*prohairesis*) (1110 b31). What makes this phrase surprising as a description of the bad man's ignorance is

---

[1] Cf. *Politics* II. 12, 1274 b18–23; *Rhetoric* II. 25, 1402 b8–12.

the fact that, in the following chapter, *prohairesis* is defined as the choice of means to a wished-for end. A bad man is one who chooses the wrong end not the wrong means to the right end. But Aristotle, although he assigns a stipulated technical meaning to *prohairesis*, also uses it in a wider sense as roughly equivalent to 'purpose'.[1] In the *EE prohairesis* is used explicitly of the adoption of an end or goal of life (*A* 1, 1214 b7-11; cf. *B* 11, 1228 a1-4). In *EN* iii. 2 Aristotle says that *prohairesis* is better evidence of character than actions are (1111 b5-6), and character is shown in ends pursued. But, even if in the phrase 'ignorance in the *prohairesis*' Aristotle has in mind the technical use of *prohairesis*, preferring a means-to-an-end, no real difficulty arises. The phrase could indicate misconception of the end as well as the failure to choose effective means. Gauthier-Jolif report that St. Albert, followed by St. Thomas, took the phrase to refer not to the man who has bad principles but to the man who is 'incontinent' (*akratēs*), i.e. fails to live up to his principles. But, even if it were necessary to distinguish 'ignorance in the choice' from the wicked man's ignorance of principles of conduct, the suggestion that 'ignorance in the choice' is the ignorance of the *akratēs* is made impossible by the fact that, in the next chapter, Aristotle says that the *akratēs* does not choose at all (1111 b13-14).

Aristotle enumerates here, and also in v. 8 (1135 a23-31 and b11-16), circumstances ignorance of which may make a man's actions involuntary: 'who he is, what he is doing, what or whom he is acting on, and sometimes also what (e.g. what instrument) he is doing it with, and with a view to what (e.g. he may think that his act will conduce to someone's safety), and how he is doing it (e.g. gently or violently)' (1111 a3-6). Aristotle's list covers a wide range of possible incidents or accidents to some of which words like 'inadvertent', 'mistake', 'accident', would apply more naturally than 'involuntary'. The list presents difficulties, e.g. the inclusion in it of 'the object in view' when the meaning which is wanted, but which cannot be accepted as a simple translation (Gauthier-Jolif) of the Greek, is 'result produced'. In some places the text needs to be emended. Again

---

[1] Cf. Ross, *Aristotle*, p. 200 and references there given.

Aristotle's brief descriptive references to exemplary instances are often cryptic. What can have been the mysterious indiscretion of the poet Aeschylus who 'did not know that it could not be said'? (1111 a9–10). Why did it matter that the stone was not pumice-stone? (a13). 'One might want to touch a man, as people do in sparring, and really wound him' (a14–15). What sort of accident was this and in what sort of contest? Perhaps some of these intriguing questions cannot be answered, and in any case the answers to them would not add to our understanding of Aristotle's general doctrine in this chapter.

Having defined the involuntary in terms of compulsion and ignorance of circumstances Aristotle concludes by formulating the implied definition of the voluntary: 'that of which the moving principle (archē) is in the agent himself, he being aware of the particular circumstances of the action' (1111 a22–4). This is followed, in our text, by a brief criticism of the view that actions 'due to anger or to appetite' are involuntary (1111 a24–b3). The view is rejected for reasons which the argumentation in the rest of the chapter would enable us to anticipate. The passage reads like an afterthought and may be out of place. Gauthier–Jolif place it immediately after the discussion of the 'mixed' actions (i.e. at 1110 b1).

IX

CHOICE AND THE ORIGINATION OF ACTION

'Now if it is in our power to do noble or base acts, and likewise in our power not to do them, and this is what being good or bad means, then it is in our power to be virtuous or vicious' (*EN* III. 5, 1113 b11–14). 'Man is a moving principle (*archē*) or begetter of his actions as of children. If this is clear, and if we cannot refer actions to moving principles other than those in ourselves, the acts whose moving principles are in us must themselves also be in our power and voluntary' (1113 b18–21). 'For we are ourselves in a sense partly responsible (*sunaitioi pōs*) for our states of character . . .' (1114 b22–3). I shall discuss Aristotle's doctrine that a man, or something in a man, is the moving principle, or responsible cause, of his actions. I shall try to make clear how I understand Aristotle's curiously unconfident statement, at the end of his discussion in chapter 5, that we are 'in a sense' and 'partly' responsible for being what we are.

Both Plato and Aristotle insist on the salutary truism that, by our actions, we form our characters and shape our lives. Both are attentive to the obvious fact that we have to work with tools, and on material, which we find and have not made. We do not choose our parents or our bodies or our innate mental aptitudes. We were not consulted about the economic resources, social customs, educational arrangements, and legal systems of the societies in which we found ourselves as children. Plato and Aristotle, being sensitive moralists, could not fail to be struck, and indeed troubled, by the fact that, in all these respects, some men and women are enormously more fortunate than others. But, while this is obvious in general, we seldom have enough information in detail to enable us to praise or blame, and to pardon, as we would if we knew more and were more thoughtful. To some philosophers, and to all men in some moods, it seems that the concept of moral merit and demerit is mistaken. Yet Plato in the *Laws* said that the powers that made us left the responsibility for being virtuous or vicious 'to our individual volitions' (x. 904 b–c). In the *Timaeus* he makes it clear that, if a man is born with an unsatisfactory set of physical and mental powers, perhaps as a woman or at the worst a non-human animal, the reason is that he misconducted himself in an earlier life (42 b–c). There were no handicaps at the start of the course of incarnations (41 e). The *Republic* says the same thing in four words: choice not God decides (617 e 4). It is significant that these over-emphatic assertions of human responsibility occur in the context of myth. Faced by a random distribution of the causes of misery and happiness, of virtue and vice, men naturally wish to tell themselves that all will be set right in the final distribution of things, or that all was fair in the original distribution. The doctrine of immortality, which Aristotle appears to have accepted when he wrote the *Eudemus*, makes it possible to veil the starker aspects of the human situation. Hence the rejection of immortality required, as R. Walzer pointed out in his book on the *MM*, a new and mature look at man's freedom and responsibility.[1] We get this new look in the *EN*, and it is one of the best things in the treatise.

To what is Aristotle referring when he speaks of 'moving principles in ourselves' (1113 b19–21)? Let us assemble some passages. In the *De Anima* he speaks of the soul as moving the living organism 'through an act of choice and thought' (*A* 3, 406 b24–5). The Greek word translated 'choice' is *prohairesis*. This is the translation used by Ross[2] in most places, but he states in a footnote (to 1111 b5) that 'sometimes "intention", "will", or "purpose" would bring out the meaning better'. In passages of which the one quoted from the *De Anima* is typical the word refers to something which happens in a man, or in the mind of a man, immediately before, or when, he acts. But it is not clear to what it refers. And we cannot make it clear since to do so would involve asking questions which Aristotle did not ask and trying out

---

[1] *Magna Moralia und aristotelische Ethik* (Berlin, 1929), p. 19.
[2] In the Oxford Translation.

distinctions which he did not make. Hence I must proceed by transliterating, and not translating, the word. This is not to evade trying to distinguish different things which Aristotle might or must have had in mind, however inexplicitly, when he used the word. Indeed such an attempt would be frustrated if we started by plumping for a translation. The passage quoted from the *De Anima* is in line with the definition of *prohairesis* in the *EN* III. 3 as 'deliberate desire' (*orexis*) of things in our power' (1113 a10–11; cf. 2, 1112 a15–16). 'When we have decided as a result of deliberation, we desire (*oregometha*) in accordance with our deliberation' (1113 a11–12). Deliberation, according to Aristotle's account in III. 3, is a process of thinking, comparable with analysis in mathematics, which starts from a desired end and works back to the discovery of a means by which it can be achieved. Hence, in the words of the *EE*, *prohairesis* is 'of something and for the sake of something' (*B* 11, 1227 b36–7; 1228 a2–3).[1]

So far a *prohairesis* would seem to be a desire for a means, derivative but distinct from the wish for a virtuous or vicious end, the means being something known or believed to be in our power to do here and now. Yet the Greek word has the strict meaning of preferential choice (cf. III. 2, 1112 a16–17), as *hairesis* means choosing or choice, e.g. the election of a magistrate. It would not be natural in English to identify, or to lump together, desiring to do something and deciding or choosing to do it. When we turn from Book III to Book VI we find Aristotle in chapter 2 speaking in a more enigmatic way about *prohairesis*. 'The origin (*archē*) of action, its efficient not its final cause (*hothen hē kinēsis all' ouch hou heneka*), is *prohairesis*, and that of *prohairesis* is desire and reasoning with a view to an end' (1139 a31–3). It is not obvious what Aristotle has in mind when he says that *prohairesis* is the efficient cause of action. But he has said in III. 1 that an action is voluntary, expresses a man's will, when 'the principle (*archē*) that moves the instrumental parts (*organika merē*) of his body is in him' (1110 a15–18). In VII. 3 he speaks of appetite (*epithumia*) as having the power directly to move parts of the body (1147 a35). He is discussing the conflict in the soul of the incontinent man

---

[1] Cf. *EN* III. 2, 1111 b5–6.

(*akratēs*), and in this conflict the antagonist of *epithumia* is *prohairesis* (III. 2, 1111 b15–16; cf. VII. 9, 1151 a5–7, a29). In view of this evidence I think it probable that in VI. 2 Aristotle is thinking of *prohairesis* as the origin (*archē*) or efficient cause of change in the body of the agent. If this is so, he is really thinking of a *prohairesis* as itself an action or the beginning of an action. For it is clear that an action, which is usually the voluntary moving, with some further object in view, of parts of a man's body, is in no case identical with the bare occurrence of the physical movements. Hence, if the *prohairesis* causes the physical movements, it must be the action, or an element in the action, and not something which is finished before the action begins and of which the action is an effect. But I am not, of course, suggesting that in all cases the *prohairesis* is the initiation of action, or issues in action. In the case of the incontinent man (*akratēs*) it can apparently be complete, though there are difficulties about this, and yet the man succumbs to passion (VII. 9, 1151 a29–33). I am suggesting only that the initiation of action is within the area covered by Aristotle's use of *prohairesis*.

A few lines later in Book VI Aristotle says that *prohairesis* is 'either desireful reason (*orektikos nous*) or reasonable desire (*orexis dianoētikē*)' and adds that 'such an origin of action (*archē*) is man' (1139 b4–5). Ross sees in Aristotle's unwillingness to say that *prohairesis* is a kind of *orexis* a step towards formulating a conception of will.[1] Burnet makes a similar remark in connection with a sentence in III. 3: 'For everyone ceases to inquire how he is to act when he has brought the moving principle back to himself and to the ruling part of himself; for this is what chooses' (1113 a5–7). 'This shows', Burnet says, 'that *prohairesis* is really what we call the will.' But what is that? I am not clear what either Ross or Burnet have in mind. I am even less clear what is in the minds of those commentators who tell us that Aristotle has no notion of will or of free will, as, for example, Gauthier and Jolif: 'dans la psychologie d'Aristote la volonté n'existe pas' (p. 219). He did not do badly without it. I must now try to say something more definite about will and action.

[1] *Aristotle*, p. 199.

I said at the outset that, while we must ask what Aristotle means by *prohairesis*, we must not assume that a definite answer can be given. A definite answer would be possible only if Aristotle had himself made and accepted the distinctions which, in asking what he meant, we have ourselves assumed. I have now suggested three things which, on the evidence of what I have reported him as saying, he might have meant or have had in mind: the desire to do an action, the decision to do an action, and the initiation of an action. The third suggestion has been left in some obscurity, and would not be made instantly clear by the use of the noun 'volition' or the verb to 'will'. But when I speak of 'willing' I am using the word as it is used when people, not only philosophers, speak of willing a bodily movement, e.g. the movement of a finger poised on the trigger of a gun. I propose, at this point in the argument, to leave Aristotle in order to consider a question which he did not ask but came near to answering, the question what an action is. I have two reasons for proceeding in this way. The first is that the vocabulary which I wish to use will make it easier for me to describe the course of Aristotle's argument about responsibility in chapter 5. The second is that, if I did not explicitly defend this way of speaking, I should be accused of simply taking for granted a concept of action which is mistaken or even unintelligible.

Before I go on to a direct discussion of will and action I shall briefly survey Aristotle's treatment of *prohairesis* and connected matters in chapters 2–4 of Book III. In chapter 2 Aristotle argues against those who say that *prohairesis* or choice is bodily appetite (*epithumia*) or anger (*thumos*) or wish (*boulēsis*) or again a kind of opinion (*doxa*) (1111 b10–12). Choice cannot be appetite or anger because these do not involve reason while choice does (b12–13). The contrast and opposition between appetite and rational choice is seen in the phenomena of continence and incontinence (b13–16). Choice is closer to wish, but wish, unlike choice, may be for what is impossible, or not under our control, and is for an end rather than a means, while what is chosen is a means to an end (b19–30). To sum up what Aristotle has said so far in this chapter, choice is not one of the generally recognized varieties of independent desire such as desires for food, drink, and sex, revenge or victory, health and happiness. Nor is it, he goes on to argue, merely an intellectual opinion or conviction. Choice is an indication of character but an opinion is not (1112 a1–3). We choose, but do not opine, to take or avoid something (a3–5). Choice is commended for being of the right object, opinion for being true (a5–7). And so on. The fact that choice is preceded or accompanied by opinion is not relevant to the question whether it is 'identical with some kind of opinion' (a11–13). Aristotle concludes by suggesting that the object of choice is 'what has been decided by previous deliberation' (*probebouleumenon*) (a15). His account of deliberation follows in chapter 3.

In the final sentence of chapter 2 Aristotle appeals, apparently in order to support his assertion that choice terminates a preceding process of thought, to the literal, or supposedly etymological, meaning of *prohairesis*: 'even the name seems to suggest that it is what is chosen before other things' (1112 a16–17).[1] So Ross translates, meaning by 'before other things' 'in preference to other things', since he has said, in a footnote to 1111 b5, that 'the etymological meaning is "preferential choice" '. It is difficult to believe that this remark of Aristotle is merely a somewhat pointless aside. But there is nothing in the immediate context to make clear what point it has. In the account of deliberation in the following chapter it is said that, when a man chooses a means to an end, he may, but need not, be choosing one course of action leading to the end in preference to others (1112 b15–20). I shall now turn to this account of deliberation and then return to Aristotle's remark on the significance of *prohairesis*.

Deliberation (*bouleusis*), the thinking which leads to the discovery and adoption of a means to an end, is described as follows in III. 3. 'They assume the end and consider how and by what means it is to be attained; and if it seems to be produced by several means they consider by which it is most easily and best produced, while if it is achieved by one only they consider how it will be achieved by this and by what means *this* will be achieved, till they come to the first cause, which in the order of discovery is

[1] Cf. *EE B* 10, 1226 b5–17; *MM A* 17, 1189 a11–16, a24–31.

last' (1112 b15–20). An example of such deliberation is given in the *Metaphysics*.[1]

This process of working back from a possibly remote end to the step which can be taken here and now is compared by Aristotle with the method of mathematical analysis. Ross explains as follows: 'Aristotle has in mind the method of discovering the solution of a geometrical problem. The problem being to construct a figure of a certain kind, we suppose it constructed and then analyse it to see if there is some figure by constructing which we can construct the required figure, and so on till we come to a figure which our existing knowledge enables us to construct.'[2] The method of geometrical analysis is a method of discovering proofs as well as constructions. In the 'analytic' stage the proposition to be proved is assumed to be true and is then shown to entail some consequence which in turn entails a further consequence and so on until a consequence is reached which is known to be true. In the 'synthetic' stage the process is reversed; starting from what is known to be true the argument terminates in the proposition to be proved. This kind of analysis presupposes that the entailments between the successive links in the chain are reciprocal. Otherwise the analysis would be a valid deduction but the synthesis not.[3]

We have seen that, in deliberation as described by Aristotle, the agent need not envisage alternative means for reaching his end.

---

[1] Z 7, 1032 b6–10, b18–26; cf. *De Motu Animalium* 701 a2–23, *De Partibus Animalium* 639 b24–640 a7.

[2] Note to 1112 b21 in Oxford Translation.

[3] Cf. *De Sophisticis Elenchis* 175 a28. The chief ancient authority on the method, Pappus, is quoted by Heath in *Mathematics in Aristotle* (pp. 270–2), and the method is fully discussed, and illustrated with an example, by Richard Robinson in *Mind* (1936). But in an article in *Phronesis* (1958), 'Greek Geometrical Analysis', N. Gulley marshals evidence that 'analysis' can be used of a movement of thought from conclusion to premisses in cases where the entailment is *not* reciprocal, i.e. the premisses cannot be deduced from the conclusion. This kind of analysis would be comparable with deliberation in cases where the means found is one of a set of alternatives. In such cases each alternative is a sufficient, but none is a necessary, condition of the achievement of the end. When only one means is possible, the means is a necessary as well as a sufficient condition and the connection is reciprocal. In this case deliberation is analogous to the method of analysis described by Robinson. Burnet's account of the method (pp. xxxiv–xxxvi; cf. p. 324, note on 1151 a17) is not clear and is made difficult to follow by his questionable assertions about the meaning of *hypothesis* in Greek geometry.

Thus it would seem that, in his choice of one thing in preference to others, the rejection of alternatives may be unconscious. But the expression 'chosen in preference to other things' (1112 a17) suggests alternatives consciously envisaged. Hence it is tempting to look for other types of practical reasoning which Aristotle might have had in mind.

In *EN* III. 1 Aristotle has referred to a kind of question which sometimes precedes action and which is not the question of what means to choose in order to achieve a desired end. The question calls for an assessment of considerations for and against some suggested line of action, a weighing of pros and cons. An action which is right or desirable in one aspect may be impossible to justify because of the cost involved (1110 a29 ff., b7–9). A father should be obeyed but not when he orders matricide (1110 a27–29). The question what should be chosen for the sake of (*anti*), or at the cost of (again *anti*), what is often difficult to decide. But there is nothing to suggest that Aristotle has this kind of deliberation in mind in chapter 2, and there would be no special propriety in describing the choice between yes and no, to act or not to act, as the choice of one thing in preference to other things.

Another interpretation of the passage (1112a15–17), and consequently another account of what Aristotle has in mind when he speaks of what is chosen as chosen 'before other things', is offered by Burnet. He connects the statement here that choice involves a rational principle (*logos*) with the doctrine in the *Metaphysics* that the same principle exhibits both an object and the deprivation (*sterēsis*) of the object (Θ 2, 1046 b7–9), e.g. the science of medicine enables a doctor either to cure a patient or to kill an enemy. This interpretation suggests that what is chosen is a means to an end in preference to a means to a diametrically opposite end. There is nothing in the context to suggest that Aristotle is here thinking of choice in this way. In the rest of his discussion he represents the object chosen as the means to an end antecedently determined or posited, the object not of choice but of wish. 'We deliberate not about ends but about means' (1112 b11–12; 1113 b3–4). Again he represents the agent not as choosing between *A* as a means to *B* and *C* as a means to *D*, but rather as saying yes or no to the means reached by deliberation (5, 1113 b6-14). For these reasons Burnet's explanation of the sense in which rational choice is of one thing before other things is unconvincing.

Thus Aristotle does not make clear his reason for the remark that the action chosen is chosen in preference to other alternatives. Perhaps he means merely that, since choice involves thought, it is appropriate that the word for it should suggest the thoughtful discrimination of alternatives. The deliberation of the agent is indeed addressed to the question, not *whether* to seek a certain end, but *how* to achieve it. But, as one acting with care and deliberation, he will be aware that, in adopting the means to his desired end, he is rejecting other steps which would lead to other ends. But, before we leave the passage, we should notice the suggestion of Joachim, followed by Gauthier-Jolif, that in the phrase *pro heterōn*, before other things, *pro* (before) has a temporal sense. Two lines earlier it has this sense as part of the word *probebouleumenon*, object of *preceding* deliberation. The adoption of the means comes before the attainment of the end. Joachim thinks that 'on the whole' Aristotle's remark is to be understood as meaning: 'the name too, *prohaireton*, seems to indicate that it is something adopted before (on the road to) other things (i.e. other steps in the series of means).' It is impossible to prove that Aristotle is not in this way playing with the ambiguity of the preposition. But the interpretation is strained, and is not supported, so far as I can see, by the parallel passages in *EE B* 10, 1226 b5–17 and *MM A* 17, 1189 a11–16, a24–31.

Aristotle has said that what is chosen is the means to an end, and that the appropriate word for the end is *boulēsis* (wish). 'We wish to be happy and say we do, but we cannot well say that we choose to be so' (1111 b28–9). But different men seek happiness in different objects, and some ends, those of bad or inferior men, appear good when they are not (1113 a31 ff.). In chapter 4 Aristotle treats these facts as raising the question whether wish is for the good or for the apparent good (1113 a15 ff.), and answers by saying that 'absolutely and in truth the good is the object of wish, but for each person the apparent good' (a22–4). He evidently thinks of the word *bouleton*, object of wish, as being ambiguous. The supposed ambiguity seems to be like that which has been found, to the confusion of J. S. Mill according to his critics, in the word 'desirable' as meaning either a possible or a suitable object of desire.

We should note, but not accept, Burnet's remark that wish (*boulēsis*) is the 'appetitive element', the *orexis*, in choice (*prohairesis*). As we have seen, Aristotle defines *prohairesis* as being a form of *orexis*. To say that *boulēsis* is the orectic element in *prohairesis* does not leave sufficiently open the question what sort of process or fact Aristotle has in mind when he speaks of *prohairesis* as *bouleutikē* (deliberate) *orexis* (desire) (1113 a10–11). He would indeed say that we choose the means *because* we wish for the end; choice depends on wish. In the words quoted earlier from the *EE* choice is 'of something and for the sake of something' (*B* 11, 1227 b36–7). Virtue directs choice to the right end (1228 a1–2). Hence Aristotle can even say in *EN* VI. 12 that virtue 'makes the choice right'.[1] It is because choice has a wished-for end in view that 'it is from a man's choice that we judge his character, not from what he does but from his object in doing it' (*EE B* 11, 1228 a2–3).[2] Virtue makes the aim right.[3] But all this is not to say that wish, which is certainly not identical with choice, is identical with an element in choice. What Aristotle has said in chapter 2 is that choice is *not* wish, 'though it seems near to it' (1111 b19–20).

Words which name actions often imply the actual occurrence of results which the agent intended to produce. A murder is an action, and it would be self-contradictory to say that *A* murdered *B* and *B* survived. There are no unsuccessful murders. Giving £1,000 to a charity is an action, and to say that the gift was made is to say that it was received. But the victim of a murderous assault does not always die. Writing a cheque does not make it certain that money will be received. Thus, it may be said, 'murder' and 'give' do not simply name kinds of actions because the very same actions, or rather the very same activities, might

---

[1] 1144 a20; but cf. 13, 1145 a4–6.   [2] Cf. above *EN* III. 2, 1111 b5–6.
[3] VI. 12, 1144 a7–8; cf. a20–2; 13, 1145 a5–6.

not have been cases of murdering or of giving. If we look for ways of talking which take account of these facts, we either use the word 'try' (or a synonym) or else redescribe the actions in terms of relatively immediate consequences. We say that A tried to murder B or that he pulled a trigger with every expectation of a fatal result. We say that C tried to make a gift or that he wrote a cheque with certain beneficent intentions. Aristotle, as we have seen, suggests that, when a man acts, what he immediately initiates is a change in a part of his body (1110 a15-18; cf. 1147 a35). But the difficulty which stopped us from defining an action as the deliberate producing of a certain result breaks out again. For the production of the relatively immediate consequences may misfire: triggers stick and pens break when we put them to paper. The next step in this regress takes us to cramp and paralysis: fingers do not always move when their owners will them to move. The conclusion suggested is that an action is to be thought of as a voluntary activity which may or may not produce results expected by the agent. It is not the causing of a change but the willing of a change. Whether willing is in fact always associated with some bodily change in the nervous system is a question, as Aristotle would say, for the physiologists.[1]

In order to avert misunderstanding I add two elucidatory comments on the proposal to describe an action as the willing of a change, or of the prevention of a change. First, the change willed is never, so far as we know, a change produced directly by the willing, but is commonly a *less* remote consequence of the willing than the consequence to which ordinary language makes primary reference; as the movement of the murderer's trigger finger is a less remote consequence than the death of the victim. Secondly, the change willed need not, at least prima facie, be the least remote of the consequences which can be envisaged by the agent as flowing from his (or her) willing, and, even when his (or her) body is involved, need not be a change in his (or her) body. This point will be readily taken by anyone who has ever instructed himself, or received oral or written instructions, in swinging a golf club. The correct position of the club at some point in the swing

[1] Cf. VII. 3, 1147 b6-9.

depends on the position of the hands but it may, nevertheless, be important for success that the objective anticipated in willing should be the position of the club and not the position of the hands. A more elaborate example is given by Miss Anscombe in support of her observation that 'the only description that I clearly know of what I am doing may be of something that is at a distance from me'.[1] She imagines a mechanism such that a pointer can be kept level by a pumping movement of my arm. What is done or willed in this example is 'keeping the thing level' not the movement of the arm. 'I am able to give a much more exact account of what I am doing at a distance than of what my arm is doing.'[1] I agree with Miss Anscombe's observation at this point; but further analysis, more refined description, is needed of 'what I am doing' in this and other cases.

In sections 29 and 30 (pp. 51-4) of her book Miss Anscombe argues that it is 'wrong to try and push the . . . act of will back to something initiating the movements that then take place' (p. vii). She expresses strong disagreement with those who 'say that what one knows as intentional action is only the intention, or possibly also the bodily movement; and that the rest is known by observation to be the *result*, which was also willed in intention' (pp. 51-2). I believe myself to have been stating and defending a form of the view which she attacks and describes as being for the following reason a 'mad account': 'for the only sense I can give to "willing" is that in which I might stare at something and will it to move. People sometimes say that one can get one's arm to move by an act of will but not a matchbox; but if they mean "will a matchbox to move and it won't", the answer is "if I will my arm to move in that way it won't", and if they mean "I can move my arm but not the matchbox" the answer is that I can move the matchbox—nothing easier' (p. 52). I think that Miss Anscombe is here claiming, in effect, to disclose a conceptual difficulty when what is needed is more detailed description of what happens when a man wills the movement of a matchbox or wills to move his leg. Perhaps, in the case of the attempted psychokinesis of the matchbox, what is willed is staring at the matchbox and the movement

---

[1] *Intention* (1957). p. 53.

is only a hope. What does Miss Anscombe think happens when a patient recovering from paralysis tries to move his (or her) leg? Staring and hoping will not do it. C. A. Campbell has argued that 'the immediate object of our willing is not the movement of our leg but certain kinaesthetic and other sensations upon which, we have learned from experience, the movement of our leg normally supervenes'.[1] Until consideration has been given to this suggestion, and to any other suggestions which introspective psychologists, if there still are any, can produce, it is too soon to decide that there is not a good sense in which we all will the movements of our own hands but not the movements of matchboxes.

Wittgenstein, quoted at this point by Miss Anscombe, declared in the *Tractatus* that 'the world is independent of my will'. 'Even if what we wish were always to happen, this would only be a grace of fate, for it is not any logical connexion between will and the world that would guarantee this, and as for the presumed physical connexion, we cannot will that' (6. 373, 6. 374). At the time when he wrote this Wittgenstein also, as Miss Anscombe tells us, wrote in his notebooks: 'I am completely powerless.' Perhaps what my discussion has suggested might be summarized, in a less sweeping formula, by saying that the only thing in the world that a man has the power to change is his mind.

Miss Anscombe has a further argument against Wittgenstein in this mood, or against anyone who says that acting is intentional willing which cannot be guaranteed to produce results. The argument is stated very briefly and starts from the proposition that an intention needs a 'vehicle', e.g. a formulation in words. The argument proceeds: 'And if so, what guarantees that I do form the words that I intend? For the formulation of the words is itself an intentional act' (p. 52). The objection is clearly intended to impute a vicious regress, as is confirmed by Miss Anscombe's use of 'nonsense' to characterize the position she attacks. Just as, when I will the movement of my leg, nothing guarantees that my leg will move, so when I will the preconditions of willing to move my leg, nothing guarantees that these preconditions will come to exist, and so on. Now it is true that voluntary activity has preconditions.

[1] *On Selfhood and Godhood* (1957), pp. 137–8.

It requires the thought of something as possible but not yet actual. This thought needs, no doubt, a 'vehicle'; it needs, perhaps, imagination, whether or not what is imagined is a formulation in words. But a regress would be involved only if the account given of willing made it necessary to assume further willing in order to explain the coming into existence of the preconditions. But that this is so has not been shown. Is any damage done if it is admitted that, unless the preconditions of willing somehow came to exist, there would be no willing? A committee cannot act without agenda, but this would lead to a regress only if settling the agenda had to be an agendum for a meeting. I cannot, therefore, find in what Miss Anscombe has said any proof that the account of acting as willing, as what 'has gone on in me', is nonsensical or, as she also says, 'a false avenue of escape' (p. 52).

I shall use the description of acting as the willing of a change, or of the prevention of a change, in the account which follows of Aristotle's discussion, in EN III. 5, of a man's responsibility for the actions which he chooses to do. I hope that the answer I have sketched to the question in what action consists will make it easier briefly to note, and avoid, some of the confusions and ambiguities which complicate the problem of free will. It would be surprising if Aristotle's pioneering exploration had produced an adequate chart of these complications.

There is a break in the argument of the chapter at 1114 a3 where Aristotle starts to consider an objection. In the first part of the chapter (1113 b3–1114 a3) he starts from the position that, whenever an agent after deliberation chooses the means to an end, his action is voluntary (*hekousios*) and according to choice (*kata prohairesin*). It is in our power (*eph' hēmin*) to do or not to do what we do deliberately, and virtue and vice are exercised in doing and not doing such actions. Hence virtue and vice are alike in our power. Thus it is untrue that no one is voluntarily wicked. To deny this is to deny that man is a moving principle (*archē*) 'or begetter of his actions as of children'. But we cannot refer our actions 'to moving principles other than those in ourselves'. As confirmation of the truism that a man, as a voluntary agent, is a 'moving principle' Aristotle adduces the use of censure and exhortation by private persons, and of rewards and punishments by legislators, to influence a man's use of his active power. No one exhorts a man not to feel pain or heat or hunger; the treatment would be ineffective. But a man is punished even for an action due to ignorance, and hence not itself voluntary, if the ignorance can be traced to his voluntary actions, e.g. in getting drunk. For it is in a man's power to take care not to get drunk (1113 b3-1114 a3).

It is important to note here what has so far been said and what has not been said. It is in a man's own power to do or not to do good or bad actions. If the assassin wills the movement of his finger, it will move; if not, not. If a man chooses to write a cheque for a charity, the cheque will be written; if not, not. It is in Caesar's power to stay at home; the cause is in his will. Nothing has been said so far which need raise the question whether a man's willing or choosing as he does can be traced to antecedents which make it certain or necessary that he should thus will or choose. And it may be thought that we need not, at least at this stage, raise such further questions in order to understand the scope and efficacy of moral exhortation and encouragement, and of the rewards and penalties prescribed by laws. These influences cause men to behave better, and this is their justification. It is enough for Aristotle's argument so far that what a man wills can be affected by what is said to him and can affect what happens in the world. Praise and blame can be justified by their consequences. Whether the whole system of ideas in which praise and blame have their place is itself valid and reasonable is a further question. In the rest of the chapter Aristotle at least approaches such further questions.

When it is said that a man can watch his step, and ought to watch it carefully, an objector may reply that perhaps he is not the kind of man to be careful (1114 a3-4). But, even if his carelessness has become a settled state of character, he can be blamed for the slack and self-indulgent actions which formed his character. The building of character is like training for a contest, and athletes never stop practising (a4-10). Again it is unreasonable to suppose that a man who acts unjustly or self-indulgently does not wish to be unjust or self-indulgent. So if a man without being ignorant does actions which make him unjust his injustice is voluntary. But, having become unjust, he cannot, by wishing it, cease to be unjust; any more than a man who has made himself ill by disobeying his doctor can cease to be ill. Aristotle points out that we blame physical faults or weaknesses, as well as faults of character, in so far, but only so far, as they result from voluntary acts (1114 a11–31).

Aristotle's argument in this section skates over some thin ice. He might have met more boldly the objector who suggests, in effect, that a man whose action expresses his character has not the power to act otherwise than he does. How has he not if it is the case that his will produces the result and that, if he had willed otherwise, the result would have been different? The agent is a moving principle and the author of his acts. He knows what he is doing and there is no constraint. Perhaps the underlying thought, not rejected by Aristotle, is that, since the action is determined by his character, the agent's activity, although a moving principle, is not an original or spontaneous principle of movement. Having tacitly conceded this ground to the objector, Aristotle suggests that a stand can be made on the distinction between the actions which express a well or badly formed character and the actions which formed it well or badly. But this move, as Aristotle here makes it, is unsatisfactory. The idea that a man is a responsible agent cannot be defended by pushing back his responsibility to a time when his character was unformed. For the objector will reply that, if the earlier actions cannot be traced to character, they can be traced to the joint efficacy of natural innate tendencies and environmental influences. Again there is no clear or sharp division of actions into those which form and those which express character. A more effective reply to the objector might have been based on the suggestion that these are two features present, in some degree, in all actions. Aristotle comes near to this line of thought in his remark that athletes are always in training (1114 a7–9). But, instead of developing it, he goes on to compare a vicious character to a disease which, once contracted, must run its course. He does not mention the dissimilarities between a bodily illness and a faulty state of character. But Aristotle would not expect to be held down to every suggestion which is made in a discussion conducted in the form of dialectical moves and counter-moves. We must go on to consider, without expecting crisp and clear-cut conclusions, the further development of his discussion in this chapter.

It may be said that all men aim at an end which seems to them good, but do not determine their own view of the good (are not *kurioi tēs phantasias*): what they think good depends on the sort of men they are (1114 a31–b1). But, if a man is responsible in a sense (*aitios pōs*) for his state of character, he will be responsible in a sense for his view of the end. Otherwise wrongdoing would be due to 'ignorance of the end'; the fact that a man aims at a certain end would not be due to his own choice (*authairetos*) but to his being born, as it were, with good or bad vision. The man with good vision will be one who is 'well-endowed by nature' (*eu-phuēs*): the greatest and fairest gift, which cannot be received or learnt from another man, will depend on what a man is by nature, and a good natural endowment in this respect will be the true and perfect natural goodness (1114 b1–12). Aristotle drives his point home by repeating four or five times in different forms the Greek word translated 'nature' (*phusis*). Goodness, the objector suggests, is a natural talent, as physical health and mental acute-ness are natural talents. The suggestion is a paradox since men are commonly blamed for cowardice and injustice as they are not blamed for being ugly or stupid. But the paradox, Aristotle seems to suggest, deserves to be debated seriously. That it was a familiar topic of debate is shown by a passage in x. 9. 'Now some think that we become good by nature, others by habituation, others by teaching. Nature's part evidently does not depend on us, but as a result of some divine causes is present in those who are truly fortunate' (1179 b20–3; cf. *EE* Θ 2). We must now see what Aristotle has to say, in the concluding sentences (1114 b12–25) of the chapter under review, about the thesis, which at a different level he rejected earlier (II. 1), that men are born good or bad, are made good or bad by nature.

His first point is that, if the view to be considered is accepted, goodness of character is no more voluntary (*hekousion*) than badness. 'To both men alike, the good and the bad, the end appears and is fixed (*keitai*) by nature or however it may be, and it is by referring everything else (i.e. the means) to this that men do whatever they do' (b12–16). This conclusion, that what is true of vice is true also of virtue, must be accepted whichever of two views is taken on the question in what sense a man is responsible for being vicious or for being virtuous. 'Whether, then, (1) it is not by nature that the end appears to each man as it does, but something also depends on him (*par' auton*), or (2) the end is natural but because the good man adopts the means voluntarily virtue is voluntary, vice also will be none the less voluntary; for in the case of the bad man there is equally present that which depends on himself (*di' auton*) in his actions even if not in his end' (1114 b16–21).

It is clear that the second alternative represents the view of those who hold that it is by nature that men are good or bad: what a man desires for itself is determined by nature but the actions which congenital desires prompt him to do are voluntary; these actions establish his character as virtuous or vicious and, in this sense, virtue and vice are voluntary. But it is not clear what view is represented by the first alternative: the end is not fixed by nature since something also 'depends on the man himself' (1114 b17). How does the agent contribute to the determination of the end? Not just by the character-forming actions done in order to achieve the end. For this is allowed by the second alternative. It might be suggested that the agent decides between seeking to achieve one end and seeking to achieve another. But this suggestion is contradicted by Aristotle's main doctrine, which is the background of the present discussion, that choice (*prohairesis*) is of means to an end laid down by wish (*boulēsis*). It is true that, in the case of continence (*enkrateia*) or incontinence (*akrasia*), the agent might be thought to be confronted by a choice between the superior end suggested by virtue and the inferior end of present pleasure. But in Aristotle's view there is choice only when the superior end is preferred; the incontinent man desires but does not choose (III. 2, 1111 b13–15). Are we to suppose, then, that Aristotle has in mind a voluntary decision which is free, in the sense of undetermined, between acting to achieve an end and not acting at all. This suggestion might seem to be supported by Aristotle's insistence, at the beginning of the chapter, that 'where it is in our power to act it is also in our power not to act, and *vice versa*' (1113 b7–8; cf. 1115 a2–3). Joachim thinks that an indeterminist interpretation of *prohairesis* is possible and that a much discussed chapter in the *De Interpretatione* (ch. 9) is evidence in its favour.[1] As we saw earlier, the choice between yes and no, to act or not to act, can be interpreted as being open only in a conditional sense: if we wish we can act; if we do not so wish, we can refrain. But the conditional interpretation leaves the objector saying that virtue and vice are ultimately determined by natural endowment. It is true that even on the conditional interpretation a man is the cause of his actions. But, in the phrase translated 'something comes also from the man himself', Aristotle perhaps draws back from closing with the conditional interpretation and suggests that choice is open in an unconditional sense, that a man is not merely the cause but the uncaused cause of his actions. But, if this is what is in Aristotle's mind, he has not made his meaning explicit or clear. He leaves us with an enigmatic and not a precise statement of the alternatives which he distinguishes in this passage (1114 b16–20). The commentators, apart from Joachim, are not helpful at this point; and they fail also to answer, or even to ask, the questions raised by the final sentence with which Aristotle now brings his discussion of responsibility to a close rather than a conclusion.

'If, then, as is asserted, the virtues are voluntary (for we are ourselves somehow partly responsible (*sunaitioi pōs*) for our states of character, and it is by being persons of a certain kind that we set before ourselves such and such an end) the vices also will be voluntary; for the same is true of them' (1114 b21–5). It is difficult here to see what is meant by the phrase translated 'somehow partly responsible'. Burnet suggests that we are partly responsible for our states of character as being responsible for them at the start (1114 b32; cf. 1114 a4–7). But responsibility for character at the beginning qualified by inability to alter it when

---

[1] Commentary, pp. 109–11; cf. *Metaphysics E* 3, 1027 a29–b16.

formed is not naturally described as co-responsibility. If we are co-responsible who or what are our partners in responsibility? Perhaps our parents or other educators? But it seems clear from the argument in the context that the other partner, or co-cause, must be nature (*phusis*). If so, the question arises whether the phrase 'somehow partly responsible', or 'co-causes in a sense', expresses the first of the alternative suggestions which have been formulated in the preceding sentence, that a man's end is not completely determined by nature but something comes from the man, or the second, that the end is determined by nature and the man contributes by his voluntary choice of means. At first sight it is natural to think the former and to understand 'co-causes in a sense' as taking up' 'something comes from the man himself'. But, as we have seen, Aristotle has given no explanation of this alternative and no reason for accepting it. The argument requires that, in this last sentence, Aristotle should not defiantly assert a position which he has not made good but rather that he should say that, even if the maximum concessions are made to the objections he has been considering, one position is intact: vice is as voluntary as virtue; if virtue deserves praise, vice deserves blame and cannot be excused as due to ignorance. Aristotle, at least provisionally and for the purpose of the present argument, accepts the doctrine that the end is determined by nature. But, even if our nature comes to us from heredity shaped by environment, it is still *our* nature. We are causes, even if not first causes, of our actions. In this sense we are 'somehow partly responsible'.

It is, perhaps, worth suggesting, as a footnote to this discussion, that co-cause, or partner in responsibility, is not the only possible interpretation of *sunaition*. The expression *sunaition pōs* occurs in a passage in the *De Anima* in which Aristotle states the doctrine that the soul is the cause (*aitia*) of growth in plants and animals (*B* 4, 416 a9–18). Only the formal element, the soul, can account for the way in which 'whatever Miss T. eats turns into Miss T.' A material element, such as fire, cannot be a cause without qualification (*haplōs aition*), although it may be, in a sense, an accompanying or subordinate cause (*sunaition pōs*). On the analogy suggested by this passage the cause proper of our virtues and vices would be nature working through us just as the cause, in the strict sense, of growth is the soul working through the material constituents of the body. Clearly this analogy cannot be pressed; it would suggest a larger concession to the deterministic criticism of responsibility than Aristotle, even in a dialectical exercise, would be likely to make. But the usage in the *De Anima* lends support to the analysis I have given of the argument in *EN* III. 5. It is possible that in the *EN* also *sunaitioi pōs* means an assisting cause rather than a cause or cause-factor which is a partner, enjoying equal status, with other co-causes.

In the account I have given of Aristotle's treatment of choice (*prohairesis*) in chapters 2–5 of Book III I have assumed that the deliberation which terminates in choice (1112 a15) immediately precedes action. 'For everyone ceases to inquire how he is to act when he has brought the moving principle back to himself and to the ruling part of himself; for this is what chooses' (1113 a5–7). The last step in deliberative analysis is the first in the order of becoming (1112 b23–4).[1] I have assumed that *prohairesis*, if distinct from action, immediately precedes it. This assumption conflicts with the view of Miss Anscombe that in Book III, as well as in Book VI, Aristotle implies that, in some cases, a choice which has been reached by deliberation is also followed by further deliberation with a view to finding how to execute it. Miss Anscombe allows that Book III does not suggest that 'wanting the more immediate means', reached by this further deliberation, 'is not itself *also*' a choice (*prohairesis*).[2]

Miss Anscombe rightly directs our attention (p. 143) to the interesting passage in VI. 9 where Aristotle speaks of the incontinent man (*akratēs*) as acting after deliberation (1142 b18–20). I cannot embark here on the complexities of Aristotle's treatment of incontinence (*akrasia*), and my only present concern is to deal with the evidence which Miss Anscombe claims to adduce for importing the idea of deliberation following choice into the interpretation of these chapters in Book III. I suggest that the

---

[1] Cf. *EE B* 11, 1227 b32–3.

[2] 'Thought and Action in Aristotle', in *New Essays on Plato and Aristotle* (1965), pp. 144 ff.

evidence vanishes under scrutiny. She adduces first a sentence in VI. 12: 'virtue makes the choice right but what should be done for the sake of it belongs not to virtue but to another faculty' (1144 a20–2). But the sentence must be understood in the light of the fuller statement in the following chapter that 'the choice will not be right without practical wisdom (*phronēsis*) any more than without virtue (*aretē*); for the one (*aretē*) determines the end and the other (*phronēsis*) makes us do the things that lead to the end' (1145 a4–6).[1] There is no suggestion in the second passage that deliberation seeks a way of executing a preceding choice. On the contrary, the passage makes it clear that choice presupposes co-operation between virtue and 'the other faculty'. As regards Book III Miss Anscombe adduces the following passage, adding her own italics at two points to Ross's translation: '. . . if a thing appears possible we *try* to do it; possible things are those which *might* come about through us' (1112 b26–7). The italics applied to 'try' and 'might' are used to suggest that, even when the choice has been made, it may still be uncertain how it is to be executed. But there is no support for this suggestion in the Greek or in Ross's unitalicized English. The word translated 'try' (*encheirousi*) means literally 'putting a hand (*cheir*)' to something and is translated 'begin' by Rackham and 'set to work' by Peters. The phrase '*might* come about through us' (*di' hēmōn genoit' an*) would be equally well rendered with 'could' or 'can' instead of 'might'. We find 'able to be performed by our agency' in Rackham and 'can be done by us' in Peters. Thus, as regards Aristotle's detailed account of deliberation and choice in these chapters of Book III, Miss Anscombe seems to be wrong in maintaining that there is any suggestion of further deliberation after a choice has been made.

[1] Cf. *EE* B 11, 1227 b38–28 a2.

X

JUSTICE

THE first sentence of Book v states what are the topics with which the book primarily deals. 'With regard to justice and injustice we must consider what kinds of actions they are concerned with, what sort of mean justice is, and between what extremes the just act is intermediate' (1129 a3–5). Aristotle has been going through the list of ethical virtues one by one in the expectation of confirming his general doctrine that ethical virtue, because it involves ranges of feelings or emotions which may be excessive or defective, lies in a mean. The principle of the mean may be expressed also in other measurable aspects, money for example, of actions which are right or wrong. In the case of justice Aristotle approaches the question what sort of mean it is by first considering just and unjust actions and the question between what extremes the just act is intermediate. His analysis of various kinds or spheres of justice leads him to the conclusion at the end of chapter 5 that 'justice is a kind of mean, but not in the same way as the other virtues, but because it relates to an intermediate amount, while injustice relates to the extremes' (1133 b32–1134 a1). Thus Aristotle does not assert, but denies, that the application of the Mean to justice is the same as its application to other virtues. But we should not be in a hurry to decide that the doctrine here breaks down or is a failure.[1] If Aristotle's treatment of justice as a mean is in some respects confusing and complicated, so also are both the facts to be surveyed and our ways of talking about the facts whether in Greek or in English.

While Aristotle's main object is to describe justice as a virtue of character, the book deals also with a number of connected topics. A citizen shows himself just or unjust most conspicuously when

---

[1] Cf. Ross, *Aristotle*, p. 214.

he serves on a jury or exercises the function of a judge or arbitrator. Aristotle could hardly not have in mind the main facts about legal processes in Athens. Book v has been described as containing a 'first endeavour to give greater exactness to some of the leading conceptions of jurisprudence'.[1] The distinctions drawn in chapter 8 between injuries caused voluntarily and involuntarily, and within the voluntary between premeditated and unpremeditated, are important for the lawyer as well as for the moralist. Some scholars have, perhaps, overstressed Aristotle's interest in legal forms, and have been rash in suggesting connections between Aristotle's divisions of justice and different types of cases in the courts at Athens. A. R. W. Harrison makes this point in criticism of Vinogradoff[2] and of Joachim. But Aristotle's interest in justice as administered in the courts is clear at many points. His contributions to jurisprudence are to be found in chapter 1 (the just as the lawful), chapter 2 (the just as the fair or equal), chapter 3 (justice in the distribution of goods), chapter 4 (justice in the rectification of wrongs), chapter 7 (natural and legal justice), chapter 8 (degrees of wrongdoing), chapter 10 (equity as a corrective supplement of legal justice). In chapter 5 (justice in the exchange of goods) Aristotle has something to say on the nature and value of a free market and the usefulness of currency. It is a short pioneering excursion into economic theory.

In chapters 9 and 11 Aristotle formulates and discusses four questions. (1) Is it possible to be voluntarily treated unjustly? (2) Is everyone who suffers what is unjust treated unjustly? (3) Is it the distributor or the recipient who is guilty of injustice in distribution? (4) Can a man treat himself unjustly? Aristotle's discussion shows that there are connections between these questions. For example, the negative answer which he gives to (1) entails a negative answer to (4) (1138 a23-4, 26-8; cf. 1134 b9-13). The question (4) whether a man can wrong himself seems to be connected in the following way with the main question at issue in Book v, what kind of mean justice is. Injustice in one sense involves a tendency to take for oneself too large a share of

[1] J. A. Smith, *Introduction to the Everyman Translation*, p. xix.
[2] See Bibliographical Note on Book v, pp. 210-11.

divisible goods (*pleonexia*). But, if justice is a mean between two vices, there should be an opposite form of injustice involving a tendency to take for oneself too small a share of divisible goods (the *meionexia* of the *elattōtikos*). The man who takes too much is unfair to someone else; the man who takes too little is unfair to himself. Thus Aristotle's negative answer to the question whether a man can treat himself unfairly seems to make it impossible for him to hold that justice is a mean in the sense of being intermediate between two vices, two opposite ways of failing to be just.

The account I have given of the contents of Book v shows that it has a dominant theme, the application of the doctrine of the Mean to justice, and that the subordinate topics are connected with this theme and with each other. But the book as it has come to us contains some repetitions which read like alternative versions of sections in a course, and the order of the sections is sometimes arbitrary and inconsequent. Thus the first lines of chapter 6 (1134 a17–23) are out of place. The discussion of the question whether a man can wrong himself and connected questions is interrupted by a digression in the later part of chapter 9 (1137 a4 ff.) and by chapter 10 on equity. In chapter 11 the argument is again interrupted by a note on the relative badness of doing and suffering injustice (1138 a28–b5). It is natural to attribute such disorders to an editor putting together material from different sources, anxious to use it all but having to decide in what order to arrange the sections and not always able to find a suitable context for a passage which in a modern book would be printed as a footnote or an appendix. Hence Gauthier-Jolif complain that double versions and editorial transpositions obscure the plan followed by Aristotle in his treatment of justice (p. 328). These editors actually print a text which incorporates their corrections of the assumed transpositions. Jackson's text (1879) also incorporated some re-arrangement. In my examination of the doctrine I shall not feel obliged to stick closely to the order of the chapters, or of the sections within each chapter; but I shall not discuss further the state of the text.[1] What has been said about the text of Book v applies, although seldom so obviously, to other books of the *EN*.

---

[1] Cf. ch. I, pp. 3–4.

After some introductory remarks on the method to be employed, Aristotle distinguishes in chapter 1 a wider from a narrower sense of 'justice' and 'injustice'. He starts from the ambiguity of 'unjust'. 'Let us take as a starting-point, then, the various meanings of "an unjust man". Both the lawless man (*paranomos*) and the grasping (*pleonektēs*) and unfair ("unequal") man are thought to be unjust, so that evidently both the law-abiding and the fair ("equal") man will be just. The just, then, is the lawful and the fair (or equal), the unjust the unlawful and the unfair (or unequal)' (1129 a31–b1). In expositions of Aristotle's doctrine justice in the sense of law-abidingness is commonly called 'universal justice'; justice in the sense of equality or fairness is called 'particular justice'. Justice as one among the other excellences of character is particular not universal. Since particular justice is the subject of Book v Aristotle does not linger long over universal justice.

Universal justice, then, is manifested in obedience to law. About the laws of a state Aristotle here makes two assertions. The first is that they aim at producing or preserving happiness or 'the common interest either of all or of the best or of those who hold power' (1129 b14–19). The second is that they prescribe conduct in accordance with the virtues, courage and moderation and good temper, or forbid conduct which is vicious; the rightly framed law does this rightly, and the hastily conceived one less well (1129 b19–25).[1] Vinogradoff gives the following paraphrase of these remarks: 'Thus in the field of General Justice the State maintains by legislation its standards of compulsory morality and political expediency; duties corresponding to virtues, crimes to vices.'[2] Aristotle concludes chapter 1 by saying that universal justice coincides with the whole of ethical virtue and universal injustice with the whole of ethical vice. As states or dispositions they are the same, but the terms 'justice' and 'injustice' convey, as 'virtue' and 'vice' do not, a relationship between a man and his neighbours (1130 a8–13). Aristotle's meaning here is unclear. Most virtues and vices are manifested in actions which affect, and often

---

[1] Cf. ch. 2, 1130 b18–24; ch. 11, 1138 a4–7.
[2] *Outlines of Historical Jurisprudence*, ii. 58.

are in their nature intended to affect, others; liberality, for example. Perhaps what Aristotle has in mind is that, when we say that an act is injurious or wrong, we are not merely saying that it manifests an ethical fault; we are saying that it is an offence or transgression against a fellow citizen of a kind which can lead to prosecution in the courts (cf. 1130 a3–5).

Aristotle starts, as we have seen, from the uses in Greek of the words we translate as 'just' and 'unjust'. The English words are not used in the wide sense, roughly equivalent to right and wrong, but only in the restricted sense proper to particular justice; and indeed in an even narrower way since we have 'just', 'fair', and 'equal' for Aristotle's *dikaios* and *isos*. There is nothing in the text to suggest that at this point Aristotle was thinking about the Athenian legal system as well as about the ambiguity of ethical language. But Joachim in his commentary accepts a suggestion of J. A. Smith (unpublished) that the distinction between universal and particular justice corresponds to the difference between public and private lawsuits. He refers to a passage in the *Rhetoric* (I. 13) where Aristotle distinguishes between offences committed against the community (*to koinon*) and offences committed against a member of the community (*hena tōn koinōnountōn*) (1373 b18 ff.). Joachim's view is that the 'general injustice' of the *EN* is shown in offences against the community and covers those 'forms of wrongdoing which rendered the agent liable to the public penal law' (p. 130). The procedure would be by indictment (*graphē*) or public suit (*dikē dēmosia*). In the *Rhetoric* Aristotle gives only one example of an offence against the community, the evasion of military service. This offence is one of those included in Aristotle's list in *EN* vi of wrong actions falling under general injustice (1129 b19–25). But the list includes also adultery and assault and these 'crimes' are classed in the *Rhetoric* as offences against particular members of the community. At the end of *EN* v. 2 Aristotle gives a list of offences which create inequalities between man and man the rectification of which belongs to particular justice: the list includes theft, adultery, poisoning, procuring, enticement of slaves, assassination, false witness, assault, imprisonment, murder, robbery with violence, mutilation, abuse, insult (1131 a6–10).

Most of these offences are examples of what Aristotle calls general injustice or wrong-doing, but they give rise to private suits for damages or redress. No doubt some of them gave rise at Athens also to public suits which any citizen could initiate.[1] But it is clear that Aristotle cannot have intended in the *EN* to suggest any correspondence, however rough, between the range of general injustice and the province of public, as opposed to private, lawsuits.

In chapter 2 Aristotle turns to particular justice. There is a kind of justice which is part of justice in the wider sense and a corresponding kind of injustice. The motive of injustice, in this limited sense, is the desire for gain (1130 a19–22). Acts which are unjust in the general sense 'are ascribed invariably to some particular kind of wickedness, e.g. adultery to self-indulgence, the desertion of a comrade in battle to cowardice, physical violence to anger; but if a man makes a gain, his action is ascribed to no form of wickedness but injustice' (1130 a28–32). Particular justice and injustice are further characterized as having to do with such good things as 'honour or money or safety' (1130 b2) which fall to be divided between citizens (1130 b32; cf. 1129 b1–4).

Aristotle would claim the support of ordinary language for defining injustice in terms of seeking a gain for oneself. It is typically 'unfair' to grab an excessive share of something. Again, we naturally think of the unjust judge as one who can be bribed. But this account of injustice raises at least two difficulties. The first is that, if excessive gain-seeking is vicious, the doctrine of the mean suggests that it is vicious also to take too small a share of something for oneself. But, as we have already noted, Aristotle finds it difficult to allow this. The second difficulty is that a judge who makes an unjust decision need not be acting from a desire for gain. He may have some other bad motive or no bad motive at all. If *A* is judging a case between *B* and *C*, only *B* and *C* have shares which are too large or too small because only *B* and *C* have shares. Aristotle does not ignore this obvious fact and the difficulty which it raises. He recognizes that a man may do justice, or fail to do justice, 'either between himself and another or between two

[1] Cf. Joachim, p. 134.

others' (5, 1134 a1–6). He does not at this point offer any solution of the difficulty. But in the following passage from a later chapter (9) he seems to be trying to answer the objection. 'But if with knowledge he judged unjustly, he is himself aiming at an excessive share either of gratitude or revenge. As much, then, as if he were to share in the plunder, the man who has judged unjustly for these reasons has got too much; the fact that what he gets is different from what he distributes makes no difference, for even if what he awards is a field, he does not actually get land but money' (1136 b34–1137 a4). This is surely only a play on the words 'getting too much'. The motive of the judge who seeks to earn favour or to gratify spite is not greed for gain. Again Aristotle does not deal explicitly with the case of the judge who simply fails to estimate reasonably the claims involved in a case without having any bad motive for judging as he does.

In the concluding sentences of chapter 2 (1130 b30–1131 a9) Aristotle distinguishes two kinds of Particular Justice: justice in the distribution of divisible goods (dianemetic justice) and the justice which 'plays a rectifying part in transactions between man and man' (diorthotic justice). Diorthotic justice is again divided according as the transactions are 'voluntary', in the sense of between two consenting parties, such as buying, selling, lending, etc., or 'involuntary', when one man receives injurious treatment from another. Involuntary transactions are again divided into the clandestine, such as theft, adultery, etc., and the violent, such as assault, murder, abuse, etc. The two kinds of Particular Justice are then explained and described in terms of elementary mathematical expressions; distributive justice in chapter 3 and rectificatory justice in chapter 4. The first part of chapter 5 deals with justice in the multilateral exchange of goods and services which is made possible by the use of money. These chapters have been found or made difficult by commentators. It is important, if unnecessary mistakes and confusions are to be avoided, to keep firmly in view what Aristotle says. In particular, confusion has been caused, as we shall see, by the unsuccessful attempts of certain commentators to locate commercial justice within one or other of Aristotle's two main divisions of Particular Justice.

Justice in distribution of goods is described by Aristotle in terms
of geometrical proportion or analogy (1131 b12–13); i.e. the
formula $A/B = C/D$. Such a proportion is said to be 'discrete' as
opposed to 'continuous' (1131 a32–3). (A continuous proportion
is of the form $A/B = B/C$ where B is the geometrical mean
between A and C.) In Aristotle's formula A and B are persons,
C and D are their respective shares of some divisible good, e.g. a
sum of money. Translated into words the formula means that A's
merit, according to some standard, stands to B's merit as the size
of A's share stands to the size of B's share. 'For all men agree that
what is just in distribution must be according to merit in some
sense, though they do not all specify the same sort of merit, but
democrats identify it with the status of freemen, supporters of
oligarchy with wealth, others with noble birth, and supporters of
aristocracy with excellence' (1131 a25–9). Aristotle points out that
$A/B = C/D$ entails $A/C = B/D$; in words, A's merit is to A's
share as B's merit is to B's share (1131 b5–7). The distribution
'couples' (*sunduazei*) the person and his share (1131 b7–9). The
original ratio of A to B is preserved by the distribution, i.e.
$A/B = A+C/B+D$ . . . 'the whole to the whole' (1131 b7–8).
'The conjunction (*suzeuxis*), then, of A with C and of B with D is
what is just in distribution, and this species of the just is intermediate . . .' (1131 b9–10). The just share is a mean in the sense
that it could fail to be according to the proportion, i.e. could fail
to be just, either by being too large or by being too small. There is
no question here of arriving at a knowledge of the mean by a
mathematical calculation, or quasi-mathematical quasi-calculation,
which starts from a knowledge of extremes. The data required for
pin-pointing the mean, the right size of the share to be assigned,
are the relative merit of the recipients and the amount to be
distributed. One further point should be noted in the account
which Aristotle gives of distributive justice in chapter 3. He says
that 'the man who acts unjustly has too much, and the man who is
unjustly treated has too little, of what is good' (1131 b19–20).
He is here either supposing that the distributor is also a recipient,
or allowing himself provisionally to speak of the man who
receives an excessive share as acting unjustly. Later (chapter 9) he

rejects the suggestion that the recipient acts unjustly, since the 'origin of the action' lies in the distributor not the receiver (1136 b25–9).

Aristotle does not in chapter 3 give examples of acts or operations which manifest justice or injustice in distribution. The passage on the different standards of merit underlying different constitutions (1131 a25–9) suggests that one thing he may have had in mind is the distribution of public money or other divisible public commodity. Some examples are suggested by Vinogradoff:[1] the payment of citizens for service as jurymen; distribution of foreign corn; the distribution of land on the foundation of a colony; public assistance for the disabled, sick, or elderly. But it is not implied in the text that funds in the hands of the state are the only 'common' funds which Aristotle has in mind as calling for justice in distribution. The common funds mentioned in chapter 4 are probably the funds of a business partnership or a benefit club; we are told that the distribution should be in proportion to the sums contributed by each member (1131 b27–32).[2] The division of an inheritance is another example of a distribution of goods which could be described as common although not public.

It is reasonable to assume, although Aristotle does not say so, that the function of an arbitrator or judge would call for important exercises of distributive justice. But Joachim goes beyond, and indeed against, the evidence when he accepts a suggestion, attributed to J. A. Smith, that 'Aristotle has primarily and mainly—if not entirely—in his mind those rights which formed the subject' of suits (*diadikasiai*) in which 'two or more parties lay claim to the same thing, or to certain shares in the same thing' (pp. 139–40). Joachim points out that in such 'declaratory' actions there is neither plaintiff nor defendant: the decision of the judge is a declaration of right. An inheritance is the commonest example; Joachim mentions others. It is difficult not to agree that Aristotle must have had such legal actions in mind. But they are not as prominently or exclusively in his mind as Joachim implies. The heirs of an estate, or the partners in a business, might distribute the

---

[1] Op. cit. ii. 51–7.   [2] Cf. VIII. 14, 1163 a30–2.

assets without taking their affairs to the courts. But the suggestion of J. A. Smith is a useful correction of the view which Joachim finds in 'many commentators' that Aristotle was thinking of 'the fundamental legislative acts by which the privileges powers and places were assigned to the constituent members or estates of the political community' (p. 138). It is one thing to frame a constitution, another to act as an administrator or judge who is bound by the standards embodied in a constitution. It is the latter which is a part, and only a part, of the field of Aristotle's distributive justice.

Stewart makes the surprising suggestion that the province of distributive justice includes 'the distribution of wealth which results from the operation of economic laws regulating wages and profits'.[1] He claims that this suggestion is supported by the MM[2] in which 'distributive justice is described as determining the returns of labour, and regulating the exchanges' which are discussed in EN v. 5. This interpretation was criticized by Stewart's reviewer in the Classical Review (1893), Herbert Richards. Stewart replied (p. 182) adducing the MM and Richards briefly answered the reply (p. 251). Stewart's suggestion is considered also by D. G. Ritchie in the course of an article on Aristotle's view of justice in the Classical Review (1894) (p. 189). I agree with these critics that the evidence is against the attribution to Aristotle of the idea that the regulation of wages and prices is part of the field, according to Stewart the most important part, of distributive justice. As Richards points out, there are no 'common funds' in commerce as such; A's property ceases to be his only when it becomes B's. The writer of the MM does not distinguish different kinds or spheres of particular justice and cannot, therefore, be adduced as assigning the regulation of commercial exchange to distributive justice. Again Aristotle's doctrine in chapter 5 that the terms on which goods are bought and sold are fixed by demand (1133 a26 ff.) implies that they are not regulated by acts of distributive justice as he has described distributive justice. It is perhaps not clear how Aristotle conceived the connection between justice and the processes by which prices are fixed in a market.

[1] Notes, i. 432; cf. 417-18, 449.   [2] A 33; 1193 b36-1194 a25.

But the commentators who have tried to allocate these processes to either of the two main divisions of Particular Justice have been unsuccessful.

The function of 'diorthotic' justice, described in chapter 4, is the rectification or correction of an injury inflicted on one man by another. The law 'treats the parties as equal' (1132 a5). When A, by fraud or violence, injures B, this equality is upset, and it is the function of the judge to restore equality (1132 a24-5). 'It is as though there were a line divided into unequal parts, and he took away that by which the greater segment exceeds the half and added it to the smaller segment' (1132 a25-7). Thus the formula of 'diorthotic' justice is not the geometrical proportion of distributive justice but what Aristotle calls 'arithmetical proportion' (1132 a1-2): 'the equal is intermediate between the greater and the less according to arithmetical proportion' (1132 a29-30). What is just, in the sense of rectification, is 'the mean between loss and gain' (1132 a18-19). The terms 'loss' and 'gain' are taken, as Aristotle points out, from the language of commerce (1132 b11-13), and he admits their apparent inappropriateness to transactions like assault and murder (1132 a10-12). The just is the mean between the impaired position of the injured party and the improved position of the injuring party (cf. 1132 a9-10). Thus the formula of rectificatory justice is $A-B = B-C$. The decision of the good judge bisects the unequally divided line (1132 a30 ff.).

The morality of the doctrine thus stated may seem, at first sight, to be as simple-minded as its mathematical expression is simple. Aristotle's elaboration of the account of rectificatory justice as an arithmetic mean (1132 a32-b9) is described by Heath as 'mathematically rather childish'.[1] What is the ethical doctrine? If A has killed B, should A be killed to square the account? If C has defrauded D of £100, should he be required to restore this sum? If not, how are loss and gain to be 'measured' (1132 a13)? According to Ross Aristotle held that account is to be taken of 'moral and intellectual damages as well as of physical and financial injury'.[2] It is true that, in the next chapter, Aristotle rejects the *lex talionis* as an account of rectificatory justice. 'For example, if

[1] *Mathematics in Aristotle*, p. 274. [2] *Aristotle*, p. 211.

an official has inflicted a wound, he should not be wounded in
return, and if someone has wounded an official, he ought not to be
wounded only but punished in addition. Further there is a great
difference between a voluntary and an involuntary act' (1132
b28–31, cf. ch. 8). These are important qualifications of the idea
that the offender should suffer what he has inflicted. But the
passage might be read as suggesting that in some cases, when
questions of status did not arise, this would be the appropriate
correction. In the *MM* (I. 33), however, we find it said explicitly
that adequate redress must always be something other than the
physical or financial equivalent of the damage inflicted. The
redress allowed to *B* must take account of the fact that *A* 'began
first'. An eye for an eye is not a sufficient penalty; justice requires
that the suffering of the offender should be more than he inflicted
(1194 a37–b2).

The account I have given of rectificatory justice agrees with
Jackson, Ross, J. A. Smith (in the Introduction to the Everyman
Translation), Vinogradoff, Joachim, and Gauthier–Jolif that it is
concerned solely with redress or the rectification of wrongs done.
Burnet, and less explicitly Grant and Stewart, take the different
view that 'diorthotic' justice is concerned with the redress of
wrong only in connection with what Aristotle calls 'involuntary
transactions' (1131 a1 ff.) and that, in connection with 'voluntary
transactions' such as purchases or loans, it is regulative. On this
view, the fairness or unfairness of the terms of a bargain would
fall under rectificatory justice, and a judge might exercise such
justice in rectifying the terms of a bargain as well as in imposing
redress for the violation of those terms. Stewart remarks that the
non-fulfilment of a voluntary contract introduces a new transaction falling under the head of the involuntary (i. 432). If this
remark is offered as an interpretation, not as a criticism, of
Aristotle, it implies the view of Burnet that chapter 4 deals with
rectificatory justice only in its application to involuntary transactions. Burnet holds that the discussion of its application to
voluntary transactions begins in chapter 5 (at 1132 b30).

This view of Burnet is unacceptable for the following reasons.
While it is true that 'diorthotic' justice is concerned with voluntary

transactions (1131 b25-6), Aristotle nowhere suggests that a new 'transaction' supervenes when the obligation voluntarily initiated (1131 a4-5) is neglected or violated. The idea that there might be legal redress for the unfairness of a bargain seems to be excluded by Aristotle's incidental admission in chapter 4 that, in matters such as buying and selling, the law offers no protection to the man who makes a bad bargain (1132 b15-16).[1] Thus the business of rectificatory justice in connection with voluntary transactions is not to regulate bargains but to restore' equality' when they are violated. Burnet's view leads him to maintain that Aristotle in chapter 4 distinguishes between justice as 'diorthotic' or directive (1131 b25) and justice as 'epanorthotic' or corrective (1132 a18), the latter being only part of the former. It is true that 'diorthotic' might in Greek have a wider meaning than 'epanorthotic'. But it can also have the narrower meaning; and the reader of chapter 4, unless warned, could only assume that they are synonyms.[2] Finally Burnet's interpretation implies that the discussion of 'diorthotic' justice is continued in chapter 5, which deals with the fixing of prices. But Ross is surely right when he says that Aristotle deals with justice in exchange not as covered by either division of Particular Justice but as an 'afterthought' or appendix.[3] Burnet looks for the 'arithmetical proportion' of diorthotic justice in Aristotle's mathematical formulations in connection with the exchange of commodities (1133 a22-4; a31-3). But the Greek in these passages cannot mean what he says it means and the meaning suggested is not intelligible as an account of Aristotle's doctrine.

Aristotle's account of judicial redress as the restoration of equality is in one respect surprising, and indeed unsatisfactory. The notions of crime and punishment are not considered; there is no discussion of the principles relevant to punishment as an act of the state. We might expect a different treatment of murder at least, especially as Aristotle was familiar with the distinction between offences against the state and offences against the individual. But,

---

[1] Cf. IX. 1, 1164 b12 ff.
[2] Cf. Joachim, p. 136; Gauthier-Jolif, pp. 358 and 364.
[3] *Aristotle*, p. 213.

if we are startled by what Aristotle says and leaves unsaid, his meaning is not, as regards the main outline of his doctrine, either doubtful or obscure.

In the interpretation of the chapter (4) in its details the student will find that there are points on which it is difficult to resolve with confidence the disagreements of the commentators. One such passage should be mentioned here. Aristotle remarks that, in the case, for example, of fraud or adultery the characters of the parties are irrelevant since 'the law looks only to the distinctive character (*differentia*) of the injury' (1132 a2–5). The phrase thus rendered by Ross is interpreted by Stewart, Burnet, and Joachim in ways different both from Ross and from each other. I shall refer here only to the view of Burnet, which involves a peculiar opinion running through his account of diorthotic justice concerning the sense in which this kind of justice is a mean. Burnet understands the phrase quoted as meaning the difference between the wrong done by one party and the loss suffered by the other. On the evidence of certain passages in the *Laws* he finds here a doctrine that 'the wrong done by one party may be much greater or much less than the damage suffered by the other'; e.g. it is greater in the case of the man who, intending to kill, in fact only wounds. Burnet implies that in this case the appropriate penalty would be half-way between the penalty for murder and the penalty for wounding. There are at least three reasons against accepting this interpretation. The first is that it could never even occur to a reader of *EN* v. 4 unless he happened to have been reading Plato's *Laws*. Secondly, the doctrine which Burnet finds here is not to be found in the section of chapter 5 (1133 b29 ff.) in which Aristotle explains the sense in which justice is a mean. Thirdly, it is only in some cases, as Burnet explains the matter, that the wrong done is different from the damage suffered. In cases where they were equal there would be no question of a mean.

After giving his account, in chapters 3 and 4, of the two kinds or spheres of Particular Justice, distributive and rectificatory, Aristotle proceeds in chapter 5 to consider the sense in which a kind of justice is involved in 'associations for exchange' (1132 b31), i.e. in the determination of the prices at which products of industry are bought and sold. But what Aristotle gives us on this subject is rather an answer to the question how prices are in fact determined than a treatment of the concept of a just or fair price. It will be best, in the analysis of this section, to start from a statement of his doctrine about economic value or price. Against this background it will be possible to separate the real difficulties presented by Aristotle's exposition from some unreal difficulties created by commentators.

Speaking of builders and shoemakers Aristotle remarks that 'there is nothing to prevent the work of one being better than that of the other, and that they must therefore be equated' (1133 a12–14). In other words, a value must be assigned to n in the equation '1 house = n pairs of shoes' (cf. 1133 a22–4). Aristotle says of the producers, as well as of their products, that they must be 'equated' (1133 a18), but the equation of the producers is only the equation of the products over again. In order to answer the question how many pairs of shoes are equal to a house it is necessary, Aristotle says, that there should be one measure for all goods (1133 a25–6). This measure is in fact 'demand (chreia), which holds all things together' (1133 a26–7), but in practice 'money (nomisma) has become by convention a sort of representative (hupallagma) of demand' (a28–9). In other words, houses and shoes and beds are equated in the market where experience and experiment show at what prices they can be sold. How can we proceed from the equating of the products to the equating of the producers? It will not do to say that one builder is worth a hundred shoemakers because the price of one house is the price of a hundred shoes. We need to have a measure, time, of the work done by both. If we know the price of a house and a pair of shoes, and the time it takes to produce both, we can compare the value of a day's work by the builder with the value of a day's work by the shoemaker. Ross, in his note on 1133 a16 in the Oxford Translation, sees rightly, as had D. G. Ritchie,[1] that the comparative values of producers must in Aristotle's view here mean the comparative values of their work done in the same time. He does not make explicitly the point that, since prices are fixed by the market, the value of

[1] *Classical Review* (1894).

the producer is only a disguised form of the demand for his product.

There is a further point or puzzle to be noticed in what Aristotle says here about the determination of prices in the market. He insists that prices should be fixed before any goods are exchanged. He expresses this by saying that 'we must not bring them into a figure of proportion', which means in effect fix prices, 'when they have already exchanged (otherwise one extreme will have both excesses), but when they still have their own goods' (1133 b1-3). This sentence is obscure. A number of interpretations are mentioned in Stewart's note and Burnet adds another. I incline to accept what Ross says in his footnote. The expression 'both excesses' is to be understood in the light of the remark in chapter 4 that, if the mean is departed from, the advantage of the gainer is twice the difference between either share and the mean (1132 a32-b2). So here, if A pays £1 too much for B's product, the inequality between A and B is £2, the sum of A's loss and B's gain. Why does Aristotle say that prices should be fixed before any exchange takes place? When else could they be fixed? Ross refers to Aristotle's suggestion in IX. 1 that a man is prone to set too low a value on something that he has received: 'the receiver should assess a thing not at what it seems worth when he has it, but at what he assessed it at before he had it' (1164 b20-1). Hence, as Ross puts it, 'the only fair method is for each to set a value on his own on the other's goods *before* they exchange, and come to an agreement if they can'. The question which Ross does not answer in his account of what Aristotle is saying is how Aristotle could suppose that people would behave in the way which, according to Ross, he disallows, viz. 'exchange goods in random amounts' and then try to fix prices.

What Aristotle has to say here about the usefulness of money, in addition to the statement already quoted that it represents demand, is contained in the following passage. 'For the future exchange—that if we do not need a thing now we shall have it if ever we do need it—money is as it were our surety; for it must be possible for us to get what we want by bringing the money. Now the same thing happens to money itself as to goods—it is not always worth the same; yet it tends to be steadier. This is why all goods must have a price set on them; for then there will always be exchange, and if so, association of man with man' (1133 b10–16). This account of money should be compared with the account in *Politics* I. 9 (1257 a6 ff.), where Aristotle makes some further points; in particular that money, in the form of bits of some precious or useful metal, is easily handled and that it can have imposed on it a stamp, indicating the quantity, which saves 'the trouble of determining the value on each occasion'.

There is nothing obscure either in Aristotle's doctrine that the relative quantities in which goods are exchanged are determined by human needs and the 'demand' which springs from these needs, or in his account of the ways in which the exchange of goods is facilitated by the use of money in the form of stamped pieces of metal. But his formulation of this doctrine of commercial 'justice' is made difficult to follow by the fact that he states it in what appears to be, and is assumed by most commentators to be, a technical mathematical idiom. 'But in associations for exchange this sort of justice does hold men together—reciprocity in accordance with a proportion (*to antipeponthos kat' analogian*) and not on the basis of precisely equal return' (1132 b31–3). The word *antipeponthos* means literally 'that which has something done to it in return' for something it has done. The chapter opens with the remark that the Pythagoreans regarded *antipeponthos*, requital (Peters) or retaliation (Welldon), as being the essence of justice. Aristotle points out, as we saw, that rectificatory justice is not simple requital (1132 b29–30). But in commercial transactions goods of different kinds are exchanged in quantities which are not indeed equal but, as measured by demand, equivalent. Aristotle expresses this idea by saying that the return is 'in accordance with proportion and not equality' (1132 b33) or by the expression *to kata tēn analogian ison*, what is equal according to the proportion (1133 a10–11). It is necessary to ask at this point whether, when Aristotle speaks here of a proportionate return (*antipeponthos kat' analogian*), he has in mind a certain technical use in mathematics of *antipeponthos* in the sense of inverse or reciprocal proportion. I think that commentators should not simply assume, as do Jackson

and Stewart, an affirmative answer to this question. Ross's rendering of *antipeponthos* as 'reciprocity' suggests that he is making the
same assumption. The assumption is questioned by Ritchie[1] and,
more explicitly, by Heath.[2]

The meaning of reciprocal proportion in mathematics is explained by Jackson (p. 43) and Stewart (i. 442), who quote the
definition in Euclid.[3] It is a geometrical proportion expressing inverse variation, and may be represented by the formula $a/b =
d/c$. Two variable quantities are said to vary inversely if, as the
one becomes larger, the other becomes proportionately smaller.
A simple instance is the principle of the lever. This is stated in a
passage quoted by Jackson from the *Mechanics* (850 a39), a work
which is thought to belong to the early Peripatetic school. 'As the
weight moved is to the weight moving it, so *inversely* (*antipepon-
then*) is the length ⟨of the arm bearing the weight⟩ to the
length ⟨of the arm nearer to the power⟩.' If we use w^1 and l^1
for the weight and length on one side of the fulcrum and w^2 and l^2
for those on the other, the formula is $w^1/w^2 = l^2/l^1$. Another
familiar case of such a proportion is the Newtonian law of gravity,
that bodies 'attract' each other directly as the product of their
masses and *inversely* as the square of the distance between them.

What makes it natural and plausible to suppose that Aristotle
here has in mind this technical use of 'reciprocity', and intends his
readers to understand this, is the fact that, in the course of his
exposition in chapter 5, he formulates proportions or 'analogies'
which have the inverted form. 'The number of shoes exchanged
for a house must, therefore, correspond to the ratio of builder
to shoemaker' (1133 a22-3). 'There will, then, be reciprocity
(*antipeponthos*) when the terms have been equated so that, as
farmer is to shoemaker, ⟨the amount of⟩ the shoemaker's
work is to ⟨that of⟩ the farmer's work ⟨for which it
exchanges⟩' (1133 a31-3). Stewart comments: 'This will be a
case of *antipeponthos*, or reciprocal proportion, for the number of
less valuable units will compensate for their qualitative inferiority'
(i. 464; cf. i. 453: '. . . the superiority of A's quality being

[1] *Classical Review* (1894).   [2] *Mathematics in Aristotle* (1949).
[3] Elem. vi, Def. 2.

200 JUSTICE

compensated for by the superiority of B's quantity; i.e. A's quantity and quality being reciprocally proportional to B's quantity and quality'). But the qualitative superiority of the producer must be defined in economic terms, as was pointed out by D. G. Ritchie.[1] Rackham indeed suggests as possible that Aristotle here 'introduces the further conception that different kinds of producers have different social values and deserve different rates of reward'.[2] But there is no evidence for this, and Aristotle's account of the determination of prices implies that the social value of a producer is measured by the demand for his product. The measurable elements in the situation are the time spent in production and the money paid for the product. The formula of reciprocal proportion, which is no more than a triviality, might be expressed as follows: the sum paid for what A produces in a given time is to the sum paid for what B produces in that time as the time which B takes to produce what is worth a given sum is to the time which A takes to produce what is worth that sum. If A earns three times as much as B in a day, B has to work three days to earn what A earns in one. The fact is that mathematical reciprocity is not needed in the formulation of Aristotle's doctrine of 'commercial justice'. J. A. Smith, speaking of Aristotle's treatment of particular justice, remarked that 'the whole treatment is confused by the unhappy attempt to give a precise mathematical form to the principle of justice in the various fields distinguished'.[3] His account of the determination of prices in commercial exchange is simple enough if I have stated correctly on p. 196 what he wishes to convey. If I am right, the mathematical formulae in chapter 5 say nothing which is not said better without them.[4]

The fact that Aristotle's doctrine can be stated without bringing in reciprocal proportion in its Euclidean sense does not settle the question whether, in his use of *antipeponthos*, Aristotle has in mind this technical sense. But I am inclined to agree with Ritchie that, even in 1133 a31–3, the word itself does not have this meaning.

---

[1] 'Aristotle's Subdivisions of Particular Justice', *Classical Review* (1894).
[2] Loeb Translation.   [3] Everyman Translation, pp. xviii–xix.
[4] The attempts of the commentators to elucidate these passages are often speculative. Burnet's notes on the passages are not, I think, intelligible.

It can be taken quite naturally as having the meaning of requital or the receiving of an equal return, which it has in the Pythagorean doctrine as reported by Aristotle at the beginning of the chapter. This interpretation is supported by the wording of Aristotle's statement that the exchange of equivalent goods will be achieved if '*first* there is proportionate equality of goods *and then* requital (*antipeponthos*) takes place' (1133 a10–12).[1] Here reciprocity, in the sense of an equivalent return, is *separated* from the determination of what is 'equal according to proportion'. This suggests that Aristotle was not here using *antipeponthos* to convey or suggest reciprocal proportion in its Euclidean sense.

In the concluding section of chapter 5 (1133 b29–1134 a16) Aristotle, on the basis of the preceding analysis of Particular Justice, gives a summary answer to the question in what sense justice, or just action, lies in a mean between extremes. 'It is plain that just action is intermediate between acting unjustly and being unjustly treated; for the one is to have too much and the other is to have too little. Justice is a kind of mean, but not in the same way as the other virtues, but because it relates to an intermediate amount, while injustice relates to the extremes' (1133 b30–1134 a1). The statement that acting justly is a mean between acting unjustly and being unjustly treated, in the obvious meaning of these words, is not only absurd but plainly inconsistent with the preceding account of particular justice. Being unjustly treated is not vicious, not a way of failing to be just (11, 1138 a34–5). Again the injustice of the unjust judge consists not in taking too much for himself but in assigning too much to one of the parties in a dispute in which he is not himself a party. Aristotle cannot be overlooking this since, in the immediate context, he refers explicitly to the case of someone in the position of the judge or arbitrator (1134 a3, 6, 11). What Aristotle must be saying, or at least what he must be meaning to say, is that the just treatment of one man by another is a mean in the sense that there are two extremes to be avoided, unfair gain and unfair loss. An unjust award which affects two parties, *A* and *B*, may go wrong either by involving undue gain (too much of the useful or too

---

[1] See on this passage Heath, op. cit., p. 275.

little of the harmful) to *A* and undue loss (too little of the useful or too much of the harmful) to *B*, or the other way round. 'Injustice relates to the extremes.' At least part of Aristotle's answer to the question in what sense the just act is related to a mean can be so stated and cannot be stated in any other way. If so, 'acting unjustly' (*adikein*) in the passage quoted must refer to the man who accepts an undue advantage. This is the interpretation, as I understand it, of Gauthier–Jolif: 'the just action, in the objective sense, represents a mean between two extremes: having more than one's share (doing injustice) and having less than one's share (suffering injustice).' We must say either that Aristotle is *deliberately* giving an unusual meaning to 'doing injustice' or that he is stating his doctrine in a way which is confusing and confused. I prefer the former alternative. But it is not easy to be certain how to construe the Greek in Aristotle's statement that acting justly is a mean. It is tempting to suggest 'a mean in relation to unjust gain and unjust loss', taking 'unjust gain and unjust loss' as a description applicable to *both* the extremes to be avoided by an adjudicator (1133 b30 ff.).[1]

The statement in this section that, while justice is a mean, it is not a mean 'in the same way as the other virtues' (1133 b32–3) is not fully explained. We are told in what way justice is a mean. We are not told explicitly what is the way in which the other virtues are means while justice is not. On the evidence of this passage a natural answer would be the one given, as Gauthier–Jolif point out, by St. Thomas. Acting justly is a mean as regards the external character of the action but not as regards the internal feelings or emotions which prompt and accompany action. This interpretation fits the case of the judge or arbitrator, who may act unjustly from a variety of bad motives,[2] or from no bad motive at all but rather from an intellectual failure to assess the relevant claims; a lack of those elements of practical wisdom (*phronēsis*) which in Book VI Aristotle describes as understanding (*sunesis*) and judgement (*gnōmē*) (chs. 10 and 11). This interpretation is

---

[1] For examples of the idiom see J. Adam on Plato, *Republic* 498 a, and R. Shilleto on Demosthenes, *De Falsa Legatione*, 181.

[2] Cf. 9, 1137 a1.

supported by the fact that, in the list of extremes and means in the
EE (*B* 3), the extremes in connection with justice appear not as
vices but as 'gain' (*kerdos*) and 'loss' (*zēmia*), the mean being not
justice but 'the just'. In all the other cases names of vices and of the
corresponding virtues are given. Justice, then, is a mean as being
'related to an intermediate amount' (1133 b33) but not as being
between two vices.

This interpretation of 1133 b30 ff. cannot, of course, be accepted as a *complete* account of what Aristotle has to say about
justice as an ethical virtue and its opposite, injustice. For, as we
saw earlier, he recognizes that 'unjust' (*adikos*) *can* be applied to
the man who is grasping, moved excessively by a desire for gain.[1]
The general doctrine of the mean implies that, if this motive is
manifested in different degrees and can be excessive, it can also be
defective. It will be an ethical defect in a man if he never, or
hardly ever, claims his share of good things.[2] Would this imply
that a man can 'voluntarily suffer injustice' or 'treat himself unjustly'? Aristotle comes to these questions in later chapters (9 and
11) of Book v.

In the first section of chapter 6 (1134 a17–23) Aristotle points
out that unjust actions, if done without deliberate intention, need
not imply a bad character. The remark, if in place here, is paren-
thetical; the doctrine is developed more fully in chapter 8. In
the following sections of chapter 6, which should be considered
along with chapters 9–12 of Book viii, Aristotle deals with
'political justice'. Political justice is justice as it exists in a state
under the rule of law not of a tyrant (1134 a35–b1), in which the
citizens 'share their life with a view to self-sufficiency', are free,
and have equal shares, or shares which are proportionate and fair,
in 'ruling and being ruled' (1134 a26–8, b15). The best life can be
lived only under such a constitution. In inferior kinds of state, in a
tyranny or in an oligarchy, as opposed to an aristocracy, there is
no political justice but only a 'likeness' of it (1134 a30).

In the concluding section of the chapter Aristotle contrasts
justice and injustice between members of a household, consisting
of husband, wife, children, and slaves, with justice and injustice

---

[1] 1129 b1, 1130 a27–8; cf. 1134 a32–4.   [2] Cf. *EE B* 3, 1221 a23–4.

between citizens. There can be no justice 'in the unqualified sense' (1134 b10) between a man and his slaves because they are part of his property. This doctrine is modified later by the remark that, while a man cannot have relations of justice or friendship with his slave *qua* slave, he can have such relations with him *qua* man (VIII. 11, 1161 b5–8). Similarly a child, 'until it reaches a certain age and sets up for itself', is 'as it were part' of the father, and there can be no justice or injustice between a man and himself or part of himself (1134 b10–13). The remark here that a man cannot be unjust to himself anticipates the detailed discussion of this question in chapter 11. Finally Aristotle recognizes to our relief that a man may be just or unjust, though not in the political sense, to his wife: 'justice can more truly be manifested towards a wife than towards children and chattels' (1134 b15–16; cf. VIII. 12, 1162 a16–29).

In chapter 7 Aristotle distinguishes, within political justice, between natural justice (*phusikon*) and conventional or legal justice (*nomikon*). Natural justice 'everywhere has the same force and does not exist by people's thinking this or that' (1134 b19–20). Its principles, as Joachim suggests, are 'based on the very nature of things or the very nature of man'. Legal justice is described by Aristotle as 'that which is originally indifferent, but when it has been laid down is not indifferent, e.g. that a prisoner's ransom shall be a *mina*, or that a goat and not two sheep shall be sacrificed, and again all the laws that are passed for particular cases . . .' (1134 b20–4). When Aristotle speaks of the principles of natural justice as 'having everywhere the same force' it is not clear whether he means that they are universally accepted or that they apply without exceptions to any dealings between one man and another.[1] He probably had both ideas in mind. Critics of the concept of natural justice urge against it that principles of justice are not in fact universally recognized and absolute (1134 b27). Aristotle admits the fact, but argues that a principle can be natural without being invariable; just as, in physics, it is natural but not invariable for the right arm to be stronger than the left (1134 b30–5).

---

[1] Cf. *Rhetoric*, 1373 b1–27.

So far Aristotle's point is clear. But I think that he fails to be clear, or to make clear, what he means by the 'legal justice' which he opposes to natural justice. The ambiguity appears if we consider the word 'convention'. Is Aristotle thinking of rights and wrongs created by conventions, like the rule of the road, or of conventional ideas about right and wrong, for example the idea, which might be prevalent in an oligarchy, that certain principles applied only to actions affecting other members of a class and not members of inferior classes? Aristotle starts, in the definition quoted from the beginning of the chapter, from the former idea. A rule which is conventional in this sense may express a principle which is natural, e.g. as the rule of the road embodies the principle that human life should not be needlessly endangered. But later in the chapter Aristotle remarks that 'the things which are just not by nature but by human enactment are not everywhere the same, since constitutions also are not the same, though there is but one which is everywhere by nature the best' (1135 a3–5). Here the distinction is between principles or rules of justice which would be observed in an ideal community and which accord with the real nature of man and the conditions of human happiness, and, on the other hand, rules observed in some community which falls short of the human ideal. Conventional morality is not determined by convention, in the sense in which the rule of the road, or the right ransom for a prisoner, is determined by convention.

Aristotle points out in chapter 8 that actions which are in accordance with justice and injustice may be done involuntarily and, if so, are not strictly acts of justice and injustice. An action is involuntary, as he has explained in III. 1, when it is done either in ignorance of circumstances, and hence without intention, or under compulsion. A man may be killed by a friendly pat on the back. But, when the result could not have been expected, it is a misadventure (*atuchēma*) not a crime (1135 b16–17). The doctrine is important but is not here developed in as much detail as in Book III. Under the head of compulsion, again, Aristotle does not consider, as he had in III. 1, the difficult case of a man who yields to a terrifying threat (1110 a23). He refers explicitly only to the simple case of physical constraint, as when a man grips the arm of another and uses it to strike a third party (1135 a27–8).

Within actions which are voluntary Aristotle distinguishes those which are chosen after deliberation and those which are not (1135 b8–11). As examples of actions done with knowledge but not after deliberation he mentions those 'due to anger or to other passions necessary or natural to man' (1135 b22). Such acts 'are indeed acts of injustice (*adikēmata*), but this does not imply that the doers are unjust or wicked; for the injury is not due to vice. But when a man acts from choice, he is an unjust man and a vicious man' (1135 b22–5). In distinguishing between voluntary and involuntary Aristotle is interested in the conditions under which, when a man is the cause of injury to another, we acquit him of responsibility. He is here interested also in the way in which we distinguish degrees of wrongdoing according as an action is or is not premeditated. His interest is that of a moralist in the correlation, or lack of correlation, between the rightness and wrongness of actions and the good or bad characters of the men who do them. But he also notes the ways in which the moralist's distinctions are reflected in legal procedures. He comments on the relevance, in different kinds of legal cases, of the question what happened and the question where justice lies (1135 b25–1136 a1).[1] The detailed difficulties raised by what Aristotle says here in referring to legal procedures need not detain us, as they are irrelevant to the understanding of his ethical doctrine.

In chapters 9 and 11 Aristotle discusses various questions which arise out of his treatment of justice and injustice, questions the answers to which are relevant, as we have seen, to the answer which he has given, or implied, to the question how the doctrine of the mean applies to justice. The discussions in chapters 9 and 11 are interrupted by chapter 10 on equity. It is not always easy to follow the thread of the argument in chapters 9 and 11 and some points are repeated. I shall try to supplement what the student will find in the text and commentaries by restating what I take to be Aristotle's main points. I shall not here follow closely the

[1] See Ross's footnotes to the Oxford Translation and Joachim's note on 1135 b31.

order of the exposition in the text as we have it, and I shall feel no obligation to refer to passages which, as not contributing essentially to the main argument, might be relegated by a modern writer to footnotes.

Aristotle starts from the question whether it is possible to be 'voluntarily treated unjustly' (1136 a15). An affirmative answer is suggested by the fact that just treatment is sometimes received involuntarily (1136 a22–3). For the corresponding answer (1136 a20) to the question about unjust treatment would be that it is sometimes received voluntarily. But Aristotle does not accept this answer. His next important move is to distinguish between being harmed and suffering injustice. If to treat someone unjustly were simply to harm him voluntarily, it would follow, as Aristotle proceeds to argue, that the incontinent man (akratēs), i.e. the man who under the influence of passion does what he knows is not for the best, would be a man who treated himself unjustly (1136 a31–4). That the incontinent man can be voluntarily treated unjustly would follow also from the fact that he may voluntarily be harmed by another who acts voluntarily (presumably in tempting him) (1136 b1–3). But Aristotle suggests that this definition of acting unjustly is wrong and requires the addition of 'contrary to the wish of the person acted on' (1136 b3–5). This amendment involves the consequence that, while a man can be voluntarily harmed, he cannot be voluntarily treated unjustly. No one wishes to be unjustly treated. Even the incontinent man acts contrary to his own wish for what is best (1136 b5–9).

Aristotle does not in this passage answer explicitly the question whether the incontinent man (akratēs) can be said to be unjust to himself. But in the concluding sentences of the book (1138 b5 ff.) he tells us that this way of speaking is only metaphorical: the conflict of desires in the man who sins against knowledge makes it natural to say, for example, that appetite is lawful or just when it obeys the 'rule' of reason. In the passage I have paraphrased in chapter 9 Aristotle notes one way in which the akratēs resembles the victim of injustice: what happens is contrary to his wish (boulēsis). In the rest of chapter 9 and in chapter 11 Aristotle does not explicitly mention akrasia. But, when the discussion of the question whether a man can treat himself unjustly is resumed in chapter 11, we are in effect given reasons for denying that this can be said of the *akratēs*. Unjust action, Aristotle says, is not merely voluntary but is deliberately chosen (*ek prohaireseōs*) (1138 a20–1). He does not deny that the *akratēs* acts voluntarily (*hekousion*). But he is always clear that an incontinent action is not done deliberately, does not proceed from choice.[1] Hence the incontinent man, since he is not in the fullest sense acting, is not acting unjustly to himself.

After raising as regards incontinence (sinning against knowledge) the question whether a man can treat himself unjustly Aristotle in chapter 9 pursues the question over firmer ground. The man who gives away what is his own, or assigns more to another than to himself, is not unjustly treated; 'for though to give is in his power, to be unjustly treated is not, but there must be someone to treat him unjustly' (1136 b11–14). Moreover the suggestion that he is unjustly treated is inconsistent with the amended definition of unjust action; for he suffers nothing contrary to his own wish and so is not unjustly treated although he suffers harm (1136 b23–5). Aristotle suggests further that, if we consider the motive of the virtuous man who takes less than his share, we may think it inappropriate to describe him as one who treats himself unjustly. 'For he, perhaps, gets more than his share of some other good, such as reputation or intrinsic nobility'; a far better thing than the material good which he relinquishes (1136 b21–2). In chapter 11 Aristotle considers the question under the separate heads of universal and particular justice. As regards universal justice, he remarks that 'no one can commit adultery with his own wife or housebreaking on his own house or theft on his own property' (1138 a24–6). The suicide acts unjustly in the sense of universal injustice, i.e. wrongly, but 'towards the state not towards himself'; for 'he suffers voluntarily, but no one is voluntarily treated unjustly' (1138 a9–12). As regards particular justice, which is achieved when gains and losses are not excessive, it is clear that 'the just and the unjust always involve more than one person' (1138 a19–20). If there were only one person, the

[1] 1111 b13–15, 1146 b22–4, 1148 a4–11, 1151 a5–7.

same thing would have to be 'subtracted from and added to the same thing at the same time; but this is impossible'.

The treatment of justice would be incomplete without a concluding section on equity (*epieikeia*). Aristotle, as often, raises the question by formulating a problem or apparent contradiction: 'it seems strange if the equitable, being something different from the just, is yet praiseworthy; for either the just or the equitable is not good, if they are different; or, if both are good, they are the same' (1137 a33 ff.). Aristotle's solution is that, while the equitable is distinct from the legally just, equity is 'a sort of justice and not a different state of character' (1138 a2–3). 'What creates the problem is that the equitable is just, but not the legally just but a correction (*epanorthōma*) of legal justice' (1137 b11–13). Legal justice requires correction because laws are universal, and about some things it is not possible to make correct universal statements (b13–14). 'The error is not in the law nor in the legislator but in the nature of the thing' (b17–19). Gaps left by the laws should be filled in the spirit of the law and the legislator. The equitable is 'what the legislator himself would have said had he been present, and would have put into his law if he had known' (1137 b22–4).

Thus the main doctrine of the *EN* is that written laws are not always specific enough to be applied as they stand to cases, so that 'a decree is needed' (1137 b27–9). Equity is discussed also in the *Rhetoric*,[1] and the treatment there makes some additional points. It is noted that the indeterminateness of a law cannot always be put down to the fact that specification would be an endless task. Sometimes legislators are forgetful and overlook a needed qualification. Again a law, because it is general, may sometimes point to a wrong conclusion, and not merely to no determinate conclusion, on a particular case. A legislator may be 'obliged to legislate as if that held good always which in fact holds good only usually' (1374 a30). Thus a law against wounding with iron objects does not merely fail to specify penalties according to the size and nature of the objects; it also makes it an offence for a man wearing an iron ring to raise his hand against another, whereas it would be inequitable to treat his action as an offence (1374 b1–2).

[1] Book I, ch. 13, 1374 a25 ff.

The passage is important because it suggests that, in the working of a legal system, equity may not be confined to the area left undetermined by the written law. It may be equitable to apply a law according to its spirit even against its letter. Vinogradoff states that, in cases about testaments and contracts, orators sometimes appealed to 'general conditions of fairness as against exact and rigid legal rules'.[1] But such an appeal, if permissible at all, would presumably be from the letter of the law to 'what the legislator himself would have said if he had been present'. In the *EN*, so far as I can see, Aristotle does not suggest that, in this sense, judges and juries should 'correct' the law. Equity steps in where the law is 'defective owing to its generality' (1137 b27). But he does say that a man may show an equitable character by waiving his strict legal rights when he has the law on his side (1137 b35–1138 a2).

In conclusion the following point is important. Aristotle's admission of the shortcomings of written laws, and his condemnation of the man who insists on his pound of flesh, might suggest the idea that he did not regard elaborate legislation as necessary in order to establish and secure justice in the state. But to say that laws cannot be made completely determinate, and should not be endlessly elaborated, is consistent with holding that they should be as determinate and elaborate as, given the nature of the subject-matter, is reasonably possible. This is the view which we should expect Aristotle to hold as a man of wisdom with a keen awareness of human weaknesses including the fallibility of judges. It is what he in fact says at the beginning of the *Rhetoric* (I. 1, § 7). Laws should be definite on every point on which definition is possible and should 'leave as little as possible to judges' (1354 a31–4; b12).

BIBLIOGRAPHICAL NOTE

The English commentators on the *EN* are not always clear and accurate on detail, particularly Burnet on Aristotle's account of Particular Justice. The edition of Book v by Henry Jackson (C.U.P., 1879) is still useful. Ross gives a short but indispensable account of Aristotle's

[1] *Outlines of Historical Jurisprudence*, ii. 66.

doctrine (*Aristotle*, pp. 209–15). D. G. Ritchie deals carefully with Aristotle's account of Particular Justice in the *Classical Review*, viii (1894) ('Aristotle's Subdivisions of Particular Justice'). It is unfortunate that Ritchie's powerful argument against the view that Catallactic Justice (commercial exchange) is part of Rectificatory Justice, or vice versa (the view of St. Thomas), is ignored in Burnet's edition.

Joachim's commentary emphasizes, and probably overstates, the connections between Aristotle's doctrine of justice and types of case in Athenian law. A. R. W. Harrison argues against this line of interpretation in the *Journal of Hellenic Studies*, lxxvii (1957) ('*NE* v and the Law of Athens'). On the significance for jurisprudence of Aristotle's doctrine reference may be made also to the following works: Vinogradoff, *Outlines of Historical Jurisprudence*, vol. ii. ch. iii ('The Legal System'), and Max Hamburger, *Morals and Law: the Growth of Aristotle's Legal Theory* (New Haven, 1951). On Vinogradoff's views see P. Shorey in *Classical Philology*, xix (1924) ('Universal Justice in Aristotle's Ethics'), and Vinogradoff's reply.

The pages (272–6) on Aristotle's mathematical formulae in Book v in Heath, *Mathematics in Aristotle*, are an important aid to understanding. Heath argues convincingly against finding Euclidean reciprocal proportion in chapter 5, but his reference to Burnet should not be understood as endorsing in detail Burnet's notes, which are at some points unintelligible.

XI

PRACTICAL WISDOM

BOOK VI of the *EN*, which deals primarily with *phronēsis*, the excellence of the practical intellect, contains, as we should expect, much that is of great importance for the understanding of Aristotle's ethical theory. But, if we are not to be misled or needlessly puzzled by what we find and fail to find in it, we should begin by recognizing that, in its literary form, the book is casual and that it does not offer us reasoned answers to all the central questions which we might expect it to answer. D. J. Allan remarks that the book has 'come down to us in a fragmentary state'.[1] But the omission of certain topics is clearly deliberate. Thus in chapter 8 Aristotle divides *phronēsis* into its main kinds or varieties; the division is set out formally by Ross.[2] 'Political wisdom (*politikē*) and practical wisdom (*phronēsis*) are the same state of mind, but their essence is not the same. Of the wisdom concerned with the city, the architectonic form of practical wisdom is legislative wisdom (*nomothetikē*) . . .' (1141 b23–5). To have legislative wisdom is to understand the nature of human happiness, including above all the life of theoretical contemplation, and to be able to frame political constitutions and laws required for the attainment of happiness. This architectonic insight is, moreover, according to Aristotle's theory, the intellectual quality exhibited by Aristotle himself in the composition of his political treatises, including the *EN*. Yet, on the subject of this, the most developed, form of *phronēsis* Book VI has nothing to offer except passing, if pregnant, remarks; in particular, the observation that perhaps the good of the individual 'cannot exist without household management, nor without a form of government' (1142 a9–10). As Allan puts it, Aristotle is 'for the most

---

[1] *The Philosophy of Aristotle* (1952), pp. 182–3.　　　[2] *Aristotle*, p. 218.

part silent about the theoretical insight of the man of practical wisdom, and seems content to present him as one who, from long experience of the moral code of the community, can judge what ought to be done in given circumstances'.[1] Commentators have sometimes involved themselves, and their readers, in needless perplexities about Aristotle's doctrine of practical wisdom, and about the so-called practical syllogism, as a consequence of not attending to the limited scope of Aristotle's remarks in particular parts of the discussion. Thus they have felt bound to try to explain away the fact that Aristotle describes *phronēsis* both as discerning means to an end determined by moral virtue (1145 a5-6) and as involving a true understanding of an end (1142 b31-3). As regards the practical syllogism they have attempted, without authority from Aristotle, to represent the whole process of deliberation as a sorites, or chain of syllogisms (e.g. Burnet and Greenwood).

The above warning is made more necessary by the fact that the introductory sections of the book contain no warning of the limited character of the discussions which follow. Aristotle gives two reasons, arising out of what has been said before, for proceeding to an examination of *phronēsis* and intellectual virtue generally. First, in the definition of ethical virtue it has been stated that the mean is 'determined by the right rule', and we need to understand more clearly what sort of rule this is (1138 b18-34). Secondly, the virtues of the soul have been classed as ethical and intellectual; we have discussed the first class, and it remains to discuss the second (1138 b35-1139 a3). These reasons for embarking on the new topic might lead us to expect a full treatment of the intellectual virtues and an attempt to show how the rules of conduct which define the various ethical virtues are required for the attainment of happiness, the ultimate human end. Book VI gives only incomplete answers to such questions, and the answers it gives might mislead us if we did not interpret them in the light of Aristotle's doctrine in other books of the *EN*.

A man seeking to know how to discipline his passions, or to spend his money, is told, under the formula of the mean, that he

---

[1] Loc. cit.

must obey the rule of right (*orthos logos*). This, Aristotle says, 'though true, is by no means clear' (1138 b25-6). It is like telling a man in need of advice about doses or diets that he must follow those treatments 'which the medical art prescribes and which agree with the practice of one who possesses the art' (1138 b29-32). These concealed tautologies leave us none the wiser. What we need to know, as regards the ethical virtues, is 'what is the right rule and what is the standard that fixes it' (1138 b34). What standard (*horos*) could there be? The answer we expect, and are given, is that the standard is the end to which the virtues contribute. 'There is a mark (*skopos*) to which the man who has the rule looks, and heightens or relaxes his activity accordingly, and there is a standard which determines the mean states . . .' (1138 b22-3). The word 'mark' (*skopos*) echoes Aristotle's formulation of the doctrine of the supreme end in the opening chapters of Book I. 'Will not the knowledge of it, then, have a great influence on life? Shall we not, like archers who have a mark to aim at, be more likely to hit upon what is right?' (1094 a22-4).

What, then, is the right rule and what is the standard that fixes it? (1138 b34). Ross, while pointing out that the question is nowhere answered 'in so many words', suggests nevertheless that Aristotle's answer is 'clear'. 'The right rule is a rule reached by the deliberative analysis of the practically wise man, and telling him that the end of human life is to be best attained by certain actions which are intermediate between extremes. Obedience to such a rule is moral virtue'.[1] But Aristotle's comment, 'true indeed but not clear', is still applicable to this formulation, as we can see from the lucid and penetrating account which Ross himself gives of Aristotle's doctrine. The statement offered of the right rule is defective because it fails to bring to light two ways in which Aristotle's doctrine is complex or, as some would say, ambiguous and confused. There is first the question whether the 'end of human life' is conceived simply in terms of egoism. Can or should a man seek as an end only his own happiness or also the happiness of his friends or of other members of a society, particularly the state, to which he belongs? The second question, which I have

[1] *Aristotle*, p. 221.

discussed earlier, is whether the end is 'paramount' and exclusive, the activity of the theorist, or inclusive, a system, or at least a plurality, of activities and enjoyments each desirable, although in different degrees, for its own sake. Aristotle certainly commits himself to the doctrine of an inclusive end. But, since this is so, the question arises whether the right rule can be represented as a rule which prescribes means for attaining an end. I shall comment, at this stage, only very briefly on these issues.

If we say of a man in English that he aims at happiness we mean his own happiness. Similarly, when Aristotle holds that a wise man has an adequate and true conception of *eudaimonia*, and makes it his end in life, he means that a wise man is an enlightened seeker of his own happiness. At the beginning of *EN* VI. 5 Aristotle refers, without any suggestion of doubt or dissent, to the opinion that it is 'the mark of a man of practical wisdom to be able to deliberate well about what is good and expedient for himself, not in some particular respect, e.g. about what sorts of things conduce to health or to strength, but about what sorts of things conduce to the good life in general' (1140 a25–8). Sometimes, in connection with this egoistic account of practical activity, the good life is narrowed to the life of theory. In both the *EE* and in the *MM* we find it stated that rules which prescribe conduct ethically virtuous have as their end and justification the contemplative activities of the agent. The end is exclusive of other goods as well as confined to the agent. I quote the concluding sentences of the *EE*:

What choice, then, or possession of the natural goods—whether bodily goods, wealth, friends, or other things—will most effectively produce the contemplation of God, that choice or possession is best; this is the noblest standard, but any that through deficiency or excess hinders one from the contemplation and service of God is bad; this man possesses in his soul, and this is the best standard (*horos*) for the soul—to perceive the irrational part of the soul, as such, as little as possible. (*EE* Θ 3, 1249, b16–23.)

The same doctrine is stated in the *MM* (*A* 34) where the relation of practical wisdom to philosophy is said to be like that of a steward (*epitropos*) to his master for whom he provides leisure; the function of wisdom is 'subduing the passions and keeping them in order' (1198 b9–20; cf. *B* 10, 1208 a5–30). The same account of the relationship is implied at the end of *EN* vi where Aristotle says that *phronēsis* does not use philosophic wisdom but 'provides for its coming into being; it issues orders, then, for its sake but not to it' (1145 a6–9). But the egoistic asceticism of these passages does not fully represent Aristotle's view. We are told in *EN* i. 2 that the end of the state is 'greater and more perfect' than the end of the individual. A statesman who provided by legislation for scientific studies might achieve his own happiness by these activities, even if he were not himself a scientist. Thus in *EN* x. 7 Aristotle speaks of the activities of the statesman as being aimed at happiness 'for himself and his fellow citizens' (1177 b12–15). If the statesman succeeded in producing happiness for others but not for himself, his insight and energy as a legislator would still be an exercise of *phronēsis*. More generally, the thesis that Aristotle's doctrine of the end for man is egoistic in some objectionable sense should not be assumed without argument. In his treatment of love or friendship in Books viii and ix Aristotle attempts to represent altruistic self-sacrifice, even in its most extreme forms, as consistent with his own theory. I do not, indeed, wish to claim that his attempt is wholly successful. But this is a question to which I shall return.

Both in *EN* vi and in *EN* x Aristotle asserts without ambiguity that theoretical activity, although more highly desirable than any other human activity, is not the only activity which is desirable for its own sake and does not by itself constitute the whole end for man. Thus in vi. 12 he says that both kinds of excellence, practical and theoretical, are 'worthy of choice because they are the virtues of the two parts of the soul respectively, even if neither of them produces anything' (1144 a1–3).[1] Somewhat more explicitly he asserts in x. 8 that activities which manifest *phronēsis* and moral virtue, although a lower form of happiness than theoretical activity, are desired for their own sake and thus constitute part of the human good or end. Aristotle, then, must

---

[1] Cf. a13–20, cf. also ii. 4, 1105 a32.

hold that the life and activity which manifests ethical virtue is desirable at most only in part because it prepares the way for contemplation and is thus a means to a further end. It is also desirable in its own right or perhaps as an essential or appropriate part of a life which as a whole is happy. Could a man be fully happy if he were not trusted and liked, and perhaps admired, by his family and his friends? But, if right conduct is desired for its own sake, because it is itself fine or noble (*hoti kalon*), its rightness cannot be dependent on the fact that it leads to an end beyond itself. The right rule will not be a rule which prescribes the means for the attainment of an end, and will not be reached by the kind of deliberation, working back from end to means, which has been described in iii. 3 (1112 b15–27). We should not, of course, find fault with Aristotle for being ready to abandon the attempt to understand all actions as the taking of means to ends; he was right to abandon it. What is unsatisfactory is that, having given an account of deliberation as the search for means to ends, Aristotle does not revise or expand this account in order to cover types of practical thinking which it does not fit. We have seen in an earlier discussion that there are types which the account does not fit; the reflection which grades ends within an inclusive end and the process of deciding whether some desirable end can properly be pursued by some undesirable means (iii. 1, 1110 a19–31). Book vi does not contain any attempt to work out an adequate account of practical thinking; it does not formally amend the account earlier given of deliberation (*bouleusis*).

Having said that further explanation is needed of 'the right rule', Aristotle reminds us of the division of the soul in *EN* i. 13 on which the classification of virtues as ethical and intellectual was based. 'We said before that there are two parts of the soul—that which grasps a rule or rational principle, and the irrational' (1139 a3–5). In i. 13 Aristotle has spoken of the connection between ethics and psychology. The students of politics must study the soul 'just to the extent which is sufficient for the questions we are discussing' (1102 a23–6). What is needed is a recognition, without theoretical refinements, of the basic distinction between the rational and the non-rational aspects of human nature.

Some things are said about it ⟨i.e. the soul⟩, adequately enough, even in the discussions outside our school (*exōterikoi logoi*), and we must use these; e.g. that one element in the soul is irrational and one has a rational principle. Whether these are separated as the parts of the body or of anything divisible (*meriston*) are, or are distinct by definition (*logō̜*) but by nature inseparable, like convex and concave in the circumference of a circle, does not affect the present question. (1102 a26–32.)

In the *De Anima* (Γ 9, 432 a22) Aristotle criticizes a twofold division of the soul into rational and irrational as well as the view of Plato that the soul has three parts. But the reference in I. 13 is not to any particular theory (e.g. that of Xenocrates, as some scholars have supposed) but rather to a general doctrine which would be accepted by Plato (to whom it is attributed in *MM* A 1, 1182 a23), by Platonists, and by Aristotle himself. Ross's rendering of 'exoteric' as 'outside our school' is misleading, as I have argued earlier,[1] since it suggests the view of Diels, adopted by Burnet and by Joachim, that the reference is to writings extraneous to those of Aristotle, usually, according to Burnet, 'the writings of the Academic school'. But most scholars would now follow Jaeger[2] in returning to the view held by Bernays in 1863[3] that the 'exoteric discourses' are the dialogues and other literary works of Aristotle himself. Bernays thought that the reference here was to the *Eudemus*. The most recent commentary on the *EN* (Gauthier–Jolif) suggests, following Jaeger, the *Protrepticus*.[4] But the fact, if it is a fact, that Aristotle here appeals to works written by himself when he was a Platonist does not imply, as Burnet seems to suggest, that he conceals from us the real foundations of his own ethical theory. Having invoked a philosophical commonplace, Aristotle is quite free to make use of more determinate doctrines similar to, or identical with, those of the *De Anima*. Already in I. 7 he has used the distinction between the soul as the principle of nutrition and growth and the soul which perceives and desires (1097 b34), and he does so again in the

---

[1] See Ch. V, p. 69 above.   [2] *Aristoteles*, p. 249.
[3] *Die Dialoge des Aristoteles*.   [4] Fr. 6 in Walzer, p. 34.

discussion which follows, in I. 13, his introduction of the exoteric
doctrine. Here, as in I. 7, the nutritive soul is dismissed as having
'by its nature no share in human excellence' (1102 b12).

The doctrine stated in *EN* I. 13 is that human virtues or excellences are either intellectual or ethical (1103 a4–5). The intellectual virtues are praiseworthy states of the soul which has a
rational principle 'in the strict sense and in itself' (1103 a2). The
ethical virtues are praiseworthy states of 'the appetitive and in
general the desiring element' in the soul (1102 b30). This element
is classed as irrational (*alogos*) but is described as 'sharing in a
rational principle' (1102 b13–14), 'in so far as it listens to and
obeys it' (1102 b31). In expounding the distinction between the
two parts or elements or principles Aristotle refers, as Plato had in
Republic IV, to the phenomena of control, and lack of control,
when passion is in conflict with a man's judgement of what it is
right to do or refrain from doing (1102 b14–28). Aristotle, as we
have seen, does not conceal from us that the psychological basis
which he offers for his division of virtue, if perhaps adequate
(1102 a24), is only rough and ready. But he does not make clear
in what ways it is rough, or in what ways its roughness is liable
to mislead us or to conceal from us questions which are important.
The following points should be noted by way of preface to our
study of Book VI.

First, notice the vagueness of the phrase used to characterize
the non-rational soul, 'the appetitive and in general the desiring
element' (1102 b30). In the *De Anima* (B 2) appetite (*orexis*) is
the genus of which desire (*epithumia*), passion (*thumos*), and wish
(*boulēsis*) are the species (414 b2). Aristotle's phrase here suggests
the generic sense; but this is too wide. The rational wish for the
highest good, whether intellectual activity or happiness in a wider
sense, is not the province of any of Aristotle's ethical virtues. On
the other hand the specific sense of the desiring faculty, covering
only desires for bodily pleasures, is too narrow even if extended,
as it was by Plato, to include desire for money. Passion (*thumos*)
must be added as the province of courage (*andreia*) and gentleness
(*praotēs*). Justice requires separate treatment; here it need only be
said that Aristotle, in his detailed analysis in Book V, does not tell

us much about the sense in which justice is to be regarded as a virtue of 'the desiring element'.

A second point to note about Aristotle's division of virtues in I. 13 is that he is here silent, where silence might mislead, on the intellectual aspects of ethical virtue. It is true and important that he does not say that a man could have ethical virtue without having any intellectual virtue. To say this would not be consistent with the doctrine of I. 7 that the characteristic excellence of man belongs to his nature as rational (1098 a3). What is unfortunate in I. 13 is the verbal suggestion that the desiring element is itself the owner of an inferior intellect which can receive suggestions but cannot initiate cogitation. 'That the irrational element is in some sense persuaded by a rational principle is indicated also by the giving of advice and by all reproof and exhortation' (1102 b33–1103 a1). The word (*pōs*) translated by 'in some sense' is an inadequate apology for the crudity of the metaphor by which one part of a man is said to listen to advice or orders from another part (1102 b25–31). The acceptance of advice or orders is as truly an exercise of the intellect as the giving of advice or of orders, although the thinking involved is simpler and more passive. Book VI supplies needed correction to what Joachim rightly calls 'the crude and simple division suggested by the present passage' (p. 69). Aristotle's view, as Joachim states it, is that 'complete moral goodness is the perfect development of an emotional and an intellectual factor' (p. 70). 'It is not possible to be good in the strict sense without practical wisdom, nor practically wise without moral virtue' (VI. 13, 1144 b30–2). It is true that what is here called practical wisdom is not the wisdom of the statesman; it does not involve the ability to formulate, or even perhaps fully to understand, the reasons for obeying the rules which are accepted. There is this element of truth, or at least of plausibility, in Aristotle's suggestion that ethical virtue is not a quality involving the rational soul 'in the strict sense and in itself' (1103 a2).

I have suggested that, in reading Book VI, we may be disappointed to find that Aristotle does not formulate, or systematically answer, the major questions in our minds. But there is another side to this. The fact that Aristotle's treatment is tentative and exploratory, even casual, may commend it, and in a way rightly, to some readers. Such readers will also be attracted, as they should be, by the interest which Aristotle shows in what men say, in the variety of the terms which they use in commending the operations of intelligence in connection with conduct. Systematic answers to large questions may do injustice to the complexity of the phenomena. J. L. Austin believed 'that our ordinary words are much subtler in their uses, and mark many more distinctions, than philosophers have realised'.[1] He suggests somewhere that we should forget about 'beautiful' and turn our attention to 'dainty' and 'dumpy'. Somewhat in the same spirit, perhaps, Aristotle chooses to forget the grand architectonic wisdom of the statesman, and undertakes instead some useful exploration of the lower slopes, not the commanding heights, of practical thinking. He turns quickly from the wisdom of the legislator to the horse sense of the plain man. He considers a range of qualities which are not specific varieties of practical wisdom, and not independent virtues, but subordinate qualities without which the main practical virtue would be incomplete. We speak of men as good counsellors (*euboulia*), as exhibiting judgement (*gnōmē*), sympathy (*sungnōmē*), and understanding (*sunesis*); as being reasonable (*nous*) or sensible (*aisthēsis*), clever (*deinotēs*), acute (*eustochia*), shrewd (*anchinoia*). Aristotle would like to make as precise as possible the distinctions marked by all these words. It is a useful inquiry, and it would be wrong to complain of the frequent changes of subject and direction which such an inquiry involves.

Having recalled the division of the soul into rational and irrational, Aristotle proceeds in chapter 1 to divide the rational soul (1139 a5–17). 'Let it be assumed that there are two parts which grasp a rational principle—one by which we contemplate the kind of things whose principles are invariable and one by which we contemplate variable things' (1139 a6–8). Aristotle, following Plato, asserts that the difference of object involves a difference of faculty, since knowledge depends on 'a certain likeness or kinship' between the mind and its objects (1139 a8–11). He

[1] *Sense and Sensibilia*, p. 3.

suggests the names 'scientific' (*epistēmonikon*) and 'calculative' (*logistikon*) for the two parts, and adds that 'to deliberate and to calculate are the same thing'; 'no one deliberates about the invariable' (1139 a11–15). We must now, Aristotle concludes, consider what is the best state, the virtue, of each of these two parts (1139 a15–16).

I propose to limit strictly the scope of my comments on the principles of the division which Aristotle here lays down between the theoretical and the practical intellect. Book VI deals primarily with the functioning of the practical intellect. Aristotle finds it necessary to point out certain resemblances and differences between practical and theoretical thinking (especially in 8, 1142 a23–30 and 11, 1143 a35–b5). In the course of chapters 3, 6, and 7 he explains briefly what he understands by science (*epistēmē*), intuitive reason (*nous*), and philosophy (*sophia*). But I shall not discuss here his views on the provinces of mathematics, physics, and philosophy. The questions which arise are best considered, so far as such consideration is needed for the understanding of the *EN*, in connection with the doctrine, stated in Book X, that theoretical activity is the supreme form of human happiness. I shall, therefore, make no comment here on the idea that knowledge depends on similarity between mind and its objects. Information about the history of the idea, and about the forms which it takes in Aristotle's accounts of sense-perception and of intellectual apprehension, is available in the commentaries on the *EN*[1] and in Ross's *Aristotle*.

Theoretical and practical thinking are here distinguished as having different subject-matters, the necessary or invariable and the contingent or variable. This raises the question to which part of the soul Aristotle would here assign what he calls 'physical' science. Theoretical wisdom, according to Aristotle, covers theology or first philosophy, mathematics, and physics.[2] But the subject-matter of physics, natural bodies, is a sphere of being in which connections sometimes are not strictly necessary but hold only for the most part.[3] In the *Posterior Analytics* (79 a21–2)

---

[1] See Stewart's note (ii. 11–15) on 1139 a8 and Joachim, pp. 169–72.
[2] *Metaphysics* 1026 a18, 1005 b1; cf. *EN* VI. 8, 1142 a17–18.
[3] Joachim, pp. 7–10, 24–5; Gauthier-Jolif on 1139 a14–15.

Aristotle recognizes that scientific demonstration in the first figure may have premisses which hold good generally but not invariably. Thus, if theoretical thinking were confined to the invariable, physics, or part of what Aristotle calls physics, would not be theoretical. But Aristotle insists that physics is a kind, though not the primary kind, of theoretical wisdom.[1] Aristotle would not assign any part of physics to the calculating or deliberative intellect.[2]

In other passages the distinction between the two kinds of intellect is based on the difference between their ultimate ends. The aim of practical science is 'not knowledge but action'.[3] But the fact, so far as it is a fact, that theoretical and practical thinking have different motives does not show that they are different kinds of thinking. The statesman, or the writer of a treatise on statesmanship, seeks to know what are the conditions of the attainment by men of the happiness they seek. Aristotle asserts that the motive of such inquiries is not intellectual curiosity but a desire to be or to do good. This, if true, would not be a good reason for saying that practical thinking is a special kind of thinking. As I have argued earlier,[4] Aristotle does not distinguish clearly between the method or logical structure of practical science and the motive for pursuing it. It is not true that questions about, or bearing on, practice can be studied only for practical or utilitarian reasons. History may have lessons to teach. But the historian may surely be disinterestedly inquisitive about the practical problems faced by the statesmen or generals whose careers he studies. Aristotle admits this in the *Politics*; interest in political science may be theoretical, not merely practical, and, if so, will extend to details which have no practical relevance.[5]

'The virtue of a thing is relative to its proper work' . . . *pros to ergon to oikeion* (1139 a16–17). Having divided the intellectual faculties of men on the basis of the objects contemplated, according as they are necessary or contingent, Aristotle proceeds in

[1] *Metaphysics* 1005 b1–2, 1025 b25–8, 1026 a6–7.
[2] Cf. Joachim, p. 169; Greenwood, pp. 23–5.
[3] *EN* I. 3, 1095 a5–6; II. 2, 1103 b26–9; X 9, 1179 a35–b2.
[4] See Ch. III above, pp. 30–1.
[5] III. 4, 1279 b12–15; cf. VIII. 2, 1338 b2–4; contrast *EN* I. 13, 1102 a18–26.

chapter 2, starting from the familiar notion of work or function (*ergon*), to a fuller account of the division. The two kinds of thinking are alike in that, in both, men make the attainment of truth their aim and business. 'The work of both the intellectual parts, then, is truth' (1139 b12). This is the conclusion stated at the end of the chapter. The difference between the two intellectual faculties, as Aristotle expounds it, is that, while the contemplative intellect aims simply at truth (1139 a27–8), the practical intellect aims at 'truth in agreement with right desire' (1139 a29–31). Practical intelligence shows itself in the choices made, after deliberation, by men of good character. If choices are to be good, 'both the reasoning must be true and the desire right, and the latter must pursue just what the former asserts' (1139 a23–6). The word *logos*, here translated 'reasoning', might be more correctly understood as referring to the rational principle or rule arrived at by the reasoning of a man seeking to decide what he should do. The word occurs again a few lines later when Aristotle says that the principle (*archē*), or efficient cause, of action is choice, while the principle of choice is desire and reasoning, or a rule (*logos*), having an end in view (1139 a31–3). But this doubt about the translation of *logos* does not affect the main question of interpretation raised by the chapter, the question how to understand the statement that practical intelligence (*phronēsis*) is shown in the grasp of 'truth in agreement with right desire' (1139 a30).

Aristotle describes deliberation as the finding of means to ends. It is natural to suppose that the true propositions affirmed by the wise man are about ends and also about means: the end which he pronounced good would indeed be good, and the means which he pronounced effective would in fact produce, or tend to produce, the end. If desire is right when it seeks a good end, and if what the practical intellect asserts or grasps is identical with the object of right desire (1139 a25–6), truth about the end must be included in the truth which is the work of the practical intellect. As confirmation we can adduce the passage, although its interpretation has been questioned, at the end of chapter 9 where Aristotle speaks of wisdom as the 'true apprehension' of the end (1142 b33). But it is no less clear that the truth achieved in practical thinking must include the truth that the means chosen will in fact conduce to the end. Aristotle represents practical thinking as the thinking which proceeds by deliberation and terminates in choice; hence it is concerned with the particular thing to be done (8, 1142 a23–30; 11, 1143 a35–b5), and, within the conceptual framework of end and means, the particular action is the taking of means to an end (cf. 12, 1144 a24 ff.).

This view of what we should understand by 'truth in agreement with right desire' is taken also, I think, by Greenwood in his note on 1139 a23 (pp. 175–6) and by Gauthier-Jolif in their notes on 1139 a21–31 (pp. 446–9). Thus Greenwood argues that 'the harmony of reason with appetite is not the same thing as the goodness of either'. There is harmony, but not practical wisdom, in the bad man who chooses an effective means to a perverted end. Gauthier-Jolif deploy the same argument (p. 448) against interpreters of Aristotle who 'wish to restrict the field of wisdom to means' (p. 446). 'Si en ce cas l'intellect pratique n'est pas vrai, ce ne peut être que parce que, outre le jugement qu'il porte sur les moyens, il implique *aussi* un jugement sur la fin; il ne dit pas seulement que la friction est le moyen de parvenir à la santé, il dit que la santé est la fin à laquelle on doit parvenir' (p. 448).

This argument is not indeed conclusive. For it has to meet the reply that, while Aristotle did not wish to identify, and believed that he could distinguish, practical wisdom and the intellectual capacity shown in the effective pursuit of a bad end, he does not succeed, especially when the question faces him in Book VI. 12 and 13, in distinguishing them. For he tells us that to have cleverness (*deinotēs*) is to be able to find the means to any proposed end (1144 a24–6), and that it is the ethical virtue of the good man which determines his end while his practical wisdom makes him do what leads to the end (1145 a5–6). Here it seems that the effect of what Aristotle says is to identify practical wisdom with cleverness. His doctrine that ethical virtue and practical wisdom are inseparable (1144 b30–2) can be reduced, it would seem, to the tautology that a man cannot be both clever and good unless he is good.

This criticism has point and force if we confine our attention to the passages adduced in its support. But we have already seen that there is much in Aristotle's account of practical wisdom which would have to be ignored by an interpretation which attributed to him the view that practical wisdom consists in the ability to devise means to antecedently defined ends. There are also other elements, still to be considered, in his doctrine which would have to be dismissed as inconsistent with his main view. At this point in my account of his doctrine I wish to stress the importance of keeping in mind what Aristotle says at the beginning of chapter 8 about the varieties of practical wisdom and the different levels at which it is manifested. Thus the legislator who has wisdom in its architectonic form (1141 b25) is a man who understands the nature of happiness, the human end, and the conditions of its attainment. His intellectual capacity is something very different from the good sense which enables a man to find ways of bringing about states of affairs which he can appreciate as good if he has been trained to ethical virtue.

The view that the truth which it is the job of practical reason to find includes true conceptions of what ends are good is supported further by reflection on the general plan, or framework, of Aristotle's treatment of intellectual virtue in Book VI, 3–11. He has explained in the first two chapters that there are two parts of the rational soul, both of which aim at truth. Then follows, in chapters 3–11, a series of discussions, strung together on no clearly visible thread, in which many different capacities and excellencies belonging to the rational soul are distinguished and described. But at the end of chapter 11 we are presented with a conclusion: practical wisdom (*phronēsis*) is the virtue of one part of the rational soul and theoretical wisdom (*sophia*) the virtue of the other (1143 b14–17). This conclusion, that in a sense there are only two intellectual virtues, implies that, just as theoretical wisdom includes or comprehends intuitive reason (*nous*), which apprehends first principles (ch. 6), and scientific knowledge (*epistēmē*), which is a capacity to demonstrate (3, 1139 b31–3), so practical wisdom includes or comprehends the various powers and qualities which may be displayed in practical thinking. It is tempting to suggest a more determinate correspondence. Theoretical wisdom is defined in chapter 7 as 'intuitive reason combined with scientific knowledge—scientific knowledge of the highest objects which has received as it were its proper completion' (1141 a18–20). Scientific capacity without the grasp of first principles would be incomplete, headless. Now what corresponds in practical thinking to the grasp of first principles in theoretical thinking is the thought of ends to be achieved. 'For the syllogisms which deal with acts to be done involve a starting-point, viz. "Since the end, i.e. what is best, is of such and such a nature"' (12, 1144 a31–3; cf. 1142 b31–3). The end, according to Aristotle, is an object of desire, and it moves us by being the object of thought or imagination.[1] Hence practical wisdom, if it is to be complete and not headless, must include the intuitive thought of the end as well as the intellectual powers required for the discovery of means. Why does Aristotle nowhere assert this in so many words? Part of the answer may be that the word *nous*, which, in its application to theory, is translated 'intuitive reason', is used in the sphere of action for the capacity to discern the particular thing to be done in a concrete situation (1143 a35 ff.), the capacity expressed in 'the undemonstrated sayings and opinions of experienced and older people or of people of practical wisdom . . .' (1143 b11–14). Hence the explicit use of the word to refer to a faculty for conceiving ends drops out of Aristotle's discussions in Book VI. But, as Greenwood points out, when Aristotle tells us that 'virtue makes us aim at the right mark, and practical wisdom makes us take the right means' (1144 a7–9), he is not to be understood as denying that the mark is discerned by the intellect. 'Since the actual stating of any proposition is an intellectual and not a moral act, the actual stating of the end . . . must be the work not of moral virtue but of practical wisdom' (p. 51). I suggest that it is the fact that Aristotle has found other uses for *nous* that makes it difficult for him to use it here for the faculty which apprehends 'the right mark'. Apart from this, the elaboration of formal analogies between the two intellectual faculties would be inappropriate to the tentative and piecemeal character of Book VI. Aristotle here shows more interest in contrasts than in correspondences

[1] *De Anima* Γ 10, 433 b10–12.

between theoretical science and the thought which reaches its conclusions in actions.

Aristotle, as we have seen, finds it helpful both to compare and to contrast theoretical reasoning with the reasoning which leads to action. Both in Book VI, and more explicitly when he discusses moral weakness (*akrasia*) in Book VII, he indicates an analogy between syllogistic proofs in demonstrative science and the application of practical rules to particular situations (VII. 3, 1147 a25–8). Hence any report of what Aristotle has to say about practical thinking must find a place for the doctrine of the so-called 'practical syllogism'. But we ought not to assume without good evidence that this place is large. The prestige of the syllogism has led some commentators to attribute to Aristotle the view that all processes of deliberation can be expressed in syllogisms. The evidence does not support this view. Commentators who take the view for granted are led into confusion. It is important, therefore, to be clear what Aristotle is and is not saying in the passages which mention, or omit to mention, the syllogism of practice.

The expression 'practical syllogism' is not used by Aristotle. The passage in the *EN* in which he comes nearest to using it is in VI. 12; 'for the syllogisms which deal with acts to be done (*tōn praktōn*) are things which involve a starting-point, viz. "since the end, i.e. what is best, is of such and such a nature whatever it may be" (let it for the sake of argument be what we please); and this is not evident (*ou phainetai*) except to the good man' (1144 a31–4). When Aristotle says here, and elsewhere, that the end to be realized is the 'starting-point' of practical thinking he is recalling the account which he has given of deliberation in III. 3: we 'assume the end and consider how and by what means it is to be attained' (1112 b11 ff.). There are references to the same account in VI. 5, 1140 b16–20; VII. 8, 1151 a15–17; and *EE B* 11, 1227 b28–32. In the passage I have quoted (1144 a31–4) no example of a syllogism is given. It is, perhaps, questionable whether 'syllogisms' here means more than processes of reasoning. But, even if the word has its technical meaning, it does not follow that a proposition of the form 'the end is such and such' is suggested by Aristotle as the form of a major premiss. There are many examples of practical syllogisms in the *EN*. In all of them the major premiss specifies means which are proper and effective for the attainment of an end, or else things to be avoided as leading to a bad end. Examples in Book VI are 'light foods are digestible and wholesome' (7, 1141 b18–19) and 'all water that weighs heavy is bad' (8, 1142 a22–3). Other similar examples will be found in VII. 3. The general form of the practical syllogism is not laid down in the *EN*. But the examples given conform to the formula in *De Anima* III, where the major premiss is 'such and such a kind of man should do such and such a kind of act' and the minor premiss 'this is an act, and I am a person, of the kind meant' (434 a16–21). The scheme does not admit a major premiss of the form 'the end is such and such'. To suppose that Aristotle was suggesting a premiss of this form is unnecessary; for it is quite intelligible to say that the 'starting-point' of a syllogism recommending the means is the thought of the end; as the end of health suggests the advice to keep to light meats. The unplausibility of making 'the end is such and such' a major premiss can be seen in the contortions of the scholars who try to construct the implied syllogisms.[1]

Although there are passages in the *EN* which compare aspects or features of scientific thinking with aspects or features of practical thinking, there is no passage which explicitly contrasts two kinds of syllogism. But there is such a passage in *De Motu Animalium* 7.

But how is it that thought is sometimes followed by action, sometimes not; sometimes by movement, sometimes not? What happens seems parallel to the case of thinking and inferring (*sullogizomenois*) about the immovable objects of science. There the end is the truth seen (*theōrēma*) (for when one conceives the two premisses, one at once conceives and comprehends the conclusion), but here the two premisses result in a conclusion which is an action—for example, one conceives that every man ought to walk, one is a man oneself: straightway one walks. (701 a7–14.)

This is not quite the contrast we expect. First, we should expect Aristotle to point out that in the scientific syllogism both premisses

---

[1] Grant, i. 265; Greenwood, p. 50; Allan, 'The Practical Syllogism' in *Autour d'Aristote* (Louvain, 1955), especially pp. 336–7; Ando, *Aristotle's Theory of Practical Cognition*, e.g. pp. 287–8. See also below, Ch. XII, pp. 250–4.

are universal, not the first only. Secondly, we should expect Aristotle to say not that the conclusion is an action but that action follows as soon as the conclusion, e.g. I ought to walk, is seen. But Aristotle speaks in a similar way in *EN* VII. 3: in scientific reasoning the soul must 'affirm the conclusion, while in the case of opinions concerned with production it must immediately act' (1147 a27–8). I think that Allan has these passages in mind when he insists that the practical syllogism offers a 'psychological account of action in accordance with principles' (p. 325); the syllogism describes 'the thought displayed in action, not that which precedes action' (p. 340). But Allan's meaning is no easier to grasp than Aristotle's. The discussion of this aspect of the practical syllogism will be in place when we consider Aristotle's treatment of *akrasia* in *EN* VII. 3. But it is worth noting that the doctrine in the *De Motu Animalium*, that the conclusion is an action, is not necessarily to be understood as denying that the agent in acting, or even before acting, affirms a conclusion. For, in one of his examples, Aristotle, having stated the premisses as 'what I need I ought to make, I need a coat', says that 'the conclusion, I ought to make a coat, is an action' (701 a19–21). The verbal conclusion, I ought to make a coat, can be distinguished from the action even if it does not precede it.

I think that I have now mentioned all the essential points in what Aristotle says about practical syllogisms. In reading what commentators say about the doctrine I have often found it hard to see any clear connection between their interpretations and what Aristotle actually says. Thus I have failed to find evidence either for the view that Aristotle regarded the practical syllogism as the form of all practical thinking or for the view that there are two main kinds of practical syllogism in one of which the major premiss defines an end and in the other formulates a rule of action. The former view seems to be asserted by Greenwood when he says that 'the reasoning that leads to choice is syllogistic' (p. 50), by Joachim when he speaks of *phronēsis* as 'an established power of reasoning or deliberating which expresses itself in syllogisms whose conclusions are . . . actions' (p. 208), and by Ando when he speaks of 'the practical syllogism as the form of deliberation' (p. 274). Aristotle's account of deliberation is open to objection, as we have seen, in so far as it suggests that in all deliberation we are searching for means to ends. But the account would be made worse by an attempt to force the search for means into the form of a syllogism or series of syllogisms. As regards the view of Allan, following Grant, that 'the practical syllogism may take two forms, according as what is expressed in the major premiss is a *rule* or an *end*' (p. 336), I have already argued that the only passage in the *EN* which seems at first sight to support it (VI. 12, 1144 a31–4) does not in fact do so. Allan (pp. 330–1) connects this interpretation with a sentence in the *De Motu Animalium* in which Aristotle says that 'the premisses of action are of two kinds, of the good and of the possible' (701 a23–5). But Aristotle is here distinguishing, not two kinds of syllogism, but two kinds of premiss. It is natural to understand him as saying that, in any practical syllogism, there will be both a normative major premiss, containing a word like *good* or ought, and a minor premiss pinpointing the fact that there is an action which is *possible* here and now. This interpretation seems to fit the examples of elementary practical reasoning which Aristotle gives in the *De Motu Animalium*, or at least those of the examples which even look like being syllogisms.

I have argued that, on the evidence of the text, the major premiss of a practical syllogism formulates a maxim of prudence, a rule to be followed in order to achieve an end, such as the rule recommending a light diet. But I do not mean by this to imply that Aristotle distinguished clearly between rules of prudent self-interest and rules of morality. I have indeed argued that there are radical questions, connected with the difference between prudent and moral conduct, on which Aristotle does not state a clear and consistent view; the question whether, or in what sense, all conduct is egoistic, and the question in what sense the theoretic life is superior to other kinds of happiness. Since Aristotle does not admit a clear distinction between rules of morality and rules of prudence, he might well have formulated, although he does not do so, a rule of morality as a major premiss in a practical syllogism; e.g. 'never act like a coward in a battle' as well as 'never get drunk the night before a battle', which can be taken as a rule of prudence. A moral injunction to be brave or just is not a counsel of prudence, a recipe for future happiness. But to act bravely or justly is to act in accordance with virtue and so, on Aristotle's principles, to achieve happiness. It is part of a life which, if lived consistently according to such rules, will be happy. It is perhaps this line of thought which leads Grant to say that the major premiss contains 'the statement of an end' (i. 265), and Joachim to say that the premiss 'defines the nature of the end or some constituent of the end' (p. 210). Greenwood says much the same thing in different language by stretching the concept of means. 'A thing may be a means to an end in either of two senses, as component part of it, or as wholly external to it' (pp. 46–7). According to this misuse of 'means', enjoying the first course of a dinner is a 'component means' to enjoying the whole dinner. No less perverse is Allan's attempt to assimilate the premiss which states a rule and the premiss which defines an end. 'There is perhaps a sense in which every rule of action may be regarded also as the statement of an end. In endeavouring to observe the rule whenever an occasion presents itself, one is, in a certain sense, making the rule real, although, since the rule is universal, the process is never-ending' (p. 337). But achieving an end and obeying a rule cannot be made to appear less different from each other by using the word 'realize' as a synonym both for 'achieve' and for 'obey'. In so far as the scholars whom I have quoted are insisting that Aristotle's interpretation of human conduct in terms of 'ends', or of a supreme 'end', contains complexities and ambiguities, I admit, and indeed maintain, that they are right. What I do not admit is that the doctrine of the practical syllogism should be inflated by importing into it these complexities and ambiguities. Aristotle does not ask us to take the practical syllogism as the form of all rational discourse in or about conduct; and he does not, so far as I can see, propose as a major premiss the definition of the ultimate end, or indeed of any end. I shall discuss the practical syllogism more fully in the following chapter.

'We ought to attend to the undemonstrated sayings and opinions of experienced and older people or of people of practical wisdom not less than to demonstrations; for because experience has given them an eye they see aright' (vi. 11, 1143 b11–14). In two passages of Book vi (8, 1142 a23–30 and 11, 1143 a35–b5)[1] Aristotle explicitly recognizes a kind of practical wisdom which enables a man to say what should be done even if he cannot produce 'demonstrations', i.e. as we may suppose, cannot relate his decision to an end by deliberative analysis or deduce it from a principle. In both passages he contrasts the unmediated practical judgement on a particular situation with the unmediated understanding of the first principles of science.[2] Nous, in the sense of intuitive reason, 'is of the limiting premisses (horoi) for which no reason can be given, while practical wisdom is concerned with the ultimate particular, which is the object not of scientific knowledge but of perception' (1142 a25–7). In the second passage the same conclusion is drawn but in a different terminology: the word nous, intuitive reason, is used both of the theoretical grasp of scientific principles and of practical intelligence. 'Nous is concerned with the ultimates in both directions; for both the first terms and the last are objects of nous and not of argument' (1143 a35–b1). The fact that practical wisdom (phronēsis) is first contrasted with nous and in the later passage said to be itself a kind of nous implies no change of view or inconsistency. Aristotle is noting the different applications of the term (nous), while making clear that what is common to them is that the proposition accepted is accepted on its merits and not as the conclusion of an inference.

Although Aristotle ascribes the intuitive judgements of the wise man to a kind of sense (aisthēsis), he is careful in chapter 8 to explain that he does not mean by this a faculty, like a sixth sense, by which we perceive a property of rightness or goodness, as we perceive colour by sight and sound by hearing. Aristotle's view that the rightness of any action, or of any rule of action, lies in the fact that it promotes, or conforms with, the end or good for man is inconsistent with any moral-sense theory of this kind. It is inconsistent also with any intuitionist doctrine that the intellect can apprehend moral rules as each self-evident in its own right. His

---

[1] Cf. also the use of 'perception' (aisthēsis) in iv. 5, 1126 b3–4 and ii. 9, 1109 b22–3.   [2] See vi. 6.

rejection of the idea that we can perceive rightness, as we see colour or taste sweetness, is conveyed in the following passage. The text and translation are not beyond doubt, but I shall state without argument the interpretation which I accept. The perception of the wise man is 'not the perception of qualities peculiar to one sense (*hē tōn idiōn*) but a perception akin to that by which we perceive that the particular figure before us is a triangle; for in that direction also there will be a limit. But this' (i.e. the 'common' sense by which we perceive shape) 'is more truly perception than practical wisdom is, although it is another kind of perception than the former' (i.e. the perception of qualities peculiar to each sense) (1142 a27–30). Aristotle divides qualities perceived by sense into those which are peculiar to one sense and those which are common to two or more. Rest and movement, number, shape, and size are common sensibles.[1] But he also attributes to 'common' sense, or to the generic faculty of sense, other functions, including the perception that we perceive and discrimination between the objects of different senses.[2] What Aristotle is saying in this passage about the wise man's faculty of 'perception' may be paraphrased as follows. It is not a faculty, comparable with the five senses, of perceiving a specific range of objects: colours, sounds, tastes. It is perception in a wide or generic sense, as is also what has been called 'common sense' in the psychological treatises. But common sense belongs to the faculty of *sense* perception and is still bound up with the five senses. The man of practical judgement shows sense in a wider use of the term; alternatively he can be described as having *nous* (1143 b5).

In the final chapters (12 and 13) of Book VI Aristotle discusses two main questions or difficulties (*aporiai*): first, what the use is of the intellectual virtues, philosophic and practical wisdom; secondly, how it is that practical wisdom, which is inferior to philosophy, can yet have supreme authority (1143 b33–5). Aristotle's answer to the second question is given at the end of chapter 13. *Phronēsis* is not supreme over *sophia*; 'for it does not use it but provides for its coming into being; it issues orders, then, for its sake but not to it' (1145 a6–9). The statesman secures

[1] *De Anima* B 6, 418 a9–20. [2] Ross, *Aristotle*, pp. 139–42.

freedom for speculation, just as he controls the externals of religion but cannot therefore be said to 'rule the gods'. This is an incomplete statement of Aristotle's view of the connections between the two intellectual virtues, and between the activities which express them; the respects in which the statement is incomplete and ambiguous have been discussed elsewhere.[1] Apart from this brief pronouncement on the second question, Aristotle is engaged, in these two chapters, in discussing the first question: how are the intellectual virtues useful, how do they contribute to happiness? Aristotle offers two main answers, or one answer in two stages. These virtues are intrinsically valuable as being the virtues of the two intelligent 'parts' of the soul, even if they 'do not produce anything' (1144 a1-3; cf. 1145 a2-4). But it is misleading to say that they produce nothing. Philosophic wisdom, as part of the complete excellence of man, is, not indeed an efficient, but a formal cause of happiness; a disposition of which the active manifestations constitute happiness (1144 a3-6). Practical wisdom is also an element in happiness because 'the work of man is achieved only in accordance with practical wisdom as well as with ethical virtue' (1144 a6-7). 'For virtue makes us aim at the right mark, and practical wisdom makes us take the right means' (1144 a7-9). This description of the parts played by thought and desire in right conduct is, as we saw earlier,[2] incomplete and misleading. Aiming at an end implies thinking of an end, and the capacity to think truly of ends is part of practical wisdom (1142 b31-3). Aristotle proceeds to develop his view of the distinction and connection between practical wisdom and ethical virtue (1144 a11-1145 a2). In the course of the discussion he attempts to make clear how his own position differs from the 'Socratic' doctrine that 'all the virtues are forms of practical wisdom' (1144 b19-20). In saying this Socrates was wrong, but on the right track; he was correct in thinking that virtue and practical wisdom are inseparable (1144 b21; cf. 1144 b28-32). It is clear that Aristotle regards this statement of his agreement, and disagreement, with Socrates as crucial and important. We shall have to see whether he makes his meaning clear.

---

[1] See pp. 214-17 above and Ch. II.   [2] See pp. 223-8 above.

'It is evident that it is impossible to be practically wise without being good' (12, 1144 a36–b1; cf. 13, 1144 b16–17; b30–2). We saw earlier[1] that this would be a tautology if cleverness in finding means to a proposed end were called wisdom when, and only when, the end proposed was good. But we saw also that, for Aristotle, the end must be an object of wise thought if it is to be an object of right desire. To have practical wisdom is to be able to envisage good ends and not only to be able to see how they can be attained. We must now look more closely at what he says in VI. 13 about the mutual implication, or inseparability, of practical wisdom and ethical virtue. The relation between cleverness and wisdom is analogous, he says, to the relation between 'natural virtue', innate tendencies to acquire and exhibit virtues, and 'virtue in the strict sense . . .' (1144 b1–4). Children and brutes have the natural dispositions which are the basis from which the various ethical virtues can be developed by training and sub-mission to the right laws (1144 b8 ff.).[2] Natural virtue, but not virtue proper, can exist without the faculty of rational discern-ment, but is liable to stumble like a blind man (1144 b10–12). Socrates, then, was partly right and partly wrong when he said that 'all the virtues are forms of practical wisdom': it was wrong to identify virtue and wisdom, but it is true that virtue cannot exist without practical wisdom (1144 b17–21).[3] This is confirmed, Aristotle says, by the fact that 'even now all men when they define virtue' say that it is 'in accordance with the right principle', i.e. in accordance with practical wisdom (1144 b21–5). So far Aristotle's meaning seems to be clear. But we come now to a crucial passage which is more difficult to interpret.

'But we must take a short further step (metabēnai). For it is not only the state which is in accordance with the right principle (kata ton orthon logon) but the state which is accompanied by the right principle (meta tou orthou logou) that is virtue; and practical wisdom is a right principle about such matters' (1144 b25–8).[4]

---

[1] See p. 225 above.   [2] Cf. x. 9, 1179 b29–1180 a10.
[3] Cf. Meno 88 a–89 a, Phaedo 69 a–b, and the note in Gauthier–Jolif.
[4] I assume that, if the text is right in 1144 b26, the repeated estin in b27 should be cut out, as it is by Burnet.

What is the contrast which Aristotle wishes to convey here by the two prepositions, *kata* and *meta*? The generally accepted interpretation seems to be that action is 'in accordance with' (*kata*) a principle if the action, in its overt aspects, is the action which the principle requires even if the conformity is only accidental. The further requirement conveyed by saying that the principle must be present (*meta*) is that the principle should be consciously accepted by the agent. Stewart agrees that Aristotle demands a further requirement, a step which brings his position closer to that of Socrates, but thinks that conscious acceptance of the principle need not be involved: he contrasts 'external rule' with 'inward principle'. This interpretation has the authority of the *MM* (*A* 34).

Wherefore Socrates was not speaking correctly when he said that virtue was reason, thinking that it was no use doing brave and just acts, unless one did them from knowledge and rational purpose. This was why he said that virtue was reason. Herein he was not right, but the men of the present day say better; for they say that virtue is doing what is good in accordance with right reason. Even they, indeed, are not right. For one might do what is just without any purpose at all or knowledge of the good, but from an irrational impulse, and yet do this rightly and in accordance with right reason (I mean he may have acted in the way that right reason would command); but all the same this sort of conduct does not merit praise. But it is better to say, according to our definition, that it is the accompaniment by reason of the impulse to good. For that is virtue and that is praiseworthy. (1198 a10–21.)

This interpretation is followed by the fourteenth-century paraphrast, and by modern commentators. Thus Burnet says that *kata* implies a 'merely external standard', while to say that virtue is accompanied by (*meta*) wisdom implies that they are inseparable.

It is quite possible that the difference which Aristotle has in mind in this passage is indeed, as the commentators say, the difference between merely acting in conformity with a principle and so acting when the principle is deliberately accepted. But Aristotle certainly does not say this: his meaning, if it is his meaning, is at most implied by the contrast between *kata* and *meta*. It was argued by J. A. Smith in the *Classical Quarterly* (1920) that this need not be, and in this passage is not, the difference which the contrasted prepositions are used to describe. He makes a grammatical point on the translation of the sentence. According to the usual interpretation Aristotle is saying that virtue is a disposition not merely in accordance with (*kata*) reason but accompanying (*meta*) reason. This makes virtue the subject of the sentence; but in the Greek text it is the predicate. What is said is that it is not only the disposition which accords with (*kata*) reason but also the disposition which accompanies (*meta*) reason that is virtue. The accepted interpretation implies that it is possible for virtue to be *kata* without being *meta*, but not vice versa. But the literal translation suggests that it is possible to be *meta* without being *kata*, but not vice versa. Thus *meta* would express a looser, and not a tighter, connection between virtue and wisdom than is expressed by *kata*. The 'short further step' would be a step taking us not back towards a position closer to the Socratic identification of virtue with wisdom but a step taking us still further away from Socrates. 'It is true that Aristotle means to go beyond Socrates, that is further in the direction of exactness, but he does so precisely by not going so far in the way of asserting coextension or identity.' Is this reversal of the accepted interpretation consistent with the meaning and use of the prepositions *kata* and *meta*? Smith argues that it is. He points out that *kata* may convey not an external or accidental connection but an intimate and causal connection, as in the expression 'in accordance with (*kata*) the grammatical knowledge in himself' in II. 4 (1105 a23–6). Again he argues that *meta* (with), or *ouk aneu* (not without), does not naturally suggest immanence or an intimate necessary connection. Indeed Aristotle himself in VI. 5 says that to define virtue as being 'with reason' does not make the connection quite close enough. 'This is shown by the fact that a state of that sort may be forgotten but practical wisdom cannot' (1140 b28–30). So far as I know, Smith's article has not persuaded students of the *EN* to give up the accepted interpretation of this passage. But I think he showed that the interpretation is an over-confident expansion of what

Aristotle actually says. If it was important for Aristotle to insist, in distinguishing his own position from that of Socrates, that not only the state of character which is *kata logon* but also that which is *meta logou* is virtue, he has left this important part of his doctrine without adequate elucidation.

XII

NOTE ON THE PRACTICAL SYLLOGISM

THE expression 'practical syllogism' is used by commentators on Aristotle as a name not for any process of thinking which leads up to, or expresses itself in, action but for a process in which a rule is applied to a concrete situation, the application consisting in the thinker's doing something, actually performing as an agent or producer. The rule prescribes things which should be done in specified types of situation; its verbal expression requires the use of an evaluative word like 'good' or 'useful' or of a prescriptive word like 'should' or 'ought'. A practical rule may be negative as well as positive, may forbid, not enjoin. A negative rule prescribes things which a man should refrain from doing in specified types of situation. What is needed to effect the due application of a rule is the perception (*aisthēsis*) by a man that he is in the kind of situation to which the rule applies. In terms of Aristotle's doctrine of the theoretical syllogism, as expounded in the *Prior* and *Posterior Analytics*, the thinking which precedes, or accompanies, practical rule-keeping can be expressed in the verbal form of a first-figure syllogism, i.e. a syllogism in which the middle term is the subject of the major premiss and the predicate of the minor. Aristotle in the *EN* compares and contrasts this kind or phase of practical thinking with theoretical thinking or syllogizing. Theoretical thinking terminates, when the premisses are considered together, in the assertion of a conclusion; in practical thinking the termination, which follows immediately when the premisses have been combined, is an action (*EN* vii. 3, 1147 a25–31). The same difference is noted in similar words in the *De Motu Animalium* (ch. 7): in theoretical thinking 'the end is contemplation (for when a man has conceived the two premisses, he immediately conceives the conclusion)'; in practical thinking 'the conclusion drawn from the two premisses becomes the action'

(701 a8–13). The statement that the conclusion 'becomes the action' sounds paradoxical. In an inference with as general premiss the prescription that acts of a certain sort should be done the conclusion to be expected is the prescription that this action as being of that sort should be done. Aristotle cannot be saying absurdly that such conclusions are never verbally formulated. Indeed in the *De Motu Animalium*, speaking of an inference which terminates in the making of a cloak, he says: 'the conclusion, the cloak should be made, is an action' (701 a19–21). The point then would seem to be that the verbal formulation of the conclusion, when there is such a formulation, is an element in the action rather than an episode which precedes it. If so, Aristotle has, of course, to face the difficulty that prima facie a man sometimes formulates the prescriptive conclusion but does not do the action. We shall see what Aristotle has to say about this when we consider, in the following section, his treatment of incontinence (*akrasia*) or weakness of will. The discussion of *akrasia* is the only place in the *EN* where he deploys fully the so-called 'practical syllogism' and states his doctrine in terms of it. What seems remarkable, if we have in mind all that commentators have said about the practical syllogism, is how little Aristotle says about it in other places.

The index to the Oxford Text of the *EN* refers to four passages in which the word *sullogismos* occurs in the singular or the plural. In the first of these (VI. 3, 1139 b27–31) the word occurs four times but Aristotle is here referring to the *Analytics* and speaking of the theoretical syllogism. Another passage is irrelevant for the same reason, that Aristotle is not speaking of a syllogism which terminates in action; the syllogism here is a sophistical argument which puts us in a difficulty (*aporia*) by seeming to prove a paradoxical conclusion (VII. 2, 1146 a21–4). Two passages remain in which 'syllogism' occurs in connection with action. The first is in VI. 9: 'but it is possible to attain even good by a false syllogism, and to attain what one ought to do but not by the right means, the middle term being false; so that this too is not yet excellence in deliberation—this state in virtue of which one attains what one ought but not by the right means' (1142 b22–6). Aristotle does not here give an example of achieving the right end by the wrong means, nor do the commentators whom I have consulted. Allan says that the middle term 'seems to be termed "false" either because the agent is mistaken in thinking that it will conduce to the end, or because it is morally unworthy, and a good end ought not to be achieved at such a price'.[1] But, as regards the first case, if the means chosen does not conduce to the end, how is it that the end is achieved? As regards the second case, why should Aristotle express the fact that the means, though effective, is morally unworthy by saying that it is false? Yet Gauthier–Jolif, in agreement with Allan's second alternative, say that Aristotle here recognizes explicitly that 'the end does not justify the means'. Aristotle does indeed recognize that not any end will justify any means. But he does so when he is discussing 'mixed actions' in III. 1 (1110 a11 ff.) and deliberation in III. 3 (1112 b15 ff.), and the practical syllogism makes no appearance in what Aristotle has to say in Book III about practical thinking. The 'false syllogism' of VI. 9 is best explained by the kind of example of practical inference which Aristotle himself offers. 'If a man knew that light meats are digestible and wholesome, but did not know which sorts of meat are light, he would not produce health, but the man who knows that chicken is wholesome is more likely to produce health' (VI. 7, 1141 b18–21). In this case experience leads to a right conclusion without any middle term. The middle term would be false if, for example, red meat were prescribed by a trainer on the ground that it is light whereas in fact it is not light. Yet the conclusion might still be right if the trainee were allergic to chicken or if he were the athletic prodigy Milo who could digest anything.[2]

The remaining passage mentioning 'syllogisms' is in VI. 12 (1144 a31–6). For reasons which will become clear I propose to defer my discussion of this passage. I shall next examine the occurrences in the *EN* of the verb (*sullogizesthai*) corresponding to *sullogismos*, and then go through the examples of syllogistic, or quasi-syllogistic, practical inference which are given in the *EN* and in the *De Motu Animalium*.

---

[1] 'The Practical Syllogism', p. 336, in *Autour d'Aristote*.
[2] Cf. II. 6, 1106 b2–4.

The verb 'syllogize' occurs, according to Bywater's index, in only two places in the *EN*, in I. 11 and in VII. 6. The first passage is in a curious discussion of the different ways in which the living and the dead are affected by what happens to their friends and near relations, and we are told that 'account must be taken' (*sullogisteon*) of this difference (1101 a34). The word here is used in a general sense not connected with the sense of 'syllogism' in logic. In the second passage Aristotle is discussing impulsive actions prompted by anger. 'For argument or imagination informs us that we have been insulted or slighted, and anger, reasoning as it were (*hōsper sullogisamenos*) that anything like this must be fought against, boils up straightway' (1149 a32–4). Here the word seems to have the general sense of reasoning but it also, by the characteristic formulation of a rule, suggests the syllogism of action as we have described it. The passages remind us that, before Aristotle connected it with syllogisms in his technical sense, the word had the general meaning of reasoning, calculation, or collection of data.[1] Bonitz reports that the noun also (*sullogismos*) is sometimes in Aristotle used in a correspondingly broader sense (711 b49–60). Ross points out that the meaning 'infer' is not uncommon in Plato, and quotes two passages where the noun is used in the sense of reasoning (*Cratylus*, 412 a; *Theaetetus*,186 d). Ross also finds both the verb and the noun used in the *Topics* and the *Sophistici Elenchi* in passages which do not imply Aristotle's developed logical doctrine of the syllogism.[2]

EN VI yields two examples of practical reasoning in syllogistic form. The first is the passage already quoted in which the ineffective knowledge of the man who knows that light foods are healthy but does not know what kinds of food are light is contrasted with the immediately applicable knowledge of the man who knows that chicken is good for you (1141 b16–21). In this example the thought of the fully informed agent could be expressed in two syllogisms; the first specifying chicken as light food and the second applying the prescription of chicken to the food in the larder with the aid of a perceptual premiss, this is chicken. The

---

[1] See Liddell and Scott; Bonitz, Index 711 b15–24.
[2] *Commentary on Prior Analytics and Posterior Analytics* (1949), p. 291.

second example is in the following chapter (8): 'further error in deliberation may be either about the universal or about the particular; we may fail to know either that all water that weighs heavy is bad, or that this particular water weighs heavy' (1142 a20–3). This example raises no new point. The interest of the passage is that in it, as in VI. 9 (1142 b22–6), Aristotle connects the practical syllogism with deliberation. But it should not be assumed that he thought that the whole process of deliberation could be expressed, or that it could only adequately be expressed, in the form of syllogisms.

Before we turn to Book VII mention should be made of the two important passages in VI where Aristotle speaks of the unreasoned insight in practical situations of the man who has experience or a certain limited kind of practical wisdom (*phronēsis*): 8, 1142 a23–30; 11, 1143 a35–b14. In these passages no examples are given of syllogisms and the word 'syllogism' is not used. The word usually translated 'premiss' (*protasis*) occurs in the second. What is to be noted here is that these passages anticipate Book VII in that they compare and contrast a power of practical intelligence with a power of the theoretical intellect. The practical power is the power to spot the thing to be done in a concrete situation: the man of sense (*aisthēsis, nous*) has a flair which enables him to jump to a correct practical conclusion without thinking of premisses or reasons. The theoretical power is the power to apprehend the basic terms or propositions in a theoretical science. What is common to the two mental powers is the immediacy of the grip or grasp: in neither is there a transition from premisses to conclusions. The fact that the same Greek word (*nous*) can be used of both reveals the analogy and conceals the differences. The passages raise problems of interpretation in detail with which we are not at present concerned.

In Book VII we have already noted one example of a major premiss: 'anything like this must be fought against' (6, 1149 a33–4). The other examples are in chapter 3. 'Dry food is good for every man.' Aristotle points out that there are two universal terms, one predicable of an object and the other of an agent. Hence a double minor premiss is required: this is dry and I am a man. If the text of this passage is sound, Aristotle complicates his example by mentioning the intermediate premiss, 'such and such food is dry' (cf. 'chicken is light' above) (1146 b35–1147 a7). The remaining examples occur in the passage in which Aristotle gives his most elaborate description of what happens when a man acts incontinently or against his own practical principles (1147 a24 ff.). Aristotle begins, as we have seen, by contrasting theoretical or factual thinking, which leads to an affirmation, with practical thinking, which issues in action. His first example of the latter describes action on a bad principle: 'if everything sweet should be tasted and this is sweet . . . the man who can act and is not prevented necessarily at the same time acts accordingly' (1147 a29–31). In the case of incontinence two conflicting syllogisms are involved. Aristotle's example of the one leading to the behaviour to be explained is: the thought that everything sweet is pleasant and this is sweet leads to the moving by appetite of our bodily parts (1147 a32–5). Unfortunately all that Aristotle tells us about the syllogism, ineffective in this case, of moral or prudential principle is that its universal premiss 'forbids us to taste' (1147 a32). According to one interpretation it prescribes explicitly the non-tasting of sweet things. If so, the two syllogisms have a common factual minor premiss (this is sweet), and what goes wrong in the case of incontinence is that the minor premiss is combined with the wrong major premiss. According to another interpretation the forbidding premiss does not mention sweet things but prescribes, for example, against drinking vintage port. The failure of the incontinent man can then be understood as due to a failure, to be explained physiologically, to activate the knowledge of the minor premiss. We are not called upon here to discuss the issue between these interpretations, or to appraise the merits and demerits of Aristotle's discussion of *akrasia*. Our concern at present is only with the form and role of the so-called practical syllogism.

In the *De Anima* (*Γ* 10 and 11) Aristotle gives an account of the initiation of movement in or by living things, i.e. in non-rational animals and in man, an animal capable of calculation and deliberation before action. The other animals have only imagination which prompts their behaviour not opinion 'based on inference' (*ek sullogismou*—434 a5–12). Aristotle here gives us not examples of syllogism but a formulation of the schema of the practical syllogism which fits the examples we have been considering in the *EN*.

The faculty of knowing is not moved but remains at rest. Since the one premiss or judgment is universal and the other deals with the particular (for the first tells us that such and such a kind of man should do such and such a kind of act, and the second that this is an act of the kind meant, and I a person of the type intended), it is the latter opinion that really originates movement, not the universal; or rather it is both, but the one does so while it remains in a state more like rest, while the other partakes in movement. (434 a16–21.)

For examples of the working of the deliberative imagination which terminates in action we turn to the *De Motu Animalium*.

The examples to be considered are formulated briefly and the list is introduced by the remark already quoted that what occurs is like what happens when 'one thinks and forms an inference (*sullogizomenois*) about immovable objects', except that the conclusion is enacted not, or not merely, contemplated (701 a8–13). We start with an open mind on the question how far the syllogism in its strict sense is indicated by the corresponding verb here translated 'inference'. We shall find that some of the examples are expressed syllogistically but that some of them are not. The first two have as their major premisses 'everyone should walk' and 'no one should walk' and as their minor 'I am a man', the conclusions being respectively the actions of walking and staying still (701 a12–15). If these examples sound insane, this is presumably because they are incompletely stated: the circumstances in which the prescriptions, to walk or not to walk, apply are not specified. Later the affirmative syllogism reappears in a different formulation, with 'walking is good for a man' as major premiss and 'walking is good for me' as conclusion (701 a26–7). The next example is not a syllogism. It sounds particularly queer, and the first premiss as formulated appears to be vacuous: 'I ought to create a good, and a house is a good, I immediately create a house' (701 a16–17). This is the only example anywhere of a practical inference formulated without a purely factual premiss. But it seems to need one all the same: here am I in a position in which housebuilding can start. The obvious incompleteness of this example is in contrast with the detailed filling of the next example, also in the sphere of productive craftsmanship. 'I need a covering, a cloak is a covering, I need a cloak. What I need I ought to make, I need a cloak, I ought to make a cloak. And the conclusion I ought to make a cloak is an action. The action results from the beginning of the train of thought. If there is to be a cloak, such and such a thing is necessary, if this thing then something else; and one immediately acts accordingly' (701 a18–23). In the last part of this example the analytic regress from the end, the existence of a cloak, to the means, something I can do here and now, recalls the account of deliberation in *EN* III. 3 (1112 b15–20). There is no suggestion that this phase of practical thinking can or should be expressed in the form of a series of syllogisms. One further instance of action, this time described as impulsive (*mē logisamenoi*), is given: 'my appetite says I must drink; this is drink, says sensation or imagination or thought, and one immediately drinks' (701 a32–3).

In the course of this enumeration of examples Aristotle makes the following remark: 'that the action is the conclusion is clear; but the premisses which lead to the doing of something are of two kinds, the good and the possible' (701 a23–5). I take this to mean that every piece of practical thinking, when set out as an inference, or in some cases a chain of inferences, contains at least one premiss of each of the kinds so named. There must be a premiss indicating a good to be achieved in a wide sense of 'good'. Men are moved to act by some form of desire,[1] and this fact is reflected in the presence of some evaluative or prescriptive word in the major premiss. But there must also be a premiss through which the desire is focused on the present situation, a premiss indicating what can be done here and now. This interpretation seems to fit both the general scheme of the practical syllogism and the particular examples given of practical inference. But Allan takes the sentence as supporting the view proposed by Grant, and criticized by Greenwood, that 'the practical syllogism may take either of two forms,

[1] Cf. *EN* VI. 2, 1139 a35.

according as what is expressed in the major premiss is a *rule* or an *end*' (p. 336). He implies that only a syllogism of the second kind contains a premiss or premisses of the 'possible' (pp. 330–1). But surely any minor premiss is of the possible. Moreover the items in Aristotle's mixed bag of examples in the *De Motu Animalium* do not fall clearly into the two supposed kinds. Allan takes 'everyone should walk' as the major premiss of a rule-type syllogism. But we walk to get somewhere or for the sake of health; in both cases we are taking steps to an end. The observation in the *De Motu Animalium* that there are two kinds of premisses does not imply that there are two kinds of syllogism. We have had no examples either of major premisses which express ends as opposed to rules to be followed in order to achieve ends or of major premisses which express rules which are not rules to be followed in order to achieve ends. A major premiss does indeed imply an end, as the word 'healthy' applied to a diet implies that health is an end. The premiss would actually mention the end if it were formulated as Greenwood proposed: 'the means to the end X ought to be done' (p. 50). I shall consider later what Greenwood has to say about the different ways in which the actions prescribed by a rule of this form may contribute, or be related, to an end.

A practical syllogism, as I said earlier, is the practical application of a rule in an actual situation. The only complication needed so far is that sometimes the rule to be applied falls under a wider rule from which it is inferred; e.g. the goodness of chicken as being light is inferred from the goodness of light food. What else have we learned from the evidence so far reviewed? First we have learned positively that, as Allan has convincingly argued, the centre of Aristotle's interest when he produces the doctrine is in the psychology, indeed the psychophysics, of action; in what happens in a man, in a besouled mindful body, when and immediately before he initiates change. This is Aristotle's concern when the doctrine appears in the *De Anima* and the *De Motu Animalium*; and in the *EN* the doctrine is elaborately deployed only in the psychological analysis of *akrasia* (weakness of will), a topic which concerns the physiologist (1147 b6–9). I agree then with Allan that the doctrine gives us a 'psychological account of

action in accordance with principles' (p. 325 n.). But it is not clear
to me why Allan should suggest that the syllogism is not even
part of a process of deliberating or discovering what to do
(pp. 325, 336–7). We have found passages in which Aristotle
connects the syllogism with deliberation (VI. 8, 1142 a20–3; 9,
1142 b21–6). There is no inconsistency, so far as I can see, in
holding both that the practical syllogism is *part* of Aristotle's
account of deliberation and, with Allan, that Aristotle intended
'that the theory shall stand or fall with its successful application
to particular problems of psychology' (p. 340). I agree that the
theory is not to be taken as the general form of all reasoning in
the sphere of action, the reasoning, for example, of the political
philosopher or the statesman; and not even as the form of all the
practical thinking of the private citizen when he seeks to decide
what to do. Much has been said about such reasoning in *EN* III:
about the weighing of pros and cons when a man has to decide
whether the price to be paid for some desired object is too high
(ch. 1) and about the working back from ends to means (ch. 3).
There was no mention in these discussions of practical syllogisms.
That the role of the practical syllogism may be humbler than has
been supposed is perhaps suggested also by the fact that the
examples given are uniformly pedestrian and unmomentous:
Guinness is good for a chap like me and here, good show, is a
Guinness; immediately the mouth waters and the hand moves.

Yet commentators commonly assert or assume that Aristotle
regards the practical syllogism as the proper form of all deliberation and practical reasoning. Burnet says that the analysis of the
Good for Man, 'though it is deliberative and not demonstrative,
will proceed through middle terms and can only be expressed
adequately in the form of a series of practical syllogisms' (p. xliii).
Joachim speaks of practical wisdom (*phronēsis*) as 'an established
power of reasoning or deliberating which expresses itself in syllogisms whose conclusions are . . . actions' (p. 208). This makes it
natural for him to say, since deliberation starts from the thought
of an end, that the major premiss 'defines the nature of the end or
of some constituent of the end' (p. 210). Ando takes 'the standard
of moral value' to be 'the highest major premiss' (p. 287), and

proposes to study 'the practical syllogism as the form of deliberation' (p. 274). One conclusion to which the study leads him is that 'the practical syllogism consists of the major premiss which orders one to purpose a value in general, and the minor premiss which recognizes the presence of a value in a particular case' (p. 278). But in Aristotle's scheme the minor premiss does not recognize a value; it merely states a fact. The practical syllogism has to be inflated in order to do the work expected by commentators, and its shape gets distorted in the process. Grant suggests as a form of the practical syllogism: such and such an end is desirable; this step will conduce to the end; taking of the step (i. 265). On this Aristotle's comment would have to be that, in the words of the *Prior Analytics*, 'the conclusion has not been drawn syllogistically (*oupō sullelogistai*); for the premisses are not in the shape required' (I. 32, 47 a30–1). Greenwood, resuming Grant's attempt to show how the syllogism covers deliberation, admits that 'X is the end' is not the form of any proposition 'fit to be the major premiss of a syllogism whose conclusion is a proposition that a particular action A ought to be done' (p. 50). He, therefore, rightly, as I think, abandons the idea that there are two different kinds of major premiss, and hence two different kinds of practical syllogism. His 'general formula' for the major is 'the means to the end X ought to be done', but he covers the retreat by remarking that this formula is, in some sense, 'equivalent' to 'X is the end'. These embarrassments, and the similar embarrassments of other scholars (e.g. Allan, p. 337), suggest that something has gone wrong.[1]

It is not difficult to say what has happened. It has been supposed, rightly or wrongly, that Aristotle has told us, in words which leave no room for doubt, that the form, or at least a form, of the major premiss in a practical syllogism is 'the end and what is best is such and such'. It is true that the form is not that of any of the examples which Aristotle gives of major premisses. Indeed no one has invented a syllogism with a major premiss of this form. These are difficulties; but they are difficulties, it is implied, created by Aristotle and not gratuitously by his commentators. Let us look

---

[1] Cf. above, Ch. XI, p. 229.

at the crucial sentence in its context. Aristotle is explaining, or attempting to explain, the difference between the cleverness (*deinotēs*) of a man who is good at finding means to (possibly bad) ends and the practical wisdom (*phronēsis*) of a man who can be trusted to make right choices. The latter, because he has ethical virtue as well as cleverness, aims at good ends. The Oxford Translation proceeds: 'And the eye of the soul acquires its formed state not without the aid of virtue, as has been said and is plain; for the syllogisms which deal with acts to be done (*sullogismoi tōn praktōn*) are things which involve a starting-point' (*archēn echontes eisin—archē* is here rendered 'major premiss' by some translators), 'viz. "since the end, i.e. what is best, is of such and such a nature", whatever it may be (let it for the sake of argument be what we please); and this is not evident except to the good man; for wickedness perverts us and causes us to be deceived about the starting-points (*archai*) of action. Therefore it is evident that it is impossible to be practically wise without being good' (*EN* vi. 12, 1144 a29–b1).

I do not wish to object to this translation, although I would not accept 'premiss' for *archē* and think that 'syllogisms' should perhaps be 'reasonings' or 'inferences'. The commentators say nothing about the two grammatical anomalies in the words which are taken to introduce the major premiss: the fact that the article is not repeated after *sullogismoi* and the participial construction *echontes eisin* (are in the position of having). I shall not consider other ways of taking the words or the possibility that there is corruption in the text since I cannot think of any alternative rendering which would make a difference to the doctrine. Moreover, on the grammatical points I have mentioned, I do not know of any investigation of Aristotle's practice.

When we are confronted by any difficult passage in Aristotle about practical wisdom (*phronēsis*) it is essential to remember that there are different kinds and levels of such wisdom (vi. 8, 1141 b23 ff.), and many different ends which a wise man (*phronimos*) may have in his sights. Here Aristotle is speaking not of his own wisdom as the writer of a political treatise, nor of the wisdom of the statesman, but of the insight displayed by any man of good

character. The end in view must then be one which the good man
has in view because he is good. A soldier, for example, knows that
courage is the supreme virtue in war. Consider the following
passage on courage in III. 7. 'Now the end of every activity is
conformity to the corresponding state of character. This is true,
therefore, of the brave man as well as of others. But courage is
noble (*kalon*). Therefore the end also is noble; for each thing is
defined by its end. Therefore it is for a noble end that the brave
man endures and acts as courage directs.'[1] It is with this kind of
passage in mind that we must read the passage before us. The end
in view is not the ultimate human good but the kind of end a
soldier has in view when he sets himself to behave well in a battle
or to inflict as much damage on the enemy as possible. He will
observe a rule forbidding retreat except under orders. It is not
for him to reason why, to locate the activities of soldiers in the
political pattern of human welfare. Ethical virtue does not entail
the presence of practical wisdom in its architectonic form. Hence
the idea that the definition of happiness is an ultimate major
premiss cannot be what Aristotle has in mind or is suggesting in
this passage. We must now consider whether the passage implies
that there is *any* end the definition of which is a major premiss.
The question is whether Aristotle here offers a new formula for
the major premiss. It is not at present the question what different
kinds of rule or principle he might wish to treat as covered by the
formula of the *De Anima* (434 a16–21).

The text of our passage suggests at least the three following
questions. (1) Should *sullogismoi* be translated 'syllogisms' or
'processes of reasoning'? (2) Is the *archē*, literally 'starting-point',
to be understood as a major premiss? (3) If it is to be understood
as a major premiss, is the form stated completely as 'the end and
what is best is such and such' or incompletely as 'since the end and
what is best is such and such . . .'? I suggest that an affirmative
answer cannot be given with certainty to *any* of these three questions, and that, unless an affirmative answer is given to *all* of them,
the superstructure which has been erected on this passage col-
lapses. (1) I have referred earlier to the evidence for a wider use of

---

[1] 1115 b20–4, Oxford Translation.

'syllogize' and 'syllogism' in Aristotle, but I do not wish to suggest as more than a possibility that we have here a case of the wider use. It seems to me probable that the *sullogismoi* here are syllogisms, that Aristotle here comes as near as he ever comes to making 'practical syllogism' a technical term. (2) The major premiss of a syllogism can be referred to as its beginning or principle (*archē*), as in *Posterior Analytics* I. 25, 86 b30–1. But we have learned in III. 3 (1112 b15 ff.) that the thought of the end is the starting-point of deliberation.[1] To say that we start from the end is not equivalent to saying that a description of the end is a major premiss even if, having viewed our end, our first step is to formulate a major premiss. For, if our major premiss were not a description of the end but a statement of conditions of its attainment, it could still be said that we started from a conception of the end. (3) But, even if the *archē* is a major premiss and not just the starting-point from which we go on to formulate a major premiss, it is not necessary, perhaps not easy, to take the words 'since the end and what is best is such and such . . .' as the complete formulation of the major premiss. The complete formulation might be 'since the end is such and such a man should act in such and such ways', the schema with which we are familiar in the *EN* and the *De Anima* (434 a16–21). My argument here brings me close to Greenwood's 'general formula' for the major premiss, 'the means to the end X ought to be done' (p. 50): the major premiss mentions an end but is not a definition or description of an end.

It should not surprise us that the sentence which we have been considering has been treated, however mistakenly, as a central and decisive passage for the interpretation of the doctrine of the practical syllogism. The elaboration of the theory of the syllogism in the *Prior Analytics* was Aristotle's major and pioneering contribution to logic; and in the *Posterior Analytics* the demonstrative syllogism in the first figure, leading to a universal conclusion through a middle term which expresses a cause or reason, is represented as the paradigm of scientific understanding. In ethical and political science the definition of happiness, the supreme human good, formulates the goal of all rational endeavour and is

---

[1] Cf. VII. 8, 1151 a15–19; *EE B* 11, 1227 b28–32.

therefore, in a sense, the supreme practical premiss. How could a statement which appears to combine the syllogism with the supreme good fail to seem of crucial importance? So it has been regarded; and, so far as seemed necessary, the other evidence has been pushed around in order to accommodate this exciting and, as was supposed, unambiguous utterance. But, if I am right, there is no basis in this passage for changing in any way the account of the practical syllogism to which the other evidence points. We can save ourselves from many of the embarrassments which have troubled commentators by keeping closely, in what we say about the practical syllogism, to what Aristotle himself has said.

The purpose of this note has been a strictly limited one: to make clear how much, and how little, is contained in Aristotle's explicit doctrine of the practical syllogism. To syllogize in action is to apply a rule of the form 'such and such a man should act in such and such ways' with a view to realizing an end and ultimately, no doubt, the supreme end, happiness. But I am not implying that all the rules which Aristotle might admit as major premisses are in fact rules which prescribe means to ends. I am not implying that Aristotle does not stretch the concept of *telos* (end) and *ta pros to telos* (means, the things that conduce or contribute to the end) more widely at least than 'end' and 'means' can properly be stretched. While it may be true that, if and only if a soldier stands firm in battle will he achieve his desire to be brave, it would be strange to say that standing firm in a battle was a means to being brave or to being happy. The appropriate embracing concept is, perhaps, price rather than means: the principle that, in an imperfect world, a man must take the rough with the smooth, make the best shoes he can with the available leather (1. 10, 1101 a2). The happy philosopher pays one price, perhaps poverty and austerity. The happy warrior pays another, the possibility of untimely death. There may be many different sorts of major premiss which could be covered by the formula: 'if', or 'if but only if a man so acts, will happiness be achieved'. The doctrine of the practical syllogism, as Greenwood rightly sees, makes no explicit provision for such variety. But Greenwood suggests a way in which Aristotle, if he had been more explicit or had thought more clearly, might have accommodated two radically different sorts of major premisses in practical syllogisms. He invents a distinction between 'external' and 'component' means, and the distinction has been welcomed by other commentators. I shall conclude this note by making some brief comments on this suggestion of Greenwood.

'A thing may be a means to an end in either of two senses, as component part of it, or as wholly external to it. To take a trivial example, fire and basin and cloth are means to a pudding in the latter sense, suet and flour and currants in the former' (pp. 46-7). Greenwood goes on to give examples more relevant to the practical syllogism. Contemplating beautiful pictures would be a component means to happiness, taking a bus to the picture gallery an external means (p. 47). Later Greenwood gives another example on the same lines: the activity of following a particular geometrical demonstration would be a component means to the happiness of the contemplative life (p. 54). We can complete the example by suggesting that taking exercise to maintain health would be an external means. Greenwood thinks that these two notions of means are 'confusedly taken into account' in Aristotle's description of practical thinking (p. 48). Hence Aristotle does not give us the form of major premiss appropriate to component means. His language and his examples usually suggest external means. Greenwood, therefore, fills the gap by stating the form of 'the practical syllogism that is suitable to reasoning about component means' (p. 54): 'the end is an aggregate of actions of the class A (i.e. every action of the class A is a component means to the end, and therefore ought to be done), but A is an action of the class A, therefore A ought to be done'. Greenwood strangely suggests as a major premiss of component means the premiss mentioned in vII. 3 which forbids the consumption of sweet but 'unwholesome' things (1147 a31-2). Here the word 'unwholesome', used by Greenwood, surely implies that the means are external. An aggregate of actions of refraining from eating or drinking things that are not good for you would be rather a dim sort of end. We now have before us Greenwood's notion of 'component means': if a man has lived a happy life, the activity filling any stretch of time within it during which the man was happy was a component means to his happiness.

The distinction between external and component means is offered, as we have seen, not as an interpretation, but rather as a needed amplification and correction, of what Aristotle says. Amplification is needed, and Greenwood's suggestion may be a part of what is needed. It is true that, as we use 'means', a means can hardly be a component. Enjoying the soup is not a means to enjoying the whole dinner. But the expression in Greek commonly translated 'means' (*ta pros to telos*) is vaguer: things that contribute or have a tendency to the end. No doubt the enjoyment of the soup contributes to the enjoyment of the dinner, although not simply, if the meal is an aesthetic whole, as a member of an aggregate of enjoyments. But not all the rules which might be major premisses of practical syllogisms would fall into one or other of the two classes, those prescribing external means and those prescribing components. When Aristotle compares the happiness of the life of contemplation with the happiness of life in accordance with practical virtue (x. 7, 8, 1178 a7–9), we need not suppose him to be thinking of the virtuous life as a series of attractive and enjoyable virtuous or heroic performances. The soldier thinks that it would be a happier fate to die than to live on as a man who has failed to keep to the rules and to do what he was trained to do, but he does not have to claim that he was happy while the battle was being fought. Aristotle's concept of *eudaimonia* takes account of this when he says that happiness must be 'in a complete life' (i. 7, 1098 a18); for he does not mean this in a sense which would imply that the worst thing that can happen to a man is to fail to survive to old age. It is clear, then, that, if Aristotle had been asked whether fighting in a battle was an external or a component means to happiness, he would have had to find some third answer. We need not understand Greenwood as denying this. He does not claim that the division of conditions of happiness into external means and component parts is exhaustive. Indeed he shows a tendency to stretch the notion of 'component means' when he suggests (p. 47) that the only place where Aristotle himself 'appears to feel' the distinction between the two kinds of means is the passage in VI. 12 where, according to Greenwood's interpretation of the passage, he speaks of the *virtues* of practical and theoretical wisdom as being, like health, 'component means' to happiness (1144 a3–6).[1] Obviously the sense in which an intellectual or an ethical virtue, or the state of being healthy, is a component of happiness is totally different from the sense in which some particular exercise or activation of a virtue, some actual performance or episode, is a component of happiness.

[1] Cf. *Rhetoric* I. 5, 1360 b19–26.

XIII

MORAL WEAKNESS

In Book VII Aristotle, making a fresh start (1145 a15ff.), distinguishes three kinds of 'moral states to be avoided': vice, incontinence (*akrasia*), and brutishness (*thēriotēs*). The opposed good states are virtue, continence (*enkrateia*), and superhuman virtue. The difference between continence and the virtue of temperance, and the difference between incontinence and the vice of the self-indulgent man, are stated as follows in chapter 9:

> both the continent man and the temperate man are such as to do nothing contrary to the rule for the sake of the bodily pleasures, but the former has and the latter has not bad appetites, and the latter is such as not to feel pleasure contrary to the rule, while the former is such as to feel pleasure but not to be led by it. And the incontinent and the self-indulgent man are also like one another; they are different, but both pursue bodily pleasures—the latter, however, also thinking that he ought to do so, while the former does not think this (*ho men kai oiomenos dein ho d' ouk oiomenos*). (1151 b34–1152 a6.)

The virtuous man, then, is described as having no bad desires; he feels no desires or emotions either more or less than he should. It is not easy to see what additional moral stature could make a man more than virtuous, more than a man. Has not Aristotle said that 'with regard to what is best' virtue itself is an extreme (1107 a6–8)? It is not surprising that Aristotle has nothing to tell us about heroic virtue. Its opposite, brutishness or bestiality, may be either inborn or a consequence of disease. 'The man who is by nature apt to fear everything, even the squeak of a mouse, is cowardly with a brutish cowardice, while the man who feared a weasel did so in consequence of disease' (1149 a7–9). Corresponding to the brutish and morbid forms of vice there are also brutish and morbid forms of incontinence: there are people who yield to such desires or impulses knowing them to be wrong (1149 a16–20).

At the beginning of chapter 3 Aristotle says that there are two main topics to be considered: a problem or problems concerning the analysis of incontinence, and a problem or problems concerning its sphere. Aristotle's main concern is with the problem of analysis, 'whether incontinent people act knowingly or not, and in what sense knowingly' (*poteron eidotes ē ou kai pōs eidotes*) (1146 b8–9). Aristotle discusses the problem of analysis as if it were primarily a question about the conduct of men who, although knowing better, indulge bodily desires. But, in asking and answering his question about the sphere of incontinence, he recognizes implicitly that the problem has a wider scope. He asks 'with what sorts of object the incontinent and the continent man may be said to be concerned (i.e. whether with any and every pleasure and pain or with certain determinate kinds), and whether the continent man (*enkratēs*) and the man of endurance (*karterikos*) are the same or different' (1146 b9–13). To take the second point first, Aristotle elucidates the difference between continence and endurance at the beginning of chapter 7: the continent man overcomes, the incontinent fails to overcome, the temptations of pleasure; the man of endurance holds out, the soft man (*malakos*) fails to hold out, against pain (1150 a13–15). It seems plain that these are different types, and that Aristotle thinks so: a hardy man might be incontinent, a continent man might be soft. The question about the sphere of incontinence is reformulated by Aristotle at the beginning of chapter 4: 'whether there is anyone who is incontinent without qualification (*haplōs*), or all men who are incontinent are so in a particular sense (*kata meros*), and if there is, with what sort of objects he is concerned' (1147 b22–1). Aristotle's answer to this question is based on the following classification of pleasures: (1) the bodily pleasures, those connected with food and sex, which are 'necessary' (*anankaia*)—these are the pleasures with which temperance (*sōphrosunē*) and intemperance (*akolasia*) are by definition concerned (b23–8); (2) pleasures which are not necessary but 'are worthy of choice in themselves but admit of excess', e.g. 'victory, honour, wealth, and good and pleasant things of this sort' (b29–31); (3) to these two classes of pleasures Aristotle adds a third in chapter 5, bestial and morbid pleasures which are not naturally felt as pleasant but can be so felt as a consequence of mutilation, bad habits, or natures originally bad (1148 b17 ff.). Aristotle's answer to his question is that unqualified incontinence is concerned with pleasures of the first class. This conclusion is stated at the end of chapter 5: 'that continence and incontinence, then, are concerned only with the same objects as self-indulgence and temperance and that what is concerned with other objects is a type distinct from incontinence, and called incontinence by a metaphor and not simply, is plain' (1149 a21–4). Aristotle goes on to argue in chapter 6 that 'incontinence in respect of anger (*thumos*) is less disgraceful than that in respect of the appetites'. In the final section (§ 7) of chapter 6 he maintains that 'brutishness is a lesser evil than vice, although it is more terrifying; for it is not that the better part has been perverted . . . they *have* no better part'. 'A bad man will do ten thousand times as much evil as a brute' (1150 a7–8).

Aristotle's treatment of the scope of incontinence is liable to strike us as perverse. He seems to be trying, somewhat arbitrarily, to narrow the scope of the term, restricting the problem as if it concerned only carnal appetites and pleasures. Surely what he ought to insist on is that the concept has application to any impulse or desire or emotion which is liable, by inappropriateness or again by its excess or defect, to conflict with a man's understanding of what is right and good. There are two points to be made in answer to this criticism. The first is that Aristotle's restriction of the term is not arbitrary but an expression of his conviction that the apparent facts should be handled with care and delicacy. In chapter 1 he makes the following important statement on method: 'We must, as in all other cases, set the observed facts [*ta phainomena*—I quote the Oxford Translation] before us and, after first discussing the difficulties, go on to prove, if possible, the truth of all the common opinions about these affections of the mind, or, failing this, of the greater number and the most authoritative; for if we both refute the objections and leave the common opinions undisturbed, we shall have proved the case sufficiently' (1145 b2–7). Among the 'phenomena' to be considered is the fact that we are prepared to apply the term *akrasia*

simply to those who are induced by carnal desires to stray from
their chosen paths, to apply it only in a qualified sense, by a conscious extension or metaphor, to those led astray by desires of
other kinds. We add the qualification 'in respect of this or that'
(*kata prosthesin*), e.g. anger (1148 a10). Somewhat similarly there
is a use in English of 'immoral' in which the word refers exclusively
to sexual irregularity. Such facts may or may not be significant,
and may be significant in different degrees. But, on Aristotle's
principles, we should assume that they are significant unless they
are shown not to be. The second point to make is that Aristotle
does not say, or suggest, that the problems raised by incontinent
behaviour are confined to *akrasia* in its proper or unqualified sense.
In particular, the questions whether, and in what sense, the incontinent man acts against 'knowledge' may be asked about all
kinds of *akrasia*, even including the *akrasia* which is a fault
(*hamartia*) rather than a vice (*kakia*) (1148 a3). Presumably the
answer which is good for *akrasia* in its unqualified sense will be
good also, *mutatis mutandis*, for other varieties.

But Aristotle's treatment of unqualified *akrasia* has incurred a
further criticism to which there is, perhaps, no satisfactory answer.
It is said that he presents too crude and simple a view of the
temptations which spring from bodily appetites. He insists on their
power to knock a man off his balance, to drive him out of his right
mind. The incontinent man is like one who is asleep or mad or
drunk (1147 a17–18). But, in the life of a being capable of complex
social and intellectual enjoyments, these appetites rarely operate
alone; the threat to virtue comes not so much from their intensity
as from their fusion with more subtle satisfactions. I quote from
T. H. Green:[1]

The conflict of the moral life would be a much simpler affair than it
is if it were mainly fought over those bodily pleasures in dealing with
which, according to Aristotle, the qualities of continence and incontinence are exhibited. The most formidable forces which right reason
has to subdue or render contributory to some 'true good' of man are
passions of which reason is in a certain sense itself the parent. They are
passions which the animals know not, because they are excited by the

---

[1] *Prolegomena to Ethics*, § 126.

conditions of distinctively human society. They relate to objects which only the intercourse of self-conscious agents can bring into existence. This is often true of passions which on first thoughts we might be inclined to reckon merely animal appetites. The drunkard probably drinks, as a rule, not for the pleasure of drinking, but to drown pains or win pleasures—pains, for instance, of self-reproach, pleasures of a quickened fancy or of a sense of good fellowship—of which only the thinking man is capable.

I turn now to Aristotle's central problem (*aporia*) about incontinence. The problem is formulated at the beginning of chapter 2. The first part of this chapter (§§ 1–5) contains a preliminary discussion of the question, and some answers to it are rejected as inadequate. The problem is reformulated at the beginning of chapter 3, and what the chapter contains is prima facie an exposition by Aristotle, in a series of stages, of his own solution. But we must not assume that this is what the chapter does contain. For Cook Wilson, whose opinion has much weight, maintained that the chapter as it stands is not a continuous discourse but a conflation of at least two similar versions.[1] Moreover Cook Wilson's thesis, as he stated it in 1879, was that neither component of the chapter can have been written by Aristotle, if Aristotle is the author of the rest of *EN* VII and of the *EE*. His reason for holding this view was that, whereas Aristotle clearly believed that men do act in ways which they know at the time of acting to be wrong, the solution reached in chapter 3 asserts or implies that Socrates was right when he said that this could not happen. In the 1912 postscript Cook Wilson adhered to the view that two parallel versions are conflated in *EN* VII. 3, but was doubtful about the adequacy of his reasons for having denied that Aristotle wrote them. He was led to this change of view by reflection on modern writings of known authorship. This convinced him 'that the possibilities of incoherence are not merely greater than what I may have thought when I wrote this study of *EN* VII, but far beyond what is usually admitted in contemporary criticism' (pp. 88, 89). But he still thought that the doctrine of the

---

[1] *On the structure of the seventh book of the Nicomachean Ethics, chapters. I–X* (1879); reissued in 1912 with a postscript on the parallel versions.

chapter should never have been held by Aristotle and that it is inconsistent with 'everything else relevant' in his writings. 'It is a question of degree; and while, in face of the facts I have observed, I would not say the thing is impossible, I do not find it easy to credit Aristotle with so grave a lapse as this' (p. 90). Cook Wilson is not alone in finding incoherence in Aristotle's treatment, as it has come down to us, of this subject. Ross complains that Aristotle's 'formal theory' fails to recognize the fact, of which he elsewhere shows himself to be aware, that 'incontinence is due not to failure of knowledge, but to weakness of will'.[1] It is clear that there is a formidable case for this criticism. I think that there is some incoherence, as well as much that is illuminating and suggestive, in Aristotle's discussion. But the difficulty has been exacerbated, mis-stated if not over-stated, as the result of a failure to notice the precise terms in which the problem is formulated by Aristotle. The misunderstanding to which I refer has arisen in fact as a consequence of a mistranslation of the first sentence of chapter 2 (1145 b21-2) and a translation which is at least highly questionable of the fourth sentence of the chapter (1145 b27-9). Our first task, then, is to look closely at Aristotle's formulation of the problem.

The problem is set, as Aristotle implies in the passage on method already quoted (1145 b2-7), by the contradictory opposition of two strongly supported opinions (endoxa): on the one hand, the universally held view that men do in fact sometimes perform actions which they know to be wrong and do not perform actions which they know to be required; on the other hand the denial, attributed to Socrates, that this could happen. 'For Socrates was entirely opposed to the view in question, holding that there is no such thing as incontinence; no one, he said, when he judges acts against what he judges best—people act so only by reason of ignorance' (1145 b25-7). The view which Socrates rejected is implicit in the meaning of akrasia as ordinarily understood. 'The incontinent man, knowing that what he does is bad, does it as a result of passion (dia pathos), while the continent man, knowing that his appetites are bad, refuses on account of his

---

[1] *Aristotle*, p. 244.

rational principle (*dia ton logon*) to follow them' (1145 b12–14). Similar descriptions of the phenomenon, none of them conveying any doubt about their own accuracy, are given by Aristotle in other passages in the *EN*[1] and in the *De Anima*.[2] Such passages made it seem obvious to Cook Wilson and Ross that Aristotle was not himself in any doubt about the occurrence of an 'active struggle' (Cook Wilson) between reason and desire in which reason might be the loser. The passage which supports this most strongly is, perhaps, the one in *EN* VII. 7 in which Aristotle distinguishes two kinds of incontinence (1150 b19–28).

Of incontinence one kind is impetuosity (*propeteia*), another weakness (*astheneia*). For some men after deliberating fail, owing to their emotion, to stand by the conclusions of their deliberation, others because they have not deliberated are led by their emotion; since some men (just as people who first tickle others are not tickled themselves), if they have first perceived and seen what is coming and have first roused themselves and their calculative faculty, are not defeated by their emotion, whether it be pleasant or painful. (1150 b19–25.)

It seems clear that, if there are facts which these sentences describe with complete accuracy, then Socrates was wrong and the assumptions or convictions which he rejected are correct.

But does not Aristotle *say* that Socrates was wrong, and obviously wrong? The words in the text which immediately follow the statement, quoted above, of the Socratic view are translated as follows by Ross: 'Now this view plainly contradicts the observed facts . . .' (*amphisbētei tois phainomenois enargōs*) (1145 b27–8). Most of the commentators offer a similar rendering of 'phenomena' or else straddle, as the Greek term can, between observed facts and accepted opinions. Grant quotes the ancient paraphrast (*tois phanerois*), translates 'manifestly at variance with experience', but sees also an allusion to the phenomena, equated with opinions, in 1145 b3. Stewart has 'plainly at variance with experience' in his summary and 'conflicts with *ta endoxa*' in his commentary. Joachim has 'the facts are plain' and Gauthier–Jolif 'données de l'expérience'. The question has helpfully been brought to a head

[1] 1102 b14–25, 1166 b6–10.   [2] 433 a1–3, 433 b5–8, 434 a12–15.

in an article by G. E. L. Owen.[1] He points out that, while there are passages in which *phainomena* seems to mean 'facts' or 'empirical observations',[2] it can hardly have this meaning in 1145 b3. Moreover Ross's rendering in 1145 b28 ('the observed facts') makes the whole sentence inconsequent. For the sentence continues: '. . . and we must inquire about what happens to such a man; if he acts by reason of ignorance, what is the manner of his ignorance?' (1145 b28–9). But, if it is false that we act 'by reason of ignorance', the question what kind of ignorance it is cannot arise. Yet Aristotle is apparently here willing to consider the possibility that conduct of the kind which would conventionally be described as sinning against knowledge might be due to some kind of ignorance. Finally the solution actually offered in chapter 3 involves attributing to the incontinent man ignorance of a kind, although not ignorance of moral principles (1147 b6–17). Owen draws the following conclusion from his examination of the passage (1145 b27–9): 'So Socrates' claim conflicts not with the facts but with what would commonly be said on the subject, and Aristotle does not undertake to save everything that is commonly said' (p. 86).

In order to make good Owen's interpretation of the passage, with which I agree, it is not, I think, *necessary* to reject Ross's translation of 'phenomena' in 1145 b28 as 'observed facts'. For there are different 'facts' with which the view of Socrates might be held to conflict. Some would claim to refute the view by saying that in fact men do wrong actions in full awareness that they are wrong. But a less drastic criticism of the view might be that, as stated by Socrates or one of his followers, the view conflicted with the fact that there are cases or stretches of human conduct which it is natural to describe, even if mistakenly, as acting wrongly against knowledge and which in fact are so described. It is convenient to use the expression 'ostensible incontinence' as an abbreviation of what I have just said. The Socratic doctrine is a direct denial that incontinence occurs . . . *hōs ouk ousēs akrasias* (1145 b25–6). But, as stated, it is inconsistent even with ostensible incontinence. In order to make it consistent it would be necessary

---

[1] *Tithenai ta phainomena*, in *Aristote et les Problèmes de Méthode.*
[2] e.g. *An. Pr.* I. 30, 46 a17–21: see Bonitz, *Index*, 809 a34.

to answer the question what manner of ignorance is involved, and this would be an amending qualification of the doctrine as first stated. I must make it clear that what I am considering at present is Aristotle's *formulation* of the problem concerning incontinence. I am not saying anything on the question whether Aristotle believes, or says that he believes, that all incontinence is merely ostensible and not actually, in a strict sense, what it seems or purports to be. Our present question is about Aristotle's question not about his answer.

We are now in a position to see why it is necessary to reject a widely accepted translation and interpretation of Aristotle's formulation of his problem in the first sentence of chapter 2, *pōs hupolambanōn orthōs akrateuetai tis*. I take this to mean that there is a problem about the sense in which the man who acts incontinently has 'right understanding'. I agree with the rendering by D. P. Chase in the Everyman Translation: 'Now a man may raise a question as to the nature of the right conception in violation of which a man fails of self-control.' F. H. Peters (1884) gives a similar translation. That *pōs* is to be taken with *hupolambanōn orthōs* is shown by the context. For Aristotle proceeds to consider whether the understanding is in the form of knowledge (*epistēmē*), opinion (*doxa*), or prudence (*phronēsis*); three possible varieties of understanding (*hupolēpsis*) according to the De Anima (Γ 3, 427 b24–6). The interpretation is confirmed by the fact that, at the beginning of chapter 3, the problem is reformulated as 'whether incontinent people act knowingly or not, and in what sense knowingly' (1146 b8–9). In chapter 2 also, as we have seen, Aristotle is prepared to *consider* the possibility that incontinence is only ostensible, that the incontinent man understands that what he is doing is wrong only in some more or less Pickwickian sense of 'understands'. And yet both Cook Wilson and Ross, as well as other scholars, understand the first sentence of chapter 2 in a way which makes Aristotle imply, inconsistently with what he goes on to say, that incontinence is certainly real and not merely ostensible. According to Cook Wilson, the question at issue is 'How is it that a man knowing the right can do the wrong?'[1] Ross translates:

[1] *Aristotelian Studies*, pp. 48–9.

'Now we may ask how a man who judges rightly can behave incontinently.' According to this formulation, there is no puzzle as to whether, or in what sense, the incontinent man knows what is right. The only puzzle is as to how, having this knowledge, he can go wrong. As we have seen, both Cook Wilson and Ross are perplexed by the fact that in chapter 3 Aristotle seems to end by defending a solution which partially vindicates the view of Socrates: 'the position that Socrates sought to establish actually seems to result' (1147 b14–15). I suggest that a factor in this perplexity is their misunderstanding of Aristotle's formulation of the problem at the beginning of chapter 2. I do not, of course, mean that there is no other evidence suggesting that Aristotle agreed with the popular view, rejected by Socrates, that the incontinent man knows very well that what he is doing is wrong. Indeed we have already seen that there is such evidence, although we have kept open the question whether it is decisive.

Cook Wilson and Ross are not alone in their failure to notice that Aristotle's question, at the beginning of chapter 2, is not how a man can go wrong when he understands correctly what is right but in what sense such a man *does* have correct understanding. The same mistake is made by the other commentators whom I have consulted, including J. J. Walsh. His rendering is 'How can a man who judges rightly act unrestrainedly?'[1] Similarly, in Gauthier–Jolif, we find: 'comment peut-on agir avec incontinence quand on juge correctement?' The same translation is followed, but not apparently after consideration of the alternative, by Grant, Joachim, Rackham, Dirlmeier. Burnet states no view. Stewart offers both views: 'How can a man have a right conception and yet act incontinently against it?' (ii. 125) and 'What is meant by the *orthē hupolēpsis* of the *akratēs*?' J. R. Bambrough, in his article 'Socratic Paradox' follows the prevailing view: 'There is a difficulty about how a man who has a right apprehension can fail in self-control.'[2] But, in spite of this perverse consensus, I think that a careful reading, with the alternative translations in mind, of the sentence in its context leaves no doubt about what it means.

[1] *Aristotle's Conception of Moral Weakness*, pp. 85, 97.
[2] *Philosophical Quarterly* (1960), p. 294.

I propose to take it as certain that Aristotle does not, from the start, so formulate the question as to beg it against Socrates.

It seemed evident to Cook Wilson, and has seemed evident to many philosophers as well as to commentators on Aristotle, that the Socratic view 'plainly contradicts the observed facts'. To the question how these facts are known the answer would be that we find them when we look into ourselves: we can observe in ourselves the 'active struggle' between our knowledge of principles and our desires; we can catch ourselves in the act of following the worse when we see the better course. Now this contention is certainly plausible, and perhaps in the end its correctness can be vindicated and accepted with confidence. In the end but not at the beginning. The victory is too easy; too easy certainly to have satisfied Aristotle, or to satisfy any contemporary philosopher. Before we go on to try to follow Aristotle's discussion in detail it may be helpful to take a quick look at some considerations which would naturally incline Aristotle to shrink from flatly contradicting the Socratic doctrine, and to take seriously the question in what sense the incontinent man knows, or is convinced, when he acts or refrains from acting, that he is wrong.

Knowledge or judgement about what it is right and wrong to do differs from knowledge or judgement on matters of historical or scientific fact in ways which can tempt plain men, as well as philosophers, to say that a man cannot really know, cannot sincerely judge, that an action is right and not do it, or that it is wrong and do it. The man who, while professing principles of moderation, drinks or smokes too much does not *know* how to behave. The very fact that he goes wrong betrays lack of *sincerity* in his conviction of right. Is it then *logically* impossible that a man who knows how to behave should misbehave? If a man who is doing wrong says that he is doing wrong, is he insincere by the *definition* of sincerity? R. M. Hare, in *The Language of Morals*, propounds stipulative definitions which would make it 'analytic to say that everyone always does what he thinks he ought to (in the evaluative sense)' (p. 169). For he proposes 'to say that the test whether someone is using the judgement "I ought to do X" as a value-judgement or not is "Does he or does he not recognize that, if he assents to the judgement, he must also assent to the command 'Let me do X'?"' (pp. 168–9). And Hare has said earlier that it is logically impossible to assent to a command and at the same time to disobey it: sincerely assenting involves doing something (p. 20). We cannot, indeed, as Hare would agree, make the Socratic paradox more acceptable *merely* by passing linguistic legislation, merely by choosing to define the 'sincerity' of belief in terms of practical conformity and thus making it impossible to *say* that the paradox is false. But the point to notice here is that there is something about 'value-judgements', their 'prescriptive' character, which makes it tempting to represent the contradictory of the Socratic view as not false, but absurd.

Does Aristotle show any inclination to yield to such a temptation? Plainly yes, in so far as he defines wisdom concerning practice as wisdom which is practical. If there is such a thing as acting contrary to our better judgement, it would be natural to suppose that the judgement involved was the faculty, *phronēsis*, of knowing right from wrong in matters of conduct. Yet in chapter 2 this supposition is dismissed as (logically) absurd.

Is it then *phronēsis* whose resistance is mastered? That is the strongest of all states. But this is absurd (*atopon*); the same man will be at once practically wise and incontinent, but no one would say that it is the part of a practically wise man to do willingly the basest acts. Besides it has been shown before that the man of practical wisdom is one who will act (1140 b4–6, 1141 b21); for he is a man concerned with individual facts (1141 b16, 1142 a24) and who has the other virtues (1144 b30–1145 a2, 1146 a4–9).

If *phronēsis* is essentially practical, it is logically impossible for a wise man to be incontinent. The doctrine is difficult, but discussion of the difficulties is proper to a commentary on Book VI rather than Book VII. But, when we come to chapter 3 of Book VII, we shall have to consider a striking, if perhaps cryptic and unacceptable, expression of the doctrine in the passage where Aristotle seems to say that what in practical thinking corresponds to a conclusion in theoretical thinking is an action (1147 a26–8).[1]

[1] Cf. *De Motu Animalium* 701 a12 . . . *ek tōn duo protaseōn sumperasma ginetai hē praxis.*

If so, then it would again be 'absurd' to suggest that we could act against a conclusion of our practical thinking.

It is suggested, then, that there is a general difficulty about holding that a practical principle can be understood and accepted without being put into practice. The general difficulty would naturally take different forms in relation to different systems of moral principles. For Aristotle the supreme principle is that a man should seek his natural end, the highest form of happiness (*eudaimonia*) of which he is capable. In its application to this principle the Socratic doctrine would be that, if a man truly understands, or judges rationally, that some course of action will be for his happiness, he will inevitably take it; if he does not, this can be due only to lack of understanding, to ignorance. It may occur to him that some other action will bring him immediate, or at least earlier, gratification or enjoyment. But *ex hypothesi* he is convinced that, if he lets this go, he will secure something better. It may occur to him that the immediate enjoyment is a bird in the hand; his calculation concerning his own future welfare may go wrong; he may not survive to enjoy the fruits of his own righteousness or prudence. But, again *ex hypothesi*, in making his original assessment of what it is best for him to do, due account has been taken of these considerations. How then can he go wrong, unless something happens which blinds, or at least dims, his moral vision?

This line of thought can be formulated in terms of Aristotle's account of the thought which leads to action. Aristotle has tried to show, in his treatment of practical wisdom in Book VI, that there is inevitably a close connection between correctness of understanding in practical matters and rightness of desire. We needs must love the highest when we see it. The man of practical wisdom has an understanding of the end which he wishes to achieve as well as the ability to make plans for achieving it (VI. 9, 1142 b31–3). There is a parallel between practical wisdom and theoretical wisdom, the excellences of the two intelligent parts (*noētika moria*) of the soul (2, 1139 b12–13). It is proper to the theorist not only to deduce conclusions from premisses supplied to him but also to grasp intuitively the first principles from which, in the theoretical sciences, deduction starts (7, 1141 a17–20). In the practical science of politics (8, 1141 b23–33) the definition of the end corresponds to the first principles in the theoretical sciences (12, 1144 a31–6).[1] The end envisaged by the wise man is the object of wish (boulēsis, III. 5, 1113 b3–4), a species of desire (orexis), and moves to action because, in being understood, it is also desired.[2] If we are not good enough to desire it, we shall not be intelligent enough to grasp it. 'For wickedness perverts us and causes us to be deceived about the starting-points of action. Therefore it is evident it is impossible to be practically wise without being good' (12, 1144 a34–b1). On the basis of these conclusions Aristotle thinks, as we have seen, that he can refute in six lines the suggestion that a man could act incontinently if he had understood what he was doing in the sense in which the man of practical wisdom understands (VII. 2, 1146 a4–9).

We must now follow the course of the discussion in chapters 2 and 3 of Book VII. James J. Walsh, who has written a book of two hundred pages on Aristotle's analysis of akrasia,[3] draws 'a distinction between narrowly contextual and broadly integrative interpretations, according to whether or not the analysis should be taken as a whole and related to wider issues in Aristotle's philosophy' (p. 118). He adopts himself the integrative method, but not in such a way as to shirk the detailed interpretation of the text. Indeed, as he puts it in his Introduction, the whole book 'amounts to the unravelling of the complexities of one small passage in the Nicomachean Ethics: Chapter 3 of Book VII' (p. 1). The conclusion, as he formulates it, of Walsh's study is 'that Aristotle supports the Socratic position', and the purpose of his book is 'to prove this case in a thorough way' (p. 2). The arguments deployed in the preceding pages are not to be understood as offered in support of this conclusion. What I have so far tried to show, on the basis of considerations of the kind which Walsh calls 'integrative', is that it would be a mistake to start an examination of Aristotle's treatment of the subject with the assumption that he sets out primarily to refute the Socratic denial of the

[1] Cf. VII. 8, 1151 a15–19. [2] De Anima 10, 433 b11–12.
[3] See Bibliographical Note, p. 292.

reality of *akrasia*. Aristotle, on the contrary, is anxious to open the proceedings in a strictly neutral way, and some eminent scholars, especially Cook Wilson, have failed to see this. It would be surprising, in view of the conflicts of opinion noted by Walsh on the interpretation of Aristotle's doctrine, if a 'contextual interpretation' of chapter 3 could demonstrate that the outcome of Aristotle's discussion is decisively either for or against the Socratic denial. Our aim can be only to get as clear as possible on the meaning of what is said, and hence to limit as closely as possible the range of legitimate disagreement on the interpretation of the doctrine.

The first part (1145 b21–1146 a9) of chapter 2 contains, as we saw earlier, a preliminary discussion of the question in what sense of 'understanding' the incontinent man understands, if he does understand, that what he is doing is wrong. In chapter 3, prima facie, Aristotle expounds his own solution in a series of stages, but we have to keep in mind the possibility that the chapter is an editor's conflation of two parallel versions. The discussion in chapter 2 is based on the division of 'understanding' (*hupolēpsis*) into three specific forms; knowledge (*epistēmē*), opinion (*doxa*), and practical reason (*phronēsis*).[1] Three different possible interpretations of *akrasia* correspond to these three kinds of understanding.

On the suggestion that the incontinent man acts against knowledge Aristotle remarks that some agree with Socrates that it would be shocking (*deinon*) if knowledge were 'overcome and dragged about like a slave' by appetite (1145 b22–4). On the other hand Socrates' unqualified denial of *akrasia* conflicts with the apparent facts (1145 b27–8). We have already discussed the interpretation of this remark. At the end of chapter 3 Aristotle says that in a sense Socrates seems to have been right after all. He was right because the knowledge against which the incontinent man acts is not 'knowledge proper' (*kuriōs epistēmē*) but perceptual knowledge (*aisthētikē epistēmē*). The meaning of this difficult, and (it seems) textually corrupt passage will be discussed when we come to it.

---

[1] *De Anima* 3, 427 b24–5.

In the next section of chapter 2 (1145 b31–1146 a4), and again in chapter 3 (1146 b24–31), Aristotle considers the suggestion that, while Socrates was right to deny that a man could yield to desire if he *knew* that it was wrong to do so, he might yield if his intellectual state were not knowledge but belief or opinion. The section of chapter 3 is repetitive, but not so much so as to make it necessary to accept Cook Wilson's view that it is a conflation of two versions. Taken together the discussions of the suggestion in the two chapters pose a dilemma. In chapter 2 Aristotle takes *doxa* (opinion) as being a judgement more tentative and less assured than that of knowledge, *ēremaia* (1146 a1). But, on this interpretation, *akrasia* would be excusable and not, as it is, blameworthy. In chapter 3 he remarks that *doxa* (belief), although not knowledge, may be held with the same degree of conviction, or the same absence of doubt, as in the case of Heraclitus.[1] The apparent fact of *akrasia* is not made easier to accept at its face value by the substitution of belief in this sense for knowledge.

We need not understand Aristotle as implying here that the distinction between knowledge and belief makes no contribution to the understanding of the facts about ostensible *akrasia*. One of the horns of the dilemma might be grasped. It may be true that when we are not quite sure, but are of the opinion, that what we are doing is wrong, the wrongdoing is excusable. Perhaps incontinent behaviour often is excusable. Who is not ready to think this of his own *akrasia*? But the excuse cannot be made in all cases. Sometimes no doubt is entertained. If so, the problem is still on our hands even if its scope is diminished.

In the next section of chapter 2 (1146 a4–9), a passage we have already considered, Aristotle rejects as absurd (*atopon*) the suggestion that the incontinent man acts against practical wisdom (*phronēsis*). For the same man would then be incontinent and practically wise. Besides, 'it has been shown that the man of practical wisdom is one who will *act*;[2] for he is a man concerned with individual facts,[3] and who has the other virtues'.[4] We might express Aristotle's doctrine here by saying that practical wisdom

---

[1] Cf. *Magna Moralia* 1201 b8–9.   [2] Cf. 1140 b4–6.
[3] Cf. 1141 b16, 1142 a24.   [4] Cf. 1144 b30–1145 a2.

necessarily involves commitment, and that an incontinent man could not count as committed to right conduct.

Aristotle's next suggestion (1146 b31–5) is that the solution of the problem might be found in the distinction between two senses in which a man may be said to 'know' something; the sense in which the geometer knows the theorem of Pythagoras when he is not thinking about geometry and the sense in which he can be said to know it only when he is actively engaged in proving it to himself or someone else.[1] It will 'make a difference whether, when a man does what he should not, he has the knowledge (*echonta*) but is not exercising it (*theōrounta*), or *is* exercising it; for the latter seems strange (*deinon*) but not the former' (1146 b33–5). The distinction which Aristotle is here applying to the problem of incontinence, the question in what sense the incontinent man understands or knows, is the distinction, familiar and fundamental in his philosophy, between a capacity or potentiality (*dunamis*), which may or may not be a state (*hexis*) acquired by training or learning, and the actualization (*energeia*), or actual exercise, of such a capacity. Aristotle here speaks of 'having' knowledge and 'using' it, and elucidates 'use' in terms of 'contemplation'. When he speaks of 'use' he means not the application of knowledge in practice but the exercise of dispositional knowledge in actual thinking.

Aristotle does not say at this point whether, in his view, the distinction between dispositional knowledge and activated knowledge solves, or contributes to solving, his problem. He goes on immediately to propound a new and more complex solution in which the distinction plays a part. The natural inference is that the distinction, even if it contributes something, does not, in Aristotle's view, solve the problem. Why not? In terms of our preceding discussion the reason must be that the distinction does not by itself account for, or 'save', the fact of ostensible *akrasia*; at least the form of *akrasia* which Aristotle calls 'weakness' (*astheneia*) as opposed to impetuosity (*propeteia*) (7, 1150 b19–28). If the whole of the knowledge to which the incontinent man failed to conform were throughout only dispositional, he would not even

[1] Cf. *De Anima* 412 a10–11.

be tempted to describe his own conduct as open-eyed wrong-doing or failure to do what he knew to be right. He might deplore his own blindness or amnesia, but his conduct would not even be ostensibly akratic.

Richard Robinson, in his essay, 'L'acrasie, selon Aristote',[1] expresses the opinion that Aristotle regards the distinction between potential and actual knowledge as solving his problem: the distinction 'contains virtually all that is needed for the explanation of *akrasia*' (p. 263). But Robinson does not overlook the objection that, if so, Aristotle would not be able, any more than Socrates, to account for ostensible *akrasia*. In effect he gives his answer when he remarks that there is an important difference between the position of Aristotle and that of Socrates: Aristotle recognized that, in the unfolding of a situation terminating in *akrasia*, the state of know-ledge might change significantly. Thus the *akratēs*, before and after his lapse, might know perfectly well the nature of his act but not at the actual moment of commission (p. 265). Similarly Robinson attributes to Aristotle the view that the weak man, 'l'acratique faible', knows as the result of deliberation that the action which he is tempted to do is wrong, but actually does it at a time, 'pendant quelques instants', when passion has driven the knowledge from his mind (p. 274). If it is the case that the know-ledge which is merely potential when *akrasia* occurs is actual at other times, this would indeed help to account for the belief that ostensible *akrasia* is not merely ostensible. But it does not answer the objection, urged by Ross against Aristotle, which Robinson is discussing when he offers his interpretation of 'l'acrasie faible'. Ross objects that Aristotle explains away the moral struggle, but that his explanation presupposes that it occurs at an earlier stage. 'And the account which explains how the wrong can be done in the absence of this knowledge cannot explain how the know-ledge has come to be absent.'[2] We shall have to consider whether the further development of Aristotle's view in chapter 3 suggests that he anticipated this objection, and, if he did, how he would answer it. The fact that, if Aristotle held the view which Robinson attributes to him, he would have been open to criticism does not

---

[1] *Revue philosophique* (1955). [2] *Aristotle*, p. 224.

show that Robinson is wrong in attributing it to him. But I think that Walsh is justified in complaining that Robinson does not seem to notice the difficulty; and does not discuss it. 'Unfortunately, Robinson does not consider the condition of the morally weak man while one of his premises is being driven out. Presumably he is in some state of conflict' (p. 120).

So far Aristotle has spoken of knowing what is better or best without saying precisely what it is that a man who has such knowledge knows. In the next section (1146 b35–1147 a10) he offers as an analysis, or partial analysis, of such knowledge the doctrine of the practical syllogism. Aristotle reintroduces this doctrine, after a section on another aspect of the problem (1147 a10–14), in the section which begins at 1147 a24. Cook Wilson holds that the earlier section on the practical syllogism is a version parallel to the later. This may or may not be a correct piece of divination. Aristotle might have wished to distinguish elements in what is known before the following section in which he distinguishes different senses of 'having' knowledge. A brief recapitulation of the doctrine of the syllogism is quite natural after the digression. Walsh is surely right when he argues that Cook Wilson's conclusions are not proved. 'Certainly the Aristotelian corpus is littered with similar digressions, and they can be explained as well by the hypothesis that they are due to the relative spontaneity of the lecture form or by the hypothesis of the accumulation of notes and partial revisions in an unfinished manuscript as by the hypothesis of compilation' (p. 186).

Two kinds of premiss (*protasis*), universal and particular, are involved in knowledge of what it is right to do. The universal premiss is a rule stating that everything of a certain sort is good; the particular premiss states that here is something of that sort.[1] Aristotle suggests that the incontinent man 'uses', i.e. actively contemplates, the universal premiss but not the particular. Without pausing to examine this suggestion he proceeds to refine it. The universal premiss contains both a personal reference to the

---

[1] The practical syllogism has been discussed in Ch. XI (pp. 228 ff) and Ch. XII. The most important texts in Aristotle are *De Anima* Γ 11, 434 a16–21; *De Motu Animalium* 7, 701 a7; *EN* VI. 7, 1141 b14–21; 8, 1142 a20–3; VII. 3, 1147 a29–b3.

agent and an impersonal reference to the object or the act; e.g. 'for every man dry food is expedient'. The elaboration of this example is complicated, if the text is sound, by the mention of an intermediate premiss, 'such and such food is dry'. But the suggestion which emerges from the example is clear: it is that the syllogism, or sorites, of action is complete, and actively known, with the exception of the particular, or singular, premiss in its reference to the action or thing as opposed to the agent; at this point the knowledge of the incontinent man is at most potential —'but whether this food is such and such, of this the incontinent man either has not or is not exercising the knowledge' (1147 a7). The incontinent man fails to recognize the application of the rule in its impersonal reference.

This suggestion, considered as an attempt to save the phenomena of ostensible *akrasia*, is an advance on the preceding solution which relied exclusively on the distinction between dispositional and activated knowing. For, if certain parts of the thinking proper to the virtuous man are actual and not merely potential, this will help to account for the fact that akratic conduct looks, or feels, like acting against knowledge, or is remembered as acting against knowledge, even if, at the moment of action, there is no actual knowledge that the action is wrong.

The solution offered in this section (1146 b35–1147 a10), that the incontinent man does not realize the truth of the minor premiss, raises questions about the location of incontinence in relation to the distinction between the voluntary (*hekousion*) and the involuntary (*akousion*) which Aristotle has elaborated in Book III. Ross points out that, according to the doctrine of Book III (1110 b31–1111 a24), an action which is due to ignorance of particular fact is involuntary.[1] The incontinent man gratifies his desire (*epithumia*) voluntarily, although his action does not spring from deliberate choice (*prohairesis*). But an action which is voluntary considered in terms of one description may be involuntary in relation to another. For, when *A* voluntarily gives *B* a drink, he may be poisoning him involuntarily. Thus Aristotle might say that, considered as a case of wrongdoing,

[1] *Aristotle*, p. 223.

the incontinent act is involuntary. But Ross points out that, in the terminology of Book III, the incontinent action is done not through ignorance (*di' agnoian*) but rather in ignorance (*agnoōn*). 'Acting by reason of ignorance seems also to be different from acting *in* ignorance; for the man who is drunk or in a rage is thought to act as a result not of ignorance but of one of the causes mentioned, yet not knowingly but in ignorance' (1110 b24–7). It is clearly true, if we follow the analysis of this section, that the incontinent man is ignorant when he acts, and the fuller analysis which follows shows that he is responsible for his ignorance as a man whose ignorance is due to drink or anger is responsible. Reginald Jackson argues against Ross that incontinence is not action in ignorance on the ground that the ignorance involved is ignorance of the minor premiss.[1] But Aristotle does not say that the description 'acting in ignorance' is applicable only when the ignorance is ignorance of principles. He implies that he has in mind also ignorance of fact. As Walsh remarks, 'a drunken man is as responsible for his inability to tell pumice from granite as he is for his inability to remember that it is wrong to throw rocks at people' (p. 116). But, if Ross is right in saying that Aristotle here represents the incontinent man as acting in ignorance, this does not mean that there are not important differences between acting in ignorance in the kind of circumstances Aristotle has in mind in Book III and incontinence. Thus the man who, because he is drunk, fails to notice that a gun is loaded would not, if he knew this fact, have any inclination to fire the gun. But the incontinent man, if he realized the consequences of drinking, would still feel a desire to drink. What is peculiar to his case, as we are to see, is that he is distracted between two different principles of action.

One further comment is appropriate at this stage. Why does Aristotle not consider, or even mention, the possibility of a failure to know effectively the universal premiss? If passion can confuse and darken the mind, make us liable to wishful thinking, we should expect the tendency to show itself in connection with

---

[1] 'Rationalism and Intellectualism in the Ethics of Aristotle', *Mind* (1942), p. 355.

either premiss. And the facts seem to confirm this expectation. The man taking a drink too many may persuade himself that the extra one will not be harmful to his digestion. But he may also lapse into thinking that it is not wrong to incur a hangover once a year. Sidgwick suggests that, in the case of anger, it sometimes happens that 'the rule is simply forgotten for a time, just as a matter of fact might be'.[1] Aristotle ought perhaps to recognize that the akratēs may fail to 'use', actively to contemplate, either the particular premiss or the universal principle.

Aristotle now goes on to distinguish different kinds of dispositional knowledge (1147 a10–24). The man who is asleep or mad or drunk 'has' knowledge in one way but in another not: his knowledge is not on tap until he wakes up, or recovers his sanity or sobriety. It is not always possible to activate a formed disposition at a moment's notice: 'a sleeping geometer is at a further remove than one who is awake, and a waking one than one who is busy at his studies.'[2] Aristotle adds that anger and physical appetite produce changes in the body similar to the changes involved in these states; they even make men mad. The condition of the akratēs is similar to these conditions. Aristotle next observes that ability to repeat moral maxims 'does not prove anything'. Men in these abnormal states may recite geometrical proofs or verses of Empedocles without, it is implied, knowing what they are saying. Two other examples are given of words used without understanding: the utterances of those who have 'just learned' something and the utterances of actors. The sequence of the argument in this section is not very clear or explicit, but I think that it is this. The drunken geometer, or the moral man drunk with passion, must first become sober before he is in a position to activate his dispositional knowledge. It would not be a valid objection to this, Aristotle is suggesting, to point out that, before he becomes sober, the geometer may recite a proof or the moral man repeat his maxim. The objection would be valid only if the hypothetical geometer and moral man knew what they were saying. So understood, the argument is consecutive. But I think

---

[1] 'Unreasonable Action', in *Practical Ethics*, p. 254.
[2] *De Generatione Animalium* 735 a9–11.

that in this section Aristotle slides from the point from which he
starts to a quite different point without making the transition fully
clear. He starts from the point that a disposition may be more or
less removed from actualization. He ends with the point that
words may be used with less or more understanding. Prima facie
the second point may have more relevance than the first to the
main problem which he is considering about *akrasia*.

'Again, we may also view the cause as follows with reference
to the facts of human nature' (*phusikōs*) (1147 a24–5). What does
Aristotle mean by a 'physical' explanation, and to what does he
oppose it? Burnet quotes passages in which 'physical' (*phusikōs*)
is opposed to 'logical' (*logikōs*).[1] The examination of a question is
'logical' if it makes use of principles or distinctions which, like the
distinction between potential and actual, have application to many
different subjects. The treatment of a topic is 'physical', at least if
the topic falls within physics, when it is in terms of principles
proper and peculiar to the topic treated. Joachim rightly points
out that the phenomena of *akrasia*, being occurrences in the
embodied soul or besouled body of a man, belong to the subject-
matter of what Aristotle calls 'physical' science. In the *Posterior
Analytics* (*A*, 84 a7–9) 'logical' is opposed to 'analytical', 'because
the science in question is the science concerned with the facts of
demonstrative knowledge' (*ta analutika*). When Aristotle states
here that the view he is about to expound is a 'physical' one he is
implying that the earlier solutions were, indeed, inadequate but
not that they were on the wrong track. As Burnet remarks, the
earlier solutions 'have gradually prepared us for this one'. There is
no sharp contrast between the logical and the physical discussion,
but rather a step by step transition from the one to the other.
It should be noted that Robinson, while he does not dissent from
the generally accepted account of what Aristotle means by
'physical' and 'logical', takes the view that the problem of *akrasia*
is primarily logical and that Aristotle, therefore, attaches relatively
little importance to the psychological or psychophysical treatment
of the question (pp. 271, 272). But it is surely clear that, in the last

[1] *Physics* 204 b4–10 and *De Generatione et Corruptione* 316 a10; cf. *Topics* 105

part of the chapter, Aristotle is offering an account which is a synthesis of suggestions made earlier. Moreover, Joachim is surely right in saying that the analysis of *akrasia* is a problem which is 'physical' in Aristotle's sense.

The section starts from a recapitulation, and development, of the doctrine of the practical syllogism. Two judgements are involved, one which is universal and another which is concerned with the particular facts and is in the sphere of perception (1147 a25–6). 'When a single judgement results from the two (*hotan mia genētai*), the soul must in one type of case affirm the conclusion (*entha men phanai*), while in the case of judgements concerned with production it must immediately act' (*entha de prattein euthus*) (1147 a26–8).[1] Aristotle proceeds to give an example of a syllogism issuing in action: 'if everything sweet ought to be tasted, and this is sweet, in the sense of being one of the particular sweet things, the man who can act and is not prevented (*mē kōluomenon*) must (*anankē*) at the same time actually act accordingly' (1147 a29–31). This, as Ross points out, is the syllogism not of an incontinent (*akratēs*) but of a profligate man (*akolastos*). Aristotle proceeds immediately to a description of what happens in the incontinent man.

So far Aristotle has distinguished two kinds of syllogism, and has said that, in the case of both, the drawing of the conclusion follows necessarily when the premisses are apprehended together. The two kinds of syllogism resemble each other in having one universal premiss and one singular premiss. When the universal premiss is factual, the conclusion is a proposition which is believed. When the universal premiss is practical, the conclusion is an action which is done. We might expect Aristotle to say that, in the case of the practical syllogism, the drawing of the conclusion, 'here is something to be done', is necessary, and is necessarily followed by the action or the decision to act. But he does not in fact say that the conclusion and the action are distinct and inseparable; he does not distinguish them. It is natural to take Aristotle's insistence here on the necessity or inevitability of the conclusion as clinching the suggestion he has made already that the incontinent

[1] Cf. *De Motu Animalium* 701 a12.

man does not know, in the sense of actively contemplating, both premises. If he did have such knowledge he would not fail, as he does fail, to act. But this is a point on which we should still, at this stage, keep an open mind in view of two phrases in the sentences rendered in our preceding paragraph: 'When a single judgement results' (1147 a26–7) and 'not prevented' (1147 a30–1). Take the second phrase first. It is natural, and probably right, to take 'prevention' as referring only to external and physical interference:[1] a man might not taste if his hand were seized or the cup dashed from his lips. But, if it could be said that an incontinent man might be 'prevented' from acting by his desire or passion, then it might be the case that he had fully grasped both premises. But I can see nothing in the text to show that 'not prevented' is to be understood in so wide a sense. The reservation indicated by the other phrase, 'when a single judgement results', must, as we shall see shortly, be taken more seriously. What it suggests is that a man might have actual knowledge of both premises and yet fail to draw the conclusion, theoretical or practical, because he did not 'put two and two together'. Some commentators, Joachim in particular, have thought that this is what happens, according to Aristotle, in *akrasia*. We shall have to say more about this interpretation in connection with the immediately following stage in Aristotle's exposition.

'When, then, the universal judgement is present in us forbidding us to taste, and there is also the judgement that everything sweet is pleasant, and that this is sweet, and the latter opinion is active (*energei*), and when appetite (*epithumia*) happens to be present in us, the one judgement bids us avoid the object (*legei pheugein touto*), but appetite leads us towards it; for it can move each of our bodily parts' (1147 a31–5). The first difficulty raised by this passage is that the last two lines, taken by themselves, would suggest that the *akratēs* succumbs to passion with his eyes open, knowing that the moral rule applies to the present situation. Thus Burnet takes the phrase 'bids us avoid the object' (*legei pheugein touto*) to imply that the moral syllogism 'may even be completed; but, in the absence of *orexis* to which it can present itself, nothing happens.

[1] Cf. *De Motu Animalium* 701 a9–16.

For *dianoia* (thought) alone moves nothing.' A more adequate statement of this interpretation would be that the moral motive, even if present, is overcome by the greater strength of passion (*epithumia*). The objection to this interpretation is that it attributes to Aristotle a view which flatly contradicts the view stated in the context, both before and after this passage, that the *akratēs* does not actually know that what he is doing is wrong. A few lines later he speaks of the *akratēs* 'regaining his knowledge' (1147 b6–7). Burnet's interpretation would also involve us in understanding 'prevent' in 1147 a31 as covering the intervention of passion, and this we have seen to be questionable. These considerations make it difficult, perhaps impossible, to accept Burnet's view. We must, therefore, follow other commentators in taking Aristotle's reference to the moral rule as 'telling' us 'to avoid this' as meaning that the rule implies this, or at least as meaning something less than the explicit application of the rule to the present case. I quote, with agreement, Robinson's statement on this point. 'But it is not necessary to hold that by these words Aristotle intends to tell us that he is now supposing the right syllogism to be completely actual. The word *legei* is vague enough to mean no more than that the right universal premiss *tends* to forbid the act, and *would* forbid it if joined to its own particular premiss in actuality' (*Essays in Greek Philosophy* p. 145).

The second difficulty to be noticed in this passage is connected with Aristotle's omission to formulate determinately the principle which 'forbids us to taste'. It is natural to take as implied, as do Burnet and Gauthier-Jolif, the formula 'sweet things should not be tasted'. This principle will be in incidental conflict (1147 b2) with the major premiss, everything sweet is pleasant, of the syllogism of appetite. But then the two syllogisms have the same minor premiss, this is sweet. This proposition must be actually known if the incontinent man is to be led astray by appetite. But it seems to be Aristotle's doctrine in the rest of the chapter that the minor premiss of the moral syllogism is not actually known. Commentators offer two different possible solutions of this difficulty. The first solution is to suppose, with Ross, that the conflicting syllogisms have different subject-terms in their major premisses and hence different minor premisses. The second solution is to suppose that there is indeed only one minor premiss, and that the *akratēs* goes wrong by connecting it with the major premiss of the appetitive syllogism and failing to connect it with the major premiss of the moral syllogism. This is on the whole the interpretation of Joachim. We mentioned it earlier[1] in our discussion of the phrase 'when a single judgment results' in 1147 a26–7.

Ross, in his brief paraphrase of the passage, formulates the moral rule as 'nothing that is X should be tasted';[2] X presumably represents a word like 'indigestible' or 'harmful'. Ross assumes that the minor premiss will be known only in the remote sense, as a drunken man may know the verses of Empedocles. The merit of this interpretation is that it agrees with the doctrine which we have found in 1146 b35–1147 a24, and which seems to be repeated in the concluding section (1147 b9–17), still to be considered, of the chapter. The demerit of the interpretation is that 'X' is not in the text but is only assumed by Ross. It is, therefore, worth while to consider whether the passage can be understood without the assumption of a second minor premiss.

Joachim maintains that Aristotle's solution of the problem of *akrasia* 'follows his treatment of error' in the *Prior Analytics* II. 21 (p. 226). 'Nothing prevents a man who knows both that A belongs to the whole of B, and that B again belongs to C, thinking that A does not belong to C, e.g. knowing that every mule is sterile and that this is a mule, and thinking that this animal is with foal: for he does not know that A belongs to C, unless he considers the two propositions together' (*mē suntheōrōn*) (67 a33–7). Aristotle explains that there are three senses in which one can 'know' a sensible thing: knowledge of a universal under which it falls, the knowledge proper to it, and the exercise of such knowledge (67 b3–5). Lacking the third kind of knowledge, a man may be deceived about the particular although he knows a major premiss which contradicts his erroneous belief, and does not affirm any opposing major premiss which would contradict the premiss he knows.

---

[1] p. 282 above.   [2] *Aristotle*, p. 223.

Nothing then prevents a man both knowing and being mistaken about the same thing, provided that his knowledge and his error are not contrary. And this happens also to the man whose knowledge is limited to each of the premises and has not previously considered the particular question. For when he thinks that the mule is with foal he has not the knowledge in the sense of its actual exercise (*to energein*), nor on the other hand has his thought caused an error contrary to his knowledge: for the error contrary to the knowledge of the universal would be a syllogism. (67 b5–11.)

This treatment of error in the *Prior Analytics* II. 21 seems to resemble in a number of respects Aristotle's account of the failure of knowledge in *akrasia*. In both analyses there is a known rule and a failure to subsume a sensible particular under the rule. In the mistake about the mule there is no acceptance of a general proposition inconsistent with the proposition that mules are sterile. Similarly the *akratēs* does not accept a general principle which contradicts the rule that sweet things should not be tasted. This is stated in the passage we are considering: 'so it happens that a man behaves incontinently under the influence, in a sense, of a rule and an opinion, and of one not contrary in itself, but only incidentally —for the appetite is contrary not the opinion—to the right rule' (1147 a35–b3). That sweet things are pleasant does not contradict the right rule although it leads to an action contrary to it. Again in the case of the mule there is no failure to know the minor premiss, this is a mule. Because the premises are not viewed together there is a failure to know the conclusion which they entail, that this animal is not with foal. Similarly the *akratēs*, while he knows that this is sweet, fails to combine the premises and conclude that to taste it is wrong. The interpretation is attractive and neatly overcomes the difficulty that the two general premises seem to require the same particular premiss. But, as we shall see, to accept the interpretation would involve us in the supposition that there is a confusion, in the final section of the chapter, between the minor premiss and the conclusion of the practical syllogism.

I have said above that Joachim 'on the whole', basing his interpretation on the *Prior Analytics*, locates the 'ignorance' of the *akratēs* in a failure to think the premises together. The qualification is required by the fact that Joachim, following the ambiguities of the text, fails to distinguish this solution sharply from a solution in terms of the suppression of the minor premiss. Thus in the following passage the two solutions are run together. 'He will know that the piece of cake is sweet but will not fully see the implications of its sweetness: i.e. his knowledge of the minor will be a mere piece of information in his mind, not in vital connection with his main thinking—he will not use his knowledge, or his knowledge will not be *theōria* but mere *hexis*' (p. 224). In a later passage Joachim formulates the knowledge which the *akratēs* fails to realize as 'this is sweet and therefore comes under the principle' (p. 228).[1] There is thus in Joachim a slide from non-realization of the minor premiss to non-realization of the conclusion. It is not clear whether he is indicating a confusion in Aristotle or merely reproducing it. The interpretation to which Joachim inclines is formulated somewhat more explicitly by Gauthier–Jolif, who also refer to *Prior Analytics* II. 21 (pp. 611–13): the *akratēs* connects the particular situation with the major premiss of appetite and fails to connect it with the moral rule. The minor premiss (this is sweet) 'peut de soi être subsumée à l'une ou l'autre des deux prémisses universelles' (p. 613).

In the concluding sentences of his discussion (1147 b9–17) Aristotle states the terms of his settlement with Socrates. But he first adds two remarks which, in a modern book, might have been appended as footnotes. Brutes (*thēria*), he says, are not incontinent 'because they have no universal judgement but only imagination and memory of particulars' (1147 b3–5). This doctrine is stated more fully in the *De Anima* Γ 11 (434 a5–21) where Aristotle distinguishes between 'perceptual imagination' and 'deliberative imagination', which involves capacity to generalize and is peculiar to man. Aristotle next refers us to the physiologists for an explanation of the way in which the ignorance (*agnoia*) of the *akratēs* is dissolved and his knowledge recovered; the explanation is the same as in the case of the man who is drunk or asleep (1147 b6–9). The physiological conditions of sleeping and waking are described in *De Somno*, chapter 3. Sleep is due to evaporations from

---

[1] Cf. Walsh, p. 107.

food which affect the central organ of sense; waking occurs when, digestion being complete, the purer blood has been separated from the thicker and concentrated in the head.[1]

Aristotle's discussion in VII. 3 of knowledge and ignorance in *akrasia* concludes as follows. I quote the Oxford Translation by Ross. The interpretation of 'last premiss' (*teleutaia protasis*) in 1147 b9 is doubtful and in 1147 b16 the homoeoteleuton (*dokousēs parousēs*) is almost certainly a corrupt reading.

Now, the last premiss both being an opinion about a perceptible object, and being what determines our actions (*kuria*), this a man either has not when he is in the state of passion, or has it in the sense in which having knowledge did not mean knowing but only talking, as a drunken man may utter the verses of Empedocles (cf. a20). And because the last term (*horos*) is not universal nor equally an object of scientific knowledge with the universal term, the position that Socrates sought to establish (cf. 1145 b22–4) actually seems to result; for it is not in the presence of what is thought to be knowledge proper that the affection of incontinence (*to pathos*) arises nor is it this that is 'dragged about' as a result of the state of passion (*dia to pathos*), but in that of perceptual knowledge. (1147 b9–17.)

A case has been stated in our preceding discussion for the view that, according to the solution offered by Aristotle in this chapter, what the *akratēs* fails to know effectively, in the sense of actual contemplation, is a prescriptive conclusion rather than a merely factual premiss: 'avoid this' or 'this is sweet and to be avoided' rather than 'this is sweet'. Can the 'last premiss' (1147 b9) be a proposition of this kind? A protasis is a proposition which is 'put forward' for acceptance, offered as a basis for argument. In the *Prior Analytics* (42 a32) we are told that a syllogism is composed of two protaseis.[2] Thus, even if *protasis* has uses which suggest 'proposition' rather than 'premiss', it is not possible, in a context where syllogisms are being considered, to defend any *translation* except 'premiss'.

Could the minor premiss of a 'practical syllogism' be an assertion which contained a moral term, an assertion which was

[1] See Ross, *Parva Naturalia*, Introduction, pp. 38-44, and Commentary, pp. 253–66.   [2] Cf. *MM* 1201 b25.

prescriptive or evaluative and not merely factual? Takatura Ando maintains that in the practical syllogism the minor premiss 'recognizes the presence of a value in a particular case.'[1] He finds fault with Teichmüller and other scholars for failing to see that the ignorance in *akrasia* is ignorance of value and not, as in action which is involuntary, ignorance of fact (pp. 300 ff.). But, although Ando's contention may represent what we are sometimes inclined to expect Aristotle to say, he makes no attempt to justify it by the detailed interpretation of what Aristotle says in VII. 3. It would be difficult for him to do so since, as Walsh remarks, 'the text of Book VII offers no clear examples of a minor premise which is itself moral and not factual' (p. 109). This is an understatement of the difficulty. For the text does offer examples of minor premisses which are factual. Ando admits (p. 280) that the fullest statement in Aristotle of the scheme of a practical syllogism is that given in the *De Anima* Γ 11, 434 a16–21, and here the minor premiss is of the form, 'this is such and such an action and I am such and such a man', the major premiss being 'such and such a man should (*dei*) do such and such an action'. The syllogism in 1147 a5–7 conforms to this pattern, and this is the pattern also of the syllogisms referred to in 1147 a29–34. So far, then, the evidence seems clear that the 'last premiss' must be factual and not evaluative. We may be reminded at this point of the suggestion in 1147 a28 that, in the case of the practical syllogism, the conclusion is not an assertion at all but an action.[2] But, even if action follows immediately, a conclusion which can be expressed in words is entailed by the assertions which are the premisses; the assertion that I ought to do this. If so, and if all the assertions which lead to the action as conclusion were called premisses, then the last premiss would be evaluative and not merely factual. But I do not think that there is any substance in this line of interpretation. A fuller account of my reasons for the views expressed in this paragraph has been given in the preceding Chapters (XI and XII).

If protasis means premiss and the minor premiss must be factual we are driven to fall back on the suggestion made earlier that, in

---

[1] *Aristotle's Theory of Practical Cognition*, p. 278.
[2] Cf. *De Motu Animalium* 701 a12.

the chapter as it stands, there is a slide, along the route indicated by Joachim, from factual premiss to moral conclusion; that Aristotle sometimes speaks of the minor premiss when he also has in mind what should properly be called the conclusion. We have seen that the treatment of mistakes concerning perceptible individuals in the *Prior Analytics* II. 21 supports this suggestion. There is further evidence in the way in which Aristotle speaks of the 'last premiss'. It is described as 'determining our actions' (*kuria*), and this phrase is appropriate to a proposition containing a word like 'right' (*dei*), or 'expedient' (*sumpherei*) and not purely factual. Similarly in VI. 11, 1143 b2–5 it is difficult to take 'the other premiss' as a bare statement of fact, since it is described as 'the starting-point for the apprehension of the end' and as apprehended by practical reason (*nous*).[1] Again in the *MM* B 6 (1201 b24–39) we find an apparently confused transition from ignorance of a particular fact to ignorance of the application of a rule to the fact: 'for it is possible for the incontinent man to possess the knowledge of the universal, that such and such things are bad and hurtful, but yet not to know that these particular things are bad, so that while possessing knowledge in this way he will go wrong (*hamartēsetai*); for he has the universal knowledge but not the particular' (1201 b35–9).

Commentators are divided on the interpretation of the contrast between 'knowledge proper' (*kuriōs*) and 'perceptual knowledge' (*aisthētikē*) (1147 b15–17). I think that the prevalent, and certainly a natural, view is that knowledge proper is knowledge of a universal rule or major premiss and perceptual knowledge is knowledge of a proposition with a singular term as its subject, whether a minor premiss or a moral conclusion. The difficulty which this view has to deal with is that the text as it stands appears to be inconsistent with what Aristotle has been saying, viz. that the knowledge which fails, and is in a sense absent, is knowledge not of the general rule but of the particular fact. But Burnet takes 'knowledge in the proper sense' to be not knowledge of the general rule but scientific knowledge in which 'all the terms are universal'. The contrast then is between the

---

[1] Cf. *EE* B 11, 1227 b32–3.

scientific syllogism and the practical syllogism, not between the two premisses of the practical syllogism. This interpretation is implied by the footnote to 1147 b17 in the Oxford Translation: 'Even before the minor premiss of the practical syllogism has been obscured by passion, the incontinent man has not scientific knowledge in the strict sense, since his minor premiss is not universal but has for its subject a sensible particular, e.g. "this glass of wine".' The interpretation is supported by the treatment of error (*apatē*) in the *Prior Analytics* II. 21; the mistake there analysed is similar to the mistake of the *akratēs* and is conditioned by the fact that the relevant knowledge involves the application of a universal principle to a singular term, i.e. it is perceptual knowledge and not scientific knowledge in the full sense.

If 'knowledge proper' is understood as knowledge of the major premiss of a practical syllogism, the text as it stands can be defended only by giving a Pickwickian meaning to the statement that this knowledge is not 'present' when *akrasia* occurs. The knowledge, Stewart suggests, is not 'immediately present', not 'near enough to the passion to be suppressed by it'. 'The true *epistēmē* which he has, and has consciously, is not in a position to be affected by *pathos*, because it is universal, and so does not enter the arena of particular action.' But Stewart feels the strain of this explanation, and he remarks also that 'the homoeoteleuton *dokousēs parousēs* is suspicious'.[1] A further point to note is that Stewart's defence of the text means that *to pathos* has two different meanings; the affection of *akrasia* in 1147 b16 and the desire or passion in 1147 b17. In view of these difficulties Stewart proposes the reading *periginetai* ('overcomes') for *parousēs ginetai* ('occurs in the presence of'): it is perceptual knowledge and not knowledge proper which is overcome by passion. With this reading 'knowledge proper' could be interpreted either, with Burnet, as scientific knowledge or as knowledge of the major premiss. Ross in his *Aristotle*[2] says that this reading 'gives the right sense' and here, inconsistently with his view in the Oxford Translation, seems to

---

[1] Burnet's suggestion that the text is 'sufficiently guaranteed by *enousēs*' in 1145 b23 is not acceptable. The earlier passage might account for the intrusion of *parousēs*.   [2] See p. 224 n. 2.

take 'knowledge proper' to be knowledge of the major premiss. Stewart's conjecture is accepted by Gauthier-Jolif.

'On the questions whether knowledge is or is not present when *akrasia* occurs, and what kind of knowledge it is that is involved, this answer must suffice' (1147 b17-19). To Cook Wilson it seemed that the answer is 'worse than no answer': 'a mental struggle is impossible, since there is no actual knowledge for appetite to struggle with' (p. 49). Somewhat similarly Ross says that Aristotle's answer is 'inadequate to his own real view of the problem' (p. 224). Aristotle should recognize that 'incontinence is due not to failure of knowledge but to weakness of will'. In the preceding discussion I have tried to do two things. First, following in detail what Aristotle says in VII. 3, I have tried, where the text is ambiguous, to make clear what interpretations are possible. Secondly, I have tried to explain Aristotle's formulation of the question and to exhibit the merits of his method. Is incontinence due to failure of knowledge or to weakness of will? We find the question difficult partly because the facts are complicated, but partly because the question has a definiteness which is delusive. Immersing ourselves in the facts, and in what we say about the facts, we become aware of a new dimension of doubt. What is to count as knowing or not knowing, accepting or not accepting, a moral principle? What are we asking when we ask whether the incontinent man has knowledge? Philosophers sometimes speak as if, once a question has been clarified, there is no longer in philosophy a question to be answered. But, if this were so, every question would be dissolved in turn into a question of higher order. And so, when we have decided what we mean or should mean by knowledge and ignorance, strength and weakness, we have still to say what descriptions match best the facts of experience. We may well doubt whether Aristotle's patterns of analysis cover all the facts. It is pertinent, for example, to ask, as Ross does, how, if the wrong act is done in the absence of knowledge, the knowledge has come to be absent (p. 224). Perhaps, if we tried harder, we could grasp our knowledge more firmly, keep a grip on ourselves.[1] The explanation of incontinence in

---

[1] Cf. VII. 7, 1150 b22-5.

terms of ignorance would be unhelpful if we had to admit that, unless we had been incontinent, we would not be ignorant. But, if we say this, we may still be puzzled by the coming to be absent of knowledge. Is it like being hit on the head and passing out? Is it like relaxing one's grip on a golf club when told to do so by an instructor? Sometimes it is not like either. For neither is like what happens when we go to sleep or fall asleep. And Aristotle has indicated that coming to be in a state in which we act incontinently is like falling asleep (1147 a17). We shall have learned something from Aristotle if, on this issue, we come to distrust, even if we must continue to seek, sharply demarcated alternatives, apparently unambiguous questions and crisply decisive answers. Any answer which is short and simple will, in Aristotle's phrase, be true perhaps, but not clear.

BIBLIOGRAPHICAL NOTE

Aristotle's account of *akrasia* (incontinence) has been much discussed. The book by James J. Walsh, *Aristotle's Conception of Moral Weakness* (1963), is comprehensive and valuable. It contains a useful bibliography (pp. 189–92).

The following articles deal with Aristotle's doctrine of *akrasia*: W. H. Fairbrother, 'Aristotle's Theory of Incontinence', in *Mind* (1897); D. G. Ritchie, 'Aristotle's Explanation of *Akrasia*', in *Mind* (1897); R. Robinson, 'L'Acrasie selon Aristote', in *Rev. Philos.* (1955). Relevant also are R. Jackson, 'Rationalism and Intellectualism in the Ethics of Aristotle', in *Mind* (1942); D. J. Allan, 'The Practical Syllogism', in *Autour d'Aristote* (1955); J. R. Bambrough, 'Socratic Paradox', in *Philosophical Quarterly* (1960).

The following references to modern discussions of Aristotle's topic may be of use. F. H. Bradley published an article, 'Can a Man sin against Knowledge?' in *Mind* (1884) (reprinted in his *Collected Essays*). The view attributed to Socrates is rejected by Henry Sidgwick in an article 'Unreasonable Action' in *Mind* (1893) (reprinted in *Practical Ethics*). C. A. Campbell also argues against the Socratic view in chapter vi of his *Scepticism and Construction*. R. M. Hare makes interesting references to the question as a 'problem of the language of the psychology of morals' in his *The Language of Morals* (1952), and has a chapter on the subject (ch. 5, 'Backsliding') in his *Freedom and Reason* (1963).

The following articles discuss the main topic discussed by Aristotle in *EN* VII. 3: H. J. N. Horsburgh, 'The Criteria of Assent to a Moral Rule', in *Mind* (1954); P. L. Gardiner, 'On assenting to a Moral Principle', in *Proceedings of the Aristotelian Society* (1954-5); C. K. Grant, '*Akrasia* and the Criteria of Assent to Practical Principles', in *Mind* (1956); Steven Lukes, 'Moral Weakness', in *Philosophical Quarterly* (1965).

For more recent work on Aristotle's doctrine of *akrasia* see now the bibliography at the end of this book.

XIV

PLEASURE

THE *EN* contains two separate discussions or discourses on pleasure (*hēdonē*): VII. 11–14 (A) and X. 1–5 (B). Following one of the commentators (Festugière) I shall refer to them as A and B. Neither discussion mentions the other, and to a considerable extent they cover the same ground and produce the same arguments. The treatment is dialectical in the familiar sense that Aristotle arrives at his own conclusions by way of an examination of views held by others; in this case views held, if not by Plato, by other disciples or associates of Plato; in particular his nephew and successor as head of the Academy, Speusippus (who said that pleasure was bad), and the astronomer Eudoxus (who said that it was good). Speusippus is mentioned by name in A (1153 b4–7), and the refutation of his view that all pleasures are bad and to be avoided is in A Aristotle's main concern. Aristotle's own view is indicated in A only by the unelaborated and undefended assertion that pleasure is not to be defined, with the anti-hedonists, as 'perceived process of becoming' (*aisthētē genesis*) but rather as 'unimpeded activity' (*anempodistos energeia*) (1153 a12–15). This definition, unless qualified as it is in B, would imply that happiness (*eudaimonia*) can be identified with pleasure, or at least, if there are pleasures which are bad, with some particular pleasure (1153 b7–14). B contains another version of the criticism of Speusippus, filling the second part of X. 2 and the whole of X. 3. Some of the weaker anti-hedonist arguments are omitted, but the treatment of the metaphysics of pleasure, in particular the argument that pleasure is imperfect (*atelēs*) because it is a process of movement (*kinēsis*) or becoming (*genesis*), is more elaborate than it was in A (X. 3, 1173 a29–b20).[1] The examination of Speusippus in B is

---

[1] Cf. VII. 11, 1152 b13–15; 12, 1153 a7–15.

preceded by an examination of the thesis of Eudoxus that 'pleasure is the good' (1172 b9–35). Eudoxus is mentioned by name (1172 b9)[1] with the comment that his advocacy of pleasure carried weight because he was himself no pleasure-lover in the vulgar sense (1172 b15–18). In A the doctrine, but not its advocate, is mentioned (1152 b25) and, as we have seen, appears to be approved, at least provisionally, without discussion or criticism (1153 b7–14). Finally B gives us an exposition of Aristotle's own doctrine on the subject: pleasure is not a movement (1174 a19 ff.); pleasure is distinct from activity but completes it 'not as a state' (hexis) but as 'an end which supervenes' (1174 b31–3); there are differences of kind between pleasures corresponding to the differences in kind between the activities which they complete (ch. 5). These statements together summarize his doctrine, and we shall find that they are all difficult to interpret.

Scholars are divided on the question whether, when he wrote A, the doctrine of B was or could have been in Aristotle's mind. So far as I can see, the question does not admit of a firm answer. In my examination of the doctrine it will be convenient to move freely between the two discussions, i.e. to divide the subject under headings rather than to go through the text, first of A and then of B, chapter by chapter. I shall not add to what I have said in Chapter I on the problem raised by the inclusion in the EN of the two parallel and unreconciled treatments. The oddity is an element in the wider set of problems raised by the fact that, according to the evidence of the manuscripts, EN v–vii are identical with EE iv–vi. The student who wishes to inform himself on these issues in their connection with Aristotle's treatment of pleasure can consult the works of two scholars who have recently written books on the doctrines of A and B and the relationship between them. The first, by A. J. Festugière, is a French translation of A and B, with introduction and notes.[2] Festugière compares the two discussions in detail and argues that A is an earlier and less searching treatment of the subject than B, both being by Aristotle. Festugière argues also for the view that A, along with the rest

[1] Cf. I. 12, 1101 b27–31.
[2] Aristote, Le Plaisir (1936, reprinted 1960).

of the disputed books, belonged originally to the *EE* and hence regards his analysis of A as confirming the view of Jaeger that the *EE* is a genuine work of Aristotle and earlier than the *EN*. The second and more recent book, by Godo Lieberg,[1] argues in greater detail for conclusions about A and B similar to those of Festugière and discusses also Aristotle's treatment of pleasure from a different point of view in the *Rhetoric*.[2] Lieberg's book appeared too late for account to be taken of it by Gauthier–Jolif (1958–9). But the comments of these editors on the problem of the disputed books include some account of the conclusions and arguments of Festugière.[3]

Aristotle's treatment of pleasure yields evidence that he and his contemporaries, all in some sense pupils of Plato, not only held different opinions on the subject but, as we should expect, discussed or debated it with each other. Debate seems to be implied when, for example, Aristotle remarks that, on a crucial point, 'the answer (*lusis*) of Speusippus is not successful' (1153 b4–7). The same debates are the background also of Plato's examination of pleasure in the *Philebus* (31 b–55 c). What were the questions at issue? No one who has tried to follow the intricate course of Plato's argument in the *Philebus* will think that a simple answer is possible. The central issue in the *Philebus* is the question whether pleasures can be 'false' and what it means to say that they are false. At least part of the difficulty of answering this question arises from uncertainty as to what, when the questions are asked, is being referred to as a 'pleasure'. Thus, while it is easy to see that, for example, the wishful thinking of a day-dreamer can be both pleasant and false, the sense in which a pleasant or painful sensation can be false seems prima facie to be derived from the falsity of a connected belief. Aristotle does not formulate the question whether pleasures can be false but he makes passing allusions to the issue (1152 b31–3, 1154 a29–31). The questions explicitly examined in A and B are of two different kinds: questions of fact or definition indicated by asking what pleasure is and questions of value or morality indicated by asking whether, it being obvious

---

[1] *Die Lehre von der Lust in den Ethiken des Aristoteles* (1958).
[2] I. 11, 1369 b30–1372 a3.   [3] Gauthier–Jolif, i. 43*–7*; ii. 781–3.

that pain is in some sense evil, pleasure is good and, if it is, whether anything else is good.

On the moral issue both Plato and Aristotle conclude by endorsing, as true even if not clear, the view of common sense that some pleasures are good and some bad. On the issue of fact or definition we may begin by asking whether the ignorance implied by the question is ignorance of the causes of pleasure and, if it is not this or not only this, what other ignorance or confusion leads to the demand for information or clarification. A rough dogmatic answer to this question may be helpful as background to our scrutiny of Aristotle's arguments. Discussion of the subject in our own time has suggested that 'pleasure' is used in at least two quite different ways. In one use or application of the word a pleasure is a feeling or sensation localized in the body, comparable with a toothache except that we like having it and dislike the toothache. The obvious example is sexual pleasure; an agreeable flavour is another. Opposed to pleasure in this sense is pain.[1] To ask for a definition of pleasure in this use of 'pleasure' can be understood as a demand for information about its causes or conditions, and cannot easily be understood otherwise. But 'pleasure' is used quite differently when we say that attending a concert or playing golf or doing philosophy or hearing good news is pleasant or a pleasure. It does not make sense to ask in what parts of the body these pleasures are felt. Golf or music or philosophy might appear in a list of a man's 'pleasures'. They would not, in the case of a man who found them unenjoyable, appear in a list of his 'pains', although he might say that he found it painful (not merely unpleasant) to read philosophy or attend concerts. The questions which puzzle us about pleasure in this sense do not seem to be questions about causes and conditions, and do seem to be questions which make it appropriate to ask what pleasure is or how we use the word 'pleasure'; and also, of course, how we use other words with similar meanings, e.g. 'enjoyment', 'gratification', and 'happiness'.

[1] But, as Mr. J. O. Urmson has recently pointed out, not all unpleasant sensations and feelings are pains; see 'Aristotle on Pleasure', in *Aristotle*, edited by J. M. E. Moravcsik, 1967, pp. 332-3.

Now Plato and Aristotle saw that what they called and we call pleasures of the body, primarily the pleasures connected with eating, drinking, and sex, are a distinct, as well as an important, class of goods, just as pains are a distinct and important class of evils. They also made some progress towards the elucidation of the difference between these pleasures and other pleasures. In particular they saw that the difference cannot be elucidated adequately in terms of the difference between body and soul. For pleasures and pains, even if they have bodily locations, are psychical and not physical phenomena. What was not clear to them, any more than it was clear to Bentham and J. S. Mill, was that it is wrong to assume that pleasures other than the bodily pleasures are other species of the same genus. Many philosophers would, I think, deny that there is a genus of pleasures of which bodily pleasures are a species. The task here of the philosopher, they would say, is not that of dividing a genus into species, but rather of sorting out the different but interconnected ways in which words like 'pleasure', 'enjoyment', 'happiness', and their opposites are used.

The purpose of these prolegomena is to distinguish from each other the radically different topics covered in Aristotle's treatment of pleasure and to make it easier to see which of them are of living interest and importance. We cannot feel much concerned about the reasons for accepting or rejecting the physiological hypotheses which he discusses concerning the conditions of bodily pleasures and pains. The place of sensual pleasures in a rational scheme of human welfare is a topic of interest to any moralist, and we look for Aristotle's views on it in his discussion of pleasure as well as in his account of ethical virtue. His polemic against anti-hedonism is a justification of pleasures other than those which are enjoyed only by the morbid or vicious. Finally, both as students of Aristotle and as students of ethics, we are interested in the similarities and dissimilarities, the bridges and the gaps, between the concepts of activity, pleasure, and happiness. Practical knowledge, in Aristotle's view, is for the sake of practice. This part of the inquiry helps us to understand what are the things in life which a reasonable man desires for their own sake and in what order of desirability he would place them. Aristotle confesses uncertainty when he says, in the part of B in which he states his own position, that we must 'dismiss for the present' the question 'whether we choose life for the sake of pleasure or pleasure for the sake of life' (1175 a18–19). He has said in the preceding chapter that 'there are many things we should be keen about even if they brought no pleasure, e.g. seeing, remembering, knowing, possessing the virtues' (1174 a4–6). It is plain, then, that he was unwilling to express in terms of unqualified hedonism his view of the supreme good for man. He was not prepared to say that to engage in enjoyable activities is the only rational pursuit. For, if it were, why should a man desire to 'possess the virtues' or to have knowledge even if 'they brought no pleasure', and why again should a life have to be 'complete' in order to be happy (I. 7, 1098 a18)?

Both A and B open with a few lines of prologue in which reasons are given for including a section on pleasure in a course on ethics or politics. In A it is said that the subject belongs to political science because the science plans for the end which is the standard of value (the standard by reference to which pains and pleasures, like anything else, are said to be good or bad), because pleasures and pains are the material of virtues and vices, and because it is generally assumed that pleasure is an accompaniment of happiness (1152 b1–8). In B there is no explicit reference to political science but, as Festugière points out (vi), a political standpoint is implied in the stress laid on the part played by pleasure and pain in education and in life (1172 a19–26). So far there is no important difference between A and B.

In both A and B the prologue or preface is followed by a brief section containing a statement of current opinions. In A the opinions listed are that no pleasure is good either essentially or accidentally; that some pleasures are good but most bad; that, even if all pleasures are good, pleasure is not the good (1152 b8–12). In the corresponding section of B the only opinions mentioned are that pleasure is the good and that pleasure is 'thoroughly bad' (1172 a26–8). B adds at this point, as a digression or footnote, that it is dangerous to maintain a doctrine not because you are convinced that it is true but because you think that its effects on people's conduct will be good. If an anti-hedonist philosopher does not practise what he preaches, his actions rather than his words are believed (1172 a29–b8). We noted earlier the main difference between the programmes of A and B. A proposes for critical discussion the varieties of anti-hedonist doctrine. B puts up for examination also the view of Eudoxus that pleasure is the good. The view that some pleasures are good and some bad, which might be taken as that of the *Philebus*, is not in the programme of B; perhaps, as Festugière suggests, because Aristotle himself in effect adopts it and develops it.

Early in A Aristotle enumerates reasons that are given for saying that 'pleasure is not a good at all' (1152 b12–20). Of these reasons the first mentioned, and the one which is most prominent in both A and B, is expressed in a definition of pleasure as 'a perceptible process to a natural state'—*genesis eis phusin aisthētē* (1152 b13). What is the theory conveyed by this definition? Aristotle assumes familiarity with it, and hence does not find it necessary to state the theory carefully before he starts to argue against it. Thus it is not made clear whether the theory is the same as the theory, considered in B, that 'pain is the lack (*endeia*) of that which is according to nature and pleasure is replenishment (*anaplērōsis*)' (1173 b7–8; cf. 1153 a2). Of this latter formula, familiar to readers of Plato's *Republic* (IX. 585 b–586 b), Aristotle says that it 'seems to be based on the pains and pleasures connected with nutrition; on the fact that when people have been short of food and have felt pain beforehand they are pleased by the replenishment' (1173 b13–15). What this means is not that people are pleased to think that their needs are being replenished but that the physical process of replenishment causes pleasant bodily sensations. Similarly the preceding pain is a bodily sensation caused by the physical hunger or thirst. The 'replenishment' formula is best regarded as a special application of the 'process to normality' formula. For it is the general formula which we find in Plato when he writes fully and carefully about pleasure in the *Philebus* and the *Timaeus*. The special formula as reported by Aristotle is not only too narrow but is unsatisfactory in another way. The proper opposite of a process of replenishment is not

a state of lacking but a process of depletion (*kenōsis*). There is
the same asymmetry in the *Republic*: being empty (*kenotēs*) not
becoming empty (*kenōsis*) is opposed to becoming full (*plērōsis*)
(585 b). This asymmetry suggests that there is an error in the
physiological explanation; prima facie being hungry is painful
even if starvation rations save the sufferer from getting hungrier.
Unless this were so, there would be no explanation of the fact
that the pains of depletion do not cease at the moment when the
process of replenishment begins.

The following is a summary statement of the theory which is
expressed by the 'process to normality' formula as we find it in
the *Timaeus* (64 a–65 b) and the *Philebus* (31 b–32 b, 42 c–d). The
theory is discussed in a long note by A. E. Taylor on *Timaeus*
64 d 7. It was held that an organism is in a normal healthy state
when a balance or proportion is maintained between its components. This view, the basis of the allopathic theory of medicine,
can be traced to Alcmaeon of Croton (probably early fifth century). Some processes of change in the organism bring it nearer
to its natural healthy state, others are in the opposite direction.
The former tend to be pleasant, the latter painful. But if the process is sufficiently slight or gradual, no pleasure or pain is felt;
hence the word 'perceptible' (*aisthētē*) in the defining formula.
Thus, for example, while a cut or a burn is painful, the slow
process of healing does not cause pleasure. The bodily processes
may be of different kinds, but what determines whether it is
pleasure or pain which ensues, if the processes are on a sufficiently
large scale and sufficiently rapid, is only the direction of the
process in relation to the normal condition of the body. 'When
the natural state of an organism is impaired by processes of combination and separation, of filling and emptying, and by certain
kinds of growth and decay, the result is pain, distress, suffering . . .
and when the organisms are being established in their natural
state . . . that establishment (*katastasis*) is a pleasure' (*Philebus*
42 c, d). Thus over-replenishment could be painful, and a needed
depletion could be pleasant. The theory is suggested by the obvious sensual pleasures, and by the pleasures of convalescence.[1]

[1] Cf. *EN* vii. 12, 1152 b32.

But it is stretched to cover other phenomena; for example the pleasures of smell and other pure pleasures of sense-experience.[1] Depletions are postulated but are said to be too slight to affect the sensitive soul.[2]

I have outlined the theory as we find it in Plato. But it should be added that Aristotle himself formulates and uses it in the *Rhetoric*: 'let it be assumed by us that pleasure is a certain movement (*kinēsis*) of the soul (*psuchē*), an intense (*athroa*) and perceptible (*aisthētē*) settling down (*katastasis*) into its natural state (*phusis*), and pain the opposite' (I. 11, 1369 b33–5). As my transliterations indicate, all the key words of the theory are here. The word translated 'intense' means literally crowded; i.e. quite a large change is packed into quite a short time. It is a reasonable, but not a certain, inference from the fact that Aristotle here states the theory without disowning it that he had not, when he wrote the *Rhetoric*, worked out the theory of pleasure which he expounds in the *EN*.

Aristotle in B, when he discusses the replenishment formula, makes explicitly the point that pleasure is not merely an organic process. He has remarked in Book I that to be pleased is something 'psychic' (8, 1099 a7–8), here using 'psychic' in a sense which implies consciousness (*aisthēsis*), and ignores the biological sense of *empsuchon* and *psuchē*. He remarks now that replenishment is something that happens to the body (*sōmatikon pathos*), and hence that to say that pleasure is a replenishment is to imply, contrary to what we all believe, that it is the body which feels pleasure (1173 b9–11). The right thing to say, therefore, is not that pleasure *is* a replenishment, 'though one might feel pleasure when it is taking place just as one might feel pain under the knife' (b11–13). Aristotle does not imply that the proponents of the theory would deny what he is here saying. As we have seen, the theory cannot be completely stated without implying the psychophysical dualism which Aristotle assumes. Pleasure is a perceived (*aisthētē*) process, and the dualistic implication is clinched by the definition of perception (*aisthēsis*) in the *Philebus* as 'the movement which

---

[1] *Philebus* 51 b, cf. 43 b, c; *Timaeus* 65 a.
[2] Cf. *Republic* 584 b, c; *Philebus* 33 d.

occurs when soul and body come together in a single affection and are moved both together' (34 a).

In both A and B Aristotle argues against the replenishment theory that there are pleasures of which it does not give a correct account. Thus he says in A that not all pleasures involve a process (*genesis*); some are activities (*energeiai*) and arise 'not when we are becoming something but when we are exercising a faculty', e.g. the faculties of sense-perception and of thought (1153 a9–11). Aristotle's distinction between a process and an activity is, as we shall find, unclear. But the respects in which it is unsatisfactory do not affect the present point, that there are pleasures in connection with which processes of the kind required by the theory are postulated only to save the theory. The corresponding passage in B gives a list of pleasures which do not involve the filling of a deficiency (as is suggested by the absence of corresponding pains): 'the pleasures of learning and, among the pleasures of sense, those of smell, and also many sounds and sights, and memories and hopes' (1173 b15–20). This seems to be a valid criticism of the theory; but, as we have seen, the defenders of the theory assume, as regards the pure pleasures of sense, organic processes too mild to register as pains. In the *Rhetoric* Aristotle himself applies the 'return to normality' formula to the pleasures of learning. To wonder and to learn, he says, are as a rule pleasant; for 'wondering implies the desire to learn, so that what causes wonder is to be desired, and learning implies a return to the normal'.[1] The passage makes an observation about the pleasures of learning which we miss in the account given in the *EN* of those godlike pleasures of intellectual contemplation which do not involve a process of transition from ignorance to knowledge and thus exclude both antecedent curiosity and the subsequent surprises of discovery.[2]

It is maintained in A, but not explicitly in B, that the process theory does not give the right account even of the bodily pleasures which suggested it, those involving a process to the normal state of the organism. 'The processes that restore us to our natural state are only incidentally pleasant' (1152 b33–5). The activity theory

---

[1] I. 11, 1371 a31–4.   [2] VII. 14, 1154 b26–8; x. 7, 1177 a25–7.

explains these pleasures also, the activities being those of the elements in the nature of the organism which have remained unimpaired (1152 b35–6; cf. 1154 b17–19). Aristotle appears to offer as a reason for accepting this account of the pleasures which accompany processes of restoration the fact that there are pleasures, such as those of contemplation, which involve no defect (1152 b36–1153 a2). This would be a good argument only if it were reasonable to assume that, if the activity theory holds of some pleasures, it must hold of all. But the assumption is not justified if the question at issue between the rival theories is about the causes of pleasure; for pleasures need not all have the same kind of cause. In view of this difficulty Cook Wilson has suggested that the existence of non-restorative pleasures is given as a reason for the statement that restorative pleasures are good only incidentally, the suggestion that these pleasures are conditioned by the activity of the unimpaired part of the organism (1152 b35–6) being in parenthesis.[1] Aristotle proceeds to find confirmation for his account of the restorative pleasures in the fact that 'men do not enjoy the same pleasant objects when their nature is in its settled state as they do when it is being replenished', e.g. convalescents enjoy sharp and bitter things which are not 'pleasant by nature or without qualification' (1153 a2–6). It is not clear whether he is claiming only that the fact adduced can be explained by the activity theory or is making also the further claim that it cannot be explained by the process theory. Even if the first claim is justified, it is difficult to see that any reason is given for accepting the second.

The process theory of the nature of pleasure is expressed in A as the proposition that pleasure is a 'coming to be'—*genesis* (1152 b13, 1153 a7–17). B also deals with the view that pleasure is a *genesis* but prefers to oppose the view held by Aristotle that it is an activity (A), or rather the completion of an activity (B), to the view that it is a 'movement'—*kinēsis* (1173 a29–31). The word *genesis*, of which the opposite is *phthora* (ceasing to be or destruction), is appropriate when attention is directed on the pleasures of replenishment and the pains of depletion; for the poles or termini

---

[1] *Classical Review*, xvi (1902).

of these processes are the continued existence and the ceasing to
exist of the living body. The word *kinēsis* is sometimes in Aristotle
a general word for any kind of change (the unambiguously general
word is *metabolē*), but sometimes is used as covering only those
forms of change in which a substance or thing exists throughout
the process (change in quality, size, place). In this narrower sense
of *kinēsis* a *genesis* is not a *kinēsis*; coming into existence is not a
change undergone by an existing substance. In the arguments of
B which we have still to consider against the process theory that
theory is expressed as the proposition that pleasure is a movement
(*kinēsis*) in this narrower sense. It is not easy to see clearly what
Aristotle means by his insistence that pleasure is not a movement,
and we shall find that the comparable doctrine of the *Metaphysics*,
while adding to the evidence, does not clear up the difficulties in
the doctrine of the *EN*. The student of the *EN* need not study in
detail Aristotle's classification, which he connects with his doctrine
of categories, of kinds of change. It is found in the *Metaphysics*
(*Λ* 1 and 2), the *Physics* (*E*) and the *De Generatione et Corruptione*.
Useful brief accounts of the classification are given by Joachim
in his commentary on the *EN* (pp. 269-75) and by Ross, especially in his commentary on the *Physics* (pp. 44-8). There is a
penetrating analysis of the difficulties raised by this part of Aristotle's doctrine in an essay by J. L. Ackrill, 'Aristotle's Distinction between *energeia* and *kinēsis*'.[1] The discussion which follows
of Aristotle's reasons for denying that pleasure is a 'movement'
owes much to this essay.

The process theory is introduced in A as being a main reason
for the denial that pleasure is good: pleasure, if it is a *genesis*, cannot be an 'end' any more than the process of building a house, as
opposed to the house, is an end (1152 b12-15). Those who hold
that pleasure is a coming to be are taken to imply that it is what
comes to be, not the process of becoming, that is the end, the end
being 'better' than the process of reaching it (1153 a7-9). The
example of building, with *kinēsis* (movement) replacing *genesis*
(coming to be), recurs in B: 'every movement, e.g. that of
building, takes time and is for the sake of an end, and is complete

[1] See Bibliographical Note, p. 316.

when it has made what it aims at' (1174 a19–21). Aristotle's account represents the antihedonist as having two theses to defend: that pleasure is a movement; that, because it is a movement, it is not good or not the only good.

Aristotle discusses only the first thesis. He admits in A that some people who have held that pleasure is good have also held that it is a process (1153 a15–17), but he does not discuss this view. His failure effectively to question the second thesis seems to be due in part to a failure to distinguish explicitly between 'end' in the sense of a planned termination and 'end' in the sense of desired for itself. That these senses are different is clear from the fact that when, for example, we occupy ourselves with a crossword puzzle or play golf, our planned termination, the solution of the puzzle or the winning of the game, may not be very seriously or at all strongly desired and is certainly not desired to the exclusion of an independent desire for the process leading to it. But the second thesis is nevertheless acceptable in the limited sense that a 'movement' which is the execution of a task is not normally the only object desired by the executor of the task. In all normal cases the termination itself, the completion of the task, will be desired. In the motive of anyone who undertakes a task, e.g. building a house or writing a poem, a desire that the task should be completed is an element, sometimes the only element and often an important element. No one wants to be the sort of man who fails to complete tasks. But to say that the completion of the task is desired for its own sake is not to say that the activity of completing it is not also desired for its own sake. Aristotle fails to notice, or at least omits to note, this point.[1]

Against the view that pleasure is a movement (kinēsis) it is argued in B that, whereas every movement, including that of the heavens, is quick or slow, pleasures are not quick or slow and cannot, therefore, be movements. We can change quickly or slowly into a state of pleasure, but 'we cannot quickly exhibit the activity (energeia) of pleasure'; we cannot be pleased quickly (1173 a31–b4). In the following chapter Aristotle argues from some further characteristics of movement that a pleasure cannot be a movement.

[1] Cf. Ch. II, especially pp. 13–14.

Every movement, he says, is 'in time' and, as in the case of the building of a house, is 'complete when it has made what it aims at' (1174 a19–21). Is he implying that, whereas a movement must begin at a time and end at a later time, this need not be true of a pleasure? This is what he seems to say: 'it is not possible to move otherwise than in time, but it is possible to be pleased; for that which takes place in a moment [in 'the now'] is a whole' (1174 b7–9). Here he seems to make the paradoxical assertion that a pleasure is at a time but need not last over a time. But he has also just made the different assertion that 'the form of pleasure is complete at any and every time' (1174 b5–6). What this statement suggests is that, whereas a movement must have duration because it involves being at different places (or in different states) at different times, this reason cannot be given for saying that a pleasure must have duration. But what follows from this is not that a pleasure need not last over a time but that it need not change during the time that it lasts.

The statement that pleasure is 'complete at any time' should be considered along with a passage in the *Metaphysics* where Aristotle expounds a distinction between a movement and an activity (Θ 6, 1048 b18–35). He gives as a distinguishing criterion of an activity that, if a man is performing one, he can at the same time be said to be performing and to have performed it.

At the same time we are seeing and have seen, are understanding and have understood, are thinking and have thought: but it is not true that at the same time we are learning and have learnt, or are being cured and have been cured. At the same time we are living well and have lived well, and are happy and have been happy. If not, the process would have had some time to cease, as the process of slimming ceases: but, as it is, it does not cease; we are living and have lived. Of these processes, then, we must call the one set movements and the other activities. For every movement is incomplete, slimming, learning, walking, building. (1048 b23–30.)

There is in this passage no suggestion that an activity, or an actual state, need not have a duration: the contrary is implied by 'it does not cease'. What is said is that it is complete at any time and that there is no time at which it is due to cease, as the building of a

house ceases when the house has been built or walking ceases
when the destination has been reached. We must now consider
what distinction Aristotle is here making and what significance it
can have in his ethical theory.

We should recall first that, in Aristotle's technical use of
energeia (actuality) as opposed to *dunamis* (potentiality), *kinēsis*
(movement) and *energeia* are not mutually exclusive; for a movement is the actuality of a capacity for movement. Both what
Aristotle here calls movements and what he calls activities
(*energeiai* in a restricted sense) are actual performances (*energeiai* in
the technical sense). We have to ask then by what criteria Aristotle
divides performances into movements (kinetic performances) and
activities (non-kinetic performances). We might try to separate
them by using the formula of the *Metaphysics* (Θ 6): 'at the same
time is —ing and has —ed'. It might be suggested that a performance is non-kinetic if the formula applies to it. Thus it is true
of anyone now feeling a pleasure, or hearing a sound, that he also
has felt the pleasure or has heard the sound. I understand Aristotle
as implying that, while however short the time (duration) over
which the pleasure has been felt there is always a shorter time
(duration) over which it has been felt, the time (instant) at which
it begins to be felt is not one of the times (instants) at which it is
felt. The formula combining the present and perfect tenses cannot, on the other hand, be applied to a movement. If a man is
building a house he has not yet built it, and if he has built it he is
no longer building it. But this criterion will not enable us to
separate two kinds of performance since the same performance
could be kinetic or non-kinetic according to the way in which it is
described. Thus a man who is occupied in building a house has
been occupied in building a house. The criterion would make
walking home kinetic but walking, in contradiction of what
Aristotle says in the *EN*, non-kinetic. Similarly hearing a symphony would be kinetic but hearing music would be non-kinetic:
a man has not yet heard the symphony, but has heard music,
when he is still hearing the symphony (music).

It might be suggested that a performance is non-kinetic if no
description of it would make it kinetic. But it could then only be

a persisting activity or state from which change was excluded. For, if there were change, all that Aristotle says about there being a succession of different stages in the kinetic performance of building a house or walking from one place to another would apply *mutatis mutandis*. For example, if a sound which a man was hearing were getting louder, its different loudnesses at its beginning and at its end and at intermediate points could be specified. The performance could then be described as a movement from one loudness to another, as walking is a movement from one place to another.

The conclusion so far reached is that the formula in the *Metaphysics* (Θ 6) gives no criterion for sorting out 'activities' and 'movements' except a criterion which would entail that, in the performance of an activity, the performer persists without changing. This conclusion is reinforced by the passage at the end of Λ which distinguishes between 'activity of movement', i.e. involving change, and 'activity of immobility' (*energeia akinēsias*), the unchanging contemplation ascribed to God: 'there is not only an activity of movement but an activity of immobility, and pleasure is found more in rest than in movement' (1154 b26–8). But Aristotle clearly wishes to hold that *human* performances can be kinetic or non-kinetic, and he implies in the *Metaphysics* that, when a *man* exercises his capacity for perception and thought, his activity is non-kinetic. What then is the distinction between one set of human activities and another which Aristotle is in effect making? Not the distinction between producing an object of art or craft, a poem or a house, and doing an action. For he would class as movements many activities not productive or technical; walking, for example, or learning a skill or a science. The distinction which he indicates is rather between activities, including productive activities, which have a definite terminus, the completion of a task, and activities which have no such definite or defined terminus, e.g. taking country walks, listening to music, or thinking philosophically. As regards the relative desirability of these two kinds of activity Aristotle, as we have seen, tends to assume that not having a terminus is a property which makes an activity more desirable, perhaps because more like that of God.

This is a mistake, even if we abstract from our natural liking for jobs done, tasks completed. Writing an article on philosophy, for example, is more worth while than reflective thinking which need not be brought to a head or conclusion. Listening to a symphony, taken as a task, is better value than music while you work. I need not add to what I have said earlier[1] about the mistaken idea that desire for productive or task-fulfilling activity is wholly dependent on desire for the existence of the product, that the only end is what comes at the end.

We saw that, in his examination of the view that pleasure is a process, Aristotle has in mind doctrines expounded in Plato's dialogues, especially the *Philebus*. The *Philebus* is probably in his mind also in the section of B, to which no section in A corresponds, which criticizes the view 'that the good is determinate, while pleasure, because it admits of degrees, is indeterminate' (1173 a15–28).[2] In the *Philebus* pleasure and pain, as admitting of degrees, are in the category of the unlimited (*apeiron*) (24 e, 27 e, 31 a), although the so-called pure pleasures are allowed a humble place among the constituents of the good life (62 e–64 a); pure pleasures of thought and sense are ranked fifth in the order of goods (66 c). Aristotle's answer in B to the argument that pleasure cannot be good because it is indeterminate states three objections. (1) If what is meant is that it is possible to feel pleasure or pain more or less intensely, it may be replied that a man may be more or less just or brave and may act more or less justly or bravely. Thus, it is implied, the argument would prove that ethical virtue is not good (1173 a17–22). In the *Categories* Aristotle recognizes that, while we certainly do speak of one man as more just than another, it is not clear in what sense a quality of the kind to which justice belongs (*diathesis* or *hexis*) admits of degrees.[3] (2) The anti-hedonist argument overlooks the distinction between 'unmixed' and 'mixed' pleasures (1173 a22–3). The mixed pleasures are those connected with bodily appetite and with the restoration of organic normality. They are liable to be preceded or accompanied by corresponding pains and are depreciated by the antihedonist,

---

[1] p. 306.   [2] Cf. II. 6, 1106 b29–30; IX. 9, 1170 a20–5.
[3] 8, 10 b26–11 a14.

in spite of their intensity, as false or impure.[1] Aristotle implies that, whatever validity there is in the charge of indeterminacy against certain bodily pleasures, the charge does not hold against the pleasures which attend virtuous activities. Further consideration of the alleged falsity or impurity of certain pleasures belongs to the study of the *Philebus* rather than of the *EN*. (3) The fact that pleasure admits of degrees does not entail that it is not determinate; for health, which is determinate, admits differences of greater and less within limits (1172 a23–8). I have already[2] considered this passage as it bears on the doctrine that ethical virtue lies in a mean.

Of the points considered in both A and B it is worth noting two on which B is clearer or more explicit than A. (1) A states but does not discuss the argument that pleasure is shown to be best by the fact that all creatures, human and non-human, pursue it (1153 b25–1154 a1). In B the argument is ascribed to Eudoxus (1172 b9–15), and against the objection that the pleasure-seekers include mindless creatures and bad men the point is made that intelligent creatures also pursue it (1172 b35–1173 a5). (2) Again B gives a fuller refutation than A of the reply ascribed in A to Speusippus to the argument from opposition, i.e. the argument that, pain being admittedly bad, its opposite, pleasure, must be good. There is evidence that Speusippus held that the good life is neither pleasant nor painful, that disturbance of either kind is to be avoided.[3] It seems to be implied in A that he argued that pleasure and pain could be opposed to each other and yet both bad, as the greater and the less are opposed to each other and both to the equal (1153 b4–6). This, Aristotle says, will not do, 'since he would not say that pleasure is essentially just a species of evil' (1153 b6–7). But Aristotle does not make clear why Speusippus should not say this. The corresponding passage in B drives the argument home by insisting on the difficulty of maintaining that pleasure and pain are alike in being as such bad and objects of aversion: 'in fact people evidently avoid the one as evil and choose the other as good; that then must be the nature of the opposition between them' (1173 a5–13).

[1] Cf. 1154 a25–31.   [2] See above, Ch. VII, p. 143.
[3] Clem. Alex., *Strom.* II. 22, 133 = fr. 57 Lang.

The view, ascribed to Eudoxus, that pleasure is 'the good' may be taken as asserting (1) that only pleasure is good in the sense of being an object desirable for its own sake, and (2) that all pleasures are good. Aristotle does not agree with either assertion, but his acceptance in both A and B of the argument that, pain being undesirable, pleasure must in general be desirable is one of the ways in which he implies the opinion that sensual pleasures, if not pursued in excess as they are by morbid or vicious men, have a place in the good life as a constituent of happiness. The doctrine of the mean, in its application to the virtue of temperance (*sōphrosunē*), rejects the ascetic view that the less we indulge in these pleasures the better. 'All men', he observes in A, 'enjoy in some way dainty foods and wines and sexual intercourse but not all men do so as they ought' (1154 a17–18). These pleasures get a bad reputation because they are pursued to excess, sometimes in order to expel pains (1154 a27), by men who are bad congenitally or from habit (a32–3). Sometimes 'they are pursued because of their violence by those who cannot enjoy other pleasures', e.g. some people deliberately make themselves thirsty (1154 b2–4). But Aristotle does not think that an effect of contrast with pain or suffering is an inevitable element in sensual pleasures. The intemperate man 'feels more pain than he should at not getting pleasant things, but the temperate man . . . is not pained by the absence of what is pleasant' (III. 11, 1118 b30–3). 'The alternative to excess of pleasure is not pain except to the man who pursues this excess' (1154 a19–21).

In the concluding chapters of B (x. 4 and 5) Aristotle expounds his own view that pleasures complete activities, and that there are specific differences between pleasures corresponding to the specific differences between the activities which they complete. He starts from a contrast between his own view and the process theory, and I have already discussed the difficulties raised by the distinction between *kinēsis* and *energeia*. His positive account (1174 b14 ff.) starts from activities of sense-perception. Perception is most complete (*teleiotatē*) and is pleasant when the perceiving subject (or the organ of perception) is in the best condition in relation to the finest of its objects (1174 b14–20). There is pleasure in connection with intellectual activity as well as with perception, and the pleasure completes (*teleioi*) the activity (b20-3). The passage which follows repeats much of what has been said about the activity of perception, and in it Aristotle tells us, or tries to tell us, in what way a pleasure 'completes' an activity (1174 b23-1175 a3). Commentators are not agreed on the meaning of the sentences in which this answer is given. The pleasure does not complete the activity 'in the same way as the object (*aisthēton*) and the sense (*aisthēsis*) . . . just as health and the doctor are not in the same way the cause of a man's being healthy' (1174 b23-6). A few lines later we are told that the pleasure completes the activity 'not as the corresponding permanent state (*hexis*) by its immanence (*enhuparchousa*), but as an end which supervenes as the bloom of youth does on those in the flower of their age' (b31-3). These sentences are separately difficult and more difficult when considered, as they must be, together.

In the former sentence Aristotle, in order to clarify the sense in which pleasure completes activity, makes use of the doctrine that there are four different senses of 'cause'. In the example of health it seems clear that the doctor is the efficient cause of healthy activity and it is natural to take health, in the sense of the condition of being healthy, as the form or formal cause.[1] As the example of health is apparently intended to illustrate the status of pleasure, it seems necessary to suppose, with Stewart, that pleasure corresponds to health as formal cause and that 'the combination of object and sense' (Ross) corresponds to the doctor as efficient cause. But the second passage contrasts pleasure as 'an end which supervenes' with the state or condition (*hexis*), and the *hexis*, if it is a kind of cause, should be the formal cause. Thus the first passage would assimilate pleasure to a formal cause, while the second would distinguish it from a formal cause and make it not any kind of cause but an epiphenomenon (supervening effect). We should then have to explain the apparent contradiction by saying that the first passage does not give a final or strictly accurate answer but is a dialectical move towards the strict answer. This must be Stewart's view, although he does not, I think, make

[1] Cf. VI. 12, 1144 a3-5.

it clear. Anyone who finds this explanation unacceptable must think again about the first sentence. Burnet understands health and the doctor as illustrating the difference between sense (*aisthē-sis*) and its object not the difference between these in combination and pleasure—'the pleasure which supervenes is something different from its efficient or formal cause'. I am inclined to think it necessary, if the sentence is to be so understood, to amend the text: Hackforth has suggested corrections (*oud' hōsper* for *hōsper oud'* and delete *homoiōs*) which would give the meaning 'nor as health and the doctor are causes . . .' for 'just as health and the doctor are not in the same way the cause . . .'. Rodier makes a similar correction but surprisingly takes sense and health as material causes. Gauthier–Jolif held that the first passage does assimilate pleasure to health but that they are both ends or final causes; for health as a final cause they adduce *EN* 1094 a8, 1145 a7–9 and *EE* 1218 b2–3, 18–22. In the second passage Gauthier-Jolif again take pleasure to be a final cause, but very strangely argue that the 'permanent state' (*hexis*) is an efficient cause. We can conclude from this review of the opinions of commentators that, if Aristotle hoped by bringing in the four causes to make clear what he wished to say about pleasure, he was unsuccessful. I think that the interpretations of Stewart and Hackforth are both possible, and I do not know how to decide between them.

In x. 5 Aristotle states the doctrine that activities different in kind are completed and promoted by pleasures different in kind and that, the better or worse the activity, the better or worse is the pleasure. The text does not raise any special problems of interpretation in detail. The doctrine looks plausible until we ask why we should accept it and what are the facts on which it is based. It recalls the no less enigmatic doctrine of J. S. Mill that pleasures differ from each other in quality as well as quantity (intensity and duration). As I suggested earlier,[1] many philosophers now would reject the doctrine as Aristotle states it and would explain his acceptance of it as due to an assumption that, when we speak of, for example, the pleasures of philosophy or music, we are referring to experiences which are not to be identified

---

[1] See pp. 207–9 above.

with the activities of doing philosophy or listening to music; just as we are referring to definite and familiar sensations when we speak of the pleasure of sherry-drinking. The philosopher and the musician, it would be said, have no such experiences to report or describe as the oenologist reports on the taste of the sherry. When we are reading without concentration or are listening to music with boredom, we may notice feelings of strain or bodily aches. When our activity flows freely, when we are enjoying the book or the music, any sensations we have, in the sense of localized bodily feelings, are unnoticed. The printed page or the music, and the intellectual processes they evoke, absorb our attention. Hence, as Aristotle observes, 'in the theatre the people who eat sweets do so when the actors are poor' (1175 b10–13). At one point Aristotle does admit that there is a question about the distinct existence of the pleasures which he has described as being the inseparable companions of our successful activities. The pleasures are 'so hard to distinguish from the activities that it admits of dispute whether the activity is not the same as the pleasure' (1175 b32–3). But, having thus opened the door to scepticism about his doctrine, he quickly shuts it again: 'still pleasure does not seem to *be* thought or perception—that would be absurd' (b34–5). The question he ought to have asked is what we are saying about, for example, a game or a theatrical performance when we assert or deny that it was pleasant. This question has the merit of not suggesting that we are bound either to assert or to deny that the pleasure we feel is the same thing as the activity we perform. Both the assertion and the denial can be misleading. The words 'activity' and 'pleasure' may not be used to refer to different experiences but they are at least used to say different things about the same experience.

BIBLIOGRAPHICAL NOTE

Much has been written on the theory of pleasure in Plato and Aristotle. It may be a convenience for readers to have a note repeating and amplifying the references I have made, other than those to editions of the *EN*, to this literature.

Two recent books are devoted to the discussion of the treatment of pleasure in the *Ethics*:

A. J. Festugière, *Aristote, Le Plaisir* (Paris, 1936, reprinted 1960).

Godo Lieberg, *Die Lehre von der Lust in den Ethiken des Aristoteles* (München, 1958).

Both these works give bibliographical information.

The views of Plato and Aristotle are compared by A. E. Taylor in his edition of the *Timaeus* (note on 64 d7, pp. 447–62).

R. Hackforth's *Plato's Examination of Pleasure* (1945) is a Translation, with Introduction and Commentary, of the *Philebus*.

J. Gosling and A. Kenny discuss acutely the doctrine of False Pleasures in the *Philebus* in *Phronesis* iv–vi (1959–61).

On Aristotle's appraisal of the *kinēsis* theory of pleasure essential reading is the essay by J. L. Ackrill in *New Essays on Plato and Aristotle* (1965), 'Aristotle's Distinction between *energeia* and *kinēsis*'. See also the Symposium ('States, Activities, and Performances') by T. C. Potts and C. C. W. Taylor in *Proceedings of the Aristotelian Society* (1965, suppl. vol.).

When I have referred to recent work on pleasure I have had in mind mainly Gilbert Ryle's chapter (iv) in *Dilemmas*, Cambridge, 1954, and his article in the *Proceedings of the Aristotelian Society*, supplementary volume, 1954. Specially helpful for the study of Aristotle are the article, 'Pleasure', by C. C. W. Taylor in *Analysis*, supplementary volume, 1963; chapter vi ('Pleasure') in *Action, Emotion and Will*, Anthony Kenny, 1963; and 'Aristotle on Pleasure' by J. O. Urmson in *Aristotle*, edited by J. M. E. Moravcsik, 1967. References to other recent discussions of pleasure are given by Taylor on p. 2.

FRIENDSHIP AND SELF-LOVE

'AFTER what we have said, a discussion of friendship would naturally follow, since it is a virtue or implies virtue, and is besides most necessary with a view to living. For without friends no one would choose to live, although he had all other goods . . .' (VIII. 1, 1155 a3–6). 'Friendship' is an inadequate rendering of *philia* which covers, as Ross points out, 'any mutual attraction between two human beings'.[1] Friends (in English) are persons outside the immediate family circle with whom interests are shared, so that conversation is easy. *Philoi* include friends in this sense but also all those who are 'dear' (*philos* is alike active and passive, 'friend' primarily active), especially wives and husbands and children and parents. There is a natural *philia* between parents and offspring 'not only among men but among birds and among most animals' (1155 a16–19). A mother's love for her children is adduced by Aristotle as a conspicuous example of the disinterestedness of friendship: sometimes she shows her love by handing her child to foster-parents, knowing that the child in ignorance 'can give her nothing of a mother's due' (1159 a28–33). Marriage is for Aristotle an important kind of friendship.

Between man and wife friendship seems to exist by nature; for man is naturally inclined to form couples—even more than to form cities, inasmuch as the household is earlier and more necessary than the city, and reproduction is more common to man with the animals. With the other animals the union extends only to this point, but human beings live together not only for the sake of reproduction but also for the various purposes of life; for from the start the functions are divided, and those of man and woman are different; so they help each other by throwing their peculiar gifts into the common stock. It is for these reasons that both utility and pleasure seem to be found in this kind of

[1] *Aristotle*, p. 230.

friendship. But this friendship may be based also on virtue, if the parties are good; for each has its own virtue and they will delight in the fact. And children seem to be a bond of union. (VIII. 12, 1162 a16–27.)

In another passage Aristotle compares the authority of the husband over the wife to an aristocracy which degenerates into an oligarchy if the man rules in everything without regard to his worth. But he adds that, when the wife is an heiress, it is sometimes she who rules (10, 1160 b32–1161 a3).

In the *Politics* as in the *Ethics* Aristotle dwells on the biological and instinctive basis of the tendency in human beings to seek each other's company. A state is a 'community of families' and 'can be established only among those who live in the same place and intermarry'. 'Hence arise in cities family connections, brotherhoods, common sacrifices, amusements which draw men together; these are created by friendship, for the will to live together is friendship.'[1] We are given a similar catalogue in the *Ethics* of forms of association in which worship of the gods is combined with social meetings: religious guilds and clubs 'assigning honours to the gods, and providing pleasant relaxations for themselves' (VIII. 9, 1160 a19–25). It is well to stress, because it is easy to overlook, this side of Aristotle's account of the good life; his insistence on the value of 'friendship' of many kinds and at many levels. A. E. Taylor in his account of the *Lysis*, Plato's dialogue on friendship, expresses a suspicion that 'those who condemn the tone of Greek ethics as "self-centred" have usually skipped these books [VIII and IX] in their reading of the *Ethics* . . .'.[2]

Aristotle's assertion that friendship 'is a virtue or implies virtue' is not to be taken as referring to the *philia* (friendliness) which appears in the list of ethical virtues in *EN* II. 7. 'The man who is pleasant in the right way is friendly and the mean is friendliness, while the man who exceeds is an obsequious person (*areskos*) if he has no end in view, a flatterer if he is aiming at his own advantage, and the man who falls short and is unpleasant in all circumstances is a quarrelsome and surly sort of person' (1108 a26–30). In IV. 6 this virtue of social intercourse is said to be name-

---

[1] *Politics* Γ 9, 1280 b35–9.   [2] *Plato*, p. 65.

less but to resemble *philia*: 'but it differs from friendship in that it implies no passion or affection for one's associates' (1126 b19–28). Aristotle is now discussing *philia* not in this restricted sense but in the sense in which it does involve 'affection for one's associates'.

The statement that friendship 'implies virtue' is not explained, but can be understood in terms of the doctrine that 'perfect friendship is the friendship of men who are good and alike in virtue' (1156 b7–8). 'Those who wish well to their friends for their sake are most truly friends; for they do this by reason of their own nature and not incidentally; therefore their friendship lasts as long as they are good—and goodness is an enduring thing' (b9–12; cf. 1159 a8–12). Aristotle has said in chapter 1 that friendship is 'not only necessary but also noble; for we praise those who love their friends, and it is thought to be a fine thing to have many friends; and again we think it is the same people that are good men and are friends' (1155 a28–31). At the beginning of chapter 2 he distinguishes three kinds of friendship on the basis of a classification of 'objects of love' (*philēta*) as good, pleasant, or useful (1155 b17–19). 'But it would seem to be that by which some good or pleasure is produced that is useful, so that it is the good and the pleasant that are lovable as ends' (b19–21). In the chapters which follow (2–6) Aristotle examines the differences and relations between these three main kinds of friendship. In my summary of what Aristotle says in these and later chapters I shall confine critical discussion to questions of interpretation which are crucial for the understanding of Aristotle's general doctrine.

The main points in Aristotle's treatment (VIII. 2–6) of the three kinds of friendship may be summarized as follows. (1) Friendship is more than 'good will when it is reciprocated'; for we should not speak of two people as 'friends' unless their mutual feelings were acknowledged and known to both (1155 b33–1156 a5).[1] (2) In the case of the inferior kinds of friendship the friend is loved not 'as being the man he is' but because he causes pleasure or is useful (e.g. in a business partnership), and such friendships tend to break up easily (1156 a10–b6). (3) When friends are 'alike in their excellence' their relationship may include the characteristics

---

[1] Cf. on *eunoia* (good will) IX. 5.

of the less perfect kinds; the friends are useful and pleasant to each other. Such friendship is rare since there are few such men, and requires also time and familiarity (1156 b7–32). (4) Friendships between bad or inferior persons belong to one or other of the inferior kinds or exceptionally and by coincidence are a combination of both (1157 a33–b5; cf. 1158 a27–33). (5) The feeling of love (*philēsis*) must be distinguished from love as a state of character (*philia*), a disposition (*hexis*) involving choice (*prohairesis*) (1157 b28–31). (6) 'Men wish well to those whom they love, for their sake, not as a result of feeling (*pathos*) but as a result of character; and in loving a friend men love what is good for themselves; for the good man in becoming a friend becomes a good to his friend' (1157 b31–4). Here Aristotle touches on the egoism of love, a theme raising questions of psychology and ethics which are his main concern in the later sections of his treatment of friendship. (7) Friendship for the sake of pleasure, as in the young, is more like true friendship than is the utilitarian kind which is for the commercially minded (1158 a18–27).

The kinds of friendship so far discussed have been regarded as friendships between equals (1158 b1). Aristotle turns in chapter 7 to friendships in which the parties are unequal; 'that of father to son and in general of older to younger, that of man to wife and in general that of ruler to subject' (1158 b11–14). He points out that there are different kinds of friendship between unequals, and that, when there is inequality, what is felt on one side is different from what is felt on the other (b14–28). Inequality may be so great as to make friendship impossible (1158 b33–1159 a5). He moves on in chapter 8 to further reflections on the reciprocity, the exchange of goods involved in such friendships. Most men desire to be loved rather than loving (1159 a12–14), and Aristotle connects this with their natural desire to be honoured: honour from good men confirms their good opinion of themselves (a22–4). For its own sake also being loved is pleasant (a25–7). But, as the example of maternal love suggests, the characteristic virtue of friends lies in loving (1159 a27–b1). Aristotle comes round again to his central truism that the best and most secure friendship is that between friends who are alike in virtue (b2–10).

Chapter 8 concludes with some remarks on friendships 'between contraries': rich and poor, learned and ignorant, lovers not alike lovable (b12–19). Aristotle adds the obscure comment that, in such cases, 'contrary does not even aim at contrary by its own nature, but only incidentally, the desire being for what is intermediate (*meson*)' (b19–21). Here he offers analogies only from speculative physics: 'it is good for the dry not to become wet but to come to the intermediate state, and similarly with the hot and in all other cases' (b21–3). These comparisons, as Aristotle says, are 'somewhat foreign to our inquiry' (b23–4).[1] He is indeed quite clear that the fancies of the poets and the speculations of pre-Socratic philosophers on strife and friendship as cosmic principles have nothing to do with the case of human friendships (1155 b9). It is unsatisfactory that he gives no examples to illustrate the sense in which friendships between unequals have in view a good which is intermediate or a 'mean'.[2] Perhaps what he has in mind is that such friendships depend on exchanges of benefits, analogous to commercial transactions, and hence seek a mean in a sense similar to the mean in commercial justice (v. 5).[3] The connections between friendship and justice are discussed in the next following section (VIII. 9–12).

'Friendship and justice seem . . . to be concerned with the same objects and exhibited between the same persons. For in every community (*koinōnia*) there is thought to be some form of justice and friendship too' (1159 b25–7; cf. 1155 a22–8). 'The extent of their community is the extent of their friendship, as it is the extent to which justice exists between them'.[4] The communities of which Aristotle speaks are 'parts of the political community' (1160 a9, a28–30). The state aims at the 'common advantage' which is what legislators call just (1160 a11–14). The aims of other associations, business partnerships and clubs and parish councils, are in different ways partial and not inclusive (a14 ff.). In the discussion which follows Aristotle has much to say about family

[1] Cf. 1155 b1–9; Plato, *Lysis* 213 e–216 a.
[2] In the *EN*, but see *EE H*, 1239 b29–1240 a4.
[3] Cf. IX. 1, 1163 b32–1164 a6.
[4] 1159 b29–31; 1160 a7–8; cf. *MM B* 11, 1211 a6–8.

relationships: parents and children, brothers and sisters, even cousins (1162 a1). I quoted earlier his assessment of marriage. He remarks that parents tend to feel closer to their children than children to their parents, and that there is an egoistic element in parental devotion: 'parents love their children as being a part of themselves' (1161 b18). In chapters 10 and 11 Aristotle expounds the doctrine that there are specific types of justice and 'friendship' corresponding to three types of political constitution, monarchy, aristocracy, and timocracy (or polity), and the perverted forms (*parekbaseis*) of these which arise when the ruling element seeks its own good instead of the good of the community. Analogies are noted between these constitutional forms and relationships within families or households (1160 b22–1161 a9). On slavery Aristotle's view is that a slave can be a friend so far as he is a man but not so far as he is a 'living tool' (1161 b2–5). 'For there seems to be some justice between any man and any other who can share in a system of law or be a party to an agreement; therefore there can also be friendship with him (the slave) in so far as he is a man' (b5–8). These chapters may be regarded as an appendix to the treatment of justice in Book v. They stress the connection between the rules and conventions of organized associations and the manifold interests which these associations promote.

The following five chapters (VIII. 13, 14 and IX. 1–3) form a section which, in the table of contents preceding the Oxford Translation, has the title 'casuistry of friendship'. The parties in each of the three kinds of friendship, friendships of the good and friendships for pleasure and for utility, may be either equal or unequal. Aristotle discusses the principles governing exchanges of benefits first in friendships between equals, next in friendships between unequals, and thirdly in friendships where the motives of the two sides are different, e.g. pleasure on one side and utility on the other. In covering this kind of ground it is not possible even for Aristotle, nor did he try, to avoid a certain amount of platitude, but the treatment is often lively and acute. It would be interesting to know how the lecture audience received the remark that no adequate return can ever be made to those from whom we have learned philosophy: 'for their worth cannot be measured against money, and they can get no honour which will balance their services, but still it is perhaps enough, as it is with the gods and with one's parents, to give them what we can' (1164 b2–6). There follows an interesting chapter (IX. 2) on conflicts of obligation: e.g. 'whether we should render a service by preference to a friend or to a good man, and should show gratitude to a benefactor or oblige a friend, if one cannot do both' (1164 b25–7). In general the payment of debts should have priority over gifts or benefactions. 'But perhaps even this is not always true; e.g. should a man who has been ransomed out of the hands of brigands ransom his ransomer in return, whoever he may be (or pay him if he has not been captured but demands payment), or should he ransom his father? It would seem that he should ransom his father in preference even to himself' (1164 b33–1165 a2). Thus in general the debt should be paid first, but the rule may be broken when the gift is 'exceedingly noble or exceedingly necessary' (a2–4). We can agree with Aristotle on this, but we may be less inclined to follow him in his next suggestion. If a man of good character who has previously borrowed money from a man whose character he does not respect is asked in return to make a loan to his benefactor, he (the good man) might be justified in refusing on the ground that, whereas the other had been able to count on getting his money back, he (the good man) could not so count (1165 a5–12). There is nothing to surprise us in the concluding chapter (IX. 3) of the section which deals with the occasions for breaking off friendships.

Chapter 4 opens as follows: 'friendly relations with one's neighbours, and the marks by which friendships are defined, seem to have proceeded from a man's relations to himself' (1166 a1–2). This thesis, expressed by Ross as 'the view that friendship is based on the love of the good man for himself',[1] is clearly regarded by Aristotle as important and it occupies him for most of the remainder of Book IX. The thesis is made difficult to interpret by the fact that the word 'self-love' (*philautia*), and comparable words in English such as 'egoism' and 'selfish', are in a variety of ways ambiguous and misleading. Aristotle's argument reaches its climax and conclusion in chapters 8 and 9. But chapter 4 is

[1] *Aristotle*, p. 231.

important because in it he is apparently trying to establish a proposition which his main argument requires as a premiss but which, as I shall suggest, is not true in the sense which the argument requires. This is the proposition expressed by saying that the good man 'is related to his friend as to himself', his friend being 'another self', an *alter ego* in Latin and *allos autos* in Greek (1166 a29–32).

Aristotle lists some defining characteristics of friendship. A friend wishes and does what is good for the sake of his friend, wishes for the sake of his friend that his friend should exist and live, lives with his friend, has the same preferences, grieves and rejoices with him (1166 a2–10). Similarly the good man is of one mind with himself, is single-minded in his desires, wishes and does what is good for himself for his own sake, wishes himself to live and to be preserved and wishes to live with himself, grieves and rejoices with himself, and finds the same things pleasant and painful at all times. In short, the good man is related to himself in the ways in which he is related to his friend (a10–33). But, as if not wholly convinced by his own queer-sounding arguments, Aristotle immediately adds: 'whether there is or is not friendship between a man and himself is a question we may dismiss for the present; there would seem to be friendship in so far as he is two or more . . .' (1166 a33–5).

We recall that in Book v Aristotle's conclusion on the question whether a man can be just or unjust to himself is that there can be justice, but only in a metaphorical sense, between different elements in his nature (11, 1138 b5–8). Ross suggests that 'the intimate nature of the relation' led Aristotle to think that reflexive friendship is more possible, or less clearly impossible, than reflexive justice. But Ross rejects this idea on the ground that the relations defining friendship 'involve two distinct selves'. That this is so, at least as regards 'grieving and rejoicing with' someone (else), is clear when we reflect that our awareness of pleasures and pains in others, however agreeable or distressing to us, is unlike our awareness of our own pleasures and pains. Aristotle adduces the intimate relation between mother and child. But, when a mother is distressed by her child's toothache, the distress which she endures, and is aware of enduring, is not toothache but her own sympathy and pity. We shall find later that the concept of self-awareness is crucial in the later development of Aristotle's argument when it is resumed in chapters 8 and 9.

In the second part of chapter 4, which need not detain us, Aristotle argues that the 'friendly' relations in which a good man stands to himself are not characteristic of bad men. Bad men are at variance with themselves and inclined to run away from themselves; they are 'full of repentance' (1166 b24-5). 'Having nothing lovable (*philēton*) in their nature they have no feeling of love to themselves' (b17-18, 25-6). Aristotle specifies incontinent people (*akrateis*) who 'choose, instead of the things they themselves think good, things that are pleasant but hurtful' (b6-10). Incontinence is the kind of badness of which Aristotle primarily speaks in this passage. But he would no doubt say that even the man who is relatively single-minded in pursuing bad or inadequate ends is likely to despise himself at times, at least if he sees that others despise him.

The three following chapters (IX. 5-7) interrupt, as I have indicated, the main course of Aristotle's argument. He proceeds (ch. 5) to distinguish friendship from 'goodwill' (*eunoia*), which does not require intimacy or even acquaintance, and (ch. 6) from unanimity (*homonoia*), which he describes as 'political friendship', holding between good men who co-operate in public services. Chapter 7 discusses the pleasures of beneficence.

It is sometimes said that Aristotle will not admit that men can feel and act unselfishly. Ross describes him as trying 'to break down the antithesis between egoism and altruism', presumably by showing that apparent altruism is really egoism.[1] D. J. Allan says of Aristotle that 'self-interest, more or less enlightened, is assumed to be the motive of all conduct and choice'.[2] G. C. Field, on the whole a fair and sympathetic critic of Aristotle, went so far as to say that, whereas morality is 'essentially unselfish', Aristotle's idea of the final end or good makes morality 'ultimately selfish'.[3] But, if these criticisms have plausibility and a measure of truth, it is

---

[1] *Aristotle*, p. 231. [2] *The Philosophy of Aristotle*, p. 189.
[3] *Moral Theory*, pp. 109, 111.

important to recognize also what confusions Aristotle avoided and what contributions he made to the clarification of the issues. I shall now describe some of the ambiguities, and possible confusions, connected with the opposition of egoism and altruism. This is necessary if we are to understand what Aristotle has to say.

The word 'egoism' can be used to refer to many different propositions about men's motives and conduct. When qualified by 'psychological' it has sometimes been used as a name for the view that human desires, widely as they may differ, all resemble each other, in so far as they are not dependent on other desires, in that the 'object' anticipated and desired is some state of the man who has the desire. Somewhat more precisely, what is suggested is that we desire pleasant or enjoyable experiences and are averse from unpleasant or painful experiences. When a man in making a will seeks to secure the happiness of his children his motive is a desire for the pleasure of thinking that his children will be happy. 'Psychological egoism' in this sense may, with slight oversimplification, be identified with 'psychological hedonism'. There is general agreement that this doctrine is preposterous and self-stultifying: a man must desire the happiness of his children if he is to find gratification in the thought that they will be happy. The evidence of introspection seems to support this criticism.

Did Aristotle think that all desires are egoistic in the sense of being desires for pleasure? Plainly not. As we have seen at many points in his account of friendship, he accepts altruistic desires at their face value.[1] Again he never suggests, and indeed denies, that a man's desire to be virtuous can be analysed as a desire for the pleasure of knowing that he is virtuous (1174 a4–8). It is true that there is one passage (in II. 3) which reads like psychological hedonism. 'There being three objects of choice and three of avoidance, the noble, the advantageous, and the pleasant and their contraries, the base, the injurious, and the painful, about all of those the good man tends to go right and the bad man to go wrong, and especially about pleasure; for this is common to the animals, and also it accompanies all objects of choice; for even the noble and the advantageous appear pleasant' (1104 b30–1105 a1). This

[1] e.g. 1155 b31, 1156 b9–10, 1159 a8–12, 28–33.

passage suggests that, as is indeed the case, Aristotle had not cleared up the concept of pleasure. If he had he might have asked himself whether what he says here is more than a tautology, whether 'appearing pleasant' is not just a synonym for 'being desired'. In view of the other evidence the passage cannot be taken as showing that he fell for the dogma of psychological hedonism.

We should note next that there are important classes of desire, familiar to Aristotle, which are in a sense egoistic but which are not desires to enjoy pleasures or to avoid pains. Thus my motive when I act from gratitude is not merely a desire that someone who has done me a good turn should receive a benefit but that he should receive it from *me*. Similarly to feel vindictive is to desire that *I* should be the person who inflicts harm on someone who has harmed *me*. These motives may be called self-referential and self-assertive. They may be grouped with desires for victory, success, fame, and less closely with desires for the welfare of *one's own* family, friends, school, college, club, nation. Such motives were grouped together by Plato in his tripartite division of the soul as belonging to the spirited element (*thumoeides*), the element which desires to win (*philonikon*) and to be honoured (*philotimon*). Men's desire to be respected is in part a desire to respect and think well of themselves: 'they seem to pursue honour in order to convince themselves that they are good' (I. 5, 1095 b26–30). Aristotle sees the power of these self-assertive motives, and he also notes a self-assertive *element* in altruistic desires, including maternal love. The feelings of benefactors for their beneficiaries are comparable with those of parents for their children and of artists for their creations. 'For that which they have treated well is their handiwork, and therefore they love this more than the handiwork does its maker' (IX. 7, 1167 b31–1168 a5).

Is Aristotle's view of human nature egoistic in the sense of asserting that men are moved to action only by desires which are either for pleasure or are self-assertive or have a prominent self-assertive aspect? The answer is negative because the motive of Aristotle's virtuous man who 'gains for himself nobility' (1169 a21–2), although Aristotle wishes to say that such a man is 'most truly a lover of self' (1168 b33–4), is not hedonistic, is not self-assertive and has no conspicuous self-assertive ingredient. Is Aristotle open to criticism on the ground that he exaggerates the extent to which human conduct is influenced by motives which are egoistic in the sense of being either hedonistic or self-assertive? The answer is a matter of opinion, but a plausible opinion is that his view is realistic rather than cynical. Aristotle has an un-Kantian appreciation of motives which are mixed and which fall short of being the highest.

We must now look more closely at the account of the motive of the virtuous man, and must consider especially the view implied by Allan that Aristotle represents even the man who lays down his life for his friend or his country as acting from 'enlightened self-interest'. The question must be approached through an examination of Aristotle's doctrine in ix. 8 and 9. Aristotle points out that the term 'self-loving' is commonly used, as is our 'selfish', in a pejorative sense: the self-lover is opposed to the virtuous man whose motive is the noble (kalon), who acts for the sake of his friend not himself (1168 a29–35). But this way of speaking conflicts with the doctrine, which Aristotle claims to have proved in chapter 4 and which is confirmed by proverbial wisdom, that the good man is his own best friend (a35–b12). Aristotle's solution of the contradiction is that what has made 'self-loving' a term of reproach is the fact that the self which is loved is often the self which desires such objects as bodily pleasures and money, the irrational part of the soul. The man who seeks what is noble and obeys his reason is not, in common speech, a lover of self but he can most truly be so described (b12–31). 'Just as a city or any other systematic whole is most properly identified with the most authoritative element in it, so is a man; and therefore the man who loves this and gratifies it is most of all a lover of self' (b31–4). Aristotle concludes that the good man ought to be a lover of self, the bad man not (1169 a11–15). 'Reason in each of its possessors chooses what is best for itself, and the good man obeys his reason' (a17–18). Thus the man who lays down his life for others, the paradigm of self-sacrifice, is achieving his own good when he gains 'nobility'. He prefers 'a short period of intense pleasure to a long one of mild enjoyment, a twelve-month of noble life to many years of humdrum existence, and one great and noble action to many trivial ones' (1169 a22–5). There seems to be something strained and paradoxical in this account of what moves a man to show heroic or saintly virtue. We can see what is wrong if we recall our earlier discussion of Aristotle's doctrine that every reasonable man aims at a final good.[1]

We found two main elements in the doctrine that a wise man has his life organized in view of some end. There is first the idea that a man should live according to *some* comprehensive plan, should observe priorities determined by the aim of living the kind of life which he thinks proper for a man like himself. This might be called the doctrine of the 'inclusive end', inclusive in the sense that there is no desire or interest which cannot be regarded as a candidate, however unpromising, for a place in the pattern of life. The second element in the doctrine consists of Aristotle's own answer to the question *what* plan will be followed by a man who is most fully a man, as high as a man can get in the scale from beast to god. This answer is that a man will make theoretical knowledge, his most godlike attribute, his main object; but that, at a lower level, as a man among men, he will find a place for the happiness which comes from being a citizen, from marriage and children and from the society of those who share his interests. Happiness (*eudaimonia*) thus conceived as the 'paramount end' is not adequately defined as the activity of the soul in accordance with the best and most complete virtue: to this definition we must add 'in a complete life'. 'For one swallow does not make a summer nor does one day; and so too one day or a short time does not make a man blessed and happy' (I. 7, 1098 a16–20).

I suggest that the morality of altruism and self-sacrifice is consistent with the doctrine of the inclusive end but not with the more determinate doctrine of the paramount end. To say that a man in arranging his life has regard to a system of priorities is not to say what these priorities are. His concept of his good in this sense need not require him to prefer self-regarding interests to other-regarding interests or one kind of self-regarding interest to

[1] See Ch. II, pp. 18, 22–3.

another. He may be selfish or unselfish in the popular sense.
Martyrdom may be part of his plan. It can hardly, at least for the
young, be part of a plan to achieve either of the kinds of happiness which for Aristotle are paramount ends. It is true that the
'completeness' of a life should not be understood in the sense of
mere survival. But completeness does seem to imply a life long
enough to permit rounded achievement and the fulfilment of
promise not just 'one great and noble action'. Aristotle might
indeed argue that the man who 'does many acts for the sake of his
friends and his country, and if necessary dies for them' (1169 a18–
20) would not gain by acting otherwise; for he would survive
without the respect and love of others which he needs to make
life worth living. In his account of courage he speaks of the motive
of the brave man not only as desire for a noble object but as
'shame' and 'avoidance of disgrace which is ignoble'.[1] This is
indeed a self-regarding reason for not seeking to survive at any
cost. But in IX. 8 the alternative to altruistic self-sacrifice is not
represented as disgrace or humiliation. What Aristotle says, as we
have seen, is that the good man prefers 'a short period of intense
pleasure to a long one of mild enjoyment, a twelve-month of
noble life to many years of humdrum existence, and one great and
noble action to many trivial ones' (1169 a22–5). A vicious circle
may be suspected in this account of the virtuous motive. The
'many years' are first made to seem 'humdrum' by contrast with
the intensity of the brief encounter, and self-sacrifice in the encounter is then justified by the 'triviality' of the alternative. Aristotle as counsellor on how to be happy though human cannot
justify the admiration which he feels as a man for the 'one great
and noble action'.

> And yet, and yet,
> These Christs that die upon the barricades,
> God knows it I am with them, in some ways.[2]

The man who, whether by good fortune or design, survives a
revolution or a war may live to experience enjoyments which are
intense not mild, to perform activities which are satisfying and

---

[1] III. 8, 1116 a28–9; cf. 18–19; cf. IV. 3, 1124 b6–9.
[2] From 'Sonnet to Liberty' by Oscar Wilde.

not trivial. He may become a professor of philosophy, or at least
a prime minister. Thus there is some justification for the remark
of Field that Aristotle makes morality 'ultimately selfish'. His
doctrine of self-love is in effect a reply to this charge. The reply
scores points and is not a complete failure, but it is not a complete
success.

In chapter 9 Aristotle deals with the question whether and why
friends are needed for happiness. He begins by adducing some
obvious considerations: friends are admittedly the greatest of
'external goods' (1169 b8–10); the good man needs friends as the
object of his well-doing (b10–13); man is political and has a
natural desire to live with his fellows (b16–19); the mistaken idea
that the good man does not need friends is due to the fact that he
has relatively little need of the inferior kinds of friendship (b22–8).
After these preliminaries Aristotle approaches a line of argument
which he seems to regard as more important and more profound.[1] He reminds us that happiness consists in life and activity
(1169 b29–33) and then makes the assertion that 'we can contemplate our neighbours better than ourselves and their actions
better than our own' (b33–5). The happy man will need friends
because 'his purpose is to contemplate worthy actions and actions
that are his own, and the actions of a good man who is his friend
have both these qualities' (1170 a2–4). The statement that we can
observe the actions of other people 'better' than we can observe
our own is not explained but can be understood in a sense in which
it is true. Detachment and externality are proper to an observer,
and it may be difficult for a man to combine acting and watching
himself act. But to say this is not to deny that there are things
about our own actions and thoughts which, as self-conscious
beings, we know directly but can only take for granted or guess
about the actions and thoughts of others. If it is obvious that there
is a sense in which we can be aware of the activities, including the
thoughts, of others more easily than we can be aware of our own,
it is no less obvious that there is a sense in which our own activities
and thoughts are the only activities and thoughts of which we
can be aware at all. In the elaboration of his argument in the rest

[1] Cf. 1170 a13.

of the chapter Aristotle ignores the difference between a man's awareness of his own thoughts and his awareness of the thoughts of his friend. He does not consider the obvious comment that, unless there were a difference, the thoughts of his friends would have to be *literally* his own thoughts. The weak link in the argument of the chapter lies in the claim that a friend is an *alter ego* in the sense that we can be aware of his thoughts as we can be aware of our own. No chain is stronger than its weakest link, and for this reason I do not propose to say more about the details of the reasoning in the second part of IX. 9, the reasoning analysed by Ross, following Burnet, as a series of five syllogisms followed by six arguments.[1]

We have seen that in the first part of the chapter (IX. 9) Aristotle speaks of friends as contemplating each other's actions (*praxeis*). In the second part he speaks of our awareness of perception and thought as they occur in ourselves and in others. Towards the end of the chapter he says that a man's consciousness of the existence of his friend 'will be realized in their living together and sharing in discussion and thought' (1170 b10–12). Sharing in discussion and thought is contrasted with merely 'feeding in the same place like cattle' (b12–14). It is likely that Burnet is thinking of this passage when he says that friendship, and friendship alone, 'can bridge the gulf between . . . the practical and the theoretic life' (p. 345). Similarly Joachim finds in Aristotle's treatment of friendship a suggestion that 'the life of action contains in itself some feature or features which point onwards to their own more perfect fulfilment in the life of thought . . .' (p. 242). But it is not clear that in this chapter Aristotle has theoretical activity in mind. His contrast of what 'living together' means for men with what it means for non-human animals suggests that he is thinking of the life of citizenship rather than of philosophy. In a similar passage in the *Politics* mere living together is contrasted with noble actions.[2] Discussion and thought belong to the life of action as well as to the life of theory. Moreover when he recommends the

---

[1] See his footnote in the Oxford Translation. In 1170 a29–33 I agree with Ross's acceptance of Bywater's emendations.

[2] III. 5, 1280 b29 ff.; cf. *EN* 1169 b30–1170 a4.

theoretic life in Book x he insists on the self-sufficiency of the philosopher who 'even when by himself can contemplate truth and the better the wiser he is' (7, 1177 a32–4). 'He can perhaps do so better if he has fellow-workers, but still he is the most self-sufficient' (a34–b1). Thus there is at least no need to interpret 'sharing in discussion and thought' as a reference to the theoretic life. But, even if there is such a reference, the fact that in the life of thought as well as in the life of action friends are a good thing would not, so far as I can see, 'bridge the gulf' in any important sense between the two lives, the two kinds of happiness.

In the books on friendship, as in his earlier detailed account of the ethical virtues and vices (III. 6–v), Aristotle is filling out in detail, as he said he would, his outline sketch of human happiness (I. 8, 1098 a20–6). In doing so he reports on the form of political society which he knew, and regarded as the best, the city state. He accepts the working morality of citizenship, and tests his general theory of the human good, which is the object of political science, by its capacity to embrace and make intelligible the moral world of citizenship while embracing also the philosophic search for truth. I have admitted that his theory is put under stress and strain by the facts to which he applies it, but it is not broken. In reply to the critic who says that he makes morality 'ultimately selfish' Aristotle can at least transfer to a deeper level the crude idea that there is merit (unselfishness) in seeking the good of others and demerit (selfishness) in seeking one's own, an idea which would place the angels on one side and Aristotle on the other. Aristotle can admit, and he describes with penetration and sympathy, man's social instincts and the intensity of his needs for his fellows. Since men have strong altruistic propensities the effective pursuit of happiness requires that these propensities should be satisfied. But it is true that, when every move has been made to reconcile ego-ism and altruism, there remains a conflict between the extreme demands of political morality, including a readiness to be killed, and the attainment of happiness in a 'complete life'. Aristotle can abandon neither, and the strain shows when he claims that in both man, as a rational being, grasps what is best for his best self. If I am right, this will not do. Some reconstruction is needed in the concept of the final good, and the case for distinguishing between 'inclusive' and 'paramount' ends shows that Aristotle fails to make clearly the distinctions which his own thinking suggests. But it is a merit in Aristotle's treatment of friendship and self-love that the problem emerges as definitely as it does. Philosophers today, aided by Aristotle's work, could perhaps find ways of stating the problem more accurately; but this is not to say that it has been resolved.

The critic who finds in the *Ethics* a defence of 'selfishness' is likely to complain also that Aristotle had an inadequate concept of 'duty'. Thus Allan says both positively that for Aristotle enlightened self-interest is 'the motive of all conduct and choice' and negatively that he 'takes little or no account of the motive of moral obligation'.[1] To the suggestion that Aristotle ignores obligations it would be reasonable to reply that the books on Justice (v) and Friendship (viii and ix) are about nothing else. They tell us about the duties which fall on judges and jurymen, on soldiers and on voters, on husbands and wives and parents and children; on men as members of clubs and fraternities, as business partners, even as belonging to a parish or local community. He is also, as we have seen, interested in the fact that these obligations are liable to conflict (ix. 2; cf. iii. 1). It will be said that laws and conventions and customs, the expectations of family and friends and neighbours, 'my station and its duties', are not what the critic means by 'moral obligation'. It is true that 'the world of claims and counterclaims' is only part, although an important part, of the province of obligation. Bradley ought not to have said that a man who tries to be better than his world is on the brink of immorality.[2] Men feel obligations to perform activities, leading them to accept poverty or even death, which often go beyond anything which anyone else could possibly 'claim' from them. They admit a duty to try to live up to their own ideals in circumstances in which no one would wish to blame them for not doing so. Aristotle does not ignore this aspect of moral conduct.

We noted, for example, his insistence that unbearable misfortunes may thwart men's efforts to achieve virtuous activity.

---

[1] *The Philosophy of Aristotle*, p. 189.   [2] *Ethical Studies*, p. 199.

'A multitude of great events if they turn out well will make life happier . . . while if they turn out ill they crush and maim happiness; for they both bring pain with them and hinder many activities' (I. 10, 1100 b25–30). Even when disaster strikes, 'nobility (*to kalon*) shines through, when a man bears with resignation many great misfortunes, not through insensibility to pain but through nobility and greatness of soul' (b30–3). 'The man who is truly good and wise bears all the chances of life becomingly and always makes the best of circumstances as a good shoemaker makes the best shoes out of the hides that are given to him' (1100 b35–1101 a5). The passage suggests that there is a fundamental obligation to make the best of bad jobs. Moral obligation is not a simple concept of which there is an agreed account so that we can ask whether Aristotle had the concept, yes or no. If we ask in what shapes the experience or fact of obligation came into his view we should consider his use of 'ought' (*dei*) and of 'right' (*dikaion*) but also what he calls the 'noble' (*kalon*). This is something which 'we divine to be proper to a man and not easily taken from him' (I. 5, 1095 b25–6). His doctrine of the final good is a doctrine about what is 'proper' to a man, the power to reflect on his own abilities and desires and to conceive and choose for himself a satisfactory way of life. What 'cannot easily be taken from him' is his power to keep on trying to live up to such a conception; to obey, as Aristotle says, his 'reason' (*nous*). It may indeed be admitted that Aristotle did not distinguish sharply, as Kant tried to distinguish, between the rationality of the moral law and the rationality of 'enlightened self-interest' or, to use Aristotle's word, 'self-love'. Aristotle did not say the last word (if there are last words in philosophy) about moral obligation, but he said some important and suggestive first words.

XVI

THEORETICAL ACTIVITY AND
THE NATURE OF REASON

IF happiness is activity in accordance with virtue, it is reasonable that it should be in accordance with the highest virtue; and this will be that of the best thing in us. Whether it be reason (*nous*) or something else that is this element which is thought to be our natural ruler and guide and to take thought of things noble and divine, whether it be itself also divine or only the most divine element in us, the activity of this in accordance with its proper virtue will be perfect happiness. That this activity is contemplative (*theōrētikē*) we have already said. (*EN* x. 7, 1177 a12–18.)

Reason or something else? If these words indicate doubts, the doubts are not further expressed in the *EN*. The doctrine of the *EN* is that 'the activity of reason which is contemplative' is 'superior in serious worth' (1177 b19–20). 'Even if it be small in bulk, much more does it in power and worth surpass everything. This would seem too to be each man himself, since it is the authoritative and better part of him' (1177 b34–78 a3). The statement of the doctrine in the *EN* is brief and unexplanatory. We are not given sufficient reasons for accepting it, and there is no discussion of the problems it raises about the relation between the divine element and other elements in the soul which, in Aristotle's account of the 'composite' nature of man, is the form or entelechy of the body. The *De Anima* offers a fuller account of reason as man's highest faculty (Γ 4 and 5), and a celebrated passage (ch. 5) seems to imply that the godlike and imperishable element in the soul of man is rather the cause of his contemplative activity than itself contemplative. The passage has generated mountains of commentary and speculation, but many of the questions it raises, or has been treated as raising, are hardly relevant to the study of the *EN*. We do not know whether Aristotle ever asked himself how this development of the doctrine would affect what is said in the *EN* about theoretical activity. But, in the hope of making the doctrine of the *EN* more intelligible, it may be helpful to consider later some of the questions raised by the discussion in the *De Anima* about the differences between reason and other faculties of men.

It has not in fact been stated explicitly in the earlier books of the *EN* that the highest and most desirable form of happiness lies in the activity of contemplation (*theōria*), and it has been suggested that in the passage quoted above Aristotle is referring to the *Protrepticus*.[1] The later treatment of the theoretic life is promised in *EN* I. 5, and its superiority is suggested by the remarks made in depreciation of its rivals, the life of pleasure and the life of political activity. The definition of happiness in I. 7 refers to the virtue which is 'best and most complete' (1098 a16–18), and theoretical wisdom (*sophia*) is one of the intellectual (*dianoētikai*) virtues listed in I. 13 (1103 a3–6). In the account given of *sophia* in VI. 7 (cf. VI. I) Aristotle makes clear that he regards it as the highest kind of human excellence. 'It would be strange to think that the art of politics, or practical wisdom, is the best knowledge, since man is not the best thing in the world' (1141 a20–2). Man may be 'the best of the animals', but 'there are other things much more divine in their nature even than man, e.g. most conspicuously, the bodies of which the heavens are framed' (1141 a33–b2). Finally, at the end of Book VI, the superiority of philosophic wisdom is asserted when it is said that 'practical wisdom does not use it but provides for its coming into being', 'issues orders for its sake but not to it' (13, 1145 a8–9). Some of the questions raised by this statement have been considered in earlier chapters.

I have quoted the most striking of the statements made by Aristotle in the *EN* about the bliss of contemplation. The concept of felicity which they convey must have seemed narrow in its scope even to Aristotle's contemporaries and pupils. It is implied that a man is in the fullest sense happy only when he is meditating, in an experience coloured perhaps by religious emotions, on

[1] Gauthier-Jolif, pp. 876–8.

theological or astronomical propositions and their proofs.[1] But Aristotle presumably regarded himself as addicted to theory, and there were stretches of his career in which it appears on the evidence that he was more engaged in the study of fish, to say nothing of men, than in that of theology. Moreover the questionable claim that the best knowledge is the knowledge of the best is not the only argument for choosing philosophy; some of Aristotle's other arguments do not point to philosophy in preference to other theoretical inquiries or cultural interests. It is disconcerting to be offered an account of happiness which seems to be tied to Aristotle's peculiar opinions about the nature and movement of the stars. We are, therefore, tempted to try to expand the doctrine beyond the narrow limits of its exposition in *EN* x. The first question to ask is whether there is any basis in Aristotle's other works for an enlargement of the doctrine.

In the *Metaphysics* Aristotle distinguishes three 'theoretical philosophies': mathematics, physics, and theology (*E* 1, 1026 a18–19). The third of these inquiries, or groups of inquiries, is elsewhere called simply 'first' philosophy and described as the universal science of 'that which exists *qua* existent and the attributes which belong to it in virtue of its own nature' (*Γ* 1, 1003 a21–6). The three sciences are distinguished in Book *E* by reference to their subject matters. 'For physics deals with things which are separable' (read *chōrista*, i.e. existing separately) 'but not immovable, and some parts of mathematics deal with things which are immovable, but probably not separable, but embodied in matter; while the first science deals with things which are both separable and immovable' (*E* 1, 1026 a13–16). Aristotle speaks of physics as 'a kind of wisdom but not the first kind' (*Γ* 3, 1005 b1–2). In the *EN* there is a casual allusion to the threefold division of science when Aristotle remarks that, because he lacks experience, 'a boy may become a mathematician but not a philosopher or a physicist' (vi. 8, 1142 a17–18). In the division of the intellect into scientific (theoretical) and calculative (practical) the former is said to deal with things of which 'the principles are invariable' (vi. 1, 1139 a6–8) and can, therefore, be taken as including mathe-

[1] Cf. vi. 6, 1141 a1–3.

matics. The position of physics in the scheme is left unclear. But in Book x there is no suggestion that mathematics or physics have a place beside divinity in the scheme of human happiness. Ross is, therefore, stretching Aristotle's doctrine when he says that the contemplative life covers 'the contemplation of truth in two, and perhaps in three departments, mathematics, metaphysics, and perhaps also natural philosophy'.[1] Ross thinks that physics can be included as being 'the study of the non-contingent element in contingent events'. But to the extent that Aristotle's case for the supremacy of 'theory' rests on the kinship between a divine spark in Man and the objects of theological and cosmological speculation, the exclusion of physics is inevitable, and of mathematics also if, as Aristotle inclines to think, mathematical propositions are about sensible substances in respect of certain of their properties.[2]

The above is the strict and restrictive answer to the question what is the scope of the 'contemplation' recommended in EN x. But the modern reader cannot start from Aristotle's metaphysical premises and is likely also to agree with Bradley's repudiation of the idea 'that in the intellectual world work done on higher subjects is for that reason higher work'.[3] He will therefore construe less narrowly than Aristotle the content of the 'theoretic life'. Moreover, as regards what we call natural science, he can quote in support of this the justly admired passage in which Aristotle himself insists that 'second philosophy', as well as divine philosophy, has its own peculiar charms.

The scanty conceptions to which we can attain of celestial things give us, from their excellence, more pleasure than all our knowledge of the world in which we live, just as a half-glimpse of persons that we love is more delightful than a leisurely view of other things, whatever their number and dimensions. On the other hand, in certitude and in completeness our knowledge of terrestrial things has the advantage. Moreover, their greater nearness and affinity to us balances somewhat the loftier interest of the heavenly things which are the object of the higher philosophy.[4]

---

[1] *Aristotle*, p. 234; cf. Gauthier-Jolif, p. 853.
[2] *Metaphysics M* 3, 1078 a2–9. [3] *Appearance and Reality*, pp. 6–7.
[4] *De Partibus Animalium* I. 5, 644 b31–645 a4.

Some commentators on Aristotle speak of 'contemplation' in terms which imply that they do not think of it as confined to the study of theoretical sciences. Stewart, for example, remarks in the course of a long note on the first sentence of the EN that happiness 'even when realised in the performance of moral actions is *theōria* or contemplation of the eternal' (i. 5). This suggestion is remote indeed from what Aristotle actually says about *theōria*. It is remote also from the spirit of his doctrine. Aristotle was not a democratic liberal, and did not shrink from the idea that happiness, at least in its best form, is for the fortunate few not the meritorious many. Bosanquet, in an interesting note on the plot of the EN, uses the phrases 'intellectual excellence and religious contemplation' and 'what the saint or the poet or the thinker may attain'.[1] Admittedly he was not here claiming to follow the text closely. But with similar freedom Burnet in his commentary speaks of 'the life of artistic, scientific or religious "contemplation"' (p. 438).

Ross deals briefly but sufficiently with the suggestion that Aristotle could allow artistic or aesthetic experience to count as *theōria*. 'There is nothing to show that aesthetic contemplation formed for Aristotle any part of the ideal life; in the *Poetics*, where he considers one particular form of aesthetic experience, that of tragedy, he makes its value lie in its medicinal effect.'[2] Apart from their effects on character Aristotle might well have classed poetry, music, painting, and sculpture as refined amusements and have applied to them his remark that 'it would be strange if the end were amusement, and one were to take trouble and suffer hardship all one's life in order to amuse oneself' (*EN* x. 6, 1176 b27–30). This is doubtless an inadequate view of the claims of the poet and the artist, but it is Aristotle's. It may be suggested, however, that some of Aristotle's reasons for commending theoretical activity, in contrast with practical and political pursuits, are applicable to artistic and aesthetic as well as to scientific interests.

The claim that Aristotle's *theōria* covers religious contemplation is ambiguous. On the one hand it might refer only to religious emotion integrated with the intellectual study of divine objects; on the other hand it might mean religion as an independent form

---

[1] *Principle of Individuality and Value* (1912), p. 402.   [2] *Aristotle*, p. 234.

of experience or as associated with activities other than theoretical science. We have evidence that Aristotle was interested in the phenomena of religion; he discussed them in one of his 'exoteric' works, the *De Philosophia*. 'Aristotle used to say that men's thought of gods sprang from two sources—the experiences of the soul and the phenomena of the heavens. To the first head belonged the inspiration and prophetic power of the soul in dreams. For when (he says) the soul is isolated in sleep, it assumes its true nature and foresees and foretells the future. So is it too with the soul, when at death it is severed from the body.'[1] Another of Aristotle's lost works was 'On Prayer' and he is reported by Simplicius as saying in it that 'God is either reason or something even beyond reason' (R. 49, W. p. 100). In the *EE* (but not in the *EN*), in a chapter on divine and natural good fortune (Θ 2), he speaks in a similar tone about divination and enthusiasm and appears to be willing to entertain a religious interpretation of the veridical dreams which come 'when reason is relaxed' (1248 a22–b7). But when he wrote his mature essays, *On Dreams* and *On Divination in Sleep*, his approach, as E. R. Dodds points out, is 'coolly rational' and, anticipating Freud, 'scientific'.[2] On this evidence it cannot be claimed that the contemplative life, as conceived by Aristotle, included either religion as something on its own or religious emotion associated with non-scientific forms of experience. We cannot attribute to Aristotle in his maturity any mystical or supra-rational interpretation of religious feelings. But he would no doubt encourage in all men the disposition to worship the author of the visibly well-ordered movements of the sun and the stars. And there is certainly a religious flavour in the language in which, in the *EN*, he speaks of the objects of philosophical study. But, as Ross points out,[3] this 'aspect of the ideal life' is more explicit in the *EE* where Aristotle speaks of 'the contemplation and worship' (*therapeuein*) of God (Θ 2, 1249 b20). Jaeger sees in this difference confirmation of his view that the *EE* represents an earlier course of

---

[1] Sextus Empiricus, *Adv. Phys.* I. 20–1 (= W. 12a); cf., on dreams, Plato, *Republic* IX. 571 d 6–72 b 1; *Timaeus* 71 a–e; *Epinomis* 985 c.
[2] *The Greeks and the Irrational*, pp. 117–21; cf. Jaeger, *Aristotle*, pp. 332–4.
[3] *Aristotle*, p. 234.

lectures which, to an extent greater than the *EN*, 'exhales the religious fervour of his youthful Platonic faith'.[1]

We have noted that Aristotle has two ways of describing the paramount theoretical science: as a universal science of being and as a science having for its subject-matter entities which are 'separable and unmovable'; God, the prime unmoved mover or first cause of change, and the intelligences responsible for the revolutions of the concentric spheres in Aristotle's celestial physics. Ross's account of the *De Caelo* gives a description of Aristotle's astronomical system.[2] The Introduction to his edition of the *Metaphysics* gives a fuller account than his *Aristotle* of the central ideas in Aristotle's metaphysical thinking, and contains also a specially valuable critical discussion of Aristotle's theology (pp. cxxx–cliv). His treatment in this discussion of the doctrine of 'active reason' stated in the *De Anima* (Γ 5) is perhaps more helpful, because less speculative, than the later treatment of the problem in his edition of the *De Anima*. In a note on the opening sentence of *Metaphysics* Γ about the universal science of being (1003 a21) Ross quotes Aristotle's apparently conflicting statements about the nature of the supreme science and concludes as follows: 'both views are genuinely Aristotelian, but the narrower view of the scope of metaphysics is that which is more commonly present in his works, and more in keeping with the distrust of a universal science expressed in the *Posterior Analytics*' (i. 251–3). It is true that the two descriptions suggest different views, and the difference may reflect a change in Aristotle's mind about the possibility and nature of a universal science. But the contrast is not sharp and clear-cut for at least the following reasons. First, as Ross points out, Aristotle's universal science is very different from the universal science conceived by Plato in the *Republic* (VI and VII), in which the principles of the special sciences would appear as conclusions. For Aristotle the first principles of the sciences cannot be deduced from more ultimate principles, and his science of being is largely an 'aporēmatic' examination of 'common principles', 'terms such as matter and form, substance and accident, quality and quantity, unity and plurality' (p. 252). Secondly, the study of

[1] *Aristotle*, p. 243.   [2] Ibid., pp. 95–9.

the highest kind of being is not like the study of some rare or specially interesting species of plants or animals, orchids or elephants. For the proof that there is a first cause is based on general facts about the nature of physical realities, and is inseparable from the analysis of such notions as form, substance, actuality, and their correlatives. Thirdly, Aristotle himself in Book *E* 1 recognizes it as a problem (*aporia*) to decide 'whether first philosophy is universal or concerned with a single kind of being' (1026 a23–5). The answer which he states, but does not elaborate, is that it is both; it is 'universal because it is first', i.e. because it deals with primary realities. 'In studying the nature of pure being, form without matter, philosophy is in effect coming to know the nature of being as a whole.'[1]

Aristotle argues that the activity which brings the greatest happiness to men must be the activity which most closely resembles that of the gods. What kind of activity can we attribute to gods? Not any activity which manifests an ethical virtue; justice, courage, liberality, temperance (x. 8, 1178 b7 ff.). 'Will not the gods seem absurd if they make contracts and return deposits and so on?' (b11–12). 'And what would their temperate acts be? Is not such praise tasteless, since they have no bad appetites?' (b 15–16). 'Still everyone supposes that they *live* and therefore that they are active; we cannot suppose them to sleep like Endymion. Now if you take away from a living being action, and still more production, what is left but contemplation? Therefore the activity of God, which surpasses all others in blessedness, must be contemplative; and of human activities, therefore, that which is most akin to this must be the happiest' (b 18–23). Since God is the best thing in the universe, the object of his contemplation must be himself.[2] For the gods the whole of life is blessed and for men 'in

---

[1] Ross, op. cit., p. 253; cf. Joachim, pp. 5–7. On Aristotle's view of metaphysics important writings include A. Mansion, 'Philosophie première, philosophie seconde et métaphysique chez Aristote', *Revue philosophique de Louvain* (1958), pp. 165–221; and two articles by G. E. L. Owen: 'Logic and Metaphysics in Some Earlier Works of Aristotle', in *Aristotle and Plato in the Mid-Fourth Century* (Gothenburg, 1960), and 'Aristotle on the Snares of Ontology', in *New Essays on Plato and Aristotle* (1965).

[2] *Metaphysics* Λ 9, 1074 b33–5; cf. MM B 15, 1212 b38–13 a4.

so far as some likeness of such activity belongs to them' (1178 b25–7). Similarly in the *Metaphysics*, speaking of the First Mover, the principle on which depend the heavens and the world of nature, Aristotle remarks that 'its life is such as the best which we enjoy, and enjoy but for a short time' (Λ 7, 1072 b14–15).

The argument in the *Metaphysics* for the existence of God as First Mover requires that he should be immaterial and unchanging (Λ 6, 1071 b4–5, 19–22). Things which change are compounded of matter and form, and the fact that they change implies that, at any given time, their state includes potentialities not then realized. But God's activity of self-contemplation is his whole nature; his nature is simple in the sense that it does not include matter as well as form. God's immunity from change has been mentioned in a passage at the end of the treatment of pleasure in *EN* VII. 'If the nature of anything were simple, the same action would always be most pleasant to it. This is why God always enjoys a single and simple pleasure; for there is not only an activity (*energeia*) of movement (*kinēsis*) but an activity of immobility (*akinēsia*), and pleasure is found more in rest than in movement' (14, 1154 b24–8). Aristotle admits that, as the poet says, 'change is sweet', but attributes this to 'vice' (*ponēria*). 'The nature that needs change is vicious; for it is not simple nor good' (b28–31). But the exclusion of change is no more descriptive of the wise and good man than of the foolish and bad. 'Research' describes the life of the student better than 'contemplation'. This point is again put aside in x. 7 when Aristotle claims that 'philosophy offers pleasures marvellous for their purity and their enduringness' and that 'it is reasonable to suppose that those who know will pass their time more pleasantly than those who inquire' (1177 a25–7). But knowing is not a way of passing time. It is reasonable rather to suppose that the philosopher, when he has enjoyed the pleasant surprise of coming to know, will be ready to move on to the next question. Gauthier–Jolif observe rightly that Aristotle implies the exclusion of discovery from the contemplative life. 'On pourrait même dire que l'idéal, pour le contemplatif aristotélien — et cet idéal le Dieu d'Aristote le réalise — ce serait de ne jamais étudier et de ne jamais découvrir . . .' (pp. 855–6). If it were said that God's unchanging self-contemplation is monotonous and might be tedious, Aristotle would no doubt object that to speak in this way of God is 'absurd' and 'tasteless'. But it is no *more* absurd to ask whether God might feel bored than it is to speak of Him as feeling pleasure. In short, the concept of God's changeless being gives us no appropriate or usable criterion for the grading of the forms of happiness open to men. To say this is not to reject Aristotle's claim that philosophers and scientists are, on the whole, exceptionally happy. It is to point out that his theological argument for this conclusion leads to an unacceptable, because incomplete, account of the characteristics of science and philosophy which make them desirable.

The paradox in Aristotle's ideal of contemplation was noted from another point of view in Chapters II and XIV when I discussed the distinction made in the first chapter of the *EN* between activities which have and have not an 'end' beyond themselves. Both gazing at an unchanging view and searching for a hidden object are, in Aristotle's language, actualizations (*energeiai*) of capacities (*dunameis*); the former of a capacity for an unchanging activity or state, the latter for a changing one. I suggested that Aristotle fails to keep steadily in view the fact that a process of working towards a planned terminus (*peras*) or end (*telos*) may itself be an end in the sense of being something desired for its own sake. But Aristotle's doctrine states a part of the truth. There is satisfaction in the static grasp of a complex argument or a general theory. In the case of a game we can distinguish the pleasure of winning from the pleasure of playing, and the pleasure of playing is the pleasure of playing to win. Similarly in intellectual inquiry the researcher desires to know the answer and not just to occupy himself in looking for it. It is not like fox-hunting in which some huntsmen may even prefer not to kill a fox. But the search for understanding is not a merely unwelcome preliminary to understanding, and may be rewarded at any stage by partial understanding. These facts distinguish the human situation from that of Tantalus, although in both there is a 'yonder to all ends'.

Aristotle's account of theoretical activity is bound up with his view that reason (*nous*), the thinking part of the soul, is 'the best thing in us' (1177 a13). It is the divine, or most divine, element in our nature (a15–16); if 'small in bulk', it is supreme in power and worth (1178 a1; cf. 1177 b19–20). Reason is 'separate', and by this is meant that its activity has no bodily aspect; it is an element in the soul which can be separated from the body (1178 a19–22).[1] In the study both of the *EN* and of the *De Anima* this doctrine presents itself as a puzzle and perhaps even as a scandal. Aristotle's physiological approach to psychology, incapsulated in the doctrine that the soul is the form (*eidos*) or actuality (*entelecheia*) of the body, is rightly regarded as one of the important and fruitful achievements of his originative genius. I have argued in Chapter V that there is no radical contrast or contradiction between the view of man's nature implied in the *EN* and the entelechy doctrine of the *De Anima*. The reader of both works is confronted in the doctrine of reason by a dualism and discontinuity which he finds hard to understand. Why does Aristotle not carry through more persistently his hypothesis that mental processes are associated with bodily conditions? The difficulty is made more acute by the fact that he insists on continuity as a feature of man's development as a thinking being. In the *Posterior Analytics* he points to intermediate stages between the confusion of mere sense-perception and the apprehension of principles.[2] In the *De Anima* discursive thinking (*dianoeisthai*) is classed with love and hate as an affection of the composite nature of the besouled body (*A* 4, 408 b25–7). Imagination and memory, as we saw, depend on physiological conditions; and much of our thinking, if not all of it, requires mental images.[3] How can the separateness of reason be consistent with these discoveries and with the experienced continuity of processes of thinking? Aristotle has not made clear what are the purely mental performances which he assigns to this entity, small in bulk and mysterious in its efficacy. Perhaps he was working towards an explanation in his doctrine of active and passive reason (*Γ* 5). But, apart from doubts about the text, the passage is too short and obscure to point clearly to any solution of the difficulty.

---

[1] Cf. *De Gen. Anim.* 736 b27, 737 a10, 744 b21; *De Anima Γ* 4 and 5, and other passages, especially *A* 1, 403 a8–10; *A* 4, 408 b18–29; and p. 72 above.

[2] *B* 19; cf. *Metaphysics A* 1.

[3] *A* 1, 403 a8–10; cf. *Γ* 7, 431 a14–17; 8, 432 a8.

One way out is to say that the entelechy theory and the doctrine of *nous* are indeed incompatible, and that the latter is a mere survival from an earlier stage in the development of Aristotle's thought. As regards the *De Anima*, this is the solution offered by Jaeger. 'Even if, therefore, the present version of the Third Book . . . is uniform and contemporary with the other two and the *Parva Naturalia* . . . that cannot alter the fact that the ideas about *nous* are earlier, while the method and execution of the rest is later and belongs to another stage of development—in fact, to another dimension of thought.'[1] Any simple hypothesis of historical stratification is faced by the difficulty that the doctrine of *nous* is not confined to the Third Book of the *De Anima* but is mentioned repeatedly in the other two. The suggestion that 'the ideas are earlier' implies that they began to be discarded, or to wither away, with the break-through to 'another dimension'. But the fact that there is no explicit repudiation, as in the case of the theory of Forms, of the supposedly earlier ideas remains a puzzle. And how do we know that the ideas, even if earlier, could not live with the later ideas? This is either obvious or a philosophical conclusion. It is not obvious. Philosophers are far even now from agreed solutions to questions about the ways in which the mind is connected with the body. We all know that we cannot see with our eyes shut, that a tooth-extraction can be painful, that our 'blood boils' when we are angry. We do not know, and physiologists do not know, how or in what sense our thinking is conditioned by processes in our heads. If we ask philosophers whether a process of thought can both be rational and be an effect of bodily causes, we shall get different answers or different reformulations of the question. The developmental interpretation of doctrines can be helpful and illuminating. But, if it is offered as a way round philosophical difficulties, it needs defence in every case. In this case there is a burden of proof to be sustained by anyone who holds that Aristotle could not have intended to defend, or could not plausibly have defended, both the physiological approach to psychology and the view that reason has a special non-physical status.[2]

[1] *Aristotle²*, p. 334.
[2] For this line of thought see also the Appendix to Ch. V above, pp. 83–93.

Perhaps they are not consistent, but prima facie Aristotle does defend both at once, and we have to see what we can make of any defence that he offers of his doctrine of *nous*.

In the *EN* the doctrine is asserted but not defended: a detailed account, Aristotle says, would be 'a task greater than our purpose requires' (8, 1178 a23). As regards the *De Anima* the work of Jaeger, and of those who have followed his lead, Nuyens for example, alerts us to the possibility that the doctrine has reached a more developed stage, and that we may even find ourselves in a different 'dimension of thought'. It is indeed true that there is no hint in the *EN* of the distinction, obscurely propounded in *Γ* 5, between a causally efficacious and a passive element within human reason (430 a10–14). But the preceding chapter of the *De Anima* (*Γ* 4), like the *EN*, treats reason as a unity and gives no hint that it is divided. And on at least one central point the *De Anima* (*Γ* 4) seems to say more fully, and with a supporting argument, what is said also in the *EN*: that reason, in contrast with other functions of the soul, is independent of the body.[1] On this point at least, therefore, the *De Anima*, if we can understand it, should throw light on the doctrine of the *EN*. I shall not attempt to comment in detail on the many problems of interpretation raised by these chapters (*Γ* 4, 5) of the *De Anima*. The question before us is whether the chapters throw any light on the teaching of the *EN* that reason, or the faculty of thought, is 'a thing apart' (1178 a22).

Aristotle's view of thinking in the *De Anima* is given in the form of a comparison, and also a contrast, between thinking and sense-perception: 'if thinking is like perceiving, it must be either a process in which the soul is acted upon by what is capable of being thought, or a process different from but analogous to that' (*Γ* 4, 429 a13–15). In sense-perception the percipient's body is affected, suffers change, by the action of the external object: a man sees when motions emanating from the object affect his eyes, or his eyes and also a single central internal organ of sense.[2] In perception

---

[1] x. 8, 1178 a14–23; *De Anima* 429 a24–b5.

[2] Ross, *Aristotle*, pp. 136 ff.; see also Irving Block, 'The Order of Aristotle's Psychological Writings', in *American Journal of Philology*, lxxxii (1961), pp. 62 ff.

the organ is assimilated to the object perceived, receives its form. Thought has no physical organ, but is analogous to perception in a way which Aristotle expresses by saying that in thinking the mind receives the intelligible form of the object (429 a15–16). Does this imply that the thinker, like the percipient, is affected, suffers change? Aristotle's answer is in terms of a distinction which he has made in an earlier passage (B 5) between different senses of 'being acted on' (paschein).

Also the expression 'to be acted on' has more than one meaning; it may mean either (a) the destruction (phthora) of one of two contraries by the other, or (b) the maintenance (sōtēria) of what is potential by the agency of what is actual and already like what is acted upon, with such likeness as is compatible with one's being actual and the other potential. For what possesses knowledge becomes an actual knower by a transition which is either not an alteration of it at all (being in reality a development into its true self or entelecheia) or at least an alteration in a quite different sense from the usual meaning (417 b2–7; cf. 429 b30).

Thus in the sense of the physical meaning of being affected and suffering change Aristotle can say that, when we think or know, we are not affected: the thinking part of the soul is 'impassible' (apathes) (429 a15–18).

When the mind comes to know, the change involved is from potentiality to actuality; before it thinks the mind 'is not actually any real thing' (429 a24). The proposition that the mind is, in the sense explained, impassible implies, in Aristotle's view, that it is, in the word used by Anaxagoras, 'unmixed' (amigēs) (429 a18 ff.; cf. b22 ff.). The argument is that the mind must be, so to speak, a transparent medium or tabula rasa (429 b31–430 a2). If it had a positive nature of its own, as opposed to an omni-receptive capacity, this nature would be a built-in source of distortion (429 a20–2). These statements, although metaphorical, can be understood and provisionally accepted.

The next step is important and difficult. It takes us from the statement that the mind is unmixed in the sense of rational neutrality, freedom from any built-in bias, to the statement that it is not 'mixed with the body'. 'For this reason it cannot reasonably be regarded as mixed (memigmenon) with the body: if so, it would acquire some quality, e.g. warmth or cold, or even have an organ like the sensitive faculty: as it is, it has none' (429 a24–7). Aristotle finds evidence for the proposition that the mind has no physical organ in an observable difference between the functioning of sense and that of intellect.

After strong stimulation of a sense we are less able to exercise it than before, as, e.g. in the case of a loud sound we cannot hear immediately after, or in the case of a bright colour or a powerful odour we cannot see or smell, but in the case of mind thought about an object that is in a high degree intelligible renders it more and not less able afterwards to think about objects that are in a lower degree intelligible: the reason is that, while the faculty of sensation is dependent on the body, mind is separable (*chōriston*) from it. (429 a31–b5.)

According to Hicks in his commentary the statement that the mind has no bodily organ 'plainly follows from the statement that mind is unmixed in the wider sense', i.e. of being neutral and free from bias. What seems to be plain is that Aristotle *claims* that it follows. But, if he were *right* in so claiming, the generally accepted belief or knowledge that thinking depends on the brain would be inconsistent with our being justified in supposing that our thoughts can achieve rationality or truth.

The key word, as we have seen, in the argument we are considering is 'mix'. What does Aristotle mean by a 'mixture'? The question is treated elaborately in the *De Generatione et Corruptione*.[1] In my summary I shall follow Joachim's commentary. In Aristotle's physics a mixture proper is a combination in definite ratios of two or more of the same 'four "simple" bodies (Earth, Air, Fire, Water) or—more precisely—of the same four "elementary qualities" (Hot, Cold, Dry, Moist)'.[2] Mere juxtaposition of bits, however small, of different stuffs (*sunthesis*) is not mixture (328 a5–10). 'If there is to be mixture in the proper sense of the term, two or more distinct and separate bodies must come together so as to form a single resultant in which they are merged. The properties of the resultant must be different from those of the constituents: and it must be uniform in its properties throughout . . . so that every part of it, however small, possesses the same

---

[1] See specially I. 10.   [2] Joachim, p. 64.

properties as the whole.'[1] It is clear that, in the case of both mix-ture proper, combination or blending, and of mechanical mixture, composition, the things said to be mixed are bodies. Thus Aristotle remarks that 'neither the art of healing nor health produces health by mixing with the bodies of the patients' (328 a22–3). The reciprocity involved in mixture is not possible when agent and patient 'have not the same matter' (a21–2). When we turn from the elaborate treatment of physical mixture in the *De Generatione et Corruptione* to the argument in *De Anima Γ* 4, the obvious comment to make is that, in this passage of the *De Anima*, Aristotle fails to note that the sense in which form and matter are combined to form a unity, as are soul and body on the entelechy theory, is different from the sense in which bodies are combined in a physical mixture. When he justifies the statement that the mind is unmixed, in the sense of neutral, he says that 'the co-presence of what is alien is a hindrance or a block' (429 a20–1). When he says that the mind is not mixed with the body, he argues that, if it were, 'it would acquire some quality, e.g. warmth or cold' (a25–6). In these passages he seems to be speaking of mind as if it were a kind of body, and to be using 'mixture' in a physical sense. If so, we can surely object that the combination of body and soul, if it is a combination of matter and form, is not a mixture in this sense. If the objection is sound, the argument, as it stands, from the neutrality of the thinking faculty to its alleged excep-tional non-physical status is invalid. But I think that the argument suggests, although unclearly, a real difficulty.

When we discussed the entelechy theory in Chapter V, we saw that, in its application to animals including men, the theory is illustrated by the dependence of sense-perception and feelings on physiological conditions, as in the hearing of a noise or the pain indirectly caused by a blow. In these cases something which hap-pens in the soul or mind is an effect of happenings in the body. Thus, if interpreted in terms of these examples, the theory could naturally come to be specified as 'epiphenomenalism': the doctrine that mental events are always effects of events in the body but never causes either of events in the body or of other

[1] Ibid., pp. 175–6.

mental events. There are obvious and weighty objections to this doctrine. There is evidence for mind–body causation of the same kind as the evidence for body–mind causation. Thus the evidence that a decision to move a limb is a factor in the cause of its movement is comparable with the evidence that processes in the body cause sensations. The idea that we do not produce effects in the world by our thoughts and decisions is contrary to a common-sense conviction shared by Aristotle.[1] No less paradoxical is the idea that, when premises lead us to a conclusion or evidence suggests a verdict, the terminal mental events have purely physical causes. The intellectual acceptance of a conclusion seems to be inseparable from the assumption that the acceptance is determined by the understanding of the premises.[2] Even the epiphenomenalist does not think that his own epiphenomenalism is the effect of processes in his own nervous system. Even Kantians who claim to have discovered that the mind, in part of its functioning, is a distorting medium cannot, without destroying their own rational scepticism, assert this of the mind which has made the discovery.[3] What I am suggesting is not that Aristotle has a good case for holding that thought, unlike sensation, has no bodily organ but that he *would* have a good case if the dependence of thought on the body were understood, and could only be understood, as epiphenomenalism understands it. The mind–body problem is puzzling, and was felt by Aristotle to be puzzling, because, while it is impossible to accept either epiphenomenalism or Platonism (the doctrine that mind and body are distinct and separable substances), it is difficult to see or state clearly what other account of the facts can be given. The fascination which the next brief chapter (Γ 5) of the De Anima has had for philosophers and scholars at different periods in two millennia may be explained in part by the idea that, on this difficult topic, Aristotle was trying to find a view less incredible than either of these extreme and too simple doctrines.

[1] Cf., for example, De Anima A 3, 406 b24–5.

[2] Cf. EN VII. 3, 1147 a25 ff.

[3] A statement of an argument on these lines will be found in the first chapter of H. W. B. Joseph's Some Problems in Ethics (cf. Spinoza, Ethics, Part iii, Proposition ii, note; William James, Principles of Psychology, i, p. 132).

Since in every class of things, as in nature as a whole, we find two factors involved, (1) a matter which is potentially all the particulars included in the class, (2) a cause which is productive in the sense that it makes them all (the latter standing to the former as e.g. an art to its material), these distinct elements must likewise be found within the soul. And in fact mind as we have described it is what it is by virtue of becoming all things, while there is another which is what it is by virtue of making all things: this is a sort of positive state like light; for in a sense light makes potential colours into actual colours. Mind in this sense of it is separable, impassible, unmixed, since it is in its essential nature activity. (430 a10–18.)

This doctrine that there is differentiation within the unity of reason (*nous*) does not appear elsewhere in the *De Anima* nor in the *EN* nor anywhere in Aristotle's surviving works. The properties of being 'separable, impassible, unmixed', which in the preceding chapter were attributed simply to reason, are now said to belong to the reason which is active or productive. We are told that active reason 'when separated appears as just what it is and nothing more' (a22–3), that it alone is 'immortal and eternal' but that 'we do not remember because, while mind in this sense is impassible, mind as passive is destructible' (a23–5). The chapter ends with a phrase which may be translated either 'without it nothing thinks' or 'without this it thinks nothing'. Nor is it clear to which element in reason each part of the phrase refers. It is difficult not to agree with the remark of Allan that, in this chapter, Aristotle succeeds in doing 'little else than record his own perplexity'.[1] It would be out of place to discuss here, even if I had the ability, the problems which have been raised about the sentences in this obscure chapter. I shall ask only one question. Can we find in *De Anima* Γ 5 any hint, however obscure, of developments in Aristotle's doctrine about reason (*nous*) which might diminish the difficulties which we have found in it as it meets us in *EN* x? On this question I have only one suggestion to offer.

A major difficulty arose from the fact that the rational cognition ascribed to the godlike reason in us was given a very restricted sphere. It was difficult to see where a line could be drawn between

---

[1] *The Philosophy of Aristotle*, p. 85.

this cognition and other cognitive states and activities of men, and difficult in particular to see how any human thinking could be separable from imagination and memory, which, as Aristotle himself teaches, depend on physiological conditions. Now when Aristotle says that passive reason 'becomes all things' (430 a14–15), he is ascribing to passive reason, as Ross points out, 'the act of apprehension'.[1] For Aristotle holds that in knowledge reason becomes identical with its intelligible objects (430 a3–5; a19–20).[2] Ross further argues that, on the analogy of art, which 'makes its objects by making the material into them', the function of active reason must be 'to make passive reason become its objects by apprehending them'. Similarly other scholars have pointed out that, in connection with human thinking, the part which Aristotle seems to give to active reason is not to think but rather to cause thinking.[3] The concluding words of the chapter, on any interpretation, suggest that in all actual human thinking both reason as active and reason as passive are involved. But passive reason is not separable from the body, and the fact that it is described as 'perishable' (*phthartos*) indicates that it is, in Aristotle's language, an entelechy, an affection of the besouled body.[4] Thus, if passive reason is engaged in all our thinking, there will be no division of our intellectual activities into those which belong to the embodied mind and others which are purely mental, the acts of a separable spiritual entity. The student of the *EN* who finds such a division and discontinuity paradoxical may be justified in regarding the *De Anima* (Γ 5) as promising the elimination of this paradox. Aristotle, it might be said, is feeling his way towards a position in which he could both claim a special status for reason and maintain his entelechy doctrine as an account of intellectual activity as well as of perception, imagination, pleasure and pain, and emotional states.[5] I suggest, therefore, that the distinction between active and passive reason, although it gives rise to new problems in the interpretation of Aristotle, might, if developed, help us to make better

---

[1] *Aristotle*, p. 149; edition of the *Metaphysics*, p. cxliv.
[2] Cf. *Metaphysics* Λ 7, 1072 b21–2.
[3] Cf. Cassirer, *Aristoteles' 'Schrift von der Seele'*, p. 177.
[4] Cf. *A* 4, 408 b25–7.   [5] Cf. *A* 1, 403 a3–16.

sense than we can without it of the doctrine of theoretical reason in *EN* x. But it is another question whether the perplexities in relation to which we find the doctrine interesting were among the considerations which suggested it to Aristotle.

The further points which Aristotle makes in Book x as reasons for expecting to find happiness in theoretical activity present no new problems of interpretation and need be mentioned only briefly. Two separate passages (7, 1177 a27–b1; 8, 1178 a23–b7) argue that the theoretic life is superior on the ground that it is in the highest degree self-sufficient (1177 a27) and is least in need of external equipment (1178 a24). The man who devotes himself to contemplation is relatively independent first of other people and secondly of money. The thinker can work by himself although 'he can perhaps do so better if he has fellow workers' (1177 a34; cf. ix. 9). The social virtues can be practised only in society. As regards material things, the philosopher needs only the necessaries of life (1177 a29; 1178 a25). But only a man with money can effectively exercise justice and liberality, and moderation implies the possibility of extravagance. It should be noted that these considerations have no tendency to show that theoretical activity has superior intrinsic worth or desirability, but only that the prizes it offers are less likely than other objectives to elude us if we make them our aim. It may be sensible to choose as a relaxation crossword puzzles rather than bridge if it is likely to be difficult over a period to assemble suitable fours for bridge. A man may choose to cultivate his garden because he cannot afford to travel. But these would not be reasons for preferring crossword puzzles and gardening if the alternatives were freely obtainable. In choosing and planning it is necessary to consider both what the possible objectives are worth and what the chances are of reaching them. Aristotle does not make sufficiently explicit the difference between these two kinds of consideration, and does not discuss the ethics of playing for safety. He claims that contemplation wins on both counts. But this is not always the case. A man attracted by the academic life, but uncertain about his prospects in it, may decide to accept an opening in business or administration. This is a frequent pattern of choice.

We are told that the toast of the higher mathematics is celebrated in Cambridge with the words 'may they never be of any use to anyone'. Aristotle took a similar line when he praised contemplation: 'nothing arises from it apart from the contemplating, while from practical activities we gain more or less apart from the actions' (1177 b2–4). The obvious comment on this line of thought was made when we examined Aristotle's arguments concerning happiness as the supreme end in EN I. He cannot be understood as asserting that activities other than contemplation are not desired for themselves. For he frequently says or implies that they are so desired, and in EN x itself he says that life lived in society in accordance with ethical virtue is a form, though not the paramount form, of happiness (1178 a9). Thus, when he suggests that theoretical activity 'alone would seem to be loved for its own sake' (1177 b1–2), what he ought to say, and must mean, is that it alone is loved for its own sake alone. But many quite trivial pleasures are pursued for their own sake alone. Aristotle might have recalled that, at the beginning of Republic, Book II, the goods said to be the fairest of all are those which are desired both for themselves and for their consequences (357 b–358 a). If we are considering in what degree some activity which we enjoy is desirable for its own sake the question whether it has desirable consequences, and how desirable these are, is ex hypothesi irrelevant. If it has desirable consequences, this is not evidence against or for its intrinsic worth, but it counts as an additional reason for pursuing the activity.

I have argued that Aristotle fails to support adequately his elevation of science and philosophy above other works of man; that his account of intellectual activity, and of what makes men desire it, is distorted by his theology; and that he gives us no satisfying explanation of the paradoxes presented to us by the doctrine of the special status of reason (nous). But these criticisms do not imply that the doctrines against which they are directed are uninteresting. When we read Aristotle we expect to find, and often we do find, valid arguments from acceptable premisses. The critic, when disappointed in this expectation, is apt to denounce a non sequitur; but he knows that, when he does this, he may only be revealing his own failure to follow the argument. Moreover my criticisms in this chapter, even when they are valid, do not touch the foundations of Aristotle's doctrine.

We may be tempted to say that on the nature of man, the problem of body and mind, Aristotle gives us no more than a set of suggestive but enigmatic apophthegms. But how many philosophers have done more than he did to illuminate the problem? It is a topic on which only the lunatic theories are comparatively clear and easy to follow. If we are as perplexed as we should be by the apparent facts we should not be surprised to find that what Aristotle says about them is also perplexing.

On the doctrine of the supreme good for man I have declined in this chapter to go along with the interpreters who would make it more acceptable by blurring or enlarging its outlines. But, if we were required to find one word and one only which best describes what is most to be desired, it would be hard to find a better word than *theōria*, contemplation. In the preceding chapter I dissented from the suggestion that Aristotle sees how to exhibit the life of theory, primary happiness, as continuous with the less exalted happiness of the non-theoretical. Nor did I find earlier in Aristotle's account of *phronēsis*, practical wisdom, any sustained attempt to bridge the gulf, to show continuity, between the principles of justice which all men must respect and the contemplative activities without which no man can be truly happy. We do not find in Aristotle's account of the nature and chief end of man acceptable answers to all the questions which he asks. But this is not to say that he was wrong to ask them, or that we need not try to answer them now.

APPENDED NOTES

I. Introductory Note: Aristotle's Ethical Writings (1–11)

pp. 1–9   This sketchy introductory chapter was written because I thought that a reader, especially one with little or no Greek, ought to know at the outset what kind of document had come down to us as the *Nicomachean Ethics* of Aristotle. I could offer only a bird's eye view, complementary aspects and impressions, of the problems it raises for Aristotelian scholarship. I had and have no solution to advocate of the major thorny problems: the 'common books'; the two treatments of pleasure; the answer or answers to the question what constitutes happiness. I hoped that my remarks would be taken as mutually complementary and corrective and not as mutually inconsistent exaggerations: the *EN* is an authoritative exposition of Aristotle's ethical philosophy but is a patchwork assembled by an editor who may or may not have been Aristotle himself or an immediate disciple and who was unprovided with many of the mechanisms of modern book-making.

On rereading the chapter I am not inclined to complain that remarks about it by at least one reviewer showed, as I think, some misunderstanding. I 'assume that the *Ethics* has no structure, but consists of a number of collocated tracts no one of which sheds light on any other', and this assumption is an 'excuse for not looking to see what structure it might have'. Of course, the sections of Aristotle's book were meant to illuminate each other and sometimes do. But it is true that, in approaching each section, I tended to think of myself simply as trying to make out what Aristotle was saying in it. Hypotheses concerning the plot or structure of the whole can be wrecked by the misunderstanding of a sentence. But questions about the consistency of the whole are important. In recent books and articles there is much discussion of structural questions, supported by minute dissection of crucial passages. Some of these Appended Notes have been prompted and guided by such discussion. I hope, therefore, that the Notes move more freely than the Chapters from one part of the *EN* to another and do something to correct any idea that what Aristotle presents us with in the book is a series of independent problems.

pp. 7–9   In these pages I refer to a number of questions which are still disputed. I had no solutions or theories of my own to defend. The past ten years have seen the publication of two important studies of the relation between the *Eudemian* and the *Nicomachean Ethics*, studies which proceed on different lines to different conclusions. (For bibliographical details see the Bibliography.)

C. J. Rowe's book (1971) 'deals with three distinct and related problems: the authorship of the *Eudemian Ethics*; the relation between the *Eudemian* and the *Nicomachean Ethics*; and the problem of the "common" books'. He agrees with Jaeger's conclusion that the *EE* is authentic and earlier than the *EN*, but is critical of Jaeger's arguments. His own main argument, based on a detailed comparison of the two works, supports the opinion that, over a range of topics, the treatment in the *EE* follows a clearer and better planned line of thought and that this fact is to be explained by the hypothesis that Aristotle in the later treatise was using the *EE* as a basis to which he added new points in revision while sometimes failing to carry the revision through. On some questions, of which the double treatment of pleasure is one, he finds the evidence insufficient for a solution. He provides clear accounts of the histories of the problems and a full bibliography.

Anthony Kenny's book was published late in 1978. He claims to prove that the affinities of the 'common books' are with the Eudemian and not the Nicomachean treatise. A number of scholars have produced particular arguments for this opinion. But in the history of the problem Kenny's books is original and epoch-making in at least two ways. First, armed with a computer and the technicalities of its use, he has carried through an elaborate statistical investigation of features of style in the disputed books and in the two sets of undisputed books. The central chapters of his book report the results of this investigation. Secondly, he has not conducted inconclusive raids but has gone into action simultaneously on many fronts. Thus he opens with a chapter on the history of the 'Aristotelian Ethics' in antiquity and a second chapter on cross-references. He ends with two philosophical chapters and a chapter on the dating of the treatises.

In my book and in these Appended Notes I have defended the substantial coherence of Aristotle's answer, in the *Nicomachean Ethics* taken as including the common books, to the question what life is best for the human animal. In a brief Postscript to the Appended Notes I survey the position on this aspect of the matter taken up by Kenny in his chapter 8 on 'Happiness in the Aristotelian Ethics'.

II. The Final Good for Man (12–27)

p. 12, l. 20   '. . . the activity itself or something produced by the activity . . .'.
A reviewer says that I 'seek to account for Aristotle's strange belief than an "incomplete" action, such as research or boat-building, is never desired or undertaken for its own sake, but only for the sake of its *telos* (discovery, a boat)'. I pointed out that, as Aristotle uses *telos*, an activity is a *telos* if it is 'desired for itself' (12–13). I referred to passages in *EN* I where Aristotle notes that an object desired may be desired both for itself and for its results (14). Thus it is an over-statement to say that I attributed to Aristotle the 'belief' that we never desire the activities of building a boat or composing a poem independently of our desire for a boat or a poem. What I said about Aristotle's depreciation of 'incomplete' (productive, goal-seeking) activities was rather that he 'tends to think' of them as not desired

for themselves, or to 'ignore', 'fail to keep steadily in view', the fact that they are or may be so desired (14; cf. 345).

But I have now come to think that the incompleteness of my treatment of *telos* in this chapter was misleading. Having pointed out that a *telos* is not the same thing as an 'end', where end is opposed to means, I did not go on to discuss what Aristotle meant by, or might include under, *ta pros ti telos*, things related or contributing to a *telos*. What prevented me from doing so was my belief, about which I am now doubtful, that both in the treatment of statesmanship in I. 1, 2 (e.g. 1094 a14–16) and in his account in III. 3 of deliberation as comparable with analysis in mathematics Aristotle was operating with a concept of *telos* and *ta pros to telos* in the sense of end and means. I, therefore, thought it better that questions about the extension beyond means of *ta pros to telos* should wait for the treatment of the practical intellect in Book VI (cf. 232, 254–7). Hence I was led to say, in view of the obvious inadequacy of means-finding as a description of the function of the architectonic science (politics), that 'Aristotle tries to make means-finding cover too large a part of practical thinking, whether of the statesman or of the private citizen' (16). In a later passage I accuse Aristotle of failing to 'revise or expand' his account of deliberation as means-seeking 'in order to cover types of practical thinking which it does not fit' (217). One of the other types I had in mind appears in my Index, under Deliberation, as 'the weighing of pros and cons'.

There was an oversight in this criticism of Aristotle. If *telos* is not equivalent to end *ta pros to telos* may not be equivalent to means. If so, the Greek pair may be applicable to rational procedures to which the English pair is not. Greenwood, in his commentary on Book VI, had suggested that this was so: he distinguished 'external means', i.e. means, from 'component means', i.e. components; the various courses are components of, not means to, a banquet. The crucial sentence in III. 3 on deliberation is translated by Ross: 'they assume the end and consider how and by what means it is to be attained' (1112 b15–16). But, as the reviewer pointed out, the Greek is less restrictive: 'positing the *telos*, they examine how and through what it shall be achieved'.

I shall refer again in later notes to the fact that practical thinking is not restricted by Aristotle to the kind of deliberation which seeks to discover the best immediately achievable means of bringing about indirectly a desired end: see the notes on III. 38–44; IX. 162; XI (on an article by David Wiggins).

p. 15, ll. 18–26   'A more definite but partial answer . . .'
It is not possible to take seriously the idea that, for Aristotle, the whole business of politics is to ensure the undisturbed pursuit of theoretical sciences by a few. It is made clear, at least in VI. 13 and more fully in X. 8, that a life lived in accordance with practical wisdom, which involves ethical virtue, is itself a form of *eudaimonia*, an end and not only a means to an end. Professor Ackrill has said, in his 1974 Dawes Hicks Lecture, 'Aristotle on *Eudaimonia*', that, in my interpretation of *EN* I, I attribute to Aristotle a 'monolithic' account of the final good, the

doctrine that it consists of 'just one valued activity', *theoria*. He quotes only from my article, 'The Final Good in Aristotle's Ethics' (1965), but implies (4²) that I took the same view in this chapter. This does not seem to me to be compatible with the distinction I made, on pp. 18–19 (cf. 22–3, 25–6), between a man's 'comprehensive' conception of the life he wants and the central or 'paramount' interest which gives it 'unity and continuity'.

I spoke of Aristotle as 'hesitating between an inclusive and an exclusive formulation' (23); I said that his 'language straddles' between the two concepts (25). By this I did not mean that he moved backwards and forwards between inconsistent doctrines, but that his emphasis shifted from one aspect to the other of a consistent doctrine. At the beginning of 1. 4 Aristotle asks 'what it is we say that political science aims at and what is the highest of all goods achievable by action' (1095 a15–17). The political end, as expounded in *EN* 1. 1, 2, is best understood as inclusive of subordinate ends, but 'the highest of all goods' suggests a paramount object. The definition of the human good (1098 a16–18) explicitly leaves open the question whether *eudaimonia* is 'activity in accordance with excellence' or 'activity in accordance with the best and most complete excellence'. If one excellence is paramount, how paramount is it? I shall discuss conflicting interpretations of the definition in a later note.

pp. 20–22   Prichard on defining happiness

A reviewer makes the following critical comment: 'Much space is given to refuting implausible pieces of cleverness on the part of Burnet or Prichard'.

The suggestion that Prichard was capable of being clever in a bad sense is itself implausible. I was perhaps wrong to refer to him only in this passage. But I included in the bibliography, in addition to the article on *eudaimonia* (1935), the posthumously published volume of articles and lectures, *Moral Obligation* (1949), in which it was reprinted. I quote here from his best-known article, 'Does Moral Philosophy rest on a Mistake?' (1913): 'the extreme sense of dissatisfaction produced by a close reading of Aristotle's *Ethics*' (p. 13). Prichard's reading was always close; his 'close reading' was very close indeed. His criticism of Aristotle (and of Plato) was complex and subtle (not 'clever') and its target was a doctrine which he interpreted as implying that a man has only one independent duty, the duty to promote his own happiness. My criticism here (20–2) is of Prichard's attempt to reinforce his general argument by an appeal to the *Posterior Analytics*. But the criticism has a wider relevance as challenging his assumption that to ask what is pleasure or happiness misleads by suggesting that we do not already know. Although I have not mentioned Prichard again, I hope that some of the passages indicated in my Index, under Egoism and Altruism, Friendship and Duty are relevant to Prichardian interpretations.

Burnet's edition has important merits. When his interpretations are unacceptable this cannot always be attributed to his cleverness. In Ch. III I criticized his important thesis that the *Ethics* is 'dialectical throughout'; and it is to this that the reviewer is evidently referring.

pp. 23–26   The *ergon* (function) of man (1097 b22 ff)

Aristotle suggests that we can clarify our concept of *eudaimonia* (well-doing) by ascertaining man's function (*ergon*) (1097 b23–5). Within the section which follows there is a transition from a first part (a) in which Aristotle tries to persuade us of the truth of the proposition that man has an *ergon* (1097 b24–33) and a second part (b) in which, starting from the conception of powers which are specific or peculiar to men as members of the class of living beings, Aristotle arrives at a tentative definition of the human good (1097 b33–1098 a20). I have come to see, with the help of Dr. Clark's sharp comments, that my treatment of this section was excessively brief. The ground is familiar, but I ought, perhaps, to have offered a more careful map. Instead I took for granted a critical acquaintance with the relevant section of Plato's *Republic* (352 d8–353 d7) between which and this section of the *EN* there is a close parallelism. I shall now look a little more closely at this parallelism.

It is convenient to have a label for this whole slice of Aristotle's exposition, (a) + (b). For this I would be happy to settle for the title of chapter II. 1 of Clark's book (*Aristotle's Man*, 1975), 'the *ergon* argument'. The label is used also by Ackrill in his Lecture, 'Aristotle on *Eudaimonia*' (pp. 16, 17). But, in the use of this label, it is important to make clear whether the reference is primarily, or even exclusively, to (a) or to (b). It will be obvious that, in my view, (a) is more misleading than illuminating. But I hope I have never said anything which would diminish the interest and importance of (b).

The objective of the argument in *Republic* I is to discover the function (and virtue) of the *psuchē* (soul), specified at 353 d as 'paying attention ruling deliberating and so on'. Plato is speaking of the rational human soul, and at this point Lee's Penguin translation gives 'conscious mind'. Socrates has led up to this statement about *psuchē* by adducing the following set, in this order, of entities which have *erga*: a horse, eyes and ears, a pruning knife made with the purpose and function of pruning vines—*epi touto ergasthenti* (352 d8–353 a5). The sentence on the *ergon* of the horse is thus translated by Lee: 'And would you define it as something that only the horse . . . can do, or, at any rate, that the horse does best?' (352 e2–3; cf. 353 a9–11). But the text speaks not of what 'only the horse can do' but of what a man can do 'only with a horse'. It thus conveys what Bosanquet mildly calls the 'very serious assumption' that the *ergon* of the horse is to be useful to man (*Companion to Plato's Republic*, p. 64). From the point of view of the horses there may be many activities useless to man which they alone, or they better than any other animal, can perform. Thus the set of entities offered as paradigms of things having functions is a set which have been made, or trained, and are used, or at least are used, as instrumental to a purpose. In this context it seemed and seems to me to be right to take Plato's formula in 353 a9–11 ('only or best') as a criterion and not as a definition (24). If so, there is no justification for the transition from the set of instrumental or quasi-instrumental entities to the soul or mind unless the soul or mind is instrumental or quasi-instrumental. Aristotle offers another example: surely, if a man has an *ergon* as a shoe-maker, he cannot not have one as a man (1097 b28–30). Why not? At this point it seemed best to abandon (a) as a preliminary and provocative flourish which serves only to inculcate the idea that the good life lies in action and activity not in passivity and inaction. (On the weakness of the *ergon* argument in *Republic* 1 cf. Cross and Woozley in *Plato's Republic*, pp. 57–60).

Clark remarks, with some severity, that I 'accept the usual translation' (of *ergon* as function) and make a 'standard response' (pp. 15–16). He does not say what is wrong with the usual translation. Both '*ergon*' and 'function' are sometimes, but not always, used to refer to a tool which is made and/or used for a purpose. Biologists do not seem to find difficulty in assigning 'functions' to 'organs' without supposing them to be products of conscious design. 'Job' would be appropriate in some cases but too colloquial for regular service. Perhaps other languages are better equipped: 'tâche' (Gauthier-Jolif), 'Leistung' (Dirlmeier). The English translators do not appear to consider alternatives to 'function'. As regards my 'standard response' to (a), Clark does not make clear what he finds wrong or confused in the substance of what I say. He expresses no wish to defend the Socratic 'introduction of the concept of an *ergon* through the examples of pruning hooks and the like' (p. 15). Moreover, in his article, 'The Use of "Man's Function" in Aristotle' (*Ethics*, 1972), while tilting against 'misunderstandings' and 'mistranslations', he tells us that 'a thing's *ergon* is whatever it alone does or it does best, its distinctive mode of activity, in which its nature is most clearly seen' (p. 272). In a reference to the *Republic* (353 a10 f.) he says, in opposition to me, that 'it seems better to suppose that he is offering a definition rather than a ground of inference' (p. 272). This interpretation is difficult to apply to the horse (or to the hen) on which man imposes functions. When he makes this suggestion Clark in effect implies what I had suggested, that Aristotle could get on with his analysis of man's nature and 'distinctive mode of activity' without any deployment of pruning knives, domesticated animals, bodily organs, arts and crafts, and professions 'and the like'.

p. 24   The definition of 'human good' (1098 a16–18)
My remark that 'only very brief comment is needed at this stage' may be justified on the ground that full comment would involve considering Aristotle's doctrine on the nature and pre-eminent desirability of theoretic activity. But, without anticipating later books, some reference is needed here to the questions which Aristotle's definition leaves unanswered: 'the activity of soul in accordance with virtue (1), and if there are more than one virtue (2), in accordance with the best (*aristē*) and most complete (*teleiotatē*), and further in a complete life' (3). It will be helpful to consider also a passage from the following chapter: '*eudaimonia* is the best, noblest, and most pleasant thing in the world ... all these properties belong to the best activities; and these or one, the best, of these we identify with *eudaimonia*' (1099 a24–30; cf. also VII, 1153 b10–12).

(1) 'Virtue' is excellence of the rational soul and has both an ethical and an intellectual component (1098 a3–8, 1144 b28–32).

(2) One virtue or many? How are we to count them? We learn in vi that the ethical virtues and *phronēsis* (practical wisdom) form a mutually conditioned set: it is impossible to have one without having them all (chs. 12 and 13). We learn also that there are two intellectual truth-finding excellencies, practical wisdom shown in deliberation and action and theoretical wisdom (*sophia*) shown in contemplation (*theōria*) (chs. 1 and 2). It is not asserted or denied that there is one-way or two-way conditionality between the two excellencies. Aristotle might have thought that *phronēsis* at its highest (architectonic) level requires *sophia* (at some level) (cf. x, 1177 a12–18). But a reasonable guess is that the answer Aristotle had in mind was that there is not only one human excellence but at least two. Neither the proposition that only a good man can be a philosopher nor the proposition that only a philosopher can be a good man has much plausibility. Whether or not mutual conditionality implies identity, non-conditionality implies difference.

(3) *Telos, teleios, teleioteros, teleiotatos. Telos* means end; to be *teleios* is to have the character of an end; according to the context the translation will be 'final', 'perfect', or 'complete'. But to say that a man has lived a complete life does not mean only, and may not mean at all, that he has lived to be an old man.

We ask now how we are to understand Aristotle when he says that, if there are more than one virtue (activity), happiness will be activity in accordance with the one which is best and most complete (*teleiotatē*). The answer accepted or assumed by most translators and commentators is that Aristotle is anticipating the doctrine of Books vi and x, that the best and most complete (final) excellence is *sophia*, the disposition which is activated in *theoria* (contemplation). When Aristotle takes up again in x. 6 the subject of *eudaimonia* he starts by recalling two cardinal doctrines of Book i: the distinction between the acquired capacity to perform an activity and the activity performed and the division of activities into those desirable for themselves and those desirable for something else (1176 a33–b9). Again he seems to echo the language of 1098 a17 when he says in x. 7 that it is reasonable that *eudaimonia* should be an activity in accordance with the highest (*kratistē*) virtue. The account in i is an outline which we expect to see 'filled in' later, and the filling must include the promised treatment of *theōria* (1098 a20, 1096 a4, 5). I can see no reason to reject this interpretation. I know of only one translator, D. P. Chase, whose rendering implies its rejection: 'if there are more than one excellence' becomes 'if excellence admits of degrees'. But this is to rewrite not to translate.

Ackrill, in his Dawes Hicks Lecture (1975), argues against the identification of the 'best and most complete virtue' of Book i with the highest virtue of Book x. The 'best' virtue, he argues, is not one virtue rather than others or another but 'total virtue, the combination of all virtues' (p. 17). So understood 'activity in accordance with the best and most complete virtue' would not differ significantly from the phrase used in the corresponding passage in the *Eudemian Ethics* where *eudaimoniā* is defined as 'the activity of a complete life in accordance with complete virtue' (1219 a38–9). It may be conceded that, taken by itself, the expression 'the best and most complete virtue' could be applied to 'the combination'. But this, of course, is not an adequate way of framing the question of translation. The question is rather whether the presence of the conditional clause, 'if there are more than one virtue', in 1098 a17 (consider also the expression 'the best of these' in 1099 a30) does not confirm in the superlatives which follow their natural selective and exclusive force. I cannot persuade myself that any other way of understanding the words is acceptable. If this is right, the other arguments in Ackrill's battery cannot help his case. He claims that, in the earlier part of the chapter (1097 a15–b21), Aristotle has 'told' readers to understand by 'the most final' (teleiotaton) as applied to a telos 'the comprehensive end which includes all partial ends' and that readers thus instructed 'will surely interpret' similarly the superlatives in 1098 a17–18. (Why have they not?) I find an implied instruction about teleioteros (more final) at 1097 a30–2, an instruction which is hardly exhaustive since an end might be said to be teleioteron simply as having a higher degree of intrinsic desirability. I find an explicit instruction about haplōs teleion (final without qualification) but not about teleiotaton. If there is an implicit instruction, I do not see what makes it obvious that it can or should be applied to later passages in which what is said seems to demand non-inclusive interpretations.

Ackrill makes the point that what 'the ergon argument requires' (p. 17) is the recognition of rationality, 'the power of thought' not 'one type of thought', as what is 'distinctive of man' (p. 10). I agree and said so. 'What is common and peculiar (idion) to man is rationality in a general sense not theoretical insight, which is one specialized way of being rational' (25–6). But this difficulty shows only that Aristotle in Book I leaves loose ends not that we must defend a forced interpretation of a crucial sentence. A man should have a 'paramount' (not 'monolithic') end which is central in an 'inclusive' plan. But by 'inclusive' I meant, both in the article (1965) and in the book (1968), 'inclusive in the sense that there is no desire or interest which cannot be regarded as a candidate, however unpromising, for a place in the pattern of a life' (291, 329). The requirement that eudaimonia should be, by itself, 'sufficient' (autarkēs) (1097 b6–21) does not imply that the man of practical wisdom will not be very choosy in his scrutiny of the candidates.

III. The Nature of the Inquiry (28–45)

p. 28   This chapter deals with a number of subjects not all closely related to each other. It may be helpful if I summarize its contents and say why it was difficult to decide how much and what to include. I wished to avert misunderstandings of a number of particular passages in EN I, especially 1095 a30–b8. But I did not wish to anticipate unnecessarily discussions appropriate to later chapters dealing with later books of the Ethics.

The contents of the chapter fall into two parts. (1) In the first (28–37) I discuss briefly various doctrines stated or implied in EN I: ethics as a political inquiry (28, 30); thinking as theoretical practical or productive (29–30); practical thinking as extending from the political and ethical thinking of the statesman and the philosopher to the good 'sense' of the morally educated citizen (30); ethics as having a practical end and Joachim's criticism (30–1); ways in which ethics has a 'variable' subject-matter (31–4); the movement of thinking to and from 'principles' (34–6); *epagōgē* ('induction') in ethics (36–7). My Index under Political Science, Phronesis, Principles, Contingency, Ethismos, shows that there is more to come, not necessarily enough, on all these matters. (2) In the rest of the chapter (37–45) I discuss the nature of 'dialectical' arguments and their importance in ethics, and give reasons for rejecting the view of Burnet that 'from the nature of the case' the *Ethics* is 'dialectical throughout'. Burnet has much to say that is true and important on Aristotle's procedures but his insight is erratic.

pp. 31–34   Variability, Imprecision, Indeterminateness

The treatment here of the doctrine that precision (*akribeia*) is not possible in ethics as it is in mathematics is supplemented by what is said in Ch. VII on the differences between the ethical mean and a mean in mathematics (134–5, 141–3; cf. 189–90). Evans has a helpful paragraph in which, adducing passages from the *Metaphysics*, he explains Aristotle's 'notion of precision . . . one by which greater precision is a function of being more simple and less in need of support from a number of additional items' (p. 86). Evans goes on to claim that, while the generality of ethics cannot 'reflect the complexity of particular cases', Aristotle is 'convinced' that there is always 'a right answer' accessible, in the particular case, to the *phronimos* (p. 87). I tried to make what may be the same point (top of 33). But I have two doubts about what Evans says here. First, as to whether the 'right reason' (*orthos logos*) of the *phronimos* necessarily achieves *akribeia*. Secondly, we must distinguish 'true' and 'correct' or 'right' from 'precise' and 'determinate': the mean may be a stretch not a point in a continuum (141–3).

pp. 38–44   Dialectic and Deliberation in the *Ethics*

J. M. Cooper, in a section of his book headed 'Ends, Intuition and Dialectic' (I. 4, pp. 58–71), refers to the opinions of Burnet which I have discussed. In the main he endorses Burnet but with qualifications and reservations. 'Burnet was the first to emphasise that Aristotle regarded the method of moral philosophy more or less explicitly as dialectical in character' (p. 69). Speaking for himself, he goes on to say that 'there seems no doubt that Aristotle conceives of his procedure as for the most part dialectical', and adds that 'particularly is this true of the first book'. He says bodly that 'the dialectical character of even the elaborate and rather formal argument by which Aristotle finally produces his definition of the best life (1097 b22–1098 a20) is beyond doubt' (p. 69). Later in his book he refers again to Burnet to say that he 'too easily allows that the dialectical "analysis" of *endoxa* is divorced from the search for truth' (p. 107 footnote). He qualifies this important criticism by saying that Burnet's 'official account of dialectic is better (pp. xxxix–xliii)'. He does not quote actual words used by Burnet. This makes it difficult to know how much of what Burnet says is regarded by Cooper as both clear and acceptable. The examples of dialectical treatment which Cooper gives on p. 69 are the obvious ones: the good for man in Book I and *akrasia* (moral weakness) in Book VII. But two of the phrases I have quoted, 'the method of moral philosophy' and 'for the most part dialectical', carry him further than I can go with Burnet.

When we say that at least some sections of the *Ethics* are dialectical with what are we contrasting 'dialectical'? This question is answered by Cooper in the sentence which immediately precedes the first mention of Burnet. 'In the case of the *Ethics* the contrast is not with demonstration but with the method of deliberation' (p. 69). This contrast might be understood in one of two different ways. (a) It might be a contrast between two different 'methods' both of which are used *within* Aristotle's moral philosophy as it is expounded in the *Ethics*. But (b) it might be a contrast *between* the methods and patterns of cogitation appropriate to moral philosophy and the thinking of the practical man, or of the casuist, which terminates in the recommendation or decision to perform a highly determinate or even an individual action.

It is difficult to say which of these two contrasts Cooper intends at this point. The main cause of the difficulty or ambiguity is, I think, that Cooper still has much, and much of value, to say in the rest of his book both about *eudaimonia* (human 'flourishing') and about the pattern or patterns of deliberation required by Aristotle's conception of *eudaimonia*.

Most of what Cooper has to say in the pages which immediately follow (pp. 70, 71), points to (b) the second interpretation of the contrast. It is perhaps sufficient to quote from the footnote (p. 71) where Cooper explains how for Aristotle moral philosophy can be 'dialectical' but also 'practical'.

He presumably thought (and reasonably so) that dialectic gives one a firmer, clearer and better articulated grasp of what the end actually is and therefore both increases ones commitment to it and makes one better able to act perceptively in its interest. Moral philosophy is a practical study, then, not because the philosopher deliberates about how to live or what to do (as the casuist does) but by providing a comprehensive and critical understanding of the basic structure and goals of the moral life.

Dialectical argumentation leads to a 'conception of good living'; deliberation shows us the means to this end or to some end which is itself a means to good living (pp. 69–70) (cf. 1140 a25–8).

But for Cooper this way of specifying the contrast of dialectical and deliberative reasoning cannot, I think, be more than itself a dialectical move. For in stating it I have implied that *ta pros to telos* (what contributes to the end) is equivalent to means, and that deliberation is always means-seeking. But Cooper has argued earlier that *ta pros to telos* 'covers more than just means' (p. 19). Moreover he is about to show admirable persistence in adhering to this conclusion and in working out its consequence in terms of 'patterns of deliberation' different from the pattern appropriate to the regressive search for means to a clearly conceived end (pp. 84–8, cf. 95–7). He formulates a scheme in which 'principles of virtue appear as steps in the deliberative argument' and the argument moves from less to more 'specific rules and precepts' (pp. 85, 86). This pattern of deliberation allows us to recognize an independent 'value inherent in moral action' and can be accommodated within 'deliberation as Aristotle understands it' (p. 87). Thus in both patterns there is a movement of the practical intellect from *telos* to *ta pros to telos*. But in the second pattern the passage is not from end to means; its function is rather to 'make explicit' what was 'vaguely grasped' in 'a strong unarticulated intuition of what morality involves, and the derivation of rules would really be the progressive articulation of the end' (p. 103; cf. p. 114 where 'progressive articulation of the end' is repeated). Here Cooper ascribes to deliberation the achievement which he had earlier ascribed to dialectic, 'a better articulated grasp of what the end actually is' (p. 71 quoted above).

I do not think that what Cooper says about dialectic on pp. 69–71 can be reconciled with his own later account of the practical deliberative function of the intellect in Aristotle's view. Nor can I interpret 'the *ergon* argument' in Book I as basing Aristotle's definition of the good life on dialectical 'premisses'. I hope I have made my own different opinions clear on pp. 38–40 and in my note above to pp. 23–6. But I agree, of course, with Cooper that the definition reached in Book I is no more than an 'unarticulated intuition' of the best life for men, an outline sketch to be filled in, or articulated, later (1098 a20–2).

IV. The Platonic Idea of the Good (46–67)

A reviewer points out that in this chapter I do not 'raise the question whether the word "good" has, in fact, more than one sense, nor whether a Platonic theory of forms, with or without revision, could accommodate it if it has'. I agree that these and other difficult questions are raised by the three pages which Aristotle here gives to his criticisms of this Platonic doctrine or these Platonic doctrines. The criticism is compressed and allusive. A commentator who seemed to himself qualified to cover the multiple ranges of questions involved and to show their relevance to these three pages would surely not attempt the task in a single chapter of a book. My aim was only, without concealing difficulties, to consider some of the more obvious questions raised by Aristotle's criticisms.

pp. 58–59 Aristotle's third argument (1096 a29–34)
Dr. E. A. Schmidt, in a review in *Gnomon* (May 1971), rightly criticizes my comments on this argument. He points out that I have no valid reason for finding Aristotle's formulation of the argument 'puzzling' in the way suggested in lines 1–9 of p. 59: 'I do not think that this expansion is permissible' (p. 242). My difficulty arose through failure to notice how closely the third argument is linked to the preceding arguments concerning the categorial multisignificance of 'good'. As Schmidt puts it in the concluding sentence of his criticism (which I paraphrase): the thought conveyed is that 'good', in addition to its categorial multisignificance

(preceding argument), is multisignificant also in another way, viz. as applied in different special sciences. Similarly Flashar: 'the good not only appears differently in the different categories—it appears in many different forms within each individual category' (p. 7).

V. The Nature of Man (68–93)

p. 68, l. 11   '... plants too have souls in the sense of being alive (empsucha)'
In the De Partibus Animalium Aristotle speaks of nature (phusis) as passing in a continuous (non-temporal) gradation from apsucha (lifeless things) to animals, and says that on the way there are living things (zōnta) which are not animals (zōa) (681 a12–15). It is natural to read this passage as suggesting that plants as well as animals are empsucha. Plato in the Timaeus (77 a, b), as also some pre-Socratic thinkers, had spoken of plants as having sensations. Aristotle said that they did not (De Anima 424 a33; cf. 415 a1–3); perception is not 'needed' for self-nutrition (De Somno 455 a2–3). But he decided nevertheless to say that plants have souls (psuchai) and hence are in a sense empsucha (414 b30; cf. 413 a20–6). This is not in fact a normal use of the word in Greek; the normal meaning is 'animate'. When Aristotle in the Rhetoric refers to the Empedoclean veto on the killing of empsucha he means animals (1373 b14–15; similarly in Plato, Laws 782 c, Thucydides VII. 29). The opposite of 'animate' is 'inanimate', and this would suggest that plants are apsucha. In Euripides apsuchos describes a vegetarian diet (Hippolytus 952). Similarly in Latin the vegetarian is content with inanimate food, inanimis contentus cibis (Apuleius). I remark later, in the appendix to Ch. V, that there is no 'psychology of plants': 'the processes which occur in them, growth for example, are not psychical but physical' (84).

It seems that for a Greek too 'plant soul' would have an odd ring, unless he happened to think it sensible to play music or to speak kindly to his growing vegetables. Even in the De Anima Aristotle slips easily into restricting the soul (psuchē) to the sphere of the 'psychical'. Thus in the first chapters of the De Anima the soul which he opposes to the body (sōma) is at least sentient or perceptual; the body which is involved in anger or fear is the living organism and, as such, might be, but here is not, spoken of as having its own more basic kind of soul (403 a16–19). The same use of psuchē is implied when he speaks of attributes which are common (koina), i.e. belong to the soul and body in conjunction (De Sensu 436 a7–8). Plato had spoken of processes in the body which, if of sufficient strength, cause pains or pleasures and of other processes which evoke the exercise, pleasant or painful or neither, of the faculties of sense-perception (Republic 584 c). In the Timaeus processes are passed on (diadidonai) from one part of the body to another 'until they reach consciousness and report the quality of the agent' (64 b, Cornford's translation; cf. 45 d, 65 a). In the Philebus the word anaisthēsia (non-perception or unconsciousness) is contrasted with aisthēsis; another word, lanthanein, which means lying hid or escaping notice, is deprecated as less appropriate

(33 e)—presumably because the fact under consideration is the non-occurrence of a perception and not an animal's unawareness of an occurrent perception (cf. *Physics* 244 b15–245 a2). Aristotle echoes this Platonic language in the *De Sensu*: perception is 'generated in the soul through the body' (436 b3–6).

p. 77, 4 lines from bottom: 'psychophysical dualism'
Some interpreters are not willing to class Aristotle's doctrine in the *De Anima* as dualistic: so to describe it is viewed as misleading since for Aristotle soul and body are not two things but elements of one thing. I agree that, if dualism is defined as a two-substance doctrine, he was not a dualist. But this admission is compatible with dualism as regards kinds of states and processes in one substance, the man. Again some have said that Aristotle had no 'concept of consciousness' or of the 'psychical'. Perhaps they are thinking of consciousness in terms of Cartesian or of Kantian doctrines. I can see no case for saying that Aristotle offered accounts of psychical states and capacities in purely biological terms. Is there any possible defence of assertions such as these: Aristotle explains perception 'simply' as an event in the sense-organ; soul is the way the body works ('that is all'); sensing is a bodily process 'thoughout'? I am quoting from three different materialist interpreters all claiming to 'dissolve mental features into body'. But sometimes verbal collisions can be averted by terminological explanations. Thus the truth of the statement that Aristotle did, or that he did not, have the concept of 'consciousness' is undecidable until we are told in what sense or senses the word is being used.

On its possible meanings I have consulted the *Dictionary of Philosophy and Psychology* (1901), ed. J. M. Baldwin and the *Encyclopedia of Philosophy* (1967), ed. Paul Edwards. 'Wherever there is not total unconsciousness, in the sense in which we attribute unconsciousness to a table, the existence of some form of mind we denote by the word "consciousness"' (Baldwin). G. F. Stout, in his *Manual of Psychology*[4] (1929), uses the word in this way: every 'kind or degree of experience', even 'the dimmer and vaguer feelings or sentience', e.g. the feel of the clothes we are wearing, counts as a manifestation of consciousness. This I take to be the use noted by Charles Landesman Jr. in the *Encyclopedia* as the 'broad use to designate any mental state or whatever it is about a mental state which makes it mental'. A linguist may not like this broad open use. He may wish to say that, when we speak properly, consciousness, like conscience, is reflexive. My conscience tells me that I have done wrong not that you have done wrong (cf. in Latin 'conscius sibi sceleris'). Thus 'consciousness' suggests that a man turns in on himself and his states. In Descartes *conscientia* is a reflexive awareness: 'But there can exist no thought of which, at the very moment that it is present in us, we are not conscious' (Adam and Tannery, vii 246; Haldane and Ross, ii. 115). The distinction between the open and the reflexive uses of 'consciousness' should save us from simply taking for granted the correctness of Descartes' doctrine that, as one of his commentators puts it, self-consciousness is the only kind of consciousness (A. Boyce Gibson, *The Philosophy of Descartes* (1932), p. 204). It is a doctrine which we are strongly inclined to accept; but also one which we are strongly inclined to reject, when we reflect on the selectiveness of attention, the difference between dreaming and waking and the difficulty of imagining the inner life of animals.

The above notes supplementary to v are shortened versions of parts of an article, 'Concepts of Consciousness in Aristotle', in *Mind* (July 1976). In it I approached Aristotle's body–mind doctrine from a lexicographical angle. I was puzzled by the tendencies for certain words to stray or straddle over the borders between four kinds of bodies which we encounter on the surface of this planet: those which are (1) non-living non-animate non-rational (rocks and machines): (2) living non-animate non-rational (plants); (3) living animate non-rational (non-human animals); (4) living animate rational (human animals). If asked to locate consciousness some would say in (3) and (4), others only in (4). Those who give the latter answer do so either because, with Descartes, they suppose non-human animals to be only physiological mechanisms (an obviously outrageous opinion) or because they think that a body which only feels and has perceptions does not qualify as 'conscious'. Thus 'consciousness' straddles because, as I have pointed out, it has uses entrenched on either side or both sides of the border between (3) and (4). I have found, by asking for off-the-cuff answers to the question whether plants are part of 'animate' or 'inanimate' nature, a certain visible vagueness, even in philosophers, and even an inclination to plump for the former. So far as I know, this inclination has no support from lexicography. The lexicographers are clear, as Byron was ('grieving if aught inanimate e'er grieves'), that trees are inanimate, though they do not always say so clearly: e.g. in *N.E.D.* 'not animated or alive; destitute of life, spec. not endowed with animal life—without sensation'. What about *empsuchos*? Ten years ago it must have been my opinion that plants as living bodies are *empsucha* in at least one sense, if not the only sense, of the Greek word. I now incline to say that *empsucha* in Greek are animate except, when he chooses, in Aristotle's Greek. I am not suggesting that the linguistic facts diminish the value of Aristotle's biological approach to the science of human bodies in the sense of human beings. But lexicography might, perhaps, be expected to restrain the excesses of materialist interpretations without unduly encouraging the Cartesians. The article contains comments on two important recent articles: 'Sensation and Consciousness in Aristotle's Psychology' by Charles H. Kahn; 'Body and Soul in Aristotle' by Richard Sorabji.

p. 81, ll. 12–14 '. . . in the sense in which the sailor is the actuality of the ship' When I wrote these pages (81–3) I had not seen, although it had been published, the note by H. J. Easterling in *Phronesis* 11 (1966) on *De Anima* 413 a8–9. Easterling points out that the comparison with the sailor and his boat can hardly be intended to suggest that the whole soul is separable from the body, since Aristotle has just asserted that the soul, as *entelecheia*, is not separable (413 a3–6). It makes sense to say that the soul as a whole is not separable but perhaps parts of it are, but it would be 'patent nonsense' at this point to suggest that perhaps, after all, all parts of it are.

This difficulty, Easterling argues, is increased by the reading, for which there is no manuscript authority, in the Oxford Text. Easterling concludes that what Aristotle is suggesting is that 'the new doctrine of *psuchē* as *entelecheia* can be reconciled with the more familiar concept of it as the ruler and controller of the body'. The doctrine of B 1 implies the idea that the soul directs and uses the body, 'because it regards the body as *organikon*, which means that there must be something to use the *organa* provided by the body'. That natural living bodies are 'organs of the soul' is stated in B 4 (415 b15–20) where Aristotle 'is still thinking of the *psuchē* in terms of the *entelecheia* doctrine'. Easterling argues that the entelechy doctrine 'can be reconciled with the sailor–boat analogy in another way': the sailor and boat is an example of a whole (*sunolon*) 'designed for a purpose which can be achieved only by the union of the two elements'. 'In the same way the *zōon* constitutes a *sunolon* (*psuchē* + *sōma*) which can exercise its function only when the *psuchē* is present in the body'.

Easterling concludes that in 413 a8–9 Aristotle 'is not introducing an alternative to the *entelecheia* doctrine', but is suggesting that 'the familiar idea of the *psuchē* as the controlling element and efficient cause . . . can be re-interpreted in terms of the *entelecheia* doctrine'.

VI. The General Nature of Ethical Virtue (94–128)

p. 119, ll. 8 f.   The particular virtues and the *megalopsuchos* (great-souled man) This paragraph goes further than I wished, or at least would now wish, towards agreeing with Ross and Burnet that Aristotle, in his description of particular virtues, was describing the moral ideals of the Greeks of his time (p. 202) or of 'the average Athenian' (Burnet, p. 163). It is true that, in his treatment of greatness of soul (*megalopsuchia*) much of what is said is a description, with many graphic strokes, of the minor attributes and demeanour of the great man and concludes, in the manner of Theophrastus, with his deep voice and unhurried movements. But, since Aristotle claims to be amplifying and verifying his own doctrine on ethical virtue (1127 a14–17), we must suppose that in general he admires the conduct and feelings which he attributes to the virtuous.

Russell, whom I have quoted, presumably means what he says about Aristotle as a moralist; it is sad to see one great philosopher write with such animus about another. Professor MacIntyre, in his *Short History of Ethics*, is even more indignant: Aristotle, he suggests, 'was not a nice or a good man' (p. 66). Even Ross cannot say more for the *megalopsuchos* than that we must take his character as being very good indeed in parts (p. 208). An earlier critic had pronounced a similar verdict. 'It is true that even in Aristotle's conception of the *megalopsuchos* may possibly be discovered some elements of good: truthfulness of character and speech, magnanimity in overlooking offences, self-respect and indifference to death' (R. L. Ottley in the article on humility in Hastings' *Encyclopaedia of Religion and*

Ethics, 1913). But these merits are compatible with unpleasing attributes; he is made to seem self-complacent, contemptuous, uninvolved, ungrateful, inactive.

When scholars think they know what Aristotle means in the chapter (IV. 3) they often come to quite different conclusions; for example on the question why it should be 'quite unfitting' for the great man to 'run away swinging his arms' (1123 b31).

Gauthier produces a battery of arguments for the surprising view that Aristotle is painting the portrait of a philosopher. This at least seems clearly wrong. There are two summits in Aristotle's account of human excellence; philosophy is one and heroic courage the other. If the *megalopsuchos* achieves either (which may seem unlikely) it can only be the latter: he has what is great in every (ethical) excellence (1123 b29–30) and, in facing great dangers, he is unsparing of his life since he knows that the price to be paid for it may be too high (1124 b6–9).

It is hardly for us possible, on reading what Aristotle says about the great-souled man, to view him as a paradigm of civilized excellence; and the problem is aggravated by the wild denunciations and speculations of commentators. Ottley, at least, goes too far when he suggests that 'indifference to death' is an attribute of the *megalopsuchos*. The text gives no warrant for this suggestion. On the contrary we should consider rather Aristotle's insistence, in his account of the highest courage, that the higher a man stands on the scale of virtue and well-doing the more agonizing is the prospect of premature death (1117 b9–11). His virtue is so great that, as a soldier, he may be less good than the 'scum of the earth' who may indeed be 'indifferent to death' (b17–20). We may, perhaps, wonder why such reluctant courage can rank as virtue rather than below virtue as merely on the level of continence (*enkrateia*). This would be a mistake. For the definition of the continent man is not that he is a struggler but that he is made so by the presence in himself of vicious tendencies. In his treatment of courage Aristotle recognizes that a virtuous character may be an impediment to (heroic) virtue, and that 'it is not the case with all virtues that the exercise of them is pleasant . . .' (1117 b15–16). I shall deal more fully with this point in a note on chapter XIII (p. 258) in which I shall try to circumvent the view of Ross, to which I adhered in the book, that Aristotle's doctrine leaves no room at the top for heroic virtue (VII. 1, 1145 a18–27). See also *Articles on Aristotle 2. Ethics and Politics* (1977), pp. 42–6.

I have discussed the character of the *megalopsuchos* in an article, ' "Magnanimity", in Aristotle's *Ethics*', in *Phronesis* (1978).

pp. 120–128 Differences between Aristotelian and modern moral ideas
It must seem arbitrary to touch on three large and distinct topics in so few pages: attitudes to slavery (120); 'ethology' (120–2); the alleged non-appearance of duty in Aristotle's 'moral scene' (122–8). It is because these subjects are so large that I could say so little about them here. But I hope that the following brief explanations may make this section seem a little less idiosyncratic.

p. 120　Attitudes to slavery

I chose to go back and quote from Green because, in long sentences, he can sometimes say with considerable precision what needs saying. He is right to face the fact that, as Barker notes in introducing his translation of the *Politics*, 'neither Plato nor Aristotle protests against any and every form of slavery' (p. lvii). Similarly Professor Dodds: 'Of all ancient institutions slavery seems to us most manifestly contrary to "nature"; but none of the major Greek thinkers dared to recognize the fact' (see his collection of essays published in 1973, p. 101). The subject has, of course, been much discussed; see K. J. Dover, *Greek Popular Morality in the time of Plato and Aristotle* (1974), and *Articles on Aristotle 2. Ethics and Politics* (1977).

pp. 120–122　'Ethology'

I have quoted Aristotle (117) as claiming that a survey of particular virtues and vices should bring, among other benefits, a better knowledge of the facts about character—*ta peri to ēthos* (1127 a15–16). What would such knowledge be like? I referred (121) to the fact that, at the end of his *System of Logic* (1843), J. S. Mill announced the arrival, or imminent arrival, of a new science of character (Ethology). As conceived by Mill, this would be a branch of psychology: popular generalizations about character, 'the common wisdom of common life', would be shown to be deducible from the system or body of causal laws constituting psychology. We are reminded, with differences, of Aristotle's distinction between the fact (*to hoti*) and the reason (*to dioti*) in 1095 b4–8. Mill's expectations were perhaps unreasonable, and somehow the new science failed to arrive. But in 1896 an article was published in *Mind* by A. F. Shand, a barrister, in which 'a theory of the sentiments' was propounded as an hypothesis required if ethology was to be launched. Shand's work was quoted with approval by G. F. Stout in his *Manual of Psychology*, and 'sentiments' found a place also in the works of William McDougall and others. In 1914 Shand published his book, *The Foundations of Character*, being a study of the tendencies of the emotions and sentiments, and promised a second volume dealing with the sentiments in detail. The book was praised, in the middle years of the First World War, in two long reviews in *Mind* (1915, 1916). The second volume did not appear; Shand was apparently still writing it at the time of his death in 1936. The suggestion I wished to make was that, if the concept of character as a system of sentiments is anticipated in Aristotle, the anticipation is to be looked for in the concept of a system or systems of ends rather than in an inventory of virtues and vices.

In this historical footnote I have reported on one explicable failure of 'ethology' to establish itself as a science. The candle was lit with difficulty and flickered out. The names I have mentioned are necessarily of philosophers who wrote also on psychology or psychologists who wrote also on philosophy. Necessarily, because it is only recently that psychology has everywhere become recognized as fully empirical and experimental. Philosophers have not been reluctant to keep their distance, to renounce the unrewarding role of non-experimental assemblers of introspectible data. The map of living systematic inquiry has to be continually redrawn. This does not mean that ethology disappears. It means rather that investigations are more wide-ranging and more specialisms are needed. There are educational psychologists and penologists and books on moral education. Conceptual clarification is part of what is needed. So scientists philosophize, and philosophers think about scientific results when they can understand them. And, as Aristotle said, we need to know for the sake of regulating our practice.

pp. 122–128   Duty and Aristotle's 'moral scene'

I hope I took enough space to state my reasons for questioning what Professor Adkins says about the absence from Aristotle's 'moral scene' of 'the related concepts of duty and responsibility'. The relations between apparently mismatching vocabularies and imperfect conceptual affinities are complex. I may not have been ready enough to consider them. I have difficulty in understanding what it is like to seek and fail to find in the *Ethics* questions about duty and responsibility and free will or about body and mind in the *De Anima*. I hope that the Index is of some use in suggesting connections between topics discussed at different points in Aristotle's treatise.

VII. Virtue is a Mean (129–151)

pp. 129–130, Introductory paragraphs

I wish to add here some brief comments on Mr. J. O. Urmson's article, 'Aristotle's Doctrine of the Mean', in the *American Philosophical Quarterly* (1973). Urmson places in an original and suggestive setting this important part of what Aristotle has to say on excellence of character (Urmson will not allow 'virtue' or 'moral virtue' as a translation) and in addition makes many acute comments in his treatment of detail. To have done all this within the bounds of a short paper is a feat of clear thinking and accurate statement. I shall not attempt to condense an article signally free from superfluous amplification. I can only pick out some points to which I think that attention can usefully be drawn.

In saying of Urmson's general account of the Mean that he presents the doctrine in a new setting I have in mind two main points. (a) He starts from Aristotle's formal definition of excellence of character (1106 b36–1107 a2), and then immediately refers us to the enumeration in VII. 1 of 'six possible states of character' and to Aristotle's statement in VII of the contrasts between the members of the three pairs in his classification, in particular between moderation and self-control and between profligacy and lack of control (1151 b34–1152 a6). (b) The second important feature of Urmson's treatment is the answer he gives to the general question what it is for emotions and actions to be in a mean. His answer is that for Aristotle an emotion or an action is in a mean if, and only if, it exhibits a settled state of character that is in a mean (p. 225). Urmson argues that what is *primarily* (my italics) in a mean is a settled state of character. What makes these points important?

(a) The reasons I now have for thinking that the doctrine of the six ethical states, three good and three bad, is an important and instructive framework for Aristotle's account of excellence and badness of character as well as of self-control and its absence were not clear to me when I wrote the book. These reasons are stated in the four-page Appendix which I was allowed to add to chapter IV of *Articles in Aristotle* 2 (1977) and have restated in my first note appended to Ch. XIII. I shall not repeat the whole argument here. I welcome the prominence which Urmson gives to the six states, but I question his acceptance of the opinion that 'Aristotle makes no serious use of the notion of heroic excellence' and that the concept can safely be ignored as 'being merely part of a Kant-like architectonic, something brought in to be the opposite of brutishness' (p. 223). Urmson points out that Aristotle's man of good character 'wants to act in the way that he does, whereas the self-controlled man does so with difficulty', has to 'struggle' because his ethical education has been faulty, 'makes himself behave properly' (pp. 223, 224). The need to 'make himself act contrary to his emotions' 'betrays a defect of character' (p. 224). But does it? Surely not when, as often, the troublesome emotions or desires are perfectly natural and normal. If ethical education makes it easier for a man to live up to his ideals it also leads him to envisage ideals more difficult to achieve. If we doubt Aristotle's awareness that struggle need not betray a defect we need only consider what he says about the response to atrocious tyranny (1110 a4–31), and the remarkable observation in his account of courage that virtue itself aggravates the difficulty of behaving properly (1117 a33–b20).

(b) 'Aristotle holds excellence of character to be a mean or intermediate disposition regarding emotions and actions, not that it is a disposition towards mean or intermediate emotions and actions' (p. 225). The points incapsulated in this summary are subtle, and I shall not try to follow Urmson in detail. But I think he is right when he suggests that it helps us to understand and defend Aristotle if we take settled dispositions rather than singular episodes and actions as the focus of his accounts both of ethical virtue and of self-control. Perhaps Urmson's most telling point here is his answer to a difficulty which has troubled commentators (my pp. 132–3). It is objected to Aristotle's doctrine that at most it is applicable to the quantitative aspects of actions and emotions and not to the non-quantitative rightness of actions—'at the right times, with reference to the right objects, towards the right people, with the right motive and in the right manner' (1106 b21–3). Urmson argues that the possibility of going wrong in either of two ways, excess and defect, arises in a variety of ways in connection with established dispositions, e.g. exhibiting an emotion 'too often or too rarely' and not only by being felt too strongly or too weakly (p. 225). Similarly he argues that the doctrine of the mean can be distinguished from 'the doctrine of moderation'. Thus, as regards using alcoholic drinks, the mean as a differentia of good character may be achieved either by never drinking very much or by drinking nothing at all except when 'making a real night of it' on very rare occasions.

The second half of Urmson's paper contains close critical discussion of three main questions about the doctrine of the mean. He argues that Aristotle does not succeed in connecting particular justice with any single range of emotion. In Hume's language justice is an 'artificial' not a 'natural virtue'. The distributor and the rectifier must have practical wisdom; and, as Aristotle states in VI, a man cannot be wise unless he has all the ethical virtues (pp. 227–8). Next Urmson analyses the difficulties which Aristotle meets when he tries to give an account of envy and spite consistent with the doctrine of the mean. Finally he criticizes Aristotle's account of courage as a mean between cowardice as one extreme and rashness as the other. He rejects the suggestion of Ross that Aristotle's triad should be replaced by two pairs, and argues that the facts require two triads. The points made by Urmson under these heads demand careful consideration.

Urmson's final verdict on the doctrine of the mean is that, while Aristotle makes mistakes, it is 'at the very least a substantial doctrine worthy of Aristotle's genius'.

VIII. The Distinction between the Voluntary and the Involuntary (152–159)

Some reviewers commented on the brevity of this chapter; one said that the 'surrounding issues' had not caught my interest, another that I had seen 'little of the virtues that Austin for one found in it' and that the penultimate paragraph (on ignorance of circumstances) was 'as cryptic as Aristotle's own remarks here are said to be'. My view of Aristotle's chapter was that much of what he means to say in it is true and clear and clearly true. Thus it is true that a man can be praised or blamed, rewarded or punished, only for his intentional actions, and hence not when overwhelming force makes him a non-actor and not when, from factual ignorance, he does not know what he is doing. But I also suggested that Aristotle's treatment is occasionally confusing in detail in a way which makes it important to be sure we know what his Greek words and our English words mean.

I now think that my chapter was defective in at least two ways. (1) First, I would have been less liable to mislead if I had said more about the translation of terms from Greek into English. (2) Secondly, I would have given a better impression of Aristotle's contribution to the study of 'pleas and excuses' if I had considered, along with III. 1, other relevant passages. I shall now try briefly to remedy these defects.

(1) In using 'voluntary' 'involuntary' for *hekōn akōn* and *hekousion akousion* I was following others. I had in mind moving a limb voluntarily (intentionally) or involuntarily (unintentionally). Of course, 'voluntary' has other meanings; when a gift is 'voluntary' (all giving is intentional) it is not made in response to any request, demand or threat. I referred to the fact that *hekōn akōn* have meanings not covered by *voluntary involuntary*. It was perhaps misleading to refer to a passage later in the chapter where *akōn* seems to mean 'unwilling' (1110 b12;

cf. 1135 b4, 7). I did not mean to suggest that the word should be so translated anywhere else in the chapter. What I did suggest was that the wider use might account for oddities like the suggestion that it is a matter of 'debate' (1110 a7) whether the jettison of a cargo in a storm is *hekousion* (of course, it is intentional). Other words on which I ought to have commented are *bia*, *biazesthai* (force, constrain), and *anankazein* (constrain, compel). I thought that the terms were equivalent, as in the *Eudemian Ethics* (1225 a2, 15). In Greek as in English the operation of force or constraint may be either to make an agent a non-agent or, more commonly, to determine (by threats) the situation in which there is (voluntary) action (1110 a5–8, a23–9; cf. *EE* 1225 a1–33).

I shall not apologize for being cryptic in my dismissal of the varieties of particular circumstances:

quis quid ubi quibus auxiliis cur quomodo quando

i.e. who, what, where, with what aids, why, how, and when. Aristotle professes only a tepid interest in the enumeration, incapsulated in the mnemonic hexameter, of the heads under which the varieties of such ignorance may be classed (1111 a3): I thought that I should not simply ignore this intriguingly Austinian material. But here, as with some passages in Book v, I have left untouched perplexities which did not seem to be crucial for the understanding and criticism of the doctrine.

(2) A more serious deficiency in my treatment of what Aristotle says about voluntary/involuntary in iii 1 is that I omitted, in connection with the distinctions between the involuntary and the non-voluntary (1110 b18–24) and between actions due to ignorance and actions done in ignorance (b24–7), to discuss them alongside of at least two later passages in the *EN*.

(a) iii. 5, 1113 b30–1114 a3. Here Aristotle remarks that, in cases where there is ignorance, punishment may be in order if the agent is responsible for his ignorance, e.g. because he is drunk. Ignorance, if it is attributable to carelessness (*ameleia*), is not a valid defence. The similar passage in the *EE* is part of the section dealing with the voluntary (ii 7–9): 1225 b11–16 knowledge may be unactivated or activated; a man may be blamed for not knowing (in either sense) something 'easy or necessary' if his not knowing is caused by carelessness (*di' ameleian*).

(b) v. 8, 1135 b11–19. Here Aristotle first speaks of all injuries done in ignorance (*met' agnoias*) of particular circumstances as mistakes (*hamartēmata*) and then divides mistakes in this wide sense into two classes: (a) mischances (*atuchēmata*) when 'the injury takes place contrary to reasonable expectation' (*paralogōs*) and (b) mistakes proper when the injury is not contrary to reasonable expectation but no vice (*kakia*) is involved; a man makes a mistake when the fault (or the ignorance?) originates in himself, but is the subject of a mischance when the origin lies outside him. (In b19 Jackson conjectured *agnoias* for *aitias*, a closer fit with 1113 b30–1, 33. Stewart is tempted by Jackson's emendation but decides against it on balance).

These later passages expand and clarify Aristotle's account in iii. 1 of the connections between ignorance and responsibility. In iii. 1 it does indeed emerge that, of actions done in ignorance, only some are strictly due to ignorance (*di'* *agnoian*), viz. when the ignorance cannot be traced as in turn due to the agent's state, for example to his being drunk or having lost his temper. In v. 8 it is suggested that an explicit distinction should be made accordingly between mis-chances and mistakes. Again in III. 5 Aristotle points out the need to move from the question whether the agent knew what he was doing when he did it to the question whether, if he did not know, he was responsible for his ignorance; and the use of the term *ameleia* (carelessness or negligence) is a development which was not explicit in III. 1. It is possible, perhaps probable, that what Aristotle says in III. 5 and v. 8 was in his mind when he wrote III. 1. But what is fuller and more explicit in the passages taken together is important for a treatment designed to be 'useful for legislators' (1109 b34-5).

The suggestion in III. 1 (1110 b18-24, 1111 a20-1) that the agent is not just the victim of a misfortune if the injury causes him to feel no distress or regret does not reappear. The statement is difficult especially if, as in the Oxford Aristotle, *metameleia* is translated as 'repentance'. But, apart from the inappropriateness of 'repentance', a pure accident is a pure accident whether or not it does distress the unwitting agent.

In my supplementary bibliography I have included the valuable article of M. Schofield, 'Aristotelian Mistakes', in the *Proceedings of the Cambridge Philo-logical Association* (1973). The focus of his discussion is v. 8: he defends the orthodox translation of *paralogōs* in 1135 b16-19 as 'contrary to reasonable ex-pectation' against Professor Daube in *Roman Law: Linguistic, Social and Philo-sophical Aspects* (1969). Professor Daube had argued against the inclusion of 'reasonable' in the translation and had denied that any legal concept of negligence is part of Aristotle's doctrine. The article illuminates the defects of Aristotle's treatment of ignorance in III. 1.

IX. Choice and the Origination of Action (160–181)

pp. 162, ll. 11-14, 165-166, Deliberation
Here reference should be made to two earlier notes: (a) the note referring to II. 12 and (b) the note referring to III. 38-44 on 'Dialectic and Deliberation in the Ethics'.

In (a) I quoted the words used by Aristotle here (III. 3), as they are translated by Ross, to describe the process of deliberation: 'they assume the end and consider by what means it is to be attained' (1112 b15-16). The translation is appropriate to the standard medical example which Aristotle gives in the *Metaphysics*: massage produces heat and indirectly a uniform temperature and so a healthy state of the body (1032 b6 ff.; references on p. 166 n. 1). But the end–means schema does not fit all examples: not the high deliberations of the statesman as he articulates his concept of the god-like well-doing (*eudaimonia*) of the state (1094 b10); not the simple syllogizing which leads to the conclusion that I need a cloak as protective covering (*De Motu Animalium* 701 a18–23). Moreover, as has been pointed out, we can improve the translation of Ross by substituting 'through what' for 'by what means'. Hopefully the amended schema will cover movements of thought from less to more determinate specification, and from whole to components, as well as from end to means. Naturally I referred on this to Greenwood's commentary on Book VI (references in my Index under 'Greenwood').

In (b) I considered J. M. Cooper's account of the difference between the parts which Aristotle assigns to dialectical and to deliberative arguments and procedures in the *Ethics*. Early in his book Cooper had argued that the expression *ta pros to telos* 'covers more than just means' (p. 19). He develops this suggestion by distinguishing different 'patterns of deliberation' which are at least implicit in Aristotle's account of the excellence of practical reason (*phronēsis*).

p. 164, ll. 18–20 '. . . to describe the course of Aristotle's argument . . .'; and p. 173 '. . . ambiguities which complicate the problem of free will . . .'
In writing IX, I found two main difficulties. The first (1) was the difficulty of making out what Aristotle meant, or what different things he was liable to mean, when he used the word *prohairesis*. The second (2) was the difficulty of making, in a reasonably brief space, a map of the 'free will problem' on which I could try to locate Aristotle. I hoped that my excursus on 'willing' was one way of alleviating both difficulties together. I hoped that it would enable me to make intelligible the statements (1) that Aristotle, when he spoke of *prohairesis*, was sometimes referring to an activity of willing and (2) that Free Will, contradicting Determinism, was the doctrine that such activity is sometimes uncaused. The terms 'willing' and 'volition' are neutral between the two doctrines.

I was unwilling to confront the second difficulty, with all its complications, directly. In making such a map it would have been necessary to add to the question (a) whether Free Will is true at least one further question (b) whether our thinking about responsibility and about moral obligation and moral goodness involves the conviction that it is true. It is natural to think of Free Will as affirming both (a) and (b) and of Determinism as denying both. But a determinist does not necessarily deny more than (a). He might, while asserting that all willing is determined, leave open the question whether this assertion is compatible or incompatible with our moral thinking or (a third possibility) required by our moral thinking. There are other complications. I was unwilling to seem to enlist Aristotle in one of only two clashing armies. And he could be enlisted at all only if he had asked the right questions.

My approach by way of 'willing' was unacceptable to some reviewers. That I was unconfident about it is, perhaps, shown by the fact that, while I was writing the book, I wrote also a short note, in reply to P. M. Huby, 'Aristotle and the Free Will Problem' (*Philosophy*, 1968), and later an article, 'Willing and Acting' (*Philosophical Quarterly*, 1971). In the article Aristotle was not mentioned. I defended those who found uses for 'willing' and for 'volitions' and tried to counter the arguments of those who found the terms useless or misleading. One reviewer met with particular incredulity C. A. Campbell's suggestion that, when I move my leg, 'the immediate objects of my willing' are 'kinaesthetic and other sensations' (p. 172). I cannot find the suggestion unplausible: cf. B. O'Shaughnessy, 'the fact that our limbs are sensitive is connected with the ability to move them' ('The Limits of the Will', *Philosophical Review*, 1956, p. 470).

Questionable reasons are sometimes given for saying that Aristotle was not in a position to take a stance on Free Will. D. J. Allan says that he was 'barely conscious of the problem': 'our notion of will is of Latin origin and the Greek ideas of wish and choice are based upon a different view of the psychology of action' (2nd edn., p. 131). But he does not say what 'our notion' is or show that there is an accepted notion. And he goes on to attribute to Aristotle the Determinist's familiar denial that responsibility and duty require Free Will: 'to say that "we" are responsible means, for him, simply that the action is not enforced but expresses our inclinations, hereditary and acquired' (p. 132). But why, then, should Aristotle make heavy weather (as I tried to show he does) of this solution in III. 5? Does Aristotle think of the soldier-citizen courting death in battle as following his 'inclinations' (III. 9)? And have we not evidence that Aristotle sometimes suggested a connection between human agency and the objectively contingent?

P. M. Huby pointed out that, if by the 'free will problem' we choose to mean the problem of 'freedom versus determinism' (we think of them as incompatible but are unwilling not to assert both), then Aristotle could not 'discover the problem' because he was not a determinist: he seems to think that some events are uncaused. Huby attributed the 'first discovery' to Epicurus. But, without denying this, it can be suggested that Aristotle had a similar problem, 'originative responsibility versus determinism in psychology'. Aristotle in psychology speaks the language of determinism but finds it problematic whether the assumption can be reconciled with his conviction that a man is the responsible originator of his own actions. The assumption that human actions are determined, at least when they express a formed and stable character, is obviously suggested by Aristotle's discussion of responsibility in III. 5. When the agent has conceived (*nous*) or imagined (*phantasia*) the end to which his virtuous or vicious character directs him and has by deliberation discovered the means to the end or the specification of the end which his situation demands, decision or action follows immediately (*euthus*) and by necessity (*anankē*). Necessitation seems to be clinched by the doctrine of the practical syllogism (1147 a25–31; cf. *MA* 701 a10–15). Alike in the movements of animals and in the conduct of men the initiation of action terminates a causally continuous process. Aristotle's detailed account, in the case of animals, of the sequence of events in the body–mind from the perceptual stimulus to the behavioral response is in the *De Motu Animalium* 6–9 (cf. *De Anima* III. 9–11).

Against this background recent interpretations of the *EN* have stressed the deterministic elements or tendency in Aristotle's analysis. I have in mind R. Loening (*Die Zurechnungslehre des Aristoteles*, 1903), D. J. Allan who finds in Loening a 'clear-headed and interesting account of Aristotle's views on freedom' (p. 74), J. L. Ackrill (in *Aristotle's Ethics*, Introduction, pp. 27–8), and D. J. Furley,

'Aristotle on the Voluntary', reprinted in *Articles on Aristotle* 2. Loening's book impresses by its thorough and orderly accumulation of evidence in support of his thesis. Nor does he fail to confront the evidence adduced by those scholars, Zeller in particular, who attribute to Aristotle an interest in the alleged (*angebliche*) freedom of the will. He rejects the evidence of *De Interpretatione* 9 on the ground that Aristotle was not yet clear about the distinction between objective indetermination and subjective uncertainty (p. 293). More importantly he finds in *EN* III. 5 only unhesitating determinism (p. 318); but, as I think, he does not follow closely the course of the argument in 1114 a31–b25 or ponder sufficiently the precise meaning of Aristotle's words in 1114 a31–2, b16–17 and b22–4.

Furley is perhaps a little over-emphatic in his repeated protestations that for Aristotle an action is not 'preceded' (who said it was?) by 'a free act of will' (p. 51), that an act is not made voluntary by being 'spontaneous' or 'freely chosen' (p. 56), that commands of the mind are not spontaneous in the sense of 'uncaused' or 'unpredictable' (p. 58), and (his final sentence) that 'we do not find in Aristotle the "free volitions" dear to later philosophers' (p. 60). The twists and turns of Aristotle's argument in III. 5 are more interesting than the precise location or non-location of his exit.

pp. 165, 168   The meaning or suggestiveness (*huposēmainein*) of the word (*onoma*) *pro-hairesis*

My treatment here of the concluding sentences of III. 2 (1112 a15–17) is unsatisfactory. I hope that the comments which follow express what I now wish to say with less tentativeness and more precision. I have no quarrel with the remark of Ross that 'the etymological meaning' of *prohairesis* is 'preferential choice'. But to say this is not to deny that Aristotle is 'playing', as I suggested, with the ambiguity of the preposition. His interest in 'etymological meaning' (cf. 1103 a17–18) seems natural when we remember the interest shown by Plato, when he wrote the *Cratylus*, in the rights and wrongs of the question whether words get their meanings from nature (*phusis*) or from convention (*nomos*). Such remarks are not necessarily to be taken seriously, as implying a considered view on the relevance of literal meaning for the analysis of concepts. Having said this I now wish to be counted along with Joachim, Gauthier–Jolif and, I think, Rackham as believing that *pro* (before) in 1112 a17 has a temporal sense, a sense determined by the preceding *probebouleumenon* and *prohairesis*: the decision, reached by prior deliberation, to take the 'means' precedes the coming into being of the 'end' which is in the agent's sights.

My doubts about this interpretation seem to have been prompted partly by Joachim's tepid 'on the whole' and partly by the fact that the interpretation is not fortified by the corresponding passages in the other ethical treatises. Thus in *MM* 1189 a12–14 the *pro* in *prohairesis* is taken as indicating preference of this to that (*tode anti toude*), the better to the worse. Dirlmeier, in his note on 1189 a13, insists on this difference and argues that, in the *MM*, the reference to the 'name' is brought in only as a minor consideration in the clarification of the distinction between a 'concrete choice' and a mere 'wish'. It is only in the Nicomachean treatise that the (spurious) 'etymology' has a decisive role in the argument; an unusual temporal sense is bestowed *ad hoc* on *pro* ('nicht wie üblich sondern zeitlich'). That Dirlmeier took the same view in his commentary on the *EN* is indicated in his note on 1112 a14. He thus vindicates Joachim's interpretation and frees me from the doubts which I confessed on p. 168. I should add that in the *EE* also there is an appeal to the literal meaning of the *pro* in *prohairesis* (1226 b5–8). It is of interest to note that the passage is in line with the *MM* and not with the *EN* in finding the suggestion not of priority in time but of preference. Dirlmeier's translation makes this clear. His succinct note on 1226 b6 seems to suggest that the 'etymological meanings' in the treatises illustrate different aspects of *prohairesis*, as means-taking or specification and as selection between alternatives.

p. 178, ll. 8–11   '. . . the choice between yes and no, to act or not to act, can be interpreted as being open only in a conditional sense . . .' (see 1113 b7–8)
I refer to (and quote from) the opening sentences of III. 5 in which Aristotle insists that virtue and vice are alike in our power (*eph' hēmin*), that the moving principles (*archai*) of our actions are in us (*en hēmin*) (1113 b6–7, b19–20), and to my comments on these claims as there formulated (173–6). Perhaps I did not state clearly enough what I meant here (178) by 'conditional' sense and 'conditional' interpretation. I now suggest the following as elucidation: 'I did intend and will what happened (e.g. my keeping of a promise) but, *if* I had desired and willed otherwise, the promise would have been broken. Nothing would have interfered with my "substitution" of a broken for a kept promise.' Almost certainly, when I used the word 'conditional', I was recalling the distinction made by C. D. Broad between 'conditional' and 'categorical substitutability' in his lecture 'Determinism, Indeterminism and Libertarianism'. So I wish here to quote, without Broad's careful elaborations and refinements, his formulation of what he calls the 'negative condition' of 'categorical substitutability': '. . . my willing of this alternative with this degree of force and persistence was not completely determined by the nomic, the occurrent, the dispositional, and the background conditions which existed immediately before and during this process of willing' (pp. 94–5). My 'elucidation' of conditional gives no answer to the question whether willing is determined but inclines, by its reference to desire, to suggest that it is. Broad's lecture, up to the last few pages, powerfully supports the 'libertarian' by conceding two of his cardinal theses: (1) that moral obligation entails 'categorical substitutability' and (2) that, in the sense of the sentence I have quoted, categorical substitutability denies determinism. But Broad argues that there is a positive as well as a negative condition of categorical substitutability. This condition (roughly) is that active willing should not be an inexplicable accident but should be fully attributable to the agent, being the exercise of his power to act in a line of greater resistence against the tendencies of his formed disposition. Broad's analysis concludes that the fulfilment of this positive condition is 'self-evidently impossible'. This denial is criticized by Campbell in his defence

of free will. The position as Broad leaves it here is paradoxical: as a moral person he accepts a proposition which his intellect rejects as absurd. But I know of no formulation of the problem more lucid than Broad's.

My account of Aristotle's anticipations of the problem finds him, as a physiological psychologist, at home with conditional substitutability and determinism but sometimes, as a moralist, speaking as if he were asserting categorical substitutability and creative agency. I have found that a number of outstanding contemporary scholars, after Loening, accept contentedly, if not aggressively, a determinist interpretation. But this hardly as yet makes their view an orthodoxy. As a philosopher Joachim had no inclination to indeterminism; but he finds indeterminism in Aristotle's treatment of ethical responsibility (pp. 109–11). When Ross says that Aristotle 'shared the plain man's belief in free will on the whole', he implies agreement with the view that a doctrine of categorical substitutability correctly interprets the plain moral man (p. 201). It is hardly heretical or overbold to suggest that Aristotle had at least an inkling of the impasse into which the problem was conducted by Broad.

The references in the preceding paragraph are to Joachim's posthumously published lectures on the EN (1951) and to Ross in Aristotle (1923). Joachim adduces the De Interpretatione 9 (19 a6–b4). He had referred similarly to the chapter (18 a28–19 a22) in the Introduction to his edition of GC (p. xxviii) (1922). I have made a number of references to DI 9 but without detailed discussion of any sentence or section. Ackrill (1963) has ten pages of commentary (pp. 132–42). He remarks that the chapter has 'provoked vigorous discussion ever since it was written and not least in the last few years'. The discussion is still in progress. The chapter is difficult: 'Aristotle's brevity and lack of sophisticated technical vocabulary make it difficult to decide what he is maintaining' (p. 132). Any uneducated person entering this field would risk being shot down by logicians. Even Ackrill only claims to be 'opening up some of the difficulties and indicating some possible lines of thought'. Anyone following up this reference should read at least the whole chapter with Ackrill's notes.

The passage in Metaphysics E 3 (1027 a29–b14) to which I referred on p. 178 n. 1 expresses the thought, similar to that in the De Interpretatione, of causes which are not effects. I was taking the doctrine of the chapter to be as formulated by Ross in the footnote to his translation (1908). But I ought not to have used the words 'clear' or 'explicit' in referring either to the De Interpretatione or to Metaphysics E 3. I have quoted above what Ackrill says about the difficulty of making out what is maintained by Aristotle in the De Interpretatione. Ross in his Commentary (1924) examines some of the difficulties in the interpretation of E 3. A similar judgement on E3 is conveyed by Christopher Kirwan's searching analysis and discussion in his Metaphysics Γ Δ E, Clarendon Aristotle Series (1971).

pp. 178–180   The interpretation of sunaitioi pōs (in a sense part-causes) in 1114 b23
Comparison between published translations does not reveal the possibility, for which I have argued, of different possible meanings. I have argued that what

Aristotle suggests by his use of *sunaitios* here is that we are causes of our dispositional states not in the sense of being one of a set of collaborative causes, equal
in 'status' if not necessarily in efficacy, but rather as subordinate or instrumental or
'accessory' causes. Two sets of considerations are relevant: (1) the usages of
sunaitios and (2) the logic of Aristotle's argument in the context. I tried to focus on
(2) and treated (1) as a 'footnote' (179). My purpose now is to supplement what
I said on (1).

I adduced as evidence the passage about the psychical cause and physical conditions of growth in the *De Anima* (416 a9–18; cf. *Metaphysics* 1015 a20–6). I
omitted to point out that this use of *sunaitios* is found in a variety of contexts in
Plato and hence would naturally be in Aristotle's mind as a standard use, if not the
standard use, of the term. In the *Gorgias* Socrates says that the real authors of the
ruin of Athens were an older generation of statesmen, Themistocles and Pericles;
Alcibiades is not a principal (*aitios*) but at most an accessory·(*sunaitios*). Dodds in
his note on 519 b 2 refers for the history of the term to Taylor's note on *Timaeus*
46 c7 (p. 291). For Plato it is a vulgar error to confuse the efficacy of the Being
who made the world with the status of the materials which he used as *sunaitia*. In
a later note (on 76 d 3–e6) Taylor notes in Hippocrates the distinction between the
cause (wind) and the predisposing conditions (*sunaitia*) of diseases (p. 539).

Dirlmeier in his translation of *sunaitioi pōs* (irgendwie Miturheber) does not
commit himself to the 'accessory' interpretation. But he refers us to the Platonic
passages as listed in Ast's *Lexicon*. Moreover by his reference to his own note on
'not without' at 1098 b25 he indicates a bridge to the concept of indispensable
condition (p. 283). As so often, students can extract from his comments all the
information which they ought to desire and use.

pp. 180–181   Professor Anscombe on choice which precedes further deliberation.
In this criticism of one point in Anscombe's essay I tried to make it clear that I
was concerned with the one limited question whether the arguments which she
had used for 'importing the idea of deliberation following choice (*prohairesis*) into
the interpretation of these chapters in III' were valid. At the end of my criticism
I repeated the crucial limiting phrase, 'these chapters of Book III'. Without the
restriction I would have seemed to be suggesting that Aristotle denied or overlooked the obvious fact that, when a man reaches after deliberation a decision to
do something, he sometimes cannot, and often does not, immediately carry out
or set about the action or course of action on which he has decided. There are
many possibilities: the agent's decision may not be firm and unconditional, and,
even if it seems that it is, much further deliberation and action may lie ahead
before withdrawal from the over-all decision becomes impossible.

There are many complications and ambiguities in Aristotle's use of the word
prohairesis. On p. 164 I mentioned some English words and phrases which are
suggested by some of the sentences in which Aristotle refers to *prohairesis*: desire,
decision, choice, initiation, or origination of action. My central concern in the
chapter was with one of the ways in which Aristotle uses the term; the way in

which it is used to refer not to a resolve to initiate action at some future date but to an intentional initiation of action now. In III. 3 the last term reached by deliberative analysis is the first in the order of becoming (1112 b23–4). It was in this context that I questioned Anscombe's translation and interpretation of 1112 b26–7.

Sorabji (*P.A.S.* 1973–4) agrees with Anscombe that *prohairesis* 'can occur well in advance of there being an opportunity for action' (p. 117). He implies that I do not. It is true that I did not at this point distinguish a decision which could be carried out here and now from a decision or resolve which, if not abandoned, would be carried out later and, in many cases, be followed by a series of connected decisions and actions.

XI. Practical Wisdom (212–239)

p. 213, l. 10 'Aristotle describes *phronēsis* . . . as involving a true understanding of an end' (1142 b31–3).
Later I adduced the same passage as 'confirming' the attribution to Aristotle of the opinion that 'truth about the end must be included in the truth which is the work of the practical intellect' while at the same time I noted that the interpretation 'has been questioned' (224). Other references to the passage are on p. 227, where I connect it with 1144 a31–3, p. 235 and pp. 270–1. My reference to a disputed interpretation (224) inadequately recorded an omission in my appraisal of the evidence. A reviewer pointed out that, if the interpretation which I omitted to confront and discuss were right, the sentence would be a difficulty for the view that *phronēsis* includes a correct grasp of the end and not a piece of confirming evidence. I thought at the time that the correctness of the interpretation which I assumed was beyond reasonable doubt. But, if this explains, it does not justify my omission. Moreover I no longer feel certain, or even confident, that 1142 b31–3 says what I thought it said, though I think it possible that it does.

'If, then, it is characteristic of men of practical wisdom to have deliberated well, excellence in deliberation (*euboulia*) will be correctness with regard to what conduces to the end of which practical wisdom (*phronēsis*) is the true apprehension' (1142 b31–3). I quote the translation by Ross of the text as printed by Bywater. The Greek words translated by 'what conduces to the end' (*to sumpheron pros to telos*) are found, as Bywater's critical note reports, in the oldest manuscript and in a medieval Latin translation, while most of the manuscripts read not *to telos* (the end) but *ti telos* (an end). Nearly all recent editors have accepted, perhaps as preferable rather than as certainly right, what Stewart calls Bywater's 'restoration' of *to telos* in place of *ti telos* in Bekker.

Whichever text we prefer, commentators face us with the question whether the antecedent of the relative clause is the end or the means. The suggestion that it is the latter was made by J. Walter in *Die Lehre von der praktischen Vernunft* (1874) and, as Gauthier tells us, accepted by Burnet with 'enthusiasm', with hestitation by Rackham and Greenwood. It has been defended by P. Aubenque in *La*

Prudence chez Aristote (1963)—see footnote 5 on p. 118 what *phronēsis* apprehends correctly is the 'utility' of the means. Aubenque elaborates his view in an article replying to Gauthier in *Revue des Études Grecques* (1965). (Aubenque, as also von Fragstein (p. 239), prefers *ti* to *to* in 1142 b33). On the other hand, the view that *to telos* is the antecedent was evidently accepted by Ross and has been defended by Stewart, Gauthier, and most recently by Cooper (p. 64 n. 84).

It is easy to see why Walter's suggestion could be welcomed by a commentator as pointing to a way out of the difficulty that elsewhere in the *EN*, including *EN* VI, *phronēsis* is presented as a faculty concerned with means: to deliberate is to seek means to prescribed and defined ends (1112 b11-16). The obvious passages to quote in VI are in Chapters XII and XIII, 1144 a6-9 and 1145 a1-5: to *phronēsis* is assigned the function of discerning means to ends prescribed by ethical virtue. No less awkward is the juxtaposition of 1142 b31-3 and 1140 a25-31: *phronēsis* is virtually defined as excellence in deliberation, the *euboulia* which finds the way to the good life generally, not to any partial or technical end. It may be said that in my chapter I have tried to overcome this difficulty by showing that *phronēsis* as the cognitive constituent of practical excellence must be essentially related to both ends and means. Otherwise there is no intrinsic difference between the *phronimos* as such and the clever non-virtuous means-finder, the *deinos* (1144 a23-9). I would still defend my general argument, but I now think that 1142 b31-3 is not a weapon to be fired in the defence; it might misfire. The sentence, as it appears in the translation of Ross but not of Rackham, too sharply distinguishes *euboulia* from *phronēsis*. Such sharpness does not match the method of Aristotelian dialectic in handling a complex matter which bristles with *aporiai*; a method exploratory, tentative, even ambiguous. Nor does it match Aristotle's apparent endorsement in VI 5 of the opinion that it is *the* 'mark of a man of practical wisdom to be able to deliberate well' (1140 a25-6).

I shall not prolong this note by reporting and discussing the arguments of the commentators who accept what Gauthier calls the 'traditional exegesis' according to which *to telos* is the antecedent of *hou* (of which). This exegesis as rendered in the translation of Ross is that the *euboulos* is one who can give correct answers to questions about how to achieve the end, human happiness, which the *phronimos* apprehends truly. The implied argument for the interpretation is that in the context the relative clause is needed to define as unqualified and not special the end which is relative to unqualified *euboulia*. A further argument is the one anticipated by Rackham and used by Cooper when he remarks that, with *to sumpheron* as antecedent, 'we have no acceptable distinction between *euboulia* and *phronēsis* itself'. What I am now inclined to say is that, on the issue between the two translations or interpretations, *non liquet*, unclear or unproven, is the right judgement.

pp. 232-234 '. . . the undemonstrated opinions—of people of practical wisdom . . .'

I have defended the attribution to Aristotle of a doctrine that *phronēsis* is sometimes manifested as a capacity for intuitive and unreasoned judgements on what it is right to do in particular circumstances. Aristotle compares this capacity with sense-perception and I considered passages in VI in which the doctrine is stated. I did not attempt an exhaustive discussion of other views. Moreover I had missed by inadvertence W. W. Fortenbaugh's article, 'Aristotle's conception of moral virtue and its perceptive role' (1964).

Fortenbaugh begins by saying that he seeks to determine 'the role of moral virtue in guaranteeing correct deliberate choice' (p. 77). Scholars give different answers to the question. He quotes as giving an inadequate answer Gauthier–Jolif: 'to help keep practical reason focused on the goal and to help realize the goal in action by controlling desire'. Such definitions err by omitting the 'perceptive role' of moral virtue. Its inclusion would contribute to the 'rehabilitation' of moral virtue.

Both Fortenbaugh in formulating his question and Gauthier–Jolif in their quoted answer naturally and rightly have in mind VI. 12 and 13, and especially the statement, which concludes the crucial discussion, that 'choice will not be right without practical wisdom any more than without virtue; for the one determines the end and the other makes us do the things which lead to the end' (1145 a4–6 Ross, and see the note in Gauthier–Jolif). We have learned at earlier stages that *phronēsis* and *aretē* in the strict sense (*kuria*) can exist only in combination, wisdom developing from cleverness in means-finding (*deinotēs*) and ethical virtue from natural (*phusikē*) virtue (1144 b1–17). The doctrine that ethical virtue is 'in accordance with (*kata*)' practical wisdom (1144 b21–5) has been anticipated in earlier books. It is foreshadowed in the definition of virtue (1106 b36–1107 a2); we are ready to learn that it is the wisdom of the good man himself that determines the mean for him (cf. 1105 a23–33). But it is in VI that Aristotle comes to grips, or at least goes through motions of coming to grips, with the question how thought and desire combine or coalesce in human action. That the union is intimate is suggested by the enigmatic statement that choice is 'desiderative reason or ratiocinative desire' (1139 b4–5). Socrates was 'on the right track' when he said that virtues are forms of wisdom (*phronēseis*). Aristotle expounds the view which he thinks right in terms of a distinction between 'with' (*meta*) and 'in accordance with' (*kata*); but, as I have argued, the meaning of this distinction is doubtful (236–9).

Fortenbaugh is right when he implies that *EN* VI leaves us unclear about the respective roles of ethical virtue and practical wisdom in ensuring right practical choices. But there is something paradoxical about both his approach and his conclusion. The natural approach is from a close scrutiny of VI. But it is only in the later part of his paper that he faces the passages in VI which appear inconsistent with his conclusion. The implication is that his case can be, or has been, successfully built up from passages in the other books of both the *EN* and the *EE*. It is, of course, true that Aristotle often speaks of the 'perception' of the man who has ethical virtue or some particular ethical virtue. I referred to two such passages in a footnote. But can they be relevantly adduced as evidence for Fortenbaugh's thesis? The virtue we are considering is that of a man of practical wisdom. We cannot assume that in all, if indeed in any, such passages the perception is being credited to one and not the other of the components of the total disposition which is activated in virtuous choices.

Consider two of the passages cited by Fortenbaugh in support of his thesis. In III. 4 Aristotle says that the good man (*spoudaios*) differs from others in that he 'sees (*hora*) the truth in each class of things, being as it were the norm and measure' (1113 a29–33). 'He can judge particulars good and bad' (p. 80). At the end of his paper Fortenbaugh says, with reference to this passage, that 'it is the morally good man and not the man possessing practical reason who is said to judge well and to see the truth' (p. 87). In X. 4 Aristotle says that 'what appears to the good man really is so'; 'virtue and the good man as such (*hē toioutos*) are the measure of each thing' (1176 a15–19). Fortenbaugh comments: 'Every perfect man possesses both moral virtue and practical reason but it is only as a possessor of moral virtue that he is a measure . . . he wishes to emphasize that it is the perfect man in one aspect only that is the measure' (p. 79). But Aristotle's 'as such' (1176 a18) is not to be understood as excluding the *phronimos* or as demoting *phronēsis* as not being here the relevant 'aspect' of 'perfection'. Both aspects are present in the discerning vision and judgement of the good and sensible man in particular circumstances. But, if there is a competition for the role of seer, it is to *phronēsis*, as the thinking aspect of practical agency, that it must be awarded.

Since the date (1964) of the article on which I have commented Fortenbaugh has published a number of papers bearing on Aristotle's account of the virtues, and most recently his book, *Aristotle on Emotion* (1975). Fortenbaugh's work is interesting and important for at least three ethical topics: the psychology of conduct, ethical education, and the concept of perfected ethical excellence. His conclusions are based on a close study, in connection with Aristotle's *Ethics*, of Plato's *Laws* as well as the *Republic*, of Aristotle's *Rhetoric* as well as the *Politics*. Commentators on the *Ethics* are bound to reconsider their interpretations in view of Fortenbaugh's findings. This cannot be done in a hurry. In the Preface of his book he speaks of 'modification, not to say abandonment, of certain previously held views and arguments'. I still find some of his views difficult to accept. But his approach is new and suggestive and thoroughly Aristotelian. He is right to take seriously Aristotle's insistence in I. 13 that psychology is as important for 'political science' as are anatomy and physiology for medical science.

The first of Fortenbaugh's four chapters is entitled 'Aristotle's analysis of emotional response' and the first of the four sections of the chapter is on 'emotion and cognition'. Ethics is concerned with *pathē* (in one sense of the word) and 'emotions' covers some of those listed in the *Ethics* (1105 b21–3) and the *De Anima* (403 a16–19). Other helpful words are 'appetites', 'likes' and 'dislikes', 'sentiments'; mainly misleading are 'feelings' and 'sensations'. Fortenbaugh, starting from Plato's *Philebus* and the *Topics*, quotes the definition of anger in the *Rhetoric* (1378 a30–2): 'a desire for revenge accompanied by pain on account of (*dia*) an apparent slight to oneself or to one's own, the slight being unjustified'. This statement of the essence is shorter in the *De Anima*, *orexis antilupēseōs*, the desire of a man hurt to hurt back (403 a29–b2). The moral suggested is that an emotional response contains cognitions ('factual and evaluative judgements') and desires of considerable complexity and sophistication, and it is cognitions rather than feelings which distinguish from each other anger, pity, fear, hate (p. 167 in the *Arethusa* article of 1969). Distinguishing them from each other is unlike distinguishing colours or flavours.

The analysis of emotional response is for Fortenbaugh the basis of a 'new political-ethical psychology' which is 'peculiarly human'. It differs from the political-ethical psychology of the *Republic* in being bipartite not tripartite (the psychology of the *Laws* tends towards bipartition). He argues that this ethical bipartition does not clash with the 'biological psychology' of the *De Anima*. He had said in *Arethusa* (1969) that the bipartition is 'between two kinds of intelligent behaviour' (p. 177); 'the alogical soul of moral psychology overlaps upon the intellectual faculty' (p. 175).

In the second half of his book Fortenbaugh draws out the consequences of Aristotle's 'political-ethical psychology' first for political and then for ethical theory. In political theory the main questions to be considered are the education appropriate for young people, and the status appropriate for slaves and for women, in a well-governed state. The questions arise because only adult human males, and only some of them, are capable of the stable practical wisdom of the ruler and the citizen. In different ways and degrees the other classes are defective in the capacity for deliberation. The treatment of education is of obvious interest to the student of the *Ethics*. According to the bipartite doctrine 'desires and emotional responses were brought together in a single psychic half' (p. 45), i.e. the part of the soul incapable of reasoned reflection and deliberation. But 'emotions are cognitive and, therefore, open to moral education' (p. 45). Fortenbaugh directs attention to passages which suggest a temporally prior stage confined to the 'alogical half' of the soul: the young acquire a disposition to feel pleasure and distress in the right objects (1104 b11–13); they need a 'training in values' (p. 48), in loves and hates (1179 b24, 29–30; cf. *Politics* 1340 a15); with the completion of the training they will be ready for 'the subsequent acquisition of total virtue' (p. 51).

The reader familiar with the *Ethics* will accept these reminders. We may indeed ask ourselves how young is too young, according to Aristotle, for readiness to consider reasons for accepting the principles (*archai*) with which the young are to be indoctrinated. Our feeling that derationalization of Aristotle's anthropology must not go too far may be stirred when we find that, in a section of Fortenbaugh's last chapter, headed 'virtuous action without calculation', the fact that a brave soldier in a crisis has not 'time for reflection and deliberation' (1117 a17–22) is taken to imply that 'the logical half of the soul does not come into play' (p. 72). Hitting the mean is a 'critical act' but 'need not be assigned to practical wisdom' (p. 73). 'Moral virtue makes correct the judgements and goals involved in emotional response' (p. 75). 'What moral virtue does not make correct is the means-end deliberation occasioned by emotional response' (p. 76). But the end which Aristotle assigns to the means–end deliberation of the *phronimos* is contrasted with limited ends; it is the comprehensive end, the good life in general. The end of a *phronimos*, when it is limited, is not the object of any art, *technē* (1140 a25–30). Fortenbaugh allows that, in addition to the 'primarily technical' role of 'end–means deliberation', practical wisdom is a capacity for reasoned reflection on 'goals of life' (p. 78). On p. 76 a footnote not merely asserts, but admirably defends the assertion, that a courageous response, unreflective perhaps at the time, 'may be made against a quite complicated background of goals and values'. Yet he insists that there is no 'exercise of practical wisdom' and that the correctness of the response is 'entirely attributable to moral virtue'. But practical wisdom is a disposition activated in practical thought and action and is 'actively exercised' in any action which, but for the disposition, would not have been what it is. It seems to me that here Fortenbaugh is clinging inconsequentially to the thesis of the 1964 article.

There are a number of passages in *EN* vi which seem to me to require qualifications of Fortenbaugh's theses. Some of these qualifications are made in numerous discerning cautions and *caveats* and footnotes. But difficult passages remain. Among them are the 'true understanding of the end' in 1142 b31–3 and the 'undemonstrated assertions' of 'wise' and sensible men in 1143 b11–14. There are 153 references in Fortenbaugh's Index of Ancient Sources to pages on which sentences in the *Ethics* are discussed or mentioned; but neither of these sentences is among them. It may be that there are places in the book where interpretations of these passages are defended or implied. But, if so, they deserved inclusion in the Index. Another perhaps surprising absentee from the Index is 1178 a16–22, the concise restatement in x. 8 of Aristotle's doctrine in vi. 13 that practical wisdom and ethical virtue are 'yoked together'.

The above comments on Fortenbaugh's views are one-sided. He has followed a new way of approaching the study of Aristotle's doctrine on ethical excellences and their acquisition. Dissent is the natural reaction of those who have been inattentive to ideas encountered in the new approach. We suppose too easily that an unfamiliar truth, if true, must be familiar after all. But familiarity with Aristotle's text does not necessarily generate thought about the differences between emotional responses which include the uttering of moral words and developed moral discriminations. No one could suppose that there are not numerous stages and different routes by way of which men may progress towards practical wisdom, whether exhibited in architectonic planning or in tactful discrimination. Plato and Aristotle desiderated and made maps of stages and routes. Modern philosophers addicted to the *Ethics* have often been more attracted by other interests, and are often more at home with the *De Anima* and the *Metaphysics* than with the *Politics* or the *Rhetoric* or with Plato's *Laws*. They have not always taken very seriously Aristotle's idea that they should study the science of human matters in order to make their characters better and to help others towards the same goal. My reading of Fortenbaugh being recent, I have only begun to ask myself how my understanding of the *Ethics* is affected by looking from his viewpoint. But I have noticed two places where I would have written differently in the light of his book.

In Chapter V I asked why Aristotle, explaining in 1. 13 the relevance of psychology for ethics, referred us to the 'exoteric' bipartition of the soul and not to 'the systematic exposition of his psychology in the *De Anima*' (69). Fortenbaugh's answer to this would distinguish between Aristotle's 'politico-ethical psychology' and his 'biological psychology'. The two overlap but seek answers to different questions. I was perhaps on the right track when I suggested that detailed physiological knowledge would not be relevant to the interest of the moralist in desires and emotions (70–1). But conversely there are questions about the emotions outside the scope of the *De Anima*. In Chapter XI I looked again, in connection with Aristotle's account of *phronesis*, at the division between ethical and intellectual excellences, as states respectively of the rational and the desiring soul (218–20). Here again I may have missed the full significance or suggestiveness of Aristotle's doctrine. I followed Joachim in regarding the bipartite politico-ethical psychology as 'crude and simple' in contrast with the doctrine that 'complete moral goodness is the perfect development of an emotional and an intellectual factor' (220). I distinguished this relatively low-level 'perfection' of the 'intellectual factor' from the wisdom of the statesman but assumed its identity with a less exalted kind or grade of *phronēsis*. I am inclined to question Fortenbaugh's opinion that *phronēsis* has a part to play only after the 'training in values' is complete.

p. 239   R. Sorabji on the role of the intellect in virtue
In his article (*P.A.S.* 1973–4) Sorabji examines critically the views of commentators who have, in a variety of contexts, minimized, or at least unduly diminished, this role. He notes Aristotle's tendency 'to present the various parts of his view in isolation', but defends effectively Aristotle's consistency in assigning a 'major role' to intellect in conduct under three heads: choice (*prohairesis*), practical wisdom (*phronēsis*), and habituation (*ethismos*). Sorabji does not accept the view of Fortenbaugh that a man can be trained to act virtuously without acquiring the capacity to discover by deliberation what he must do to achieve *eudaimonia*, the capacity which Aristotle calls *phronēsis*. He argues cogently that the earlier books do not leave us 'unprepared for the account of practical wisdom' in VI. His article will be helpful to those who find it difficult (and who does not?) to envisage Aristotle's moral philosophy as a whole.

Article by David Wiggins, 'Deliberation and Practical Reason', (*P.A.S.* 1975–6) The article, as its title suggests, has a wide range. The questions at issue are difficult and central in Aristotle's philosophy of practice. Writing from his own 'neo-Aristotelian' (p. 43) point of view, Wiggins finds in Books III and VI the framework of a theory of deliberation different 'from that pseudo-rationalistic irrationalism, insidiously propagated nowadays by technocratic persons, which holds that reason has nothing to do with the ends of human life' (p. 36). He knows that he has more to say than can be said in one article; and, at some points, shortage of space has disconcerting consequences. For example, he expresses the controversial opinion that 'Aristotle allows the problem of incontinence to confuse and disrupt his whole theory of practical reason' but is compelled 'to adjourn all discussion of *akrasia*' (p. 42). But the difficulty of the article will not discourage readers already puzzled by the imperfections in Aristotle's treatment of the topic.

We are invited to consider three contentions which 'taken singly are 'familiar enough in Aristotelian exegesis'. They are: (1) that in Book III Aristotle expounds a 'restricted and technical' concept of deliberation as being 'never of ends but always of means'; (2) that in Books VI and VII we find the analysis of 'a much less restricted notion of deliberation and choice' and the recognition of 'two irreducibly distinct modes of practical reasoning, *means–end* deliberations and *rule–case* deliberations'; (3) that the 'supposed modification of view' is a 'radical change' and an advance towards a more adequate account. The article argues that the conjunction of these three theses constitutes an interpretation which is 'substantially and damagingly mistaken' (p. 30).

Wiggins observes that the conjunction 'represents something of a conflation or contamination of what I have read or heard people say'. Who are these people? A note at this point suggests that Professor Allan is viewed as the prime expositor of the 'overall picture' which the conjunction paints. But the note does not quote either from Allan's influential and justly praised paper on Aristotle's account of 'the origin of moral principles' (1953) (reprinted as Ch. 7 of *Articles on Aristotle 2. Ethics and Politics*) or from 'The Practical Syllogism' (1955). Moreover in Wiggin's formulation of (2) the distinction drawn between 'means–end deliberations' and 'rule–case deliberations' (whatever these are) cannot be identified with or derived from Allan's distinction between two allegedly different kinds of 'practical syllogism' as having respectively utilitarian or deontic rules as major premisses. Indeed at the end of the note Wiggins himself tells us that Allan did not regard the new doctrine in VI and VII as significantly affecting the analysis of deliberation in III. It seems likely that Wiggins had in mind the passage in the earlier article where Allan describes as alike 'masterly' the analysis of end–means thinking in III and the deployment in VI and VII of the subsumption of a particular case under a general rule (p. 75). Allan's final paragraph speaks of the latter as the distinctive work of 'practical reason': 'not a reasoning process which precedes action, but rather thought expressed in action and controlling it' (p. 78).

Wiggins proceeds to an examination and rejection of the 'first thesis', that in Book III Aristotle 'set out to analyse a restricted notion of deliberation' (pp. 30–6). I agree with the rejection and with some of the arguments used by Wiggins. But I do not think that we need describe Aristotle as 'setting out' to analyse either an unrestricted or a restricted notion of deliberation. An unrestricted notion might be expected to involve specifying modes and varieties of the cogitation which issues in action. The natural place for such an analysis would be the treatment of the intellectual excellencies. In III he is setting out to answer primarily the question how a rational agent initiates rational action. In III. 1 he starts with a discussion of behaviour which is voluntary but not necessarily rational, deliberated or deliberate. Men perform actions by moving parts of their own bodies (1110 a15–18). These are the only changes which it is in their power to originate directly. This generalization is clearly true over at least a wide area, including the use of written language, and can easily be elaborated a little to include also oral speech-acts. Still in III. 1 Aristotle analyses ways in which factual ignorance often brings it about that our initiations have effects which could not have been foreseen and intended; such actions are 'involuntary' and hence not expressions of character. These are the facts which Aristotle has in mind in the statement which opens III. 2, that choices (*prohaireseis*) are a better criterion of character than actions (1111 b5–6). The point is put more neatly, and perhaps more accurately, in the *Eudemian Ethics*: our criterion is not what a man does (*ti*) but what he does it for (*tinos heneka*) (1228 a3–4). It seems to me that what Wiggins says round this point on p. 31 is confusing.

I have suggested that in Book III Aristotle's interest in the content of deliberation is subordinate, even incidental, to his interest in the concept of action as a mind–body transaction, performed with a view to anticipated effects. For, from this angle, it is possible to view the bare transaction, the last step in the analysis and the first cause of what ensues (1112 b19–20, 23–4), as a means to a future state of affairs, the object of the agents intention and wish, his end. The momentous transaction is productive of something; but Aristotle is talking of practical life not of the practice of a technique. The geometrical analogy illustrates a contrast between direct and indirect causation. It has perhaps obsessed commentators more than Aristotle himself. What is there in it which resembles the agonizing deliberations which Aristotle has mentioned in III. 1 (1110 a29–30) or in III. 3 itself the choice between alternative means (1112 b16–17)? If the geometrical example has unduly dominated the interpretation of deliberation, this is also true of the 'practical syllogism': its interest for Aristotle emerges primarily in connection with 'the mind-body transaction'. (Cooper may not be far wrong when he asserts that the syllogism is not even part of Aristotelian deliberation).

Wiggins goes on to discuss Aristotle's repeated insistence in III. 3 that 'we do not deliberate about ends but about things which are towards ends' (1112 b11–24, b34–5, 1113 a11–12). He remarks that the difference between means and constituents has become a 'commonplace of Aristotelian exegesis': what is 'towards an end' in Greek need not be a means in English. But it remains disconcerting to be told flatly by Aristotle that 'we do not deliberate about ends': the doctor, orator, statesman do not deliberate whether to cure, persuade, promote law and order but only how and through what (1112 b11–16). Deliberation, we may add, must start somewhere; it cannot always start at or near the top, as in *EN* i. The 'positing' of an end (b15) defines a sphere of deliberation here and now, a situation. So it is helpful to be told firmly how absurd it would be 'to suppose that a man could not deliberate about whether to be a doctor or not' (p. 35). We accept the assurance that the absurdity is not in Aristotle. But criticism is not easily silenced. Aristotle, we think, should have had more to tell us about the differences between the executive deliberation which terminates in an action, or in a resolve for action in the near future, and the 'architectonic' thinking of the statesman or the political philosopher articulating his comprehensive plans for political societies (I. 1, 1094 a26–8; cf. VI. 8, 1141 b23–8). It is not surprising that acute commentators have seen confusion and error in the proposition that deliberation is never about ends or the end. H. W. B. Joseph, for example, called it 'a capital mistake' which springs from the 'connected error' of 'regarding as a means to some whole its contributory or constituent factors' (*Essays*, pp. 183, 185).

Wiggins claims that his discussion of the First Thesis makes 'fairly smooth' the transition from Book III to Book VI (p. 36). Practical wisdom is concerned both with 'questions of general policy' and with 'specific objectives' (p. 37). But 'standard problems' are different in 'technical' and non-technical deliberation (pp. 37–8); the latter seeks not means to a determinate end but 'the best specification' of a vaguely described end. There follows a criticism of Allan's attempt to connect the abandonment, or extension, of the strict means–end concept with the distinction drawn by Aristotle in the *De Motu Animalium* between premisses of the good and premisses of the possible (701 a23–5) (pp. 39–41). I made somewhat similar comments on this suggestion of Allan (247–8). This section of the article (pp. 36–42) ends with some remarks on Aristotle's doctrine that, in ethical science, all rules have exceptions, and with the claim that Aristotle's doctrine in Book VI 'was nothing remotely resembling what has been ascribed to him by his Kantian and other deontomaniac interpreters' (p. 42). The 'deontomaniacs' are not named; but the fact that in Gauthier's Index of Names there are four references under 'Kant' to places in his commentary on Book VI may possibly be a clue.

The last section of the article (pp. 42–9) is about 'deliberative specification', so far as Aristotle sketches it, and propounds 'a general framework for its interpretation and evaluation'. It is claimed that, while Aristotle's ideas on the matter are expressed only 'sketchily and obscurely', they are 'of more fundamental importance than anything to be found now in utility theory, decision theory, or other rationality studies' (p. 42). Practical decisions are made in response to particular contexts, contexts having features which are the basis of 'competing and inconsistent claims'. What is needed, therefore, is 'a high order of situational appreciation, or as Aristotle would say perception' (*aisthēsis*). Sets of relevant concerns are not closed, and their pattern is a shifting pattern; planning procedures should 'make room' for 'stepping back and re-evaluation'. But there are no 'formal criteria' for comparing competing claims (pp. 43–5). In the last pages of the article (pp. 46–9) Wiggins tries to show that his concept of 'situational appreciation' and Aristotle's intuitive *phronēsis* (*nous*) are akin and mutually illuminative by giving expanded paraphrases, with brief comments, of two difficult passages in Book VI, 1142 a23–30 and 1143 a25–b14. He anticipates two difficulties in this move: that he may seem to choose disputable interpretations which suit his case (perhaps at 1142 a28–9 of *to eschaton trigōnon*—the ultimate particular is a triangle) and that too little is said, or perhaps can be said, either about situational appreciation or about intuitive practical wisdom. He counters this second objection by expressing the 'unfriendly suspicion' that those who ask for something more scientific do so because they desire 'a system of rules by which to spare themselves some of the agony of thinking and all the torment of feeling that is actually involved in reasoned deliberation' (p. 49).

XII. Note on the Practical Syllogism (240–257)

(1) In what I said on this topic in Chapters XI and XII I argued against interpretations which seemed to go beyond what Aristotle had said or implied. I agreed with D. J. Allan's remark, at the beginning of his paper on the subject (1955), that the practical syllogism is 'a psychological account of action in accordance with principles'—in a wide sense of principles (*archai*). When I was preparing these notes I read an article by Sanford G. Etheridge, 'Aristotle's Practical Syllogism and Necessity' (*Philologus*, 1968) in which he defended a similar thesis. He suggested that the 'term . . . which in any case is not Aristotelian, be reserved to designate the use of the syllogism (in a metaphorical sense) to analyze the psychology of moral action', or indeed of 'voluntary action in general' (pp. 34, 37). He pointed out that, if we thus insist on the action as the 'conclusion', we avoid the 'needless' dispute whether 'such and such a food is dry' (1145 a5–7) is a major or a minor premiss; it is the minor premiss of a prosyllogism, i.e. a syllogism the conclusion of which becomes a premiss of another syllogism (*An. Pr.* 42 b5).

J. M. Cooper (1975) has much that is useful to say on the practical syllogism. He argues that it is not a 'part of deliberation' but rather the link between deliberation and action. He complains more than once that Allan and I are 'mistaken' when we 'assert' that the major premiss is a 'rule' (pp. 25–6). Perhaps 'rules', like 'principles' (and 'syllogisms'), are not the best words to describe the non-verbalized patterns of behaviour in the animals observed by Aristotle as they got moving.

(2) Aristotle's *De Motu Animalium*, Text with Translation, Commentary, and Interpretive Essays by Martha Craven Nussbaum (1978), Princeton University Press. This is a book of 400 pages containing, after a brief Introduction (xv–xxiii): I Two chapters on Text Transmission and Manuscripts (3–17); II Greek Text and Translation (pp. 20–54); III Five Interpretive Essays (pp. 59–269): 1. Teleological Explanation (pp. 59–106), 2. Scientific Method (pp. 107–42), 3. Soul and Body (pp. 143–64), 4. Practical Syllogisms and Practical Science (pp. 165–220), 5. The Role of *Phantasia* in Aristotle's Explanations of Actions (pp. 221–69); IV Commentary (pp. 273–385); Bibliography (pp. 387–400), Indexes (pp. 401–30).

I first saw this book early in 1979 when I had completed the typescript of the Appended Notes. The book would have helped me at many points if I had seen it earlier. I note it as a major contribution to Aristotelian studies by a scholar who, as is evident from the briefest acquaintance with her book, is as critically familiar with the writings of distinguished contemporary philosophers on metabiology and on the philosophy of mind and of action as with Aristotelian texts. The titles of the five essays show that they are all closely relevant to the interpretation of the *Ethics*. I shall now comment briefly on the treatment of the practical syllogism in Essay 4. The practical syllogism, being an integral part of Aristotle's answer to the question which he puts by asking how the soul moves the body, is the central doctrine of the *MA*. It is also one of Aristotle's central doctrines in the *Ethics*.

(3) I start from a passage in which the difficulty which concerns me comes to the surface (pp. 179–80). Nussbaum quotes from Aristotle's medical example in *Metaph.* VII (1032 b6–9, b18–31) of his familiar model for analytic deliberation (*EN* 1112 b15 ff., *MA* 701 a20–2). Aristotle insists that 'if the agent really has desires and beliefs of this form, he must of necessity act' (p. 179). Nussbaum says that Aristotle was 'evidently puzzled' about the 'logical status' of this 'practical necessity'. Here her exposition is moving very fast, and it is best to pause at this point before we are transported to some paradoxical pages in von Wright's Gifford Lectures which speak of practical syllogisms as 'patterns of valid inference' with actions not propositions as their conclusions and 'an enlargement of the province of logic' (*Varieties of Goodness*, pp. 166–71).

'He must of necessity act.' It seems plain that the 'practical necessity' (*anankē*) to which Nussbaum here refers is the same as the necessity to which Aristotle refers as he approaches the end of his analysis of *akrasia* in *EN* VII. 3 (1147 a27, 30; cf. *Metaph.* 1048 a14), the 'immediate' necessity familiar in the *MA* examples. The necessity may be called 'practical' because what is necessitated is the behaviour of a human or non-human animal. But it might less misleadingly be called 'factual' or 'causal' to distinguish it from the 'logical' necessity apprehended in demonstrative inference. To distinguish necessities as practical and theoretical can be misleading. For, on the one hand, logical necessities, entailments, are apprehended in the course of practical thinking (as in the prosyllogism about the lightness of chicken). On the other hand, the factual issues of theoretical processes in which a mind comes to apprehend a complex entailment are naturally viewed as being predictable effects of causes. In mathematics the teacher has no doubt that his bright pupil will shortly and *necessarily* realize that the square on the hypotenuse of a right-angled triangle is *necessarily* equal to the sum of the squares on the other two sides and will *necessarily* exhibit the kind of pleasure which *necessarily* caused Pythagoras to sacrifice an ox and *necessarily* moved Russell to throw his pipe in the air on coming to think that the ontological argument is *necessarily* valid. We have no difficulty here in distinguishing the two necessities which are logical from the four which are factual.

(4) After quoting the testimony of von Wright to the logical respectability of the practical syllogism Nussbaum remarks that it was 'very important' for Aristotle to distinguish between the 'theoretical necessity' of valid deduction and 'the necessity of his teleological patterns' of inference. What made this important is the fact that 'he does not want to grant that an efficient-causal explanation that makes no reference to the agent's goals and intentions could ever provide an entirely satisfactory account of the action (cf. Essays 1 and 3) . . .' (p. 180). This

sentence could be interpreted in more than one way. (A) It might mean that a causal explanation of an action could not be 'entirely satisfactory' if it did not embrace as causes 'the goals and intentions' of the agent. (Goals and intentions can be causes because, while they look to the future, they are present facts.) So understood, the sentence could be taken as an ironical understatement of a firm commonsensical conviction; with Aristotle ready to reinforce and save common sense. But (B) the sentence could also be read in a sense more sophisticated, less sensible and more disputable. It might mean that an 'efficient-causal explanation' is as such incapable of any 'reference to the agent's goals and intentions' and hence can give only an incomplete account, even if a complete causal account, of an action. The efficient-causal explanation would be, perhaps, exclusively in terms of physical and physiological causes. It would be supplemented, not contradicted, by the teleological explanation, a different but not competing story, in terms of goals and intentions, feelings and cogitations. But can we make sense of this? Have we not to protest that the two explanations refer not to different worlds but to the same world and the same events within it and to the causes of the events which are actions? The suggestion that the practical syllogism offers not a causal account but a 'pattern of valid inference' is disturbing; and the reference to the earlier essays invites further probing. I shall quote a few passages which reveal complexities in Nussbaum's thinking about causation in biology and psychology.

(5) It is not a matter for surprise or fault-finding if, in metabiological discussion, it is sometimes unclear whether 'teleological' explanations are to be understood as correcting or as supplementing or as replacing 'causal' explanations. If a plant is a self-maintaining system (pp. 76–80) the thought of such a system may well aid and guide the search for types of structure which would promote self-maintenance, A teleological approach, as Nussbaum indicates, is not to be thought of by the botanist as involving either 'a mysterious *a fronte* causal power' in 'ends' or some extra cause in the shape of 'some non-physiological entity which interacts' with physiological causes, the 'material factors' (p. 90). We expect a comparison, and are prepared for a distinction, between biological and mechanical causation. But sometimes what seems to be disparaged by Nussbaum is 'any account in terms of an antecedent efficient-causal sequence' (p. 74). The practical syllogism looked like a causal account of the movements of animals in terms of their desires and beliefs. But, 'if the proposed causal account in terms of antecedent desires and beliefs is to be a genuine alternative to teleology, it must be possible to identify the desire and belief independently of the goal' (p. 88). Why? 'The desire and the belief are not genuine Humean causes' (p. 88). Are they not antecedent causes?

In other passages Nussbaum elucidates by defining errors and crudities which Aristotle and teleology will help us to avoid: '... no mysterious non-empirical entities ... no efficient causal gaps ...' (p. 60); 'desire ... is a functional state of matter and not some Cartesian incorporeal agent, quite literally using the body as a tool to effect changes in the world' (p. 146); 'the power of soul-events to cause body-events' (p. 152). These passages suggest imperfect sympathy with the opinions of those who, if 'isms' were in order, would call themselves dualists and interactionists. But arguments are needed to show that the opinions shot at really involve the physiological gaps, the Cartesian incorporeal agents and the efficacy of unenmattered soul-events. In what I said about 'Bodies which have Souls' I was trying to anticipate and avert these interpretations (Chapter V, Appendix).

(6) I have quoted Nussbaum as saying that 'the desire and the belief', the premisses of the practical syllogism, are 'not genuine causes' (p. 88). The quotation goes on: 'The connection between them and the goal is a logical or conceptual one'. Obviously there is a conceptual connection in the sense that we identify the desire by saying what it is the desire for. What is difficult is the suggestion that this conceptual connection is not also causal: the necessity which was causal on p. 179 is apparently on p. 180 given the 'status' of a logically necessary demonstration. At this crucial point we are referred to a passage in chapter VII of von Wright's *The Varieties of Goodness* (see pp. 160–77, especially 166–71). Does his argument effectively support the thesis that we should take 'literally' (Nussbaum p. 186 n. 35) Aristotle's statement that an action (not a proposition) is the 'conclusion' of a 'logically conclusive' sequence?

Von Wright's verbalization of the syllogism he discusses (pp. 167 ff.) is:
    x wants to reach the train in time
    Unless x runs, he will not reach the train in time
    ∴ x has to run

Is there here, von Wright asks, any proposition which would be a fitting conclusion (p. 168)? A conclusion is a proposition seen to be necessitated by premisses. The only 'insight' he can see is that formulated in the second premiss. But then the first premiss would be irrelevant. At this point he abandons the search for a propositional conclusion. Why does he not suggest 'Unless he runs X will not get what he wants'? Instead von Wright tells us that 'in one place' Aristotle says that the conclusion is an action and that 'his saying this is not at all odd'. In saying it Aristotle 'is *almost* right—but not *quite* right' (p. 168). The 'correct' verbalization of the conclusion is that the agent 'puts himself in motion', 'sets himself to do the act', 'embarks on the road to the actual performance' (p. 169). This suggests that the agent does not draw a propositional conclusion before he starts to act. But, if the agent uses language, he often does first draw a propositional conclusion. It is as if von Wright did not expect us to be wholly convinced by his defence of Aristotle. He goes on to admit that it is 'peculiar' to 'regard practical syllogisms as logically conclusive arguments', but he suggests that to do so helps us to shape the 'concepts' involved and to 'meet the philosopher's craving for clarity in these matters' (p. 170).

I have left as a loose end Nussbaum's remark that, if desires and beliefs are to be 'genuine causes', it 'must be possible to identify them' independently of the goal (p. 88). This is a strange demand. If we take them to be 'realized in physiological states', functions of enmattered consciousness or besouled body, how else could they be identified, unless by the brain scientist who might hope to tell us in due course what is going on when and where inside our heads? We all know what it is like to want a drink. Nothing is odder in 'physicalism', a doctrine which Nussbaum seems to find Aristotelian and acceptable (p. 89 n. 38), than the way its adherents speak of the familiar non-physical aspects of facts as if they were ghostly, mysterious, mentionable only in negative terms. There are passages in Nussbaum's book other than those already mentioned which refer to the 'picking out' of 'Humean causes' and to the coexistence in the syllogism of causal and logical connections: Aristotle asserts 'both a causal and a conceptual relationship among desire, belief and action' (pp. 188–9); desires and beliefs are after all Humean causes—but only under their descriptions in bodily terms as physiological changes (p. 188). 'Aristotle never, I believe, even claims that the two descriptions are related in any constant or predictable fashion'—sometimes 'it seems simply to be an act of faith with Aristotle for which he has no evidential support' that there is a 'physiological description' of desire (p. 188). But did Aristotle regard as inconstant or unpredictable the unity of form and matter in the emotions of anger or fear (*DA* 403 a24–b2)?

(7) Nussbaum's candour and acumen do not allow her to conceal either her omissions or her qualms. Thus she refers at the end of the final essay to 'complicated problems' concerning 'action and responsibility' in which she has not had 'the time to become enmeshed' (p. 268). An earlier passage had alluded to 'the muddy issue of Aristotle's position on agency and determinism' (p. 206 n. 52). The latter passage continues: 'If he [Aristotle] does not want to introduce any randomness into the ante-action psychological sequence—and if he believes that each psychological process is, under another description, a physiological change—can he in fact avoid the consequence he considers untenable in *DI* 9, that deliberation and planning are merely epiphenomenal?' I think that Aristotle did see or glimpse a problem about determinism and responsibility; but I have not been enmeshed in it in this note. But my objection to Nussbaum's 'double account' interpretation of Aristotle's doctrine on 'desire belief and action' is indeed that it is epiphenomenalist. For she attributes to Aristotle the view that our perceptions desires beliefs deliberations and ratiocinations, considered as Humean, i.e. antecedent, causes of actions, are to be described exclusively in physiological terms. As they are experienced by the agent, in their psychical character, they are epiphenomenal, effects but not causes. Epiphenomenalism so understood is unintelligible to common sense and incompatible with Aristotle's view of the way in which actions are originated in human and other animals.

(8) Finally two notes on passages where what I said is not taken by Nussbaum quite in the sense I intended.

(a) 1144 a31–4 'Syllogisms that deal with the acts to be done . . .'. I commented on this passage on pp. 228–9 and 249–54. It is the passage which comes nearer than any other to being a use of the term 'practical syllogism'; and it has misled many commentators, including Nussbaum, into using the term much more widely than Aristotle does. Nussbaum's references on pp. 183–4 to what I said about the sentence are not quite accurate. I did not say that *sullogismos* here was used in a wide sense (process of reasoning) and not in its technical sense. I suggested this as a possibility in one place (228) and rejected it as improbable in another (253). I also argued that the narrower interpretation was compatible with the schema in the *De Anima* (434 a16–19), provided that 'the end is such and such' is not taken as by itself the form of a major premiss. Of course a premiss which specifies a means or a constituent might, in a subordinate clause, name or define the end in view. I do not know whether Aristotle thought it specially fitting that a deliberative chain should be exhibited as having syllogisms for its links. He does not say so. The links could not be practical syllogisms if these always lead, through a singular minor premiss, to a present action or decision to act. Only the last syllogism in the chain could be practical.

(b) p. 207 n. 53. I am said to be one among others who find the syllogisms in the *MA* 'far too trivial in subject-matter . . . to provide anything like a schema for all deliberation'. We are rebuked for forgetting that simple examples can happily elucidate implicit complexity. But I did not say 'too trivial'; I said 'unmomentous' (249), e.g. drinking when thirsty not signing a covenant or pulling a trigger. Aristotle's subject here is the psychophysics of the perhaps non-linguistic behaviour of animals not 'all deliberation' with higher and lower 'levels' in its 'hierarchies'. 'I should make something good; a house is something good; at once he makes a house' (701 a16–17). What 'stage of the deliberative process' is this (p. 185 n. 34)? It might be the speech of a bird, if a bird could speak, when it starts to build a nest. Nussbaum's book contains much admirable discussion of questions about 'rules of practice' including 'a rule-like major premise for a lion' (see her Index and p. 198).

XIII. Moral Weakness (258–293)

p. 258 Introduction to the treatment of moral weakness and its opposite: the three kinds of ethical states to be avoided and their opposites (1145 a15–b2)
I now think I was wrong not to show more interest than I did in the doctrines stated or suggested in this brief introduction. In particular, following Ross, I dismissed Aristotle's 'heroic virtue' on the ground that the concept of such virtue was incompatible with Aristotle's account of virtue as a mean. But, when the Editors of *Articles on Aristotle* desired to reprint part of my Chapter VII (on *The Mean*), my dissatisfaction with what I had said and omitted to say in it came to a head. I had come to think it important to face the question whether the ethical hero was as much of a stranger in Aristotle's ethical scene as had been supposed. The editors kindly allowed me to add a four-page Appendix, 'Continence, Virtue, Heroic Virtue', to the reprinted extract. This note is a variation on the theme of the Appendix. But first a word about the treatment by the commentators of this passage at the beginning of *EN* vii.

'Aristotle's doctrine as it is worked out leaves no room for anything higher than virtue. Temperance . . . is described as involving the entire absence of bad desires (1152 a1–2), and there is no room for a superhuman virtue beyond this'

(Ross, *Aristotle*, p. 222). 'The absence of bad desires': a curiously negative phrase for the man who faces pain which 'overstrains human nature' (1110 a23–31) or experiences the 'brief intense delight' which rewards death for friends or country (1169 a18–26). Stewart, Burnet, and Dirlmeier ignore the embarrassing phantom. This suggests agreement with the view of Ross that there is nothing to be said about 'heroic virtue' and Aristotle says it. Grant, failing to find the hero on earth, translates him to another place: Aristotle is showing a 'scale of moral states' with 'divine virtue or pure reason' at the top and 'bestiality or pure passion at the bottom'. But the godlike man falls short of the simplicity of a god as the bestial man of the innocence of the beast. Both are 'rarely found among men' but they are found (1145 a27–30). Gauthier–Jolif suggest that heroic virtue has 'only a very modest place' in Aristotle's thought; that it is merely posited as the counterpart of brutishness—certainly a modest place; and that 'the whole passage, far from being an appeal in favour of heroic virtue, on the contrary invites a man to be truly himself'. But the hero is exceedingly, not excessively, virtuous. Aristotle was certainly 'in favour' of such virtue (that of Hermias) when he wrote his poem in its praise.

The commentators, then, are in mutual disagreement. They are not a team building a cumulative case for the negative conclusion to which their negations and evasions and silences all point. So it is reasonable to ask whether nothing more positive can be concluded. But the present passage suggests that we should begin with the opposition of the hero to the brute.

Bestial vice, and the unnatural or unnaturally strong appetites which are its basis, may be innate, chiefly in barbarians. It may also be the effect of constitutional abnormality or of mutililation or disease or madness (1145 a30–2). Some extreme examples of morbidity are given later (VII. 5). Here Aristotle adds another variety: 'also such men as exceed in vice all ordinary measures we designate by this opprobrious term' (1145 a32–3, Chase). Evidently the 'bestial state' covers a wide range of abnormalities and horrors, and these in turn raise a wide range of questions. But for his scheme of six states it is reasonable to suppose that it is this last use of the term which Aristotle has in mind. So we have to look for the character which most sharply distinguishes the exceedingly good man from the exceedingly bad man.

Thus we are told that the highest virtue, the virtue which is 'beyond us' ordinary persons (1145 a19), is in polar opposition to the most abysmal vice (a32–3). But now we should look at heroism from another angle; not as contrasted with bestiality but as compared with the two good states below it on the scale, standard virtue and below virtue continence (*enkrateia*). Note that the terms *enkrateia* and *akrasia*, while in their specific sense they have as their sphere the pleasures and pains proper to *sōphrosunē* (temperance) and *akolasia* (intemperance), are extended by analogy to the provinces of other virtues and vices (1145 b19–20 etc.; 259–61).

(i) 'Both the continent man and the temperate man are such as to do nothing contrary to reason (*logos*) on account of the bodily pleasures, but the former has and the latter has not bad desires (*phaulas epithumias*), and the latter is such as not to feel pleasure contrary to reason, while the former is such as to feel pleasure but not to be led by it' (VII. 9, 1151 b34–1152 a3). When we consider this definition of the difference between continence and temperance, or generally between moral strength and moral virtue, it is important to keep firmly in mind what Aristotle has said about virtuous action in earlier books.

(ii) He has said in II. 4 that a virtuous action must satisfy three conditions: (a) the agent must know what he is doing; (b) he must choose the action for its own sake; thirdly (c) the action must be the expression of a firm and unchangeable character (1105 a28–33).

(iii) In III. 1 Aristotle considers the case of a man required, under threat of an unpleasant death for himself and/or others, to betray (let us say) some political or military secret. Aristotle remarks that it is sometimes 'difficult to determine what should be chosen at what cost, or endured for what gain, and yet more difficult to abide by (*emmeinai*) our decisions' (1110 a29–31). What makes it 'difficult' to hold firm is the strength of the desires and aversions which are motives for giving way. Let us speak of actions which are difficult in this sense, a sense familiar but not easy to analyse, as 'effortful'.

Now, when we report what Aristotle says in (i) VII. 9, we may slip into saying something like this: an action manifests continence not virtue (1) if it is both right and effortful and (2) only if it is both right and effortful. But, while (i), as stated by Aristotle, is clear and explicit, (1) and (2) are both false and Aristotle implies that they are false. That he implies the falsity of (1) is clear when we consider the conjunction of (i) and (iii). An action which is both right and effortful manifests continence only if what makes it difficult is the fact that the agent has 'bad' desires, i.e. desires which he would not have if he were virtuous. But the desires which make right action difficult for the tyrant's victim are not bad, the desire not to die too soon or the desire to save a hostage. I shall quote in a moment another passage which clinches this point in a more emphatic way. That (2) is a misrepresentation both of the facts and of Aristotle's view of the facts can be seen if we reflect on an implication of (ii): an action which qualifies as virtuous as satisfying the first two conditions, (a) and (b), may fail only because it fails to satisfy the third (c), that the ethical state which it manifests should be firm and constant. We do not give credit for temperance when we have seen someone enjoy a good meal without seeming to enjoy it too much. We do not give credit for courage when someone shows no inclination to panic at the first hint of danger. When we know them better we may feel confident that they have achieved at least continence; when we know them better still we may be in a position to decide whether they are continent persons or virtuous persons or neither. A single act is not diagnostic of a dispositional state. We are now in a position to correct the too facile statement of Aristotle's distinction between continence and virtue from which this paragraph started. What can be said is that there are classes of right actions which are normally effortless, and so far pleasant, for the virtuous but more or less effortful, and so far distressing, for the non-virtuous but continent.

For our present purpose, the location in Aristotle's scheme of extra-ordinary virtue, the point which is important is that virtuous action can be difficult and distressing. This is said explicitly about courage in III. 9.

Death and wounds will be painful to the brave man and against his will, but he will face them because it is noble to do so or because it is base not to do so. And the more he is possessed of virtue in its entirety and the happier (*eudaimonesteros*) he is, the more he will be pained at the thought of death; for life is best worth living for such a man, and he is knowingly losing the greatest goods, and this is painful. But he is none the less brave, and perhaps all the more so because he chooses noble deeds of war at that cost. It is not the case, then, with all the virtues that the exercise of them is pleasant, except in so far as it reaches its end. But it is quite possible that the best soldiers may be not men of this sort but those who are less brave but have no other good; for these are ready to face danger, and they will sell their life for small gains. (1117 b7-20)

'Aristotle's doctrine as it is worked out leaves no room for anything higher than "virtue".' So Ross (p. 222); and I was following him when I said that it was difficult to find the 'additional moral stature' which would raise Aristotelian virtue from the ordinary to the extra-ordinary. But what we are given in the *Ethics* is not always a 'worked out doctrine'. Sometimes it may be something which could be more interesting: a report of work in progress or the work itself. Certainly Aristotle has not worked out an account of 'heroic' virtue. What he is mainly working on in VII. 1-10 is the difference between virtue-vice and continence-incontinence. We praise the continent man for the firmness of his effort to stick to the right principles; we praise the virtuous man for the acquired dispositions to follow these principles without effort. Naturally Aristotle's discussion invites out attention to situations in which this difference is obvious to the agent if not to the spectator. But I hope I have shown that Aristotle can and does state his doctrine without implying either that right action is always difficult for the non-virtuous or that it is always easy for the virtuous. I hope it is also clear that both these propositions are contradicted by common sense. I do not wish to suggest that Aristotle had worked out a doctrine on heroic virtue. I claim only to have shown that he had left himself 'room': he could look in territory in which virtue is difficult. The extra-ordinary man might be one on a level superior both to the continent man as having only innocent and moderate propensities and to the man of humdrum virtue for whom rightly desired ways of living are not difficult to attain.

pp. 264, 266.   (1) Is it possible to sin against knowledge? (2) Did Aristotle think it possible?
A reviewer says that I am 'inclined' to answer 'no' to both questions. As to (1) I am indeed inclined to answer 'no'; but I am more inclined to answer 'yes' (268, 291-2). As to (2) I agree that my answer is 'no', with the reservations (a) that Aristotle required anyone answering 'no' to (1) to account for the strongly held opinion that the correct answer is 'yes', and (b) that I could not deny, as the reviewer denies, that 1150 b19-25 is evidence against my 'no' to (2), and (c) that I was impressed by the remark of Ross that to explain how a wrong act can be

done in the (temporary) absence of complete knowledge is not to explain how knowledge has come to be absent (224). The force which I found in Ross's remark tends to reflect doubt on the firmness of Aristotle's 'no' to (1) and to illuminate the difficulty of saying 'no' to (1).

I have a few particular disagreements with the reviewer.

1145 b21–2 '... having correct understanding in what sense?' The reviewer rejects the argument for my rendering (266–8). I suggested that, if the context is considered, no other translation is possible; this should be clear when we read the next line (b22–3). It is clinched by 1146 b8–9 (cf. 1145 b28–9). It is alleged that my translation rests 'on the perverse ground' that the translation against which I argue implies that 'Socrates' is mistaken (1147 b14–15). But it is surely not 'perverse' to think (and hope) that Aristotle does not formulate the main question for discussion in terms which would beg it against Socrates. If the rejoinder were made that my translation also begs the question against Socrates since it implies that in the continent action the *akratēs* knows in some sense that he is doing wrong, the answer would be that the knowledge which the *akratēs* must have if his having it is to imply that the Socratic view is erroneous is knowledge which is occurrent (activated) and not only dispositional. But I have not succeeded in believing that the Greek is ambiguous in spite of the weight to be attached to the opinion of those with whom, on this point, I disagree.

1147 b1–3. The reviewer thought I took the 'correct principle' (*orthos logos*) in b3 to be 'to taste this is wrong' and not the general rule against consuming sweet things (as bad for health). The factual proposition that sweet things are pleasant is consistent with, not contrary to, this rule; but it evokes a desire and hence leads to a violation of the rule (283, 285). The principle followed by the profligate (*akolastos*) permitting or enjoining the consumption of sweet things is contrary to the right rule.

1150 b19–25. While I could not agree with Ross or Cook Wilson that Aristotle again and again states or implies an anti-Socratic view of *akrasia*, I found this passage difficult to interpret as admitting only ostensible *akrasia*. My reason was that the description of what it is like to screw determination to the sticking place seemed to imply that an incontinent action was more like open-eyed unscrewing or non-screwing, or at least receptiveness of excuses for unscrewing, than like a sudden uncheckable onset of anaisthesia. That is why I quoted fully on p. 264 and referred on p. 275 to the critical comment of Ross and on p. 276 to Walsh's similar criticism of Robinson, and mentioned the difficulty again on pp. 291–2. The reviewer refers to nothing of this and rejects my opinion that the passage ought to trouble anyone who attributes to Aristotle a negative answer to (1).

p. 279 Dispositional knowledge (1145 a11–13): Dr. Kenny on 'half-having' and 'pseudo-exercising' knowledge.

Kenny's article, 'The Practical Syllogism and Incontinence', *Phronesis* xi (1966) was included in the bibliography (Select List) of my first edition (1968). I have reread it along with Kenny's most recent book on Aristotle's ethics, *Aristotle's*

Theory of the Will (1979). In a footnote to the fourteenth chapter, 'The Breakdown of Ethical Reasoning', Kenny says that he is restating with modifications 'the principal conclusions of the article' on Aristotle's *akrasia* doctrine. The effect of reading together the book and the article must be to increase admiration for the depth of the analysis and the penetration shown in Kenny's anticipations of hesitations and difficulties which may be suggested by his conclusions.

The article is a critical analysis of *NE* VII. 3 and concludes that Aristotle does justice both to Socrates' doctrine of knowledge and to the reality of a 'full-blooded conflict between reason and desire' (182). The conclusion is at least prima facie paradoxical in view of what sounds like an admission by Aristotle that the argument has reached 'the position which Socrates sought to establish' (1147 b14–15); an admission supported by the second entry of the drunkard reciting the verses of Empedocles (1147 a20, b12). In this note I wish to suggest some points on which Kenny's exposition seems to me to need correction or clarification. My references are to the pages of the article in *Phronesis* except when I refer explicitly to the book.

(1) p. 164. 'Aristotle's first and principal problem is this: how can a man be incontinent in action while making a correct judgement? (1145 b22)'. I have argued (a) that this is a mistranslation and (b) that it begs the question against Socrates (pp. 266–8). But the second contention is not given as a reason for accepting the first. (See the preceding note.)

(2) p. 165. Kenny says that in Aristotle *agnoia* (ignorance) commonly means 'not just ignorance' but 'positively mistaken belief' and that in the *Topics* (148 a8) 'he even says that *agnoia* is never merely non-possession of knowledge, else infants would have it'. The point in the *Topics* is that *agnoia* is a privative term: infants, lacking capacity for knowledge, cannot be ignorant just as trees or stones cannot be blind.

(3) p. 168 ff. At 1146 b31 Aristotle introduces into the discussion of *akrasia* the distinction, met earlier in his treatment of *eudaimonia* and of *arete*, between a *hexis* (disposition), which is a kind of *dunamis* (power), and the 'exercise' of a *hexis*. It is a distinction which, in English as in Greek, is commonly nailed down by the use of pairs of semi-technical words or expressions: potential actual, dispositional occurrent, and, more dangerous because less technical and therefore more ambiguous, disposition or state and exercise or activity. In the treatment here by Aristotle of the knowledge which the incontinent person grasps or fails to grasp or lets slip Kenny finds 'three pairs of expressions'; *echein* (having) and *chrēsthai* (using) knowledge; *hexis* (disposition) and *energeia* (actualization or activation); *echein* (having) and *theōrein* (contemplating). *Energeia* is sometimes used in the sense of 'activity', a use which reflects Aristotle's view that *theōria* (contemplation) is an activity. But there are dispositional states the *energeiai* of which are passivities, e.g. brittleness and irritability. Now Kenny says: 'With these three pairs of expressions Aristotle is making a single contrast' (168). If this means, as it surely must, that the three pairs express an identical concept, he is surely right. It is, therefore, a surprise when he goes on to suggest that, when *theōrein* is used in contrast with

APPENDED NOTES

407

echein with reference to knowledge, what it means is 'to apply knowledge to a particular instance', and that 'to use a general principle is to apply it to a particular instance' (170). Moreover this interpretation of the 'single contrast' has a part to play in Kenny's valiant decoding of the concluding sentence of VII. 3: the universal ethical premise 'does operate, i.e. is applied to the less general case' (184).

Kenny next points out that prima facie anyone holding that to 'use' knowledge is to apply it would be reducing to incoherence the suggestion in 1147 a1 that the *akratēs* 'has' both premises but 'uses' only the universal major. How could the application of the major not involve the use of the minor (170)? The answer lies 'in the nature of the practical syllogism'. In the next stretch of his argument, which I need not report in detail, Kenny argues that the minor premise may be a composite proposition inclusive of a proposition which, while less general than the major premise, is universal: thus at 1147 a6–7 'such and such food is dry' represents part of the particular premise, and at 1131 a31–3 we have only one syllogism and 'everything sweet is pleasant' is part of the minor premise. Thus the major premise can be applied over a narrower but still general extension while its application to singular terms, myself or this comestible, is only potential. It is surprising how much miscellaneous information scholars are able to extract about the practical syllogism from Aristotelian treatises. Kenny notes that Aristotle never uses the expression and that he is liable to use the technical term for a premise (*protasis*) when he seems to be referring to the conclusions of a piece of practical thinking.

(4) pp. 176–7. In 1147 a26–8 *entha men* (in one type of case) is commonly understood as introducing a contrast between theoretical and practical reasoning: the taking together of the two premises issues respectively in the assertion (*phasis*) of a conclusion and the performance of an action. Of course, this is a difficult doctrine to interpret. But the same contrast is stated in similar language in *M.A.* 701 a7–15. In the article Kenny says that a reference to theory would be quite 'irrelevant', and takes *men* and *de* to 'mark the contrast between the general case and a specific instance': there is affirmation of the conclusion in all practical cases but action as well when the conclusion is affirmative. In the book, while endorsing the rejection of the common interpretation, he takes *poiētikai* as marking 'the usual contrast between production and action' (157 n. 2). He does not refer to *M.A.* 701 a7–15.

(5) pp. 181–2, 1147 a31–b3. Kenny interprets the crucial passage as describing the kind of *akrasia* which Aristotle later calls *astheneia* (weakness) (1150 b19–23). He takes the words in a34, *hē men oun legei pheugein touto*, to mean that the right conclusion is drawn from the combined premises although desire prevents the action which should follow. I shall not repeat, and do not withdraw, what I said against this interpretation on pp. 282–4. But I may not be right in supposing that I really disagree with Kenny. For the interpretation which I attribute to him seems to me to be contradicted when he says on the next page (183) that the conclusion (I must not indulge my desire) is 'drawn verbally but has no more effect on action than the babblings of a drunkard'. 'Verbally' must surely be deleted if it is part of what is claimed to be the description of a 'genuine conflict'. Drawing

a conclusion verbally should mean uttering the words expressive of the proposition which is the conclusion without apprehending the necessitation of the conclusion by the premisses. In the article Kenny clearly does not think that, in Aristotle's final description of incontinent behaviour, the drawing of the conclusion is merely verbal. For he says that 1147 b6–9, which refers to the ignorance (*agnoia*) of the *akratēs*, is 'clearly out of place' (183). The word 'verbally' and the reference to 'babbling' in the final sentence of the paragraph are thus at best inappropriate. But in the book Kenny withdraws the proposal to remove 1147 b6–9. He goes so far as to say that the text of *NE* VII, now seems to be perfectly in order, and the reorganisations proposed by scholars to be quite unnecessary' (163 n. 1). The footnote explains his change of view: 'I now realise that even in this case there is a minimum degree of *agnoia*: the conclusion, though drawn, is only half-had as a piece of knowledge'. Surely, if so, the verbal drawing of the conclusion really is babbling or 'stringing phrases' (1147 a21) and the incontinent act itself *is* something done in ignorance.

Aristotle does not speak of 'half-having' either dispositional or activated knowledge. Having distinguished dispositions from their activations he starts at 1147 a10 to consider different ways of having dispositional knowledge: he argues for 'the possibility of having knowledge in a sense and yet not having it', as when a man is asleep or drunk (perhaps in a drunken sleep) or mad. These are states which resemble each other, and resemble also the states of those under the influence of rage or lust, in being causally involved with physiological changes (a14–18). What is the difference between having and having-and-not-having 'a piece of knowledge'? It is the difference between knowledge which can be immediately activated and knowledge which cannot be made available without time and/or treatment. It is a matter of comparative accessibility, of the distance from activation. But at 1147 a18 Aristotle abruptly turns his attention to a fresh point: the utterance of words which might express knowledge is no proof of activated knowledge or perhaps even of progress towards it (a18–19). The levels of dispositional knowledge are now compared not merely in terms of distance from activation but by comparing the actual manifestations or ostensible manifestations of dispositional knowledge at different levels. Aristotle does not describe the marks or notes which may distinguish the more or less incompletely formed and the more or less precariously established *hexis* such as degrees of attention and concentration, sustained continuity heedfulness and clarity and, perhaps, as Kenny supposes, movement from the general to the particular or more specific. But the variety of Aristotle's examples, which he deploys with a minimum of analytic description, shows his awareness of the complexity, not to say obscurity and elusiveness, of the phenomena: someone who knows by rote, by heart but not by brain, a geometrical proof or a passage from Empedocles; someone who has just learnt or is still learning a lesson; the utterances of actors on the stage. Such, we must suppose, is the linguistic behaviour of men in an incontinent state (1147 a19–24).

'Only half-had as a piece of knowledge' (163 n. 1). The phrase I have quoted from Kenny is puzzling: 'half-*had*' suggests dispositional knowledge, but what is under consideration is the 'actual drawing' of a conclusion and this must be an occurent actualization of the disposition. Two pages earlier half-having is a point 'on a scale of increasing actualization of potentiality' (160–1). But, as I have pointed out in this note, there are different ways of constructing a scale of part-havings. One way is by comparing them in respect of the close or distant accessibility of an exercise: sobering up normally takes longer than waking up but not so long as getting cured of mental illness. Corresponding to any point in the scale of dispositions there will be an appropriate set of actualizations comparable with other sets as more or less coherent consequent or in focus. Kenny remarks that half-having, in Aristotle's view, is 'compatible with a pseudo-exercise of knowledge' (162). The babbler mouthing lines from Empedocles pseudo-exercises knowledge but genuinely exercises pseudo-knowledge. Such is the answer which Aristotle gives to his 'first and principal' question: in what sense of 'correct understanding' does a man have it when he acts incontinently 1145 b21–2)?

XIV. Pleasure (294–316)

pp. 312–15 'The pleasure completes (*teleioi*) the activity' (1174 b23–1175 a3)
The critical account in this chapter of the two treatments of pleasure, VII. 11–14 (A) and X. 1–5 (B), in the *Nicomachean Ethics* is incomplete and inconclusive. I cannot here attempt a radically new discussion. There are questions, and disagreements, as to both the interpretation of the Greek text and the critical appraisal of Aristotle's doctrine, on which the search for conclusive answers will go on. But I hope in this note to do something to modify the overt inconclusiveness of the three final paragraphs of the chapter. (1) In the first two of these paragraphs I failed, or omitted, to express a preference between the view of modern commentators who have claimed to interpret the received text of the passage (1174 b23–1175 a3), e.g. Stewart, Festugière, Gauthier, and those who would amend the text on the ground that, without emendation, Aristotle is inconsequent, e.g. Burnet and Hackforth. (2) In recent discussions Aristotle's treatment in B has usually been given better marks than his treatment in A. Those who make this judgement do not necessarily agree about the reasons for making it. Aristotle's doctrine that each kind of activity is made perfect by its own proper pleasure has been thought to be, if not a correct account, suggestive of a correct account. His use of a linguistic argument for the distinction between a movement or end-seeking process and an activity has been commended. The reader of my third paragraph (314–15) together with the earlier pages to which it refers (297–9) is not told clearly what conclusions I wish to suggest. I shall try, starting from what I would now say under (1), to be less tentative about (2).

(1) In the Preface to his *Contributions to the Textual Criticism of Aristotle's*

Nicomachean Ethics (1892) Bywater said that 'by adopting into the text the various excisions and transpositions which have been, or might be, suggested to correct structural anomalies, we run some risk of marring what we have without recovering anything better or more authentic' (p. vii). This general caution seems to me applicable to this passage. I agree now with Festugière's unwillingness to 'correct' the text. I agree also with Stewart (1892) and Hackforth (in the *Classical Review* 46 (1932)) and with Festugière (1936, 1960) that what Aristotle says in 1174 b23–27 is that the difference between the way in which on the one hand the pleasure and on the other the combination of the object perceived and the faculty of perception perfect (*teleioi*) the activity is analogous to the difference between the ways in which a man's health (as a *hexis*, i.e. a kind of potentiality) and his doctor are causes of his actual health.

Hackforth says that there are 'two fatal difficulties' in the way of attributing this comparison to Aristotle. The first (a) is that the combination of sense-perception and the object of perception is 'nowhere else spoken of by Aristotle as an efficient cause'. But is this surprising? In the *Metaphysics* the doctor, or his art, is an example of the 'moving' 'external' cause (of a cure) distinct from internal causes, *enuparchonta* (1070 b22–8, cf. *EN* 1174 b32). In the *Ethics* the standard example of an external moving cause is a purposive will (1110 a15, 1113 b17–19). Aristotle found it more difficult than we do to look for causes and causal laws without looking for 'ends'. But this is not to say that he did not assume physical moving causes to be at work when a man hears a noise or smells a smell. Hackforth makes the surprising remark that Aristotle 'is not thinking here of *aisthēton* and *aisthēsis* as producing an actual sensation: the sensation theory of the *De Anima* is beside the point . . .' But, of course, Aristotle is considering the actual perceptions and cogitations enjoyed by men.

Hackforth's second 'fatal difficulty' is, as we expect, that the analogy represents pleasure as a formal cause, a dispositional state (*hexis*), which is just what Aristotle goes on to say that it is not since it is rather a 'supervening end' (1174 b31–3). The apparent reversal is a real difficulty but it is faced and overcome by Festugière. Aristotle's answer to the question how pleasure 'completes' is reached in two stages: first by saying that it does so not as an external cause and secondly by correcting the answer suggested at the first stage to the question what kind of non-external completion it is. The fact that Aristotle's final statement is to be read as a correction of something said actually confirms, as Festugière suggests, the received text.

But what Aristotle is saying is not limpid: 'an end which supervenes as beauty comes with the years' (1174 b33). 'Is the enjoyment something different from the activity or the same?' I suggested that a better question might be what we mean when we say that we enjoy our best performances and happiest experiences. Dirlmeier's comments are suggestive (p. 582). He reminds us that a *telos* is both a completion and a goal ('schillert ja immer zwischen Vollendung und Ziel'); that to supervene (*epiginesthai*) is not quite the same as to accrue (*prosginesthai*) or to be placed along with (*prostithesthai*) (cf. 1172 b23f.)—'no, the pleasure is not added to the activity'. What enhances the 'good minute' and makes it perfect is not anything additional to the actualities which constitute its perfection: that it is an activity, whether perceptual or cognitive, of the best-conditioned subject in relation to the finest object, an activity at once, and in the highest degree, undistracted absorbed intense acute (1174 b18–23, 1175 a31–5). To gild refined gold or paint the lily is, the poet states, 'ridiculous excess'. We can interpret on these lines much of what Aristotle says in x. 4, 5: we can come near to eliminating a supervenient actual happening which 'follows' the activity (1175 a5). But it remains difficult, so far as I can see, to explain away what Aristotle says when he develops in x. 5 the doctrine that, corresponding to the many different kinds of activity, there are correspondingly different kinds of pleasure; when he says that an activity is promoted, made more intense, by its own proper pleasure (1175 a30–1, 36) but interfered with by alien pleasures. For this opposition seems to represent the enjoyment as an experience distinct, if inseparable, from the activity which it completes.

(2) I shall now mention three recent articles devoted to the analysis and appraisal of Aristotle's treatment of pleasure in the *Nicomachean Ethics*. They are (i) J. O. Urmson, 'Aristotle on Pleasure' in *Aristotle* (1967), a collection of essays edited by J. M. E. Moravcsik; (ii) G. E. L. Owen, 'Aristotelian Pleasures', *P.A.S.* 1971–2, reprinted as chapter 9 of *Articles on Aristotle* 2. *Ethics and Politics* (1977); (iii) J. C. B. Gosling, 'More Aristotelian Pleasures', *P.A.S.* 1973–4. Urmson's paper was listed in my bibliographical note (316), but I had completed the book when the article was published. I cannot attempt in this postscript to describe in detail or to criticize the contents of these important articles. But there may be those trying to understand and assess Aristotle's doctrine who will find helpful even a brief descriptive reference to philosophical work in progress on Aristotle's sympathetic rejection or qualified acceptance of apparently hedonistic contentions.

(i) Urmson praises the acuteness of Aristotle's account in v. 4, 5 of what makes an activity in the highest degree enjoyable, and endorses the account as 'surely at least in general correct' (pp. 323, 327). But Aristotle goes wrong in so far as he offers this analysis as 'an account of pleasure in general' (p. 327). For the analysis does not apply, although Aristotle thinks it does, to cases where what is enjoyed is not the perception or thought of interesting objects but, to take the prime example, feelings which we locate in our bodies produced in connection with touch and taste, the sphere of temperance (1118 a26–33, 1153 b33–5, 1154 a8–10). These pleasures are not to be construed as 'the enjoyment of activities of sense-perception' (pp. 325, 328). There are, indeed, important activities of looking and listening which are 'happily covered by Aristotle's account', and perhaps also unimportant enjoyments of tasting and 'sniffing at things' which are not just 'having a taste in one's mouth or an odour in one's nostrils' (p. 329). A vulgar error treats all pleasures as feelings. Aristotle's less damaging error is to treat all pleasures as enjoyed activities.

(ii) Commentators have tried to explain the presence in the *EN* of two separate treatments of the question what pleasure is; they have questioned their compatibility but have tended to 'play down' their differences. Owen argues that what the commentators have failed to see is that the two accounts neither compete nor co-operate, being 'answers to two quite different questions' (p. 136/93). The difference between the two questions is connected with the fact that 'pleasure' (and similarly *hēdonē*) is used in two different ways. It is used in one way when we say that bridge or bird-watching are among our pleasures, in the other way when we say that they give us pleasure (we enjoy them). Corresponding to the first use is the question what is common to the things men enjoy; corresponding to the second what it is to enjoy something. Owen examines the assumption which Aristotle seems to make that there must be some common feature in all the things which men seem to enjoy, noting that in x Aristotle admits incidentally that end-directed processes may be pleasant. When Aristotle turns to the question 'what enjoying is', the verb or verbs used in the vocabulary of pleasure 'take the stage'. At cardinal points, which Owen reviews, 'the argument turns directly on the behaviour of the verb' (p. 147/101). Owen argues persuasively that the question which, unconsciously at least, Aristotle had in view in x but not in vii is of a 'different type'. It is less clear how near, in Owen's view, Aristotle came to a correct formulation of this question and of the answer he was commending.

(iii) Gosling's paper examines the thesis of Owen's and defends his own views on the interpretation of the discussions in vii and x. He argues that 'the proposed contrast of problems' could be interpreted in different ways. Aristotle in x can be understood as saying that pleasure, as it is distinct from what it is taken in, is 'an added bonus', the activity and the pleasure being 'two occurrences or experienceable features of occurrences'. Gosling thinks that any view which can be so expressed would be regarded by 'those of a Rylean turn of mind' as a 'philosophical dead end'. He suggests that Owen's approval of x needs further justification and that 'the logic of the verb can be overvalued' (pp. 17–19). Gosling next discusses 'an alternative version' of the contrast between the two uses of 'pleasure', and its connection with Aristotle's apparent refusal at 1175 b30–5 to identify any pleasure with the activity from which it is inseparable (pp. 20–4). Gosling is seeking an interpretation of Aristotle's final formula (1174 b33) which can be construed as consistent with this refusal. Aristotle does not speak of the activity as the necessary and sufficient causal condition of the pleasure, and such a connection would not be close enough to account for the opinion that the activity *is* the pleasure. The pleasure is 'added to the activity but not, of course, to the perfect activity'. 'Perfect activity is what pleasure is' (pp. 27, 28). The activity 'has a further perfection as an activity of its kind, and it is this glory whose presence we note when we know that we enjoy something' (p. 27). The differences between vii and x do not mean either that vii is rejected or that Aristotle is 'involved in a different project'. Aristotle's principle and practice is to 'bring out the truth in well-received positions'. Hence his concessions to hedonism, which 'should be sweet to the hedonist's ears so long as he only looks at the score and does not face the music' (p. 34).

XV. Friendship and Self-Love (317–335)

pp. 322–323 'It would be interesting to know how the lecture audience received the remark that no adequate return can be made to those from whom we have learned philosophy. . .'

The last phrase should read 'those with whom one has studied philosophy'. At the end of her article, 'Plato and Aristotle on Friendship' (*Mind*, 1977), Julia Annas refers to this question: commentators generally leave Aristotle's remark (1164 b2–6) 'in embarrassed silence' (p. 554). I had noticed the silence, Dirlmeier being an exception. Annas suggests: 'But the audience would surely hear this not as a vain puff on Aristotle's part but as a tribute to his own philosophy teacher, to whom his work on friendship owed so much, Plato.' I was not suggesting any 'vain puff on Aristotle's part'. Rather the passage suggested the sort of thing a lecturer might try out in a dead pan way on an audience to see if they were listening. But Annas may well be right, in view of her argument for Aristotle's indebtedness to the *Lysis*, about Aristotle's intention in this 'notorious little passage'.

In the article it is argued that Aristotle 'regards it as simply a fact that altruism is possible': 'people can in fact come to like others and regard their interests as they do their own' (p. 543). When Aristotle says that the good man's friend is 'another self' (1166 a30–2) he is not importing 'absurdities about thinking of his pains as if they were my pains; what is meant in the context is clearly regarding his *desires*, and their fulfilment, as I do my desires and their fulfilment—that is, attaching as much importance to them, making as great efforts to fulfil them, and so on' (p. 542). This direct interest in others is 'explained as derivative' from the good man's relation to himself 'but it is not explained away' (p. 542). More non-committal is the treatment later in the article (pp. 548, 550–1) of Aristotle's argumentation in IX. 9, which starts from 'the extremely counter-Cartesian statement that we can contemplate the activities of others better than our own' (1169 b33–5). It is not clear how Annas understands this certainly extreme statement or whether she encourages us to hope to salvage from 'deep waters in Aristotelian psychology' an interpretation which makes sense in spite of being counter-Cartesian.

'The course on friendship is self-contained and gives the impression of having been originally a separate lecture course' (p. 532). At the end of the article Annas argues that, on an important matter, the moral psychology of vice, Aristotle's treatment of *philia* 'fails to fit into the *Ethics*' (pp. 553–4). A similar comment seems appropriate to what is said in IX. 9 about 'living together and sharing in discussion and thought' (1170 b10–12). The insistence on the notion of the extension of self-awareness seems inconsistent with the claim in X. 7 that the self-sufficiency (*autarkeia*) of the philosopher elevates his activity above all others; the greater his wisdom the less his need for collaborators. The tentativeness of the admission that perhaps he does better if he has them ignores the argument for the extension of self-awareness (1177 a32–b1).

p. 332 '. . . the reasoning in the second part of ix 9 . . .'
My discussion of Aristotle's chapter took two pages. I was unwilling to use
further space in quoting or restating the analysis in the footnote of Ross of the
five prosyllogisms, one lemma and six arguments deployed in 1170 a14–b19. I
hoped that readers would agree that I had concentrated on 'the weak link'.

A reviewer attributes to me an unargued refusal to admit that Aristotle's claim
that a good man 'is related to his friend as to himself' is 'true in the sense that the
argument requires'. At this point the reviewer is quoting words which I had used
eight pages earlier when discussing ix. 4 (324) instead of the more determinate
wording when discussing ix. 9 (332). He goes on to say that my 'refusal' to
'examine the argument as a whole' makes it impossible for me to tell 'what the
required sense' is. For me (he says) it is that in which one man might feel another's
toothache', whereas Aristotle, in a passage which I 'ignore', 'makes it plain that
he thinks the sense required is that in which two men can think the same thought'.
But the reviewer stops short of saying what that sense is in Aristotle's opinion or
in his own. And in fact I quote fully the passage I am alleged to ignore (332): 'He
needs, therefore, to be conscious of the existence of his friend as well, and this
will be realized in their living together and sharing in discussion and thought; for
this is what living together would seem to mean in the case of man, and not, as in
the case of cattle, feeding in the same place' (1170 b10–14). The reviewer concludes that I do not 'come to grips with Aristotle's position at all'. For himself he
seems to claim a viewpoint from which he can locate thought-sharing at 'the
heart of the *Ethics*'.

On rereading these pages I regret not having been able to say more on Aristotle's
after all bold and interesting assertion that we can observe the thoughts and
actions of our neighbours or good friends or fellow-students as well as we can our
own. The reviewer may be right in a way about thought-sharing. But what is the
sense in which 'two men can think the same thought'? If *A* tells *B* that he (*A*) is
rehearsing a Pythagorean proof *B* can be sure that he thinks *A*'s thought because
both are familiar with the mathematical necessitations. *B* may be equally free from
doubt that *A* is feeling a pain, especially if *A* tells him so. But *B*'s assurance does
not, therefore, resemble either his assurance about his (*B*'s) own pain or his
assurance about *A*'s thought. If anyone feels, after reading what Aristotle says, and
says well, on the importance of 'friendship', that he needs to come to earth again
he may be referred to the judicious assessments of Ross (pp. 230–2) and Allan (p.
138). We should not ignore signs of caution in Aristotle's references to altruism:
paraplēsiōs (almost so) on the friend as 'another self' (1170 b8); *isōs* (perhaps) on
the contribution of 'collaborators' to the happiness of the philosopher (1177 a34).

XVI. Theoretical Activity and the Nature of Reason (336–357)

pp. 340–2   Aristotelian *theōria* and religion
This paragraph is too brief and allusive, and would be misleading if it suggested

an intention to support conclusions about Aristotle's philosophical development or about his significance for the study of Greek religion and of the philosophy of religion. These topics are tangential to the scope of this book. My purpose in the present note is to amplify what I said in the paragraph about Aristotle's concern with the phenomena of religion and my references to the evidence which has been found in the 'fragments' of Aristotle's non-surviving works.

The fragments were collected by Valentine Rose (Teubner, 1886) and have been added to by the labours of later scholars. They embrace references, as well as verbatim quotations, in ancient writers. In the interpretation of the evidence there is often room for differences of opinion. For the student of the *Ethics* R. Walzer's volume of selections (1934), mainly from the *Eudemus*, the *Protrepticus*, and the *De Philosophia*, is very helpful. A larger selection is translated by Ross in vol. XII (the last) of the Oxford Aristotle (1952).

Chapter VI (pp. 124–66) of Jaeger's *Aristoteles* (1923; translated 1934, second edition 1948, paperback 1962) has the title 'The Manifesto *On Philosophy*' and is a reconstruction of the *De Philosophia* and a discussion of its significance in Aristotles philosophical development and in the history of philosophy. Towards the end of the chapter (p. 161) Jaeger quotes the passage which I quoted at the top of p. 341, Aristotle's answer to the question about the origin 'in men' of the notion (*ennoia*) of gods. I ought to have noticed the surely questionable comment by Jaeger which immediately follows the quotation: 'This derivation is not to be understood historically; it does not refer to the men of primitive times; it is a pregnant juxtaposition of the two great wonders that all the enlightenment of the enlightened cannot explain, the residue that the system of rationalistic physics cannot reduce' (p. 161). Aristotle's central interest, on this interpretation, is not in the question what phenomena put into men's heads the idea that there are gods but what are the phenomena which support the idea, and his answer is a formula which incapsulates 'simply the attitude of Plato's circle towards the universe'. Substitute Stoic duties for mantic dreams and we should be still closer to Kant's celebrated dictum on the starry heavens above and the moral law within. Jaeger's interpretation of the fragment needs a more fully argued defence than he offers by his reference to the *Laws* (966 d). The interpretation helps him to draw a sharp contrast between Aristotle's philosophy when he wrote the *De Philosophia* (expressed also, as Jaeger argues, in the *Eudemian Ethics*) and 'his complete break with the Platonizing view' in his later essays on *Sleep* and on *Divination in Dreams*: 'completely non-ethical and purely scientific—this new and completely unmystical attitude' (p. 333).

There is a further reason for doubting whether the Aristotelian fragment on prophetic dreams gives significant support to Jaeger's general view of Aristotle's philosophical development. This is the lack of evidence for the suggestion that, on the significance of dreams, Plato held a mystical and Aristotle an unmystical, in the sense of rationalistic, view. I referred, in the first footnote on p. 341, to passages in the *Republic* and the *Timaeus*. Comparison with Aristotle's mature essays does not support a sharp contrast between the views of the two philosophers.

Both are interested primarily in physical or physiological causes and explanations; according to the *Timaeus*, dreams originating in the rational soul appear as distorted reflections, requiring expert interpretation, on the smooth surface of the liver; neither philosopher denies that some dreams may be 'heaven-sent'; neither claims that they are sent to the best and wisest recipients. Plato's account is given in an artful idiom and with the framework of a myth. Aristotle's remarks are severely argumentative: other animals too have dreams; the resemblance between a dream and a future event may be coincidental; some dreams may be related to future apparently precognized events as causes to effects; lack of intelligence in the recipient might facilitate paranormal communications by leaving comparatively vacant access. Dodds doubts whether, on dreams, modern science has 'advanced very far beyond Aristotle' (p. 120). Taylor, in his commentary on the *Timaeus*, concludes that the significance which Plato ascribed to dreams 'is mainly what would be admitted by physicians and psychiatrists of our own time' (p. 515).

'Purely scientific . . . and completely unmystical'. When he contrasts the later Aristotle's dedication to empirical inquiries and 'the organization of research' with his 'youthful Platonic faith' Jaeger does not mean to imply that religious conviction and emotion ceased to be manifested in Aristotle's philosophy. It took a different form. 'According to Plato the spiritualization of man's whole life could be attained only by turning away from appearances to the archetype; according to Aristotle it is in the end identical with the specialization of knowledge as here understood' (p. 340). Identical? Jaeger's explanation is at least eloquent: '. . . every new discovery of a form . . . that of the lowest insect—or the tiniest part of human art or speech is a step onward in the task of making mind supreme over matter and thus giving meaning to reality' (p. 341). A recent book about Aristotle by A.-H. Chroust devotes a chapter to his 'religious convictions'. The writer starts by pointing out that 'scholars, often motivated by their own religious commitments, have come up with a great variety of widely conflicting suggestions and interpretations with regard to the religious content of the *Corpus Aristotelicum*. These suggestions range all the way from an allegedly complete "religious indifferentism" on the part of Aristotle to his fervent affirmation as well as deeply felt awareness of certain fundamental religious problems faced by all thoughtful people' (*Aristotle* i, ch. XVI, 1973). This being so, it might seem that, on the question whether religious convictions and emotions have a place in the best human life as Aristotle conceives it, the first, if not the only, thing to say is that we do not know. Yet the writer proceeds at once to assert that 'much of his philosophy was inspired and determined by his innermost religious convictions' (pp. 221–2). In a letter written in old age Aristotle is reported as saying that, in his loneliness and isolation, he has become more and more a lover of myths, *philomuthoteros* (fr. 668). We are to understand by 'mythical' not 'fictitious' or 'irrational' but rather 'metarational', and to remind ourselves of a passage in the *Metaphysics* (982 b17). 'A man who is puzzled and wonders thinks himself ignorant. Hence even the lover of myths is in a sense a lover of wisdom, for the myth is made up of wonders' (p. 402). Aristotle was 'profoundly religious'. It may be so. Chroust strangely says that Aristotle's religious life was 'hidden not only from the world at large, but seemingly also from his friends and more intimate associates'. Surely, then, his warning against subjectivity is applicable to his own claim to have detected this secret.

There is a good treatment of the *De Philosophia* in the second chapter of D. J. Allan's *The Philosophy of Aristotle* (pp. 17–22). In Gilbert Murray's *Five Stages of Greek Religion* (1925) we can appreciate concise comments, from an agnostic angle, on the impact of Plato and Aristotle on religion. 'The successors of Aristotle produced rather a school of progress in science, those of Plato a school of refined scepticism. The religious side of Plato's thought was not revealed in its full power till the time of Plotinus in the third century A.D.; that of Aristotle, one might say without undue paradox, not till its exposition by Aquinas in the thirteenth' (p. 17). Aristotle's school 'took the existing world and tried to understand it instead of inventing some intense ecstatic doctrine which should transform it or reduce it to nothingness'. Its members 'instead of passionately saving souls diligently pursued knowledge and produced . . . scientific results which put all their rivals into the shade' (p. 145). Murray discusses the attractions of 'the Porch and the Garden' for 'thoughtful men' and the practical influence on kings and governors of these philosophies. 'Aristotle was not lacking in religious insight and imagination, as he certainly was not without profound influence on the future history of religion . . . If he had not written his other books he might well be famous now as a great religious teacher . . .' (p. 143).

p. 345 (bottom)   '. . . the best thing in us (1177 a13 . . . the excellence of reason is a thing apart (1178 a22) . . .?
I was trying in this chapter to do two things. The first was to make clear that the main doctrine which it discusses, that theoretical knowledge, while not the only constituent, is far the most desirable constituent of human well-being, is one which must seem to most of us intrinsically implausible, especially when presented by Aristotle as a deduction from his own view concerning the special status of reason in man's soul and from his own cosmology and theology, which for us is a museum piece. I may have expressed this negative opinion rather too strongly when I said that the doctrine of separable reason, as we find it in the *De Anima* and the *Ethics*, 'presents itself as a puzzle and perhaps even as a scandal' and confronts us with a 'dualism and discontinuity' which is 'hard to understand' (346).

But I qualified my endorsement of this line of criticism. For my second aim was to suggest that the criticism, unless presented with circumspection, would be less than fair and objective. I, therefore, explored tentatively a number of ways in which its too sharp edge could be filed down.

(a) Aristotle's account of the theoretical intellect did not confine it to metaphysics but was extended to include mathematics and what Aristotle called 'physics'. Thus his account of happiness is not tightly tied to his opinions about the nature and movements of the heavenly bodies (338).

(b) Some have suggested that Aristotle's concept of *theōria* could be fitted, beyond theory, to artistic and aesthetic activity, to religion and even to morality. But the evidence for such applications by Aristotle is hard to find (340–2).

(c) Aristotle claims that philosophy 'offers pleasures marvellous for their purity (*kathareiotēs*) and enduringness (*bebaiotēs*)' (1177 a25–6). This and other arguments deployed by Aristotle are no less applicable to any life which requires and permits continuous intellectual or artistic activity.

(d) Confronted in *EN* x (1178 a19–23) with the notion that *nous* (reason) is 'a thing apart' from 'our composite nature', and not the form of any bodily matter, it is reasonable that commentators should turn for further explanation to the similarly formulated doctrine in the *De Anima* and particularly to the treat-. ment of *nous* in *Γ* 4 and to the remarks on active and passive *nous* in *Γ* 5. But my account of what I found raises more questions than it answers (348–55). The doctrine is frequently obscure, sometimes unconvincing and can be fitted only very loosely to what is said in the *Ethics*. The consistency of the two works on the matter is open to question. The *EN* seems to imply that, in *theōria*, the element of the soul which is active is of a different kind from the soul involved in other human activities. This echoes phrases earlier in the *De Anima*: 'a different kind of soul, differing as what is eternal from what is perishable and alone capable of existence in isolation' (413 b24–7). But I did not see how to reconcile this concept with what is said about passive reason (*nous pathētikos*) in *Γ* 5. I note that Cooper, with whose 'intellectualist' interpretation of *EN* x in the last section of his recent book I cannot wholly agree, admits the difficulty: 'the question is further complicated by the theory of the *nous pathētikos* which seems to connect even some intuitive thinking with the body' (p. 176).

I shall now try to carry a little further my discussion of the status of theoretical reason in Aristotle's *Ethics*; not by dwelling further on the subtle profundities of the *De Anima*, but by being more explicit about the difficulties raised by Aristotle's insistence in the *Ethics* that *eudaimonia* has a primary and a secondary form (1178 a9–10). What are the difficulties? Did Aristotle see them? If he did, and if they are as radical as has been thought, how could he not try to do more than he did to overcome or diminish them?

Ackrill has given helpfully definite answers to these questions in the concluding pages (pp. 20–3) of his British Academy Lecture, 'Aristotle on *Eudaimonia*' (1975). Aristotle says that *theoria* and virtuous action are independently, but not equally, valuable forms of activity. The question how they should be combined in 'the best possible human life' is 'crucial for his project in the *Ethics*' (p. 21). Ackrill says that Aristotle signally fails even to attempt an answer. For 'the question is incapable of even an outline answer that Aristotle could accept'. What is the ground for asserting this incapacity? Ackrill's answer is 'that *theoria* is the incommensurably more valuable activity' (p. 21). The weight of this argument is carried by 'incommensurable'. In the *EN* the word is used in its mathematical sense of 'the diagonal and side' of a square, $\sqrt{2}/1$ (1112 a21–3). The mathematical sense seems inappropriate for Aristotle in an ethical context if only because it is mathematical. Moreover to deny commensurability is not to deny quantitative comparability: $\sqrt{2}$ is greater than 1 and less than 2, greater than 4/3 and less than 3/2. More helpful and relevant is Aristotle's use of 'commensurate' with reference to the use of money as a medium of exchange: 'in truth it is impossible that things so different should become commensurate (*summetra*), but with reference to need (*chreia*) they may become so sufficiently' (1133 b18–20). Can we attribute to Aristotle the suggestion that, while *theōria* and virtuous action are indeed very different, yet with reference to the need and desire of men for *eudaimonia* they become sufficiently comparable? To say this would be to allow a 'trading relation'. Ackrill substitutes 'incomparably more important' for 'incommensurably more valuable', but reaffirms his statement of the issue. 'But how can there be a trading relation between the divine and the merely human? Aristotle's theology and anthropology make it inevitable that his answer to the question about *eudaimonia* should be broken-backed' (p. 22). 'But, if the nature of man is thus unintelligible, the best life for man must remain incapable of clear specification even in principle' (p. 22).

The two sentences just quoted, and others in the same paragraph, are not wholly clear and convincing. Aristotle may have said, and not only when speaking of *theōria*, that a man could be godlike, but not that he was or could become a god. As regard *theōria*, did the questions raised about divine self-contemplation in the *Magna Moralia* (B 15) never trouble Aristotle? As to the anthropology of the *De Anima*, was his own dedication to philosophy made irrational by the fact that, even after the explanations in *Γ* 4 and 5, the nature of man 'remains obscure and mysterious' (p. 22). 'Incapable of clear specification even in principle'; either 'clear' or 'even in principle' should be omitted since we do not know whether the denial of 'clear specifiability in principle' is to be understood as compatible with 'specifiability in principle'; presumably not.

The alleged impossibility of 'trading between *theōria* and virtuous action' should be considered in the context of Aristotle's general account of decision-making in man's thoughtful pursuit of *eudaimonia*. These two potentially rival trades are not, presumably, to be viewed as interests normally incompatible; perhaps rather they are mutually helpful and promotive. But this is hardly relevant since choices do have to be made between Aristotle's primary and secondary kinds of well-doing. But is it right to pick out such choices as alone having grounds 'incapable of clear specification'? Are there no choices within the closed boundaries of 'theory' or of 'practice' the grounds of which are comparably unclear? Objective A, perhaps, has greater intrinsic and derivative desirability than B, but the probability of success in achieving A is less. On what principle can we decide what sorts of chances to take? When is it rational to seek a reason in determining priorities or resolving a conflict of values? Clark suggests in one place that, when ideals conflict, we decide between them on the basis either of 'immediate impulse' or of 'some over-riding value', a value which is 'the reasonable man's reason for his ordering of ends' (pp. 148–9). But what of a decision reached after careful comparison and weighing of pros and cons? 'It is difficult sometimes to determine what should be chosen at what cost, and what should be endured in return for what gain' (1110 a29–30). Difficult indeed; but Aristotle's words suggest neither some 'over-riding value', which would threaten an indefinite regress, nor leaving the determination to 'immediate impulse'. The determination is agonizing as well as difficult when the course which seems best involves the certain or probable death of the agent. The 'over-riding value' can only be the pattern of life which seems best. But this value will not answer, since the solution would be circular, the question on what principle priorities are to be determined. For the pattern is itself built up by character-forming decisions between conflicting desirables.

In the *De Partibus Animalium* (I. 5) Aristotle sets out the pros and cons, the rival attractions, in a choice between 'the philosophy which contemplates the things that are divine' (of which we have only fleeting glimpses) and the study of plants and animals, the things that perish (about which anyone who takes trouble can learn much). Each has its own attraction (*charis*): 'detail and certitude, nearness and affinity to us, balance somewhat the loftier interest' (644 b22–645 a4). Aristotle's appraisal seems to be uninhibited and uncomplicated by mysteries concerning divine self-contemplation and the efficacy of a separable soul in man. Our sense-faculties and bodily organs are directly involved in the study of plants and animals; in astronomy theology and first philosophy much less. 'How can there be a trading relation between the divine and the merely human?' Aristotle seems to be looking quite calmly at a question which Ackrill thinks he ought to find unanswerable.

In the market-place, armed with money, we compare and measure incommensurables by walking round and exposing ourselves to our awareness of our needs and desires. Our decisions may, but need not, be impulsive. In the life-determining and death-determining decisions which shape their lives men weigh against each other the advantages and disadvantages of possible actions and inactions. Ackrill agrees that 'compromises are made and . . . nobody need feel guilty' (p. 23). Yet he suspects Aristotle of 'giving absolute priority to *theōria*', of entertaining the notion that 'one should do anything however seemingly monstrous if doing it has the slightest tendency to promote *theōria*' (p. 22). Surely, if this had been said to Aristotle, his answer could only have been the one which he gave to 'those who say that the victim on the rack or the man who falls into great misfortunes is happy if he is good'; he would have agreed that those who say such a thing 'are, whether they mean it or not, talking nonsense' (1153 b19–21).

p. 357, ll. 1–3   '. . . criticisms . . . do not touch the foundations of Aristotle's doctrine'

What did I mean by this? It might be retorted that what, following other critics of Aristotle, I had been trying to do in this chapter was to remove, and not merely to touch, the foundations. I hope that in the preceding note I have spoken, if tentatively, for the defence of Aristotle not the prosecution. But I think that there is more to be said for Book x than I have tried to say. The book states, perhaps extravagantly, the case for the 'theoretic life'. It was not an easy case to state. 'The career of the savant', as Stewart drily remarks, was 'his own career' (ii. 443). It is easy to think of words which disapprove more than they applaud: 'intellectualist', 'élitist', 'inegalitarian', or even (absurdly) 'undemocratic'. But there is a case for the theoretic life. And, on the whole, Aristotle is able to state it in terms which to readers, or to some readers, seem more realistic than they are offensive. I shall conclude by pointing out some possibilities of misunderstanding and distorting crucial sentences in x.

'For man . . . the life (bios) according to reason (kata noun) is best, since reason more than anything else is man (anthrōpos). This life, therefore, is also the happiest (eudaimonestatos). But in a secondary degree (deuterōs) the life in accordance with the other virtue (kata tēn allēn aretēn) is happy; for the activities in accordance with this (kata tautēn) befit our estate (anthrōpikai)' (1178 a6–10). The philosopher, 'so far as he is a man (anthrōpos) and lives with a number of people', chooses action 'in accordance with virtue' (kat'aretēn) and will need many aids to living a human life—pros to anthrōpeuesthai (1178 b5–7).

There is, of course, an element of verbal paradox in the stance which Aristotle here takes: man is divine reason and his life is that of embodied rational soul; man is more than man but man for all that. There is no suggestion that for any man the possession of primary excellence and happiness can make secondary excellence and happiness unimportant. It is unfortunate that secondary happiness usually appears in the commentators under the disguise of chilling phrases like 'the life of morally good action'. So Joachim. But on the same page he at least has an ampler expression for the excellent state of man as a suntheton (composite being): 'the best states of his feeling and desiring self in unison with the best state of his reason so far as that controls action' (p. 187).

I do not think that, in the passages I have quoted, Aristotle fails to make his meaning clear to readers of the Ethics. But there are traps in the Greek words for the unwary and for the over-ingenious. Aretē, nous, eudaimonia have known complexities. As to bios and bioi we have to watch the slide from the lives of the philosopher and the non-philosopher as individuals to the lives which a man lives as a philosopher and as a citizen. And even deuterōs (in a secondary degree) and kata (in accordance with) may lead a commentator astray. I refer to the note in Gauthier–Jolif on deuterōs (1178 a9) and to Cooper's interpretation of kata.

The note in Gauthier–Jolif insists that Aristotle is not distinguishing two 'separable' kinds of happiness: they are conjoined in one man who is both philosophical and political (1178 b5–7). But Aristotle does not deny that a non-philosopher may possess and practice 'the other virtue'. More startling is the interpretation of deuterōs which follows: 'without doubt' the word is to be understood in terms of homonymy and 'focal' meaning; the sense in which the good citizen is eudaimōn is related to the sense in which the philosopher is eudaimōn as the sense in which a 'healthy' diet is related to a 'healthy' man. It follows, as these commentators point out, that the good citizen-soldier can be said to be eudaimōn in a sense if, but only if, his good activities protect some philosopher and thus *produce eudaimonia* for somebody. This, as it seems to me, must be the meaning of the note on 1178 a9 (pp. 891–2). The note is difficult to follow because it incapsulates earlier expositions and discussions by these commentators of Aristotle's doctrine on *eudaimonia* in VI and X. We are properly referred to these earlier passages (pp. 542–7, 560–78, 860–6); at least thirty massive pages in all.

They revolve round the fact that Aristotle seems to say of virtuous actions both that they are means to a final end and that they have 'the character of absolute moral values' (p. 575). The ideal 'mixed life' involves both contemplation as end and virtuous activity as means (p. 863). Every reader is aware of this tension. I was trying to relax it when I distinguished 'comprehensive plans' from 'paramount objects'. Sometimes Gauthier–Jolif speak as if the tension were an inconsistency which Aristotle failed to see or failed to face: il n'a pas eu conscience' (p. 575). I am not here resuming this discussion.

What I am saying is something simpler. Aristotle sometimes writes quite clearly and in lapidary Greek. Here (especially 1178 a4–14, b5–7) he says something we can understand: most of all to be felicitated are philosophers (cf. 1101 b23–25); they are on the heights; while they are a minority, the life they choose accords with man's nature; in the second place as candidates for felicitation come good citizens and family men (a life from which philosophers, if human, are not excluded), practising the virtues, probably seeking public offices, escaping disasters, having the benefit of all the aids (*chorēgia*), such as health and money and friends, which a man needs if he is to act and fare well. We can disagree, but we can hardly fail to understand. If so, we are not bound to submit the 'second place' (*deuterōs*) to Procrustean treatment as the 'vocabulary of homonymy' (p. 892); nor can we digest the news that the word 'ought' (*dein*) in the *Ethics* occurs 'about 170 times' in 'a sense incontestably moral' and only about 100 times ('une centaine') with a non-moral significance (p. 569). We might, if we followed these leads, be passing from daylight into a more crepuscular region.

Aristotle says that the philosopher, as a man among men, 'chooses actions in accordance with virtue', *kat' aretēn* (1178 b5–7). Cooper finds a way of avoiding the conclusion that Aristotle regards 'secondary happiness' as part of his philosopher's human happiness. 'He says only that the theorizer may *perform* various virtuous actions—that in so far as he remains involved with other people he may conform his conduct to the requirements of the virtues. But there is a large difference between this and being a virtuous person' (p. 164). A philosopher might think it prudent to do just or courageous acts but 'they would not be the acts of a just or courageous person' (p. 165). But then, as Aristotle has said in II, they would not be virtuous acts (1105 a23–33). Has Cooper sufficiently considered this passage and others, including the other three occurrences of *kata* in the passages I have quoted? Even if Cooper's interpretation were possible, we should be loth to accept it if the natural and generally accepted interpretation were possible, as it plainly is.

Before we attribute to Aristotle, on the evidence of his words, opinions which we find repugnant we have to be sure that we know what his words mean.

Before we attribute to him edifying opinions with which we should like to agree we must be able to point to the sentences in which such alleged opinions are stated. In this note I have quoted with agreement words of two commentators, Stewart and Joachim. But, in their treatments of Book X as a whole, both seem to me to give occasion for criticism in this second way.

In his note on 1178 a10 Stewart points out that the 'theoretic life' is closed to 'the bulk of mankind', 'all but a very few'. Most citizens come no nearer to the happier life than by the contributions they make, brilliant or obscure, to 'the *eudaimonia* of a city in which savants are produced and held in honour'. But in a long note a few pages earlier (on 1177 a27) we find, alongside this one, another interpretation: Aristotle 'does not distinguish two lives, but rather two points of view'; the theoretic life is not here 'a separate career' but 'the form of the political life', the form without matter of 'man's life as a whole'. 'But these two ways of looking at the theoretic life scarcely present themselves to him as two'. Stewart admits that the result is 'a confusion of expression'. So indeed it is. But perhaps the confusion arises through reading into Aristotle's text a meaning that is not there.

In Joachim's commentary we find a similar suppression of the 'two lives', unqualified by Stewart's admission of the philosopher's 'separate career'.

The ideal for all men, therefore, is the life of morally good action; but all men, in so far as there is in them an element of the divine, are capable of entering into and sharing a higher and more perfect felicity, the life of God. The answer to the question 'What *energeia kat' aretēn* constitutes *eudaimonia*?' is, therefore, '*theoria*—the life in which the *aretē* of *nous* is manifested' (pp. 287–8).

Joachim's next sentence tells us that 'the style of this portion of the *Nicomachean Ethics* is beautifully clear and transparent, and it did not seem necessary to follow the movements of Aristotle's thought in detail' (p. 288). But surely it was necessary.

Stewart and Joachim belong to an older tradition. But it is interesting to find in the Commentary of Dirlmeier a tribute to the lasting worth of the speculations to which Stewart is prompted by *EN* X. 7 and 8: 'wertvoll noch immer' (still valuable) Stewart ii. 443–5, 451. Dirlmeier finds in Stewart a denial, with which he agrees, of an 'essential chasm' ('eine wesenhafte Kluft') between the activities of theoretical wisdom (*sophia*) and those of practical wisdom (*phronēsis*) (p. 593). 'The philosopher too realizes ethical virtue, but it is given to him to approach nearer to God than other worthy persons can'. It is, perhaps, the persistence of this desire to find a bridge across a seeming chasm in Aristotle's moral philosophy which has provoked Ackrill's insistence that the chasm is plainly insurmountable.

We now have in Clark's book a renewed attempt to vindicate the unity of Aristotle's thought in the *Ethics*, the coherence of his complex concept of man. 'It is the Aristotelian saint who is most especially human, in that it is his life which gives sense to human structure and society—and also, as I shall argue, to the world' (p. 27). 'Civil and theoretic good meet in this, that both are a service to the divine in man' (p. xi). The generality of these claims makes it difficult to dissent. But, as with Joachim, we expect to hear something said about the way in

APPENDED NOTES

which the divine in man is present in the 'civil good'. More vulnerable is the following: 'We practice virtue, we concern ourselves with what is worthwhile, in order to clear the way to the knowledge of the god, and having reached that end we act correctly in the world' (p. 197). Can theology suggest or authenticate practical decisions other than perhaps a decision to study or not to study theology? The student of the *Ethics* recalls the coldly sober passage which concludes Aristotle's attack on the Platonic Good. 'Perhaps, however, someone might think it well to have knowledge of it with a view to the goods which *are* attainable and achievable; for having this as a sort of pattern we shall know better the goods that are good for us, and if we know them shall attain them. This argument has some plausibility, but seems to clash with the procedure of the sciences' (1096 b35–1097 a4).

'To understand a philosophy is to understand a man . . . not to be confronted by any sort of distinguishable object, but rather to inform, reform oneself' (p. 11); '. . . philosophy is essentially a way of life, and hears the voice of the god' (p. 13). These sentences from Clark's Introduction tell us something important about the study of a great philosopher and about *theōria*. They help me to understand, to endorse and to qualify, what was in my mind when I said that criticisms of *theōria* 'do not touch the foundations of Aristotle's doctrine' (357). For the doctrine is religious or has religious overtones. I thought this then (340–42). I would suggest it more firmly now and with fewer restrictive qualifications. I would not now suggest that, in Aristotle's view and in his experience, religious emotion was exclusively 'integrated with the intellectual study of divine objects' (340) and not 'associated with non-scientific forms of experience' (341). I did not then think, as I do now, that there is a place for 'heroic virtue' in Aristotle's anthropology; philosophers are not alone in hearing 'the voice of the god'. It is true that religious emotion, like other emotions, is not a mere sensation or bodily feeling. It is defined and dignified by its own propositions and concepts. But philosophers of religion can admit, and can recognize that religious men can admit, that conceptual formulations, so far as they express determinate positive doctrines, are inadequate and analogical. We cannot assume that, if Aristotle had come to see a need to reconstruct his cosmological theology and the anthropology of the *De Anima*, the consequences for his view of the best life for men and for his religious attitudes would necessarily have been radical. Dirlmeier, commenting on 1177 b33 ('we should make ourselves immortal so far as we can'), recalls that Aristotle near the end of his life is said to have been threatened with prosecution for impiety, the charge being that he celebrated the heroic death of Hermias by giving him honours due only to one who was a hero and immortal. Doubtless the charge ('absurd' Ross, 'preposterous' Allan, 'trumped up' Lloyd) was an excuse for a politically motivated attack. (E. Dérenne, *Les Procès d'impiété intentés aux philosophes à Athènes au Vième et au IVième siècle* (1930).) But the report that Aristotle took the trouble to compose the defence which he could have offered against the reproach (*Vorwurf*) of impiety (*asebeia*) should not surprise any student of the *Nicomachean Ethics*.

Postscript to the Appended Notes

Dr. Kenny's Book (Anthony Kenny, *The Aristotelian Ethics* (1978), A study of the relationship between the *Eudemian and Nicomachean Ethics* of Aristotle) is 'an attempt to solve a long-standing problem of Aristotelian scholarship on the basis of historical and philosophical arguments and a statistical study of features of style' (Preface, 1st sentence). The problem arises from the fact that the two treatises have three of their Books in common: *EE* IV–VI and *NE* V–VII are identical. In order to avoid seeming to take sides on the question which treatise has the stronger claim to the common books Kenny uses '*NE*' and '*EE*' for the respective undisputed books and '*AE*' (*Aristotelian Ethics*) for the three disputed books. His conclusion, as he states it at the end of chapter 6 on the basis of 'external evidence' and 'statistical stylistics', is (1) that there is 'close resemblance between the *AE* and the *EE* and a much more distant relationship between *AE* and *NE*'; (2) that it is 'in the highest degree improbable' that the 'over-all picture ... could be seriously disturbed by further stylistic investigation, however sophisticated'; (3) that the 'most plausible and economical explanation of this result is that the *AE*, just as they now stand, belonged originally to the *Eudemian Ethics*' (pp. 159–60). The two chapters which follow contain philosophical arguments and deal respectively with the topics wisdom (*phronēsis*) and happiness (*eudaimonia*) in the *AE*. The final chapter 9 deals generally with 'the dating of the Aristotelian treatises'. The conclusions reached at the end of chapter 6 are re-stated in chapter 9 in a more surgical idiom: the books of *AE* should be 'restored ... to their rightful place as part of *EE*' (p. 223), 'replaced in the framework of *EE*' where they 'fit very much better'. Presumably we should cease to think of them as the central books of the *Nicomachean Ethics*. But Kenny remarks that, after the transplant, the *EE* must be 'studied as the *NE* has been for centuries' so that we 'shall be able to make an unclouded judgement about their comparative worth' (p. 238). Kenny's argument is both (a) for the superiority of *EE* to *NE* in argumentative tightness and finish and (b) for its superiority as a 'framework' for *AE*. So the inclusive comparison of 'worth' must be between $(AE + EE)$ and $(AE + NE)$.

Kenny's book was published in September 1978. I had then completed but not relinquished the typescript of my appended notes. Before the publication date of this revised reissue his conclusions and arguments would be under review by classical scholars and philosophers. I thought I should state now that Kenny's book had not been available when I was writing the notes. I was uncertain whether I had either a right or a duty to ask for time in which to reconsider or revise the notes. But objections were obvious: I could not make my own assessment of Kenny's book as a whole because I had not the most elementary knowledge of statistics and knew very little about the use of the computer in the scrutiny of either ancient or modern texts; I could not delay my reading of his philosophical chapters, but it would be unseemly to start arguments on details before I had taken the time I would need to absorb what I could of the book as a whole. Further reflection confirmed these objections. But I was troubled by one question which I wish to formulate explicitly before leaving my own book. It arises on the assumption that qualified opinion will concede to Kenny, with admiration and gratitude, the achievement of showing, by historical arguments and stylometry, that the components of $(AE + EE)$ are more like each other than are the components of $(AE + NE)$. Let us concede further the fact or probability that AE and EE are both later than NE, as Kenny gives reasons for believing. These propositions raise collectively a difficulty for those, of whom I am one, who have thought of $(NE + AE)$ as being the more comprehensive and mature exposition of Aristotle's ethical doctrines and an exposition in essentials self-consistent. I wish to face the question how strongly the set of propositions which I have quoted as what Kenny claims to be the outcome of his inquiry ought to incline us to doubt or deny the persistent, but perhaps too complacently accepted, assumption that $(NE + AE)$ is superior.

I have formulated the question or doubt in general terms; its force can be seen more clearly when we consider how it arises in connection with Kenny's chapter 8, 'Happiness in the *Aristotelian Ethics*' (pp. 190–214). He argues that on *eudaimonia* the doctrine of AE is in positive harmony with EE but inconsistent with NE. His opening statement of the contrast contains reservations and implicit admissions which seem to be faded out later in the chapter.

The NE sees happiness as constituted essentially by the contemplative activity of *nous*: this is the only happiness really worthy of the name, and the life of wisdom [i.e. *phronēsis*] and the moral virtues is a second-rate kind of happiness. In the EE on the other hand happiness consists in the ideal functioning of every part of the soul: the activity of contemplation is only one, admittedly the highest one, among a family of activities which constitute the happy life. (p. 190)

Later in the chapter the single-minded and fanatical intellectualism of the Nicomachean eudaimonics is asserted more starkly: NE I, as contrasted with EE I, II, 'identifies happiness with a single dominant end, the activity of the highest virtue; whereas the latter views happiness as an inclusive end, the activity of all the virtues of the rational soul in the broadest sense' (p. 203). The highest virtue is *sophia*, the capacity which determines theoretical activity, as Kenny confirms later in the chapter when he contrasts 'the EE view of happiness as a whole with parts' with 'the NE view of happiness as a single dominant activity' (p. 209). Kenny goes on (1) to argue that in AE II (i.e. NE VI = EE V) happiness includes practical as well as theoretical activity ('an inclusive, not a dominant conception of happiness') and (2) to assert that, in being 'inclusive', NE VI 'is in perfect accord with the doctrine of EE I and EE VIII, but in flagrant contradiction with that of NE X and more muffled contradiction with that of NE I (pp. 209–11). I agree with (1) but disagree with (2).

I do not suggest that, on this topic, Kenny's interpretation of the NE, if paradoxical, is new or unplausible or even heretical. Most recently he finds some, if qualified, support from both Ackrill and Cooper. In his introductory formulation of the interpretation he makes, as we have seen, two incidental statements in a way which makes it natural to call them admissions: (1) Aristotle asserts in the *NE* that 'the life of practical wisdom and the moral virtues' is a 'kind of happiness'; (2) Aristotle asserts in the *EE* that contemplation is 'the highest' of the 'activities which constitute the happy life'.

(1) Aristotle not only asserts this but explains it lucidly in *NE* x. 8. He does not say that this happiness is 'unworthy' of the name. It is the happiness which men hope and strive to obtain 'as they are men and live with a number of people' (1178 b5–7). I find, as I have said, no suggestion here 'that for any man the possession of primary excellence and happiness can make secondary excellence and happiness unimportant'. The doctrine of the *NE* agrees with the doctrine which Kenny finds in the *EE*: 'brave temperate and generous living is an end in itself, chosen for its own sake, and as a part of happiness in its own right' (p. 208).

(2) I do not deny that in the *EE*, as in the *AE*, Aristotle thinks of contemplative activity as higher than any other in the scale of happiness. But Kenny does not claim that this is stated fully and clearly. It would be difficult to make such a claim in view of the fact that there is no explicit mention of the 'theoretic life' in (*AE* + *EE*). He finds it in the 'excessively laconic' conclusion of the *EE* (1249 b6–25) and refers to his own admirable treatment of its difficulties as 'decoding a cryptogram' (pp. 173–8). The comparable passage is in the last two sentences of *AE* II (*NE* VI = *EE* V) where again we seem to find cryptic overstatement. But the doctrine, when it has been extracted, accords with *NE* I and x and with the *Politics* VII. 1–3. Kenny asserts in chapter 7 that in *NE* practical wisdom (*phronēsis*) 'does not appear as the handmaid of learning, but only as the yokemate of the moral virtues' (p. 180). Is this proposition applicable to the 'architectonic art' of *NE* I. 1 (cf. x 7, 1177 b12–15)? I suggest that some of the inconsistencies and anomalies which Kenny claims to find in (*NE* + *AE*) are merely apparent. This, if true, is not a reason for doubting the conclusions of his stylometry. It may be a reason for not expecting an easy victory for either *NE* or *EE* in their various claims and counterclaims to be the better framework for *AE*.

How does Kenny come to play down, and even ignore or deny, Aristotle's doctrine in the *NE* that 'secondary' happiness is independently desirable? I think that I can answer this question in one sentence. I suggest that (a) he extracts too much from the difference between the definitions of *eudaimonia* in *EE* II. 1 (1219 a35–9) and 'the human good' in *NE* I. 1 (1098 a11–18); that (b) he misinterprets the way in which the distinction between primary and secondary *eudaimonia* (1178 a7–9) offers a choice between 'alternative careers' (pp. 208–9); and that (c) these misunderstandings, as I believe them to be, are made more difficult to detect by his repeated use of the distinction between 'dominant end' and 'inclusive end' without making explicit the multiple ambiguity of this confused and confusing terminological invention.

(a) The difference is that between 'activity of complete life in accordance with complete virtue' (*EE*) and 'activity of soul in accordance with virtue, and if there are more than one virtue, in accordance with the best and most complete' (*NE*). Aristotle does not tell us here or elsewhere in *NE* I how he understands the question whether virtue is one or many or how he answers it or which of the virtues is the best. But we can take it from *NE* x, as from *AE* (*NE* vi = *EE* v), that there are at least two 'virtues of the rational soul', and that *sophia*, which determines theoretical activity, is the more perfect. This gives us a premiss which, in conjunction with the Nicomachean definition, entails the identification of *eudaimonia* with theoretical activity. But, until we have been given the elucidation in *NE* x, we are not in a position to interpret in so determinate a sense the unelucidated definition of *NE* i. 7. We can interpret the best activity as a component necessary, but not therefore both necessary and sufficient, for the worthwhile life attainable by an appropriately gifted and fortunate man. For Aristotle slides easily from one formulation of a question to another: what life is best, what are the components of the best life, what is the most worth while of all activities (1095 a16–17). Of course, the sense in which a kind of life is happy is not the same as the sense in which a continuous clockable stretch of activity is happy; but the ambiguity is systematic—roughly a life is more or less happy as its central or paramount interest is an activity which is happy and there are no Priamic disasters. So Book x gives us a natural specification of the definition in i. 7. Kenny interestingly concludes his chapter 8 with the admission that 'a person who organized his life entirely with a view to the promotion of philosophical speculation' would be a vicious and ignoble character (p. 24). Is it Aristotle's doctrine or a misinterpretation of his doctrine which is here reduced to absurdity?

(b) On primary and secondary happiness (*NE* x. 7–8) Kenny insists that they are not parts of one life but alternative 'careers', one 'first-class' and the other 'second-class' (pp. 208–9). He states that, in stating this, he is agreeing 'with Cooper (1975) pp. 157–60 against Gauthier-Jolif (1959), pp. 893–6' (p. 209 n. 1). The sentences quoted (1178 a6–10) are no more 'crucial' than the later sentence (1178 b5–7) which tells us that, as a man living with a number of others, the philosopher needs external goods and 'the other excellence'. The passages in Gauthier to which reference should be made are the notes on 1178 a9 (891–2) and on 1178 a22 (pp. 893–6). I think that, in their interpretations here, each of these scholars, Kenny, Cooper, Gauthier, is right on some points and wrong on others. I agree with Kenny and Cooper that Aristotle speaks of alternative lives (or 'careers') as well as of different activities: the difference between a life in which activities determined by *sophia* are a paramount interest and a life in which they are not is indeed important. I find surprising Kenny's inability to reject as impossible Cooper's interpretation of 1178 b6 (Kenny, p. 214 n. 1).

(c) In discussions of Aristotle's eudaimonics, his view of what is good for man, the expressions 'inclusive end' and 'dominant end' are sometimes used, as by Kenny, to designate two incompatible kinds of life-plan. Kenny finds in the *NE* a 'single dominant end'; here 'single' explicates 'dominant'; to be a dominant aim is to be the only aim the achievement of which is desired for its own sake. The expression 'inclusive end' is seldom defined or explained. Kenny speaks of it as 'the sum total of goods sought for their own sake' (p. 204). One objection to this way of using the terms is that it may induce temporary blindness to the fact that any man who really opted for either of these kinds of life-plan would have to be mad or bad or both. But there is another use of the terms in which every man, unless mad and/or bad, has both an 'inclusive end' and at least one 'dominant end': he has a comprehensive plan which includes a number of objectives or interests and, as part of what is included, one, or perhaps more than one, major interest for which many adjectives are available less dangerous than 'dominant'—'paramount', 'primary', 'central', or, if two interests are paramount, 'focal'. If we want a substitute for 'dominant' in the sense which implies that non-dominant interests are included only as means to the dominant end, we could use Ackrill's 'mono-lithic'. It is natural to identify a kind of life by mention of its paramount objective. It is not to be supposed that in a life so identified, e.g. as philosophic or *kata sophian* non-paramount interests are admitted always for their effects only and never for their intrinsic worth.

I return to the question raised earlier in this note. How far do the conclusions of Kenny's historical arguments and his investigation of stylistic features require us to reassess the merits of (*NE* + *AE*) as a statement of Aristotle's moral philosophy? At the end of chapter 9 he suggests, but only as a conjecture compatible with the evidence, that (*NE* + *AE*) could be 'a collection of material from various periods of Aristotle's life' and may not have existed 'in a collected form' before the second century A.D. (p. 239). Kenny insists that further study, including work on stylistic features of individual books of the *NE*, is needed before such a conjecture could be supported. He does not say in what form the items collected might have pre-existed the collection; perhaps a lecturer's notes for a number of courses. Some of such courses, perhaps not all, might have existed in more than one version. If so, the parts of the collection might not all have been written in the same 'period of Aristotle's life'. Hence the stylometric arguments cannot settle the rival claims of *NE* and *EE* to be the more fitting owner of *AE*. Kenny does not suggest that they can. His philosophical arguments for the proposition that *AE* fits within the framework of *EE* 'very much better' than it fits within the framework of *NE* are independent of his other (historical and philological') arguments. The subject of his chapter 8, 'Happiness in the *Aristotelian Ethics*', is one where we are bound to look very hard at the closeness of the fit. I have tried to show that, in his treatment of this corner of his complex problem, he has not made a conclusive case for the incoherence of (*NE* + *AE*).

BIBLIOGRAPHY

(Books and articles referred to in the Bibliographical Notes at the ends of Chapters I, X, XIII, XIV are not, as a rule, named again in this Bibliography.)

The *Nicomachean Ethics* is translated, in *The Works of Aristotle translated into English* (Oxford, 1910–52), by W. D. Ross (1925). The translation in the Loeb Classical Library is by H. Rackham (1934). The translation in Penguin Classics by J. A. K. Thomson (1953) has been revised with Notes and Appendices by Hugh Tredennick and in addition a lively Introduction and informative Bibliography by Jonathan Barnes (1976).

The Greek text was edited by I. Bywater (Oxford 1890) with a usefully comprehensive Index of Greek words (pp. 225–64). His *Contributions to the Textual Criticism of Aristotle's Nicomachean Ethics* (1892) supplements his edition. His references are, of course, given by page, column (a, b), and line of the Greek text of Aristotle prepared for the Berlin Academy by I. Bekker (1831). Volume V of Bekker's edition contains the *Index Aristotelicus* by H. Bonitz (Berlin 1870).

The Commentaries in English on the ten books of the *EN* are: A. Grant, *The Ethics of Aristotle*[4] (1885); J. A. Stewart, *Notes on the Nicomachean Ethics of Aristotle* (1892); J. Burnet, *The Ethics of Aristotle* (1900); H. H. Joachim, *The Nicomachean Ethics* (posthumously published lectures delivered 1902–17) ed. D. A. Rees (1951); J. L. Ackrill, *Aristotle's Ethics* (1973) (most of the *EN* with extracts from other works, an introduction and brief notes).

The fullest Commentary is in French: R. A. Gauthier and J. Y. Jolif, *Aristotle: L'Éthique à Nicomaque*[2] (Louvain, 1970). The first part of vol. i of the second edition contains a new enlarged Introduction (pp. 5–314) and a Bibliographical Supplement (pp. 315–34) covering 1958–68 and supplementing the Bibliography in vol. ii (pp. 917–40). Each volume has two separately printed parts. The second part of vol. i contains a Translation into French.

F. Dirlmeier is the author of a Translation and a splendidly detailed informative Commentary in German, *Nikomachische Ethik* (Berlin, 1956, 1969). Dirlmeier has similarly translated and commented on the *EE* (1969) and the *MM* (1966). Access to these stores of learning and judgement is made more difficult than it should be by very small print on very large pages and the absence of indexes.

Other treatises of Aristotle are relevant at many points to the *EN*. A number of these are edited, with revised texts, introductions and commentaries by W. D. Ross: *Metaphysics* (1924); *Physics* (1936); *Prior and Posterior Analytics* (1949); *Parva Naturalia* (1955); *Rhetoric* (text only) (1959); *De Anima* (1961).

Other standard commentaries are: E. M. Cope, *Rhetoric* revised by J. E. Sandys (1877); W. L. Newman, *The Politics of Aristotle*, 4 vols. (1887–1902);

R. D. Hicks, *De Anima* (1907); H. H. Joachim, *De Generatione et Corruptione* (1922); E. Barker, *Politics* (translation, introduction, notes, appendices) (1946); Martha Craven Nussbaum, *De Motu Animalium* (Princeton 1978).

J. L. Ackrill is the editor of the Clarendon Aristotle Series, and himself the author of the translation and commentary for *Categories and De Interpretatione* (1963). The series achieves scrupulous closeness of its translations to the Greek and subtle dissection of philosophical arguments.

There are many good accounts of Aristotle's thought. The following four books are interestingly different from each other in what they aim at and achieve: W. D. Ross, *Aristotle* (1923); W. Jaeger, *Aristoteles. Grundlegung einer Geschichte seiner Entwicklung* (1923), English translation of second edition by R. Robinson, paperback (1962); I. Düring, *Aristoteles* (1966); D. J. Allan, *The Philosophy of Aristotle*[2] (1970).

The following volumes assemble and reprint previously published articles in or connected with Aristotle's ethical theory: (1) J. J. Walsh and H. L. Shapiro (edd.), *Aristotle's Ethics: Issues and Interpretations* (1967); (2) J. M. E. Moravcsik (ed.), *Aristotle. A Collection of Critical Essays* (1967) (four of the essays on ethical subjects); (3) P. Moraux and D. Harlfinger (edd.), *Untersuchungen zur Eudemischen Ethik* (Berlin, 1971); (4) F.-P. Hager (ed.), *Ethik und Politik des Aristoteles* (1972); (5) Jonathan Barnes, Michael Schofield, Richard Sorabji (edd.), *Articles on Aristotle. 2. Ethics and Politics* (1977). This is the second volume to be published of a series of four with the same main title and produced by the same editors with extensive indexes and informative reasoned bibliographies. The first of the series, 1. *Science*, was published in 1975.

The bibliography in my first edition (1968) took the form of a 'Select List of Books and Articles' with the names of authors or editors in alphabetical order in each main section. This was supplemented by brief bibliographical notes after Chapters I, X, XIII, XIV. These notes have been left as and where they were; this Bibliography replaces the Select List. The composition of bare lists of items in alphabetical order is not the best way of presenting bibliographical information, especially when the information has to be highly selective. I shall, therefore, present my suggestions in this second and final part of the Bibliography under the titles of the successive chapters of the book. I shall also continue to allow myself very occasional and very brief explanations.

I. Introductory Note: Aristotle's Ethical Writings

The bibliographical note on pp. 10–11 briefly compared the English commentators with each other but omitted to emphasize the weight and value of the more recent Commentaries in French and German. I hope that this imbalance has been corrected by what I have said about these commentators earlier in this Bibliography.

I referred in this chapter to 'questions to which experts have given different answers' concerning 'the common books' and the comparative merits and dates of the *EN* and the *EE*. Two important books have since been published on these issues: C. J. Rowe, *The Eudemian and Nicomachean Ethics—a Study in the Development of Aristotle's Thought, Proceedings of the Cambridge Philological Society*, Suppl. 3 (1971); Anthony Kenny, *The Aristotelian Ethics—a Study of the Relationship between the Eudemian and Nicomachean Ethics of Aristotle* (Oxford, 1978). In the second of the Appended Notes to Chapter I I have described very briefly the contents of these two books.

On the influence on Aristotelian studies of Jaeger's book see the following articles: W. D. Ross, 'The Development of Aristotle's Thought', *British Academy* (1957); G. E. L. Owen, 'The Platonism of Aristotle', *British Academy* (1965). These two articles are reprinted as the first two chapters of *Articles on Aristotle 1. Science* (1975).

II. The Final Good for Man

In the paragraphs which follow I shall arrange books and articles or chapters in two separate lists, both in chronological order. Any reference to an item previously listed will usually be by the name of the author or editor.

Books: G. C. Field, *Moral Theory* (1921); J. Léonard, *Le Bonheur chez Aristote* (Brussels, 1948); G. H. von Wright, *Varieties of Goodness* (1963); S. R. L. Clark, *Aristotle's Man* (1975); J. M. Cooper, *Reason and Human Good in Aristotle* (1975).

Articles: H. A. Prichard, 'The meaning of *agathon* in the *Ethics* of Aristotle', *Philosophy* (1935), reprinted ed. Moravcsik (1967); K. von Fritz and E. Kapp, 'The Relation between Aristotle's Treatise on the Constitution of Athens and his Political Philosophy', III from Introduction to edition of *The Constitution of Athens* (New York, 1950), reprinted as chapter 2 of *Articles on Aristotle 2* (1977); B. Williams, 'Aristotle on the Good: a formal sketch', *Philosophical Quarterly* (1962); W. F. R. Hardie, 'The final good in Aristotle's *Ethics*', *Philosophy* (1965), ed. Moravcsik (1967); Anthony Kenny, 'Aristotle on Happiness', *P.A.S.* (1965–6), ed. *Articles on Aristotle 2* (1977); J. L. Austin, '*Agathon* and *Eudaimonia* in the *Ethics* of Aristotle', ed. Moravcsik (1967); C. Kirwan, 'Logic and the Good in Aristotle', *Philosophical Quarterly* (1967); J. L. Ackrill, 'Aristotle on *Eudaimonia*', *British Academy* (1974); W. F. R. Hardie, 'Aristotle on the best life for a man', *Philosophy* (1979).

See also on 'function' and 'good'. P. T. Geach and R. M. Hare in *Analysis* (1956–7) and A. M. MacIver in *Analysis* (1957–8).

III. The Nature of the Inquiry

Two of the volumes containing the proceedings of the triennial (since 1957)

'Symposia Aristotelica' (titles in *Articles on Aristotle* [30]–[34]) are about Aristotelian methodology: ed. S. Mansion, *Aristote et les Problèmes de Méthode* (1961); ed. G. E. L. Owen, *Aristotle on Dialectic. The Topics* (1968). In the former of these volumes the articles of special interest in relation to the *Ethics* are: G. E. L. Owen, 'tithenai ta phainomena' (reprinted in *Articles on Aristotle* 1 and in Moravcsik); Pierre Aubenque, 'Sur la notion aristotélicienne d'aporie'; three articles about method in the ethical treatises by J. D. Monan, W. G. Rabinowitz, and D. J. Allan.

See also J. D. Monan, *Moral Knowledge and its Methodology in Aristotle* (1968); J. D. G. Evans, *Aristotle's Concept of Dialectic* (1977).

IV. The Platonic Idea of the Good

Aristotle's criticisms of Plato's Theory of Ideas raise questions which are often difficult to understand. The books and articles in which these questions have been discussed are very numerous. All I shall do here is to list some recent articles which have discussed arguments stated or mentioned in *EN* I. 6: G. E. L. Owen, 'Logic and metaphysics in some earlier works of Aristotle', in *Aristotle and Plato in the Mid-fourth Centruy* (1960); D. J. Allan, 'Aristotle's criticism of Platonic doctrine concerning goodness and the good', *P.A.S.* (1963/4); W. W. Fortenbaugh, '*Nicomachean Ethics* I, 1096 b26–9', *Phronesis* (1966); H. Flashar, 'The Critique of Plato's Theory of Ideas in Aristotle's *Ethics*'; J. L. Ackrill, 'Aristotle on "Good" and the Categories'. The last two articles are reprinted as chapters 1 and 2 of *Articles on Aristotle* 2 (1977).

V. The Nature of Man

On conceptual problems about besouled bodies or embodied minds much is said in short space by broadcasting scientists and philosophers in *The Physical Basis of Mind*, edited by Peter Laslett (1952). Much more is said by Karl R. Popper and John C. Eccles in *The Self and its Brain* (1977).

On Aristotle's doctrine I list the following books and articles:

Books: H. Cassirer, *Aristoteles' Schrift von der Seele* (Tübingen, 1932); F. Nuyens, *L'Évolution de la psychologie d'Aristote* (Louvain, 1948); D. W. Hamlyn, *Aristotle's de Anima*, Clarendon Aristotle Series (1968); R. Sorabji, *Aristotle on Memory* (1972); G. E. R. Lloyd and G. E. L. Owen (edd.), *Aristotle on Mind and the Senses* (Cambridge, 1978).

Articles: 1. Block, 'The Order of Aristotle's Psychological Writings', *American Journal of Philology* (1961); W. F. R. Hardie, 'Aristotle's Treatment of the Relation between the Soul and the Body', *Philosophical Quarterly* (1964); H. J. Easterling, 'A note on *De Anima* 413 a8–9', *Phronesis* (1965); C. H. Kahn, 'Sensation and Consciousness in Aristotle's Psychology', *Archiv für Geschichte der Philosophie* (1966); J. Barnes, 'Aristotle's Concept of Mind', *P.A.S.* (1971–2);

J. L. Ackrill, 'Aristotle's Definitions of Psuchē', *P.A.S.* (1972–3); R. Sorabji, 'Body and Soul in Aristotle', *Philosophy* (1974); W. F. R. Hardie, 'Concepts of Consciousness in Aristotle', *Mind* (1976); H. M. Robinson, 'Mind and Body in Aristotle', *Classical Quarterly* (1978).

VI. The General Nature of Ethical Virtue

I hope that this chapter with its Annexed Notes reflects my awareness that the choice of topics is here arbitrary. It is natural that this fact should be reflected in the corresponding section of the Bibliography:

Books: T. H. Green, *Prolegomena to Ethics* (1883); W. James, *Principles of Psychology* (1890); C. D. Broad, *Mind and its Place in Nature* (1925); B. Russell, *History of Western Philosophy* (1946); H. V. Jaffa, *Thomism and Aristotelianism. A Study of the Commentary of Thomas Aquinas on the Nicomachean Ethics* (Chicago, 1952); A. W. H. Adkins, *Merit and Responsibility* (1960); E. R. Dodds, *The Ancient Concept of Progress and other Essays in Greek Literature and Belief* (1973); K. J. Dover, *Greek Popular Morality in the Time of Plato and Aristotle* (1974); W. W. Fortenbaugh, *Aristotle on Emotion* (1975).

Articles: E. A. Schmidt, 'Ehre und Tugend', *Archiv fur Geschichte der Philosophie* (1967); D. A. Rees, '"Magnanimity" in the *Eudemian* and *Nicomachean Ethics*' in P. Moraux and D. Harlfinger (edd.) (1971); W. F. R. Hardie, '"Magnanimity" in Aristotle's *Ethics*''', *Phronesis* (1978).

VII. Virtue is a Mean

Articles: J. L. Stocks, '*Logos* and *Mesotēs* in the *De Anima* of Aristotle', *Journal of Philology* (1914); 'The Test of Experience', *Mind* (1919); H. W. B. Joseph 'Aristotle's Definition of Moral Virtue and Plato's Account of Justice in the Soul', VI in *Essays in Ancient and Modern Philosophy* (1935); E. Harris Olmsted, 'The "Moral Sense" Aspect of Aristotle's Ethical Theory', *American Journal of Philology* (1948); W. W. Fortenbaugh, 'Aristotle and the questionable mean-dispositions', *American Philological Association* (1968); J. O. Urmson, 'Aristotle's Doctrine of the Mean', *American Philosophical Quarterly* (1973); W. F. R. Hardie, 'Continence, Virtue, Heroic Virtue' printed, as Appendix with pp. 129–143 from my chapter VII, in *Articles on Aristotle* 2, pp. 42–6 (1977).

VIII. The Distinction between the Voluntary and the Involuntary and
IX. Choice and the Origination of Action

Books: R. Loening, *Die Zurechnungslehre des Aristoteles* (1903); G. E. M. Anscombe, *Intention* (1957); ed. Ted Honderich, *Essays on Freedom of Action* (1973); Anthony Kenny, *Aristotle's Theory of the Will* (1979).

Articles etc. H. A. Prichard, chapters 10 and 11 in *Moral Obligation* (1949); Vinit Haksar, 'Aristotle and the punishment of psychopaths', *Philosophy* (1964), reprinted in Walsh and Shapiro; C. A. Campbell, *In Defence of Free Will* (1967), chapters I, II, III; P. M. Huby, 'The first discovery of the free-will problem', *Philosophy* (1967); W. F. R. Hardie, 'Aristotle and the free will problem', *Philosophy* (1968); F. A. Siegler, 'Voluntary and Involuntary,' *Monist* (1968); C. D. Broad, '*Broad's Critical Essays in Moral Philosophy* (1971), chapter IV 'Determinism, Indeterminism and Libertarianism' (1934); W. F. R. Hardie, 'Willing and Acting', *The Philosophical Quarterly* (1971), cf. 'My own free will', *Philosophy* (1957); M. Schofield, 'Aristotelian Mistakes', *Proceedings of the Cambridge Philological Society* (1973); D. J. Furley, 'Aristotle on the Voluntary', chapter 5 in *Articles on Aristotle* 2 (1977). On the comparison of deliberation with mathematical analysis, see the articles by R. Robinson and N. Gulley referred to in footnote 3 to p. 166.

X. Justice

To the literature mentioned in the bibliographical note on pp. 210–11 I add: H. Kelsen, 'Aristotle's Doctrine of Justice', reprinted in Walsh and Shapiro (1967) from *What is Justice?* (1960); M. I. Finley, 'Aristotle and Economic Analysis', chapter 13 in *Articles on Aristotle* 2 (1977). Relevant also are Urmson in VII above and Schofield in VIII/IX above. Henry Jackson's edition (with commentary) of *EN* v (1879) has been reprinted (1973).

XI. Practical Wisdom and XII Note on the Practical Syllogism

Books: J. Walter, *Die Lehre von der praktischen Vernunft in der griechischen Philosophie* (1874); L. H. G. Greenwood, *Nicomachean Ethics Book Six* (Cambridge, 1909); T. Ando, *Aristotle's Theory of Practical Cognition* (1958, 1965); P. Aubenque, *La Prudence chez Aristote* (Paris 1963); G. H. von Wright, *The Varieties of Human Goodness* (1963); A. von Fragstein, *Studien zur Ethik des Aristoteles* (Amsterdam, 1974); J. M. Cooper, *Reason and Human Good in Aristotle* (1975).

Articles: J. A. Smith, 'Aristotelica', *Classical Quarterly* (1920); R. Jackson, 'Rationalism and Intellectualism in the *Ethics* of Aristotle', *Mind* (1942); D. J. Allan, 'Aristotle's Account of the Origin of Moral Principles' (1953), chapter 7 in *Articles on Aristotle* 2; 'The Practical Syllogism' in *Autour d'Aristote* (Louvain 1955); W. W. Fortenbaugh, 'Aristotle's conception of moral virtue and its perceptive role', *American Philogical Association* (1964); G. E. M. Anscombe, 'Thought and Action in Aristotle' (1965), chapter 6 in *Articles on Aristotle* 2; P. Aubenque, 'La prudence aristotélicienne porte-t-elle sur la fin ou sur les moyens', *Revue des études grecques* (1965); S. G. Etheridge, 'Aristotle's Practical

Syllogism and Necessity', *Philologus* (1968); C. J. Rowe, 'The meaning of *phronēsis* in the *Eudemian Ethics*' in Moraux and Harlfinger (edd.) (1971); R. Sorabji, 'Aristotle on the role of Intellect in Virtue', *P.A.S.* (1973–4); D. Wiggins, 'Deliberation and Practical Reason', *P.A.S.* (1975–6); A. Kenny, 'Wisdom in the Aristotelian Ethics', chapter 7 in *The Aristotelian Ethics* (1978); M. C. Nussbaum, 'Interpretive Essays' in edition of *Aristotle's De Motu Animalium* (1978).

XIII. Moral Weakness

Books: J. Cook Wilson, *On the Structure of the Seventh Book of the Nicomachean Ethics* (1879, reprinted with Postscript 1912); J. J. Walsh, *Aristotle's Conception of Moral Weakness* (1963); G. W. Mortimore (ed.), *Weakness of Will* (1971). On Plato Mortimore prints part of the *Protagoras* and G. Santas, 'Plato's *Protagoras* and Explanations of Weakness', *Philosophical Review* (1966). See also C. C. W. Taylor, *Protagoras*, translated with notes (1976) in Clarendon Plato Series.

Some of the articles and chapters listed in my bibliographical note (pp. 292–3) are reprinted by Mortimore, viz. those by P. L. Gardiner, R. M. Hare, H. J. N. Horsburgh, and Steven Lukes. To my list add A. Kenny, 'The Practical Syllogism and Incontinence', *Phronesis* (1966); G. Santas, 'Aristotle on practical inference, the explanation of action and akrasia', *Phronesis* (1969). The article of R. Robinson in *Revue Philosophique* (1955) is reprinted as chapter 8 ('Aristotle on Akrasia') of *Articles on Aristotle* 2 (1977).

XIV. Pleasure

See the Bibliographical Note on pp. 315–16.

At least two later articles are important: G. E. L. Owen, 'Aristotelian Pleasures', *P.A.S.* (1971–2) reprinted as chapter 9 of *Articles on Aristotle* 2; J. C. B. Gosling, 'More Aristotelian Pleasures', *P.A.S.* (1973–4).

XV. Friendship and Self-Love

Book: J.-C. Fraisse, *Philia: La Notion d'amitié dans la philosophie antique* (Paris, 1974).

Articles: A. W. H. Adkins, 'Friendship and self-sufficiency in Homer and Aristotle', *Classical Quarterly* (1963); J.-C. Fraisse, '*Autarkeia* et *Philia* en *EE* VII. 12, 1244 b1–1245 b19' in Moraux and Harlfinger (edd.) (1971); J. Annas, 'Plato and Aristotle on Friendship and Altruism', *Mind* (1977).

XVI. Theoretical Activity and the Nature of Reason

See also II and V above.

Books: G. Rodier, *Aristote: Éthique à Nicomaque*, livre X (1897); Trond Berg Eriksen, *Bios Theoretikos*, Notes on *EN* x 6–8 (Norway, 1976).

Articles: W. K. C. Guthrie, 'The Development of Aristotle's Theology', *Classical Quarterly* (1933, 1934); P. Defourny, 'Contemplation in Aristotle's *Ethics*' (1937), reprinted in *Articles* 2; G. Müller, 'Probleme der aristotelischen Eudaimonielehre', *Museum Helveticum* 1960, reprinted in F.-P. Hager (ed.) (1972); R. Norman, 'Aristotle's Philosopher God', *Phronesis* (1969); W. J. Verdenius, 'Human Reason and God in the *Eudemian Ethics*', in Moraux and Harlfinger (edd.) (1971).

INDEX OF ARISTOTELIAN PASSAGES

GENERAL INDEX

Ackrill, J. L.: on the category of quality, 96–8; on *energeia* (activity) and *kinēsis* (movement), 305; on eudaimonia, 360, 364–5, 418; on *De Interpretatione* ch. 9, 384.

Adkins, A. W. H., on responsibility, virtue, duty, 123–8, 375.

Akrasia (weakness of will, incontinence): Chapter XIII; dialectical form of the discussion, 37, 39, 40; question whether the *akratēs* is unjust to himself, 207–8; the scope of *akrasia*, 259–61; the 'phenomena', 264–6; the meaning of Aristotle's main question, 266–8; question whether *akrasia* is logically possible, 268–70, 273; suggestion that the *akratēs* has belief not knowledge, 273; dispositional and actual knowledge, 274–5, 279; the practical syllogism in *akrasia*, 241, 244–5, 248, 276–91; logical and physical analyses, 40, 280–1; the 'last premiss', 287–9; the *akratēs* his own enemy, 325. See also 404–5, 405–9.

Akribeia (precision), 31–4, 366.

Allan, D. J.: on the mean, 145; on the practical syllogism, 229–31, 242, 248; on the major premiss, 232, 247–8, 395, 396; on self-interest, 325, 328; on moral obligation, 334.

Altruism, *see* Egoism.

Ameleia (carelessness), 173–5, 378–9.

Analogia (analogy, proportion): analogical predication, 62, 64, 65–7; continuous and discrete proportion, 146; geometrical and arithmetical proportion, 146–7; in distributive (dianemetic) justice, 189–90; in rectificatory (diorthotic) justice, 192; reciprocal (inverse) proportion, 198–201.

Analysis in mathematics, *see* Deliberation.

Ando, T., on the practical syllogism, 249–50, 288.

Anger (*orgē*): its definition, 74–5, 79, 90, 112; may be dispositional or occurrent, 95. See also 389–90.

Anscombe, G. E. M.: on final ends, 17; on the concept of willing, 170–3; on deliberation (*bouleusis*) and choice (*prohairesis*), 180–1, 385–6.

Archai (beginnings, principles), *see* Principles.

Aretē (virtue, excellence), *see* Virtue.

Arnim, H. von, on the *MM*, 6.

Art, as a final end, 340, 418.

Asceticism, rejected by Aristotle, 25, 312.

Aubenque, P., on *phronēsis*, 386–7.

Austin, J. L.: on an argument in the *EE*, 55; on ordinary words, 221.

Block, I., on the development of Aristotle's psychology, 73.

Bosanquet, B.: on *theōria* (contemplation), 340; on what a horse is for, 362.

Bradley, F. H.: on moral obligations, 334; on metaphysics, 339.

Broad, C. D.: on dispositional properties, 110–11; on 'categorical substitutability', 383–4.

Brutishness (*thēriotēs*), 258–60, 402.

Burnet, J.: on the *MM*, 5; on the *EE*, 6, 7; on the common books, 8; on starting points in ethics, 34–5; on the dialectical character of the *EN*, 38–44, 70, 361, 366; on the exoteric writings, 69, 218; on the mean as a ratio, 151; on will, 163; on rational choice (*prohairesis*), 167–8, 169; on responsibility for character, 178–9; on justice and price-fixing, 193–4; on the mean between gain and loss, 195; on the practical syllogism, 249; on *akrasia* (weakness of will), 280, 282–3, 289–90; on friendship (*philia*), 332; on *theōria* (contemplation), 340.

Campbell, C. A., on willing, 172, 380–1, 383–4.

Case, T.: on the *MM*, 5; on the *EE*, 7.

Categories: natural priority, 52; on synonyms and homonyms, 62; the kinds of quality, 94–9.

Character, *see Hexis*.

Choice, *see Prohairesis*.

Clark, S. R. L.: on function, 362–3; on the good, 423–4.

Cleverness (*deinotēs*), shown in finding means, 221, 225, 236.

Consciousness; concept of, 370–1.

Contemplation, *see Theōria*.

Contingency, suggestion that actions are uncaused, 33–4, 103, 115–16, 177–8, 380–1, 383–4.

Cooper, J. M.: on dialectic and deliberation, 366–8, 379–80, 387; on *eudaimonia*, 422, 428.

Courage (*andreia*): political courage, 106, 330; as a mean, 118, 140, 145; the end in courage, 252; not effortless, 373, 376, 404.

De Anima: how related to the *EN*, 69–77, 218, 348; on the *pathē* (affections), 75, 112; on the mean (*mesotēs*) in sensible qualities, 147–8; on originating cause (*aitia*) and assisting causes (*sunaitia*), 179–80, 384–5; on the practical syllogism, 229, 245–6, 288; on the division of understanding *hupolēpsis*), 272; on the status of reason (*nous*), 72, 74, 112, 345–51.

De Generatione et Corruptione, on mixture, 149–51, 350–1.

De Interpretatione, on contingency, 33, 103, 116, 178, 384.

De la Mare, W., quoted, 179.

De Memoria, physiological conditions of memory, 75, 113.

De Motu Animalium: the origination of movement, 82; on practical thinking, 229–30, 240–1, 246–8, 396–400.

De Partibus Animalium, on the knowledge of terrestrial things, 339, 420.

Deliberation (*bouleusis*): as the finding of means, 162, 214, 217; compared with analysis in mathematics, 165–6; as the weighing of pros and cons, 167, 217; and *prohairesis* (choice), 180–1; how connected with the

practical syllogism, 249, 252–3. *See also* 366–8, 379–80, 394–5, 397.

Demand (*chreia*), determines prices, 196–7.

Desire, *see Orexis, Pathos*, Wish.

Dialectic: dialectical arguments in ethics, 37–45; *endoxa* (received opinions) as starting-points 37–8; *topoi* (commonplaces) as logical tools, 38–9, 41; Burnet on the dialectical character of the *EN*, 38–44; 'dialectical' opposed to 'physical', 40, 42, 280–1; the dialectical advance ·to principles, 41–2. *See also* J. M. Cooper.

Dirlmeier, F.: 6, 382–3, 384–5, 410, 423.

Disposition, *see Dunamis, Hexis*.

Dodds, E. R., on Aristotle and Freud, 341; on slavery, 374.

Dualism, psychophysical: in general, 82–93; in Aristotle, 77–9, 351–2, 369–70.

Dunamis (power, potentiality) (*see also Hexis*): as a kind of quality, 95, 96–7; in a wider sense, 98, 100; natural and acquired powers, 100–1; virtues as rational powers, 101–2; dispositions as hypothetical facts, 107–8; the Megarian view, 108; dispositions as secondary qualities, 108–10; acquired dispositions and physical traces, 110–13; dispositional and actual knowledge, 274–5, 279, 405–9; opposed to *energeia* (actuality), 308, 345.

Duty and Duties, 123–8, 323, 334–5.

Easterling, H. J.: on the soul, 371–2.

Education (*paideia*), in logic, 31–2.

Egoism and Altruism (*see also* Friendship (*philia*)): Aristotle's general doctrine, 214–16, 320, 322–4, 327–8, 333–4; psychological egoism, 326–7; self-assertive desires, 327; self-sacrifice, 329–31. *See also* 413–14.

Emotion, *see Pathos*.

End (*telos*) and Means (*ta pros to telos*) (*see also* Happiness, *Theōria*): two kinds of end, 12–13; two meanings of 'end', 13–14, 305–6, 309–10, 345; superordinate and subordinate ends, 14–16; the supreme end, 16–18,

213–17, 234–5; happiness (*eudaimonia*) as the end, 19–27; comprehensive plans and paramount objects, 18, 22–3, 25–6, 329–31, 359–60, 364–5, 394–5, 425–9; the end of the city-state (*polis*), 18–19; ends and virtues, 122; virtue and vice determine ends, 169, 181, 225, 235; '*telos*' wider than 'end', 252, 254–7.

Endoxa (received opinions), see Dialectic.

Energeia (actuality, activity), see Dunamis, End, Happiness, Hexis, Pleasure, Theōria.

Epagōgē (induction), in understanding principles (*archai*), 37.

Epistēmē (knowledge, science): the sphere of the necessary, 221–3; included in *sophia*, 226; cannot be sinned against, 272, 286–7; the theoretical sciences, 338–9.

Epithumia (desire, appetite), see Orexis, Pathos.

Equity (*epieikeia*), 209–10.

Etheridge, S. G., 396.

Ethics, see Political Science.

Ethics, Eudemian (*Ethica Eudēmia*): meaning of the title, 6–7; Books common to the *EE* and the *EN*, 8–9, 295–6; on the final good, 17–18, 215, 364, 425–9; on endoxa (received opinions), 38; on the Form of the Good, 49; on Platonic Forms, 50; on two kinds of good, 50; on the priority of the Form, 52; on the idea of number, 53–5; no single science of goods, 58; on the multisignificance of *philia* (friendship), 63–5; on the mean in action, 133–4; on the meaning of *prohairesis*, 158, 162, 165; on justice as a mean, 202–3; on enthusiasm, 341–2.

Ethics, Nicomachean (*Ethica Nicomacheia*): arrangement of its contents, 1–3; literary characteristics and style, 3–5; disorder in the text, 2–4, 184; meaning of the title, 6–7; Books common to the *EN* and the *EE*, 8–9, 295–6, 425–9.

Ethismos (habituation) (*see also* Principles): required for understanding ethical principles, 36–7; distinguished from instruction, 99–100; function

of the laws, 100, 106, 236; the paradox of ethical habituation, 104–5; Aristotle as educationist, 122, 390–1.

Eudaimonia, see Happiness.

Eudemus: views of W. Jaeger, 7; Platonic view of the soul, 71–2.

Eudoxus, on pleasure, 294, 311.

Exoteric writings (*exōterikoi logoi*), views on their nature, 69–70, 218.

Festugière, A. J., on Aristotle's treatment of pleasure, 295, 299, 300, 409–10.

Field, G. C., on self-interest, 325, 331.

Fortenbaugh, W. W.: on moral perception, 388–9; on emotional response, 389–91.

Friendship, Friendliness (*philia*): Chapter XV (*see also* Egoism, Duty); active and passive senses of '*philos*', 317; forms of social organization, 318, 321–2; friendliness as an ethical virtue, 318–19; three kinds of friendship, 319–20, 322; friendship and justice, 321; the friend as 'another self', 323–4, 331–2; good and bad kinds of self-love (*philautia*), 328–9; friendship as an extension of self-consciousness, 331–2, 414.

Function (*ergon*): of man, 23–4; 362–3, 365; of the intellectual virtues, 223–4.

Furley, D. J., on Aristotle's determinism, 381–2.

Gauthier, R. A., and Jolif, J. Y.: on method in ethics, 36; on the views of F. Nuyens, 73, 77; on justice as a mean, 202; on practical wisdom, 225; on akrasia (weakness of will), 267; on theōria (contemplation), 337, 344–5, 373.

God: his activity, 309–10, 343–4; as pure form and first mover, 344–5.

Good (*agathos, agathon*) (see also End): Chapter IV on the Platonic Idea; as object of desire, 12–13, 21; as a Platonic Form, 47–50; different for fish and men, 50; no single science of goods, 58; intrinsic goods and instrumental goods, 61–2, 356; the multisignificance of 'good', 62–7;